Contrastiveness in Information Structure, Alternatives and Scalar Implicatures

Studies in Natural Language and Linguistic Theory

VOLUME 91

More information about this series at http://www.springer.com/series/6559

Chungmin Lee · Ferenc Kiefer
Manfred Krifka
Editors

Contrastiveness in Information Structure, Alternatives and Scalar Implicatures

Springer

Editors
Chungmin Lee
Seoul National University
Gwanak-gu, Seoul
Republic of Korea

Ferenc Kiefer
Research Institute for Linguistics
Hungarian Academy of Sciences
Budapest
Hungary

Manfred Krifka
Department of General Linguistics
Humboldt University of Berlin
Berlin
Germany

ISSN 0924-4670 ISSN 2215-0358 (electronic)
Studies in Natural Language and Linguistic Theory
ISBN 978-3-319-10105-7 ISBN 978-3-319-10106-4 (eBook)
DOI 10.1007/978-3-319-10106-4

Library of Congress Control Number: 2016947480

Printed on acid-free paper

This Springer imprint is published by Springer Nature
The registered company is Springer International Publishing AG
The registered company address is: Gewerbestrasse 11, 6330 Cham, Switzerland

Preface

This volume consists of selected papers from the CIL (International Congress of Linguists) 18 Workshop on *Contrastiveness and Scalar Implicatures* organized by Ferenc Kiefer and Chungmin Lee, and the CIL18 Symposium on *Information Structure* organized by Manfred Krifka, and some additional papers. CIL 18 was held in Seoul. Korea, July 21–26, 2008. The papers by Kratzer and Shimoyama, by Krifka, and by Keshet were separately invited to be included and we express our gratitude to the authors for their generosity.

Seoul, Republic of Korea	Chungmin Lee
Budapest, Hungary	Ferenc Kiefer
Berlin, Germany	Manfred Krifka

Contents

Introduction

Over the past decades, semantics and pragmatics have made a great deal of progress in understanding information structure, polarity and implicatures. This volume provides a forum for exploring their core issues by carefully selecting papers dealing with Topic and Focus, Contrastivc Topic and Contrastive Focus, Focus Alternatives and Exhaustivity, Implicatures and Scalar Implicatures, and Polarity and Question. All the topics are closely interwoven with each other and some cross-linguistic facts are provided for theoretical claims. One outstanding question, for example, is how to characterize contrastiveness in information structure. Although "kontrastiveness" is claimed to be orthogonal to informational thematicity and rhematicity (Vallduvi and Vilkuna 1998) and Contrastivc Topic has been fairly well established, Contrastive Focus is less commonly received but is understood to be distinct from Information Focus. A recent issue is epistemic indefinites and related points of alternatives, (scalar) implicatures, ignorance and identification, modified numerals, and free choice (Alonzo-Ovalle and Menendez-Benito 2015). Another issue is the elaboration of expressives as conventional implicatures (Potts 2005, Gutzmann 2015, McCready 2014). Some relevant edited volumes were also published (such as Lee et al. (Eds.) 2007 and Féry and Ishihara (Eds.) 2016).

The chapters in the volume fall into four parts. Those in the first part discuss aspects of information structure such as contrastiveness in Contrastive Topic and Contrastive Focus, along with Topic and Focus. This part includes Yabushita on Contrastive Topic by partition semantics with questions and answers, Lee on Contrastive Topic with scalar conventional implicatures and Contrastive Focus by alternative questions, Kiss on structural Focus by movement in Hungarian, van Rooij on Topic and Focus with exhaustivity, Gyuris on a focal "contrast-marking" particle analogous to 'only' in Hungarian, and McCoy-Rusanova on multiple discourse particles including Contrastive Topic with scalar implicatures in Russian.

The second part includes those dealing with polarity, alternatives, exhaustivity and implicatures such as Kratzer and Shimoyama on indefinites, disjunction and alternatives, J. Choi on free choice in Korean without domain widening, Y. Choi and Lee on expletive negation and polarity, Lim on the focus particle *-lato* in Korean, Liu on negative polarity items with negative implicatum and positive implicatum, Sauerland on disjunction and scalar implicatures with globality/localitiy, and Keshet on scalar implicatures with functional application in alternative semantics.

The third part comprises chapters discussing quantificational expressions with implicatures such as Horn on 'almost' with scalar implicatures, Yeom on numerals, Nakamura on *-mo* and numerals with scalar implicatures, and Paltiel-Gedalyovich and Schaeffer on scale and non-scale words by experiment in Hebrew child language.

The fourth part comprises chapters by Krifka on negated questions as denegation of assertion speech act, and by Ishihara on the intonation of question speech acts in Tokyo Japanese.

I. Information Structure and Contrastiveness

The chapter by Lee (Contrastive Topic, Contrastive Focus, Alternatives and Scalar Implicatures) is concerned with how to obtain Contrastive Topic and Contrastive Focus in natural language. By providing cross-linguistic data in English, Korean, Japanese, and Chinese, the author proposes that Contrastive Focus as well as Contrastive Topic can be derived on the basis of Question under Discussion (QUD), suggested by Roberts (1986). CT, as part of Potential Topic, is claimed to generate conventional scalar implicature, not cancellable. Constant (2012) shares this 'conventional' view for English. CT but not 'list CT' has unresolved sub-questions. CF is shown to occur via alternative question (AltQ), which has the exhaustivity condition that exactly one disjunct holds. CT and CF constructions are claimed to be cross-linguistically witnessed.

The chapter by Katsuhiko Yabushita (Partition Semantics and Pragmatics of Contrastive Topic) reviews two existing approaches to Contrastive Topic: one is viewing Contrastive Topic as an information-structural discourse-regulating device on a par with focus, the other one analyzes a contrastive marker as a focus-sensitive operator with its inherent semantic and pragmatic content. The former approach is claimed to be not general enough as a theory of contrastive topic because it cannot be extended to non-canonical examples of Contrastive Topic such as sentences that have more than one instance of Contrastive Topic and/or no focused phrase (this multi-CT was previously discussed (see Lee's chapter); furthermore, it does not address the implicational/presuppositional features of Contrastive Topic. In contrast, the alleged imlicatures and/or presuppositions proposed by the latter approach in the literature can easily encounter counterexamples or are found to be easily cancellable. Therefore, the author proposes a new analysis based on Stokhof's and Groenendijk's partition semantics of questions and answers, which he claims is empirically more adequate. In particular, the new analysis characterizes a Contrastive Topic sentence as a direct answer to a sub-question and accounts for the implicational/presuppositional features of Contrastive Topic in terms of 'conversational' (as opposed to 'conventional' (see Lee's chapter for the 'conventional' claim)) implicatures arising as the addressee infers the reasons why the speaker opts to answer the sub-question derived from the question under discussion, which may be explicit or implicit, instead of the question itself.

Katalin É. Kiss's chapter (Deriving the Properties of Structural Focus) is centrally concerned with focus. It proposes a theory of structural focus derived via focus movement which can account for all the focus-related facts attested in Hungarian. Focus movement is analyzed as the establishment of a syntactic predicate-subject structure which expresses quantificational predication. The subject of the specificational construction determines a set which the predicate (the focus-moved constituent) identifies referentially. It is the referential identification of the set determined by the background which is predicted to entail the exhaustive listing of its members. The subject of the predication is associated with an existential presupposition and the referential identification of the set consists in the exhaustive listing of its members. Consequently, the exhaustivity feature of the focus is not asserted but entailed. Furthermore, the background is predicted to be associated with an existential presupposition. The specificational predicate-subject of predication (i.e. the focus-background) articulation of the sentence does not correlate with the division into new and given information since the background can also be new and the listing of the members of the set (i.e. the focus) can also be given. Moreover, the paper also claims that there is no direct correlation between focus-background articulation and the stress pattern of the sentence. The analysis proposed accounts for properties of the focus movement construction in Hungarian that current alternative theories cannot explain. It remains to be seen to what extent this account can be extended to cover focus construction in other languages.

Robert van Rooij's chapter (Topic, Focus, and Exhaustive Interpretation) proposes how to interpret focus exhaustively. It argues that exhaustive interpretation is sensitive to the denotation of discourse referents and that also 'topics' (Contrastive Topics, actually) should be interpreted exhaustively. As the author notes, it is now generally assumed that a difference should be made between non-contrastive thematic topic (with no focal component) and Contrastive Topic with focal component. This holds for topical expressions in general, whether they have a 'referential' or a 'quantificational' reading. The author shows that the different kinds of accents reflect the way the speaker economically encodes the information she wants to communicate, and proposes that topical accent gives rise to an extra implicature on top of the one due to exhaustive interpretation. This extra-topical implicature accounts for relevant scope data.

The chapter by Beáta Gyuris (The Interpretation of a "Contrast-Marking" Particle) is devoted to the interpretation of a "contrast-marking" particle in Hungarian, *csak*. This particle has developed from a focus-sensitive particle with an exclusive interpretation analogous to English *only*. It is shown that the necessary and sufficient conditions for the appearance in discourse of the "contrast-marking" particle indicate that it has the function of an adversative context marker. The semantic change in the course of which the exclusive particle acquired this meaning is due to a process of semantic reanalysis assumed to have taken place in order to avoid pragmatic overload. The adversative context marker can appear in structures where its exclusive counterpart can never show up. This meaning has spread to all three sentence types where it can appear in contemporary Hungarian (declaratives, yes–no interrogatives and imperatives), including structures where the particles cannot have an exclusive reading at all.

The chapter by Svetlana McCoy-Rusanova (Scalar Implicatures, Presuppositions, and Discourse Particles: Colloquial Russian *–to*, *že*, and *ved'* in Combination) tackles the problem of interaction between multiple discourse particles in colloquial Russian. It examines how presuppositions and/or implicatures contributed by individual particles are combined to account for connotations which arise in utterances containing multiple particles. It is shown that the context-invariant meaning of individual particles is preserved in utterances containing particle combinations. With respect to the sets evoked by combined particles, the result is not a simple intersection or union of sets since one of the particles assumes narrow scope on a contrastive/focused term, while the other takes a wide, sentential scope. The author points out that a question still to be settled has to do with the exact nature of the connotations expressed by multiple discourse particles. A promising solution is to account for them—at least partly—in terms of scalar implicatures. The characterizaion of the connotation could also benefit from contrastiveness research. Contrastiveness within closed sets versus that operating in open sets and the properties that result from the intersections of these sets (the particle combinations) lend themselves well to the discussion of the nature of contrast.

II. Polarity, Alternatives, Exhaustivity and Implicatures

The chapter by Kratzer and Shimoyama (Indeterminate Pronouns: The View from Japanese) (a reprint of their 2002 paper with the abstract newly added for this volume) treats the quantificational system in Japanese, making use of so-called indeterminate pronouns along with German *irgendein* indefinites, which take on existential, universal, interrogative, negative polarity, or free-choice interpretations depending on what operator they associate with. Such systems are claimed to be cross-linguistically witnessed. This chapter provides a first step toward answering the question why such systems look so different from more familiar systems by presenting an analysis of the German determiner *irgendein* from a Japanese point of view.

It uses Hamblin question semantics, extended to indefinite phrases, particularly Japanese indefinites. Indefinite phrases denote sets of individual alternatives, and most lexical items denote a singleton set. For instance, in the Japanese interrogative sentence *Dare(-ga) nemutta* (who slept), *dare* 'who' denotes the set of all humans whereas the verb *nemutta* ('slept') denotes a property (Lee 1997 indicates a *wh*-indefinite has the same domain as its corresponding *wh*-word domain adopting a Hamblin semantics). Alternatives can via 'pointwise' functional application expand to a higher type, which results in a set of propositional alternatives of the form {'*a* slept', '*b* slept', '*c* slept', etc.}. The alternatives keep expanding until they meet a propositional operator. This Hamblin style semantics becomes an essential part in the relation between free-choice indefinites and modals. They claim that free-choice indefinites induce maximal widening of the set of alternatives. However, unlike Kadmon and Landman (1993), where 'domain widening' always creates a stronger statement, the purpose of domain widening of free-choice indefinites in modal contexts can also be 'weakening'. For instance, the statement 'you can borrow the algebra book or the biology book' is weaker than the statement 'you can borrow the biology book'. Weakening is to avoid a false exhaustive inference. They also introduce a notion of 'distribution requirement,' which says that 'for every proposition in the alternative set, there has to be an accessible world in which it is true.'

This work remains influential, although there is some resistance to the above overall 'propositional move' replacing the treatment of indefinites as Heimian variables (Giannakidou and Quer 2013).

The chapter by Jinyoung Choi (Free Choice Without Domain Widening) attempts to clarify the notion of domain widening (DW) to discover the source(s) of polarity sensitivity. The author claims that two distinguishable phenomena, i.e. "proper domain widening" and "domain not-narrowing", have been commonly discussed under the notion of DW in the previous literature. The "proper domain widening" is Kadmon and Landman's (1993) DW, where a polarity item widens the contextually salient domain and includes contextually marginal entities, and the other one is Kratzer and Shimoyama's (2002, and this volume) DW, where a polarity item prohibits its domain to be narrowed down to any subset of the given domain. By showing that Korean polarity sensitive items do not necessarily involve the indefinite root *amwu-*, which the author argues to be the morphological incarnation of proper DW, the author suggests "domain not-narrowing" is more crucial to create polarity sensitivity, and presents as two independent sources for polarity sensitivity in Korean, the particles *-na* 'or' and *-lato* 'even' that *amwu-* or the other indefinite root *wh-* combines with. As for the semantics of *-na* 'or', she builds on Dayal's (1997) and von Fintel's (2000) accounts of *-ever* free relatives, and her analysis of *-lato* 'even' extends the scope theory of *even* items in Guerzoni (2003, 2005).

The chapter by Yoonhee Choi and Chungmin Lee (Expletive Negation and Polarity Alternatives) investigates the role of expletive negation (ExN) and its relation to licensing predicates. ExN has been analyzed based on two views in the literature: the expletive view (J. Dubois 1994; Rey-Debove Josette and Alain Rey 1993 among others) and the negative view (Jespersen 1917: Damourette and Pichon's discordance analysis 1911–1940; Martin 1987; van der Wouden 1994 among others). The expletive view, however, does not comply with the principle of compositionality (Frege). The negative view cannot account for cross-linguistic variation of ExN either. For instance, in Korean and Japanese, ExN is licensed by positive predicates. An alternative explanation is that ExN-licensing predicates form a subcase of nonveridicality (Knüppel 2001; Choi and Lee 2009; Yoon 2009; 2013 among others), which introduces polarity alternatives (p and $\neg p$) of an embedded complement (Hamblin 1973; Martin 1987; Giannakidou 1997 among others). In this chapter, Choi and Lee adopts this nonveridical analysis and extend it to ExN-licensing predicates in Korean, Japanese and French (cf. Giannakidou 1997).

The under-generation problem of nonveridicality in Korean and Japanese is solved by means of veridicality-suspension raised by the Qcomp. The over-generation problem of nonveridicality is accounted for by restricting the predicates to neg-raisers or neg-raiser holders in their lexical meaning. The chapter thus overcomes Giannakidou's 'veridical' problem and also provides a new theoretical perspective in studies of ExN: the interpretation of ExN exhibits the same pattern as that of positively biased negative questions both in syntactic makeup and in pragmatic implicature. The ExN and its interaction with licensing predicates is necessitated to capture the process of the expletive interpretation. However, pragmatically, ExN implicates that the attitude holder has a higher belief toward p than $\neg p$.

The chapter by Lim (On the Distribution and the Semantics of the Korean Focus Particle *–lato*) is about the Korean focus particle *-lato*, which is usually translated as 'even'. Since Karttunen and Peters (1979) and Rooth (1985), many scholars have paid attention to the peculiar nature of the focus particle 'even' and its cross-linguistic counterparts: the implication (which is assumed as conventional implicature according to Karttunen and Peters 1979, but is assumed as presupposition by many consequent studies) introduced by 'even' seems to be unexpectedly changed under negation and downward-entailing environments. To account for this, two major theories are proposed: the scope theory, according to which 'even' must take wide scope over negation or elements introducing downward-entailing environments, and the lexical ambiguity theory, according to which there are two 'even's, the positive polarity item 'even' and the negative polarity item 'even'. One of the suggested evidence which allegedly supports the lexical ambiguity theory is that in languages other than English there are lexical items which can be translated as 'even' but can appear only under downward-entailing environments: German *auch nur* and Italian *anche solo*. Against the lexical ambiguity theory, however, Guerzoni (2003, 2006) argues that these items can be decomposed into the part corresponding to the additive particle (German *auch* and Italian *anche*) and the part corresponding to the exclusive particle (German *nur* and Italian *solo*), and that the apparent NPI-like behavior of these particles is due to the fact that the additive particle and the exclusive particle take different scopes with respect to negation or downward-entailing operators, to avoid the presupposition clash between the exclusive particle and the additive particle. Lim's analysis is basically based on Guerzoni's: like Guerzoni (2003, 2006), he claims that *-lato* can be decomposed into the covert exclusive particle (similar to English *merely*) and the additive particle *-to* (similar to English *also*). In addition to this, the author further focuses on the unique distributional properties of *-lato*: that is *-lato* is acceptable under the scope of attitude report predicates and modals, unlike *auch nur* or *anche solo*. To account for this, he proposes that the additive presupposition that *-to* in *-lato* introduces is weaker than that of *auch* in *auch nur*, which then does not clash with the other presuppositions of the covert exclusive particle and thus successfully contributes to the interpretation of *-lato* in attitude predicates and modals.

Mingya Liu's chapter (Negative Entailment, Positive Implicature and Polarity Items) proposes a novel account of *only*, *all* and *no* as (anti-)licensors of polarity items. The author shows that polarity items can be pragmatically licensed, 'pragmatically' meaning that they can appear in one sentence but be licensed by another one with appropriate logical properties. Negative polarity items (NPIs) are licensed both in and outside the focus of *only*. Following Horn (2002), the author assumes that *only* is semantically conjunctive and that it licenses NPIs by its exclusive entailment that is negative. Without turning to Horn's distinction of asserted/inert entailment, the author shows that it is not to the prejacent but to the exclusive entailment that NPIs such as *any*, *ever* and minimizers contribute their domain widening (Kadmon and Landman 1993) function. Thus, she attributes the challenge of *only* for NPI theories not to lie in the notion of downward monotonicity but in the compact packaging of two propositions with different monotonicity properties in one single sentence. In the case of positive polarity items (PPIs), the author argues that they can co-occur with the anti-additive quantifier *no N* if intonation or enriched context makes it a contrastive negation or denial. The anti-licensing fails due to a positive implicature (PI) that performs pragmatic licensing and it is to this PI that PPIs contribute their meaning. In the case of *all Ns*, the occurrence of NPIs in its restriction renders the weak (negative) implicature more prominent, whereas that of PPIs does not. This argues for a bi-directional view on polarity effects, that is, there is a pragmatic effect, e.g., the strengthening of a conversational implicature (in the case of universal quantifiers *all Ns*) or a negative entailment (in the case of *only*) by NPIs. The author suggests that future research should also pay attention to the question of how the presence of polarity items in discourse affect sentence processing and reasoning.

Uli Sauerland's chapter (Disjunction and Implicatures: Some Notes on Recent Developments) discusses the interaction of scalar implicatures and disjunction. He focusses on two domains that have played a role in the debate between the pragmatic and grammatical approaches to scalar implicatures: multiple disjunctions and free-choice phenomena. He shows that at present the grammatical approach predicts an unattested reading for multiple disjunctions, namely one that would be derived by treating each disjunction as exclusive xor. Such an interpretation of "a or b or c" would exclude scenarios where exactly two disjuncts are true, but should admit the one where all three disjuncts are true. While it is easily derivable on the grammatical implicature approach, it is clearly unavailable. Sauerland therefore suggests that other data where local implicature computation has been shown to be available in the scope of disjunction, namely, the cases of so-called Hurford's disjunction, could be analyzed as a metalinguistic repair strategy.

A second problem of the grammatical approach, Sauerland discusses comes from free-choice phenomena. Sauerland introduces the analysis of free-choice inferences by Fox (2007). In Fox's approach, free-choice inferences arise from the recursive computation of scalar implicatures. However, Fox's analysis is challenged by scope data that point to a difference between scalar implicatures and free-choice inferences. In particular, free-choice inferences seem to more strongly require narrow scope than scalar implicatures when they are embedded under a universal quantifier. Instead Sauerland suggests that free-choice disjunction lexically encodes the free-choice meaning, but that this disjunction is furthermore a positive polarity item.

The chapter by Ezra Keshet (Scalar Implicatures with Alternative Semantics) examines several challenges to the standard Horn-Scale analysis of scalar implicature and proposes a new system based on the alternative semantics of Kratzer and Shimoyama (this volume). Following the early proponents of embedded implicatures (Chierchia 2002, Fox 2004, 2006), it proposes an embeddable exhaustive operator *Exh*, akin to the overt word "only". The key insight is that *Exh* operates over alternative propositions generated via Kratzer and Shimoyama's system of indefinites (extended to disjunctions by Alsonso-Ovalle 2005). Such propositions each include a specific plural individual, rather than a quantification over individuals; for instance, "*Exh* Paul read The New York Times or The Boston Globe" is equivalent to "Paul only read The New York Times or Paul only read The Boston Globe."

This system avoids problems (pointed out by Chierchia 2002) arising in the combination of disjunction and quantification, as well as problems in complex quantifiers like "more than two" (Krifka 1999). In essence, reducing these cases to propositions containing only individuals, not quantifiers, prevents the issues inherent in other systems. For instance, "Paul read more than two books" operates over alternative groups comprising more than two books and asserts that for one such group, Paul only read the books in that group.

This analysis can also properly treat Contrastive-Topic-like scalar implicatures (see Lee 2006), unlike other systems relying on an exhaustive operator.

III. Quantificational Expressions

The chapter by Lawrence Horn (*Almost* et al.: Scalar Adverbs Revisited) examines the proximal and polar components of *almost*, *barely* and other proximatives and presents a solution by *assert*, reviewing Sadock's (1981) and other competing analyses. Sadock proposed that *a almost Ø'd* is true if a in fact Ø'd: *Chris almost died* entails that Chris approached dying and conversationally implicates that Chris didn't die. Given that *barely* = *almost not*, *Dana barely survived* would likewise implicate, not entail, that Dana in fact survived. One persistent problem is the resistance of the *almost* $\varphi \rightarrow$ *not* φ implication to cancelation. Assertability involved in addition to entailment is presented as a new solution.

The chapter by Jae-Il Yeom (Interpretations of Numerals and Structured Contexts) explains how numerals get the meaning of 'at least' or 'at most'. Neo-Griceans claim that numerals constitute a semantic scale and that the semantic meaning of each numeral 'n' is 'at least n'. In the traditional analysis, the 'exactly' meaning is derived with the help of the scalar implicature that no stronger alternative with a larger number is true. However, it has been observed that numerals do not behave like other scalar terms. To account for the observations, Krifka (1999) and Geurts (2006) take a semantic approach, assuming that a numeral has the semantic meaning of 'exactly' and that it can get the 'at least' meaning pragmatically. Still, they cannot explain, Yeom claims, how a numeral can get the 'at most' meaning. Carston (1998) and Breheny (2008) take a pragmatic approach and claim that the meaning of a numeral is determined by the context. But they do not explain precisely how the actual meaning of a numeral is determined and how the meaning of a numeral is restricted. Yeom also takes a pragmatic approach. He shows that numerals do not constitute a semantic scale, and that numerals themselves do not have the meaning of 'at least' or 'at most', just like other scalar terms. He claims that a numeral gets such a reading in the scope of a quantifier. He assumes that there are two kinds of scalarity involved in interpreting numerals: the basic scalarity among numerals and the scalarity of unlikelihood. The basic scalarity is involved when each member in the domain of a quantifier is considered. It requires us to consider only the maximal numbers of elements involved in the interpretation of the numeral. The scalarity of unlikelihood, which is determined by background knowledge, orders alternative sentences with a different numeral. The two scales determine the ordering among alternative sentences with respect to the maximal numbers of elements involved in the quantifier domain. Then the numeral mentioned in the sentence is considered an upper limit or lower limit value. This leads to the 'at most' reading or 'at least' reading of the sentence uttered. The 'at least/most' reading of a sentence can be converted to the 'at least/most' interpretation of the numeral in the sentence in some cases, but not in others, depending on what quantifier is involved. When there is no explicit quantifier involved in a sentence, a universal quantifier over epistemic alternatives is provided by the support conditions of a statement.

The chapter by Chidori Nakamura (Focus Particle *Mo* and *Many/Few* Implicatures on Numerals in Japanese) aims to show that it is possible to give a single formal semantic content to the many/few 'mo', and various 'many/few' interpretations, which have been mentioned in the descriptive literature (Numata 1986 etc.), are proposed to be explained by scope differences of the mo phrases. For the semantics of the many/few mo, the chapter gives mo in a sense a lexical meaning, using Fernando and Kamp's (1996) formalization of the quantifier 'many,' which employs the possible world semantics. And together with the substitution mechanism of alternatives, the many/few *mo* phrases are unified as a single 'quantifier-*mo*.' This 'Q-*mo*' correctly predicts various co-occurrence restrictions of 'mo' (e.g. 'one-person-*mo*' in affirmation/negation). The semantic description of *mo* here, which contains a value c within the transitive order of probabilities, reveals the nature of the notion 'unlikely' (Rooth 1985)/'unexpectedness' (Numata 1986)/'less probable' (Krifka 1991) formally.

On the other hand, the numeral+classifier+*to*'even' (including 'a half/middle'+'even') construction in Korean functions as a negative polarity minimizer, whereas its positive counterpart requires a surprise/mirative particle *-ina* 'as many as' instead of *to*'even' after a numeral+classifier. Even in Japanese, the positive counterpart, although with the same morpheme *mo*, has a different prosody, with emphatic focus on the numeral (Lee 2002). A. debate between lexicalists (or NPI theorists) (Rooth 1985, Rullmann 1997 a.o.) versus scope theorists (Wilkinson 1997 a.o.) cannot be said to have been settled.

The chapter by Leah R. Paltiel-Gedalyovich and Jeannette Schaeffer (Scales and Non-scales in (Hebrew) Child Language) reports adult and child knowledge of the generalized scalar implicature (GCI) of disjunction, the non-scalar 'Allover' GCI and the particularized No-contrast implicature. The contributions of scales, generalization and relational complexity to the developmental difficulty of phenomena at the semantic–pragmatic interface are discussed. Results show that children as old as 9-years do not demonstrate adultlike knowledge of the scalar GCI of disjunction or the No-contrast PCI, while the 'Allover' GCI is demonstrated at 5 years. The authors conclude that the quaternary-level relational complexity of the later developing implicature and the ternary-level complexity of the earlier developing implicature, and that the pattern is not dues to the involvement of scales or the generalized versus particularized nature of the implicature.

IV. Questions and Speech Acts

The chapter by Manfred Krifka (Negated Polarity Questions as Denegations of Assertions) takes up a long-standing problem in the interpretation of negation in questions, first pointed out in 1981 by Robert Ladd. Questions can contain an "inner", or propositional, negation, as in *Did John NOT come to the party?* Such questions ask whether the proposition 'John did not come to the party' is true or not. They also can contain an "outer" negation, as in *Didn't John come to the party?* This results in a biased question; in typical uses, the speaker believes that John came to the party, but wants to give the addressee the occasion to confirm that. This outer negation has been a long-standing problem for semantic analysis. Krifka recapitulates the various accounts that have been developed, which typically involve scoping of negation over an operator outside of the proposition, like a *verum* operator (roughly, 'Is it not true that John came to the party?'). Krifka, too, proposes that negation has scope over an extra-propositional operator, but for him, this is a speech act operator. For this to work, he has to develop a theory in which speech acts, which are not propositions, can be negated, which he relates to the known case of denegation of speech acts as in *I don't promise to come to your party*. In this case, the speaker makes it clear that he or she refrains from making the speech act: *I promise to come to the party*. Krifka suggests that in an outer negation question sentence like *Didn't John come to the party?* the speaker checks whether the addressee refrains from making the assertion, *John came to the party*. He argues that the biased interpretation of such questions (in contrast to a regular question like *Did John come to the party?*) can be derived from the kind of situation where such checking is a rational move by the speaker. In order for this proposal to work, Krifka has to develop a semantic framework in which speech acts are changes in so-called commitment spaces. A question changes a commitment space insofar as it invites certain reactions by the addressee, and for such changes the formal operation of negation can be defined in the usual way, as set complement.

The chapter by Ishihara (The Intonation of *wh*- and Yes/No-Questions in Tokyo Japanese) is an experimental study on the intonation patterns of *wh*- and Yes/No questions in Tokyo Japanese. It aims to provide insights into the semantic and phonological theories of focus. The experiment results show that the *wh-* question exhibits an F_0-prominence on the *wh*-phrase, while the Yes/No-question displays an F_0-prominence on the verb. The author proposes that a focus is assigned to the *wh*-phrase and to the V-T complex in each of *wh-* and Y/N questions, and shows that this unified account is compatible with the semantic theories of question and focus (Hamblin 1973, Rooth 1992). Furthermore, the author suggests that the prosodic effects of focus (focal F_0-rise and post-focal reduction) and the prosodic effect of givenness (F_0-reduction) are independent, by comparing the results with the ones in Féry and Ishihara (2007).

References

Alonzo-Ovalle, Luis and Paula Menendez-Benito 2015. eds. *Epistemic indefinites: Exploring modality beyond the verbal domain.* Oxford: Oxford University Press.

Féry, Caroline and Shinichiro Ishihara. 2016. eds. *The Oxford handbook of information structure.* Oxford: Oxford University Press.

Fox, Danny. 2007. Free Choice and the theory of Scalar Implicatures. In *Presupposition and Implicature in Compositional Semantics*, ed. Uli Sauerland and Penka Stateva, 71–120. Palgrave-Macmillan.

Giannakidou, Anastasia and Josep Quer. 2013. Exhaustive and non-exhaustive variation with free choice and referential vagueness: Evidence from Greek, Catalan, and Spanish. *Lingua* 126: 129–149.

Gutzmann, Daniel. 2015. *Use-conditional semantics.* Oxford: Oxford University Press.

Hamblin, C. 1973. Questions in montague english. *Foundations of Language* 10: 41–53.

Kadmon, Nirit and Fred Landman. 1993. *Linguistics and Philosophy* 16(4): 353–422.

Lee, Chungmin. 1997. Negative polarity and free choice: Where do they come from? In *Proceedings of the 11th Amsterdam Colloquium*, ed. P. Dekker, M. Stokhof and Y. de Venema.

Lee, Chungmin. 2003. Negative polarity in Korean and Japanese. *Bilingual Research* 22: 1–48.

Lee, Chungmin, Matt Gordon and Daniel Buring (Eds.) 2007. *Topic and focus: Cross-linguistic perspectives on meaning and intonation.* Springer.

McCready, Eric. 2014. Expressives and expressivity. *Open Linguistics* 1: 1, 53–70

Potts, Christopher. 2005. *The logic of conventional implicatures.* Oxford: Oxford University Press. (Revised version of 2003 UCSC dissertation 2005).

Roberts, Craige. 1996. Information structure in discourse: Towards an integrated formal theory of pragmatics, slightly revised from the version. In *OSU Working Papers in Linguistics*, ed. JaeHak Yoon and Andreas Kathol. Vol 49: *Papers in Semantics.* (It was re-published in *Semantics and Pragmatics* 5 (2012): 1–69).

Roberts, Craige. 2011. Information structure: Afterword. *Semantics and Pragmatics.*

Rooth, Rutz. 1985. Association with focus. University of Massachusetts Doctoral Dissertation.

Rullmann, H. 1997. Even, polarity, and scope. In *Papers in Experimental and Theoretical Linguistics*, ed. Martha Gibson, Grace Wiebe, and Gary Libben, vol. 4, 40–64. Department of Linguistics, University of Alberta.

Vallduvi, Enric and Maria Vilkuna. 1998. On Rheme and Kontrast. In *Syntax and semantics 29: The limits of syntax*, ed. Peter Culicover and Louise McNally, 79–108. San Diego: Academic Press.

Part I
Information Structure and Contrastiveness

Contrastive Topic, Contrastive Focus, Alternatives, and Scalar Implicatures

Chungmin Lee

Abstract This chapter attempts to establish Contrastive Topic (CT) and Contrastive Focus (CF) in relation to how their alternatives are evoked via their focal components involved and Question under Discussion (QUD) in discourse. CT, as part of Potential Topic, is claimed to generate conventional scalar implicature, not cancellable. CT but not 'list CT' has unresolved sub-questions. CF is shown to occur via alternative question (ALT-Q), which has the exhaustivity condition that exactly one disjunct holds. CT and CF constructions are cross-linguistically witnessed. CF, in parallelism with ALT-Q, may shed some light on the problematic exceptions to suspension of scalar implicatures in DE contexts such as antecedents of conditionals, and similar problems as well.

Keywords Contrastive topic • Contrastive focus • Potential topic • QUD • Conventional scalar implicature • Alternative question (ALT-Q) • Exhaustivity

1 Contrastive Topic

Sentential utterances in discourse are structured to optimize the exchange of information. Several dimensions of information structure have been identified by various authors: Topic and Focus, Topic and Comment, Topic (=Link), Tail and Focus, and finally Contrastive Topic and Contrastive Focus. As for topic-comment, the speaker of a sentence identifies something to talk about as a topic, and then

I would like to express my gratitude to Manfred Krifka for his comments on and improvement of style of part of an earlier version and an anonymous reviewer at ESSLLI 2013 for his/her comments on the workshop abstract. I also thank the series editor's (Marcel den Dikken) comments on style. Infelicities are mine. This work was funded by the Korean government through the National Research Foundation (Excellent Scholar) Grant No. 100-20090049.

C. Lee (✉)
Department of Linguistics, Seoul National University, Seoul 151-742, Republic of Korea
e-mail: clee@snu.ac.kr

C. Lee et al. (eds.), *Contrastiveness in Information Structure, Alternatives and Scalar Implicatures*, Studies in Natural Language and Linguistic Theory 91, DOI 10.1007/978-3-319-10106-4_1

makes a comment about it. Within the comment, there is a Focus that induces alternatives relevant for the interpretation of expressions. Information structure, particularly Focus, has the pragmatic purpose to improve discourse coherence, but it also can affect truth conditions.[1] This occurs if intonational focus is in reason clauses or if it is associated with adverbial operators such as *only*, *usually/always,* and *fortunately*.

Contrastive Topic (CT) and Contrastive Focus (CF) are natural as answers to explicit or implicit questions, and do not occur naturally in discourse initial sentence. Roberts (1996/2012) has introduced the notion of Question under Discussion (QUD), to explain the function of CT (and CF). The notion of QUD seems to be better equipped linguistically than the notions of simple 'Goal' in Ducrot (1972) and Merin (1999).[2] To illustrate, let us assume that there are people named Fred, Sue, and Kim, and things to eat such as beans, peas, and kimchi in the discourse settings (cf. Jackendoff 1972; Carlson 1983; von Fintel 1994).

(1)	a. Who ate what?	QUD
	b. What did *Fred, Sue and Kim* eat?	Potential Topic
	A: *They*$_{TOP}$ ate kimchi. (answer to (b))	Topic[3]
	c. Well, what about FRED? What did HE eat?	Sub-Q under (b)
(2)	FRED$_{CT}$ ate the beans.	CT

The QUD is recursively broken down into sub-questions. A sub-question is a strategic move to get a CT answer from a dominating QUD for Roberts. But what we crucially need is the stage of replacing a *wh*-question in QUD by a **Potential Topic**[3] (Lee 2006, 1999) consisting of a set of relevant alternatives, e.g., *Fred, Sue, and Kim* for (1b) or *beans*, *peas,* and *kimchi*, replacing *what* in the QUD. According to Büring (2003), the CT value of the CT utterance (2) is like a set of question meanings such as (3) or equivalently a set of a set of propositions such as (4).

(3) {What did Fred eat? What did **Sue** eat? What did **Kim** eat?}

(4) $[[\text{FRED}_{CT} \text{ ate the beans}]]^{ct} = \{\{x \text{ ate } y \mid y \in De\} \mid x \in De\}$ (Büring 2003)

A CT answer to either (1b) or (1c) has its alternatives minus the CT individual itself **unresolved**. Its neighboring relevant sub-questions have not been resolved, and so the unresolved part gives rise to a **conventional scalar implicature**.

---

[1]See a scenario of truth-conditional reason clauses. [Pat had two daughters Bertha and Aretha. Aretha is indispensable to him in his business. He had made a commitment to marry one of the daughters one of the sons of a man who once saved his life. There were two such sons, the elder son Clyde and the younger son Derek. Because of a custom of seniority, an elder son had to marry before his younger brothers. The best thing to do was to marry Bertha to Clyde, as he actually did.] Evaluations: (1) The reason he married Bertha$_F$ to Clyde was that Aretha was indispensable in the business. **true** (2) The reason he married Bertha to Clyde$_F$ was that Aretha was indispensable in the business. **false** (Dretske 1972, Rooth 1999). This has to do with Contrastive Focus to be treated shortly. For adverbial operators, see Rooth (1992, 1995, 1999).

[2]Their Argumentative Goal has a similar function but it seems to go afar, in a linguistically less predictable way. See a recent discussion by Roberts (2012).

[3]This is a definite anaphoric pronoun. As a sentential Topic, a proper noun and other definite nouns including a generic subject can appear.

A question is asked to resolve decision problems (van Rooij 2003; Merin 1999). A Topic answer, as in (1b), is anaphoric to the Potential Topic as a whole and leaves nothing unresolved. I claim that the questioner faces a decision problem that involves a Potential Topic as a frame in the context. The question with a Potential Topic is not resolved completely by a CT answer. A question as its set of resolving answers must provide an *exhaustive* list of individuals or predicates in the Potential Topic set[3]; a CT answer in (2) is just a *partial* answer. Of course, if we provide a **list CT** (Lee 2000) answer as (5) (with a final fall in English and with an intonation different from the regular CT in Korean), it can be complete and there is no need for an implicature.

(5) FRED_{CT} ate the beans, SUE_{CT} the peas, and KIM_{CT} kimchi. (In pondering.)

A partial CT answer leaving the Potential Topic question only partially resolved forces the generation of an implicature concerning the rest of the Potential Topic set. Büring did not investigate the conveyed meaning part in detail.[4] He and some other researchers conceive of the implicature thus generated as simply "**conversational." But CT marking cross-linguistically is a marked "linguistic device"** with its special CT intonation, like the B accent or L + H * LH% in English and other CT intonations in German (T accent) and French (C accent, Marandin et al. 2002) or lexical CT markers in Korean, Japanese, Chinese, Vietnamese and Aymara. Korean *–nun* and Japanese *–wa* with a high tone for CT nominals, predicates, adverbials, and sentences and no high tone for non-contrastive Topic. In contrast, Vietnamese *–ty*, Aymara *–sti* and Chinese *–ne* are used exclusively for CT, not for Topic at the same time. For the French C accent CT, a high tone starts at the beginning of the CT phrase (to avoid a conflict with a natural phrase end rise in French presumably). See an analogous S initial rise in a CT S in Lee (2000). Lambrecht's (1996) denial of "contrastive" topic and Chiarcos's (2011) degree of salience in context may not treat these morphologically distinct CT markers and/or equivalent intonations.[5] Hence we should assume that this implicature is in fact a **conventional** implicature, an implicature that is tied to certain linguistic form features and cannot be canceled (Constant 2012 joins my conventionality claim). To see this, observe the contrast that we get in case we remove that linguistic form feature; in this case we end up with a mere conversational scalar implicature that can be canceled. This is happening in (6), whereas in (7) the implicature generated

[4]Buring presents a CT sentence with information focus in it following the German pattern but we can have just a CT phrase without a focal part in its sentence in other languages such as English, Korean and Japanese. *She* $\textit{APPLIED}_{CT}$ is a CT utterance with no separate focal part in it. *She* is a Topic. VP CT will be discussed.

[5]In Ngwo, a Bantu language, an utterance initial rising tone occurs for a CT, although the contrasted element (ηε^m 'meat') is located at the end. This shows that in our mind the contrast is preplanned. Observe: (15) ma/ nde⁻ ηε^m 'I ate meat_{CT}' (but not vegetables) (Lee 2000).

by the CT-marked utterance cannot be canceled (Lee 2000, 2007 = 2002, 2006 for English, Korean and other languages; Constant 2012 for English).[6]

(6) Most of the roommates ate kimchi. In fact, all of them did.
(7) MOST_{CT} of the roommates ate kimchi. #In fact, all of them did.

The CT intonation with its high boundary tone H% at the end of an intonational phrase signals the speaker's **uncertainty** (Ward and Hirschberg 1985) in the partial CT answer. (2) is partial with regards to the predicate meanings of the entire Potential Topic set and (7) is partial with regards to those of the entire Potential Topic set of scalar values on the quantificational scale. The partial CT assertion is concessively admitted by the speaker, and the unresolved part is left as a semantically elliptical proposition starting with a concessive *But*. (2) can be continued by a stronger version of the conventional implicature in (8a) and a weaker version by (9). Alternatives cannot co-occur with an additive, as in (8b).

(8) a. *But Sue and Kim did not eat kimchi.*
b. # *Sue and Kim ate kimchi, too.*
(9) ***I do not know*** *what Sue and Kim ate.*
(see Sauerland (2004) about conversational scalar implicatures; Grice (1975))

People seem to manipulate or exploit the implicature of negating stronger alternatives. If an investigator asks (10), (11) is used by the suspect. Hirschberg (1985) established a wide range of scalar implicatures by extending Horn's entailment scale to pragmatic scale, but she has no notion of CT crucially involved here. Not only individuals but also a predicate of type <*e*, *t*>, a modifier of type <<*e*, *t*>, <*e*, *t*>>, and a proposition of type <*t*>, I claim, can be CT-marked and form scales (to be discussed). Therefore, not only arguments but also functions and propositions can be asked by *wh*-words in QUD: *What did he do about the food? What happened?* CT in root clauses is speaker-oriented, and even a CT embedded in the complement of *say* and *believe* shows the speaker's attitude, not the attitude of the matrix subject. (11a) is about the speaker's own actions and the CT is meant to convey (11b). The weaker implicature version ~ KspP, that is, that it is not the case that the speaker knows P, is not an adequate representation. If a negative CT

---

[6]Hara (2006) also views the J CT *–wa* as generating 'conventional' implicature and Vermeulan (in Neelman and Vermeulan 2012) is in support of it, although Oshima (2002) differently views it as generating 'presupposition.' Lee (2007 = 2002) indicated that cancelation of CT implicatures would be possible only with heavy epistemic hedge, which can connect even contradictory sentences. This is contra Yabushita in this volume. Yabushita's "secrecy" issue sounds interesting (*$Mary_{\text{CT}}$ came but I cannot tell about others*) but its expression is somewhat against sincerity condition or cooperative principle and cannot be in the realm of conveyed meanings and the 'secrecy' is still negative to the hearer, who remains ignorant about other alternatives. Partitively quantified CT expressions in Korean take *–nun*: *Roommate-tul-ey/cwung taypwupwun/celpan isang/sey myung-**un** kimchi-rul mek-ess-ta* 'Most/more than half/three of/among the roommates ate kimchi' like (7) but non-partitive counterparts take *-ka* in Korean like (6). The same happens in Japanese.

utterance is given as a reply, a polarity-reversed weaker affirmative implicature arises, as in (12b).

(10) Did you give money to the Governor?
(11) a. [I made a few phone calls to her]$_{CT}$ (*–nun* is attached to the verb *–kel* "make" in K)
b. ~> But I did not even meet her. How can I give money to her?
(12) a. [I did not give money to her]$_{CT}$
b. ~> But I just offered some golf plays.

There can be multiple CTs in a sentence. A multivariable CT operator has been proposed (Lee 2000): $CT_{x,\ y,\ z}$ [DP_x DP_y DP_z give]—each CT-bound DP has its own contextual set of alternatives and respective conventional scalar implicature. In Japanese and Korean, up to three CTs tend to be barely possible due to a processing constraint, as follows:

(13) emeni-nun$_{ct}$ tongsayng-hanthey-nun$_{ct}$ cangnankam-un$_{ct}$ sa-cwusi-ess-e
'Mother$_{CT}$ bought my younger brother$_{CT}$ a toy$_{CT}$.'

But English allows for only two CTs due to intonational restrictions (Lee 2007), as in (14).

(14) a. Sam$_{CT}$ ate kimchi$_{CT}$. (But others ate cheese.)
b. Mary$_{CT}$ just applied$_{CT}$. (But Judy has been accepted.)

In Korean, a relative clause can contain a CT but not a non-contrastive Topic (*Sue-nun*$_{CT}$ *cohaha-nun yenghwa* "a movie Sue$_{CT}$ likes"; its head nominal is already topical in derivation (Lee 1973), but a complement clause can contain both. A CT in a relative clause also generates conventional scalar implicatures. A set of multiple CT contextual alternatives resists an easy interpretation, requiring expensive processing costs with calculation of alternatives in proper contexts. [CT + **Focus**] in a sentence is not required in most languages (except in German). A partition semantics approach with cells and blocks is a possibility (Yabushita 2016) but the exact nature of the involved implicature is not easily characterized by this model.

Answers involving a complete sub-question CT look like pair-list interpretations of universal quantifier in a question responding to conjoined speech act questions (Krifka 2003). The universal quantifier as a generalized conjunction is employed here. But the more typical partial CTs lack information on other conjoinable alternatives in a Potential Topic set, except by implicature. A Potential Topic phrase consists of conjuncts (as in *Fred, Sue, and Kim* in (1)) but not disjuncts (Lee 2006; Onea and Steinbach 2012). For (10), there must be a (scalar) series of alternative conjoinable acts such as *make a call, meet her,* and *offer a golf ticket*, leading to the strongest act of *give*ing *money to the Governor*, as a Potential Topic. The stage of QUD with Potential Topic is most relevant to CT, and the questioner at that stage must have a *goal* (as in Ginzburg 1995 and van Rooij 2003, resolving levels of specificity in the context, etc.) and the goal can involve Potential Topic. Ducrot (1972) and Merin's (1999) *goal* is useful in explaining the concessive *But* (and general causal relations), although it is sometimes linguistically distant, involving nonlinguistic orientational acts. Although contextual dependency is heavy for CT, the presence of implicature is mandatory, hence it is conventional.

We already observed the scalar nature of CT implicatures in the examples. Remember the totality of a Potential Topic set, with regards to which CT is established. Even in the case of list-like examples such as I_{CT} *passed* in the context of you and I, a scale <I, you and I> is formed and the implicature negates the higher value "both you and I," leaving "you" to be negated because "I" has been affirmed in the utterance. The totality or sum in quantity (of individuals) by Potential Topic is always a higher value than a CT-marked referent. In the case of predicate CTs involving quality/property, different alternative predicates already form scales, no matter whether they are Horn's entailment scales such as <possible, necessary> or Hirschberg's pragmatic scales such as <date, be engaged, be married>, <apply, be admitted>, etc. Observe an example, as in (15).

(15) Mary applied$_{CT.}$ ~> But she was not admitted.
Apply she did. (CT meaning; bombastic meaning)

Our Potential Topic is conjunctive and not disjunctive, i.e., not inquisitive (in the sense of the term in Inquisitive Semantics (InqSem), see Groenendijk et al. 2011; Ciardelli et al. 2013). My claim that Topics are conjunctive (2006) is supported by Onea and Steinbach (2012), and that is why (16a Cf. <1>) and (17d) are non-felicitous.[7] In contrast, in the *As for* CT construction ('CT' I say because it is with B accent in Jackendoff 1972), the *not both* implicature of *or* is suspended, as in (16), no matter whether the predicate is individual-level or not, unlike in DP Topics without *as for* in English. As in (17a), if the original object is in the *as for* CT, its pronominal copy *them* must remain, whereas an object Topic without *as for*, leaves no pronominal copy, as in (17b). A disjoined DP object, as in (17c), with the "not both" scalar implicature, gives rise to a sluiced clause with *which*, requiring a choice between the previous two alternatives out of the inquisitive object. An inquisitive object can be a disjoined DP or an epistemic *wh*-indefinite positive polarity item (PPI) such as *someone/something* and *which*. The latter generates a sluiced clause with *which*. (17c) has: *I don't know which of the alternatives {oranges, bananas} Mary carried -> Did Mary carry oranges*$_{CF}$ *or bananas*$_{CF}$ (ALT-Q). However, if the disjunctive object is topicalized to function as a Topic, as in (17d), it results in an anomaly. In the *as for* CT construction, other monotone-decreasing elements such as *any* are not permitted, as in (17d). Apart from *as for*, what about is a CT-eliciting *wh*-question, as shown in (1c) above.

(16) a. As for linguists **or** philosophers, they are stubborn.<"not both" suspended: meaning 'both'>
Cf.<1>?*Linguists or philosophers are stubborn.
<2> Are linguists or philosophers stubborn?
b. As for the oranges **or** the bananas, they are next to the door. <"not both" suspended: meaning "both">

[7]I thank Darcy Sperlich and Luke Bates for confirming the judgments for (16) and (17). I also thank Greg Ward (at CLS 40) and Manfred Krifka (reading my draft) for appreciating my finding of anomaly in (17d).

(17) a. As for the oranges, Mary likes *(them).
b. Oranges, I like.
c. Mary carried oranges or bananas, I don't know which. (Cf. (45) with *neg> or*)
d. ?* Oranges or bananas, Mary carried.
e. *As for *any* linguists, they are stubborn. (Lee 2006)

The proposition which is partially admitted as a concession in a CT utterance may be incorporated into the Common Ground (CG), as we discussed mutual or public belief, being incorporated into the CG. But we cannot be quite sure about the non-at-issue proposition, which we call (conventional) implicature (but not presupposition). Therefore, it is not clear if this situation is what Baltag and Smets (2009) calls "uncertain information." It is just partially certain and uncertain for the rest and as a whole it may still be called "uncertain." The answerer's partial plus implicational meaning is conveyed to the questioner.

Some researchers including Roberts (2011) rarely admit CT to constituents other than subject (-like) nominals, predicates, and (temporal) adverbials and some are reluctant to admit even predicate CTs, which are cross-linguistically prevalent in various forms. Kuroda (1965) used the term "contrastive," which cannot distinguish between CT and CF. However, we notice a recent exception such as Jasinskaja's admission of predicate CT (2016) or "predicate doubling" in Slavic, which Lee (2002) investigated, using Russian data. Some simply confuse CT with CF, e.g., Choi (1999) calls *-nun* here (in VP) in [1] "Contrastive Focus," which is a misnomer. It is a typical CT in-situ, generating alternatives in contrast and evoking scalar implicatures (denying [Potential Topic total minus Inho = 'others']). Observe.

[1] Sohi-ka Inho-nun manna-ss-ta
S –NOM I –nun meet-PAST-DEC
"Sohi met Inho (but not others)"

[2] Inho-nun Sohi-ka manna-ss-ta
I –nun S-NOM meet-PAST-DEC
"*As for* Sohi, Inho met" (her translation has the CT marker *As for* before the Topic DP).

The sentence in [2], on the other hand, has a topicalized *–nun*-marked object, which she calls "Topic," apparently having CT in mind with 'prominence' underlined. This part is understandable but the topicalized (fronted) *–nun* DP can also function as a real, non-contrastive Topic. The CT in the Topic position gets a more marked CT intonation (to distinguish it from a non-contrastive Topic possibility) than that in mid-sentential (VP) position, as experimentally shown. Her discussion of German and English data may also need to consider CT intonations as well in addition to word ordering.

I also noticed an erroneous treatment in some other work that calls subject CT a "CF" erroneously in the following context:

[3] A: "Who came?"
nwu-ka w-ass-ni?
who-NOM come-PAST-DEC
B: Sohi-nun w-ass-e
S-nun come-PAST-DEC
'Sohi came.'

In [3A], the question has the subject *wh*-phrase, *nwu-ka*. Therefore, B's reply in [3B] with -nun is initially non-congruent because A expects a Focus subject exhaustively and the initially expected reply ought to be *Sohi-ka*$_{FOC}$. Some may mark the *-nun*-marking in [3B] as a little unnatural in this context. For B's reply with *–nun* to be properly interpreted, the DP should be a CT and B should have some relevant alternative nominals in mind to be contrasted with *Sohi* and A must be cooperative with B to understand each other. Otherwise, A may remain puzzled because of B's non-congruent reply with CT. CF cannot step in here; no ALT-Q (to be discussed) or immediately relevant alternative given in the context. A normal *wh-Q* simply evokes a Focus, pragmatically exhaustive. A Southern Ryukyuan has a Focus marker *du* for *wh-Q* subject and object and their corresponding answers consistently (Davis 2014). with the NOM and FOC markers separately in a declarative answer as in *Sohi-n*$_{Nom}$*-du*$_{Foc}$—for *taa*(who)*-du*$_{Foc}$ *suba-ba*$_{Acc}$ *fai*(ate)? 'Who ate soba?' and with the ACC and FOC markers as in *Sohi-ja*$_{Top}$ *suba-ba*$_{Acc}$*-du*$_{Foc}$ *fai* 'Sohi ate soba' for 'What did Sohi eat?'. In Korean, *wh-Q* subject and object and their answers happen to have subject and object markers with Focus on the core arguments. That's why the initially congruent question and answer pairs in [3A, B] must have the subject/NOM marker *-ka*$_{FOC}$. A CT is a sort of Topic with topicality as its subcategory, although it is topical and focal at the same time. Because of its focal component (scalar) alternatives are present. If it happens to be located at the default focus position in an utterance, it tends to give some more focal flavor (that is why some people like to have "foci") and if located at the topic position it tends to give more topical flavor. A CF is a sort of Focus with focality, as its subcategory. We must pay attention to the head nouns of 'Contrastive *Topic*' and 'Contrastive *Focus*.'

2 Contrastive Focus

Focus is marked typically by pitch accent to indicate new information (about Topic or CT), correct existing information, or make choice between alternatives. The first category is Information Focus (IF) and the other two categories belong, we claim, to Contrastive Focus (CF). IF is induced by a *wh*-question and CF by a disjunctive alternative question (ALT-Q, see below).

CF typically invokes a closed set of disjunctive alternative possibilities. Previous studies (Bolinger 1961; Chafe 1976; Rooth 1992, 1995; Schwarzschild 1999; Selkirk 1984, 2002; Kratzer and Selkirk (K&S) 2010; Katz and Selkirk 2011) all show different aspects of CF intuitively and innovatively but **explicit "CF-marking"** has rarely been proposed, analogous to "F-marking." We propose it via ALT-Q, arguing that CF-marking requires both semantic (/pragmatic) motivations and phonetic prominence. Cho and Lee (2012) experimentally showed that CF in English has significantly longer duration and greater intensity than information

(a) [[φ]] (b) [[?φ]]

Fig. 1 Simple propositions visualized

focus, though pitch was primarily affected by prosodic position (phrase initial versus noninitial). Various cases of CF, including correction, clefts, and CF-reduplication in English need CF-marking, correlated with ALT-Q. Cross-linguistic manifestations also require CF. ALT-Q is based on **immediately relevant alternatives** in the dynamic hearer–speaker information exchange. This may well be compatible with Pruitt & Roelofsen's (P&R) (2011) alternative disjunctive questions in Inquisitive Semantics. They show how *Sue drank wine* (φ) is simply informative with a single possibility (Fig. 1a) and *Did Sue drink wine* ($?\varphi$) is inquisitive with two possibilities of Sue's drinking wine and her not drinking wine, requesting a response (Fig. 1b) ($[[\varphi]]$ is inquisitive iff info(φ) $\notin [[\varphi]]$). A disjunctive YN-Q *Did Sue drink wine-or-beer*↑? (YN?Φ) is shown in Fig. 2a. A prototypical ALT-Q is: *Did Sue drink wine*↑*or did she drink beer*↓? (ALT?Φ) and its exclusive strengthening is represented in (Fig. 2b). From φ, 11 in a circle in Fig. 1 is a world in which Sue drank both wine and beer, 10 a world in which she drank wine but no beer (See Collins et al. (2014) for the inquisitive potential of appositive content with an indefinite NP antecedent for sluicing).

CF is argued to come overtly or covertly from ALT-Q, as an intermediate QUD in question–answer interlocution. ALT-Q consists of two or more underlyingly full interrogative clauses cross-linguistically, the first with a Q final rising high tone and the second (or last) with a Q final falling contour, joined by disjunction in English

(a) YN-Q [[Φ]] (b) ALT-Q $[[\Phi]]^{s}$ (S: strengthened)

Fig. 2 Disjunctive questions

and Korean. ALT-Q also manifests itself in other unique characteristics in various languages, distinct from a yes/no question with constituent disjunction in it. In English, the second clause can be elliptical except the element with CF but in many languages including K ellipsis is harder. In K, as a head-final language, clause-final Q marker is required for each disjunct clause of TP or VP at least. Observe an ALT-Q in (18).

(18) a. Did she dance$_{CF}$↑ or sing$_{CF}$↓?
b. kunye-ka chwum-ul chwu$_{CF}$-ess-ni↑ (animyen) noray-rul pwul$_{CF}$-ess-ni↓?
she-NOM dance-ACC dance-PAST-Q (if not) song-ACC sing- PAST-Q
c. 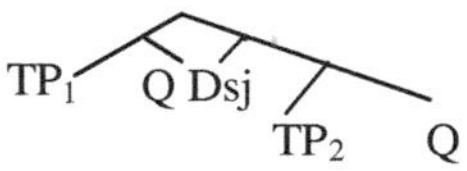

AltQ as disjoined polar Qs: Lee (2003), Pruitt et al. (2011), Uegaki (2012), similarly Krifka (2017); but not like Han and Romero (2004) or Guerzoni and Sharvi (2013), who have the highest Q.

Under total ellipsis, based on the common ground, just the two categorically disjunctive elements in CF with the core prosody of rise ↑ and fall ↓ (e.g., 'This↑ or this ↓?') can convey an ALT-Q. A final boundary tone H% in an ALT-Q signals something unresolved and a final falling contour in the second (or last) disjunct in an ALT-Q in E and K signals closure and 'exclusive strengthening,' proposed as an operator E by P&R, assimilated to some LF lexical meaning. Intonation is compositional (Pierrehumbert and Hirschberg 1990). Its conventional, "imposed" meaning is accepted by default, resulting in the exhaustive consequence "**exactly one** disjunct holds." Typically, if one disjunct holds, other disjuncts do not hold or are excluded. The exclusive component of an ALT-Q is not directly challengeable and thus constitutes a non-at-issue implication of a conventional implicature (Karttunen and Peters 1976) (or presupposition (Aloni and Egŕe 2008)). However, an ALT-Q may have the atypical forms of [P_{CF}↑ R_{CF}↑ or both$_{CF}$↓], [P_{CF}↑ R_{CF}↑ or neither$_{CF}$↓], or [P_{CF}↑ R_{CF}↑ both$_{CF}$↑ or neither$_{CF}$↓]. If 'both' or 'neither' holds, exclusion/inclusion becomes different.

If one CF-marked alternative is accepted in the reply and not challenged by the questioner, the question is resolved and the chosen possibility becomes mutual or public belief, being incorporated into the CG. The answer assertion commits the speaker to the proposition expressed and we can separate out the beliefs publicly attributed to each participant, as in (19) (adapted from Gunlogson 2003). Let $CG_{\{a,b\}}$ be the CG of a discourse in which a and b are the individual discourse participants (PB = public belief).

(19) a. PB_a of $CG_{\{a,b\}} = \{p: B_a p \in CG_{\{a,b\}}\}$
b. PB_b of $CG_{\{a,b\}} = \{p: B_b p \in CG_{\{a,b\}}\}$
c. CG of a discourse = $\{p \in \wp(W)$: p is a mutual belief of the participants of the discourse$\}$

In sharp contrast, a disjunctive yes/no Q (= YN-Q) (Q > ∨) rises at the end, as in (20).

(20) a. Did she drink coffee or tea↑?
b. kunye-ka coffee-*na* cha-rul masi-ess-ni?
she –NOM c -or tea-ACC drink-PAST-Q
Same as (20a).

The YN-Q (20) has no rise on the pre-disjunction element and has a single final rise in English and analogously in K. The disjunction marker *-na* in (20b) in K only functions as an operator of constituent disjunction in a YN-Q but not in an AltQ.

Strikingly in Chinese, the ALT-Q disjunction marker *haishi* (its associated core alternative constituents being CF-marked) and the YN-Q constituent disjunction marker *hou* are lexically distinct and the latter ends with the yes/no Q ending *ma*, unlike in AltQ.[8] Observe an ALT-Q in (21), both in matrix Q and embedded/indirect Q, as opposed to the latter in (22a). Korean has the predicative (YN-Q) disjunction marker *–kena*, distinct from nominal disjunction marker *–na*, as in (22b).

(21) a. ta shi tiao-wu le haishi chang-ge le?
she CF dance ASP AltQ-or sing ASP
'Did she dance or sing?' like (18a) in English.
b. caicai ta shi tiao-wu le haishi/*hou chang-ge le.
guess she FOC dance ASP AltQ-or/or sing ASP
'Guess whether she danced or sang.'
(22) a. ta shi tiao-wu le hou chang-ge le **ma**?
she FOC dance ASP or sing ASP YN-Q
"Did she dance or sing↑?'
b. ku yeca-ka chum-ul chwu-kena noray-rul pwul-ess-ni↑? (Korean)
the woman-NOM dance-ACC dance-or song-ACC sing-PAST-YN-Q
'Did she dance or sing↑?' (with the predicative disjunction *–kena*)

A YN-Q such as [1] *Is it raining*? has been considered as equivalent to an ALT-Q [2] *Is it raining or (is it) not (raining)*? but as syntactically *degenerate* (Karttunen 1977). However, the YN-Q [1] itself is foregrounded (by the **highlight** operation InqSem) and can readily generate relevant conversational implicatures such as *I may have to take an umbrella*, whereas the ALT-Q [2] (the YN-Q predicative disjunction *–kena* cannot be employed here in Korean: **Pi-ka o-kena an o-ni*↑? *"Is it raining or not raining↑?") directly expects an alternative between *It is raining* and *It is not raining*. Therefore, the ALT-Q between positive and negative has quarreling effects in most languages. Interestingly, however, the frequently used Chinese A-not-A question has no such quarrelling effects, except the mild effect of narrowing down the interlocutors' attention to the given utterance. A polarity ALT-Q like (23) cannot occur with the regular YN-Q ending *ma* or extrasentential Yes/No (*shi/bu-shi*) responses. For English, *no* seems to be possible in this particular case, as in Farkas and Roelofsen.[9] It has no bias regarding truth or polarity in Chinese.

[8] Krifka (p.c.) directed me to Karttunen (1977) for a similar distinction, *vai* in ALT-Q and *tai* elsewhere, in Finnish.

[9] Krifka (p.c.) drew my attention to the paper for this possibility in English.

(23) ni bu ni (*ma)? (as opposed to *ni ma*? "Is it greasy?")
greasy not greasy
'Is it greasy or not?'

A negative question must also come from two possibilities by highlighting, as in (24). But, whereas a positive question *Is she married?* is rather neutral, a negative question is biased towards its positive counterpart, particularly in its contracted form. This biased belief needs modeling, which InqSem currently lacks. Declarative questions (Queclaratives) such as *It's raining?* have been analyzed by modeling a bias involved in terms of commitment sets, contextual bias, controversiality (Gunlogson 2003). A commitment set, as a representation of an individual's dynamic *public* commitments rather than that of the individual's doxastic state should be relevant here. The addressee's commitment via a question in negation to prevent the neutral inquisitiveness of the positive question is the speaker's way of leading the conversation to the enriched CG. We also argue that expletive negation is rooted in the positive bias of negative question with matrix modal attitude verbs (often DE) such as 'fear' (Choi and Lee 2017).

(24) Isn't she married?—*Biased towards* "She is married."

The correction type of CF is phonetically most prominent but it is simply F-marked by Schwarzschild (1999) and Rooth (1992, 2007), although givenness is well appreciated by K&S. K&S reports, "The duration of a contrastive focus constituent is greater than the duration of a new constituent in the same sentential position." The notion of CF is semantically plausible and phonetically supported.

CF is licensed if a pair or more of **immediately relevant alternatives** are available in the discourse context. Typically one is given in the preceding context, and the other proposed by the speaker from the context, as an alternative not challengeable by the addressee and they together form an overt or covert ALT-Q. The representation for *RITA* in (25B) as (22b) is not enough. The focus value for IP_1 in (18b) is the set of alternatives to the proposition that *Rita married John*, where *Rita* is replaced by alternative individuals of type <*e*> in (25). But it is not simple replacement by any alternatives in the domain for a *wh*-Q. The immediately relevant pair of alternatives in rivalry and contrast matter here with an accommodated CF-accompanying ALT-Q, as in (28). It is a stage of speaker–hearer conflict on the contrastively focused issue elements. To form an ALT-Q, the answerer must have an immediately relevant alternative to impose, which the questioner may not challenge. In (25B), a refuting negation "**Sue** did not marry Sam" is implicated (to be in *no*). For simple F-marking, there is no restricted, explicit pair or list of immediately relevant alternatives of any corresponding constituent types. Such correctives and all explicitly refuting constructions form CF-marked ALT-Qs. [*not X but Y* (*X, Y* are identical sub-clausal categories)] (Lee 2009, in press) is a typical CF construction constituting metalinguistic negation (see also Horn 1989). (25) and (26) can also be effective with an anaphoric proposition from the context but we must make sure that we set up a list of **immediately relevant alternatives** to CF-mark them in an overt or covert ALT-Q. One alternative appears in the surface answer, CF-marked by inheritance from the previous ALT-Q. The possibility of **SUE**$_{CF}$ is rejected. A simple *wh*-information Q 'Who married Sam?' is different in replacing the *wh*-word with F-marked alternative from a set of contextually more open (though loosely relevant) alternatives in (27).

(25) A: Sue married Sam?
B: No, RITA married Sam.

(26) a. $[_{IP}$ Sue married Sam$]^1$
b. $[_{IP2} \sim 1$ C $[_{IP1}$ **Rita**$_F$ married Sam]]

(27) $[[IP_1]]^f = \{\lambda w\text{: marry}_w\ (x, \text{Sam}) \mid x \in De\}$
(cf. Mayr 2010, adopting Rooth 1992)

(25) A: Sue married Sam?

(28) Did **SUE**$_{CF}$ marry Sam↑ or did **RITA**$_{CF}$ marry Sam↓?
(From the **immediately relevant alternatives** set:
{**Sue** married Sam, **Rita** married Sam}) (Exactly one alternative holds.)

(25') B: No, RITA$_{CF}$ married Sam. ("No" is licensed by the highlighted/profiled question involving the denied alternative "**Sue**$_{CF}$ didn't marry Sam.")

A D-linked alternative *wh*-Q can be CF-marked, with clear alternative possibilities to reject, as in "Which lady married Sam, SUE↑ or RITA↓?" equivalent to (28). It is possible only if there are **immediately** relevant alternative referents presupposed in the context. It is distinct from ordinary *wh*-Qs that denote a set of multiple alternative possibilities, out of which one individual (say, *Rita*) that corresponds to the *wh*-word is chosen in the answer. It is simply F-marked. Observe (29).

(29) Who got married to Sam?
{λw. Mary got married to Sam in w, λw. Cindy got married to Sam in w, λw. Sue got married to Sam in w, λw. Rita got married to Sam in w...}

In the following discourse, a corresponding constituent in the parallel structure can be in CF:

(30) Q: Sam drove Mary's red convertible. What did he drive before that?
A: He drove her **BLUE**$_{CF}$ convertible.

(31) Did he drive her RED convertible or her BLUE convertible?

The CF-marked ***BLUE***$_{CF}$ in (30A) comes from an AltQ like (31). CF is on ***RED*** and ***BLUE***. CF avoids given information, "given" here. Exclusive (exhaustive) focus bears CF in context, as in (32). Similarly, a CF-marked "I" in English in (32) comes from an AltQ in speech context, as in (33).

(32) Pago **IO**$_{CF}$ 'I'$_{CF}$ll pay'

(33) ['Will YOU$_{CF}$ pay or shall I$_{CF}$ pay?'].

A reciprocal CF such as (34) comes ultimately from a reciprocal ALT-Q like (35).

(34) I told you: CARL$_{CF}$ sued the COMPANY$_{CF}$.

(35) I did not get it. (ALT-Q) Did CARL$_{CF}$ sue the COMPANY$_{CF}$ or did the COMPANY$_{CF}$ sue CARL$_{CF}$?

A clefted constituent in a cleft sentence also has CF if it is used for correction or contrast (cf. Prince 1978; Hedberg 2013). It comes from an ALT-Q again, as in (38).

(36) Did Sam break the window?
(37) No, it was SUE_{CF} who broke the window.
(38) Did SAM_{CF} break the window or did SUE_{CF} break the window?

The marker *–no-ho* in Japanese appears in various CF contexts such as the *yori* comparative and cleft-S.[10] Observe (39).

(39) *Meari-ga tabeta-no-wa piza-**no-ho**-da*
"What Mary ate was pizza, (not a hamburger)."

Yet another interesting CF phenomenon in English and a few other languages is CF-Reduplication, as in *salad*$_{CF}$*-salad*, *drink*$_{CF}$*-drink*, etc. It is viewed as a dynamic prototype (see Song and Lee 2011). Its denotation is determined as context changes and it is not so obvious and must be a probabilistic interactive decision problem.

(40) A: I want a drink.
B: Here, have some coke.
A: No, I want a *drink*$_{CF}$*-drink*.
[Do I want a drink like COKE_{CF} or do I want a *drink*$_{CF}$*-drink*?]
(immediately relevant alternatives?)

The denotation of the *drink*$_{CF}$*-drink* in contrast with *coke* (soft drink—nonalcoholic) is an 'alcoholic drink' by default (when a *drink* is offered, it is predominantly an alcoholic drink). But if beer or wine is offered, the same *drink*$_{CF}$*-drink* by the hearer may denote a "strong alcoholic drink," for example, whisky (a salient type of alcoholic drink) (but a prototypical nonalcoholic drink such as "water" for few people, depending on special context). *Salad*$_{CF}$*-salad* is not a marked salad such as meat salad or fruit salad. It is green vegetable salad for most native speakers of English as a "prototype." But still for some people it is "Ceaser salad" and for Russian-American community it is "potato-salad."

Interesting consequences of CF-marking appear in various ways. See its metalinguistic negation (MN) effect in (41). Cardinals forming an entailment scale normally invoke scalar implicatures, but not here in (41a). MN requires a separate scale.

[10] Yukaghir is reported to show subject nominal focus marking, which functions as a cleft-construction with the meaning of "It's me who sit," as in (1). The focus marking here must be CF. It has an infinitival (nominal) predicate source, suspending subject agreement (Malchukov 2013).

(1) Met-ek moda-l
I FOC sit-INF
'**I** sit.'

(41) a. Sam does not have $[2]_{CF}$ kids; (*but) he has $[3]_{CF}$ kids. (MN in Horn's definition, from ALT-Q)
b. A: Are you happy? B: (i) Are you happy or not? (Descriptive negation)
B': (ii) Are you happy or ecstatic?
'I am not happy; I am ecstatic.' (An MN reply; a surprise because A expected B answer. For surprise effects of CF, see Zimmermann 2007)

Downward-entailing (DE) contexts such as antecedents of conditionals, restriction of *every*, and even nonveridical contexts such as questions and imperatives typically suspend scalar implicatures. But the embedded question one can postulate would be an ALT-Q for QUD, as in (43), to derive the CF-marked cardinal $[two]_{CF}$. CF-marked alternatives in an ALT-Q are in contrast and mutually exclusive (choice of one negating the other), superseding scalarity between them. Exclusion of the other alternative turns out to be equivalent to making an exception to suspension of scalar implicatures but the processes involved are different. Such exhaustivity effects in DE contexts can be explained by conventional CF semantics, rather than by conversational implicature. CF-marking can occur virtually in all DE contexts. For this phenomenon, the explanation that localists such as Chierchia (2004) offer seems less intuitive.

(42) If John has $[two]_{CF}$ *cars*, the third one parked outside must be someone else's.
(43) Does he have $[two]_{CF}$ ↑ or $[three]_{CF}$ ↓ cars?

Similarly, Sevi (2005) offers some echoic *wh*-Q such as (44), having wide-scope over other possible scope-bearers or quantifiers.

(44) Whom did not Sue meet?

Then, the relevant answer part corresponding to the *wh*-constituent will have narrow focus with wide scope over negation for him, as in (45).

(45) She did not meet Hugo **or** Theo (I do not know which).

But it is crucial for ***or*** to get CF-marked for prosodic support with its prominent pitch accent.

The so-called Krifka's puzzle (Krifka 1999) such that (46a) does not scalarly implicate (46b) (whereas *Sam has two kids ~> Sam does not have three kids*) also seems to have to do with CF. The covert ALT-Q does not allow for scalar alternatives (scales of humans do not need to be dense (Lee 2009); humans have individuation cognition) and it may be 'Does Sam have more than two kids or (just) two kids?'

(46) a. Sam has more than two kids.
b. ~> *Sam does not have more than three kids.

An ALT-Q is distinct from both a YN-Q and a *wh*-Q in that in the former both of the nouns/verbs connected by *or* are stressed and the second ones fall in intonation (↓) in English; two separate interrogative sentences rising and falling appear in Korean; possibly doubly focused-marked by *ne* (before the alternative constituents) in Kikuyu (Schwarz 2003). An ALT-Q can be answered properly by affirming an alternative and negating the other, denoting the unit set containing the affirmed proposition (P_1 or P_2). If both alternatives are negated, the ALT-Q denotes the empty set and if both alternatives are affirmed, it denotes the set containing both of these alternative propositions. The last two cases are against the speaker's expectation and the hearer's felicitous responsiveness that exactly one (one and only one) alternative holds/is true. This cannot easily be treated model-theoretically (Karttunen 1977). However, relying on the presupposition-like conventional meaning attached to the linguistic device of ALT-Q, we can go ahead with CF (see Gutzmann 2014 for conventional semantics possibility).

3 Concluding Remarks

A conjunctively conceived CT is distinct from CF, conveying an un-cancelable conventional scalar implicature, due to the unresolved partial information (except a list CT). The meaning a CT denotes is partial because Potential Topic in a sub-QUD is typically total. CF and ALT-Q with disjunction are correlated in exhaustivity effects. (Particularly, ALT-Q seems better characterized in InqSem, where question–answer and connectors such as disjunction are explored in terms of proposed possibilities in dynamic exchange.[11]) We showed how CT is distinct from CF consistently cross-linguistically. CT implicatures pose the question of certainty in answerhood, although CT and CF are, as I argue, linguistically universal phenomena to be explored further. Our discussion alluded to the speaker—addressee public beliefs to be incorporated into the Common Ground, which is a far way to go. CF, in parallelism with ALT-Q, may shed light on the problematic exceptions to suspension of scalar implicatures in DE contexts such as antecedents of conditionals, and similar problems as well.

References

Aloni, M., and P. Egŕe. 2008. Alternative questions and knowledge attributions. *Philosophical Quarterly*.

Baltag, Alexandru, and Sonya Smets. 2009. Learning by questions and answers: from belief-revision cycles to doxastic fixed points. In *LNAI Lecture Notes in Computer Science*, ed. Makoto Kanazawa, Hiroakira Ono, en Ruy de Queiroz, 124–139, Vol. 5514.

Bolinger, Dwight. 1961. Contrastive accent and contrastive stress. *Language* 37: 83–96.

Carlson, Lauri. 1983. *Dialogue games: An approach to discourse analysis*. Synthese Language Library, Vol. 17. Dordrecht: D. Reidel Co.

Chafe, Wallace. 1976. Givenness, contrastiveness, definiteness, subjects, topics, and point of view. In *Subject and topic*, ed. Charles N. Li. New York: Academic Press.

[11]The core ideas such as exclusively disjoining relevant interrogative sentences are seminal in Lee (2003).

Chierchia, Gennaro. 2004. Scalar implicatures, polarity phenomena, and the syntax/pragmatics interface. In *Structures and beyond*, ed. A. Belletti. Oxford: Oxford University Press.

Chiarcos, Christian. 2011. The mental salience framework: context-adequate generation of referring expressions. In *Salience: Multidisciplinary perspectives on its function in discourse*, ed. Christian Chiarcos, Berry Claus, and Michael Grabski. Berlin: Mouton de Gruyer.

Choi, Hye-Won. 1999. *Optimizing structure in context: scrambling and information structure*. Stanford: CSLI.

Cho, Heysun, and Chungmin Lee. 2012. Phonetic prominence of contrastive focus in English across multiple types and its semantic implication. *English Language and Linguistics* 18: 1–29. Seoul.

Choi, Yoonhee, and Chungmin Lee. 2017. Expletive negation and polarity alternatives. In *Contrastiveness in information structure, alternatives and scalar implicatures*, eds. Chungmin Lee, Ferenc Kiefer, and Manfred Krfika, 175–201. Springer.

Ciardelli, Ivano, Jeroen Groenendijk, and Floris Roelofsen. 2013. Inquisitive semantics: A new notion of meaning. *Language and Linguistics Compass* 7(9): 459–476.

Collins, James N., Daria Popova, Ivan A. Sag, and Thomas Wasow. 2014. Sluicing and the inquisitive potential of appositives. In *Parenthesis and ellipsis: Studies in generative grammar 121*, ed. M. Kluck, D. Ott, and M. de Vries, 47–73. Berlin: De Gruyter.

Davis, Christopher. 2014. The Role of Focus Particles in Wh-Interrogatives: Evidence from a Southern Ryukyuan Language. In *Proceedings of the 31st WCCFL*, ed. R.E. Santana-LaBarge, 124–133.

Ducrot, O. 1972. *Dire et ne pas dire: Principes de sémantique linguistique*. Paris: Hermann.

von Fintel, Kai. 1994. *Restrictions on quantifier domains*, Doctoral Dissertation. University of Massachusetts, Amherst.

Ginzburg, Jonathan. 1995. Resolving questions. *I', Linguistics and Philosophy* 18: 459–527.

Grice, Paul. 1975. Logic and conversation. In *Syntax and semantics*, vol. 3, ed. Peter Cole, and Jerry Morgan. New York: Academic Press.

Groenendijk, Jerome, and Floris Roelofsen. 2011. Inquisitive Semantics. ESSLLI lecture handouts.

Guerzoni, E., and Y. Sharvit. 2013. *Interrogatives, negation and negative polarity*. Talk given at KSLI.

Gunlogson, Christine. 2003. True to Form: Rising and Falling Declaratives as Questions in English. New York: Routledge.

Gutzmann, Daniel. 2014. Semantics vs. Pragmatics. In *The companion to semantics*, ed. Matthewson, Lisa, Cécile Meier, Hotze Rullmann, Thomas Ede Zimmermann. Oxford: Wiley.

Han, Chunghye, and M. Romero. 2004. The syntax of whether/Q—Or questions. *NLLT* 22: 527–564.

Hara, Yurie. 2006. Implicature unsuspendable: Japanese contrastive *wa*. In *Proceedings of Texas Linguistics Society* 8, Cascadilla Press.

Hedberg, Nancy. 2013. Multiple focus and cleft sentences. In *Cleft Structures*, ed. Katharina Hartmann, and Tonjes Veenstra. Linguistik Aktuell series: John Benjamins.

Hirschberg, Julia. 1985. A theory of scalar implicature. PhD Diss., University of Pennsylvania.

Horn, Lawrence. 1989. *A natural history of negation*. Chicago: University of Chicago Press.

Jackendoff, Ray. 1972. *Semantic interpretation in generative grammar*. MIT Press.

Jasinskaja, Katja. 2016 (in press). Information Structure in Slavic. In *The Oxford handbook of information structure*, ed. Caroline Féry, and Shinichiro Ishihara. Oxford: Oxford University Press.

Karttunen, Lauri. 1977. Syntax and semantics of questions. *Linguistics and Philosophy* 1: 3–44.

Karttunen, Lauri and Stanly Peters. 1976. Conventional implicature. In *Syntax and Semantics* 11. Academic Press, San Diego.

Zona, Katz, and Elisabeth Selkirk. 2011. Contrastive focus vs. discourse-new: Evidence from phonetic prominence in English. *Language* 87(4): 771–816.

Krifka, Manfred. 1999. At least some determiners aren't determiners. In *The semantics/pragmatics interface from different points of view (CRiSPI) 1*, ed. Ken Turner, 257–291. London: Elsevier.

Krifla, Manfred. 2003. Quantifiers in questions. *The Korean Journal of English Language and Linguistics* 3: 499–526.

Krifka, Manfred. 2017. Negated polarity questions as denegations of assertions. In *Contrastiveness in Information Structure, Alternatives and Scalar Implicatures*, eds. Chungmin Lee, Ferenc Kiefer, and Manfred Krfika, 359–398. Springer.

Kuroda, Sige-Yuki. 1965. Generative grammatical studies in the Japanese language. MIT Dissertation.

Lambrecht, Knud. 1996. *Information structure and sentence form: Topic, focus, and the mental representations of discourse referents.* Cambridge University Press.

Lee, Chungmin. 1973. *Abstract syntax and Korean with reference to English.* Indiana University Dissertation. (Online Kyobo.).

Lee, Chungmin. 1999. Contrastive topic—A locus of the interface. In *The semantics/pragmatics interface from different points of view* (Current Research in the Semantics/Pragmatics Interface 1), ed. Ken Turner, 317–342, Elsevier.

Lee, Chungmin. 2000. *Contrastive predicates and conventional scales*. Ed. Okrent, Arika and John Boyle. *CLS* 36–1: 243–257.

Lee, Chungmin. 2002. Contrastive topic and proposition structure. In *Asymmetry in Grammar*, ed. Di Sciullo, Anne-Marie. (John Benjamins, Asymmetry Conference, UQAM, 2001).

Lee, Chungmin. 2003. Contrastive topic and/or contrastive focus. In *Japanese and Korean Linguistics*, ed. Bill McClue, Vol. 12, CSLI.

Lee, Chungmin. 2006. Contrastive topic/focus and polarity in discourse. In *Where semantics meets pragmatics,* ed. K. von Heusinger and K. Turner, 381–420. CRiSPI 15. Elsevier.

Lee, Chungmin. 2007. Contrastive (Predicate) topic, intonation, and scalar meanings. In *Topic and focus*: *Cross-linguistic Perspectives on Meaning and Intonation*, ed. Lee, Gordon, and Buring, 151–176. Springer. [Presented at the 2001 UCSB LSA Institute Workshop on the same topic and included in the Institute course package. "Conventional scalar implicature meanings" explained.].

Lee, Chungmin. 2009. Information structure in PA/SN or descriptive/metalinguistic Negation: With reference to scalar implicatures. In *Contrasting meaning in languages in languages of the East and West*, ed. D. Shu, and K. Turner. Berne: Peter Lang.

Lee, Chungmin. (in press). Metalinguistic negation vs. descriptive negation: Among their kin and foes. In *Pragmatics of negation*, ed. Malin Roitman. Amsterdam: John Benjamins.

Malchukov, Andrej. 2013. Verbalization and insubordination in Siberian languages. In *Shared grammaticlaization: With special focus on Transeurasian languages*, ed. Martine Robbeets, and Hubert Cuyckens, 177–208. Amsterdam: Benjamins.

Marandin, Jean-Marie, Claire Beyssade, Elisabeth Delais-Roussarie, and A. Rialland. 2002. Discourse marking in French: C accents and discourse moves. *Speech Prosody* 471–474.

Merin, Arthur. 1999. Information, relevance, and social decision-making: some principles and decision-theoretic semantics. In Logic, language, and computation, ed. L. Moss, J. Ginzburg, and M. de Rijke, 179–221. CSLI.

Neelman, Ad, and Reiko Vermeulan. (eds.) 2012. The syntax of topic, focus, and contrast: an interface-based approach. In *Studies in generative grammar*. De Gruyter.

Onea, Edgar, and Markus Steinbach. 2012. Where question, conditionals and topics converge. Selected Papers of the Amsterdam Colloquium 2011.

Oshima, David Y. 2002. Contrastive topic as a paradigmatic operator. Handout for Workshop on Information Structure in Context. Universität Stuttgart.

Pierrehumbert, J. and J. Hirschberg. 1990. The meaning of intonational contours in the interpretation of discourse. In *Intentions in Communication*, ed. P. Cohen, J. Morgan, and M. Pollack, MIT Press, Cambridge MA. 271–311.

Prince, Ellen. 1978. A comparison of wh-clefts and it-clefts in discourse. *Language* 54: 883–906.

Pruitt, Kathryn, and Floris Roelofsen. 2011. Disjunctive questions-prosody, syntax and semantics, ESSLLI Ms.

Roberts, Craig. 2011. Topics. In *Semantics: International handbook of natural language meaning*, 33–42.

Roberts, Craige. 2012. Information structure: Afterword to Roberts (1996). *Semantics and Pragmatics* 5(7): 1–19. doi:10.3765/sp.5.7.
Rooth, Matz. 1992. A theory of focus interpretation'. *Natural Language Semantics* 1(1): 75–116.
Rooth, Matz. 1995. Indefinites, adverbs of quantification and focus semantics. In *The generic book*, ed. Greg Carlson, and Francis Pelletier, 265–299.
Schwarz, Florian. 2003. Focus marking in Kikuyu. *ZAS Papers in Linguistics* 30: 41–118.
Schwarzschild, Roger. 1999. Givenness, Avoid F, and other constraints on the placement of accent. *Natural Language Semantics* 7: 141–177.
Selkirk, Elisabeth O. 1984. *Phonology and syntax. The relation between sound and structure*. MIT Press, Cambridge MA.
Selkirk, Elizabeth. 2002. Contrastive *FOCUS* versus presentational *focus*: Prosodic evidence from RNR in English, *Speech Prosody*.
Sevi, Aldo. 2005. *Exhaustivity: a Semantic Account of Scalar Implicatures*, Doctoral Dissertation, Tel-Aviv University.
Song, Myoung Hyoun, and Chungmin Lee. 2011. CF-Reduplication in English: Dynamic prototypes and contrastive focus effects. *Proceedings of SALT* 21: 444–462.
Uegaki, Wataru. 2012. Japanese/Korean alternative questions are disjunctions of polar questions. Poster session, Japanese/Korean Linguistics (JK) 22. NINJAL, Tokyo.
Van Rooij, Robert. 2003. Questioning to resolve decision problems. *Linguistics and Philosophy* 266(6): 727–763.
Ward, Gregory, and Julia Hirschberg. 1985. Implicating uncertainty: The pragmatics of Fall-Rise intonation. *Language* 61: 747–776.
Yabushita, Katsuhiko. This volume. Partition semantics and pragmatics of contrastive topic.
Zimmermann, Malte. 2007. Contrastive Focus. In *Interdisciplinary studies on information structure* 6: *The notion of information structure*, ed. by Fery, C., G. Fanselow, and M. Krifka, 147–159.

Partition Semantics and Pragmatics of Contrastive Topic

Katsuhiko Yabushita

Abstract Two existing approaches to the semantics and pragmatics of contrastive topic (CT) will be examined, and it will be shown that neither of them is adequate because one cannot account for what the other can; moreover, there is a garden-variety class of CT sentences that is problematic for both of them. Against this backdrop, an alternative approach will be proposed couched in the (dynamic) partition semantics of questions and answers proposed by Groenendijk and Stokhof. The alternative approach will be demonstrated to be able to handle the class of CT sentences in question as well as capture the insights of both existing approaches, thus having the best of both worlds, so to speak.

Keywords Contrastive topic (CT) · Semantics · Pragmatics · Partition semantics of questions and answers

1 Introduction

For the semantics and pragmatics of contrastive topic, two approaches have been proposed in the literature: one is to take contrastive topic as an information-structural discourse-regulating notion on a par with focus (Roberts 1996; Büring 1999; Kadmon 2001) and the other is to analyze a contrastive marker, phonetic or morphological, as a focus-sensitive operator with its inherent semantic and pragmatic content (Lee 1999, 2006; Hara 2006; Oshima 2002). In the current work, we will review the two approaches and show that both of them have empirical problems; then, we will present an alternative analysis of contrastive topic couched in the so-called partition semantics of questions proposed by Groenendijk and Stokhof (1984) and Groenendijk (1999). It will be seen that the proposed analysis has the

K. Yabushita (✉)
Naruto University of Education, Naruto, Tokushima 772-8502, Japan
e-mail: yabuchan@naruto-u.ac.jp

C. Lee et al. (eds.), *Contrastiveness in Information Structure, Alternatives and Scalar Implicatures*, Studies in Natural Language and Linguistic Theory 91, DOI 10.1007/978-3-319-10106-4_2

best of both worlds, so to speak, being empirically more adequate than either of the existing analyses. A word is in order about the marking of contrastive topic. Crosslinguistically, there is more than one way of marking CT: by means of, e.g., a morpheme like—*wa* in Japanese and—*nun* in Korean, and H * LH % or L + H * LH % tone in English (Pierrehumbert 1980). In the following, a CT-marked constituent is marked with a subscript CT or a CT-marker morpheme.

2 Two Existent Approaches to Contrastive Topic

2.1 CT as an Information-Structural Discourse-Regulating Device (Roberts 1996; Büring 1999; Kadmon 2001)

Consider the question-answer discourse in (1). It is intuitively clear that CT has as much to do with the fact that the questions and the answer are congruent with each other as with the fact that they occur in the order in which they do. The congruence can be described as follows: (1c) directly answers (1b), and (1b) is a sub-question of (1a), or to use Roberts' terms, (1b) is part of a "strategy of inquiry" aimed at answering (1a).

(1) a. Who kissed whom?
 b. Well, who did Larry kiss?
 c. [Larry]$_{CT}$ kissed [Nina]$_F$

Büring (1999) proposed that a contrastive topic induces a third type of semantic value besides ordinary and focus semantic values, called *topic* semantic value. He proposed that the topic semantic value of an expression is the set of alternatives of the focus semantic value in the sense of Rooth (1985, 1992). Then, the topic semantic value of a declarative sentence is a set of sets of propositions, i.e., a set of questions; the topic semantic value of (1c) is (2).

(2) {'Who did Larry kiss?', 'Who did Bill kiss?', 'Who did John kiss?', ...}

Kadmon (2001) argued the focus and the topic semantic values for (1c) can account for the congruence in question; first, the focus semantic value of (1c) being equal to the ordinary value of (1b) is considered to be a formal semantic characterization of (1c) being a direct answer to (1b), and second, (1b) being an element of the topical semantic value of (1c), which is the set of the sub-questions of (1a) accounts for the intuition that (1c) answers (1b) as part of a "strategy of inquiry" aimed at answering (1a).

The above analysis of CT as an information-structural discourse-regulating device seems to be very successful as long as it is applied to sentences with one instance of CT and one instance of focus, like (1c). However, in Japanese, there are simply garden-variety examples with instances of CT but no instance of focus as in (3).[1] Here are some example sentences, all of which have at least one instance of CT but no focus.[2]

(3) a. John-wa hashitte-imasu.
John-CT running-is
'John$_{CT}$ is running.'

b. John-wa Mary-wa aishiteimasu.
John-CT Mary-CT loves
'John$_{CT}$ loves Mary$_{CT}$.'

c. John-wa Mary-wa Bill-ni-wa shookai-shi-ta.
John-CT Mary-CT Bill-Dat-CT introduction-do-Past
'John$_{CT}$ introduced Mary$_{CT}$ to Bill$_{CT}$.'

Let us present a congruent question-answer discourse in which there appear a sentence with two instances of CT but no instance of F, (4), and a similar but incongruent one, (5), which is minimally different from (4) in that *Larry* and *Nina* in the second sentence are not contrastive-topic marked (or focus-marked):

[1]Constant (2014) has English examples of multiple CT, i.e. sentences with more than one instance of CT (but along with a focus phrase). One of which is (iB) with the following background scenario. Person B is practicing a diet called "ABC diet", which is something like this. Every day, eat the following three meals: one avocado, one burrito, and one cheesecake in any order you like. Person A is interested in B's diet and asks B to tell her more about it, saying (iA), to which B responds starting with (iB).

(i) (= Constant (2014: (26), p. 76)
A:For each day of the week, tell me what time you have each food.
B:On [SUNDAYS]$_{CT}$ … [the BURRITO]$_{CT}$ … I have for [LUNCH]$_{Exh}$.
L+H* L-H% L+H* L-H% H L-L%

[2]Japanese particle *-wa* has two uses: "thematic" and "contrastive", the latter of which is the case relevant to the current issue, i.e. CT. It is the general understanding in the literature since Kuno (1973) that all the occurrences of *-wa* phrases in a sentence can be interpreted as contrastive, while only the first (left-most) occurrence can be interpreted as thematic; that is, the first occurrence is ambiguous. From which, all the instances of *-wa* phrases in (3) can be interpreted as instances of CT.

(4) a. Dare-ga dare-ni kisu-o-shita no.
who-Nom who Dat kiss-Acc-did Q
'Who kissed who(m)?'

b. Dewa, Larry-wa Nina-ni-wa kisu-o-shita no
well, Larry-CT Nina-Dat-CT kiss-Acc-did Q
'Well, did Larry_{CT} kiss Nina_{CT}?'

c. Hai, Larry-wa Nina-ni-wa kisu-o-shita
yes Larry-CT Nina-Dat-CT kiss-Acc-did
'Yes, Larry_{CT} kissed Nina_{CT}.'

(5) a. Dare-ga dare-ni kisu-o-shita no.
who-Nom who-Dat kiss-Acc-did Q
'Who kissed who(m)?'

b. #Dewa, Larry-ga Nina-ni kisu-o-shita no
well, Larry-Nom Nina-Dat kiss-Acc-did Q
'Well, did Larry kiss Nina?'

c. #Hai, Larry-wa Nina-ni-wa kisu-o-shita
yes Larry-CT Nina-Dat-CT kiss-Acc-did
'Yes, Larry_{CT} kissed Nina_{CT}.'

I will argue that the Roberts-Büring-Kadmon analysis of CT cannot characterize the incongruence of (5) as a discourse, or the difference in congruence between (4) and (5).

For a critical review of Kadmon's analysis, the formal rendition of the above regulations on question-answer discourses will be presented here. Kadmon formulated the conditions on the discourse congruence as two constraints, *the Question-Under-Discussion constraint on FOCUS-focus* and *the Question-Under-Discussion constraint on TOPIC-focus*, which are (F-1) and (F-2) in Kadmon (2001: 389).[3] The constraints can be represented in our terms as (6a) and (6b), respectively.

(6) a. An utterance B is felicitous only if the focus semantic value of B is identical to the ordinary semantic value of the immediately preceding interrogative sentence.
b. An utterance B is felicitous only if the topic semantic value of B is identical to the focus semantic value of the immediately preceding interrogative sentence.

[3]Kadmon's *FOCUS-focus* and *TOPIC-focus* correspond to our *focus* and *contrastive topic*, respectively.

Now, let us see if the proposed constraints account for the (in)congruence of (4) and (5). First, (6a) is supposed to capture the relation of being-a-direct-answer-to. The relevant semantic values here are the focus semantic value of (4c) (= (5c)) and the ordinary semantic values of (4b) and (5b). The focus semantic value of (4c) (= (5c)) is considered to be as follows: As (4c) (= (5c)) has no instances of focused phrase, the focus semantic value is considered to be the singleton set containing the ordinary semantic value, i.e., the proposition that Larry kissed Nina, denoted {kissed(l, n)}. On the other hand, the ordinary semantic values of (4b) and (5b) as interrogatives are both {kissed(l, n)}, as they do not have instances of focused phrases. Consequently, both (4) and (5) satisfy constraint (6a); however, as is shown, the continuation from (4b) to (4c) is felicitous while that from (5b) to (5c) is infelicitous. One might argue that (6a) is a necessary condition, not a sufficient condition, for the felicitousness. That is true, but since, as it stands, Kadmon's analysis does not have other relevant conditions or constraints, it cannot but be said to be inadequate for an account of the relation of being-a-direct-answer-to. Second, (6b) is supposed to account for the relation of being a direct answer for a question as a sub-question for another question, as in the relation among (1c), (1b) and (1a). Let us see if (6b) is effective in characterizing the relevant relation in (4). The topic semantic value of (4c) is {{kissed(x, y)}: x $\in$ D and y $\in$ D} and the focus semantic value of (4b) is a singleton set containing its ordinary semantic value, i.e.{{kissed(l, n)}} as (4b) does not have an occurrence of focused phrases. That is, (4) does not satisfy (6b); nonetheless, the questions and the answer in (4) are congruent with one another; specifically, (4b) is a sub-question of (4a). From this, it can be said that (6b) is inadequate in characterizing the relevant relation in (4). We have reviewed Kadmon's (2001) analysis of contrastive topic as an information-structural discourse-regulating device to see that it cannot adequately characterize the congruence and incongruence of question-answer discourses (4) and (5).

I argue that the inadequacy is due to the fact that the analysis is not designed to deal with examples where there are no focus phrases along with contrastive-topic phrases like (4) and (5), and that the analysis based on the three types of semantic values is too "rigid" for a flexible treatment of examples with contrastive topic phrases but no focus phrases. One might argue that the alleged problem with Kadmon's analysis is merely due to the non-canonicity of examples like (4) and (5) and that, thus, it is not a problem with the analysis itself. To that refutation of my argument, I would say that (4) and (5) are genuine data of contrastive topic, whose (in)congruence needs to be accounted for by any reasonable analysis of contrastive topic.

In this section, we have reviewed an approach to contrastive topic in which contrastive topic is analyzed as a discourse device regulating the congruence among sentences in a discourse along with focus; specifically, Kadmon's (2001) analysis based on Roberts (1996) and Büring (1999). And we have found that the basic setup of the analysis is tailor made for "canonical" examples in which there is exactly one instance of contrastive topic and exactly one instance of focus;

however, the analysis is not flexible enough for the treatment of "non-canonical" examples in which, for example, there are two instances of contrastive topic but no instances of focus, as in (4c).

2.2 *CT as a Focus-Sensitive Operator*

2.2.1 Lee (1999, 2006) and Hara (2006)

The other approach takes CT to be a focus-sensitive operator on a par with particles like English *even*, *only*, and *also*, or their counterparts in the other languages. Lee (1999, 2006) and Hara (2006) proposed the following analysis of CT:

(7) Semantics and Pragmatics of CT as a Focus-Sensitive Operator

a. $CT(\langle \beta, \alpha \rangle)$ (semantic representation)
b. $\beta(\alpha)$ (assertion)
c. $\exists$ x [x $\neq \alpha \wedge \neg[\beta(x)]$] (conventional implicature)

A word is in order about the notations in (7). First, in (7a), which is the semantic representation of a sentence with a CT, $\langle \beta, \alpha \rangle$ is the structured meaning of the sentence, with β and α being the background and the focus parts, respectively. Second, in (7b), which is the assertion of the sentence, $\beta(\alpha)$ is the result of function-applying β to α—or α to β, whichever is possible—and is the ordinary semantic meaning of the sentence. (7c) is supposed to capture the so-called "Reversed Polarity Implicature" (RPI) of CT; a sentence with a CT-marked constituent tends to imply a "contrasting" sentence with the constituent replaced by an alternative of the opposite polarity. In fact, however, the alleged implicature can be absent, as seen in (8), which should not be the case if it were really a conventional implicature.[4]

(8) John-wa kita ga sonohokano hito-nikanshite-wa shira-nai.
John-CT came but the other people-about-CT know-not
'[John]$_{CT}$ came, but as for the other people, I don't know whether they came.'

2.2.2 Oshima (2002)

The above problem, in fact, can be got around by Oshima's (2002) variant in which the pragmatic feature of a CT sentence is not a conventional implicature, but rather the presupposition that there is some alternative to the CT-marked constituent such that it is not known if it has the property denoted by the background part, formalized as in (7c′).

[4]Despite evidence like (8), Lee (2017) maintains that implicatures associated with CT are conventional, not conversational.

(7) c′. $\exists x[x \neq \alpha \wedge -[\beta(x)]]$ (presupposition), where – is a weak negation in three-valued logic.

However, it is doubtful that (7c′) is a presupposition of a CT sentence. Consider the following question-answer dialog:

(9) Q: Dare-ga paatii-ni ki-mashi-ta ka.
who-Nom party-to come-Polite-Past Q
'Who came to the party?'

A: Jon-wa ki-mashi-ta (kedo).
John-CT come-Polite-Past (but)
'John$_{CT}$ came.'

According to (7c′), at the time of the utterance of (9A), it would be presupposed that somebody other than John is not known if she came to the party. From this, it follows that the questioner is required to have the presupposition. But the utterance of (6A) is perfectly felicitous in contexts where she does not have the presupposition, and is rather more natural without the presupposition.

Independently of Oshima (2002), Hara and van Rooij (2007) proposed a very similar analysis. They proposed that CT should have as its pragmatic component the following implicature, which is reformulated in our terms as in (7c″):

(7) c″. $\exists x[x \neq \alpha \wedge \neg K_{sp}[\beta(x)]]$ (implicature)

In (7c″), K_{sp} is an epistemic operator and '$K_{sp}\phi$' is read as "the speaker knows that ϕ". (7c″) is different from (7c′) only in that the absence of the relevant knowledge is required only of the speaker and the requirement is a conventional implicature, not a presupposition. However, it is as easy to find counterexamples for Hara and van Rooij's version as for Oshima's. Consider the following scenario. A test was administered to a class of pupils; the teacher knows, for all the pupils, whether they passed the test or not, and the father of Mary, a pupil, who is rather nosy, asks the teacher who passed the test in such a way that it is clear he would like the teacher to supply him with an exhaustive list. To the question, the teacher can answer perfectly felicitously as in (10).

(10) Mary-wa goukakushimashi-ta ga,
Mary-CT pass (the test)-Past but

hokano seito nikanshite-wa iemase-n.
other pupils as-to-CT can-say-not
'Mary$_{CT}$ passed the test, but I can't say as to the others if they passed it or not.'

In (10), the speaker, i.e. the teacher, knows of all the students including Mary whether they passed the test or not, but she can felicitously utter "Mary$_{CT}$ passed the test", which is contradictory to Hara and van Rooij's prediction. The use of CT in (10) is not so much characterized as ignorance on the part of the speaker as confidentiality, or secrecy.[5]

The fact that the implicational/presuppositional features of CT sentences are very elusive or hard to identify, I claim, suggests that they are not inherent attributes of the meaning of CT, but are epiphenomena arising from some unique feature of CT in conjunction with their particular uses. Along the line of this view, I will propose a novel approach to CT in the following section. Before we move on to the new approach, let us demonstrate that sentences with more than one instance of CT are problematic to the currently reviewed approach as well.

Let us restate (4c) (= (5c)), actually the version without the sentence-initial *hai* 'yes', as example (11).

(11) Larry-wa Nina-ni-wa kisu-o-shita
Larry-CT Nina-Dat-CT kiss-Acc-did
'Larry$_{CT}$ kissed Nina$_{CT}$.'

In the approach currently under review, which views CT as a focus-sensitive operator, (11) will necessarily be taken to have two instances of the operator, so the semantic representation will be alleged to be something as in (12).

(12) $CT(\langle \lambda x.CT(\langle \lambda y.KISSED(x, y), Nina\rangle), Larry\rangle)$

What implicature or presupposition is associated with the semantic representation? Whichever analysis we adopt, the implicature or presupposition in question will have the following schematic form:

(13) $P/I.\exists x[x \neq Larry \wedge Op[P/I.\exists y[y \neq Nina \wedge Op[KISSED(x, y)]]]]$

The implicature or presupposition predicted to be associated with (11) by Lee (1999, 2006) and Hara (2006); Oshima (2002), and Hara and van Rooij (2007) will be the result of replacing 'Op' in (13) with '$\neg$', '$-$', and '$\neg K_{sp}$', respectively and choosing P or I depending on whether the formula following it is analyzed to be a presupposition or a (conventional) implicature, respectively. Let us see what (13) says using a specific example from e.g. Lee (1999, 2006) and Hara (2006), which is the following:

(14) $I.\exists x[x \neq Larry \wedge \neg[I.\exists y[y \neq Nina \wedge \neg[KISSED(x, y)]]]]$

In words, (14) reads "It is implied that it is not implied that somebody other than Larry didn't kiss somebody other than Nina". The predicted content in itself is

---

[5]An anonymous reviewer suggested that we could save the approach to CT as a focus-sensitive operator by "adding an intentional operator to specify the option of 'Speaker wants not to disclose the information' for capturing the case of secrecy to the semantics in (7)". That kind of move, I'm afraid, would make the semantics of contrastive topic, or Japanese *wa* too specific, not general enough for the various uses. For example, if the semantics were modified to have the content the reviewer suggested, the resulting interpretational rules would make the speaker using a contrastive-topic marker always secretive. However, the use of contrastive topic is not always motivated by secrecy; for example, recall that in the case of (8), it is rather ignorance.

rather senseless, and more crucially, is not implicated by the utterance of (11) at all. The contents predicted by the other two analyses by Oshima (2002) and Hara & van Rooij (2007), i.e., "It is presupposed that it is not presupposed that it is not known if somebody other than Larry kissed somebody other than Nina" and "It is implied that it is not implied that the speaker does not know if somebody other than Larry kissed somebody other than Nina", respectively, are equally senseless and implausible.

One could argue that the resulting senseless pragmatic contents are due to the implicit assumptions that a CT operator can be embedded in another one, as is manifested in (12), and that pragmatic operator 'I/P' can occur as part of a logical formula, especially under the scope of logical negation, as in (13). Alternatively, we could assume that contrastive-topic operator CT is an *n*-ary operator that simultaneously binds all the argument places corresponding to the CT-marked constituents on analogy to *binary quantifiers* or *binary wh-operators* proposed by Higginbotham and May (1981), instead of a unary operator that binds one argument place for each CT-marked constituent, which will be iterated over another. With CT as an *n*-ary operator, the semantic representation for (11) will be as shown in (15), where (x, y) is a sequence of variables and (Larry, Nina) is a sequence of constants, instead of that shown in (12).

(15) $CT(\langle\lambda(x, y).KISSED(x, y), (Larry, Nina)\rangle)$

Consequently, the implicature or presupposition that is predicted by the analyses will be something of the following schematic form, (16) instead of (13).

(16) $P/I.\exists x, y[x \neq Larry \wedge y \neq Nina \wedge Op.KISSED(x, y)]$

Now that we have come up with a way to give a reasonable semantic representation for a sentence with multiple CT phrases and its implicature or presupposition, the question is if the predicted implicature or presupposition is empirically correct. The implicature or presupposition of (11) predicted by (i), Lee (1999, 2006) and Hara (2006); (ii), Oshima (2002); and (iii), Hara & van Rooij (2007) now will be something like, (i), "It is (conventionally) implied that someone other than Larry didn't kiss someone other than Nina"; (ii), "It is presupposed that there is someone other than Larry and someone other than Nina such that it is not known if the former kissed the latter"; and, (iii), "It is (conventionally) implied that there are someone other than Larry and someone other than Nina such that the speaker does not know if the former kissed the latter", respectively: sentences with multiple CT phrases are expected to be in this respect analogous to sentences that contain only one CT phrase. It is easy to find a felicitous discourse that is a sweeping counterexample to the predicted implicatures and presupposition. The following sentence can be felicitously uttered by someone who is perfectly knowledgeable about who kissed whom (of the contextually relevant pairs of people):

(17) Larry-wa Nina-ni-wa kisu-o-shita ga
Larry-CT Nina-Dat-CT kiss-Acc-did but
'Larry$_{CT}$ kissed Nina$_{CT}$, but...'

sono hoka no hitotachi nikanshite-wa i-e nai.
the other of people about say-can not
'(but,) as for the other (pairs of) people, I cannot say (about who kissed whom).'

In this section we have seen that the approach to contrastive topic that analyzes contrastive topic as a focus-sensitive operator is empirically inadequate, by demonstrating that (i) the implicatures and presuppositions for sentences with a contrastive topic-marked phrase that are predicted by the analyses along this line of approach are empirically wrong and furthermore, (ii) the analyses as they are cannot be applied to sentences with multiple instances of contrastive topic-marked phrases, and even if they are modified to be applicable to those sentences, the predicted implicatures and presuppositions will be empirically wrong again. In the next section, we will propose an alternative approach to CT that can capture the insights of both of the existing approaches, yet will remain free of the problems they encounter.

3 Alternative Approach: Partition Semantics and Pragmatics of Contrastive Topic

3.1 Partition Semantics and Pragmatics of Question and Answer: Groenendijk (1999), Groenendijk and Stokhof (1984)

In this section, we will briefly review a semantic framework in which our current analysis of CT will be couched. It is a dynamic-semantic analysis of question and answer; specifically, one presented in Groenendijk (1999). The gist of the analysis is that not only indicative sentences but also interrogative sentences are interpreted as context change potentials (CCP). To accommodate interrogative sentences, contexts cannot be simply sets of possible worlds as in Stalnaker (1978); instead, they are now defined as equivalence relations on a set of possible worlds as follows:

(18) Definition (*Context*)
A context is an equivalence relation on a subset of the set of possible worlds.

To define the CCP of an interrogative sentence we first specify the *abstract*, or *predicate* meaning of the interrogative sentence.

(19) Definition (*Abstract, or Predicate Meaning of an Interrogative*)
The predicate meaning of an interrogative sentence is a lambda abstract binding the variables substituted for the WH-phrases in the interrogative sentence. (When there is no WH-phrase, i.e., the interrogative sentence is a YES-NO question, the predicate meaning is a proposition denoted by the corresponding declarative sentence.)

The predicate meanings of interrogative sentences will be illustrated with the following examples:

(20)

	Interrogative sentences	Predicate meanings
a.	'Who came to the party?'	λx.came-to-the-party′(x)
b.	'Who bought what?'	λyλx.bought′(x, y)
c.	'Who ate what at which place?'	λzλyλx.ate-at′(x, y, z)
d.	'Did John come to the party?'	came-to-the-party′(j)

In general, when there are *n* WH-phrases in an interrogative sentence, the predicate meaning of the interrogative sentence is an *n*-place predicate; notably, when there is no WH-phrase, i.e., the interrogative sentence is a YES-NO question as in (20d), the predicate meaning is a 0-place predicate, i.e., a proposition. In terms of the structured meaning approach to focus, the predicate meaning of an interrogative sentence coincides with the background part of the background-focus meaning.

Now that contexts and predicate meanings of interrogative sentences have been defined, we can proceed to define CCPs of interrogative sentences.

(21) Definition (Context Update by Interrogatives)
Suppose that $\lambda\vec{x}\phi$ is the abstract meaning of an interrogative and C is a context. The update of C by the interrogative, denoted $C + \lambda\vec{x}\phi$, is defined as follows:

$$C + \lambda\vec{x}\phi = \left\{ \langle w, w' \rangle \in C \colon [[\lambda\vec{x}\phi]]^{w} = [[\lambda\vec{x}\phi]]^{w'} \right\}.$$

In prose, given a context C and an interrogative sentence whose predicate meaning is $\lambda\vec{x}\phi$, updating C with the utterance of an interrogative sentence turns C into an equivalence relation between possible worlds with respect to their extensions of $\lambda\vec{x}\phi$. In terms of partition, C will be partitioned into the cells of possible worlds such that every possible world in each cell has the same extension of $\lambda\vec{x}\phi$ as do the others.

Let us illustrate how the update works, diagrammatically. Suppose that C is a context in which w_1, w_2, and w_3 are compatible with what is known so far, i.e., $C = \{\langle v, u \rangle : v, u \in \{w_1, w_2, w_3\}\}$, which is represented as in (22).

$$(22)\ C = \left\{ \begin{array}{lll} \langle w_1, w_1 \rangle & \langle w_2, w_1 \rangle & \langle w_3, w_1 \rangle \\ \langle w_1, w_2 \rangle & \langle w_2, w_2 \rangle & \langle w_3, w_2 \rangle \\ \langle w_1, w_3 \rangle & \langle w_2, w_3 \rangle & \langle w_3, w_3 \rangle \end{array} \right\}$$

Suppose, furthermore, that John came to the party in worlds w_1 and w_2 and he didn't in w_3. Then, the update of C with the utterance of 'Did John come to the party?', whose predicate meaning is **came-to-the-party′(j)**, results in the following context, C′, which is diagrammed as in (23).

$$(23)\ C + \text{came} - \text{to} - \text{party}'(j) = C' = \left\{ \begin{array}{lll} \langle w_1, w_1 \rangle & \langle w_2, w_1 \rangle & \\ \langle w_1, w_2 \rangle & \langle w_2, w_2 \rangle & \\ & & \langle w_3, w_3 \rangle \end{array} \right\}$$

In the form of a partition, C′ is diagrammed as in (24).

(24)

C + came-to-the-party′(j) = C′ =

(the set of possible worlds where) John came to the party
(the set of possible worlds where) John didn't come to the party

Having reviewed how a context is to be updated with an interrogative sentence, let us move on to the case of indicative sentences. The CCP of an indicative sentence is defined as in (25).

(25) Definition (Context Update by Indicatives)

Suppose that ψ is the meaning of an indicative sentence and C is a context. The update of C by the indicative sentence denoted C + ψ is defined as follows:

$$C + \psi = \{\langle w, w' \rangle \in C\colon [[\psi]]^{w} = [[\psi]]^{w'} = 1\}.$$

What the utterance of an indicative sentence does to a context is to eliminate from C the ordered pairs of possible worlds in which the indicative sentence is false in one or both of the possible worlds. In terms of partition, it eliminates from a partition the cells of possible worlds in which the indicative sentence is false.

Let us illustrate the update of a context with the utterance of an indicative sentence as defined in (25), by going over some examples. Recall context C′, which has been updated with 'Did John come to the party?', i.e. (24), a set of ordered pairs of possible worlds, or equivalently, (25), a partition of a set of possible worlds. The update of C′ with e.g. (26) '(Yes,) John came to the party' (**came-to-the-party′(j)**) will be illustrated in (27) and (28), where John came to the party in possible worlds w_1 and w_2, but not in w_3.

(26) (Yes,) John came to the party: came-to-the-party′(j)

(27) $$C': \left\{ \begin{matrix} \langle W_1, W_1\rangle & \langle W_2, W_1\rangle & \\ \langle W_1, W_2\rangle & \langle W_2, W_2\rangle & \\ & & \langle W_3, W_3\rangle \end{matrix} \right\} + (26) = \left\{ \begin{matrix} \langle W_1, W_1\rangle & \langle W_2, W_1\rangle \\ \langle W_1, W_2\rangle & \langle W_2, W_2\rangle \end{matrix} \right\}$$

(28)

C′:

John came to the party
John didn't come to the party

+ (26) =

John came to the party

Next, let us go over the case of a WH-question. (In the following, we will adopt the partition format solely for ease of illustration.) Suppose that C is to be updated with e.g. (20a), an interrogative sentence with one occurrence of a WH-phrase, reproduced here as (29). This results in C″, shown in (30). There, it is assumed that John and Mary are the only relevant party-goers, and that the block with $\{a_1, a_2, \ldots, a_n\}$ represents the cell for the set of possible worlds in which $a_1, a_2, \ldots,$ and a_n and only $a_1, a_2, \ldots,$ and a_n came to the party.

(29) 'Who came to the party?': λx.came-to-the-party′(x)

(30)

C″ =

{John, Mary}	{John}
{Mary}	∅

The results of updating C″ with e.g. (31) and (32) are as shown in (33).[6]

(31) Mary to John ga ki-mashi-ta.
Mary and John Nom come-Polite-Past
'Mary and John came.'

(32) Jon-ga ki-mashi-ta.
John-Nom come-Polite-Past
'John came.'

[6]Here it is assumed that sentences (31) and (32) are interpreted exhaustively as they share the same focus structure with (29).

(33)

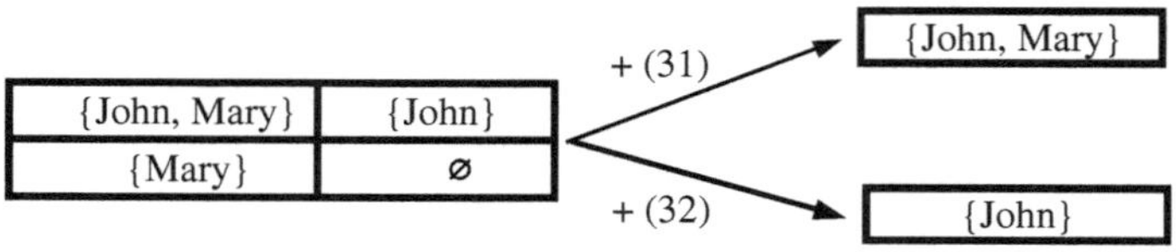

Following is the case of a WH-question with two WH-phrases:

(34) Dare-ga nani-o tabe-mashi-ta ka.
who-Nom what-Acc eat-Polite-Past Q
'Who ate what?'

Suppose that the domains of the eaters and the eatens relevant here are {John, Mary} and {hamburger, salad}, respectively. Then, the context resulting from updating C with (34) will be something as in (35) in terms of partition, where each cell represents the set of possible worlds in which, for each ordered pair, the person of the first coordinate ate the foods of the second coordinate and no other eating events obtained.

(35)

⟨j,{h, s}⟩,⟨m,{h, s}⟩	⟨j, {h}⟩,⟨m, {h, s}⟩	⟨j, {s}⟩,⟨m, {h, s}⟩	⟨j, ø⟩,⟨m, {h, s}⟩
⟨j, {h, s}⟩,⟨m, {h}⟩	⟨j, {h}⟩,⟨m, {h}⟩	⟨j, {s}⟩,⟨m, {h}⟩	⟨j, ø⟩,⟨m, {h}⟩
⟨j, {h, s}⟩,⟨m, {s}⟩	⟨j, {h}⟩,⟨m, {s}⟩	⟨j, {s}⟩,⟨m, {s}⟩	⟨j, ø⟩,⟨m, {s}⟩
⟨j, {h, s}⟩,⟨m, ø⟩	⟨j, {h}⟩,⟨m, ø⟩	⟨j, {s}⟩,⟨m, ø⟩	⟨j, ø⟩,⟨m, ø⟩

3.2 Partition Semantics and Pragmatics of Contrastive Topic

Now that we have reviewed the partition semantics of questions and answers presented in Groenendijk (1999), I will propose to apply it to a novel analysis of contrastive topic. The thesis is intuitively as follows. The use of a sentence with contrastive topics "presupposes" a question under discussion (QUD), explicit or implicit; however, the sentence does not directly answer the QUD, but rather a "sub-question" derived from the QUD by restricting the values of the WH phrases to the denotations of the contrastive topics. The implicational/presuppositional features observed surrounding CT are to be attributed to the reasons why the speaker opts to answer the sub-question instead of the QUD.

Following is our analysis of the semantics and the pragmatics of CT. First is the semantic component:

(36) *Semantics of CT*

Suppose that

(i) γ is a sentence with CT-marked phrases,
(ii) ?-γ is the interrogative sentence directly corresponding to γ in that only the focused phrases are replaced by the corresponding WH-phrases and, if there is no focused phrase, ?-γ is a polar interrogative sentence;
(iii) the sequence of the semantic representations of the CT-marked phrases and that of the variables for the WH-phrases are denoted $\vec{t}$, and $\vec{x}$, respectively;
(iv) the predicate meaning of ?-γ is $\lambda\vec{x}$.R, where R is the semantic representation for γ;
(v) *wh*-γ is the interrogative sentence resulting from γ by replacing the CT-marked phrases as well as the focused phrases if any with the corresponding WH-phrases; and,
(vi) the sequence of variables for the WH-phrases corresponding to the CT-marked phrases is denoted $\vec{y}$.

Then,

(vii) the predicate meaning of *wh*-γ is $\lambda\vec{y}\lambda\vec{x}.R[\vec{t}/\vec{y}]$, where $R[\vec{t}/\vec{y}]$ is the result of replacing $\vec{t}$ in R with $\vec{y}$.

Next is the pragmatic component:

(37) *Pragmatics of CT*

(i) Sentence γ, indicative or interrogative, explicitly or implicitly assumes interrogative sentence *wh*-γ as QUD;
(ii) When γ is an indicative sentence, the answerer, or the utterer of γ opts to answer ?-γ instead of *wh*-γ *for some reason.*

Let us illustrate the current analysis by going over (1), which is reproduced here as (38).

(38) a. Who kissed whom?
b. Well, who did Larry kiss?
c. $[\text{Larry}]_{CT}$ kissed $[\text{Nina}]_{F}$

The CT sentence in question here, (38c), is γ in (36). Then, (38b) and (38a) are ?-γ and *wh*-γ in (36), respectively. For the characterization that (38c) is a "direct" answer to (38b) and (38b) is a "sub-question" of (38a), relevant notions have already been worked out in the theory in which the current analysis is couched, i.e., the semantic theory of questions and answers by Groenendijk and Stokhof (1984) and Groenendijk (1999). The relevant notions are *complete answer* and *partial answer*. Given a partition of the set of possible worlds induced by the predicate meaning of an interrogative sentence as in (21), each block of the partition as a proposition represents a *complete* (and exhaustive) answer to the question, while the union of some but not all blocks is a *partial* answer, eliminating some blocks as not being the case. In terms of those semantic notions of answerhood, the following fact holds of ?-γ and *wh*-γ:

(39) Every complete answer to ?-γ is a partial answer to *wh*-γ.

It is reasonable to take *complete answer* to be a formal rendition of "direct answer" and to define that question Q_1 is a "sub-question" of Q_2 when every complete answer to Q_1 is a partial answer to Q_2. From this and (39), it follows that γ (as interpreted exhaustively) is a direct answer to ?-γ and ?-γ is a sub-question of *wh*-γ; in particular, (38c) is a direct answer to (38b) and (38b) is a sub-question of (38a). In this sense, the current semantic analysis of CT is as adequate as the Roberts-Büring-Kadmon analysis in characterizing the congruence among the sentences in (38).

In fact, I contend that the current analysis is superior in that it is applicable to the "non-canonical" examples of CT sentences like (3) as well. Note that in the semantic rules of CT in (36), there is no restriction on the number of CT phrases (other than that there be at least one); there is also no restriction on the number of focused phrases in a sentence (and there can be none). Thus, CT sentences with more than one instance of CT and no apparent focused phrase, as in (3), will not be a special case in the current analysis, unlike in the Roberts-Büring-Kadmon analysis.

We have seen that Kadmon's (2001) analysis has difficulty characterizing the (in)congruence of (4) and (5), or the difference between them in terms of congruence. In our currently proposed analysis, (4) and (5) will be analyzed as follows. In terms of the semantic content, or CCP, (4b) and (5b) have the same content; given a partition of a set of possible worlds, they will induce a two-cell partition such that one cell contains the possible worlds in which Larry kissed Nina and the other one consists of the possible worlds in which Larry didn't kiss Nina. In our proposed analysis, consequently, the sentences in (4) and the corresponding sentences in (5) will be predicted to have exactly the same semantic content. In fact, in terms of our current definitions of direct answer and sub-question based on the notions *complete answer* and *partial answer* of Groenendijk and Stokhof (1984), (4c) is analyzed to be a direct answer to (4b), and (4b) is a sub-question of (4a), as is the case for (5c), (5b), and (5a); that is, there is no difference between (4) and (5) with respect to semantic content.

Does that mean that the proposed theory is no more adequate than that proposed by Kadmon (2001) in its analysis of the (in)congruence of discourses (4) and (5)? As far as semantic content is concerned, the current analysis indeed cannot tell (4) from (5). But remember that there is a pragmatic component to the current theory of CT, i.e. (37). Specifically relevant here is (37i), which specifies that (4b) and (4c) both assume (4a) as QUD while, although (5c) (= (4c)) assumes (5a) (= (4a)) as QUD, (5b) does not, as *wh*-(4b), *wh*-(4c), and *wh*-(5c) are (4a) (= (5a)) while *wh*-(5b) is (5b) itself as (5b) does not contain any CT or focused phrase. Our theory predicts differences between (4) and (5) with regard to the commonality of QUD between the second and third sentences. In (4), (4b) and (4c) share the same question, (4a), as their QUD while in (5), (5b) and (5c) do not share their QUDs.

I propose that given an indicative sentence and an interrogative sentence, it is necessary for them to share a question as QUD such that they can form a congruent discourse in such a way that the indicative answer is a direct answer to the interrogative sentence as a sub-question to the QUD. To the extent that it can characterize the difference in congruence between (4) and (5), the current analysis couched in terms of the partition semantics of questions and answers is superior to that of Kadmon (2001).

We have shown that our current analysis of CT can capture Roberts' original insights of CT as a discourse regulator as adequately as the Roberts-Büring-Kadmon approach can; in fact, our approach is superior in that it can deal with the "non-canonical" examples as well as the "canonical" ones. Next, we will see how the current analysis fares alongside the other existent approach to CT: specifically, we will examine how our analysis accounts for the implicational/presuppositional features surrounding CT. In Sect. 2.2, we reviewed existing analyses that take CT to be a focus-sensitive operator with some implicature or presupposition attached. For all of these, we have demonstrated that it is easy to find a counterexample to the alleged implicational/presuppositional contents, or that they are cancelable. Of course, this fact alone does not invalidate the approach per se, but we also have pointed out that "non-canonical" examples of CT sentences will be problematic for the approaches in question, as well, for they deal with sentences that have only one instance of contrastive topic, and their interpretational rules are not equipped to handle the "non-canonical" examples. I have demonstrated that, even if the interpretational rules are modified to accommodate the "non-canonical" examples according to reasonable assumptions, the resulting implicatures and presuppositions do not make sense empirically.

In the current approach we take the position that there is no implicational or presuppositional content that is hard-wired in the meaning of a CT sentence. Rather, we propose that what seem to be implicational or presuppositional features characteristic of CT are actually conversational implicatures arising from the use of a CT sentence instead of its corresponding non-CT version. Relevant here is (37)—specifically, (37ii)—which says that the use of a CT sentence indicates that instead of answering the QUD directly, the speaker opts to answer one of its sub-questions directly, for some reason. My contention is that what have been observed and claimed to be (conventional) implicatures and presuppositions of CT sentences are actually conversational implicatures that arise from the speaker's choice to answer a sub-question instead of the QUD itself. At this point, I don't know if there is any fixed number of reasons for the use of a CT sentence or that, if there is, how many of such there actually are. We will not attempt to resolve this issue, for it is not directly relevant to the point of the paper.

In the following I will put forward some, but enough, reasons to cover what has been proposed to be the implicational/presuppositional features of CT in the literature. For illustration, let us use the following CT sentence and interrogative sentences for γ, *wh*-γ, and ?-γ in (37).

(40)	γ:	Jon-wa	paatii-ni	ki-mashi-ta.	
		John-CT	party-to	come-Polite-Past	

'John$_{CT}$ came to the party.'

(41)	*wh*-γ:	Dare-ga	paatii-ni	ki-mashi-taka	ka
		who-Nom	party-to	come-Polite-Past	Q

'Who came to the party?'; λx.came-to-the-party′(x)

(42)	?-γ:	Jon-wa	paatii-ni	ki-mashi-taka	ka
		John-CT	party-to	come-Polite-Past	Q

'Did John come to the party?'; came-to-the-party′(j)

According to the current theory, the utterance of (40) "presupposes" interrogative sentence (41), or the question denoted by it, as QUD; however, instead of directly answering the question, the speaker answers interrogative sentence (42), for some reason. As in Sect. 3.1, suppose that the relevant domain of discourse is {John, Mary} and assume the diagrammatic conventions for partitions adopted there. Then, the partition representing the context updated with (41) is C″ in (30), which is reproduced in (43).

(43)

C″ =

{John, Mary}	{John}
{Mary}	∅

On the other hand, the partition for the context updated with (42) is C′ in (24), which is equivalently reproduced as in (44) to highlight its contrast with C″. In C′, the upper block and the lower one represent the set of possible worlds where John came to the party and that where John didn't, respectively, and both of the blocks are noncommittal about whether the other people, in this case, Mary, came to the party or not.

(44)

C′ =

{John, Mary}	{John}
{Mary}	∅

The question here is why the speaker opts to resolve the issue represented by C′ instead of that by C″.

Possible Reason 1: Lack of Information

As for John, the speaker knows for sure that he came to the party, but as for the other people, in this case, Mary, the speaker doesn't know if they came to the party. So she restricts her assertion only to the fact that John came, shying away from the issue as to whether the other people came to the party or not. This will nicely account for the continuation displayed in (45).

(45) Jon-wa/#-ga paatii-ni kita ga,
John-CT/-Nom party-to came but

sonohokanohito nikanshitewa shira-nai.
the-other-people about know-not
'John$_{CT}$ came to the party, but I don't know about the other people.'

This feature of CT, i.e., that it can be used when the speaker doesn't have enough information to resolve the original question under consideration, is what Oshima (2002) and Hara and van Rooij's, (2007) took special notice of and tried to capture. If the answerer uttered (46) instead of (40) in the state of information described above, she would be taken by the hearer to imply that no other people came to the party due to the exhaustification mechanism (see van Rooij & Schulz 2006 for a formal formulation). Her response would violate the Grice's Maxim of Quality.

(46) Jon-ga paatii-ni ki-mashi-ta.
John-Nom party-to come-Polite-Past
'John came to the party.'

Possible Reason 2: Secrecy, or Confidentiality

Suppose that the question under discussion is who came to the party and furthermore, the answerer is willing to proffer only the information as to whether John came to the party or not, keeping secret the information about the other people. What she can do in terms of question and answer will be that instead of answering the question 'Who came to the party?' directly, she will answer a restricted version of the question in which 'who' is restricted to 'John'—i.e., 'Did John come to the party?'—directly. This is exactly what the current theory specifies a CT sentence can be used for. The proposed use of CT motivated by secrecy is validated by the natural continuation observed between the first and the second sentences in examples like (47).

(47) Jon-wa/#-ga paatii-ni kita ga,
John-CT/-Nom party-to came but

sonohokanohito nikanshitewa ie-nai.
the-other-people about can-say-not
'John$_{CT}$ came to the party, but I can't say about the other people.'

The counterexample presented above against Hara and van Rooij's theory, example (17), is just another example of the use of a CT sentence motivated by secrecy, or confidentiality.

Possible Reason 3: Extension Specification by Positive and Negative Instances

When the extension of a one-place predicate is queried by an interrogative sentence like (41), one way to specify the extension is to specify the positive instances of the extension and let exhaustification (see again van Rooij and Schulz, 2006) imply that the rest of the domain is in the negative extension of the predicate. Another way is to specify both the positive and the negative instances of the extension separately (and not necessarily exhaustively). Specifically, for the positive instances of the predicate, the answerer specifies that it is true that they are in the extension of the predicate, and for the negative instances, she specifies that it is not true that they are in the extension of the predicate. This can be seen as an act of answering a WH-question by answering two Yes-No questions.

To use (40) as an example, in our current analysis, (40) can be seen as part of specifying the positive instances by answering the (implicit) question 'Did John come to the party?' in the two-part way of specifying the extension of the predicate under discussion. Then, (40) is expected to be followed by a sentence specifying some of the negative instances. For example, suppose that John, but not Mary came to the party. In terms of the partition of C″ in (48), the speaker could choose the shadowed block to be the case by uttering (46) plus exhaustification, 'Only John came to the party', or 'John and nobody else came to the party'.

(48)

C″ =

{John, Mary}	{John}
{Mary}	∅

Alternatively, she can utter first (49a) and then (50a) to choose the shaded blocks in (49b) and (50b), respectively, which has the same effect as designating the shadowed block in (48) to be the case directly.

(49) a. Jon-wa ki-ta.
John-CT come-Past
'John$_{CT}$ came.'

b.

C′ =

{John, Mary}	{John}
{Mary}	∅

(50) a. Mearii-wa ko-naka-tta.
Mary-CT come-not-Past
'Mary$_{CT}$ didn't come.'

b.

C‴ =

{John, Mary}	{John}
{Mary}	∅

This use of CT sentences–i.e., to specify positive instances, followed by a separate CT sentence to specify negative instances (or vice versa), in identifying the extension of a predicate, is considered to be a feature of CT sentences that was discussed as Reversed Polarity Implicature (RPI) in Sect. 2.2.1.

In the above, we have examined what the current theory of CT can say about the implicational/presuppositional features of CT that have been taken to be essential properties of CT in the approach that views CT as a focus-sensitive operator. We have demonstrated that these features can be seen as conversational implicatures, arising as the addressee infers the reason why, given a QUD, *wh*-γ, the speaker opts instead to answer one of *wh*-γ's sub-questions, ?-γ with sentence γ.

4 Conclusions

We have reviewed two representative existent approaches to CT, one that views CT as an information-structural discourse-regulating device–specifically, it characterizes a CT sentence as a direct answer to a sub-question of a QUD–and another that takes a CT to be a focus-sensitive operator with conventional implicatures or presuppositions. The former approach–or, strictly speaking, the particular analysis on this approach–we have demonstrated, is not general enough as a theory of CT because it cannot be extended to "non-canonical" examples of CT sentences that have more than one instance of CT phrase and/or no focused phrase; furthermore, it does not address the implicational/presuppositional features of CT. As for the latter approach, the alleged implicatures and the presuppositions for CT proposed in the literature have all been shown to be easy to find counterexamples to or to be cancellable, which strongly suggests that those are not hard-wired in the pragmatics of CT. Furthermore, the "non-canonical" examples have turned out to be problematic to the approach as well.

We have proposed a new analysis of CT couched in the partition semantics of question and answer presented in Groenendijk and Stokhof (1984) and Groenendijk (1999) and demonstrated that the new analysis can capture the insights of both of the above approaches and yet is free from the problems for them. That is, the new analysis can characterize a CT sentence as a direct answer to a sub-question of a QUD whether it is a "canonical" or a "non-canonical" example and will analyze the implicational/presuppositional features of CT as conversational implicatures arising as the addressee infers the reason why the speaker opts to answer the sub-question instead of the QUD. In this sense, the current analysis can be said to have the best of both worlds of the existent approaches, and more.

There are certainly many things about CT that have not been touched upon in this paper, among which is the fact that CTs can also occur in other types of sentences than declarative sentences: at least in Japanese, interrogative, imperative, exhortative, and performative sentences can contain CT elements, as was pointed out by Tomioka (2007). The issue of whether the current analysis can be extended to the occurrences of CT in non-declarative sentences is left for future research.

Acknowledgments I would like to thank two anonymous reviewers for their useful comments and suggestions, and one of them in particular, for rightly pointing out some critical loose ends in the previous version. I hope that they have been tied up in the current version, but of course, all the remaining errors are mine. And I am very grateful to the editor of the current volume, Professor Chungmin Lee, for his patience with my slow revision of the paper and for constantly encouraging me to finish the job. Without his encouragement, this paper might not be here. And I would like to thank the series editor, Professor Marcel Den Dikken for his finishing-touch suggestions and requests for clarifications. Last but not least, I would like to express my sincere gratitude to Kathy Hoyt for a very careful proofreading of the manuscript, which has resulted in a tremendous improvement in readability.

References

Büring, Daniel. 1999. Topic. In *Focus: Linguistic, cognitive, and computational perspectives*, ed. P. Bosch, and R. van der Sandt, 142–165. Cambridge: Cambridge University Press.

Constant, Noah. 2014. *Contrastive topic: meanings and realizations.* Amherst, MA: University of Massachusetts, Amherst Ph.D. dissertation.

Groenendijk, Jeroen. 1999. The logic of interrogation. In *Proceedings of the ninth conference on semantics and linguistic theory (SALT 9)*, ed. T. Matthews, and D.L. Strolovitch, 109–126. Ithaca: CLC Publications, Cornell University.

Groenendijk, Jeroen, and Martin Stokhof. 1984. *Studies on the semantics of questions and the pragmatics of answers.* Amsterdam: University of Amsterdam Ph.D. dissertation.

Hara, Yurie. 2006. Implicature unsuspendable: Japanese contrastive *wa*. In *Proceedings of the 2004 Texas linguistics society conference: issues at the semantics-pragmatics interface*, ed. P. Denis, E. McCready, A. Palmer, and B. Reese, 35–45. Somerville, MA: Cascadilla Press.

Hara, Yurie, and Robert van Rooij. 2007. Contrastive topics revisited: A simpler set of topic-alternatives. Talk given at the 38th Meeting of the North East Linguistic Society.

Higginbotham, James, and Robert May. 1981. Questions, quantifiers and crossing. *The Linguistic Review* 1: 41–80.

Kadmon, Nirit. 2001. *Formal pragmatics: Semantics, pragmatics, presupposition, and focus.* Malden, Massachusetts: Blackwell Publisher.

Kuno, Susumu. 1973. *The structure of the Japanese language.* Cambridge, MA: MIT Press.

Lee, Chungmin. 1999. Contrastive topic: A locus of the interface—Evidence from Korean and English. In *The Semantics/Pragmatics Interface from Different Points of View*, ed. Ken Turner, CRiSPI 1. Elsevier Science.

Lee, Chungmin. 2006. Contrastive topic/focus and polarity in discourse. In *Where Semantics Meets Pragmatics* (CRiSPI 16), eds. K. von Heusinger, & K. Turner, 381–420. Elsevier.

Lee, Chungmin. 2017. Contrastive topic, contrastive focus, alternatives and scalar implicatures. In *Contrastiveness in Information Structure, Alternatives, and Scalar Implicatures*, eds. Chungmin Lee, Ferenc Kiefer, and Manfred Krfika, 3–21. Springer.

Oshima, David, Y. 2002. Contrastive topic as a paradigmatic operator. Handout for Workshop on Information Structure in Context. Universität Stuttgart.

Pierrehumbert, Janet B. 1980. *The phonology and phonetics of English intonation.* Cambridge, MA: MIT Ph.D. dissertation.

Roberts, Craige. 1996. Information structure: Towards an integrated formal theory of pragmatics. In *OSUWPL Volume 49: Papers in Semantics*, eds. Jae Hak Yoon, & Andreas Kathol. Columbus, OH: Department of Linguistics, The Ohio State University.

Rooij, Robert van, and K. Schulz. 2006. Pragmatic meaning and non-monotonic reasoning: The case of exhaustive interpretation. *Linguistics and Philosophy* 29: 205–250.

Rooth, Mats. 1985. *Association with focus.* Amherst, MA: University of Massachusetts, Amherst Ph.D. dissertation.

Rooth, Mats. 1992. A theory of focus interpretation. *Natural Language Semantics* 1: 75–116.
Stalnaker, Robert. 1978. Assertion. In *Syntax and Semantics 9: Pragmatics*, ed. P. Cole, 315–322. New York: Academic Press.
Tomioka, Satoshi. 2007. Contrastive topic, speech acts, and (anti-)exhaustivity. Talk given at Stony Brook University, February 16, 2007.

Deriving the Properties of Structural Focus

Katalin É. Kiss

Abstract The paper has proposed a theory of structural focus which analyzes focus movement as the establishment of a syntactic predicate–subject structure, expressing specificational predication. The subject of the specificational construction, an open sentence, determines a set, which the predicate (the focus-moved constituent) identifies referentially. The subject of predication is associated with an existential presupposition (only an existing set can be referentially identified). The referential identification of a set consists in the exhaustive listing of its members—hence the exhaustivity of focus. It is claimed that this analysis also accounts for properties of focus movement constructions that current alternative theories cannot explain.

Keywords Focus • Focus movement • Exhaustivity • Existential presupposition • Specificational predication

1 Goal

This paper proposes a theory of structural focus derived via focus movement which can account for all the focus-related facts attested in Hungarian, among them facts which other current theories cannot explain. It will claim that focus movement serves the purpose of creating a predicate–subject structure, in which the focus-moved constituent functions as a specificational predicate. The properties of both the focus and the background follow from the independently established properties of specificational predication constructions.

Section 2 of the paper briefly introduces two recent theories of focus movement: the 'movement for stress' theory of Szendrői (2003), and the 'movement for the checking of the exhaustive identification feature' theory of Horvath (2005), pointing out the problems which they cannot handle. Section 3 presents the

K.É. Kiss (✉)
Research Institute for Linguistics of the Hungarian Academy of Sciences, Benczúr utca 33, Budapest 1068, Hungary
e-mail: ekiss@nytud.hu

C. Lee et al. (eds.), *Contrastiveness in Information Structure, Alternatives and Scalar Implicatures*, Studies in Natural Language and Linguistic Theory 91, DOI 10.1007/978-3-319-10106-4_3

proposal argued for. Section 4 demonstrates how the problems observed in Sect. 2 receive a natural solution in the proposed framework. Section 5 discusses a further consequence of the proposed theory, involving the definiteness effect attested in presentational constructions.

2 Some Current Theories of Structural Focus

2.1 *Structural Focus as a Phonological Phenomenon*

A type of language, represented, e.g., by Hungarian, has a designated focus position in the left periphery of sentence structure, as illustrated in (1b,c):

(1) a. Péter fel hívta Évát.

Peter up called Eve-ACC

'Peter called up Eve.'

b. Péter ÉVÁT hívta fel.

'It is Eve that Peter called up.

c. Évát PÉTER hívta fel.

'It is Peter who called up Eve.'

This type of structural focus, called identificational focus by Kiss (1998), has a number of properties that prosodic focus does not necessarily share, among them: (i) it is derived by movement (also accompanied by V-movement in Hungarian); (ii) it is interpreted exhaustively; (iii) the background is associated with an existential presupposition; (iv) the focus is subject to selectional restrictions (universal quantifiers cannot be focussed). Theories of structural focus, among them the best know theories of these days, Szendrői's (2003) focus theory, and Horvath's (2005) exhaustive identification theory, face the challenge of accounting for these properties without ad hoc stipulations.

Szendrői's (2003) influential theory of structural focus aims to provide a unified analysis of English-type prosodic focus, and Hungarian-type structural focus. Both types of foci are claimed to be motivated by the stress–focus correspondence principle (Reinhart 1995; Zubizarreta 1998), according to which the focus of a clause is any constituent containing the main stress of the intonational phrase, as determined by the stress rule. Whereas in an English-type language the stress–focus correspondence is usually attained by stress shift, in a Hungarian-type language it is claimed to be achieved by the movement of focus into the position of main stress, at the left edge of the verbal projection. (Szendrői analyzes the Hungarian sentence as a VP. Topic constituents are claimed to be extrametrical adjuncts, which are skipped by the stress rule.) The V-movement accompanying Hungarian focus movement serves the purpose of establishing a functional projection the specifier of which provides a landing site for focus movement.

Szendrői's 'movement for stress' theory of focusing raises several questions, among them

(i) The structural focus in Hungarian does not necessarily bear main stress. If it is preceded by a universal quantifier (preposed to the left edge of the VP via overt Q-raising), or certain types of adverbs, it can lack primary stress—as pointed out by Horvath (2005). In the following examples, the initial quantifier and adverb bear primary stresses, whereas the focus (spelled in capital letters) can be unstressed:

(2) a. **'Mindenkit** [$_{\text{FocP}}$ JÁNOS hívott meg]

everybody-ACC John invited PRT

'JOHN invited everybody. [For everybody, it was John who invited him.]''

b. **'Valóban** [$_{\text{FocP}}$ JÁNOS késett el]

indeed John was.late PRT

'Indeed it was John who was late.'

The focus is unstressed if it is presupposed; e.g., (2b) would be felicitious in a context of the following type:

(3) a. Azt gyanítom, hogy [$_{\text{FocP}}$ JÁNOS késett el]

'I suspect that it was John who was late.'

b. **'Valóban** [$_{\text{FocP}}$ JÁNOS késett el]

'**Indeed** it was John who was late.'

The intuition is that (3b) involves a second-occurrence prosodic focus, with the first focus presupposed, hence destressed—however, Szendői does not give any hint regarding how such an analysis could be executed in the framework outlined by her.

(ii) A more severe problem is that the uniform treatment of the English-type prosodic focus and the Hungarian-type structural focus hides their interpretational difference. It remains unaccounted for why structural focus—and only structural focus—has exhaustive interpretation; why (2a), unlike its English counterpart, is true if and only if everybody was invited only by John.

The exhaustivity of structural focus was first demonstrated by Szabolcsi (1981), on the basis of solid evidence often quoted in the literature ever since.[1] Here let me only present two little known arguments.

According to Horn (1972), Levinson (2000), Kadmon (2001), and others, the basic meaning of a numerical modifier *n* in natural language is 'at least *n*'. Indeed, this is the meaning a Hungarian numerical modifier is associated with whether the modified expression is in postverbal argument position (4a) or in prefocus topic

[1]See also Kiss (1998, 2009), and Horvath (2005, 2006). For a somewhat different view, treating the exhaustivity of focus as an implicature, see Wedgwood (2005).

position (4b). (Pragmatic factors can impose an upper limit on *n*—however, the upper limit is always a mere implicature which can be easily canceled.) In the preverbal focus position, however, the numeral *n* can only mean 'exactly *n*' (4c), no matter what the pragmatic conditions are—which is derived from the [+exhaustive] feature of focus, i.e., the exclusion of all alternatives but the one denoted by the focused constituent in Kiss (2009).

(4) a. János [$_{\text{PredP}}$ meg keres **egy milliót** havonta]
John PRT earns one million-ACC monthly
'John earns a/one million a month.' (one million or more)

b. [$_{\text{TopP}}$ **Egy milliót** [$_{\text{PredP}}$ meg keres János havonta]]
'A/one million, John earns a month.' (one million or more)

c. János [$_{\text{FocP}}$ EGY MILLIÓT keres meg havonta]
'It is one million that John earns a month.' (exactly one million)

As shown by Szabolcsi (1981), *ha* 'if' clauses are also interpreted differently in and out of focus. Conditionals, like other types of embedded clauses in Hungarian, have a pronominal head. When focused, the embedded clause is obligatorily extraposed, leaving only the pronominal head in the focus position of the matrix clause (5c). Whereas a *ha*-clause functions as a simple conditional both in postverbal position and in topic position, it is a biconditional (an *if and only if* clause) in focus position, which is again derived from the exhaustivity of focus by Szabolcsi (1981).

(5) a. Fel-hívlak [(**akkor**$_i$) [ha János megérkezett]$_i$]
up call-I-you then if John arrived
'I will call you **if** John has arrived.'

b. [[Ha János megérkezett]$_i$ (**akkor**$_i$)], fel-hívlak.
'I will call you **if** John has arrived.'

c. [$_{\text{FocP}}$ AKKOR$_i$ hívlak fel, [ha János megérkezett]$_i$]
then call-I-you up if John arrived
'I call you **if and only if** John has arrived.'

If focusing is merely movement for stress, as claimed by Szendrői (2003), the interpretational differences between (4a, b) and (4c), and between (5a, b) and (5c) cannot be predicted.

(iii) Szendrői's theory cannot handle the acceptability difference between (6b) and (6c). Both sentences intend to answer the question *What happened?,* i.e., both are all new sentences. In the English equivalents, the object bears primary stress in both cases. If focusing is movement for stress, the object should be focusable in both sentences. In (6c), however, the focus movement of the object is unacceptable.

(6) a. Mi történt? 'What happened?'

b. McCAINT választották elnökjelöltnek a republikánusok az USÁ-ban.

McCain-ACC elected candidate-DAT the republicans the USA-in

'Republicans elected McCain presidential candidate in the USA.'

c. %BENAZIR BHUTTÓT gyilkolták meg a fanatikusok Pakisztánban.

Benazir Bhutto-ACC murdered PRT the fanatics Pakistan-in.

'Fanatics murdered Benazir Bhutto in Pakistan.'

This example is problematic for the focus theory of Fanselow (2006), as well, according to whom focus movement is nothing but the movement of an accented constituent, and the focus position is not associated with any special semantic or pragmatic function.

(iv) According to Szendrői (2003: 37) the focus of an answer is the constituent that is questioned. In question–answer pairs like that in (7), however, it is the other way round: it is the familiar, nonquestioned constituent of the question that has to undergo focus movement in the answer—contrary to prediction.

(7) a. Ki volt Fleming?/Mit tudsz Flemingről?

'Who was Fleming?/What do you know about Fleming?'

b. Ő/FLEMING fedezte fel a penicillint.

he/Fleming discovered PRT the penicillin

'It was him/it was Fleming who discovered penicillin.'

A proper theory of structural focus should also account for examples of this type.

2.2 *Structural Focus as a Constituent with an Exhaustive Identification Operator*

In reaction to Szendrői's theory of focus, Horvath (2005, 2006) has developed an alternative theory intended to account for the exhaustivity of the Hungarian focus, while maintaining the unified treatment of English and Hungarian focus. She claims that structural focus is an XP with an invisible Exhaustive Identification operator (EIOp) in its specifier, attracted to the specifier of an Exhaustive Identification Phrase in order to check the Exhaustive Identification features of its head. The EIOp requires association with focus.

This theory only eliminates problem (ii) of the stress-driven theory of focus movement, and also raises new problems, among them

(v) The theory—correctly—acknowledges the structural difference between sentences of type (8a) and those of type (9a), which becomes transparent under negation. In (8a), *orvos* 'doctor' occupies the specifier of EIP, where it precedes the verb also when negated:

(8) a. Az apám [$_{EIP}$ ORVOS [volt]].
my father doctor was
'My father was a doctor.'
b. Az apám [$_{NegP}$ nem [$_{EIP}$ ORVOS [volt]]
my father not doctor was
'My father wasn't a doctor.'

In (9a), on the other hand, *jó orvos* 'good doctor' occupies the position of the verbal modifier (identified here as Spec, PredP), where it is preceded by the V, undergoing head movement, in negative sentences:

(9) a. Az apám [$_{PredP}$ *jó orvos* [$_{Pred'}$ volt]].
my father good doctor was
'My father was a good doctor.'
b. Az apám [$_{NegP}$ nem [volt [$_{PredP}$ *jó orvos*]]]
my father not was good doctor
'My father wasn't a good doctor.'

What Horvath's theory leaves unexplained is why *orvos*—as opposed to *jó orvos*—is to be focused in the unmarked case.

(vi) In the framework of the EIOp theory, the object in (10) is associated with an EI operator, the effect of which is canceled by the expression *többek között* 'among others'. It seems uneconomical to introduce an operator and immediately neutralize it.

(10) Többek között JÁNOST hívtam meg. / JÁNOST hívtam meg többek között.
among others John-ACC invited-I PRT
'It was John, among others, that I invited.'

(vii) Hungarians tend to move to focus position also constituents whose interpretation is inherently exhaustive.

(11) Andrásnak [$_{FocP}$ DECEMBER 13-ÁN van a születésnapja]
Andrew-DAT December 13th-on is the birthday-his
'It is on December 13th that Andrew has his birthday.'

December 13th exhausts the set of days of Andrew's birth. It seems redundant, hence uneconomical, to mark its exhaustivity also with an EI operator.

(viii) It does not follow from the theory why universal quantifiers cannot be focussed

(12) *MINDEN FIÚT hívtam meg.
every boy-ACC invited-I PRT
'I invited everybody.'

(ix) It is unexplained why a bare nominal, ungrammatical in argument position, becomes perfectly acceptable if focussed:

(13) a.*Évát fel-kérte szőke fiú.
Eve-ACC PRT asked[for a dance] blond boy-NOM
b. Évát SZŐKE FIÚ kérte fel.
'It was a blond boy that asked Eve for a dance.'

3 The Proposal: Focus as a Specificational Predicate

The present proposal adopts Higgins's (1973) analysis of the English pseudo-cleft focus, and Huber's (2000) analysis of the Swedish and German cleft focus to Hungarian structural focus.[2] In the theory developed by Higgins and Huber, pseudo-cleft and cleft sentences instantiate a type of predication structure called specificational predication. The wh-clause represents the subject of predication, and the (pseudo-)cleft constituent, identified as the focus, represents the predicate. In specificational predication constructions, neither the subject, nor the predicate is claimed to be referential.[3] In the formulation of Huber (2000), the subject determines a set, and the predicate referentially identifies it, by listing its members. The predicate, i.e., the (pseudo-)cleft focus, is exhaustive because the referential identification of a set consists in the exhaustive listing of its members. The subject is associated with an existential presupposition because only an existing set can be referentially identified.

I claim that focus movement in Hungarian—and presumably in other languages, as well—serves the purpose of establishing a predicate–subject articulation to be interpreted as a specificational predication construction. The focus-moved constituent functions as the specificational predicate, and the postfocus sentence part

[2]For previous formulations of this proposal, see Kiss (2006a, b). For an extension of Higgins' (1973) analysis to English truncated clefts, see Mikkelsen (2004).

[3]Mikkelsen (2004) argues that the predicate of a specificational construction is, nevertheless, more referential than its subject.

(the background) functions as the subject of predication.[4] The subject of predication, an open sentence, determines a set, which the focus identifies referentially. The referential identification of the set determined by the background is predicted to entail the exhaustive listing of its members. Furthermore, the background is predicted to be associated with an existential presupposition.

4 The Facts Explained

From the proposed analysis, all the properties of the Hungaria focus construction fall out, including the problematic facts enlisted under (i)–(ix) above.

Focus movement is triggered by the need of creating a predicate–subject structure, with the predicate and the subject mutually c-commanding (or m-commanding) each other.

The fact that focus movement goes together with V-movement seems to be independently motivated, as focusless negated sentences and for e.g., imperatives also involve V-movement. Apparently, a neutral predicate, with its preverbal position occupied by the secondary predicate: a verbal particle, a predicative NP or a predicative AdvP (see, e.g., (14)) cannot be further extended by an operator; it can merely be merged with Q-raised quantifiers, adverbials, and topics. The neutral predicate can only be combined with a further operator if it becomes V-initial, i.e., if it undergoes V-movement (see, e.g., (15)). Thus V-movement signals a kind of type-shift: the predicate phrase becoming the argument of a higher predicate.

(14) PredP

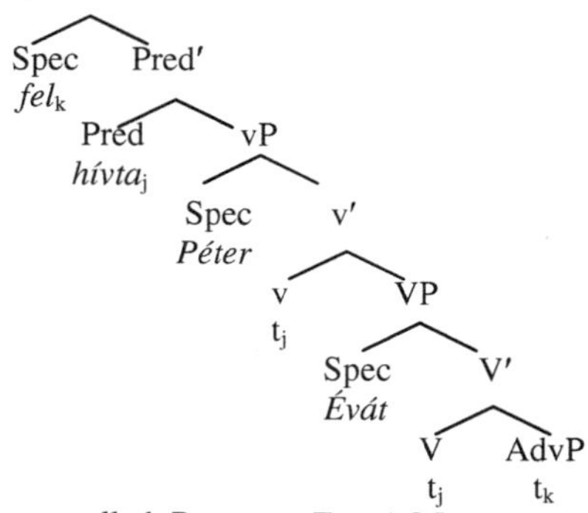

up called Peter Eve-ACC
'Peter called up Eve.'

[4] Although in subsequent stages of the derivation, Q-raising and topicalization can remove certain constituents of the postfocus unit (the subject of predication), they remain represented by their copies in postverbal position.

(15)

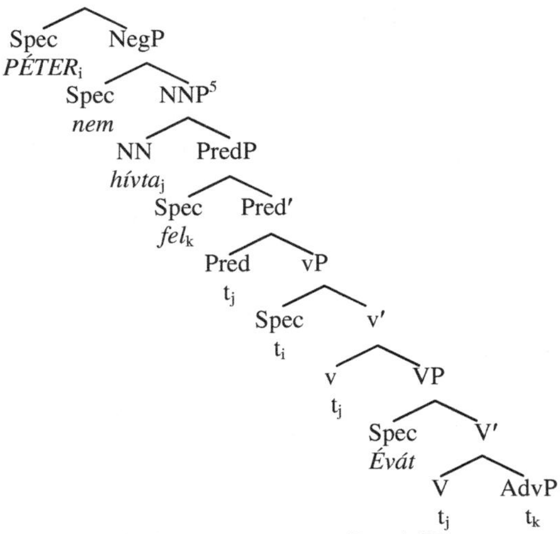

Peter not called up Eve-ACC
'It was Peter who did not call up Eve.'[6]

This is how the proposed analysis accounts for problems (i)–(ix).

Problem (i), illustrated by examples (1a, b), concerns the question why the structural focus of the Hungarian sentence does not always bear main stress. In the proposed framework, there is no direct relation between structural focus and stress. In Hungarian, Nuclear Stress is assigned to the leftmost constituent in a phrase. There is also a stress-reduction rule which destresses given (anaphoric) constituents. If the filler of Spec, FocP is preceded by quantifiers and/or adverbials adjoined to FocP, they are also assigned Nuclear Stresses, as shown in (1a) and (1b). Any of the constituents marked as 'strong' by the Nuclear Stress Rule can also be destressed, if it is anaphorically given. This is what happens to the focus in both (1a) and (1b).

Problems (ii), (vi), and (vii), related to the exhaustivity of structural focus, are explained by the specificational predicate function of focus. Specification means the referential identification of a set by listing its members, hence it is understood to be exhaustive, as illustrated by examples (5) and (6). However, exhaustivity is not asserted in focus constructions; it is a mere entailment. That is why focusing is not redundant whether exhaustivity appears to be neutralized right away by the overt expression *többek között* 'among others' (cf. (10)), or whether it is also lexically entailed, as in (11). Sentences (10) and (11) are not formulated as specificational constructions in order to mark the exhaustivity of focus. (11) serves the purpose of identifying the day when Andrew has his birthday, whereas (10) serves the purpose of

[5]NNP stands for Non-Neutral Phrase; it is a term of Olsvay (2000).

[6]The postverbal section of the Hungarian sentence, i.e., the vP in (14), and the PredP in (15), can be freely linearized. The optimal postverbal order is that observing Behaghel's (1932) Law of Growing Constituents—see Kiss (2008).

specifying the set of those I invited. This set is specified in part by an R-expression (*János*), in part by a kind of pronominal expression (*többek (között)*' (among) others').

Examples (6), and (8)–(9), illustrating problems (iii) and (v), show that specificational predication is licensed if the background is associated with an existential presupposition.[7] Although both (6b) and (6c) are all new sentences answering the question *What happened?*, in the case of (6b) it is part of the knowledge base of the speaker and the listener that there is someone that the Republicans will elect, or have already elected, presidential candidate in the USA.[8] In the case of (6c), the focus-background articulation is impossible because the background lacks an existential presupposition: When Benazir Bhutto was murdered, it was not shared knowledge that there was someone that fanatics would murder or had already murdered in Pakistan.

The minimal pair in (8) and (9) illustrates the same point. In the case of a grown-up person it is presumed that he has an occupation; when asking (8a) we are merely interested in the specification of this occupation. Thus (8a) amounts to asking 'is it true that the profession that your grandfather had is the profession *doctor*?' Being a good doctor, on the other hand, is not the specification of a generally held assumption.

Problem (iv) is also related to problems (iii) and (v). The question is why we have to focus *Fleming/he* in (7b), when *Fleming/he* represents the only given element in the sentence. Observe another question–answer pair illustrating the same point:[9]

(16) a. Who was Jack Ruby?

b. [$_{\text{FocP}}$ Ő lőtte le Lee Harvey Oswaldot]

he shot PRT Lee Harvey Oswald-ACC

'It was him who shot Lee Harvey Oswald.'

Both (7b) and (16b) are clear instances of specificational predication: their background determines a set associated with an existential presupposition (the sets 'who invented penicillin', and 'who shot Lee Harvey Oswald', respectively), which the focus referentially identifies. It is not a requirement that the set to be specified must be given information, and the listing of its member(s) must be new; it can just as well be the other way round, as happens in (7) and (16).

The focus-background articulation of the answer is not licensed if the background is not associated with an existential presupposition; thus the discourse in (17) is unacceptable—unless there has already been discussion about a certain man who shot his wife.

---

[7]According to Geurts and van der Sandt (2004), the background is associated with an existential presupposition in all types of focus constructions. They call the following rule 'the null hypothesis'
(i) The Background-Presupposition Rule

Whenever focusing gives rise to a background $\lambda x.\varphi(x)$, there is a presupposition to the effect that $\lambda x.\varphi(x)$ holds of some individual.

[8]Delin and Oberlander (1995) make a similar claim about the subordinate clause of cleft sentences: they count as presuppositional also when they convey information that is expected to be known.

[9]The English equivalents of (7b) and (16b) are called comment-clause clefts by Delin and Oberlander (1995).

(17) Who was John Smith?

%[$_{FocP}$ Ő lőtte le a feleségét]]

he shot PRT his wife

'%It was him who shot his wife.'

Problem (viii) was the question why a universal quantifier cannot be focussed. Partee (1987) has shown that universal quantifiers cannot be used as predicate nominals, in other words, as nominal predicates. If the focus functions as a predicate, the impossibility of focussing a universal quantifier is predicted.[10]

---

[10]Puskas (2000:342) claims that this does not hold in Hungarian, on the basis of examples like.

(i) Emőke (volt) minden örömöm.
Emőke (was) all joy-my
'Emőke is/was all my joy.'

According to Surányi (2002), the constraint formulated by Giannakidou and Quer (1995) does not apply to *all*-type universal quantifiers. However, in Hungarian, *every* and *all*-type quantifiers do not seem to differ in the relevant respect (neither of them can be focussed). In my analysis, *Emőke* is the predicate nominal in (i), and *minden örömem* is the subject. If *minden örömem* were a predicate nominal, it ought to be able to precede the verb *volt* (occupying first Spec, PredP, and then Q-raised into a PredP-adjoined position). Furthermore, if *Emőke* were the subject, it ought to be able to undergo topicalization, i.e., to occupy an unstressed clause-initial position. Both of these moves are impossible

(ii) *Emőke 'minden örömöm volt.
Emőke all joy-my was
'Emőke was all my joy.'

Cf.

(iii) Minden örömöm Emőke volt.
'All my joy was Emőke.'

A reviewer mentions that if *Emőke* is the predicate of this sentence, it will reject a nonrestrictive relative clause. This is, indeed, the case:

(iv) ?* Emőke, akit gyerekkorom óta ismertem, volt minden örömöm.
Emőke whom childhood-my since know-I was all joy-my
'Emőke, who I had known since my childhood, was all my joy.'
(v) *Emőke t_i volt minden örömöm, [akit gyerekkorom óta ismertem]$_i$.

The reviewer also mentions that in the English *She is my every dream*, where the quantifier occurs inside (rather than on the edge of) the predicate nominal, the noun phrase *my every dream* is not outwardly quantificational: *Someone made my every dream come true* does not support a distributive reading. This does not hold for Hungarian; in example (vi), the noun phrase is Q-raised, and is interpreted distributively

(vi) Minden álmomat valóra váltotta valaki.
every dream-my-ACC true-to rendered somebody
'Someone made every dream of mine come true.'

Problem (ix), illustrated by example (13), also represents a consequence of the predicate status of focus. A bare NP, which cannot function as an argument,[11] is grammatical as a predicate in Hungarian:

(18) a. Éva vőlegénye szőke fiú (volt).
Eve's fiancé blond boy (was)
'Eve's fiancé is/was a blond boy.'

b. A tettest szőke fiúnak hitték.
the offender-ACC blond boy-ACC believed-they
'The offender was believed to be a blond boy.'

In (13b), the bare nominal subject is grammatical because the focus position it occupies is associated with a (specificational) predicate interpretation.

5 A Further Consequence of the Proposal

The proposed analysis is further supported by the fact that it has good consequences in other areas of grammar, as well. For example, it can explain a curious correlation between focusing and definiteness effect.

As is well known from the literature (Szabolcsi 1986; Kiss 1995; Piñón 2006a, b; Peredy 2009, and the references therein), verbs of (coming into) being and creation require a nonspecific theme. Compare:

(19) a. Született egy baba.
was.born a baby
'A baby was born.'

b.*A baba született.
the baby was.born
'The baby was born.'

(20) a. János szerzett egy autót.
John obtained a car-ACC
'John obtained a car.'

b.*János minden autót szerzett.[12]
John every car-ACC obtained
'John obtained every car.'

[11]In fact, a semantically incorporated theme or goal argument occupying Spec, PredP, the position of secondary predicates, can be represented by a bare nominal.

[12]Hungarian verbs of (coming into) being and creation also have particle verb counterparts, which denote the change of their theme, whose existence is presupposed. These particle verbs, as opposed to their bare V equivalents, select a [+specific] theme

(i) a. A gyerekek meg-születtek.
the children PRT were.born
'The children were born.'
b.*Gyerekek meg-születtek.

(ii) a. János meg-szerezte az autókat.
John PRT obtained the cars
'John obtained the cars.'
b.*János meg-szerzett autókat.

Interestingly, the focusing of an adjunct, or the focusing of the agent neutralizes the 'definiteness effect', i.e., the nonspecificity requirement on the theme; the focusing of the theme, on the other hand, has no such neutralizing effect

(21) a. A baba TEGNAP született.
the baby yesterday was.born
'The baby was born YESTERDAY.'

b.*A KISLÁNY született.
the little.girl was.born
'THE LITTLE GIRL was born."

(22) a. Minden autót JÁNOS szerzett.
every car-ACC JOHN obtained
'Every car was obtained by JOHN.'

b. János minden autót ILLEGÁLISAN szerzett.
John every car illegally obtained
'John obtained every car ILLEGALLY.'

Szabolcsi (1986) derived the (in)definiteness effect illustrated in (19) and (20) from the meaning of the verbal predicates: they assert the (coming into) being of their theme argument; hence the existence of their theme cannot be presupposed; that is why they cannot be associated with a determiner eliciting a [+specific] reading. In (21) and (22), both the verb expressing coming into being and the theme whose coming into being it denotes constitute (part of) the background of a focus-background construction, in other words, (part of) the subject in a specificational predication construction. (More precisely, in (22) it is the variable bound by the Q-raised universal quantifier that represents the theme argument in the background/subject of predication). Recall that the subject of a specificational predication construction is associated with an existential presupposition, i.e., the event of the theme's coming into being is presupposed in both cases; that is why also a [+specific] theme is licensed. However, if the theme is the focus/specificational predicate, no existential presupposition is assigned to it, hence the (in)definiteness effect is not neutralized.

6 Conclusion

The paper has proposed a theory of structural focus which analyzes focus movement as the establishment of a syntactic predicate–subject structure, expressing specificational predication in the sense of Higgins (1973) and Huber (2000). It is claimed that this analysis also accounts for properties of focus movement constructions that current alternative theories cannot explain. The subject of a specificational construction, an open sentence, determines a set, which the predicate (the focus-moved constituent) identifies referentially. The crucial properties of a specificational predication construction are the existential presupposition associated with the subject of predication (only an existing set can be referentially identified), and the exhaustivity of the focus (the referential identification of a set consists of the exhaustive listing of its members). Hence the [+exhaustive] feature of the focus is not asserted, but is always present as an entailment. The specificational predicate–subject of predication (in other words, the focus-background) articulation of the sentence does not correlate with either the new–given division of the information conveyed (the open sentence determining the set to be identified (i.e., the background) can also be new, and the listing of the members of the set (i.e., the focus) can also be given). There is no direct correlation between the focus-background articulation and the stress pattern of the sentence, either (e.g., a given focus can be destressed).

References

Behaghel, Otto. 1932. *Deutsche Syntax IV*. Heidelberg: Carl Winters.

Delin, Judy J., Jon, Oberlander. 1995. Syntactic constraints on discourse structure: the case of *it*-clefts. *Linguistics* 33/3.

É. Kiss, Katalin. 1995. Definiteness effect revisited. In: *Levels and structures. Approaches to Hungarian,* ed. István Kenesei, Vol. 5, 65–88. Szeged: JATE.

É. Kiss, Katalin. 1998. Identificational focus versus information focus. *Language* 74: 245–273.

É. Kiss, Katalin. 2006a. Apparent or real? On the complementary distribution of identificational focus and the verbal particle. In: *Event structure and the left periphery. Studies on Hungarian*, ed. É. Kiss, Katalin, 201–224. Dordrecht: Springer.

É. Kiss, Katalin. 2006. Focussing as predication. In *The architecture of focus*, ed. Valéria Molnár, and Susanne Winkler, 169–193. Berlin: Mouton de Gruyter.

É. Kiss, Katalin. 2008. Free word order, (non–)configurationality, and phases. *Linguistic Inquiry* 39: 441–475.

É. Kiss, Katalin. 2009. Structural focus and exhanstivity. In *Information structure: theoretical, typological, and experimental perspectives*, ed. Caroline Féry, and Malte Zimmermann. Oxford: Oxford University Press.

Fanselow, Gisbert. 2006. On pure syntax. In *Form, structure and grammar*, ed. P. Brandt, and E. Fuss. Berlin: Akademie Verlag.

Geurts, Bart, and Rob Sandt. 2004. Interpreting focus. *Theoretical Linguistics* 30: 1–44.

Higgins, Roger F. 1973. The pseudo-cleft construction in English. PhD diss., MIT

Horn, Laurence R. 1972. On the semantic properties of logical operators in English. Ph.D. diss., UCLA

Horvath, Julia. 2005. Is "Focus Movement" driven by stress? In: *Approaches to Hungarian 9. Papers from the Düsseldorf Conference,* eds. Christopher Piñón and Péter Siptár, 131–158. Budapest: Akadémiai Kiadó.

Horvath, Julia. 2006. Separating "Focus Movement" from focus. In *Clever and Right: A Festschrift for Joe Emonds*, ed. V.S.S. Karimi, et al. Berlin: Mouton de Gruyter.

Huber, Stefan. 2000. *Es-Clefts und det-Clefts*. Stockholm: Almquist and Wiksell.

Kadmon, N. 2001. *Formal pragmatics*. Oxford: Blackwell.

Levinson, S.C. 2000. *Presumptive meanings*. Cambridge, MA: MIT Press.

Mikkelsen, Line H. L. 2004. Specifying who: on the structure, meaning, and use of specificational copular clauses. PhD diss., University of California Santa Cruz

Olsvay, Csaba. 2000. Formális jegyek egyeztetése a magyar nemsemleges mondatokban. In *A mai magyar nyelv leírásának újabb módszerei IV*, ed. László Büky, and Márta Maleczki, 119–151. Szeged: SZTE.

Partee, Barbara. 1987. Noun phrase interpretation and type-shifting principles. In: *Studies in discourse representation theory and the theory of generalized quantifiers*, GRASS 8, eds. J. Groenendijk, D. de Jongh, and M. Stokhof, 115–143. Dordrecht: Foris

Peredy, Márta. 2009. Obligatory adjuncts licensing definiteness effect constructions. In: *Adverbs and adverbial adjuncts at the interfaces*, ed. Katalin É. Kiss, 197–230. Berlin: Mouton de Gruyter

Piñón, Christopher. 2006a. Definiteness effect verbs. In: *Event structure and the left periphery*, ed. Katalin É. Kiss, 75–90. Dordrecht: Springer

Piñón, Christopher. 2006b. Weak and strong accomplishments. In: *Event structure and the left periphery*, ed. Katalin É. Kiss, 91–106. Dordrecht: Springer

Puskás, Genovéva. 2000. *Word order in Hungarian: the syntax of A-bar positions*. Amsterdam: John Benjamins.

Reinhart, Tanya. 1995. *Interface strategies*. OTS Working Papers (TL-95-002).

Surányi, Balázs. 2002. *Multiple operator movements in Hungarian*. Utrecht: LOT.

Szabolcsi, Anna. 1981. The semantics of topic–focus articulation. In: *Formal methods in the study of language*, eds. J. Groenendijk et al., 513–540. Amsterdam: Matematisch Centrum.

Szabolcsi, Anna. 1986. From the definiteness effect to lexical integrity. In *Topic, focus, and configurationality*, ed. Werner Abraham, and Sjaak de Meij, 321–348. Amsterdam: John Benjamins.

Szendrői, Kriszta. 2003. A stress-based approach to the syntax of Hungarian focus. *The Linguistic Review* 20: 37–78.

Wedgwood, Daniel. 2005. *Shifting the focus. From static structures to the dynamics of interpretation*. Amsterdam: Elsevier.

Zubizarreta, Maria. 1998. *Prosody, focus, and word order*. Cambridge, Mass: MIT Press.

Topic, Focus, and Exhaustive Interpretation

Robert van Rooij and Katrin Schulz

Abstract In this paper, we propose that a sentence like *John*$_T$ *ate broccoli*$_F$ should pragmatically be interpreted as follows: (a) Focus should be interpreted exhaustively; John ate only broccoli; (b) Topic must be interpreted exhaustively: Only John ate (only) broccoli; and (c) The speaker takes it to be possible (or even knows, if he is competent) that at least one alternative of the form *x ate y* not entailed by the sentence is true. It will be shown that in terms of this analysis we can also account for all the scope-inversion data of Büring (Linguist Philos 20: 175–194, 1997), without giving rise to some of the problems of the latter analysis.

Keywords Topic · Focus · Exhaustive interpretation · Dynamic semantics · Economic encoding · Questions

The ideas in Sects. 1–4 and 6 of this paper were presented during the 2007-Contrastiveness and Scalar Implicatures workshop of CIL 18 in Seoul. The ideas and even the writing of Sects. 2–5 date back to 2004. The ideas presented in Sect. 6 were developed in cooperation with Yurie Hara to improve on some ideas of Hara (2005) and discussed in a joint draft that was never published. We would like to thank Yurie Hara for her 'intellectual' contribution to this paper. Furthermore, we would like to thank Chungmin Lee, an anonymous reviewer, and the participants of the workshop for their comments.

R. van Rooij · K. Schulz (✉)
FNWI ILLC (Institute for Logic, Language and Computation), Universiteit van Amsterdam (University of Amsterdam), P.O. Box 94242, 1090 GE Amsterdam, The Netherlands
e-mail: k.schulz@uva.nl

R. van Rooij
e-mail: r.a.m.vanrooij@uva.nl

C. Lee et al. (eds.), *Contrastiveness in Information Structure, Alternatives and Scalar Implicatures*, Studies in Natural Language and Linguistic Theory 91, DOI 10.1007/978-3-319-10106-4_4

1 Introduction

Consider the following sentence with a typical topic-focus, or hat-contour:

(1) $[\text{John}]_T$ ate $[\text{broccoli}]_F$.

In this paper we argue that the (strong) pragmatic interpretation of this sentence is as follows:

(a) Focus should be interpreted exhaustively: John ate only broccoli.
(b) Topic must be interpreted exhaustively: Only John ate (only) broccoli.
(c) The speaker takes it to be possible (or even knows, if he is competent) that at least one alternative of the form *x ate y* not entailed by (1) is true. From (a) it follows that this alternative cannot be *John ate y*, with *y* different from broccoli; from (b) it follows that this alternative cannot be *x ate broccoli*, with *x* different from John. Thus, the alternative must be something like *Mary ate the beans*.

In Sect. 2 of this paper we will propose how to interpret focus exhaustively. In Sect. 3, we will defend claim (a), despite the existence of sentences like '$[\text{Some boys}]_T$ ate $[\text{broccoli}]_F$', by making use of *dynamic exhaustivity*: exhaustive interpretation is sensitive to the denotation of discourse referents. In Sect. 4, we will defend (b) mainly on empirical grounds. But we also suggest that claim (b) already makes sense for conceptual reasons. Section 5 deals with topic accent and the economic encoding of information. Section 6 discusses claim (c), and it will be shown that in terms of it we can account for all the scope-inversion data in Büring (1997), without giving rise to some of the problems of the latter analysis. Section 7 concludes this paper.

2 Bare Focus, Circumscription, and Exhaustivity

Consider the following sentence:

(2) John introduced $[\text{Bill}]_F$ to Sue.

In this sentence the item *Bill* is focussed. In what types of contexts can we appropriately use a sentence like (2) with this focal accent, and what is its effect? The central intuition implemented by most theories of focus (e.g., Jackendoff 1972; Rooth 1985) is that (2) can only be used appropriately in a context in which the question expressed by *Who was introduced by John to Sue?* was at issue and in which (2) was not yet common ground. Many theorists (e.g., Rooth 1992; Krifka 1995) have proposed that focal stress, in addition give rise to Gricean Quantity implicatures. In the case of example (2), to the implicature that for none of the other individuals under discussion it is true (as far as the speaker knows) that John introduced this other individual to Sue.

There are two popular theories of focus-dependent interpretation on the market that can account for these intuitions: Rooth's (1985, 1992) alternative semantics, and the structured meaning approach of Jacobs (1983), von Stechow (1991) and Krifka (1995).[1] To start with the latter, assume that a sentence is represented as a Background-Focus pair $\langle B, F\rangle$, and that the item in focus gives rise to a set of alternatives $Alt(F)$. The background B indicates that a question of the form *Who has property B?* is at issue. Then, we can describe Krifka's analysis in terms of Jacob's assertion operator as follows[2]:

(3) $[\![\mathbf{Assert}(\langle B, F, Alt(F)\rangle])]\!] = [\![B(F)]\!]$ iff $B(F)$ is assertable and for all $F' \in Alt(F)$ such that $B(F') \neq B(F)$, the speaker has reasons not to assert $B(F')$.

Krifka explicitly states that there might be various reasons for not asserting alternative propositions $B(F')$: it might be that $B(F')$ is weaker (entailed by) $B(F)$, or that the speaker may know that $B(F')$ is false or lacks sufficient evidence for it. In particular, it might be that $B(F')$ is stronger than (entails) $B(F)$, and that the speaker knows that this stronger proposition is false. In the latter case, Krifka notices that the assertion operator can account for many scalar implicatures. This is such an important special case of the assertion operator that he defines it as a special operator called 'Scal.Assert':

(4) $$[\![\mathbf{Scal.Assert}_1(\langle B, F, Alt(F)\rangle)]\!] = \{w \in [\![B(F)]\!] | \neg\exists F' \in Alt(F) : w \in [\![B(F')]\!] \wedge [\![B(F')]\!] \subset [\![B(F)]\!]\}$$

We will assume in this paper that neither 'Assert,' nor 'Scal.Assert' is meant as a *syntactic* operator—e.g., like a hidden *only*—as some recent authors (e.g., Chierchia et al. 2012) seem to favor. No, both should be thought of as *pragmatic* interpretation rules. According to the latter interpretation rule, any world that verifies the sentence is excluded for which there is an alternative F' in $Alt(F)$ such that replacing F in the sentence by F' gives rise to a statement that is true in this world and more informative than the actual assertion given. Obviously, for this analysis to have any effect for a sentence like (2), Krifka has to assume that denotations of conjunctive noun phrases like *Bill and Mary* can be alternatives to (the denotation of) *Bill*, and that the background predicate B is *distributive* in nature. But if we do so, we can conclude from (2) that John did not introduce d and Bill to Sue, for any $d \neq$ Bill, which, in combination with the semantic interpretation of (2), gives rise to the intuitively correct prediction that John introduced only Bill to Sue.

Another nice feature of interpretation rule (4) is that it predicts correctly for an example such as (5):

(5) John introduced $[\text{Bill and Mary}]_F$ to Sue.

In particular, it does not pragmatically rule out the truth of (2) just because there are alternatives to *Bill*, namely *Mary* and *Bill and Mary*, for which the sentence is true as well.

---

[1] Only later we will discuss another theory that is perhaps not so popular.

[2] This rule slightly differs from the one given explicitly by Krifka in that we assume that $Alt(F)$ is closed under conjunction (group-forming), instead of Krifka's assumption that F' can be any subset of $Alt(F)$. This does not seem to make any difference, though.

Krifka's analysis is stated in terms of a Background-Focus structure. A very same pragmatic interpretation rule can be stated, of course, in terms of Rooth's (1985, 1992) alternative semantics as well.[3]

(6) $[\![\textbf{Scal.Assert}_2(\phi)]\!] = \{w \in [\![\phi]\!] | \neg\exists\psi \in Alt(\phi) : w \in [\![\psi]\!] \wedge [\![\psi]\!] \subset [\![\phi]\!]\}$

The only difference between (4) and (6) is that for the latter we do not assume that the operator 'Scal.Assert' has immediate access to its focused and backgrounded parts. Instead, it is assumed that we can give a recursive definition of the set $Alt(\phi)$. As far as the analysis of examples like (2) is concerned, it does not matter whether we take (4) or (6), as long as also for the latter case, we limit ourselves to distributive predicates, and assume that $Alt(\phi)$ is closed under conjunction.

Unfortunately, even if we limit ourselves to distributive predicates, the pragmatic interpretation rules (4) and (6) have some serious flaws. They give rise to wrong predictions if the item in focus is of a disjunctive or existential form. Both interpretation rules have the effect that (7a) and (7b) pragmatically denote the impossible proposition.

(7) a. John introduced $[\text{Bill or Mary}]_F$ to Sue.
    b. John introduced $[\text{one person}]_F$ to Sue.

The reason is that one can infer from neither the semantic meaning of (7a) nor that of (7b) that any of the standard alternatives is true. Therefore (4) predicts that all these alternatives are false, resulting in the impossible proposition. Assuming that in these cases the alternatives involve generalized quantifiers obviously does not help: the original alternatives remain alternatives when we make this shift, and the problems remain as well.

It is easy to see that changing (4) and (6) to interpretation rule (8) does not really help. For our purposes, this rule comes down to the same as the earlier ones.

(8) $[\![\textbf{Scal.Assrt}_3(\phi)]\!] = \{w \in [\![\phi]\!] | \forall\psi \in Alt(\phi) : w \in [\![\psi]\!] \rightarrow [\![\phi]\!] \subseteq [\![\psi]\!]\}$.

Also this pragmatic interpretation rule gives rise to the false prediction that (7a) and (7b) pragmatically denote the impossible proposition: neither the alternative that John introduced Bill to Sue nor the alternative that John introduced Mary to Sue is entailed by (7a) and both are thus predicted to be false.

We have seen that it is wrong to assume that disjunctive sentences rule out worlds where the *stronger* propositions obtained by the disjuncts themselves are false, and assuming that now (suddenly) these disjuncts are not alternative propositions anymore also doesn't seem to be natural. According to us, Gricean reasoning should just rule out worlds where more of the relevant alternative propositions are true than demanded to verify the sentence. This intuition is directly expressed in the following interpretation rule. For reasons to become obvious soon, we will call this interpretation rule one of *exhaustive interpretation*.

---

[3]In this rule, and later, we could replace $Alt(\phi)$ by a contextually given subset of $Alt(\phi)$ as suggested by Rooth (1992), Roberts (1996), and others. We will leave these changes to the reader.

(9) $[\![Exh(\phi)]\!] = \{w \in [\![\phi]\!] | \neg\exists v \in [\![\phi]\!] : \{\psi \in Alt(\phi) | v \in [\![\psi]\!]\} \subset \{\psi \in Alt(\phi) | w \in [\![\psi]\!]\}\}$

Notice that (9) does not give rise to any of the (potential) problems discussed above for sentences (5), (7a), and (7b). It is predicted that the sentences can be true in worlds in which John introduced Bill to Sue, because such worlds are among the ones that verify the embedded clauses that make only a minimal number of elements of $Alt(\phi)$ true. For (5) they are predicted to be the only ones, while (7a) and (7b) allow other worlds as well. But (9) predicts that (7a) and (7b) are only true in worlds in which John introduced only one person to Sue.

Obviously, if we define the following (partial) ordering relation between worlds, '$<_{Alt(\phi)}$' in terms of the sets of alternative sentences that are true in those worlds, $v <_{Alt(\phi)} w$ if and only if $\{\psi \in Alt(\phi) : v \models \psi\} \subset \{\psi \in Alt(\phi) : w \models \psi\}$, we can define (9) equivalently as $[\![Exh(\phi)]\!] = \{w \in [\![\phi]\!] | \neg\exists v \in [\![\phi]\!] : v <_{Alt(\phi)} w\}$. Suppose now that ϕ is of the form '$P(\alpha_F)$' and that we define $Alt(\phi)$ in terms of predicate P as follows: $Alt(\phi) =_{def} \{P(\mathbf{d}) | d \in D\}$, with **d** a name for d. In that case (9) comes down to interpretation rule (10):

(10) $[\![Exh(\phi, P)]\!] = \{w \in [\![\phi]\!] | \neg\exists v \in [\![\phi]\!] : P(v) \subset P(w)\}$

In Rooij and Schulz (2004, 2006) it is explained that if in addition we assumed a *ceteris paribus* condition for considering alternative worlds, (10) actually comes down to Groenendijk and Stokhof's (1984) principle of exhaustive interpretation, or to McCarthy's (1980) rule of predicate circumscription.

Interpretation rules (9) and (10) make strong predictions. For (2) for instance, it predicts that John introduced no-one else to Sue than Bill. A complaint often heard against interpretation rules like (4), (6), and (10) has it that all we can conclude by standard Gricean reasoning is that the speaker *only knows* of Bill that he was introduced by John to Sue, leaving it open that he does not know that anyone else was so introduced as well.[4] The Gricean interpretation of ϕ that the speaker only knows ϕ can be formalized by the following interpretation rule $[\![\mathbf{Grice}(\phi)]\!] = \{w \in [\![\Box\phi]\!] | \forall\psi \in Alt(\phi) : w \in [\![\Box\psi]\!] \rightarrow [\![\phi]\!] \subseteq [\![\psi]\!]\}$, with '$\Box\phi$' meaning that the speaker knows that ϕ. The strengthening from *not know* to *know that not* is then mostly contributed to the extra assumption that the speaker knows who John introduced to Sue. We fully agree with this intuition, and in Spector (2003), Rooij and Schulz (2004, 2006) it is even shown how exhaustive interpretation rules (9) and (10) can be inferred and thus motivated by this type of Gricean reasoning.

3 Exhaustive Interpretation and Discourse Referents

It is standardly assumed that the focal phrase of a sentence is marked phonologically by falling intonation. But phrases can also receive a rising intonation and the use of this intonation also seems to have interpretational effects. The denotation of

[4]This complaint goes back at least to Soames (1982) and has been taken up by recent defenders of the Gricean picture such as Rooij and Schulz (2004), Sauerland (2004), and Spector (2003).

the phrase with rising intonation was called the 'independent focus' by Jackendoff (1972), but is more often referred to as the (sentence, or contrastive) *topic* of the sentence, as in the work of Büring (1997, 2003), Lee (1999), Kadmon (2001) and others.[5] In this section, we will say that such phrases have topical accent and limit ourselves to example sentences with a *hat*-contour, or a bridging accent, i.e., examples with both topical and focal accentuated phrases. Before we discuss how to interpret phrases with topical accents, however, it will prove instructive first to discuss a problem observed by Eckardt (p.c.) for the analysis of focus hitherto assumed.

Consider a sentence like (11)

(11) $[\text{Half}]_T$ of the children wore $[\text{green}]_F$ shirts.

Intuitively, this sentence is true if half of the children wore green shirts, and the other half red shirts. Unfortunately, as noted by Eckardt, this does not come out if we interpret the focal expression exhaustively by using a strong notion of exhaustivity. For if we would do so in the straightforward way, we would predict that for all alternative colors C to *green*, the sentence *Half of the children wore shirts with color C* has to be false, which we don't want.

We have noticed in the previous section that pragmatically interpreting focal accent strongly exhaustive does not always correspond with the facts, and that in general we should interpret focus in a weaker way, saying that of the alternative sentences the speaker does not know that they are true. Perhaps the problem disappears when we assume this weaker notion of exhaustivity. Indeed, in that case, we would rightly predict that (11) can still be used truthfully in the situation sketched above. Unfortunately, however, this cannot be the whole solution to the problem. To see this, notice that a speaker might naturally answer a question like *What kind of shirts did the children wear?* with (11) immediately followed by (12):

(12) and the $[\text{other half}]_T$ of the children wore $[\text{red}]_F$ shirts.

And now we do not want to conclude after (11) that the answerer does not know that (12) is true. Thus, even if we assume that focus should be interpreted in a weakly exhaustive way we would end up with a wrong prediction.

From Eckardt's discussion it might seem that the problem discussed above is due to the very particular quantificational expression *half*. In fact, however, the problem is of a very general nature. Consider sentences like (13b) and (13c) as answers to question (13a).

(13) a. What did the boys eat?
b. $[\text{Some boys}]_T$ ate $[\text{broccoli}]_F$.
c. $[\text{One boy}]_T$ ate $[\text{broccoli}]_F$.

[5] As stressed by Chungmin Lee (1999, and personal communication), it is now generally assumed that a difference should be made between non-contrastive thematic topic (with no focal component) and contrastive topic with focal component. In this paper, we always refer to the latter type of topical construction.

If we would interpret *broccoli* in a strong exhaustive way, and *some* or *one* as *at least some/one*, it would mean for (13c) that for all alternatives x distinct to broccoli, the sentence *(at least) one boy ate x* has to be false. But this gives the wrong result that from (13b) we can conclude that *none* of the boys ate anything else than broccoli (replacing *one* in (13c) by *some* gives the same result). Again, weakening exhaustive interpretation by interpreting it as 'minimal knowledge' does not really help: it would falsely predict that one cannot continue answer (13c) by something like *and two boys ate the beans*.

In the discussion, above we completely ignored the fact that in the sentences that gave rise to the problems the 'quantified' expression received a contrastive topical accent. Taking this into account, one obvious solution to the problem seems to be that (at least) in topic-focus constructions, the expression with focal accent should not receive an exhaustive interpretation. But notice that this would be a pity! Among other things, we would have to give up the general rule that the item with focal accent should always be interpreted exhaustively.

In contrast to the above suggestion, in this paper, we would like to argue that focus should always be pragmatically interpreted in an (at least weakly) exhaustive way, and that the above observations indicate that topical expressions should pragmatically be interpreted somewhat differently than standardly assumed.

To discuss the standard theories of topical accent, let us take a look at the following dialogue.

(14) a. Who ate what? What did Larry eat?
b. $[\text{Larry}]_T$ ate $[\text{broccoli}]_F$.

Just as it is standardly assumed that by our use of focal, or falling, accent we indicate something about the context in which the sentence is used (i.e., what is the question under discussion) and about how the sentence should be interpreted (i.e., exhaustive with respect to the focal accent), something similar is standardly taken to be the case for our use of rising, or topical accent. First of all, our use of topical accent is taken to indicate that a set of alternatives is relevant, and that some kind of (general) question is under discussion. Second, it is generally agreed that the topical accent indicates that the sentence that contains the topical phrase does not by itself completely resolve the relevant question for all alternatives under discussion. We share those intuitions, but we do not think that the ways these intuitions are accounted for are fully appropriate.

The perhaps best-known theory of topical accent is due to Büring (1997, 2003). Büring builds his theory of topic on top of Rooth's theory of focus. Just as Rooth (1985) assumed that any sentence ϕ has a focus-semantic value, $[\![\phi]\!]^F$, the value that we denoted so-far by $Alt(\phi)$, Büring assumes that all sentences also have a *topic-semantic value*, $[\![\phi]\!]^T$. Consider sentence (14b). We know already that its focus semantic value, $Alt((14b))$, is the following set of propositions: $\{\lambda w[\![\text{Larry ate } f \text{ in } w]\!] : f \in F\}$, where F is the set of relevant kinds of food. Hamblin's (1973) identifies this set of propositions as the meaning of the question *What did Larry eat?*. Büring (1997) proposes that the topic-semantic value of (14b) is the following set of Hamblin-questions:

(15) a. $[\![(14b)]\!]^F = \{[\![Ate(larry,f)]\!] : f \in F\} \approx$ What did Larry eat?
b. $[\![(14b)]\!]^T = \{\{[\![Ate(d,f)]\!] : f \in F\} : d \in D\}$
$\approx$ For each individual of set D, what did that individual eat?

To account for the first intuition discussed above, Büring proposes that (14b) can be used appropriately only if both questions (15a) and (15b) are under discussion. Obviously, this immediately explains the felicity of the sequence (14a)–(14b): the second question of (14a) is identical to (15a), while if one wants to know the complete answer to the first question of (14a), one has to address all questions in (15b). To account for the second intuition that all relevant issues are not fully resolved by a sentence like (14b), Büring demands that the interpretation of (14b) leaves open some issues addressed in (15b). And this comes out appropriately as well in case D contains other elements than 'Larry': whether we interpret the focus in (14b) exhaustively or not, the sentence only *partially* addresses (15b) and leaves open the possibility that Bill, for instance, ate something else than broccoli.

Although Büring notices that topical accent many times gives rise to a partitive reading, he does not suggest that as a consequence we should interpret phrases with topical accent in a nonstandard way. But, as we saw above, if we interpret the phrases with topical accent in (11), (13b), and (13c) in a standard quantificational way, the analysis makes the wrong predictions for these examples once we interpret focus exhaustively. As for (11), Eckardt herself provided us already with the right intuition: what gives rise to the problem is the assumption that the noun phrase *half of the children* should be interpreted *quantificationally*, and this not only in the sentence (11) itself, but also in all the focal-alternatives that are supposed to be excluded by exhaustive interpretation. Instead, she suggests, we should look at the actual set of children that constitute this half, and assume that by exhaustification it is excluded that any of the other children also wore green shirts.

One natural way to account for this intuition is to assume that the speaker had a particular group of children in mind when she used (11), and referred to this group by her use of the topical noun phrase *half of the children*.[6] In this paper, we do not want to be committed to such a referential analysis of certain noun phrases, and we want to show that using any form of dynamic semantics will already help us to solve this problem.

Instead of looking at Eckardt's original example, we will consider the examples (13b) and (13c). What we want to account for is the intuition that the (contrastive) topical accent on *Some/One boy(s)* in (13b) is used to indicate that more than some boys (one boy) are (is) under discussion, with the result that (13c) and (13c) can at most be *partial* answers to question (13a). Following the suggestion of Eckard, we propose that in (13c), for instance, we have to exhaustify the focal expression not with respect to the quantifier *one boy*, but with respect to the *denotation* of the discourse referent introduced by *one boy*.[7] Thus, if this denotation is S, the alternatives that are excluded by exhaustive interpretation are all of the form S *ate* f, where f is some kind

[6]Recall that already Reinhart (1981) proposed a referential analysis of sentential topics.

[7]The suggestion that for the interpretation of topical accent, we need to make use of diccourse referents is not new. Vallduvi (1994, p. 7), for instance, claims that "[...] the internal structure of

of food different from broccoli. The easiest way to state exhaustive interpretation when discourse referents are crucial, we feel, is by using exhaustification rule (10) or its weakly epistemic variant. In that case, we can represent (13c) simply as something like (16).[8]

(16) $\exists X[Boy(X) \wedge Exh(card(X) = 1 \wedge Ate(X, Broccoli), \lambda y.[Ate(X, y)])$

Sentence (13C) is now predicted to mean that one boy ate broccoli, and, depending on whether the speaker is taken to be competent on the subject matter of discourse, either that this one boy is known to have eaten nothing else, or that the speaker does not know that this one boy ate anything else. As a consequence, the idea to interpret topical quantificational expressions with respect to denotations of discourse referents allows us to interpret (as a default) focus exhaustively also in hat-contours without the undesired consequence: it is still possible that non-members of the denotation of the discourse referent X ate something else besides broccoli, i.e., beans.

Combining the ideas that focal phrases must be interpreted exhaustively and topical phrases referentially has an extra appealing consequence. Representing (17a) by (17b):

(17) a. and [three boys]$_T$ ate [pizza]$_F$
b. $\exists Z[Boys(Z) \wedge Exh(card(Z) = 3 \wedge Ate(Z, Pizza), \lambda y.[Ate(Z, y)])]$

we correctly predict that if the speaker indicates that he is knowledgeable about the subject matter of the discourse and that the answer is complete after sequence (13C)–(17a), that four boys were under discussion. Thus, we predict that the topical phrases have *disjoint* denotations, as is natural in partitive constructions. The reason is that if all members of X have only property P (among the relevant ones) and all members of Y only property Q and $P \neq Q$, it follows that X and Y have mutuallydisjoint denotations. Notice that this doesn't follow solely from our proposal to interpret the topical phrases in (13C) and (17a) 'referentially,' as the interpretation of a discourse referent, we needed the extra assumption that the focal phrases must be interpreted exhaustively as well.

(Footnote 7 continued)
information states which is, in fact, crucially exploited by the different information-packaging strategies used by speakers in pursuing communicative efficiency is at least a system of file cards connected by pointers."

[8]In this explicit representation, '*Exh*' is used as an operator that can be used freely in the representation of the sentence. This way of representing things here is only for convenience, however. In Rooij and Schulz (2006) a *dynamic exhaustivity operator* is defined that takes scope over the whole sentence (and in particular over the existential quantifier), but is interpreted just as (16) should intuitively be interpreted. Thus, our proposal is still completely compatible with a Gricean *global* analysis of implicatures.

4 Exhaustive Interpretation of Topics

Eckardt (p.c.), however, shows that topical phrases do not always have mutually disjoint denotations. Consider the following sequence:

(18) a. At different days of my measles, an increasing numbers of red spots appeared on my face:
b. [One spot]$_T$ had appeared by [Monday]$_F$,
c. [two spots]$_T$ by [Tuesday]$_F$,
d. and [three spots]$_T$ had appeared by [Wednesday]$_F$.

Now we do not conclude that we are talking about six different spots. The reason is, intuitively, that in contrast to (13C) and (16) the only thing that is crucial for the interpretation of the numerical expressions here is the *quantity* of spots involved, not their identity. In accordance with many others making use of dynamic semantics, we suggest that phrases like *one N* can have both a *'referential'* reading—where discourse referents are introduced immediately—and a *quantificational*, one, where discourse referents are introduced only after the interpretation of the whole sentence. Thus, we propose in contrast to Reinhart (1981) and others that some expressions with topical accent—some numerical ones—receive a quantificational, and thus non-denotational meaning. An exhaustive reading of the focal expressions in (18b) now does not have the effect that the specific spot introduced had appeared only by Monday, but rather just that only on Monday had one spot appeared. This has the result that the topical expressions in (18b) and (18c) need not denote mutually disjoint sets of spots anymore.

But the resulting proposal that at least some numeral expressions with topical accent receive a quantificational interpretation gives rise to some wrong predictions. First, and worst, we are back to our original problem: on a quantificational reading of *one spot* (and the assumption that focus should be interpreted exhaustively) we falsely predict from (18b) that on all other days than Monday no spot appeared. Second, the analysis does not predict the inappropriateness of a sequence like (13C) followed by (19):

(19) and [three boys]$_T$ ate [broccoli]$_F$.

Intuitively, sequence (13C)–(19) is out because the speaker could have coded the expressed information more economically by just saying that *all* boys ate broccoli. But the proposal under discussion has to stipulate an extra constraint to account for this. Similarly, we do not account for the intuition that (18b) implicates that on Monday *only* one spot appeared.

To account for these problems we propose/suggest that in sentences with a hat-, or bridge-contour, not only the item with focal accent, but also the one with topical accent should (by default) be interpreted exhaustively (with respect to the relevant domain).

There are at least two reasons why a uniform analysis of focal and topical accent is at least prima facie desirable. First, it would be unnatural to propose quite different meaning contributions to a supposed phonetic distinction that can hardly, if at all, be observed experimentally.

> How much 'meaning' do you have to attach to specific accent types, if it turns out that it is hard to make a phonetic distinction among them?
>
> Experiments have shown that every speaker realizes a sentence in a different fashion. However, hearers *are* able to determine whether a phrase is accented or not [...]. Our working hypothesis, then, is that it does not matter *what* accent is used by a speaker, but *that* he uses an accent. (Krahmer et al. 2007)

A second reason for why a uniform analysis of focal and topical accent is desirable is given by Féry (1992, p. 60): "As a matter of fact, it is nearly always possible to replace a hat pattern by a sequence of two falling accents." But she mentions two restrictions, however, on when this replacement is appropriate. First, the replacement is in order only if the two accents have approximately the same prominence. Second, the hat pattern is necessary and cannot be replaced by a sequence of two falling accents in case of explicit contrast and gapping. To illustrate the case of contrast, Féry (1992) points out that (20a) is acceptable, but (20b) is not:

(20) a. John is often sick, [Mary]$_T$ [never]$_F$.
b. *John is often sick, [Mary]$_F$ [never]$_F$.

For a simple sentence with a hat-contour like (14b) our proposal that not only the item with focal accent, but also the one with topical accent should (by default) be interpreted exhaustively means that in case the speaker is taken to be competent about the subject matter of discourse, it is interpreted not only as saying that Larry ate only broccoli, but also that only Larry ate (only) broccoli. When the topical phrase is of a more complex nature, like in (13c), with a denotational reading of *one boy*, the proposed analysis predicts that (the speaker knows) only (of) the boy introduced (that he) ate only broccoli, while (18b), with a quantified reading, implicates that on Monday (as far as the speaker knows) only one spot appeared. Note that we also make the intuitive correct prediction for

(21) a. A: Did your wife kiss other men?
b. B: [My wife]$_T$ [didn't]$_F$ kiss other men.

Just as Büring (1997) we predict that the reply (21b) gets the reading that the speaker knows only of his own wife that she did not kiss other men, suggesting that he is not so sure of A's wife.

In general, we predict that not only topical phrases that are interpreted referentially, but also the ones we interpret quantificationally give rise to *contrastive* readings. The prediction that topical phrases involve a contrast is behind almost any analysis of topical accent. According to Bolinger (1986),

> [...] contrast involves cases where one or more individual items are singled out from a larger (but limited) set as being true regarding some relationship whereas others in the same set are untrue.

There are some doubts, however, whether not only focal, but also topical accent really has this strong contrastive effect. We have seen already that we predict such a contrastive reading only in case we take the speaker to be competent about the subject matter. But even then this seems to be too strong a prediction. First, it seems possible that one can answer question (22a) appropriately by a sequence like (22b)–(22d):

(22) a. Who ate what?
b. Let's see.... $[\text{Larry}]_T$ ate $[\text{broccoli}]_F$.
c. $[\text{John}]_T$ ate $[\text{broccoli}]_F$.
d. And $[\text{Bill}]_T$ had $[\text{the beans}]_F$.

We agree, but are also convinced that this can be done appropriately only in case the speaker has to check for herself with respect to each individual (Larry, John, and Bill) what he ate, and does so just before she uttered (22b), (22c), and (22d), respectively. Thus, we think that the answerer cannot have uttered (22b) appropriately when she already had the plan, or strategy, to continue the answer with (22c) and (22d). But in that case the sequence is not a counterexample to our assumption that both focal and topical expressions should be interpreted exhaustively also in topic-focus sentences: if we interpret both exhaustively with weak epistemic force, we receive the correct prediction (or so we feel) that at the moment the speaker utters (22b), she does not know yet whether someone else (i.e., John) also ate (only) broccoli.

A second, though very similar, kind of example that seems problematic for our assumption that topical accent involves a strong form of contrast that follows from our proposal that also topical phrases be interpreted exhaustively are sequences like (23a)–(23b).

(23) a. Where can I find the cutery?
b. The $[\text{forks}]_T$ are in [the cupboard]F, and the $[\text{knives}]_T$ and $[\text{spoons}]_T$ too.

At first it seems that these examples cannot be 'explained away' in a similar way as we dealt with (22a)–(22d): the topical phrases are now mentioned in the same sentence. Still, we feel that there is something special about (23b): if one wants to give an answer like this, one is *required* to use an additive focus particle like *too* in the second conjunct (as stressed by Henk Zeevat, p.c.). Indeed, it seems that an answer like (23b) without the focus particle is fully inappropriate. We would like to suggest here that this is because by the use of such an additive focus particle in the second conjunct, the speaker suggests that the hearer is not allowed to interpret the first conjunct exhaustively, i.e., that he should *cancel* the implicature induced by exhaustive interpretation.

Although we propose that both topical and focal expressions should be interpreted exhaustively, this does not mean that we predict that it is irrelevant how a phrase is accentuated, as long as it is accentuated. If we would claim that, we would end up with the wrong prediction that there is no difference in meaning between sentences with bridging accent and sentences with double focal accent. We propose, however, that the function of using the second topical accent, instead of a second focal accent, is that the sentence should receive an exhaustive reading with respect to *two predicates* (or two sets of alternative sentences), and not with respect to *one relation*, which would (or at least could) be the result if the sentence contains a double focal accent.[9] To illustrate, for a double focal example such as *[Larry]$_F$ ate* [pizza]$_F$, we only minimize the sentence *one* time, with respect to relation *ate*, and conclude that (as far as the speaker knows) only one eating event took place and that the answer was complete; for bridging accent with a topical accent on 'Larry,' however, we minimize with respect to focus *and* topic. In the latter case, we end up with the interpretation that only Larry ate only pizza, and it is left open whether Bill, for instance, ate broccoli. The double focus sentence is interpreted as (24a), the topic-focus sentence as (24b):

(24) a. Exh(John ate Pizza, $\lambda xy[Ate(x, y)]$)
b. $Exh(Exh$(John ate Pizza, $\lambda y[Ate(j, y)]$),
$\lambda x[Exh(Ate(x, p), \lambda y[Ate(x, y)])]$)

Notice that as a consequence we predict that in contrast to a sentence with a double focal contour, a sentence with bridging contour is allowed if the speaker only *partially* answers the question under discussion. In Sect. 6 we will discuss whether giving a partial answer should be associated with topical accent.

5 Strategic Economic Encoding

According to the above analysis, topical, and focal items are both interpreted exhaustively, but we exhaustify the topical expression 'later' than the focal one.[10] What is the reason for this difference? We believe that it reflects the strategy of how to *economically encode* the to be transmitted information.

Roberts (1996), Kadmon (2001), and Büring (2003) correctly propose that a topical accent indicates that a set of questions is under discussion and that a *strategy* is at stake. However, we feel that they underestimate the role of the answerer. It is the *answerer* who has to decide how to economically encode the complete information she has to convey such that the hearer can still process it. In this section we want to propose that the information structure of the sentence, or its topic-focus structure, reflects the strategy of the speaker to economically encode the information to be transmitted.

Consider multiple *wh*-question (25).

(25) Who ate what?

Let us adopt a partitional analysis of questions. If we now assume that only John and Mary and only broccoli and pizza are under discussion, it follows that the seman-

[9]This seems compatible with Féry's first constraint on when we can replace a hat-pattern with two times focus accent.

[10]This does not mean that as a result the topical expressions should always have wide scope. If so, it would give rise to the prediction that *[Alle]$_T$ Politiker sind [nicht]$_F$ korrupt.* receives the small-scope reading of negation, which is wrong as made clear by Büring's (1997). We will come back to this example in the next section.

tic meaning of (25) is identical to the intersection of the semantic meanings of (26a) and (26b), and also to the intersection of the semantic meanings of (27a) and (27b).

(26) a. What did John ate?
b. What did Mary ate?

(27) a. Who ate broccoli?
b. Who ate pizza?

More concretely, if we denote the partition that represents the meaning of interrogative sentence S by $[\![S]\!]$, and if we define $Q \sqcap Q' = \{q \cap q' : q \in Q \;\&\; q' \in Q' \;\&\; q \cap q' \neq \emptyset\}$ for two partitions Q and Q', we see that $[\![(25)]\!] = [\![(26a)]\!] \sqcap [\![(26b)]\!] = [\![(27a)]\!] \sqcap [\![(27b)]\!]$. Now suppose that John ate only broccoli, and Mary only pizza. We believe that (25) can in these circumstances equally well be answered by the sequence (28a)–(28b) as by the sequence (29a)–(29b) with the respective topic-focus patterns:

(28) a. $[\text{John}]_T$ ate $[\text{broccoli}]_F$,
b. and $[\text{Mary}]_T$ ate $[\text{pizza}]_F$.

(29) a. $[\text{broccoli}]_T$ was eaten by $[\text{John}]_F$,
b. and $[\text{pizza}]_T$ was eaten by $[\text{Mary}]_F$.

Roberts (1996) proposes that a sentence like (28a) presupposes both (30a) and (30b), while Kadmon (2001) and Büring (2003) argue that it rather presupposes both (30a) and (30c).

(30) a. What did John eat?
b. For each individual, what did that individual eat?
c. Who ate what?

Notice that although (30b) and (30c) differ in that whereas the former denotes a set of questions, the latter denotes only one question, on a partitional analysis of questions the two are closely related: as we have seen above, $[\![(30c)]\!]$ is just the intersection of the set of questions denoted by (30b), i.e., $[\![(26a)]\!] \sqcap [\![(26b)]\!]$.

Similarly, a sentence like (29a) presupposes both (31a) and (31b) according to Roberts (1996), while it presupposes both (31a) and (30c) according to Kadmon (2001) and Büring (2003):

(31) a. Who ate broccoli?
b. For each kind of food, who ate it?

Obviously, if these questions have a partition semantics, and if we take the intersection of the whole set of questions, then both (30b) and (31b) will correspond with the question (30c).

Now suppose that John and Mary are still the only relevant individuals, but they not only had a main dish, but also a dessert, either an ice cream or a cake. Then, we think, the only natural way to answer (25) is to 'go by individuals':

(32) a. $[\text{John}]_T$ ate $[\text{broccoli and an icecream}]_F$,
b. and $[\text{Mary}]_T$ had $[\text{a pizza and a cake}]_F$.

One might think that this is just because 'going by individuals' is more natural than 'going by food'. This does not seem to be the crucial factor, however, because the same effect seem to occur with a question of the form *Who kissed whom?* where only individuals are involved. How this latter question is typically answered also typically depends on how many kissers versus kissed ones there are. A more natural reason why in the above case we answer question (25) by 'going by individuals' is because of the form of the question: *who* was mentioned before *what* in (25). What has to be explained now, though, is why the questioner didn't ask (33).

(33) What was eaten by whom?

We believe that (33) should be asked instead of (25) if there were more people than kinds of food, because in that case the answer can most economically be given by first mentioning the food, as in answers like:

(34) a. $[\text{Broccoli}]_T$ was eaten by $[\text{John, Paul and Mary}]_F$,
b. and $[\text{pizza}]_T$ was eaten by $[\text{Bill, Sue, and Peter}]_F$.

Our suggestion is related to a proposal made recently by Komagata (2003). Komagata proposes that the information structure of a sentence is a means to *balance* the information load carried by the theme (topic) and the rheme (focus) of an utterance. It is natural to measure the information load of a question as the average information load of its answers. Using information theory and a natural balancing principle, he shows that the ordering of an expected theme followed by a surprising rheme is more desirable than the ordering of a surprising theme followed by a expected rheme.[11] We will not make use of information theory in this paper to make Komagata's suggestion more precise. But already our informal description explains why the natural way to answer (25) is to 'go by individuals' if John and Mary are the only relevant individuals, but they not only had a main dish, but also a desert, either an ice cream or a cake. If, however, there are more people than kinds of food, Komagata's balancing principle explains why the answer to (25) should 'go by food.'

6 Topical Implicatures

We have not yet discussed Büring's (1997) demand that the use of topical accent implicates the existence of an open question. As is well known, it is in terms of this extra constraint that he explains a number of interesting scope data as observed, among others, by Féry (1992). Let us inspect the best-known example, (35a), which in principle could have two readings, (35b) of form $\neg\forall$ and (35c) of form $\forall\neg$:

[11] However, if the theme is totally predictable (i.e., has zero entropy), the ordering does not affect the information balance. Examples like *Q: Who knows the secret? A: Peter$_F$ knows it*, which are problematic for more naive 'old things first'-hypotheses, can now be accounted for.

(35) a. $[\text{Alle}]_T$ Politiker sind $[\text{nicht}]_F$ korrupt.
all politicians are not corrupt.
b. It is not the case that all politicians are corrupt.
c. No politician is corrupt.

The empirical observation is that only the first reading is observed. It is worth pointing out that we cannot yet explain this observation. A natural explanation would be that only one of the readings is compatible with the exhaustive inferences we have proposed above. It is easy to see how the implicatures of the $\neg\forall$ reading are computed: exhaustive interpretation due to *[nicht]*$_F$ does not give rise to any additional inference (because the alternative $\forall x[P(x) \rightarrow C(x)]$ is already entailed to be false), but exhaustive interpretation due to *[Alle]*$_T$ leads to the implicature that (the speaker thinks it is possible that) at least some politicians are corrupt (the alternative $\neg\exists x[P(x) \wedge C(x)]$ is not (known to be) true). This implicature is consistent with the assertion, meaning that there is nothing to prevent (35a) to receive the $\neg\forall$ reading. On first thought it seems that for the $\forall\neg$ reading, on the other hand, a problem will occur, because now one of the exhaustivity inferences will be in conflict with what is asserted. The exhaustive interpretation due to *[Alle]*$_T$ leads now to the implicature that it is not the case that (the speaker knows that) there is a politician who is not corrupt ($\neg\Box\exists x[P(x) \wedge \neg C(x)]$, or equivalently $\Diamond\forall x[P(x) \rightarrow C(x)]$), which is incompatible with what is asserted (on the $\forall\neg$-reading). On second thought, however, this is not really the case: the alternative $\exists x[P(x) \wedge \neg C(x)]$ is already entailed by (and thus weaker than) what is asserted (if it is presupposed that there are politicians), so this sentence is *not* implicated to be (possibly) false. So, nothing is implicated that is inconsistent with the $\forall\neg$ reading, and we cannot yet explain the observation that this reading does not exist.

Just as Büring (1997), we propose to explain these empirical observations by an extra implicature triggered by the topical accent. However, we would not adopt Büring's proposal, because that gave rise to the so-called 'last-answer problem' (see below). Instead, like Wagner (2007), we make a *weaker* proposal, namely that a contrastive topic used in hat-contour comes with the following felicity condition.

(36) Topic Felicity Condition:
There exists at least one alternative that is derived from substituting topic and focus values for other salient objects that is (i) not entailed by the assertion, and (ii) compatible with what the speaker knows.

In case, the speaker is taken to be knowledgeable, condition (ii) is strengthened from $\Diamond\psi$ to $\Box\psi$. Notice that condition (36) gives rise to the pragmatic inference, or implicature, that some non-entailed alternative has to be (possibly) true, and in terms of this implicature we propose to account for Büring's (1997) scope data. To see the working of condition (36), consider the example we started out with:

(37) a. Who of John and Mary ate broccoli and pizza?
b. $[\text{John}]_T$ ate $[\text{broccoli}]_F$ and $[\text{Mary}]_T$ ate $[\text{pizza}]_F$

The first conjunct of (37b) gives rise to the focus-exhaustive inference that John did not eat pizza, and the topical-exhaustive inference that Mary did not eat broccoli.[12] On the strong version of our new felicity condition of topic marking, it must be the case that one of the following alternatives must be true: {Ate(j,p), Ate(m,b), Ate(m,p)}. Because the first two are ruled out by the focus- and topic-exhaustive inferences, it immediately follows that the last one has to be true: Mary ate pizza.

But if this is the inference, why is it still appropriate to assert the second conjunct of (37b)? The reason is that exhaustive interpretation is based on (i) standard *Gricean interpretation*, and (ii) the assumption that the speaker is (maximally) *competent*. In general, the competence assumption cannot be assumed, and all that is left is the Gricean interpretation. According to the Gricean interpretation, the first conjunct of (37b) gives rise to the focus-based inference that it is not known that John ate pizza, and to the topic-based inference that it is not known that Mary ate broccoli. The felicity condition is weaker as well: at least one of the following alternatives is not ruled out: {Ate(j,p), Ate(m,b), Ate(m,p)}. Notice that in this case all three of them are still possible, which means that the second conjunct from (37b) cannot yet be derived from the first conjunct and its (weak) pragmatic implicatures. Only in case it is assumed that the speaker is competent—i.e., knows the extension of the question-predicates of *what did John eat?* and *who ate broccoli?*—we can derive from the first conjunct of (37b) given as answer to question (37a) that Mary ate pizza, and thus that the second conjunct is superfluous.

As already indicated above, Büring's (1997) original proposal of how to interpret topical accent gives rise to the *last answer problem*. If it is assumed that after the interpretation of a clause with a topical accent there still must be an open question, it is predicted that after the second conjunct of (37b) is asserted, it should be an open question what John ate, or an open question whether Mary ate broccoli. Intuitively, however, this is not the case: after the second conjunct of (37b) is interpreted we know exactly who ate what. Despite the fact that our proposal is very close to Büring's (1997) analysis, it is easy to see that this 'last answer problem' does not arise on our analysis.[13] The reason is that we predict only that (at least) *one* possibility statement must be true, which is weaker than Büring's requirement that an issue is unresolved, meaning that (at least) *two* possibility statements must be true. In our case, the topical condition predicts that the second conjunct of (37b) can be felicitously uttered only if one of the following propositions must be (possibly) true: {Ate(j,b), Ate(j,p), Ate(m,b)}. But this condition is obviously satisfied, because it is

[12]The most obvious way to formally account for our extra topical inference of ϕ = "[John]$_T$ ate [broccoli]$_F$" is as follows: $\exists\psi \in \{Ate(x,y) : x \in T \;\&\; y \in F \;\&\; \phi \not\models Ate(x,y)\} : \Diamond\psi$, with T and F the set of topical and focal alternatives to John and broccoli, respectively. However, there are reasons to prefer the following formulation of basically the same idea: $\exists\psi \in \{Ate(x,y) : x \in (T - \{j\}) \;\&\; y \in (F - \{b\}) \;\&\; \phi \not\models Ate(x,y)\} : \Diamond\psi$. The main reason for preferring this alternative is that in this way we can easily explain why a sentence like "John did [not]$_T$ eat [five]$_F$ apples" seems to implicate that John ate at least one apple (without it being required that he ate exactly four apples). The reason is that the predicted topical inference is now that the speaker thinks it is possible that John ate at least one apple, which after strengthening gives the desired result.

[13]Of course, the problem doesn't show up in Büring's (2003) newer analysis either. But the explanation in this latter paper is rather different from the one adopted in Büring (1997), while the one we proposed is very similar in spirit to this earlier proposal, it is just weaker.

explicitly asserted by the first conjunct of (37b) that the proposition expressed by the first element of this set is true.

Let us now return to the scope-data, and in particular to (35a). We have seen already before that none of the exhaustivity implicatures can rule out one of the two possible readings of this sentence. However, the new topical implicature *can* do so. The new topical implicature for oeadings of the sentence will now be that (the speaker thinks it is possible that) at least some politicians are corrupt ($\Diamond\exists x[P(x) \wedge C(x)]$). This implicature is compatible with the $\neg\forall$ reading of the sentence, but *incompatible* with its $\forall\neg$ reading. For this reason, or so we propose, example (35a) does not have the latter reading.

Our approach can also account for further German data discussed by Büring (1997). (1), for instance, is predicted to be infelicitous since it fails to have any extra topical-implicature in any scope ordering. Thus, condition (i) of rule (36) is not met.

(38) *[Alle]$_T$ Politiker sind [immer]$_F$ betrunken.
all politicians are always drunk

The two orderings (all>always and always>all) are semantically equivalent. The assertion in either ordering entails all the alternatives. Hence, (38) cannot be uttered with the topic-focus contour.

The following example, (1), is claimed to have only the surface (No>always) reading.

(39) [Kein]$_T$ Politiker ist [immer]$_F$ betrunken.
no politician is always drunk

In the non-surface reading (always>no) the extra topical inference that (the speaker thinks it is possible that) $\exists t \exists x[P(x) \wedge B(x,t)]$ is incompatible with what is asserted ($\forall t[\neg\exists x[P(x) \wedge B(x,t)]$), and thus is ruled out. On the other hand, the surface reading (No>always) is available, because this time the extra topical inference is compatible with and not entailed by what is asserted. Intuitively, (39) uttered with a topic-focus contour indeed induces an interpretation that some politicians are sometimes drunk. The predicted implicature is attested.

By similar reasoning, one can show that we predict in accordance with Büring (1997) that (40) and (41) are ambiguous between their two scopal readings: the proposed extra topical implicature that (the speaker thinks it is possible that) some politicians are sometimes drunk is not entailed but still compatible with what is asserted on both of their readings.

(40) [Kein]$_T$ Politiker ist [nie]$_F$ betrunken.
no politician is never drunk

(41) [Alle]$_T$ Politiker sind [selten]$_F$ betrunken
all politicians are rarely drunk

What this shows is that our analysis can predict the scope data discussed in Büring (1997).

7 Conclusion

In this paper, we proposed that a sentence like (1), $[\text{John}]_T$ ate $[\text{broccoli}]_F$, should pragmatically be interpreted as follows:

(a) Focus should be interpreted exhaustively: John ate only broccoli.
(b) Topic must be interpreted exhaustively: Only John ate (only) broccoli.
(c) The speaker takes it to be possible (or even knows, if he is competent) that at least one alternative of the form '*x* ate *y*' not entailed by (1) is true. From (a) it follows that this alternative cannot be 'John ate *y*,' with *y* different from broccoli; from (b) it follows that this alternative cannot be '*x* ate broccoli,' with *x* different from John. Thus, the alternative must be something like 'Mary ate the beans.'

In Sect. 2 we argued in favor of an exhaustivity rule that differs somewhat from some better-known standard alternatives. In Sects. 3 and 4 we considered some problems for this rule, and argued that exhaustive interpretation should be sensitive to discourse referents and that also topics should be interpreted exhaustively. This holds for topical expressions in general, whether they have a 'referential' or a 'quantificational' reading. Our unified interpretation of topical and focal expressions does not predict that the accents are interchangeable: in Sect. 5 we argued that the different kinds of accents reflect the way the speaker economically encodes the information she wants to communicate, while in Sect. 6 we proposed that topical accent gives rise to an extra implicature on top of the one due to exhaustive interpretation. It as shown that this extra topical implicature is weaker than a similar implicature proposed by Büring (1997), but still can account for the relevant scope data.

References

Bolinger, Dwight. 1986. Intonation and its parts: Melody in spoken English. London: Edward Arnold.

Büring, Daniel. 1997. The great scope inversion conspiracy. *Linguistics and Philosophy* 20: 175–194.

Büring, Daniel. 2003. On D-trees, beans, and B-accents. *Linguistics and Philosophy* 26: 511–545.

Chierchia, Genaro, Dany Fox, and Benjamin Spector. 2012. The grammatical view of scalar implicatures and the relationship between semantics and pragmatics. In *An International Handbook of Natural Language Meaning Semantics*, eds. P. Portner, C. Maienborn and K. von Heusinger, Mouton de Gruyter.

Féry, Caroline. 1992. *Focus, Topic and Intonation in German*. SFB papier 340, Stuttgart/Tübingen.

Groenendijk, Jeroen and Martin Stokhof. 1984. *Studies in the Semantics of Questions and the Pragmatics of Answers*. Ph.D. thesis, University of Amsterdam.

Hamblin, Charles. 1973. Questions in Montague English. *Foundations of Language* 10: 41–53.

Hara, Yurie. 2005. Contrastives and gricean principles. In *Fifteenth Amsterdam Colloquium*, ed. Paul Dekker and Michael Franke, 101–106. Universiteit van Amsterdam.

Jackendoff, Ray. 1972. *Semantic interpretation in generative grammar*. Cambridge, MA: MIT Press.

Jacobs, J. 1983. *Focus und Skalen*. Niemeyer, Tübingen: Zur Syntax and Semantik von Gradpartikeln im Deutschen.

Kadmon, Nirit. 2001. *Formal pragmatics*. Oxford: Blackwell.
Komagata, Noga. 2003. Contextual effects on word-order. In *Modeling and Using Context*, ed. P. Blackburn et. al., vol. 2680/2003, 190–203. Berlin/Heidelberg, Lecture Notes in Computer Science: Springer.
Krahmer, Emiel and Marc Swerts. 2007. Perceiving Focus. In *Topic and Focus: Cross-linguistic Perspectives on Intonation and Meaning*, ed. C. Lee, M. Gordon and D. Bring (eds.), 121–138. Kluwer Academic Publishers, Studies in Linguistics and Philosophy Series.
Krifka, Manfred. 1995. The semantics and pragmatics of polarity items linguistic. *Analysis* 25: 209–258.
Lee, Chungmin. 1999. Contrastive topic: a locus of the interface evidence from Korean and English. In *The Semantics/Pragmatics Interface from Different Points of View*, vol. 1, ed. K. Turner. Elsevier Science.
McCarthy, J. 1980. Circumscription—a form of non-monotonic reasoning. *Artificial Intelligence* 13: 27–39.
Reinhart, Tanya. 1981. Pragmatics and linguistics. *An Analysis of Sentence Topics. Philosophica* 27: 53–94.
Roberts, Craige. 1996. Information Structure: Towards an integrated formal theory of pragmatics. In *OSUWPL Volume 49: Papers in Semantics*, eds. Jae Hak Yoon and Andreas Kathol, The Ohio State University: Ohio.
Rooth, Matts. 1985. *Association with Focus*. Doctoral Dissertation, University of Massachusetts at Amherst.
Rooth, Mats. 1992. A theory of focus interpretation. *Natural Language Semantics* 1: 75–116.
Sauerland, Uli. 2004. Scalar implicatures in complex sentences. *Linguistics and Philosophy* 27: 363–391.
Schulz, Katrin, and Robert van Rooij. 2006. Pragmatic meaning and non-monotonic reasoning: the case of exhaustive interpretation. *Linguistics and Philosophy* 29: 205–250.
Spector, Benjamin. 2003. Scalar implicatures: exhaustivity and gricean reasoning. In *Proceedings of the ESSLLI'03 Student Session*, ed. B. ten Cate.
Soames, Scott. 1982. How presuppositions are inherited: A solution to the projection problem. *Linguistic Inquiry* 13: 483–545.
Valduvi, Enrich. 1994. The dynamics of information packaging. In *Integrating information structure into constraint-based categorial approaches*, ed. E. Engdahl, 4–26. University of Edinburgh: HCRC Publications.
van Rooij, Robert, and Katrin Schulz. 2004. Exhaustive interpretation of complex sentences. *Journal of Logic, Language and Information* 13: 491–519.
von Stechow, Arnim. 1991. Focusing and background operators. In *Discourse particles*, ed. W. Araba, 37–84. Amsterdam: John Benjamins.
Wagner, Michael. 2007. *A Compositional Analysis of Contrastive Topics*. Handout presented at NELS 38.

The Interpretation of a "Contrast-Marking" Particle

Beáta Gyuris

Abstract The paper discusses the interpretation of the obligatorily stressed *csak* discourse particle in Hungarian that is often referred to in the literature as a marker of contrast. It is argued that this particle has the function of an adversative context marker, defined in Zeevat (Presupposition triggers, context markers or speech act markers, 91–111, 2003, A dynamic approach to discourse particles, 133–148, 2006). The discourse particle use of *csak* is contrasted to its older, exclusive particle use, whose interpretation is described in terms of Beaver and Clark's (Sense and sensitivity: how focus determines meaning, 2008) proposal. It is shown that the meaning change in the course of which *csak* acquired its adversative context marker interpretation can be accounted for in terms of semantic reanalysis, along the lines of Eckardt's (Meaning change in grammaticalization: an inquiry into semantic reanalysis, 2006) theory.

Keywords Context marker • Discourse particle • Exclusive particle • Contrast • Semantic reanalysis

1 Aims

This paper[1] analyses the interpretation of the obligatorily stressed *csak* discourse particle in Hungarian, which has been claimed to be a marker of contrast (Kocsány 1986). After providing an empirical characterization of the necessary and sufficient

[1]Research for the paper was supported under projects No. F 68139 and NF 84217 by the Hungarian Scientific Research Fund (OTKA). I thank the editors of the volume, three anonymous reviewers, and series editor Marcel den Dikken for suggestions for improving on previous versions the paper, the participants of the CIL18 (2008) workshop *Contrastiveness in Information Structure and/or Scalar Implicatures*, particularly Laurence Horn, as well as audiences in Berlin (ZAS), Budapest (RIL HAS) and Szeged (SZTE) for discussion and criticism, Tonjes Veenstra for the discussion of some Dutch data, and Mark Newson for checking the language of the paper.

B. Gyuris (✉)
Research Institute for Linguistics, HAS Benczúr u. 33, Budapest 1068, Hungary
e-mail: gyuris@nytud.hu

C. Lee et al. (eds.), *Contrastiveness in Information Structure, Alternatives and Scalar Implicatures*, Studies in Natural Language and Linguistic Theory 91, DOI 10.1007/978-3-319-10106-4_5

conditions for the appearance of this particle in Hungarian sentences (Sect. 2.1), we will formalize them in the framework proposed by Zeevat (2003, 2006), relating the interpretation of stressed *csak* to the interpretation of accented Dutch *toch* and German *doch* (Sect. 2.2). The particle *csak* in Hungarian has a much more prominent and older use as a focus sensitive particle with an exclusive interpretation analogous to English *only*. In Sect. 3 of the paper we will look at the contribution of this exclusive *csak* to the presuppositions and truth conditions of Hungarian sentences, proposing that they are best accounted for in the framework of the theory proposed by Beaver and Clark (2008). It will then be argued in Sect. 4 that the latter approach also leads naturally to an account of the meaning change in the course of which *csak* acquired its discourse particle use in terms of semantic reanalysis, assumed to have taken place in order to avoid pragmatic overload (cf. Eckardt 2006). The paper ends with a summary of the conclusions. In what follows, in the text and in the constructed examples we will refer to the obligatorily stressed discourse particle under investigation as *CSAK*.[2] However, the examples from the written corpus will be reproduced in their original form, for easier reference.[3]

2 The Discourse Particle *CSAK*

2.1 Some Data

Example (1) below illustrates a context where a sentence containing an obligatorily stressed *CSAK* particle can appear in Hungarian:[4]

(1) A: *I don't think John will be invited.*

B: *I've just heard Mary invite him.*

A: *Szóval/Tehát #(CSAK) meghívták Jánost.*

so CSAK VM:invited:3pl John:ACC

"So, John did get invited (after all)."

Although leaving the particle *CSAK* out from A's second sentence would not make it ungrammatical or alter its truth conditions, it would definitely make the sentence inappropriate in the context, since the speaker would have to be attributed beliefs that are normally felt to be incompatible on standard assumptions (even though they are strictly speaking not contradictory). Thus, (1) suggests that the

[2]There are several discourse particle uses of non-stressed *csak*, most of which are analogous to the discourse particle uses of German *nur* 'only' (cf. Gyuris 2007).

[3]The historical texts are reproduced here in the form found in the source referred to in the corresponding footnotes.

[4]VM refers to the category 'verbal modifier', which includes, among others, the class of verbal prefixes in Hungarian (cf. É. Kiss 2002).

contribution of the particle to the interpretation of the sentence is to mark that the speaker is aware that the propositional content of his present utterance is in conflict with the propositional content of a previous utterance of his. The above example is thus a typical case where the use of a particle serves the aim of indicating the "speaker's epistemic attitude" towards the truth of the proposition (Zimmermann 2011: 2013), thus ensuring the coherence of the discourse. The latter interpretational features have been attributed in the literature to the so-called *modal* or *discourse particles* (cf. Kiefer 1988, Thurmair 1989, Meibauer 1994, Zimmermann 2011, among others), whose characteristic features on the formal side include the fact that they cannot be negated, do not answer any questions, cannot be coordinated, and do not form a constituent with other expressions. In the rest of this section we will look more closely at what the presence of *CSAK* signals about the context and in exactly what cases its presence is necessary for the coherence of the discourse.

As (2) illustrates, the acceptability of an utterance containing *CSAK* does not depend on whether it is uttered by an interlocutor who made a previous utterance with the conflicting propositional content or by somebody else.

(2) A1: *I think John will be invited.*

B: *I don't think so, Mary does not like him.*

C: *I've just heard Mary invite him.*

A2:	*(Szóval/Tehát)*	*#(CSAK)*	*meghívták*	*Jánost.*
	so/thus	CSAK	VM:invited:3pl	John:ACC

"(So,) John did get invited (after all)."

The fact that in the Dutch counterpart of (2A2), the presence of the accented *toch* particle, referred to as *TOCH*, is required for the well-formedness of the discourse (T. Veenstra, p.c.), suggests that the latter particle and *CSAK* have similar interpretations:

(3) *(Dus,)*	*Jan*	*is*	*#(TOCH)*	*uitgenodigd.*	(Dutch)
so	John	is	TOCH	invited: PTCP	

"(So,) John got invited (after all)."

The contrast between a Dutch example by Zeevat (2000), repeated in (4), and an analogous Hungarian example in (5) points, however, to the need for attributing *CSAK* a different "epistemic commitment" (Zimmermann 2011) from that attributed to *DOCH* by Zeevat, discussed below:

(4) *Jan droomde dat hij was gezakt voor het examen,* (Dutch)
maar hij had het TOCH gehaald.
"Jan dreamt he would fail the exam, but he passed after all." (Zeevat 2000: 88 (28))

(5) *János azt álmodta, hogy veszíteni fog a csapata,*
John that:ACC dreamt:3sg that lose:INF will:3sg the team:his
de (#CSAK) győztek.
but CSAK won:3pl
"John dreamt that his team would lose but they won after all."

Although the Hungarian translation of (4) is impeccable, as shown in (6), I believe it has to do with certain cultural assumptions, superstitions about the impact of bad dreams on one's performance:[5]

(6) *János azt álmodta, hogy meg fog bukni a vizsgán, de*
John that:ACC dreamt:3sg that VM will fail:INF the exam:on but
(CSAK) átment.
CSAK VM:passed:3sg
"John dreamt that he would fail the exam but he passed after all."

There are two further facts to be observed concerning the use of *CSAK*. First, as (7) shows, the propositional content *p* of a *CSAK*-sentence does not have to be in conflict with the propositional content of one single sentence in the previous discourse.[6]

(7) *Zsuzsi: Hisz' ez azé a kis tolvajé! oly kegyetlen volt*
but this that:POSS the small thief:POSS:3sg so cruel was
nagyságod, hogy elvette tőle?
your:majesty that VM:took from:him
"But this belongs to that small thief! Was your majesty cruel enough to take it away from him?"
Countess: CSAK nem hagyhattam a karján![6]
CSAK not leave:could:1sg the arm:POSS:on
"I could not leave it on his arm after all!"

[5]M. den Dikken (p. c.) remarks that he finds the following version of (4), where the verbs for *fail* and *pass* are exchanged, awkward with TOCH:

i) *Jan droomte dat his was geslaagd voor het examen, maar hij was (TOCH) gezakt.*
"John dreamt that he would pass the exam but he failed after all."

H. Zeevat (p. c.), however, does not find the above example unacceptable, which might point to a dialectal difference that we cannot discuss here any further.

[6]Source: *Figaro's Wedding*, by Ede Paulay (1877). (Hungarian Historical Corpus, http://www.nytud.hu/hhc).

What the propositional content of the second speaker's sentence is incompatible with in the case of (7) is the proposition expressed by the first speaker's first sentence, the presuppositions introduced by her second sentence ('the countess took the thing referred to'), and default inferences based on the latter two together ('one should leave the things that belong to a person with him').

Second, *CSAK* is not only licensed in discourse by previous utterances whose propositional contents or presuppositions are in conflict with the propositional content of the *CSAK*-sentence. The felicity of the following discourse, for example, is ensured by the existence of shared beliefs regarding the normal (expected) consequences of not preparing for an exam between the interlocutors (which are viewed to be in conflict with the content of A's sentence):

(8) A: *John did not prepare for the exam.*
B: *CSAK átment.*
CSAK VM:went:3sg
"He still passed."

The *yes-no* interrogative in (9) below, which would also be appropriate as the third sentence of the discourse in (1) above, and the second, imperative sentence of the discourse in (10) illustrates that *CSAK* is not restricted to the declarative sentence type:

(9) A: *(Szóval) #(CSAK) meghívták Jánost?*
so CSAK VM:invited:3pl John:ACC
"(So) did John get invited after all?"

(10) A: *I don't think John would come to the party even if he got an invitation.*
B: # *(CSAK) hívjuk meg!*
CSAK invite:IMP:1pl VM
"Let us still invite him!"

The conditions under which *CSAK*-sentences belonging to the latter two sentence types can or must appear in a discourse are analogous to those under which the corresponding declaratives are licensed: there is a conflict between the propositional content of the *CSAK*-sentence and the propositional contents of previous utterances in the discourse, the presupposition of the latter, and/or certain general default assumptions. The following example shows that in addition to (negated) verb phrases, *CSAK* can also precede an immediately preverbal focus constituent (cf. Section 3 for further discussion), indicating a contrast between the focus denotation and its alternatives with respect to some property:

(11) A: *They said that the person they invite would be Mary.*

B: *CSAK (csak) Jánost hívták meg.*

CSAK only John:ACC invited:3pl VM

"Still, it was John whom they invited."

Having illustrated the basic facts about the use of the *CSAK* discourse particle, in the next section we will make a proposal to capture its meaning in terms of Zeevat's (2003, 2006) theory.

2.2 CSAK *as a Context Marker*

Zeevat (2003, 2006), investigating the interpretation of a number of discourse particles in various languages, including English *indeed*, Dutch *immers, toch, wel*, or German *ja* and *doch*, argues for considering them so-called *context markers* instead of nonstandard presupposition triggers, particularly due to the fact that this allows a more uniform treatment of a larger number of particles in his opinion. As Zeevat (2006) explains, a potential analysis of the semantic/pragmatic contribution of discourse particles based on the assumption that they introduce a presupposition appears less attractive because it cannot provide an explanation for certain nonstandard properties shared by the majority of them. These include the following: the purported presuppositions cannot be accommodated, they are not optional, the particles "have a rather minimal meaning apart from their presuppositional properties," and that some of them "can occur in contexts that are not accessible from the position of the trigger in the sense of discourse representation theory" (Zeevat 2006: 136–137).[7] Context markers are seen by Zeevat (2006: 138) as "markers of a relation of the content of the current sentence to the context (or to another parameter of the utterance context)," and their presence is attributed by him to "functional necessity"[8] or "a universal principle that requires the marking of the relationship." The relations Zeevat considers relevant for marking include the following: the propositional content of the sentence they are situated in is viewed by the speaker as being part of the *common ground* (*CG*, containing the propositions that represent the mutual knowledge of speakers, cf. Stalnaker 1978), it is viewed as having been suggested to be false in the context, as having been denied in the common ground, or as addressing a topic that has been addressed before. He considers the existence of context markers to be motivated by the existence of the difficulties that hearers face when attempting to integrate recent information with information already available.

[7]Zeevat (2006: 146) remarks, nevertheless, that not all particles can be analyzed as context markers, either.

[8]Functional necessity means that "if the relation in question is unmarked, wrong interpretations result." (Zeevat 2006: 138).

Zeevat assumes that the obligatory presence of such context-marking particles can be modeled in optimality-theoretic syntax by postulating a constraint requiring that if the relation *R* obtains between context parameters and the current utterance, the particle *P* should be added to the utterance (2006: 140), referred to as *max(R)*, which would overrule a constraint against special devices referred to as **Particle*. The order of the above two constraints thus guarantees that a context-marking particle is present if and only if the particular relation holds between the content of the sentence and the context parameter.

Zeevat (2003, 2006) argues that German accented *DOCH* and Dutch accented *TOCH*[9] are *adversative context markers*, signaling that "the content of the current utterance goes against material that was already present in the common ground" (Zeevat 2006: 141). (12) contains the formal definition:

(12) ADVERSATIVE(CG, φ), iff CG $\models$ *presumably(not-φ)* or CG $\models$ *suggested(not-φ)*
(Zeevat 2006: 141)

Given a proposition *p*, *presumably(p)* is true in an information state if there are a set of propositions $\psi_1, \ldots, \psi_n$ in the common ground that "together constitute a reason for thinking that" *p*, but there are no set of propositions that support a similar argument for *not-p* (Zeevat 2006: 141). The proposition *suggested(p)* is defined in a recursive manner, as follows:

(13) $suggested(p) \Leftrightarrow may\ p \wedge (p \vee O_1\, p \vee \ldots \vee O_n\, p \vee suggested\,(p))$ (Zeevat 2006: 141)
where the set $\{ O_1, \ldots O_n\}$ contains operators like *x dreams that, x suggests that, x believes that.*

(13) means that *suggested(p)* is true if and only if *p* is possible, and either *p* itself, *suggested(p)* or any $O_i\, p$ are true, where O_i is an element of a set of operators.

The data presented in Sect. 2.1 suggest that Hungarian *CSAK* should be analyzed as an adversative marker along with Dutch accented *TOCH* and German accented *DOCH.* This explains why the licensing of *CSAK* in a sentence can depend on the propositional contents and presuppositions of previous utterances plus the joint assumptions of the interlocutors, which all are assumed to be included

---

[9]Note that Zeevat (2003, 2006) distinguishes between "accented" *TOCH/DOCH,* which he classifies as adversative markers and "contrastively stressed" *TOCH/DOCH,* which he considers corrective markers together with Dutch *WEL* and *NIET* and English *DO* and *DON'T*, all with contrastive stress. Corrective markers intend to change the common ground by indicating the "retraction of (the reasons for) $\neg\varphi$ and the addition of φ as a replacement." (Zeevat 2003: 104) A typical context for a corrective marker thus appears to be i), which is incompatible with the use of *CSAK:*

i) A: *John wasn't invited.*
B: *#CSAK meghívták Jánost.*
CSAK VM: invited:3pl John:ACC
Intended: "John WAS invited."

in the *CG*, as illustrated in (1)–(2) and (5)–(6) above, and why the particle is not excluded from non-declaratives, as shown in (9)–(10).

However, the contrast between (4) and (5)–(6) above, points to a difference: *CSAK*, as opposed to Dutch accented *TOCH*, does not automatically get licensed in a sentence with propositional content *p* where *suggested(not-p)* is entailed by CG but *presumably (not-p)* is not. Given these findings we will assume that Hungarian *CSAK* belongs to a subtype of adversative context markers that are inserted into a sentence with propositional content *p* if and only if CG |= *presumably(not-p)*. In other words, it indicates that there is a set of propositions in the common ground that constitute a reason for thinking that *not-p* is true, but that an analogous requirement does not hold for *p*.

Having illustrated the contribution of the discourse particle *CSAK* to the meaning of Hungarian sentences, we consider the interpretation of its homonym, the exclusive particle *csak,* in order to find out how the adversative particle use came about.

3 The Meaning of the Exclusive Particle *Csak*

The Hungarian exclusive particle *csak* appears to be a close counterpart of the exclusive particle *only* in English, illustrated in (14) below, whose semantic-pragmatic properties have been studied intensively in the last decades:

(14) Only John made a perpetuum mobile.

Although there is general agreement concerning the fact that (14) simultaneously conveys that "John made a perpetuum mobile" (the "prejacent," cf. Horn 1969) and that "Nobody other than John made a perpetuum mobile" (the "exclusive proposition"), it is a hotly debated issue in the literature what the status of the latter two propositions are, whether they are entailed, presupposed or implicated.[10]

Regarding the interpretation of Hungarian exclusive *csak*, a further challenge presents itself, due to the fact that constituents situated in the immediately preverbal position are attributed an exhaustive reading (cf. Szabolcsi 1981, 1994 and É. Kiss 1998, among others, for the discussion and analysis of the relevant data): sentences containing preverbal focus constituents and those containing *csak* (associated with focus) cannot replace each other in all contexts, particularly, they cannot substitute for each other under negation. Szabolcsi (1994) makes a proposal (based on Kenesei 1989) that accounts for the contrasts between the interpretation of these two structures, illustrated in (15)–(16) and (17)–(18) below, by proposing that *csak*-sentences presuppose their prejacent and assert that no alternative propositions are true that are not entailed by the latter, whereas sentences containing a preverbal focus introduce

[10]In the current paper, we cannot even start to provide an account of the major results in the quest for the most adequate analysis of the meaning of *only*. In order to get a glimpse of the issues at stake and the various options of resolving them, the reader is advised to turn to Atlas (1993), Beaver and Clark (2008), Geach (1962), Geurts and van der Sandt (2004), Horn (1969, 1996), Ippolito (2007), Rooth (1992), and van Rooij and Schulz (2007), among others.

an existential presupposition and assert that the focus denotation is identical to the entity whose existence is presupposed. This account can successfully derive the truth conditions of (15)–(18) (as well as those of their negative counterparts), where capital letters mark the syllables bearing the heaviest stress within the sentences (which are equivalent to the information-structural focus here):[11]

(15) *JÁnost hívták meg.*
John:ACC invited:3pl VM
"JOHN got invited."

(16) *Csak JÁnost hívták meg.*
only John:ACC invited:3pl VM
"Only John got invited."

(17) *KÉT diákot hívtak meg.*
two student:ACC invited:3pl VM
"TWO students got invited."

(18) *Csak KÉT diákot hívtak meg.*
only two student:ACC invited:3pl VM
"Only two students got invited."

Szabolcsi's (1994) account can successfully explain why (16) is considered false if there is a true proposition among the alternative propositions generated by replacing the denotation of the focus for all of its alternatives (e.g., "Mary got invited"),[12] but why the truth of (18) is compatible with the truth of the nonidentical proposition 'There is a student who got invited.'

The above approach, however, runs into difficulties when it comes to the question of why *csak* is not superfluous in (19) in contexts where it is presupposed that everyone has one single occupation:

(19) *Mari csak egy DIák volt.*
Mary only a student was
"Mary was only a student."

Intuitively, the presence of *csak* in the previous sentence seems to indicate that the speaker expected Mary to have an occupation situated higher within the

[11]In these examples, information-structural foci are all identical to or included in the constituent situated in the syntactic focus position, referred to as [Spec,FP] in É. Kiss (2002), which is not necessarily always the case. (See Gyuris 2012 for further discussion).

[12]Note the string-identity and the simultaneous interpretational difference between (11) above and (16). The latter parallels the contrast betweeen their prosodic forms.

hierarchy of alternative occupations, like being a lecturer or being a professor, etc. The same meaning component, referred to as *mirativity* in the literature (cf. Beaver and Clark 2008 and Zeevat 2009) is also present in the case of (16) and (18): (16) suggests that the expectation was that more people in addition to John would be invited, and (18) that more than two students would be invited.

It appears that the intuitions about the interpretation of *csak* described above can be captured successfully with the help of the proposal made by Beaver and Clark (2008) for formalizing the meaning of exclusives, which equally takes into account their truth-conditional impact (excluding higher values on a scale) and their mirative function. Beaver and Clark's definition, shown in (20) below, assumes an ordering on the set of possible true answers to the Current Question (the question that the particular utterance addresses), which includes the prejacent of the sentence containing the exclusive particle, from weak to strong. The ordering creates a structure on the set of true alternatives that can either be a preorder or a partial order, and it is either based on entailment or some relevant pragmatic notion, e.g., newsworthiness.[13]

(20) *Meaning of exclusives*

The lexical meaning of exclusives is exhaustively described by:

Discourse function: To make a comment on the Current Question (CQ, [...]), a comment which weakens a salient natural expectation. To achieve this function, the prejacent must be weaker than the expected answer to the CQ on a salient scale.

Presupposition: The strongest true alternatives in the CQ are at least as strong as the prejacent.

Descriptive Content: The strongest true alternatives in the CQ are at most as strong as the prejacent.

(Beaver and Clark 2008: 251)

By adopting Beaver and Clark's (2008) proposal for the analysis of *csak* we can correctly account for why none of its occurrences are predicted to be superfluous in (15)–(19): each of them introduces a presupposition saying that among the alternative true answers that the speaker would have found appropriate to the Current Question beforehand, all are stronger or at least as strong as the prejacent. Given the descriptive content attributed to exclusives, the proposal correctly predicts that in cases where the alternative propositions do not exclude each other, the truth of a *csak*-sentence entails the falsity of alternative answers stronger than the prejacent, but does not exclude the truth of weaker alternative answers.[14]

---

[13]In the CIL18 talk that this paper is based on I made a suggestion for capturing the contribution of scalar *csak* to the presuppositions of Hungarian sentences that resembled Beaver and Clark's (2008) proposal very much, without having been aware of the latter.

[14]Zeevat's (2009) proposal, which analyses *only* as expressing low quantity mirativity ("less than expected"), and attributes exhaustivity not to the semantics of *only*, but to the prejacent containing a focus seems to be a viable candidate for capturing the interpretation of Hungarian *csak* as well. Since by the time Zeevat's paper appeared the present paper was already submitted for publication, detailed discussion of the above approach will have to be left for another occassion, as well as the discussion of Balogh's (2009) treatment of *csak*, which closely follows the latter.

Having discussed the interpretation of exclusive *csak* in Hungarian, in the next section we will argue that assuming an interpretation of the type shown in (20) for exclusive *csak*, it is possible to put forth a reasonable explanation for how it acquired the discourse particle interpretation described in Sect. 2 historically.

4 From Exclusive Particle Use to Discourse Particle Use: Historical Development Through Semantic Reanalysis

In this section, I would like to show that by assuming the interpretation proposed by Beaver and Clark (2008) for exclusives in (20), we can account for the problem of how the adversative discourse particle use described in Sect. 2 developed for *csak*, to which no fully convincing solution has been proposed in Hungarian historical linguistics so far.[15,16] The explanation offered here is based on the idea that the semantic change in the course of which the particle *csak* acquired its adversative context marker interpretation was a consequence of semantic reanalysis, which took place in order to avoid *pragmatic overload*, an important motivation for meaning change, according to Eckardt (2006).

Eckardt (2006) claims that when an expression is used in a particular type of construction where the information necessary to compute the presuppositions/implicatures introduced by it is not readily available to the hearers, and therefore too much pragmatic accommodation is required in order to understand the meaning of the construction, semantic reanalysis takes place. What this means is that the hearers redistribute the parts of the meaning of the whole sentence (which they are assumed to understand in full) among the constituents in a way that frees the relevant constituents from the pragmatic overload.

The earliest appearance of *csak* as an exclusive particle is found in a codex written in the 14th–15th centuries (Jókai codex, cf. Pólya 2008). The earliest occurrences of the particle where it clearly has the adversative discourse marker interpretation I found in texts dating from the middle of the seventeenth

---

[15]Cf. Pólya’s (2008) overview of the various interpretations of *csak* that it acquired historically, which, incidentally, contains only one example for adversative *csak*, from 1737.

[16]Although the question of how frequently the homonymy between an adversative discourse marker and an exclusive particle is attested in other languages would need further investigation, the cases of adversative particles turning to mirative markers discussed by Malchukov (2003) indicate that it is not an isolated phenomenon. Cf. also Zeevat (2009) for the claim that only-type mirative particles have a tendency to turn into adversative particles in Dutch or English.

century.[17,18] (21)–(22) below show two examples from the above period where *csak* can only be given an adversative interpretation. (Speakers of present-day Hungarian only find this example grammatical if the particle is pronounced stressed.)

(21) *Kedveseb jószágunk nincsen az életnél*
more:dear value:our be:NEG:3sg the life:than
Halálnak sarcoló pénzt ha fizethetnél
death:DAT ransom money:ACC if pay:could:COND:2sg
Van-é oly kedves jód, mellyet kimilhetnél,
is-E[19] such dear good:your that:ACC save:could:COND:2sg
Az mig kedved tartya, csak addig élhetnél.
that as:long liking:your hold:3sg CSAK that:until live:could:COND:2sg

"We have nothing more valuable than our lives / If you could pay ransom to death / Is there any of your dearest properties that you would not sacrifice / To be able to live just as long as you wish?"[20]

(from the poem *Murány Venus conversing with Mars,* by István Gyöngyösi, 1664[21])

[17]Benkő (1993–1997) argues that the first occurrence of *csak* having an interpretation that is to be translated into German with the help of the particle *doch* (which would correspond to the adversative discourse marker interpretation) dates back to the middle of the 16th century. There are, however, strong reasons to debate the accuracy of the author's interpretation of the use of the particle he provides as an example. Szabó T. (1978: 12) cites an example from 1608 that he translates as *doch* into German, but which cannot be analyzed properly due to lack of information about the preceding context.

[18]The electronic corpus of the Hungarian Generative Diachronic Syntax project at the Research Institute for Linguistics of the Hungarian Academy of Sciences, which contains 47 codices, 24 shorter texts, and 244 letters (2.2 million words) from the Old and Middle Hungarian periods (until the beginning of the 16th century) does not include any occurrences of *csak* where it has the adversative discourse marker interpretation. The Hungarian Historical Corpus, also at the Research Institute for Linguistics, collects texts from 1780 onwards, and includes many occurrences of the adversative context marker *csak.* Since at the time of collecting material for the paper there were no searchable databases of texts written between the beginning of the 16th and the end of the 18th centuries, I was relying on the investigation of printed texts constituting the corpus of the (non-generative) historical grammar of Hungarian, Benkő (1991, 1992) (http://www.nytud.hu/oszt/nyelvtort/abcrendeskkforras.pdf).

[19]Interrogative particle marking *yes/no* interrogatives in Hungarian.

[20]Literal translation, B. Gyuris.

[21]Source: Gyöngyösi, István 1664. *Márssal társolkodó Murányi Vénus*, strophe 216. Available at: http://mek.niif.hu/05900/05940/05940.pdf

(22) …	*egy*	*darabig*	*mind*	*igyekezénk*	*a*	*szelet*
	one	while:for	continually	tried:1pl	the	wind:ACC

megcsalni	*oldalfélt*	…	*való*	*mesterséges*	*evezésekkel,*
cheat:INF	sideways		being	artificial	rowing:PL:with

…	*de*	*hiába,*	*csak*	*meg*	*kelle*	*fordulni…*
	but	in:vain	CSAK	VM	must:PAST	turn:INF

"… for a while we continually tried to cheat the wind by rowing sideways artificially, … but in vain, we had to turn round after all…"
(from a letter by Miklós Bethlen, 1672[22])

Assuming that the normal preference of humans is to live forever, the exclusive interpretation of *csak* in (21), which would convey that the preferred length of the life of the addressee is ordered lower on some (unspecified) scale than alternative lengths is rather unlikely. However, on the adversative reading of the particle the *yes/no* interrogative is taken to ask whether the addressee would make all possible sacrifices to live as long as s/he wishes, which is taken to be in opposition to what follows under normal circumstances from the common ground, namely, that the length of somebody's life does not depend on how long that person wishes to live. The latter seems to be the only correct reading of the sentence.

Turning to (22), on the exclusive reading of *csak*, the sentence would convey that the only thing, the least significant or the least newsworthy thing that happened was that the speaker and his company had to turn round. By considering the wider context, it becomes clear that the turning round was quite a newsworthy and significant thing, because they fought quite hard to avoid it. On the adversative reading, the sentence is interpreted as saying that the speaker and his company had to turn round, which is in opposition to what would follow from the common ground under normal circumstances. This seems to be the correct reading given the huge efforts described in the preceding text that the company made to avoid turning round.

The following example, which can, however, be interpreted by assigning an exclusive reading to *csak*, illustrates that the position of the particle in front of the verb phrase does not automatically give rise to an adversative reading:

[22]Source: Bethlen, Miklós et al. 1987. *Bethlen Miklós levelei*. Budapest: Akadémiai Kiadó.

(23) … *és mikor észrevevém magamat, csak elhűlék nagy*
and when realized:1sg myself:ACC CSAK VM:be:amazed:1sg big
álmélkodással…
surprise:with
"…and when I realized my position, I was just struck dumb with amazement…"
(Miklós M. Tótfalusi Kiss, 1698[23])

On the exclusive reading of *csak* (23) thus means that the only thing the speaker did after realizing his position was being struck dumb with surprise (instead of obvious alternative actions like shouting, quitting, crying, etc.), which seems to be a reasonable interpretation.

I believe that the semantic reanalysis in the course of which the adversative interpretation of the *csak* particle came about was initiated by constructions that shared the following properties. First, the set of alternative answers to the Current Question is not made explicit, except for the prejacent. Second, based on the lexical meaning of the focus within the prejacent or on the wider context, all theoretically possible alternatives to the prejacent mutually exclude the latter. Third, based on the lexical meaning of the focus within the prejacent or on contextual information, the prejacent is considered to be ordered lowest among these alternatives. Fourth, there is reason to assume the opposite of the prejacent under normal circumstances given the content of the common ground. Below we illustrate two examples for the case under consideration:

(24) … *mert engemet csak héában igyekezel hozzád hajtani.*
because I:ACC CSAK in:vain strive:2sg towards:you bend:INF
"… because your efforts to bend me in your direction are in vain after all."
(Bálint Balassi, 1589[24])

(25) … *ha a lovak magokban mind sánták, ha öszve*
if the horse:PL alone:PL:in all lame:PL if together
fogjákis tsak sánták.
harness:3pl:also CSAK lame:PL
"… if the individual horses are all lame, they are still lame if they are harnessed together."
(from the *Sárospatak Dispute*, 1660[25])

[23]Source: M. Tótfalusi Kiss, Miklós 1698. *M. Tótfalusi K. Miklósnak Mentsége.* Kolozsvár.

[24]Source: Balassi, Bálint 1589. *Szép magyar komédia.* Available at: http://mek.oszk.hu/00600/00610/00610.htm

[25]Source: Kulcsár, Árpád 1999. A sárospataki hitvita 1660. szeptember 30. - október 1. In Csaba Fazekas (ed.) *Fiatal egyháztörténészek írásai.* Miskolc: Miskolci Egyetem BTK Újkori Magyar Történeti Tanszék, 21-46. Available at: http://mek.oszk.hu/02000/02082/html/kulcsar.htm.

Let us consider first the interpretation of (24) before the reanalysis. The wider context does not make it clear what alternatives of the prejacent are assumed by the speaker. The use of *csak* introduces the presupposition that the strongest true alternatives are at least as strong as the prejacent. Given that the focus of the prejacent is *héában* 'in vain', the theoretically possible alternatives to the prejacent in the CQ include the propositions 'your efforts will lead to mild success,' 'your efforts will lead to medium success,' 'your efforts will lead to great success,' etc., among which the prejacent, equivalent to 'your efforts will lead to no success,' is ordered lowest according to the most natural ordering imaginable. The descriptive content introduced by *csak* says that none of the alternatives stronger than the prejacent are true, which, again, follows from the fact that none of the alternatives can be true simultaneously with the prejacent. Given that both the presupposition and the descriptive content follows from the meaning of the sentence already, in the lack of explicit reference to alternative answers to the CQ, interpreters have the problem of identifying the reason for the use of *csak*. After the reanalysis, the interpretation of the prejacent is retained, and *csak* conveys that this interpretation is the opposite of the proposition that the common ground constitutes a reason for assuming under normal circumstances. This is supported by the fact that the common ground contains information about how hard the addressee has tried to gain the heart of the speaker.

The meaning (25) before and after the reanalysis can be calculated in an analogous way: here again all alternative answers to the CQ are incompatible with the prejacent (since they all entail that the horses harnessed together are not lame), which is ordered lowest among the alternatives on every natural ordering.

The only remaining question regarding the latter interpretation then is why the particle must obligatorily be stressed. I suggest that it is due to the fact that stressing some constituent of the prejacent is prohibited given that the whole of the latter is considered given information, whereas on the exclusive reading the focus constituent is not given, thus available for being stressed. Since there has to be a constituent that bears the main stress of the sentence, on the adversative reading the particle receives it as a last resort.[26]

The only analysis in the literature of the relation between the exclusive and the adversative interpretations of *csak* is provided by Simonyi (1881). According to him, the adversative interpretation of the particle, which he illustrates with the example in (27) below, developed from another discourse particle use of non-stressed *csak*, to be paraphrased as "without interruption," illustrated in (26) (Simonyi 1881:193). (Interestingly, this latter interpretation is not discussed either by Benkő 1993–1997 or Szabó T. 1978.)

[26] I thank Manfred Krifka for suggesting this explanation.

(26) *csak beszélek, csak beszélek neki, de hiába*
only talk:1sg only talk:1sg he:DAT but in:vain.
"I keep talking to him, but in vain."

(27) *Akármint ragyogjon a nap, de csak nem lát a vak*
no:matter:how shine:SUBJ:3sg the sun but CSAK not see:3sg the blind
"No matter how strongly the sun shines, the blind cannot see."
(*Proverb*, cited in Simonyi 1881: 193)

The scarcity of the relevant data available does not allow one to decide whether this explanation is on the right track. I believe that to be able to do so, one should have proof for the use of non-accented *csak* on which it is to be paraphrased as "without interruption" being earlier than the adversative use. Also, the number of constructions where *csak* is followed by an activity or a state verb (phrase) should be higher than the number of those where the particle is followed by accomplishment or achievement verbs, immediately after the adversative interpretation arises. In any case, I have not been able to find any examples for the reading of *csak* where it means "without interruption" in the seventeenth century sources I have consulted and where the examples in (21)–(22) and (24)–(25) illustrating the adversative reading come from.

It is assumed that the interpretation of *csak* as an adversative context marker spread to all three sentence types where it can now appear (declaratives, *yes-no* interrogatives and imperatives), including structures where *csak* cannot have an exclusive reading at all, illustrated in the contemporary examples below. In (28), stressed *CSAK* is followed by a universal noun phrase, and in (29) by a negated noun phrase, neither of which can be interpreted as being the focus associating with an exclusive particle:

(28) *CSAK mindenki Jánost hívta meg.*
CSAK everybody John:ACC invited:3sg VM
"Everybody invited John after all."

(29) *CSAK nem Jánost hívták meg.*
CSAK not John:ACC invited:3pl VM
"It wasn't John who got invited after all."

5 Conclusions

In this paper, the interpretation of the Hungarian stressed *CSAK* discourse particle was investigated. It was argued that the necessary and sufficient conditions for its appearance in discourses indicate that it has the function of an adversative context marker, as proposed by Zeevat (2000, 2003, 2006). It was shown that a plausible motivation for the meaning change in the course of which the exclusive particle *csak* acquired this discourse particle use can be given by assuming Beaver and Clark's (2008) analysis for the interpretation of exclusive *csak,* and a process of semantic reanalysis due to pragmatic overload, a process of semantic change, described by Eckardt (2006).

References

Atlas, Jay David. 1993. The importance of being 'only': Testing the neo-gricean versus neo-entailment paradigms. *Journal of Semantics* 10: 301–318.

Balogh, Kata. 2009. *Theme with variations. A context-based analysis of focus.* Doctoral Dissertation, University of Amsterdam.

Beaver, David I., and Brady Z. Clark. 2008. *Sense and sensitivity: How Focus determines meaning.* Chicester: Wiley-Blackwell.

Benkő, Loránd. (ed.). 1991. *A magyar nyelv történeti nyelvtana I. [A Historical Grammar of the Hungarian Language.]* Budapest: Akadémiai Kiadó.

Benkő, Loránd. (ed.). 1992. *A magyar nyelv történeti nyelvtana II. [A Historical Grammar of the Hungarian Language.]* Budapest: Akadémiai Kiadó.

Benkő, Loránd. (ed.). 1993–1997. *Etymologisches Wörterbuch des Ungarischen I-III.* Budapest: Akadémiai Kiadó.

Eckardt, Regine. 2006. *Meaning change in Grammaticalization: An inquiry into semantic reanalysis.* Oxford: Oxford University Press.

Katalin, É.Kiss. 1998. Identificational focus versus information focus. *Language* 74: 245–273.

Katalin, É.Kiss. 2002. *The Syntax of Hungarian.* Cambridge: Cambridge University Press.

Geach, Peter. 1962. *Reference and generality.* Ithaca: Cornell University Press.

Geurts, Bart, and Robert van der Sandt. 2004. Interpreting focus. *Theoretical Linguistics* 28: 1–44.

Gyuris, Beáta. 2007. Contrasting expectations: The Hungarian modal particle *csak.* Paper presented at the 3rd Workshop on Contrast, 4 May 2007, ZAS, Berlin.

Gyuris, Beáta. 2009. A hangsúlyos *csak* diskurzuspartikula interpretációja. [The interpretation of the stressed *csak* particle.] In *A mai magyar nyelv leírásának újabb módszerei VII.* [New Methods for the Description of the Hungarian Language.] ed. Márta Maleczki, and Enikő, Németh T. Szeged: Szegedi Tudományegyetem Általános Nyelvészeti Tanszék, 157–178.

Gyuris, Beáta. 2012. The information structure of Hungarian. In *The expression of information structure,* ed. Manfred Krifka, and Renate Musan, 159–186. Berlin: Mouton de Gruyter.

Horn, Laurence R. 1969. A presuppositional analysis of *only* and *even. Papers from the Fifth Regional Meeting of the Chicago Linguistics Society,* 98–107. Chicago: University of Chicago.

Horn, Laurence R. 1996. Exclusive company: *Only* and the dynamics of vertical inference. *Journal of Semantics* 13: 1–40.

Ippolito, Michela. 2007. On the meaning of *only. Journal of Semantics* 25: 45–91.

Kenesei, István. 1989. Logikus-e a magyar szórend? [Is Hungarian word order logical?] *Általános Nyelvészeti Tanulmányok* XVII: 105–152.

Kiefer, Ferenc. 1988. Modal particles as discourse markers in questions. *Acta Linguistica* 38: 107–125.

Kocsány, Piroska. 1986. *A mondás mint szövegtípus*. [*The saying as a text form.*] DSc dissertation, MTA, Budapest.

Malchukov, Andrej. L. 2003. Towards a semantic typology of adversative and contrast marking. *Journal of Semantics* 21: 177–198.

Meibauer, Jörg. 1994. *Modaler Kontrast und konzeptuelle Verschiebung. Studien zur Syntax und Semantik deutscher Modalpartikeln*. Niemeyer: Tübingen.

Pólya, Katalin. 2008. A *csak* partikula történeti változásaihoz. [On the historical changes characterizing the particle *csak*.] In László Büky, Tamás Forgács & Balázs Sinkovics (eds.) *A nyelvtörténeti kutatások újabb eredményei V. [New results in diachronic research.]* Szeged: Department of Hungarian Linguistics, SZTE, 177–184.

Simonyi, Zsigmond. 1881. *A magyar kötőszók*. [*Hungarian Conjunctions*.] Budapest: A Magyar Tudományos Akadémia Könyvkiadó Hivatala.

Stalnaker, Robert C. 1978. Assertion. In *Pragmatics. Syntax and semantics*, Vol. 9, ed. Peter Cole, 315–332. New York: Academic Press.

Szabolcsi, Anna. 1981. Compositionality in focus. *Folia Linguistica* 15: 141–161.

Szabolcsi, Anna. 1994. All quantifiers are not equal: The case of focus. *Acta Linguistica Hungarica* 42–43: 171–187.

Szabó T., Attila. 1978. *Erdélyi magyar szótörténeti tár II*. [*Transsylvanian Hungarian Historical Dictionary Vol. II.*]. Bukarest: Kriterion Könyvkiadó.

Thurmair, Maria. 1989. *Modalpartikeln und ihre Kombinationen*. Niemeyer: Tübingen.

van Rooij, Robert, and Katrin Schulz. 2007. *Only:* Meaning and Implicatures. In *Current research in the semantics/pragmatics interface*, ed. Maria Aloni, Alastair Butler, and Paul Dekker, 193–223. Oxford and Amsterdam: Elsevier.

Zeevat, Henk. 2000. Discourse particles as speech act markers. *LDV-Forum* 17: 74–91.

Zeevat, Henk. 2003. Particles: Presupposition triggers, context markers or speech act markers. In Reinhart Blutner & Henk Zeevat (eds.) *Optimality Theory and Pragmatics*. Basingstoke & New York: Palgrave Macmillan, 91–111.

Zeevat, Henk. 2006. A dynamic approach to discourse particles. In *Approaches to discourse particles*, ed. Kerstin Fischer, 133–148. Oxford & Amsterdam: Elsevier.

Zeevat, Henk. 2009. "Only" as a mirative particle. *Sprache und Datenverarbeitung* 33(1-2): 179–196.

Zimmermann, Malte. 2011. Discourse Particles. In *Handbook of semantics*, ed. Paul Portner, Claudia Maienborn, and Klaus von Heusinger, 2012–2038 (= Handbücher zur Sprach- und Kommunikationswissenschaft). Berlin: Mouton de Gruyter.

Scalar Implicatures, Presuppositions, and Discourse Particles: Colloquial Russian *–to*, *že*, and *ved'* in Combination

Svetlana McCoy-Rusanova

Abstract This paper tackles the problem of interaction between multiple discourse particles in the same utterance. It examines how presuppositions and/or implicatures contributed by individual particles are combined to account for connotations which arise in utterances containing multiple particles. The subject of study is free combinations of set-evoking colloquial Russian particles ***–to***, ***že***, and ***ved'***. The data are drawn from constructed minimal discourses. The study integrates the theories of information structure (Vallduví, The informational component, 1992), scalar implicatures (Hirschberg, A theory of scalar implicature, 1985/1991), and discourse organization (Büring, On D-trees, beans, and B-accents, 2000). The current approach to decomposing the meaning of particles by examining them in combination sheds new light on the context-independent interpretations of the particles and makes another step toward understanding their complex roles in discourse.

Keywords Discourse particles • Colloquial Russian • Scalar implicature • Presupposition

1 Introduction

The meaning of so-called *discourse* (alternatively, *modal*, or *pragmatic*) *particles* in various languages has been notoriously difficult to capture. In recent decades some progress has been made in moving away from describing and cataloguing their context-dependent meanings to more formal approaches capturing semantic and discourse contributions of individual particles. (For cross-linguistic studies see, for example, volumes edited by van der Wouden et al. 2002 and Fischer 2006; for German and Dutch particles see Zeevat 2000, 2002; Karagjosova 2001a, b; Eckardt 2006, etc.; for the colloquial Russian particles see Bitextin 1994; Parrott 1997;

S. McCoy-Rusanova (✉)
Appen Linguistic Consulting, Department of German, Russian, and E. European Languages and Literatures Russian Program, Rutgers University, 172 College Avenue, New Brunswick, NJ 08903, USA
e-mail: smccoy@rci.rutgers.edu; svetgmcc@yahoo.com

C. Lee et al. (eds.), *Contrastiveness in Information Structure, Alternatives and Scalar Implicatures*, Studies in Natural Language and Linguistic Theory 91, DOI 10.1007/978-3-319-10106-4_6

Feldman 2001; McCoy 2001; Marshall 2002; Hagstrom and McCoy 2003; Bolden 2005; Post 2005, etc.) However, the problem of interaction between multiple particles in the same utterance has not yet been adequately addressed (for a notable exception see Parrott 1997).

The subject of this paper is three colloquial Russian particles ***–to***, ***že***, and ***ved,'*** which were traditionally called *emphatic*, *emotive, expressive, intensifying,* etc, and more recently labeled as *set evoking*, or *set generating*. The goal is to examine how presuppositions and/or implicatures contributed by individual particles are combined to account for connotations which arise in utterances containing multiple particles. The study integrates the theories of information structure (Vallduví 1992) and discourse organization (Roberts 1996; Büring 2000).

For the purpose of comparing the contributions of each particle first in isolation and then in combinations, let us hold the discourse setting as constant. Speakers A and B are discussing a particular book, for example, some bestseller that everybody else in the group has read, except for A and B. Speaker A recommends that B read this book, while B utters (1) – a sentence containing either a single particle ***–to***, ***že***, or ***ved'*** or a combination of these particles:[1]

(1) Situation: A recommends that B read a particular book. B replies:

Ty	***–to/že/ved'***	eë	ne	čital!
You	***Particle(s)***	it	NEG	read

'You haven't read it!' [+ *additional meaning(s) contributed by the particle(s)*]

All of the resulting sentences share the same assertion (i.e., *the hearer has not read the book*). However, each of them is unique in the set of implicatures and/or presuppositions that arise due to the particular particle(s) being used, which will be tackled individually below.

The decision to draw data from a constructed discourse rather than natural language corpora is motivated by the need to isolate and compare the contribution of each particle without accounting for multiple variables that are necessarily

[1]This situation is adapted from Vasilyeva (1972: 179) where a proposition in the preceding discourse, shown in (i), is followed by an utterance in (ii):

(i) Oni vse čitali etu knigu.

They all read this book

'They've all read this book.'

(ii) Ty ***–to*** eë ne čital ***že***!

You ***–to*** it NEG read ***že***

'But as for you, you haven't read it!'

But you haven't read it, have you?' (Vasilyeva's translation)

present in recordings of natural speech (for a study based on data drawn from colloquial Russian corpora, see McCoy 2001).[2]

The paper is structured as follows: Sect. 2 summarizes context-independent meanings of each of the three particles. Section 3 discusses all possible combinations of ***–to***, ***že***, and ***ved'*** and examines how their invariant meanings are preserved and combined with each other. Finally, Sect. 4 comments on the nature of the additional meaning contributed by the particles.

2 Background on the Colloquial Russian Particles *–to, že, and ved'*

This section draws primarily on the insights developed in McCoy (2001) and Hagstrom and McCoy (2003), where the particles ***–to***, ***že***, and ***ved'*** are analyzed as set-evoking/set-generating/'kontrastive' (after Vallduví and Vilkuna 1998) lexemes, which means that the use of such particles by the speaker makes the hearer generate a set of alternatives, essentially in the same way as Focus alternatives (in the sense of Rooth 1985) are generated in English by the use of certain intonation contours. The particles, however, differ with respect to the types of sets that are being evoked.

2.1 The Particle –to

The particle ***–to*** has high frequency in colloquial speech; it is an enclitic and thus it is always unstressed. It is etymologically related to the distal deictic/demonstrative pronoun *to(t)* 'that' in its neuter/singular form *to*, as opposed to the proximal deictic *èto(t)* 'this.' It can cliticize to practically any notional part of speech or phrasal category—NP, AP, PP, VP, AdvP—with its most frequent host being a nominal.

The tendency of this particle to occur more frequently at the beginning of the clause might give a false impression that ***–to*** can be analyzed as a 'second position' clitic (see Halpern 1995 for terminology). However, this is not supported with

[2]The presence of negation in the tested sentence should not affect conclusions on the contributions of each particle. The constructed discourse situation could be reversed: A and B could be talking about a bestseller that nobody in the group except A has read; and B would be soliciting A's advice by uttering a sentence which asserts *You have read it* and contains the particle(s). However, I am finding this situation slightly more unnatural than in (1) above, especially with particles ***že*** and/or ***ved'*** which add the tone of contradiction to the utterance. This issue is worth discussing in more detail in the future.

naturally occurring data on ***–to*** (see McCoy 2001 for multiple examples). Since ***–to*** is a clitic, its host can be only a phonological word.[3]

It has been claimed in the literature that ***–to*** cliticizes to a thematic (or 'old/given' information, in other terms) element of the clause (Bonnot 1987; Bitextin 1994, among others) or serves as a marker of a contrastive topic (Lee 2002). While these analyses are basically correct, it would be more accurate to treat this particle, first of all, as set evoking, or set generating, or 'kontrastive' (see McCoy 2001 for examples of ***–to*** cliticizing to contrastive rhemes).

The particle ***–to***, as in (2), cliticizes to a contrastive theme/topic (or 'kontrastive' link, after Vallduví 1992; Vallduví and Vilkuna 1998), shown in (3), and marks **a set of sets of propositions** (same as **a set of questions**), shown in alternative ways in (4–5). The placement of ***–to*** at the clausal level is a direct consequence of its essential kontrastive property as a marker of a set of sets of propositions (or a set of questions). In order to satisfy this essential property, the default position of ***–to*** at the clausal level is encliticized to the (kontrastive) link: the kontrast on the link value results in the set of alternatives, which is a set of sets of propositions. (By comparing links to each other, the hearer has to consider the rheme value for each of these links; so the kontrast on the link produces, or forces, kontrast on the rheme.) Thus, the usual position of ***–to*** is an enclitic to the (kontrastive) link:[4]

(2) Situation: A recommends that B read a particular book. B replies:

Ty-***to*** eë ne čital!

You ***-to*** it NEG read.

'As for you [*compared to the other people*], you haven't read it [*although you may have done something else with it, such as browsed through it/bought it/etc.*].'

(3) [$_{+K/Link}$ You] (***-to***) [$_{+K/Rheme}$ haven't read] it

(4) M(***-to***)={{**You haven't read it**; You've browsed through it; You've bought it;}
{They haven't read it; They've browsed through it; They've bought it}
{I haven't read it; I've browsed through it; I've bought it;...}}

(5) M(***-to***)={{What have **you** done with it?}
{What have **they** done with it?}
{What have **I** done with it?};...}

---

[3]For example, short prepositions, like *v* 'in' cannot host ***–to***, while it can cliticize to phonetically longer ones, such as *vnutri* 'inside' (see McCoy 2001: 160–162).

[4]However, the essential property of ***–to*** as a marker of a set of sets of propositions will also be satisfied when the link is marked as kontrastive by some other linguistic means (prosody, other lexical expressions that mark kontrast, etc.) and ***–to*** encliticizes to the (kontrastive) rheme. In this case, which is not the default option, the set of sets of propositions is still marked by ***–to*** (however, with additional help of some other linguistic expression marking the kontrastive status of the link).

Sentences with *–to* generate scalar implicatures in the same way as sentences with contrastive topics do (see, for example, Lee 2006). Essentially, *–to* creates two points of contrast: *you* vs. *they/I/*etc. and the property of *not having read the book* vs. other context relevant properties, such as *browsing through it* or *buying it*.[5] The latter set forms a pragmatic, contextually relevant, scale: <*read the book, browse through the book, buy the book*> (following Hirschberg 1985/1991). While it is asserted that the truth value of the proposition *read-it(you)* is false, the truth values of the other propositions are not determined. However, the discourse could naturally proceed in that direction or truth values of some propositions could already be part of common ground. This is graphically represented in (6), which utilizes the Question Under Discussion (QUD) discourse model (Roberts 1996; Büring 2000):

(6) D-tree for an utterance with *–to*, (2):

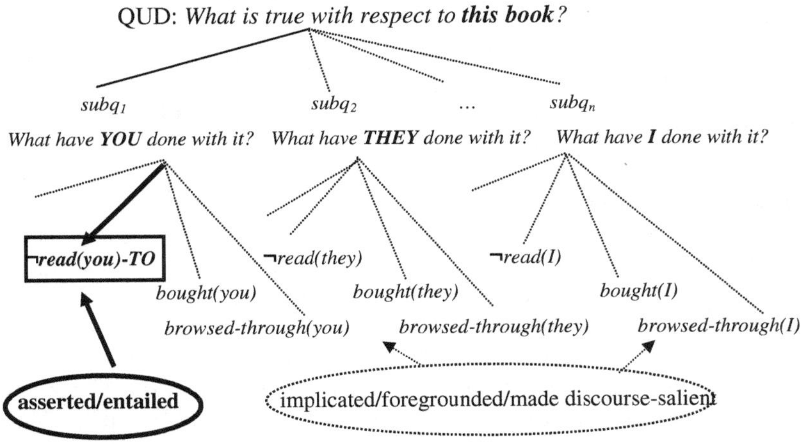

2.2 The Particle *že*

The particle *že*, the origin of which is traceable to Proto-Indo-European *ghe, has been described in the literature as truly multifunctional: the diversity of its usage ranges from being a purely "modal/affective" particle to playing only the organizational role in discourse, from being a marker of focus to marking thematic elements, from having scope over a phrase-level category to having clausal scope, etc. Additionally, it can be used in utterances of various pragmatic types and it poses no restrictions on the host with respect to its syntactic category.

[5]The position of *–to* in the sentence is determined by which element plays the role of a contrastive topic/theme/link: if, for example, *–to* were cliticized to *eë* 'it/this book,' the generated set of questions (or the set of sets of propositions) would be organized around the contrast on *this book* versus *that book* or *this book* versus *this article* versus *this dissertation* and the respective properties of each of these entities (the property of *not having been read by you* versus other relevant properties).

Here we will discuss only the sentential ***že*** (in the sense of Parrott 1997, as opposed to the phrasal ***že***), as in (7)—the modal/pragmatic/discourse particle which adds the tone of aggressiveness, contradiction, combativeness to the utterance:

(7) Situation: A recommends that B read a particular book. B replies:

Ty ***že*** eë ne čital!

'But you HAVEN'T read it!

[*even though you believe and/or act as if the opposite is true*]'

The meaning of statements containing ***že*** can be rendered into English with the help of the so-called "contradiction contour" (Liberman and Sag 1974; Pierrehumbert and Hirschberg 1990).[6] Parrott (1997: 120) points out that English translations of statements containing ***že*** "should, in general, be read with an argumentative pitch, one that is high overall and that rises toward the end of the utterance."[7]

The possible placement of ***že*** in the clause is shown in (8): even though it can appear in different positions, the resulting sentences have the same meaning.

(8) Ty *(**že**)* eë *(**že**)* ne čital *(**že**)*!

This particle has been analyzed as a so-called *verum focus marker*: it creates contrast on the polarity of the proposition. Thus, in (7–8) the proposition *the hearer has not read the book*, uttered by the speaker, is contrasted with the contextually relevant proposition *the hearer has read the book*, which may be attributed (possibly erroneously) by the speaker to be true of the hearer on the basis of the hearer's behaviour and/or presuppositions or implicatures of the hearer's previous utterances. To elaborate on the discourse situation in (1) when A recommends that B read a particular book: what may have made B utter (7) is B's knowledge that A has just bought this book and, therefore, has not had any time to read it. While the fact of A's buying the book is true, B's conjecture that A has not read the book may or may not be true (a couple of possible scenarios: A had previously read a library copy of the book and decided to buy a copy to own; or A already owns a copy and has read it and is buying another one for a gift to somebody else, etc.). The natural way for the discourse to proceed is in the direction of finding out which of the two mutually exclusive propositions is true: either *the hearer has read the book*, or *the hearer has not read the book*.

To summarize, the set evoked by ***že*** in (7) consists of two propositions, only one of which can be true, as shown in (9). Proposition *p* marked with ***že*** asserts *p* and

[6]In Pierrehumbert's (1980/1988) notation this intonation contour is "analyzed as beginning with a prenuclear L* + H followed by one or more prenuclear L* accents before the nuclear L*" (quoted from Ladd 1996: 296).

[7]The particle ***že*** also occurs in wh-questions (and quasi-questions with wh-words). One possible way to render their meaning into English is by a phrase *(who/what/...) in the world* or its synonyms in the 'familiar' mode of communication *(who/what/...) the hell....*

presupposes that the hearer believes, or acts like, $\neg p$ (cf. Hagstrom and McCoy 2003). The discourse tree for (7) is shown in (10).

(9) M(*že*) = {**You haven't read it;** *You've read it*}

(10) D-tree for the utterance with *že*, (7):

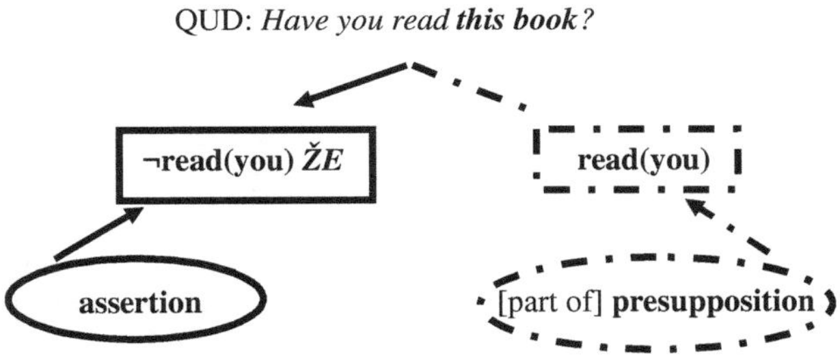

2.3 The Particle *ved'*

The particle ***ved'***, which is historically related to the verb *vedat'* 'to know,' was probably used as a parenthetical before it was fully grammaticalized into a particle. Its word order properties, more flexible than those of ***že*** or ***–to***, have been attributed to its verbal origin. Another property of ***ved'*** that has been traced to its etymology is that ***ved'*** is rather restricted with respect to modality: it occurs only in affirmative statements (including statements of possibilities or probabilities); questions containing this particle lack the illocutionary force of questions and are usually perceived as rhetorical questions (Bitextin 1994). The use of this particle not only activates the background knowledge that the speaker assumes the interlocutor shares, but also implies the indisputability of this knowledge (Vasilyeva 1972; Grenoble 1998).

Utterances with particle ***ved'*** are perceived as a polite reminder and not as a verbal attack, as with ***že*** (Parrott 1997). This difference in positive/negative connotations is grounded in the status of information marked by the two particles. While ***ved'*** refers to information known to the hearer but not necessarily activated in the discourse yet and, therefore, reminds the hearer to retrieve an important piece of information and perform the necessary reasoning, particle ***že*** refers to information which is or should already have been activated in discourse and which the hearer—according to the speaker's assessment—ignores and thus fails in reaching the conclusion preferred by the speaker.

The interpretative meaning of particle ***ved'*** can be paraphrased as *I know that you know about this though you are not thinking about this now, nevertheless this information is really relevant now.*

So, in our discourse situation that is being held constant, the utterance with ***ved'***, as in (11), is perceived to be less argumentative and more of a polite reminder or advice to the addressee, compared with ***že*** being a verbal attack on the addressee:

(11) Situation: A recommends that B read a particular book. B replies:
Ty ***ved'*** eë ne čital!
'You haven't read it, you know!
[*while others have read it and I'm reminding/advising you to do so*]'

Notice that unlike the other two particles, it can also be placed at the beginning of the clause, as in (12):

(12) ***(ved')*** Ty ***(ved')*** eë ***(ved')*** ne čital ***(ved')***!

The discourse situation in (11–12) can be elaborated in the following way to make for the felicitous use of the particle ***ved'***: A recommends B to read some bestseller; B knows that A hasn't read it yet but takes A's recommendation as echoing or endorsing the opinion of others (if it is a bestseller, it should be good). There is no disagreement between A and B that A has not read the book: both know it as a fact. What B is implicating is that A's advice may not be as valid as the advice of those who have read the book (or could be perceived more valid after A reads the book in the future).

(13) M(***ved'***)= { {**You haven't read it**}
{They HAVE read it} }

Similarly to ***že***, the particle ***ved'*** marks the polarity of the proposition: the property of having read the book versus not having read it. However, ***ved'*** lacks the presupposition that the hearer believes or acts as if ¬*p* is true. Instead, by using ***ved'*** the speaker indicates that s/he is aware that the hearer knows *p* but is not thinking about it at the moment (cf. Parrott 1997; McCoy 2001) and contrasts it with attributing the opposing property to another referent. In this sense the particle ***ved'*** works similarly to the particle ***–to***: both go beyond their immediate QUD and build a super question above it (as opposed to ***že*** which operates under a single QUD where the truth value of one proposition is being determined):

(14) D-tree for an utterance with ***ved'***, (11):

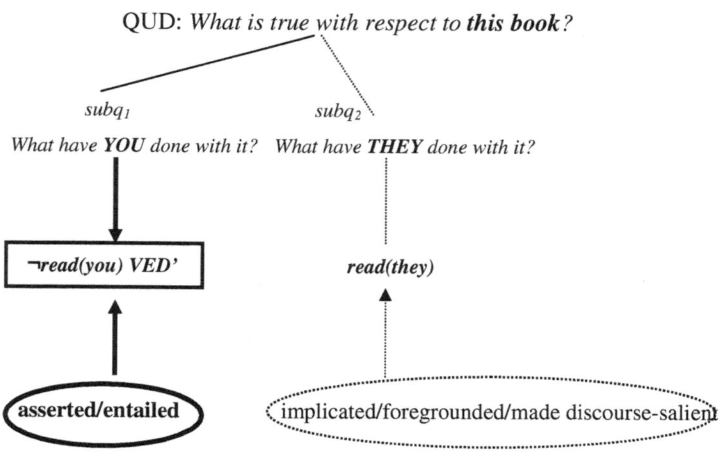

2.4 Summary on the Particles *–to*, *že*, and *ved'*

The particle ***–to*** generates a set of sets of propositions, or alternatively, a set of questions, shown in (15–17), in which the proposition marked by the particle ***–to*** is asserted, while the other propositions are implicated, foregrounded, or made discourse salient:

(15) M(-***to***)={ {**A(x)**, *B(x)*, *C(x)*, …};
{*A(y)*, *B(y)*, *C(y)*, …};
{*A(z)*, *B(z)*, *C(z)*, …};…}

(16) M(-***to***)={ What is true of *x*?;
What is true of *y*?;
What is true of *z*?; …}

(17) D-tree for utterances with ***–to***:

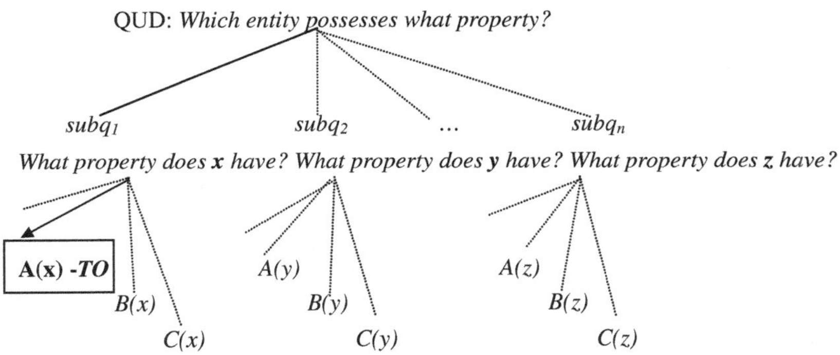

The particle ***že*** generates a set of mutually exclusive propositions, only one of which could be true, shown in (18–19). The proposition marked by ***že*** is asserted by the speaker, the other proposition is attributed by the speaker to be a part of the addressee's knowledge or belief set

(18) M(***že***) = {**A(x)**; ¬***A(x)***}
(19) D-tree for the utterance with ***že***:

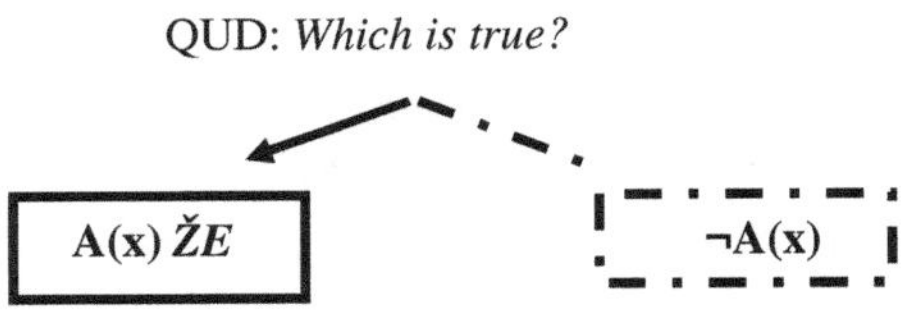

The particle ***ved'*** evokes a set of sets of propositions (resembling ***–to*** in this respect), where two opposing properties are predicated of two different entities, shown in (20–21). The proposition marked by ***ved'*** is asserted by the speaker and is in the addressee's knowledge set but not currently activated at the moment:

(20) M(***ved'***)= { {**A(x)** }
{¬*A (y)*} }

(21) D-tree for an utterance with ***ved'***

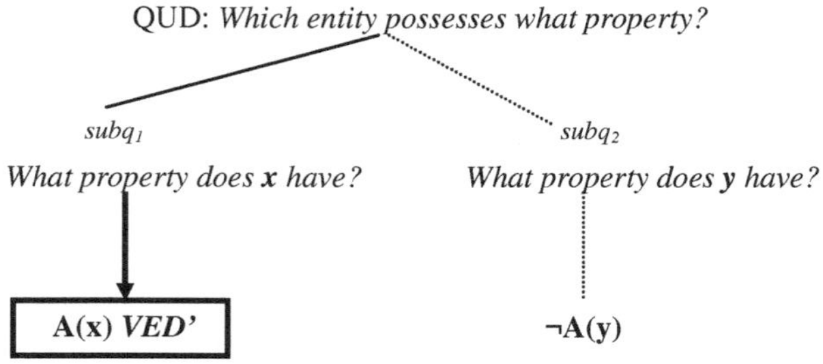

Now let us proceed to examine whether these context-invariant meanings of the particles are preserved in utterances containing combinations of these particles.

3 Particles in Combination

When the particles are freely combined in one utterance, we should expect that all the properties they bring with them—evoked sets, presuppositions, implicatures, etc.—are preserved and combined into one whole that has features of its individual contributors. In the sections below I will demonstrate that this is indeed the case and show the mechanisms that are involved. First I will tackle the particles that have similar characteristics: the two adversarial particles ***že*** + ***ved'*** will be discussed in Sect. 3.1; the two particles evoking a larger discourse tree ***–to*** + ***ved'*** will be handled in Sect. 3.2. Section 3.3 will focus on ***–to*** + ***že***, the particles that have fewer properties in common. And Sect. 3.4 will handle the combination of all three particles in one utterance.[8]

3.1 A Combination of že + ved'

When ***že*** and ***ved'*** co-occur, ***že*** assumes a narrow scope on the term, while ***ved'*** has a wide, sentential, scope, as in (22): one of them contrasts *you* versus *they*, while the other one brings up contrast on the polarity/veracity of the propositions.[9] The resulting set for ***že*** + ***ved'*** is shown in (23):

[8]For a previous attempt to analyze particles in combination see McCoy-Rusanova (2008).

[9]The same happens with two occurrences of ***že*** in one clause. Parrott (1997:166ff.), however, points out that multiple ***že*** is functionally identical to its single use besides its occurrence in emotional speech and the flavor of being somewhat substandard. She also calls attention to the existence of the marginal colloquial form ***žež*** (which is common in Belorussian).

(22) Situation: A recommends that B read a particular book. B replies:
(***ved'***) Ty ***že*** (***ved'***) eë (***ved'***) ne čital (***ved'***)!
'As opposed to the other party involved, you haven't read it, you know! [*while they have!*]'

(23) M(***že*** ***+ved'***)= { {**You haven't read it;** ***You've read it*** }
{They haven't read it; *They've read it* } }

An utterance with a combination of ***že*** + ***ved'*** is perceived less adversarial than the one with ***že*** by itself, however, its tone is slightly more aggressive than of an utterance containing only ***ved'***. In our discourse situation these two particles can be felicitously used in the following circumstances: the speaker knows that the hearer hasn't read the book and is surprised by the hearer's behaviour, thus asking for an explanation, a solution to this puzzle. The clash in polarity that is brought by the presupposition triggered by ***že*** still needs to be resolved (*You haven't read the book*—although you behave as if *you have read it*). The contribution of ***ved'*** here is contrasting this unresolved conflict with some other evoked proposition, in which the negated property of the statement asserted by ***že*** is predicated of some other referent, such as *They have read it*. The truth value of such evoked proposition is indisputable: it is accepted by both the speaker and the hearer that the other people have definitely read the book before writing good reviews about it, which motivated more people to buy and read this book, since it is a bestseller, after all. With the help of ***ved'***, the speaker goes beyond determining the truth value of whether the hearer has read the book (which is the function of ***že***) and reaches out into a larger discourse tree by hinting at the indisputable fact that other people have read the book, thus they may be more qualified to give advice about it. Thus, an utterance with a combination of ***že*** + ***ved'*** is at the same time a reproach by the speaker to the hearer and a suggestion to do otherwise. This is graphically represented in a discourse tree in (24):

(24) D-tree for an utterance with ***že*** and ***ved'***:

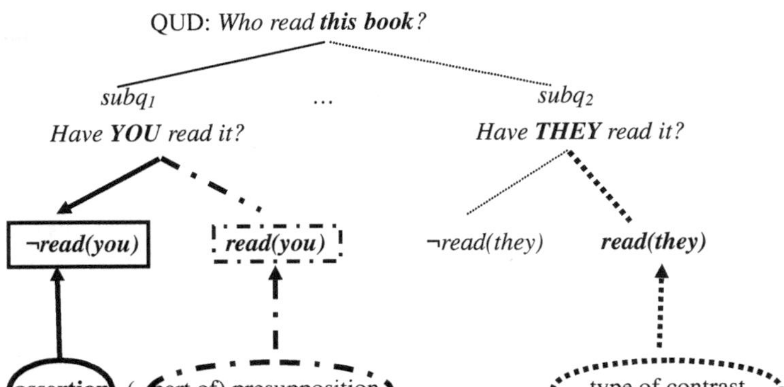

3.2 A Combination of –*to* + *ved'*

In this combination, the particle ***–to*** cliticizes to the contrastive topic/theme/link and ***ved'*** takes a sentential scope, as in (25). The resulting set is shown in (26).

(25) Situation: A recommends that B read a particular book. B replies:
(***ved'***) Ty-***to*** (***ved'***) eë (***ved'***) ne čital (***ved'***)!
'As compared to the other people involved, you haven't READ it, you know!'
[*I am sure that you will like it, too, when you do read it!*]

(26) M(-***to***+***ved'***)={{ **You haven't read it**; You've read it; You bought it;…}
{ They haven't read it; *They've read it;* They bought it;…}
{ I haven't read it; *I've read it;* I bought it;… } }

The membership set evoked by the combination of ***–to*** + ***ved'*** has features of both sets generated by the individual particles, as shown above in (4–5) for ***–to*** and in (9) for ***že***. The particle ***–to*** is responsible for foregrounding contextually relevant propositions which are organized around a certain pragmatic scale of properties, such as *<browse through the book, buy the book, read the book, write a book review, …>*. And the particle ***že*** 'highlights' in that evoked set the propositions which are negated properties predicated of other entities: since it is asserted that *You haven't read this book*, the important issue is that *They have read this book* or *I have read this book*, etc.

Neither of these particles questions the veracity of the asserted proposition (as the particle ***že*** does), thus the utterance does not have aggressive overtones but instead can be perceived as a revelation on the speaker's part that the hearer hasn't read the book, on the commonly agreed upon background that others have read it. One possible scenario of our discourse situation where the combination of ***–to*** + ***ved'*** could be appropriately used is the following: the speaker and the hearer bump into each other in a checkout line at a bookstore on the eve of some major holiday (New Year's Eve in Russia, Christmas in the US, etc.) when at least some people go to buy copies of their favorite books as gifts to others. The speaker assumes that the hearer is buying the book for the others, while from other contextual or situational cues it becomes clear to the speaker that the hearer hasn't actually read the book and is perhaps buying it for him/herself.[10] The relationship between the propositions in the ***–to*** + ***ved'*** evoked sets is graphically represented in the diagram in (27).

---

[10]The implicatures of the utterance in (25) can be made even more explicit when other linguistic elements are added to the sentence, such as certain interjections (*a* 'oh'), reflexive pronouns (*sam* 'yourself'), adverbs (*eschë* 'yet/still'), as shown in (i) below. Such linguistic elements work in concord with the particles and highlight the contrasts brought up by them. The interaction of the particles with other linguistic means and the requirements for their compatibility are worth exploring in the future:

(i) A, ***ved'*** ty-***to*** sam eë eschë ne čital!
Oh, ***ved'*** you-***to*** yourself it yet NEG read
'Oh, and you, yourself, haven't READ it yet!''

(27) D-tree for an utterance with ***–to*** and ***ved'***

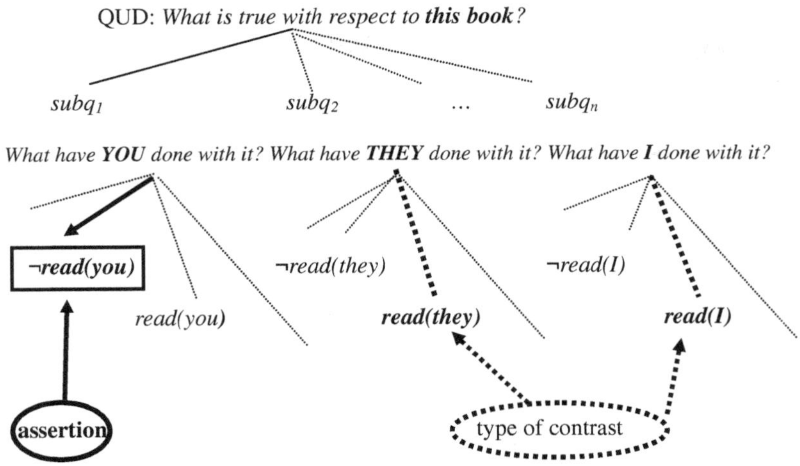

3.3 A Combination of *–to* + *že*

In this combination, shown in (28), the particle ***–to*** is cliticized to the term which functions as a contrastive topic/theme/link, while ***že*** takes a wider, sentential, scope:

(28) Situation: A recommends that B read a particular book. B replies:

Ty-***to*** (***že***) eë (***že***) ne čital (***že***)!

'As compared to the others, you HAVEN'T READ it!'

[*Other activities you may have done with it do not count; what is relevant is that you haven't read it - while the others may have read it and/or have done something else with it, such as writing a review!*]

The result of adding the ***že***-type of contrast to the set of sets of propositions evoked by ***–to*** is the following: in the '*you*'-subset, the asserted proposition **You haven't read the book** is contrasted with the proposition ***You have read the book***, which is a part of the ***že*** presupposition *[you believe or act as if **you have read the book**]*. This, however, has a consequence for certain propositions in the remaining subsets within the ***–to*** implicature set, namely those that share the property of *having read the book*: *read-it(they)* and *read-it(I)*, which become foregrounded. This accounts for the connotations of utterances with ***–to*** + ***že***: the most salient contrasts in (29) are between ¬*read-it(you)* and *read-it(they):*

(29) M(***-to+že***)=

{ { **You haven't read it**; ***You've read it***; You've bought it;}
{ They haven't read it; *They've read it*; They've bought it}
{ I haven't read it; *I've read it;* I've bought it;...} }

(30) D-tree for an utterance with ***–to*** and ***že***

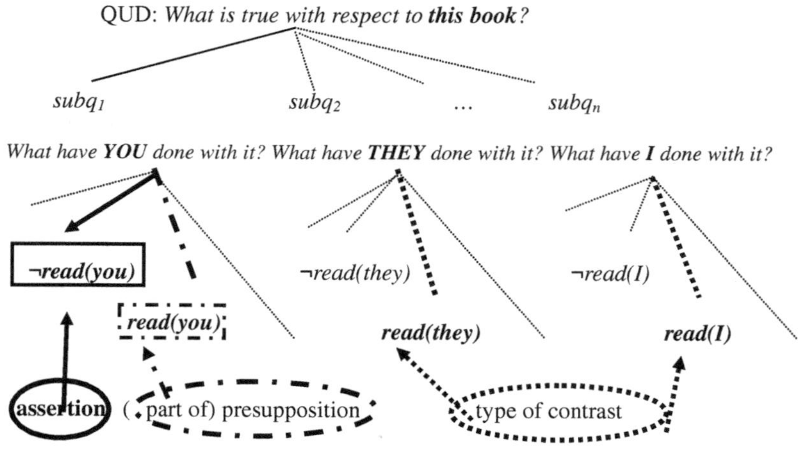

3.4 A Combination of –to + že + ved'

The combination of all three particles in one utterance generates connotations that appears to be very close to those produced by the previously discussed union of ***–to*** + ***že***: in both cases it is a reproach that A behaves as if s/he read it, although s/he knows that s/he hasn't, while other people may be more qualified to give advice:

(31) Situation: A recommends that B read a particular book. B replies:
(***ved'***) Ty-***to*** (***že***) (***ved'***) eë (***že***) (***ved'***) ne čital (***že***) (***ved'***)!
'As compared to the others, you HAVEN'T READ it and you know that!'
[*Other activities you may have done with it do not count; what is relevant is that you haven't read it - while the others may have read it and/or have done something else with it, such as writing a review!*]

The fact that the connotations of an utterance with all three particles, as in (31), are difficult to distinguish from those in an utterance with the ***–to*** + ***že*** combination, as in (28), could be explained in the following way. First, the particle ***–to*** generates a set of sets of propositions, which are built on two points of contrast: the contrastive themes/topics/links and the contrastive rhemes, as in (4–6) or (15–17): **You haven't read the book** *but you may have done something else with it AND others may have done something with it.* When the particle ***že*** is added to the utterance with ***–to***, it brings along the presupposition that the speaker believes that the hearer acts as if the opposite is true: **You haven't read the book** ***but you behave is if you have read it*** *while others may have done something with it.* The result of this unresolved conflict contributed by ***že*** (*Have you read the book or not?*) on the background of the scalar set of properties contributed by ***–to*** (*Others doing other things with the book*) is that the property that the speaker believes the hearer lacks becomes more foregrounded with respect to other individuals in that contextual set: the most prominent contrast is on *They've read it* or *I've read it*. This is the set for ***–to*** + ***že*** that is shown in (29–30) above.

When the particle ***ved'*** is added to the mix, the main contrasts that it would have foregrounded—**You haven't read the book** versus *They/I have read it*—are already highlighted by the union of the other two particles' sets (cf. the ***–to*** + ***ved'*** set in (26–27) above). Thus, a logical explanation for the implicatures created by ***–to*** + ***že*** being the same as those generated by the ***–to*** + ***že*** + ***ved'*** is that the union sets of these combinations are identical, shown in (32):

(32) M(***-to+že+ved'***) =
{{ **You haven't read it**; ***You've read it***; You've written about it;}
{ They haven't read it; *They've read it*; They've written about it}
{ I haven't read it; *I've read it;* I've written about it;...} }

It is not accidental that the discourse tree generated by the combination of all three particles, as shown in (33) below, is the same as the one for the ***–to*** + ***že*** set in (30):

(33) D-tree for an utterance with ***–to*** + ***že*** + ***ved'***:

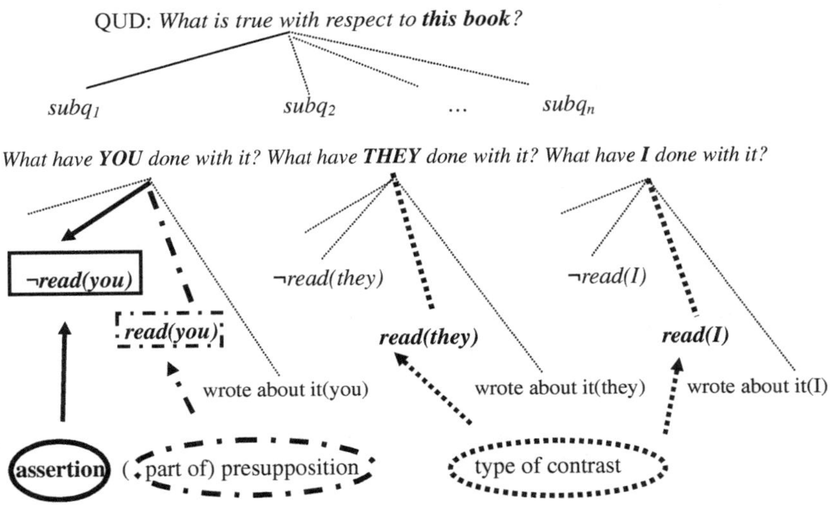

The equivalence in generated sets between combinations of ***–to*** + ***že*** and ***–to*** + ***že*** + ***ved'*** does not necessarily mean that the two utterances are identical in all other respects. In the future it would be beneficial to examine, for example, cognitive statuses of referents (in the sense of Yokoyama 1986) evoked by combinations of these particles (see Parrott 1997 and McCoy 2001 for analyses of such properties by individual particles).

4 Conclusion

The particles ***–to***, ***že***, and ***ved'*** occur in colloquial Russian in free combinations rather frequently. Based on the very fact of their co-occurrence, it would be natural to assume that the principles determining their usage are compatible with one another. This paper makes an attempt at uncovering these principles by examining how membership sets and discourse trees that are generated by each of these particles contribute to the meaning of an utterance with more than one particle. It demonstrates how presuppositions and/or scalar implicatures contributed by individual particles are combined into a more complex meaning.

To summarize, the membership sets evoked by utterances containing combinations of these three particles are shown below in (34) through (37): in each of them the proposition $\mathbf{A(x)}$ is asserted/entailed (that is the speaker's utterance which contains the particles; shown in bold). The proposition $\neg \boldsymbol{A(x)}$ is (a part of) the presupposition contributed by the particle ***že*** (shown in bold italics). The proposition $\neg A(y)$ alone or in combination with $\neg A(z)$ represent most salient contrasts within the implicatures evoked by the particles (shown as italics highlighted in gray):

(34) $$M(\textit{\textbf{že+ved'}})=\{\{\mathbf{A(x)}, \boldsymbol{A(x)}\}\ \{A(y), \neg A(y)\}\}$$

(35) $$\begin{aligned} M(\textit{\textbf{-to+ved'}}) = \{ & \{\mathbf{A(x)}, \neg A(x), B(x), C(x), \ldots\};\\ & \{A(y), \neg A(y), B(y), C(y), \ldots\};\\ & \{A(z), \neg A(z), B(z), C(z), \ldots\};\ldots\} \end{aligned}$$

(36) $$\begin{aligned} M(\textit{\textbf{-to+že}}) = \{ & \{\mathbf{A(x)}, \boldsymbol{A(x)}, B(x), C(x), \ldots\};\\ & \{A(y), \neg A(y), B(y), C(y), \ldots\};\\ & \{A(z), \neg A(z), B(z), C(z), \ldots\};\ldots\} \end{aligned}$$

(37) $$\begin{aligned} M(\textit{\textbf{-to+ e+ved'}}) = \{ & \{\mathbf{A(x)}, \neg \boldsymbol{A(x)}, B(x), C(x), \ldots\};\\ & \{A(y), \neg A(y), B(y), C(y), \ldots\};\\ & \{A(z), \neg A(z), B(z), C(z), \ldots\};\ldots\} \end{aligned}$$

It has been found that the resulted merged sets are identical for the combinations of ***–to*** + ***že*** and ***–to*** + ***že*** + ***ved'***: the contrasts that are brought up by ***ved'*** are already in place in the set created by the other two particles, as shown in (36–37) above.

Certain issues, however, have not yet received adequate treatment and have to be left for future research. For example, the relationships among the propositions within the evoked sets are still on a rather intuitive level and would benefit from further formalization. It would be illuminating to sort out layers of connotations and determine their exact nature; i.e., whether these added meanings are actually presuppositions (see Hagstrom and McCoy 2002 for the discussion of ***že***), or conversational implicatures (Grice 1975), or conventional implicatures (Potts 2005), or some combination of the above. Thus, the idea of utilizing the notion of scalar implicature (Hirschberg 1991) with respect to the connotations that arise with the use of the particle ***–to*** sounds promising.

This data would also benefit from being examined from another angle, i.e., with respect to the notion of contrast that is currently being developed (Molnar 2001; de Hoop and de Swart 2004, etc.). Contrastiveness within closed sets (***že***) versus the one operating in open sets (***–to***) and the properties that result from the intersections of these sets (the particle combinations) lend themselves well to the discussion on the nature of contrast.

Another promising avenue for future development would be to explore the interaction of these particles with other discourse elements they work together with, such as contrastive conjunctions ***a***[11] and ***no*** (nonconcessive and concessive 'but,' respectively) in Russian. Finally, the tools of tackling 'particle concord'[12] in colloquial Russian developed in this article could potentially be useful in exploring similar phenomena in other languages (German, Dutch, etc.)

Acknowledgments I am grateful to Paul Hagstrom for support and encouragement and to Emily Diehl for another pair of attentive eyes. Previous versions of this talk were presented at SURGE (Rutgers Semantics Research Group) and as a poster at FASL 2007 (Formal Approaches to Slavic Linguistics, Stony Brook University). I would like to thank the organizers (especially Professor Chungmin Lee) and the participants of the Workshop on Contrastiveness in Information Structure and/or Scalar Implicature at CIL 18, two anonymous reviewers, and the audiences at previous venues, for helpful comments. All remaining errors are mine, of course.

References

Bitextin, Aleksandr Borisovič. 1994. *Časticy -to, že, ved' i vvodnye konstrukcii tipa kak izvestno kak sredstva ukazanija na izvestnost' propozicional'nogo soderžanija predloženija slušajuščemu*. MGU: AKD.

Bolden, Galina. 2005. Delayed and incipient actions: the discourse markers "-to" and "so" in Russian and English conversation. Doctoral dissertation, UCLA.

Bonnot, Christine. 1987. *To* Particule de Rappel et de Thematisation. *Les Particules Enonciatives en Russe Contemporain* 2: 113–171.

Büring, Daniel. 2000. On D-trees, beans, and B-accents. Ms., UCLA.

de Hoop, Helen, and Peter de Swart. 2004. Contrast in discourse: Guest editors' introduction. *Journal of Semantics* 21: 87–93.

Eckardt, Regine. 2006. Was noch? Navigating in question answer discourse. In *Interface and interface conditions*, ed. Andreas Spaeth, 77–97. Berlin: Mouton DeGruyter.

Feldman, Anna. 2001. Discourse markers—accessing 'hearer-old' information: the case of the Russian že. *In* Proceedings of the 27th LACUS Forum *(*Speaking and Comprehending*), ed. Brend, Ruth M., Melby, Alan K., and Lommel, Arle R., 186–201. Montréal, Canada: Université du Québec à Montréal.*

Fischer, Kerstin (ed.). 2006. *Approaches to discourse particles*. Amsterdam: Elsevier.

[11]See McCoy (2002) for an analysis of a colloquial Russian construction "X-*to* X, *a*…" which has both the particle ***–to*** and the conjunction ***a***.

[12]Thanks to an anonymous review for the suggestion.

Grenoble, Lenore A. 1998. *Deixis and information packaging in Russian discourse*. Amsterdam/Philadelphia: John Benjamins Publishing Company.
Grice, H.P. 1975. Logic and conversation. In *Speech acts: syntax and semantics 3*, ed. Peter Cole, and Jerry Morgan, 41–58. New York: Academic Press.
Hagstrom, Paul, and Svetlana McCoy. 2003. Presuppositions, *wh*-questions, and discourse particles: Russian *že*. In *Annual workshop on Formal Approaches to Slavic Linguistics: the Amherst Meeting. 2002*, ed. Browne, W., et al., 201–218. Ann Arbor: Michigan Slavic Publications.
Halpern, Aaron. 1995. *On the placement and morphology of clitics*. Stanford, CA: Center for the Study of Language and Information (Dissertations in Linguistics).
Hirschberg, Julia. 1991. *A theory of scalar implicature*. New York: Garland.
Karagjosova, Elena. 2001a. Modal particles and the common ground: meaning and functions of German *ja, doch, eben/halt* and *auch*. In *BI-DIALOG* 2001, ed. Kühnlein, P., Reiser, H., and Zeevat, H., 201–209. Bielefeld, Germany: ZiF, Bielefeld University.
Karagjosova, Elena. 2001b. Towards a comprehensive meaning of the German *doch*. In *Proceedings of the sixth ESSLLI student session*, ed. Striegnitz, Kristina, 131–141. Helsinki: University of Helsinki.
Ladd, D.Robert. 1996. *Intonational phonology*. Cambridge, UK: Cambridge University Press.
Lee, Chungmin. 2002. Contrastive topic and proposition structure. In *Asymmetry in grammar*, ed. Di Sciullo, Anne-Marie, 345–372. Amsterdam: John Benjamins.
Lee, Chungmin. 2006. Contrastive topic/focus and polarity in discourse. In *Where semantics meets pragmatics*, ed. Klaus von Heusinger, and Ken Turner, 381–420. Amsterdam: Elsevier.
Liberman, Mark, and Ivan Sag. 1974. Prosodic Form and Discourse Function. *Proceedings of the Chicago linguistic society* 10: 416–427.
Marshall, Todd Alden. 2002. Connotations and functions of Russian discourse markers *ved'*, *že* and *-to*. Doctoral dissertation, Cornell University.
McCoy, Svetlana. 2001. Colloquial Russian particles *–to*, *že*, and *ved'* as set-generating ("kontrastive") markers: a unifying analysis. Doctoral dissertation, Boston University.
McCoy, Svetlana. 2002. Semantic and discourse properties of colloquial Russian construction of the form "X-*to* X, *a…*" In *Glossos* 3, spring 2002. http://slaviccenters.duke.edu/uploads/media_items/3mccoy.original.pdf.
McCoy-Rusanova, Svetlana. 2008. Decomposing particles in combination: colloquial Russian *–to, že,* and *ved.* In *Annual workshop on Formal Approaches to Slavic Linguistics: the Stony Brook meeting. 2007*, ed. Antonenko, Andrei, Bailyn, John F., Bethin, Christina Y., 282–296. Ann Arbor: Michigan Slavic Publications.
Molnár, Valeria. 2001. Contrast from a contrastive perspective. Paper presented at the 2001 ESSLLI workshop on information structure, discourse structure, and discourse semantics. Helsinki, August 2001.
Parrott, Lillian. 1997. Discourse organization and inference: the usage of the Russian particles *zhe* and *ved'*. Doctoral dissertation, Harvard University.
Pierrehumbert, Janet B. 1980/1988. *The phonology and phonetics of English intonation*. Ph.D. dissertation, MIT. Published in 1988 by IULC.
Pierrehumbert, Janet, and Julia Hirschberg. 1990. The meaning of intonational contours in the interpretation of discourse. In *Intentions in communication*, ed. Philip R. Cohen, Jerry Morgan, and Martha E. Pollack, 271–312. Cambridge, Mass.: MIT Press.
Post, Margje. 2005. The Northern Russian pragmatic particle *dak* in the dialect of Varzuga (Kola Peninsula): an information structuring device in informal spontaneous speech. Doctoral dissertation, University of Tromsø, Norway.
Potts, Christopher. 2005. *The logic of conventional implicatures*, vol. 2. New York: Oxford University Press.
Roberts, Craige. 1996. Information structure in discourse: towards an integrated formal theory of pragmatics. In *OSU working papers in linguistics: papers in semantics*, vol. 49, ed. Yoon, Jae-Hak, and Kathol, Andreas, 91–136. The Ohio State University Department of Linguistics, Ohio State University.

Rooth, Mats. 1985. *Association with focus*. Doctoral dissertation, UMass, Amherst.

Vallduví, Enric, and Maria Vilkuna. 1998. On rheme and kontrast. *Syntax and Semantics* 29: 79–108.

Vallduví, Enric. 1992. *The informational component*. New York: Garland.

van der Wouden, Ton, et al. (eds.) 2002. *Particles*. Special edition of *Belgian Journal of Linguistics* 16. Amsterdam: John Benjamins.

Vasilyeva, A.N. 1972. *Particles in colloquial Russian: manual for English-Speaking students of Russian*. Moscow: Progress Publishers.

Yokoyama, Olga Tsuneko. 1986. *Discourse and word order*. Amsterdam/Philadelphia: John Benjamins.

Zeevat, Henk. 2000. Discourse particles as speech act markers. *LDV Forum* 17: 1/2, 74–91.

Zeevat, Henk. 2002. Particles: presupposition triggers or context markers. Ms.

Part II
Polarity, Alternatives, Exhaustivity and Implicatures

Indeterminate Pronouns: The View from Japanese

Angelika Kratzer and Junko Shimoyama

Abstract The quantificational system in Japanese makes use of so-called indeterminate pronouns, which take on existential, universal, interrogative, negative polarity, or free choice interpretations depending on what operator they associate with. Similar systems are found crosslinguistically, which raises the question as to what makes such system look so different from more familiar determiner quantification systems. This paper takes a first step toward answering this question by presenting an analysis of the German indeterminate pronoun or determiner *irgendein* from a Japanese point of view.

Keywords Indeterminate pronouns • Indefinites • Free choice • Quantification • German • Japanese • Alternative semantics

1 Cross-Linguistic Variation

The traditional view on natural language quantification is that languages have determiner quantifiers projecting DPs that scope overtly or covertly, subject to the usual constraints on movement. The quantification system in Japanese does not seem to conform to this picture. In Japanese, quantifier phrases are built using what

This paper was written in 2002 and has circulated through Semantics Archive. It appears here unchanged, except for some minor editorial changes. A slightly shorter version of this paper appeared in Yukio Otsu (ed.): *The Proceedings of the Third Tokyo Conference on Psycholinguistics*. Tokyo (Hituzi Syobo), 2002, 1–25. We would like to thank the audiences at the 13th Amsterdam Colloquium, the Third Tokyo Conference on Psycholinguistics, UCLA and UMass Amherst for helpful comments.

A. Kratzer (✉)
University of Massachusetts, Amherst, USA
e-mail: kratzer@linguist.umass.edu

J. Shimoyama
McGill University, Montreal, Canada
e-mail: junko.shimoyama@mcgill.ca

C. Lee et al. (eds.), *Contrastiveness in Information Structure, Alternatives and Scalar Implicatures*, Studies in Natural Language and Linguistic Theory 91, DOI 10.1007/978-3-319-10106-4_7

scholars of Japanese commonly refer to as 'indeterminate pronouns' (Kuroda 1965):

(1) dare 'who' doko 'where'
nani 'what' itu 'when'
dore 'which (one)' naze 'why'
dono 'which' (Det) doo 'how'

Depending on the operator they 'associate with', Japanese indeterminate phrases can take on existential, universal, interrogative, negative polarity, or free choice interpretations. (2a) is an example of the universal construction, and (2b) is an example of a wh-question.

(2) a. [[**Dono hon**-o yonda] kodomo] **-mo** yoku nemutta.
which book-ACC read child -MO well slept
'For every book x, the child who read x slept well.'

b. Taro-wa [[**dare**-ga katta] mochi]-o tabemasita **ka**?
Taro-TOP who-NOM bought rice cake-ACC ate Q
'Who is the x such that Taro ate rice cakes that x bought?'

A first connection between quantification in Japanese and in English was established by Nishigauchi (1986, 1990). Nishigauchi argued that some Japanese quantifiers are adverbial quantifiers, and that they can unselectively bind variables made available by indeterminate phrases and bare NPs, as proposed in Heim (1982). The semantic part of Nishigauchi's analysis was criticized by Ohno (1989) and von Stechow (1996). Von Stechow (1996) also attempted to provide an explicit analysis of the syntax-semantics mapping. However, his analysis relies on assumptions for Japanese that are idiosyncratic and ad hoc (see Shimoyama 2001), hence moves us away from a possible explanation for how apparently different types of quantifiers can be acquired by children.

In his typological survey of indefinite pronouns (Haspelmath 1997) shows that indeterminate pronouns in the Japanese sense constitute a unified class cross-linguistically. An example is Latvian (Haspelmath 1997, p. 277, diacritics omitted):

	Interrogative	**kaut**-series	**ne**-series	**jeb**-series
person	**kas**	**kaut kas, kads**	**ne-viens**	**jeb-kads**
thing	**kas**	**kaut kas**	**ne-kas**	**jeb-kas**
place	**kur**	**kaut kur**	**ne-kur**	**jeb-kur**
time	**kad**	**kaut kad**	**ne-kad**	**jeb-kad**
manner	**ka**	**kaut ka**	**ne-ka**	
determiner	**kads, kurs**	**kaut kads**	**ne-kads**	**jeb-kads, jeb-kurs**

The Latvian 'bare' series has interrogatives. The *kaut*-series has existentials. The *ne*-series appears under the direct scope of negation, and the *jeb*-series is found in indirect negation contexts, in comparatives, and also with a free choice interpretation. If indeterminate phrases form a natural class crosslinguistically, the question arises as to what it is that makes Japanese quantifier and interrogative constructions look so different from their counterparts in Indo-European languages. In this paper, we will take a first step toward answering this question by presenting an analysis of the German indeterminate pronoun/determiner *irgendein* from a Japanese point of view. We will show that the Japanese perspective allows us to explain some puzzling properties of *irgendein* and free choice indefinites more generally. We will also address the differences between Indo-European and Japanese indeterminate pronouns and speculate that they might ultimately reduce to the presence or absence of uninterpretable features that give Indo-European indeterminate pronouns their selective look.

2 A Hamblin Semantics for Indeterminate Pronouns in Japanese

Hamblin (1973) originally designed his alternative semantics for run-of-the mill questions in English. As far as we are aware, the first extension to quantification in languages other than English is Ramchand (1997). Hagstrom (1998) applied Hamblin's semantics to existentially quantified sentences in Japanese.

Shimoyama (1999, 2001) established the connection with universally quantified sentences, and argued, moreover, for an in situ interpretation of indeterminate phrases. The guiding idea behind a Hamblin semantics for indeterminate phrases is that they introduce sets of alternatives that keep 'expanding' until they meet an operator that selects them. The alternatives can be of different semantic types, such as individuals, properties, and propositions, and consequently, we expect the existence of quantifiers that can operate over alternatives of different semantic types. Determiner quantification falls out as a special case, the case where the alternatives are individuals.[1] On such an analysis, the Japanese universal quantifier *mo* can be analyzed as a regular generalized quantifier, and the semantics of sentence (2a), for example, can be sketched as in (3).

---

[1]Thanks to Akira Watanabe for bringing to our attention the fact that Japanese lacks a quantificational particle meaning **most** that takes indeterminate phrases. Here is how 'most' is expressed in Japanese (the 'floated' versions are also possible). NO = pre-nominal modification marker.

(i) Hotondo-no	gakusei-ga	utatta.
most-NO	student-NOM	sang

'Most students sang.'

Watanabe pointed out that the question of whether the above fact is an accident in Japanese, or it holds across languages that has Japanese-type systematic indeterminate phrase quantification, should have consequences in the validity of the claim that determiner quantification is reduced to a special case.

(3) All members of A slept well: A = {the child who read book a, the child who read book b, the child who read book c, ...}

A second important consequence of a Hamblin analysis for indeterminate phrases in Japanese is that while allowing for long-distance association between indeterminate phrases and particles as in (2), it automatically derives the locality conditions for this association without any stipulations. Indeterminate phrases in Japanese must associate with the closest available operator:

(4) * [....[.... **ind** .... **ka/mo**]......]-**ka/mo**

On a Hamblin analysis, the alternatives created by an indeterminate phrase can expand across relative clause boundaries as illustrated in (2). They are, however, caught by the first relevant operator in their way. In (4), which illustrates a typical intervention effect, the alternatives created by the indeterminate pronoun must associate with the lower *ka/mo*. It could not be otherwise. The intervention effects follow from the very architecture of the interpretation system, in interaction with structural configurations. No locality principles have to be stated in the grammar.

Here is a brief illustration of how the interpretation of the simple sentence *Dare(-ga) nemutta* '(lit.) who(-NOM) slept' is computed in a Hamblin semantics. We give an overview of the essential definitions of the interpretation system in the Sect. 3, which can be skipped by readers who are not interested in the technical parts of our proposal. In a Hamblin semantics, all expressions denote sets of 'traditional' denotations. These are the alternatives. Most lexical items denote singleton sets. The main innovation comes with indeterminate pronouns and phrases. Those denote sets of individuals. We have to think of those sets as individual alternatives, rather than as properties. This is the major conceptual shift in Hamblin's system. Via pointwise functional application, the alternatives created by indeterminate phrases can 'expand'. More formally, we have (for all possible worlds w and variable assignments g):

[[**dare**]]^{w,g} {x: human(x)(w)}
[[**nemutta**]]^{w,g} {λxλw'. slept(x)(w')}
[[**dare nemutta**]]^{w,g} {p: ∃x [human(x)(w) & p = λw'. slept(x)(w')]}

Dare ('who') denotes the set of all humans. The verb *nemutta* ('slept') denotes a singleton set—it introduces just one alternative, a property. The denotation of the sentence *Dare(-ga) nemutta* is a set of propositions of the form {'a slept', 'b slept', 'c slept', etc.}. To compute this set, we apply functional application 'pointwise'. The alternatives can expand until they meet an operator that selects them. Here is an overview of the most common operators. The propositional ones operate over propositional alternatives, the generalized quantifiers operate over individual alternatives.

Propositional quantifiers

Where A is a set of propositions, we have:
[∃](A) {the proposition that is true in all worlds in which some proposition in A is true}
[∀](A) {the proposition that is true in all worlds in which every proposition in A is true}

[Neg] (A) {the proposition that is true in all worlds in which no proposition in A is true}
[Q](A) A (or other denotations, see Sect. 3)

Generalized quantifiers
Where A is a set of individuals, we have:
[∃] (A) {the property of properties that is true of any property if some individual in A has it.}
[∀] (A) {the property of properties that is true of any property if every individual in A has it.}

And so on, for the others.

3 The Semantic Interpretation System

This section gives an outline of the components of a Hamblin semantics, listing the major composition principles. In line with much recent work on the topic, we assume that composition principles are largely type-driven, and apply freely whenever they can.

Hamblin Functional Application
If α is a branching node with daughters β and γ, and $[[\beta]]^{w,g} \subseteq D_\sigma$ and $[[\gamma]]^{w,g} \subseteq D_{<\sigma\tau>}$,then $[[\alpha]]^{w,g} = \{a \in D_\tau\text{: } \exists b\, \exists c\, [b \in [[\beta]]^{w,g}\ \&\ c \in [[\gamma]]^{w,g}\ \&\ a = c(b)]\}$.

Sentential quantifiers[2]
For $[[\alpha]]^{w,g} \subseteq D_{<st>}$:

(i) $[[\exists\alpha]]^{w,g} = \{\lambda w'.\ \exists p\, [p \in [[\alpha]]^{w,g}\ \&\ p(w') = 1]\}$
(ii) $[[\forall\alpha]]^{w,g} = \{\lambda w'.\ \forall p\, [p \in [[\alpha]]^{w,g} \rightarrow p(w') = 1]\}$
(iii) $[[\text{Neg } \alpha]]^{w,g} = \{\lambda w'.\ \neg\exists p\, [p \in [[\alpha]]^{w,g}\ \&\ p(w') = 1]\}$
(iv) $[[Q\alpha]]^{w,g} = [[\alpha]]^{w,g}$ or (Groenendijk and Stokhof 1984)

$$[[Q\alpha]]^{w,g} = \{\lambda w'.\ \forall p\, [p \in [[\alpha]]^{w,g} \rightarrow [p(w) = 1 \leftrightarrow p(w') = 1]]\}$$

Generalized quantifiers
For $[[\alpha]]^{w,g} \subseteq D_e$:

(i) $[[\exists\alpha]]^{w,g} = \{\lambda P \lambda w'.\ \exists a\, [a \in [[\alpha]]^{w,g}\ \&\ P(a)(w') = 1]\}$
(ii) $[[\forall\alpha]]^{w,g} = \{\lambda P \lambda w'.\ \forall a\, [a \in [[\alpha]]^{w,g} \rightarrow P(a)(w') = 1]\}$

Etc.

Predicate abstraction
If α is a branching node whose daughters are an index i and β, where $[[\beta]]^{w,g} \subseteq D_\sigma$, then $[[\alpha]]^{w,g} = \{f\text{: } f \in D_{<e\sigma>}\ \&\ \forall a\, [f(a) \in [[\beta]]^{w,g[a/i]}]\}$[3].

Pronouns and traces
For any index i, $[[i]]^{w,g} = \{g(i)\}$.

[2]There should be a choice for the world index with respect to which α is to be evaluated in (i) to (iv), an issue we will neglect here and below.

[3]There is a question about the correctness of the definition for Predicate Abstraction. It does not quite deliver the expected set of functions. As far as we can see, however, no wrong predictions are actually made, as long as we only use the definition for generating propositional alternatives.

4 A Japanese-Style Analysis of German *irgendein*

In the first part of our paper, we introduced a theory of quantification where determiner quantifiers and propositional quantifiers fall out as special cases. Such a theory captures three-distinctive properties of Japanese indeterminate phrases: their interpretational variability, apparent locality violations, and the intervention effects. In what follows, we present a case study of a single indefinite: German *irgendein*. Next to a Japanese indeterminate phrase, *irgendein* looks like a rather dull existential that is unlikely to contribute any new insights into the properties of quantification. It doesn't show any quantificational variability at all. Moreover, it doesn't seem to have exceptional scope properties. When we look closer, however, we discover that *irgendein* has other properties that consistently show up with quantifiers in the languages of the world: It triggers free choice effects in the scope of modals and displays what we might describe as 'polarity sensitivity'. We will show that a Hamblin semantics for *irgendein* explains why it can have those properties in addition to its quantificational and scope characteristics. Moreover, by arguing for a Hamblin semantics for both *irgendein* and indeterminate pronouns in Japanese, we hope to motivate a unified theory of quantification that has the right architecture to account for the core properties of quantifiers, including categorial variability (e.g. determiners vs. sentential operators), interpretational variability (e.g. interrogative, existential, universal), scope properties, polarity sensitivity, free choice effects, and intervention effects.

The typical properties of *irgendein* are illustrated in (5)–(7). In (6), we see a subtle epistemic effect. By using *irgendein*, Hans conveys that he doesn't know or care about who called, or thinks the identity of the speaker is irrelevant. Maria's question is pragmatically inappropriate, then. Choosing *irgendein* in (7), Maria expresses indifference as to the choice of guests. Anybody in the universe of discourse would be fine with her. *Jemand* would be pragmatically inappropriate. The simple indefinite, would merely repeat what the question already presupposes.

Epistemic effects[4]

(5) Hans: Jemand hat angerufen.
Somebody has called.

Maria: Wer war es?
Who was it

(6) Hans: **Irgendjemand** hat angerufen. Ignorance
Irgend-one has called or Indifference

Maria: # Wer war es?
Who was it?

[4]Examples (5) and (6) are due to Haspelmath (1997).

Modals[5]

(7) Hans: Wen soll ich einladen?
Who shall I invite?

Indifference

Maria: **Irgendjemand** / # Jemand.
Anybody. Somebody.

For reasons of space, we will primarily discuss the non-epistemic effects of *irgendein* in this paper. Our analysis should carry over to the epistemic cases, however, assuming that declarative sentences have assertoric operators that might trigger implicatures relating to the common ground of the conversation. When experimenting with the properties of *irgendein*, we have to be aware of the epistemic interpretation, however. Sentence (8) is ambiguous, for example:

(8) Mary musste **irgendeinen** Mann heiraten.
Mary had-to irgend-one man marry.

(a) There was some man Mary had to marry, the speaker doesn't know or care who it was.
(b) Mary had to marry a man, any man was a permitted marriage option for her.

As illustrated in (5)–(8), *irgendein* indefinites have a special relation with modals and the options they provide, be they epistemic, deontic, or what not. The special link with modality is a well-known property of free choice indefinites and plays a crucial role in the analyses of free choice indefinites proposed in Dayal (1998), Giannakidou (2001), and Saebø (2001). The connection with modality provides the key to an understanding of the free choice effect. However, existing accounts of the free choice effect struggle with the traditional assumption that modals select propositions, hence can't really 'see' a free choice indefinite buried somewhere in their scope. There is currently no compositional account of the link between free choice indefinites and modals, nor an explanation why there should be such a link. Our analysis of the free choice effect is based on the idea that free choice indefinites—like all indeterminate phrases—create Hamblin sets, hence alternatives. Those alternatives keep expanding until they meet an operator that can make use of them. In this way, a local link between an indefinite and a modal can be established. The alternatives created by the indefinite can then be 'distributed over' the set of accessible worlds, as Dayal and Giannakidou envisaged. On our account, the alternatives to be distributed grow into propositions, and are not individuals any longer. This is what makes a compositional semantics for free choice indefinites possible.

[5]Example (7) is from the Akademiegrammatik (1981), p. 667 f.

5 What is the Relation with Modality?

To see how the alternatives created by an indefinite can relate to the accessible worlds introduced by a modal, let us look at two scenarios and how to describe them. First scenario: Mary has to marry a doctor, and any doctor is a permitted option. Her deontic options look as follows, then:

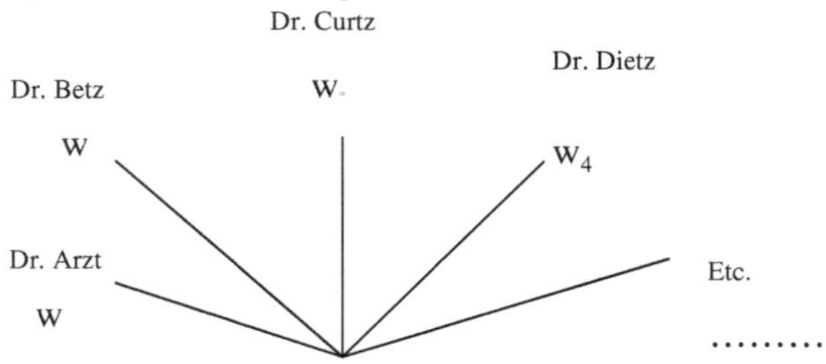

Sentence (9) can felicitously describe such a situation.

(9) Mary muss **irgendeinen** Arzt heiraten.
Mary has to irgend-a doctor marry
'Mary has to marry a doctor, any doctor is a permitted option.'

Second scenario: Mary has to marry one of two doctors, Dr. Heintz or Dr. Dietz, and those are the only permitted options for her. This time, her deontic options look as follows:

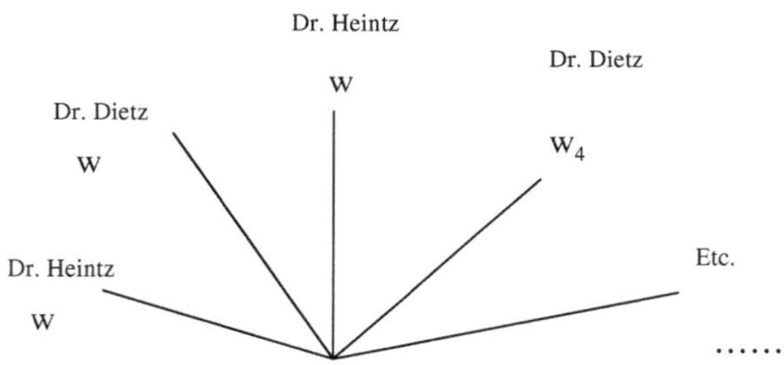

(9) cannot felicitously describe such a situation, so long as our universe of discourse contains more than two men. Using (10) would be fine in both cases.

(10) Mary muss **einen** Arzt heiraten.
Mary has to a doctor marry
'Mary has to marry a doctor'

The examples illustrate what it means for the propositional alternatives created by a free choice indefinite to be 'distributed over' the accessible worlds introduced by a modal. *Irgendein*, unlike simple *ein*, induces maximal widening of the domain, as Kadmon and Landman have observed for English *any*. In our example, there has to be a propositional alternative 'Mary marry x' for each and every man x. The meaning of the modal *muss* 'must' requires that in every accessible world, one of those alternatives be true. All by itself, however, this requirement is still compatible with Mary marrying the same man in every accessible world. To get the free choice effect, we need the additional requirement that there be an accessible world for every alternative created by *irgendein*. The challenge we are facing is to explain where that second requirement, the distribution requirement, should come from. The following section will show that the distribution requirement is not part of the meaning of the modal. If it was, it would have the status of a logical implication. We'll argue that it is a conversational implicature. It completely, but predictably, disappears in certain environments.

6 The Distribution Requirement is a Conversational Implicature

That the distribution requirement is not a logical implication, suggested by the fact that it can be canceled.

(11) Du musst **irgendeinen** Arzt heiraten, und das darf niemand anders
You must irgend-one doctor marry and that may nobody else

sein als Dr. Heintz.
be than Dr. Heintz

'You must marry some doctor or other, and it can't be anybody but Dr. Heintz.'

A second and more reliable indication that the distribution requirement is a conversational implicature is the fact that it disappears in downward entailing contexts (Gazdar 1979; Horn 1989; Chierchia 2001). You need a special focus particle or emphatic stress (as in (14)) to retain it.

(12) Niemand musste **irgendjemand** einladen.
Nobody had to irgend-one invite
'Nobody had to invite anybody'.

(13) Ich bezweifle, dass sie je **irgendjemand** einladen durfte.
I doubt that she ever irgend-one invite could
'I doubt that she was ever allowed to invite anybody.'

(14) Sie darf nie einfach nur **IRGENDjemand** einladen.
She may never just only irgend-one invite.
'She is never allowed to invite just ANYbody.'

If the distribution requirement was part of the meaning of *muss* 'must', sentence (12), for example, could be true in a situation where people had to invite a particular person, hence weren't given any options. This is clearly not so. We should now be able to derive the distribution requirement pragmatically in interaction with a plausible semantics for *irgendein* and the modals. We'll present the semantics of *irgendein* and the modals *muss* 'must' and *kann* 'can' in the following section, and will then illustrate in Sect. 8 how the distribution requirement can be derived via Gricean reasoning.

7 Deriving the Special Relation with Modality. A Hamblin Semantics

For comparison, we will start with the semantics of simple indefinites: For all possible worlds w and variable assignments g we have:

$g(\mathbf{D}) \subseteq D$ (D is the set of possible individuals)
$[[\mathbf{ein_D\ Mann}]]^{w,g}$ $\{x\text{: x is a man in w \& x} \in g(\mathbf{D})\}$

DPs headed by *ein* denote subsets of their common noun set. *Ein Mann*, then, denotes a subset of the set of men. Which subset depends on the domain variable *D*, whose value might be provided by the context. In the limiting case, *ein Mann* might denote a singleton with a single man in it. We would have a singleton indefinite, then, as Roger Schwarzschild has called them (Schwarzschild 2000). As for *irgendein*, the main effect of *irgend-* is to widen the domain. This is the signature of a free choice indefinite. Following Chierchia 2001, the semantics of widening looks as follows:

For $[[\alpha]]^{w,g} \subseteq D_e$:
$[[\mathbf{irgend\text{-}}\ \alpha]]^{w,g}$ $\{x\text{: } \exists g'[x \in [[\alpha]]^{w,g'}]\}$
$[[\mathbf{irgend}\text{-}\ [\mathbf{ein_D\ Mann}]]]^{w,g}$ $\{x\text{: } \exists g'[\text{x is a man in w \& x} \in g'(\mathbf{D})]\}$
$\{x\text{: x is a man in w}\}$

In contrast to *ein Mann, irgendein Mann* has to denote the set of all men. It cannot denote a proper subset of the men. As long as there is more than one man, then, *irgendein Mann* cannot be a singleton indefinite. As for the modals, it is tempting to take them to be operators over sets of propositional alternatives. In this way, they can be sensitive to the alternatives introduced by indeterminate pronouns in their scope:

Modal [............ **Irgendein** NP ....]

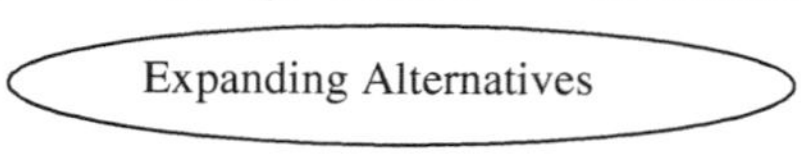

Another possibility would be to let modals operate on singleton sets of propositions, but assume that their scope is immediately closed by the operator ∃. What we have described as an interaction between an indefinite and a modal, would then technically be an interaction between a modal + ∃ combination and an indefinite. We 'll see shortly that this second possibility is correct, but we'll carry on with the first possibility for illustration. A possibility modal, then, says that some proposition in the alternative set it operates over is true in some accessible world. A necessity modal requires that for every accessible world, there be some proposition in the alternative set that is true in it. The distribution requirement is the same in both cases: For every proposition in the alternative set, there has to be an accessible world in which it is true.

Possibility Modals: Meaning
For $[[\alpha]]^{w,g} \subseteq D_{<st>}$: $[[\text{kann } \alpha]]^{w,g}$ $\{\lambda w'.\exists w''[w'' \text{ is accessible from } w' \ \& \ \exists p \ [p \in [[\alpha]]^{w',g} \ \& \ p(w'') = 1]]\}$

Necessity Modals: Meaning
For $[[\alpha]]^{w,g} \subseteq D_{<st>}$: $[[\text{muss } \alpha]]^{w,g}$ $\{\lambda w'.\ \forall w''[w'' \text{ is accessible from } w' \rightarrow \exists p \ [p \in [[\alpha]]^{w',g} \ \& \ p(w'') = 1]]\}$

Distribution Requirement (to be derived as an implicature, see below)
$\{\lambda w'.\ \forall p \ [p \in [[\alpha]]^{w',g} \rightarrow \exists w''[w'' \text{ is accessible from } w' \& \ p(w'') = 1]]\}$

The t(ruth-conditional)-content of the modals is thus standard and weak. The distribution requirement distributes the propositional alternatives generated by *irgendein* over the accessible worlds. The task ahead is to derive that requirement.

8 The Pragmatic Derivation of Free Choice Implicatures

Irgendein, like any free choice item, induces maximal widening of the set of alternatives as part of its lexical meaning. An important insight of Kadmon and Landman (1993) is that this widening should be for a reason. Since they were dealing with *any*, the obvious reason in their case was strengthening of the statement made. This will not do for us. With a 'pure' existential, widening usually makes your statement weaker. That there is some man in the whole world, for example, is a weaker thing to say than there is some man in this room. Strengthening cannot always be the purpose of domain widening, then. Sometimes, weakening is what is called for to avoid a false claim. With existentials, then, widening might help avoid a false claim. To those two possible reasons for domain widening we propose to add a third, that's intimately tied to any semantics based on alternatives: Avoidance of false exhaustivity inferences. Exhaustivity inferences have been discussed for the semantics of questions by Groenendijk and Stokhof (1984), and for lists of possibilities by Zimmermann (2000). Zimmermann's work is particularly relevant, since it concerns the interaction between modals and *or*, which is likely to parallel the interaction between modals and indefinites. Here is a simple example of an exhaustivity inference:

(15) Two books are under discussion. An algebra book and a biology book.
I say to you: You can borrow the algebra book.
Exhaustivity inference: You cannot borrow the biology book.

My mentioning of the algebra book might trigger an inference about the biology book, given that it was among the alternatives under discussion. The inference is that I don't want you to borrow the biology book. It's an exhaustivity inference based on the assumption that by mentioning one book option for you exhausted your options. The reason why exhaustivity inferences are expected to play a major role in a semantics based on alternatives is that if alternatives are created in the semantics, they have to be reckoned with no matter what. They can't be 'contextualized away'. Let us assume, then, that domain widening might serve any of the following reasons: (a) strengthening of the claim, (b) avoiding a false claim, (c) avoiding a false exhaustivity inference.[6] We can now derive the distribution implicatures triggered by *irgendein* via Gricean reasoning. Here is the strategy: We are trying to reconstruct why the speaker chose to widen the domain by using a free choice existential like *irgendein*. We are assuming that widening could in principle serve any one of the three reasons we have mentioned. If we can figure out which one of those reasons led to the widening of the domain, we can use what we found to strengthen the statement that was actually made. As we will see, it can also happen that the reason for the widening is already logically implied by the claim made. In that case, the claim cannot be strengthened by figuring out why it was made, and no implicature is generated. This is when we say that the implicature is "canceled." For ease of exposition, we'll illustrate the pragmatic derivation of the distribution implicature for the case of just two alternatives, and we will work through three representative examples in some detail.

Possibility

(16) Du kannst dir **irgendeins** von diesen beiden Büchern leihen.
You can you(dat.) irgend-one of those two books borrow.
'You can borrow one of those two books, it doesn't matter which.'

Alternative set chosen:	**Can** {A, B}.
T(ruth-conditional) content:	P (A v B)

Figuring out the implicature

She picked the widest set of alternatives, {A, B}. Why didn't she pick {A}, which would have led to a stronger claim? Suppose P(A) is false. Then she should have made the stronger claim P(B). Why didn't she? It couldn't be because the exhaustivity inference ¬P(A) is false. Assume, then, that P(A) is true. The reason why she nevertheless made the weaker claim P(A ∨ B) would now have to be that the exhaustivity inference ¬P(B) is false. We infer P(A) → P(B). Parallel reasoning for why she didn't pick {B} leads to P(B) → P(A).

Computing the total meaning of (16)

P(A ∨ B)	T-content of claim
P(A) ↔ P(B)	Implicature
P(A) & P(B)	Total meaning

[6]There is some discussion in Groenendijk and Stokhof's and Zimmermann's work concerning the status of exhaustivity inferences. Staying agnostic with respect to this issue, we are using the neutral term "inference".

Necessity

(17) Du musst dir **irgendeins** von diesen beiden Büchern leihen.
You must you(dat.) irgend-one of those two books borrow.
'You must borrow one of those two books, it doesn't matter which.'

Alternative set chosen: **Must** {A, B}.

T(ruth-conditional) content: N(A v B)

Figuring out the implicature

She picked the widest set of alternatives, {A,B}. Why didn't she pick {A}, which would have led to a stronger claim? It might be that N(A) is false. Or else, it might be that N(A) is true, but its exhaustivity inference ¬N(B) is false. We infer N(A) → N(B). The same kind of reasoning can be given for why she didn't pick {B}, and we infer N(B) → N(A).

Computing the total meaning of (17)

N (A ∨ B)	T-content of claim
N(A) ↔ N(B)	Implicature
N (A ∨ B) & (N(A) ↔ N(B))	Total meaning
N (A ∨ B) & P(A) & P(B)	Implication of total meaning

Negated Possibility[7]

(18) Du kannst dir auf keinen Fall **irgendeins** von diesen beiden
You can you(dat.) in no case irgend-one of those two

Büchern leihen.
books borrow.
'In no case can you borrow any one of those two books'.

Alternative set chosen: ¬**Can** {A, B}.

T(ruth-conditional) content: ¬P (A v B)

Failed attempt to derive an implicature

Why didn't she pick the smaller set of alternatives {A}? Avoiding a false claim? This can't be, since ¬P(A) follows from what she said, so she can't think it is false. Could widening have served the purpose of strengthening? Yes, but we know that without making any further factual assumptions. Could widening have served the purpose of avoiding a false exhaustivity inference? Yes, but, again, we know that without making any further factual assumptions. What she said implies that the exhaustivity inference of ¬P(A) is false. The same kind of reasoning applies to {B}, the other smaller alternative set.

[7]In (18), *auf keinen Fall* was chosen, since *irgendein* can't be in the scope of sentential negation.

Computing the total meaning of (18)
Since there is no implicature, the total meaning is the same as the T-content of the claim: ¬P (A ∨ B). Reconstructing why the widening took place doesn't yield any statements that are not already implied by what she said. The implicature is "canceled".

We have seen that a Japanese-style Hamblin semantics can account for two properties of free choice indefinites. It explains how indefinites can interact with far-away modals in a compositional way, and also why the distribution requirement that is responsible for the free choice effect is in force in some environments, but not others. A Japanese-style alternative semantics was essential for those explanations. Expanding Hamblin alternatives can bridge the distance between indefinites and their operators, and exhaustivity inferences that come with those alternatives play an important role in producing the free choice effect. A semantics based on alternatives also establishes an immediate connection to existing accounts of negative polarity items, in particular English *any*. A number of authors, including Krifka (1994, 1995), Lee and Horn (1994), and Lahiri (1998) have argued that negative polarity items of the *any* NP-type are best understood as consisting of an indefinite NP and an affective component comparable to English *even*. Krifka (1994, 1995) develops this idea within an alternative semantics where negative polarity items introduce individual alternatives that can expand to propositional alternatives via the same semantic mechanism used in a Hamblin semantics. Krifka is assuming a multidimensional semantics, a difference that is irrelevant for our present concerns. What is important is that the long-distance relation between the *even*-part and the indefinite part of *any* NPs is established via expanding alternatives, just as in our account of the free choice effect. Moreover, the meaning contribution of the *even*-part essentially relies on alternatives. While there are minor divergences in detail, it is exciting to see how different courses of inquiry all converge on the same semantic architecture for indeterminate phrases. In the remaining sections of this paper, we will demonstrate that if we look at the behavior of *irgendein* under the new perspective we have gained, we'll find more Japanese behavior. We'll also find some differences that have to be explained.

9 Long-Distance Relations and Selectivity

If a Japanese-style semantics is right for *irgendein*, we should find long-distance relations between possibly multiple occurrences of *irgendein* and 'their' modal. We do. (19) has meanings (a) and (b).

(19) Mary <u>muss</u> **irgendeinen** Mann heiraten, der **irgendwo**
Mary must irgend-one man marry who irgend-where

in Bayern wohnt.
in Bavaria lives.

a. There is a man who lives somewhere in Bavaria who Mary has to marry, (the speaker doesn't know or care who it is and where he lives in Bavaria.)
b. Mary has to marry a man who lives somewhere in Bavaria, (any man who lives anywhere in Bavaria is a permitted marriage option for Mary).

On both readings, *irgendwo* associates with a modal across a relative clause boundary. Interestingly, reading (c) is absent (for reasons we'll discuss shortly):

c. * There is a place in Bavaria (the speaker doesn't know or care what place it is) and Mary must marry a man from that place, (any man from there is a permitted choice for Mary).

In contrast to its Japanese cousins *irgendein* is selective. It cannot associate with [∀], for example ([∀] presumably contributes to the generic reading):

(20) **Irgendeins** von diesen Kindern kann sprechen.
Irgend-one of these children can talk.

a. 'One of those children can talk' (the speaker doesn't know or care which one it is).
b. 'One of those children is allowed to talk' (any one is a permissible option).
c. * Any one of those children can talk (in the sense of 'any one of those children has the ability to talk.')

Irgendein NPs can't associate with [Neg] either, nor with [Q]:

(21) * Ich **hab'** <u>nicht</u> **irgendwas** gelesen.[8]
I have not irgend-what read
'I didn't read anything.'

(22) Der Lehrer hat gefragt, <u>ob</u> Hans **irgendein** Buch gelesen hat.
The teacher has asked whether Hans irgend-one book read has.
'The teacher asked whether Hans read any book.'

Impossible reading
The teacher asked whether {Hans read book a, Hans read book b, Hans read book c, ...etc. for all books in the universe of discourse}

It seems that the only operator *irgendein* indefinites can associate with is [∃]. This is the reason why, as alluded to earlier, we do not want *irgendein* indefinites to associate directly with modals. Assuming a traditional semantics for modals plus [∃]-closure of their scope will deliver the right result without any further changes. [∃]-closure of the scope of certain operators has been argued for in Heim (1982), and is a common assumption in Discourse Representation Theory. It is needed in other cases we have discussed. Compared (21) with sentences (12) and (18) above:

[8]If *irgend* is stressed, you get the reading 'I didn't read just ANYthing.'

(12) Niemand musste **irgendjemand** einladen.
Nobody had to irgend-one invite
'Nobody had to invite anybody'.

(18) Du kannst dir auf keinen Fall **irgendeins** von diesen beiden
You can you(dat.) in no case irgend-one of those two

Büchern leihen.
books borrow.
'In no case can you borrow any one of those two books'.

(21) is ungrammatical because it has sentential negation. *Irgendein* is entirely acceptable in the scope of *niemand* ('no body'), *auf keinen Fall* ('in no case'), or *nie* ('never'), showing that German makes a distinction between sentential negation and negative quantifiers. Assuming that sentential negation is [Neg], but negative quantifiers close their scope with [∃] accounts for the difference.

Why is it that *irgendein* and many of its Indo-European relatives can be so selective? A property we can't overlook is that they look selective. Existential *irgendein*, does not resemble its interrogative or negative siblings *wer* and *niemand*. The pronouns in the Latvian paradigm we introduced at the beginning of this paper show a common core, but there are clearly marked differences also. We mentioned already that the *kaut*-series has existentials, and that the *ne*-series appears under the direct scope of negation. The *jeb*-series occurs in indirect negation contexts, in comparatives, and with a free choice interpretation. In contrast, the Japanese indeterminate pronouns do not change shape when they associate with different kinds of operators. They always look the same.

Following much work in the minimalist tradition, suppose that selective indeterminate phrases like the German *irgendein* series or the Latvian *kaut, ne*, or *jeb*-series have uninterpretable, but pronounceable features [∃], [∀], [Neg], or [Q]. It's those features that give them their distinctive look. The interpretable versions of those features would be the operators [∃], [∀], [Neg], [Q], most likely carried by inflectional categories like 'episodic' or 'generic' aspect, sentential negation, and wh-complementizers. The uninterpretable features would have to be checked against their interpretable counterparts, and this should trigger movement of either the features alone or the whole DPs, as suggested in Chomsky (1995) and Pesetsky (2000). Pesetsky's work is very relevant, since he argues that feature movement is not merely the proper way of analyzing covert movement. If Pesetsky is right, we expect three types of movements in the realm of quantification: Overt scope shifts, covert scope shifts, and feature movement. Both overt and covert scope shifts are amply attested in German. The syntactic expression of the relation between an indeterminate phrase and its operator could now be feature movement.

Assuming, as is natural, that feature movement is stopped by nonmatching operators, the ungrammaticality of (21) and the Beck Effects (Beck 1996) in (23) fall out.

(23) a. *Was hat sie nicht **WEM** gezeigt?
What has she not to-whom shown
'What didn't she show to whom?'

b. *Was hat sie nie **WEM** gezeigt?
What has she never to-whom shown
'What didn't she show to whom?'

c. *Was hat niemand **WEM** gezeigt?
What has nobody to-whom shown
'What did nobody show to whom?'

d. * Was hat fast jeder **WEM** gezeigt?
What has almost everybody to-whom shown
'What did almost everybody show to whom?'

e. * Was hat (irgend)jemand **WEM** gezeigt?
What has somebody to-whom shown
'What did somebody show to whom?'

f. Was hat der Hans **WEM** gezeigt?
What has the Hans to-whom shown
'What did Hans show to whom?'

g. Was hat sie damals **WEM** gezeigt?
What has she then whom shown?
'What did she show whom at the time?'

In (21), uninterpretable [∃] bumps into interpretable [Neg]. In the examples of (23), movement of uninterpretable [Q] from the *wh*-phrase in situ is blocked by intervening operators. In 23(a), the culprit is [Neg]. For *(irgend)jemand* in 23(e) to be acceptable it has to be in the scope of interpretable [∃]. But then *WEM* would be in the scope of that [∃] as well, and its [Q] feature would run against [∃]. Assuming that *niemand* ('nobody'), *nie* ('never'), and *fast jeder* ('almost everyone') close their scope with [∃], that [∃] will block the [Q] feature of *WEM* as well. A covert scope shift seems to be ruled out, presumably because the blocked item could shift over its intervener overtly in this configuration via object shift or scrambling:

(24) a. Was hat sie **WEM** nicht gezeigt?
What has she to-whom not shown
'What didn't she show to whom?'

b. Was hat sie **WEM** nie gezeigt?
What has she to-whom never shown
'What didn't she show to whom?'

c. Was hat **WEM** niemand gezeigt?
What has to-whom nobody shown
'What did nobody show to whom?'

d. Was hat **WEM** fast jeder gezeigt?
What has to-whom almost everybody shown
'What did almost everybody show to whom?'

e. Was hat **WEM** (irgend)jemand gezeigt?
What has to-whom somebody shown
'What did somebody show to whom?'

There are intriguing interactions between scope shifts and feature movement. The possibility of overt and covert scope shifts produces three possible readings for (25), for example:

(25) Hans will, dass Mary **irgendeinen** Mann heiraten darf.
Hans wants that Mary irgend-one man marry may

(a) There is a man who Hans wants Mary to be allowed to marry (the speaker doesn't know or care who it is).
(b) Hans wants there to be a man who Mary is allowed to marry (any man would be fine with him).
(c) Hans wants Mary to be allowed to marry a man (she should be allowed to pick any man).

All scope shifts seem to respect islands and this is why the reading (19c) above is ruled out. (22) from above illustrates how the components of our analysis work together to produce rather subtle semantic facts. (22) has a single reading. Moreover, there is a 'feeling' that there is 'no free choice effect'.

(22) Der Lehrer hat gefragt, ob Hans **irgendein** Buch gelesen hat.
The teacher has asked whether Hans irgend-one book read has
'The teacher asked whether Hans read any book.'

(i) √ *irgendein* stays within the domain of ∃ within the *ob*-clause.
(ii) * *irgendein* scopes over ∃, but stays within the *ob*-clause.
(iii) * *irgendein* scopes out of the *ob*-clause.
(iv) * The alternatives created by *irgendein* expand beyond ∃.

On our account, (ii) produces a feature clash with [Q], (iii) violates scope constraints, and (iv) can't happen because the expanding alternatives are caught by ∃. Our derivation of the free choice effect in Sect. 8 was based on the assumption that domain widening has to be for a reason. The reasons we came up with were reasons applying to assertions. They can hardly be expected to carry over to questions. Questions do not make claims. What purpose might domain widening serve in questions, then? Does 'strength' play a role in any way?[9] (22) ascribes a slight bias to the teacher's question. The bias could go either way. The teacher might be kind and try to elicit a positive answer. Domain widening can bring in marginal reading materials, comic books, and computer manuals that might establish Hans as a reader. By asking the question the way he did, the teacher made sure that even the weakest positive answer would be considered. But the teacher might also be evil, knowing very well that Hans hasn't read anything at all. Anticipating a negative answer, he hopes that widening the domain will increase the public embarrassment for Hans. If Hans hasn't even read comic books or computer manuals, he is hopeless. In this case, the teacher was shooting for the strongest negative answer. That's the kind of things that widening could do in questions. Given the way we derived the free choice implicature earlier, we expect it to be "canceled" in questions. Of course, "canceled" is the wrong word to use.

In this section, we have focused on a salient difference between 'typical' Indo-European indeterminate pronoun paradigms and the Japanese series, their visible selectivity. We suggested that this difference might be represented by the presence or absence of pronounceable, but uninterpretable features corresponding to the interpretable operators [∃], [∀], [Neg], [Q]. If uninterpretable features carried by DPs have to be checked against interpretable counterparts carried by inflectional heads, we expect that Indo-European style indeterminate phrases might be able to scope, and we might also find the signs of feature movement. Overt or non-overt scoping is a well-investigated phenomenon, maybe the most studied phenomenon in the area of quantification. Overt scoping can be seen or heard, and covert scoping can be easily identified, too, because it affects semantic interpretation. Feature movement is harder to detect, as documented in Pesetsky (2000). Feature movement is likely to be at work when an indeterminate phrase is stuck in the scope of a nonmatching operator it can't covertly skip over for some reason, as in examples (21) and (23). It produces Beck effects. Negative concord and certain cases that are traditionally classified as polarity sensitivity may turn out to be special cases of the same effect. In all of those cases, ungrammaticality is produced when a DP finds itself in the scope of an 'incompatible' operator. If our speculations are on the right track, we might eventually understand how complicated syntactic behavior may be triggered by a rather insubstantial difference affecting lexical items.

There are many consequences to follow up on. One would be to explore whether even within a single language, morphological differences between indeterminate pronouns lead to the expected differences in syntactic behavior. After all, the kind of property that we held responsible for scoping and intervention effects is a morphological property of individual lexical items or paradigms, and not a

[9]See Krifka (1994, 1995) for an assessment in the same spirit as the following rather sketchy remarks.

parameter affecting a language as a whole. We hope to inspire more work on quantification in different languages by raising those questions at the end of our own investigation.

10 Outlook

In this paper, we have pursued an approach to cross-linguistic variation that relies on what Matthewson (2001) has called "The No Variation Hypothesis". The hypothesis assumes that there is no cross-linguistic variation in semantics, "there are certain fundamental semantic structures or properties which all languages should share" (p. 156). Adopting this hypothesis as aresearch strategy has led us to an analysis of the German *irgendein* series that we could not have dreamed of otherwise. It has helped us solve a tough puzzle concerning the interaction of free choice indefinites and modals that establishes the expected parallel with *or*, for which (Zimmermann 2000) has already proposed a semantics based on alternatives. Moreover, we were able to connect our results with existing work on negative polarity items. We also confirmed the view that indeterminate phrases do not have their own quantificational force, not even those which, like *irgendein*, do not exhibit any quantificational variability. In this sense, we have preserved the pioneering insights of Kamp (1984), Heim (1982), and Nishigauchi (1986, 1990).

References

Autorenkollektiv. 1981. *Grundzüge einer deutschen Grammatik*. Berlin: Akademieverlag.
Beck, Sigrid. 1996. Quantified structures as barriers for LF movement. *Natural Language Semantics* 4(1): 1–56.
Chierchia, Gennaro. 2001. Scalar Implicatures, Polarity Phenomena, and the Syntax/Pragmatics Interface. Manuscript, University of Milan, Bicocca.
Chomsky, Noam. 1995. *The minimalist program*. Cambridge, MA: The MIT Press.
Dayal, Veneeta. 1998. *Any* as inherently modal. *Linguistics and Philosophy* 21(5): 433–476.
Gazdar, Gerald. 1979. *Pragmatics*. New York: Academic Press.
Giannakidou, Anastasia. 2001. The meaning of free choice. *Linguistics and Philosophy* 24: 659–735.
Groenendijk, Jeroen, Martin, Stokhof. 1984. *Studies on the semantics of questions and the pragmatics of answers*. Universiteit van Amsterdam Ph.D. Dissertation.
Hagstrom, Paul A. 1998. *Decomposing questions*. MIT Ph.D. Dissertation.
Hamblin, Charles L. 1973. Questions in montague English. *Foundations of Language* 10: 41–53.
Haspelmath, Martin. 1997. *Indefinite pronouns*. Oxford: Oxford University Press.
Heim, Irene. 1982. *The Semantics of Definite and Indefinite Noun Phrases*. UMass Ph.D. Dissertation.
Horn, Laurence R. 1989. *A natural history of negation*. Chicago: Chicago University Press.
Kadmon, Nirit, Fred, Landman. 1993. Any. *Linguistics & Philosophy* 16: 353–422.
Kamp, Hans. 1984. A theory of truth and semantic representation. In *Truth, interpretation, and information*, ed. J. Groenendijk, T. Janssen, and M. Stokhof, 1–41. Dordrecht: Foris.

Krifka, Manfred. 1994. Some remarks on polarity items. In *Semantic universals and universal semantics*, ed. D. Zaefferer, 150–189. Dordrecht: Foris.
Krifka, Manfred. 1995. The semantics and pragmatics of polarity items. *Linguistic Analysis* 25(3–4): 209–257.
Kuroda, S.-Y. 1965. *Generative grammatical studies in the Japanese language*. MIT Ph.D. Dissertation.
Lahiri, Utpal. 1998. Focus and negative polarity in Hindi. *Natural Language Semantics* 6(1): 57–123.
Lee, Young-Suk, Laurence, Horn. 1994. *Any* as Indefinite plus *Even*. Manuscript, Yale University
Matthewson, Lisa. 2001. Quantification and the nature of crosslinguistic variation. *Natural Language Semantics* 9(2): 145–189.
Nishigauchi, Taisuke. 1986. *Quantification in syntax*. UMass Ph.D. Dissertation.
Nishigauchi, Taisuke. 1990. *Quantification in the theory of grammar*. Dordrecht: Kluwer.
Ohno, Yutaka. 1989 *Mo*. In: *Papers on quantification*, NSF Grant Report, Department of Linguistics, UMass, Amherst, GLSA Amherst, eds. E. Bach, A. Kratzer and B. H. Partee, 224–250.
Pesetsky, David. 2000. *Phrasal movement and its kin*. Cambridge/Mass: The MIT Press.
Ramchand, Gillian C. 1997. Questions, polarity, and alternative semantics. *Proceedings of NELS* 27, GLSA Amherst, 383–396.
Saebø, Kjell Johan. 2001. The semantics of Scandinavian free choice items. *Linguistics and Philosophy* 24: 737–787.
Schwarzschild, Roger. 2000. Singleton indefinites. Manuscript, Rutgers University
Shimoyama, Junko. 1999. Complex NPs and Wh-quantifiers in Japanese. *Proceedings of NELS* 29, GLSA Amherst, 355–385.
Shimoyama, Junko. 2001. *Wh-constructions in Japanese*. UMass Ph.D. Dissertation.
von Stechow, Arnim. 1996. Against LF pied-piping. *Natural Language Semantics* 4(1): 57–110.
Zimmermann, Thomas Ede. 2000. Free choice disjunction and epistemic possibility. *Natural Language Semantics* 8: 255–290.

Free Choice Without Domain Widening

Jinyoung Choi

Abstract This paper questions the explanatory power of the notion of "Domain Widening" proposed in Kadmon and Landman (1993) by observing that Korean polarity sensitive items (PSIs) do not necessarily involve the indefinite root *amwu-*, which I argue to be the morphological incarnation of domain widening in Korean. By showing that the non-widening root *wh-* can successfully form a PSI in Korean, I analyze how the particles *-na* 'or' and *-lato* 'even' that *amwu-* and *wh-* combine with function as the two independent sources for free choiceness. I build on Dayal's (1997) and von Fintel's (2000) accounts of *-ever* free relatives for the semantic of *-na* 'or,' and my analysis of *-lato* 'even' extends the scope theory of *even* items in Guerzoni (2003, 2005). It will be shown that both of the particles commonly yield, directly or indirectly, a "Domain Not-Narrowing" or "No singling out" effect (Jayez and Tovena 2005) as an inference. This inference that reads as "*no matter wh-*," triggered by the two particles, forms the common core of free choice (FC) in Korean. Finally, I discuss the contrastive properties of the two types of Korean FC items in terms of their quantificational force and the orientation of FC effects (external locus vs. agent), while as for their common property, I point out that their FC-ness is never cancelable.

Keywords Free choice • Domain widening • Domain not-narrowing • No singling out • External indifference • Agent indifference • Scope theory of *even*

1 Introduction

For the past few decades, many lexical-semantic approaches have been made to address the question, what is the lexical-semantic property that derives polarity sensitivity.[1] One of the most successful accounts among them seems to be Kadmon

[1]To name a few, Lee and Horn (1994), Krifka (1995), Lahiri (1998), Giannakidou (1998), Lee et al. (2000), Farkas (2005), and Kadmon and Landman (1993).

J. Choi (✉)
multi-LEARN Institute, Luxembourg, Luxembourg
e-mail: choi.jinyoung@gmail.com

C. Lee et al. (eds.), *Contrastiveness in Information Structure, Alternatives and Scalar Implicatures*, Studies in Natural Language and Linguistic Theory 91, DOI 10.1007/978-3-319-10106-4_8

and Landman's (1993), which has been followed by a great number of researchers (Kratzer and Shimoyama 2017; Chierchia 2006; among others). In dealing with English *any*, a representative example of polarity sensitive items (PSIs, including negative polarity items (NPIs) and free choice items (FCIs)), Kadmon and Landman (1993) (K&L, henceforth) proposed that the property of domain widening (DW, henceforth) inherent to *any* gives rise to polarity sensitivity of the item. For instance, *any* in *any potatoes* widens the domain of the indefinite noun *potatoes* along a contextual dimension, so that *any potatoes* even includes contextually marginal potatoes, say, inedible potatoes. According to K&L, the purpose of DW is to make a statement strengthened, and *any* is licensed only if its DW function creates a stronger statement. K&L's account has three advantages. First, they find from the lexical property of *any* what motivates its polarity sensitivity. Second, they account for the distribution of *any* also from the lexical characteristic of the item. Finally, they nicely make a unified account of the FCI use of *any* and the NPI use of *any*.

In this paper, I question the explanatory power of the notion of DW in K&L (cf. Krifka 1995; Giannakidou 2001; Szabolcsi 2004; Jayez and Tovena 2005). More specifically, I point out that two different phenomena have been dubbed with the same label "Domain Widening" in the previous literature on polarity sensitivity. The first one is the K&L-style DW, which I call "Proper Domain Widening"; as we saw above, Proper DW leads the regular or salient domain of an indefinite to be replaced by a much bigger one, namely, one of its supersets. On the other hand, the other line of DW accounts, which is suggested by Kratzer and Shimoyama (2017) and Chierchia (2006) (among others), considers DW to be similar to the widening of disjunction; just as disjunction reads as conjunction in some modal contexts, a FC indefinite makes an indefinite denote a set of all members of the contextual domain D, but not its subset. However, this kind of DW, in fact, has nothing to do with including contextually marginal entities as proposed in K&L. Rather, as Jayez and Tovena (2005) put it, this account simply suggests that a FC prevents the contextual domain D from getting narrowed down, and thus any particular member or any particular subset of the members of D is not singled out. I call this type of widening "Domain Not-Narrowing" or "No Singling out" in order to distinguish it from "Proper DW" of K&L.

In this paper, I will argue that Proper DW cannot be the culprit to induce polarity sensitivity, based on Korean PSIs. I will show that Korean PSIs do not necessarily involve the indefinite root *amwu-*, which I argue to be the morphological incarnation of Proper DW *per se* in Korean; but rather, the non-widening indefinite root *wh-* can successfully form a PSI in Korean.[2] Then, I will present that the particles *-na* 'or' and *-lato* 'even' that *amwu-* or *wh-* indefinites combine with serve to not narrow down their domains and thus create polarity sensitivity.

In Korean PSIs, it is transparent from the morphology which part is common to PSIs. As shown in (1), Korean PSIs are composed of one of the two indefinite roots *amwu-* and *wh-* and one of the three particles, *-to* 'also/even,' *-lato* 'even,' and *-na*

[2]Lee (1996) mentions that Korean polarity items can be based on *wh-* indefinites as well as indefinite *amwu-*.

'or.' A common noun can be inserted between the indefinite root and the particle. Thus, the possible ways of combination result in the following six items, all of which correspond to English *any*.

(1) Formation of Korean polarity sensitive items

Particles / Ind roots	*-to* 'also/even'	*-lato* 'even'	*-na* 'or'
Amwu-(N)	***Amwu*-(N)*-to***	***Amwu*-(N)*-lato***	***Amwu*-(N)*-na***
Wh-(N)	***Wh*-(N)*-to***	***Wh*-(N)*-lato***	***Wh*-(N)*-na***

Tables (2) and (3) display the licensing environments of each PSI.[3] The environments in the tables are divided into four sub-groups. The first group is episodic negation. The second group consists of downward entailing (DE) contexts such as the antecedent of a conditional and the restrictor of a universal quantifier. Episodic negation does not belong to this group although it is also downward-entailing. The third group includes so-called FC contexts where FCIs typically appear across languages, such as generic contexts, possibility and necessity modal contexts, and imperatives. The last group contains affirmative episodic sentences.

(2) Licensing environments of *amwu*-PSIs

***Amwu*-PSIs** / Contexts	***AMWU*-(N)*-TO***	***AMWU*-(N)*-LATO***	***AMWU*-(N)*-NA***
Negative episodic	√	*	*/√[4]
DE contexts other than negation	*	√	√
FC contexts	*	√	√
Affirmative episodic	*	*	*/√

[3]Relevant examples are not illustrated in this paper due to lack of space. Refer to Choi (2007) for examples and more extensive analyses of those.

[4]The "*/√" marks in the first and last rows indicate that the *-na* FCIs can be rescued in an episodic sentence via rescuing strategies such as subtrigging (LeGrand 1975; Dayal 1995, 1998) and agentivity. For example, when *wh*-(N)*-na* is modified by a relative clause (i.e., subtrigged), it can appear in an episodic sentence like (iia). Also, both *wh*-(N)*-na* and *amwu*-(N)*-na* are licensed in an episodic sentence when they occur with a volitional agent, as in (iib). For more discussion and detailed analyses of these two rescuing strategies, see Choi and Romero (2008).

(i) *John–un **amwu-/nwukwu**-hako-**na** macuchi-ess-ta.
J.-TOP AMWU-/WHO-with-OR run.into-Past-Dec
'(Lit.) John ran into anyone.'

(ii) a. John-un ke-ipkwu-lo tuleo-nun **nwukwu**-hako-**na** macuchi-ess-ta.
J.-TOP the-entrance-by enter-Rel WHO-with-OR encountered
'(Lit.) John ran into anyone who was coming in by the entrance.'

b. John-un **amwu/mwusun** -chayk-**ina** cip-ese ku-wi-ey olyenoh-ass-ta.
J.-TOP AMWU/WHAT-book-OR take-and the-top-LOC put-PAST-DEC
'(Lit.) John took a random book and put it on the top (of the pile).'

(3) Licensing environments of *wh*-PSIs

Contexts \ ***Wh***-PSIs	***WH*-(N)-*TO*[5]**	***WH*-(N)-*LATO***	***WH*-(N)-*NA***
Negative episodic	√	*	*/√
DE contexts other than negation	*	√	√
FC contexts	√	√	√
Affirmative episodic	*	*	*/√

These distributional restrictions are a typical characteristic of a PSI. Given the fact that both the *amwu-* root and the *wh-* root can form PSIs, as shown in (2) and (3), I argue that Proper DW (of *amwu-*) cannot be the common core of polarity sensitivity in Korean.

After showing that Proper DW is not a necessary condition to create polarity sensitivity, I will propose that it is the particles *-to* 'also/even,' *-lato* 'even,' and *-na* 'or' that give rise to polarity sensitivity in Korean. Focusing on FCIs[6] due to lack of space, I will briefly demonstrate how each particle generates free choiceness by giving a compositional analysis. From this, we identify that there are two independent sources for FC-ness (and polarity sensitivity, more in general); the inherent meaning of the disjunctive particle *-na* that produces "Domain Not-Narrowing" or "No Singling Out" as a presupposition, on the one hand, and the combination of scalar and existential presuppositions of the scalar focus particle *-lato*, on the other

[5]One reviewer raised a question that *encey-to* 'when-even' and *eti-to* 'where-even' do not pattern with the other *wh-to* items in that they do not appear in FC contexts. However, I find many instances of them serving as FCIs, as illustrated in (i) and (ii).

(i) kolphu ka-nun nalcca-nun **encey-to** coh-supnita.
Golf go-REL date-TOP when-EVEN good-DEC
'Any date is good to go play golf.'

(ii) Na-nun **eti-se-to** ne-lul ciciha-kess-ta-ko malha-l.swu.iss-e.
I-TOP where-LOC-EVEN you-ACC advocate-will-DEC-COMP say-can-DEC
'I can say anywh ere that I will advocate you.'

[6]Considering their licensing environments, I characterize Korean PSIs as in (i). This paper will focus on the *-lato*-based items (i.e., *amwu-*(N)*-lato* and *wh-*(N)*-lato*) and the *-na*-based items (i.e., *amwu-*(N)*-na* and *wh-*(N)*-na*) in the shaded areas of the following table.

(i) Characterization of Korean PSIs

Ind roots \ Particles	***-to*** 'also/even'	***-lato*** 'even'	***-na*** 'or'
Amwu-(N)	**NPI**	**FCI**	**FCI**
Wh-(N)	**NPI/FCI**	**FCI**	**FCI**

hand.[7] Our lexical-semantic and compositional approach will lead to the more detailed observation that the FC-ness of the two sources is not exactly the same, though similar, because the mechanism by which each source makes a FCI is determined by distinct lexical-semantic properties of each source. I will discuss the similarities and differences of the FC-ness between the two sources at the end of this paper.

This paper is organized as follows. We will first investigate the roles of the two indefinite roots *amwu-* and *wh-* in Sect. 2. Following Choi (2005, 2007), I will show that Korean *wh-*(N) ranges over a regular domain that is either explicitly stated or implicitly understood, whereas *amwu-* induces Proper DW, as K&L proposed for English *any*. Given that both *amwu*-based items and *wh*-based items create polarity sensitivity, I conclude that the common source of their polarity sensitivity cannot be DW. In Sect. 3, I will propose that it is the particles *-na* 'or' and *-lato* 'even' that are responsible for deriving FC-ness. As for the particle *-na*, I will apply and extend von Fintel's (2000) account of English *-ever* free relatives (FRs), and argue that the particle *-na* introduces the presupposition of counterfactual variation, which provides FC-ness for the *-na*-based FCIs. As for the particle *-lato*, I will adopt Guerzoni's (2003, 2005) decompositional account of German PSI *auch nur* and show how the *-lato* FCIs' FC-ness is derived from the particle's lexical meaning and combination with the indefinite roots. Section 4 discusses the similarities and differences of the two types of free choice. Section 5 concludes this paper.

2 Is Domain Widening Essential?[8]

This section addresses the question whether DW proposed by K&L is an indispensable property for polarity sensitivity. After briefly discussing K&L's analysis, I will introduce Choi's (2007) proposal that the notion of DW cannot be the common core of polarity sensitivity (at least) in languages like Korean. It is because not only the widening root *amwu-* but also the non-widening root *wh-* can form a PSI, as long as they combine with one of these three particles, *-to* 'also/even,' *-lato* 'even,' and *-na* 'or.'

[7]Chierchia (2006) argues for two independent sources for polarity sensitivity in Italian, i.e., domain-widening and *even*. In this paper, I emphasize that examining Korean PSIs reveals not only that there can be two independent sources for the same effect, but also that those sources are represented compositionally by the micro-pieces of Korean PSIs.

[8]This section is previously presented in Choi and Romero (2008).

2.1 Domain Widening in Kadmon and Landman (1993)

Kadmon and Landman (1993) argue that "*any* CN (common noun)" is basically an indefinite noun like "*a* CN." However, unlike "*a* CN," *any* introduces additional semantic and pragmatic characteristics, namely, widening the interpretation of "*a* CN" along a contextual dimension. For instance, the generic sentence (4a) that contains a plain indefinite has meaning (4b): *An owl* ranges over a regular domain, that is, a set consisting of owls with the regular or normal properties. In contrast, sentence (5a) that contains *any owl* instead of *an owl* has a DW effect applied to it. Then the normality is defined in a broader sense, as shown in (5b).

(4) a. An owl hunts mice.
b. Every owl that is "normal"—in a sense that it includes being healthy—hunts mice.

(5) a. Any owl hunts mice.
b. Every owl that is "normal"—in a sense that it is compatible with being healthy or being sick—hunts mice.

Imagine that the two sentences (4a) and (5a) are uttered in a context with a "healthy-sick" dimension involved. While in (4a), the definition of the normality of an owl includes the property of being healthy, this property of being healthy is eliminated from defining the domain in (5a) and then both "healthy" and "sick" become compatible with "normal" after DW is applied by *any*. As a result, the domain of *any owl* is larger than the domain of *an owl*. Importantly, the essence of a DW action is to replace the set denoted by "*a* CN" by one of its supersets. The choice of the superset is determined by contextual factors.

2.2 Domain Widening Is not Necessary: Evidence from Korean

In this section, I will show that the Korean indefinite root *amwu-* morphologically marks DW. The root *amwu-*(N) ranges over a maximally widened domain or an open domain, whereas Korean *wh-*(N) ranges over a regular domain that is explicitly stated or implicitly understood in the context, as depicted in (6).[9] I will propose that DW cannot be considered a core value for PSIs, because without the DW effect of *amwu-*, all of *wh-*PSIs can also convey polarity sensitivity.

[9] Kim and Kaufmann (2006) propose a similar account of *wh-* indefinites in Korean, saying the domain of quantification of *wh-* is restricted to contextually salient entities. However, they differ from my analysis in an account of the widened domain of *amwu-*. For them, *amwu-* is an intensional and counterfactual indeterminate that can create a scalar reading.

(6) Domains of the Korean indefinite roots

Amwu-(N)	*Wh*-(N)
Widened domain	Regular or contextually salient domain

Previously, Lee et al. (2000) claimed that *amwu-* evokes a least-likely scalar implicature on a quantity or a quality scale of likelihood. This is very similar to Lee and Horn's (1994) analysis of *any*, where *any* is analyzed as having a hidden *even* meaning which introduces a quantity or quality scale. In Lee et al.'s example (7), *amwu-* is taken to denote the least likely person to be able to do the job, yielding a derogatory reading such as "Even an idiot can do the job."

(7) **Amwu-lato/-na** ku-il-ul ha-l.swu.iss-ta.
AMWU-EVEN/-OR the-job-ACC do-can-DEC
'Anyone can do the job.'

I agree with their intuition that only *amwu-*, but not *wh-*, usually triggers such a derogatory reading. But the question is whether that reading really comes from *amwu-*'s denoting a minimal value on the likelihood scale, or from another characteristic, namely, DW.

Now I will introduce several pieces of evidence from Choi (2007) that strongly suggest that Korean *amwu-* is a DW indefinite à la K&L (1993). In contrast to *amwu-*(N), *wh-*(N) ranges over a normal or salient domain. The evidence to be presented combines the two roots with one of the three particles *-na* 'or,' *-lato* 'even,' and *-to* 'also, even' from (1), to show that the proposed semantic difference stems from the roots alone and cross-cuts the choice of suffixed particles.

First, the contrast between (8a) and (8b) indicates that the domain of *amwu-*(N)-*na* is wider than the domain of *wh-*(N)-*na*. In (8a), while *wh-*(N)-*na* only includes normal people, i.e., people who received the appropriate education or have average I.Q., *amwu-*(N)-*na* ranges over a larger domain that includes contextually marginal people as well, that is, people who have not received any education or are severely handicapped. If the positions for *wh-*(N)-*na* and *amwu-*(N)-*na* are switched as in (8b), the sentence does not make sense due to the difference in domain size.

(8)
a. Ku il-un **nwukwu-na** ha-l.swu.iss-ciman, **amwu-na** ha-l.swu-iss-ci.ahn-ta.
The job-TOP WHO-OR do-can-but AMWU-OR do-can-NEG-DEC
'(Lit.) As for the job, anyone can do it, but not just ANYone can do it.'
b. #Ku il-un **amwu-na** ha-l.swu.iss-ciman, **nwukwu-na** ha-l.swu-iss-ci.ahn-ta.
The job-TOP AMWU-OR do-can-but WHO-OR do-can-NEG-DEC
'(Lit.) As for the job, just ANYone can do it, but not everyone/anyone can do it.'

Second, *wh-*(N) is usually linked to a contextually salient domain, whereas *amwu-*(N) is not restricted to such a salient domain. Consider the scenario in (9) and suppose that the mother thinks John's future wife being a doctor is better than her having any other job and says one of the sentences in (10) and (11). Note that in sentences (10), the particle *-na* 'or' is kept constant: it combines with *wh-*(N) in

(10a), and with *amwu*-(N) in (10b). In (11), the particle *-lato* 'even' is constant: it combines with *wh*-(N) in (11a), and with *amwu*-(N) in (11b).

(9) Mother: You've been having a lot of blind dates so far. Now is the time to decide.
John: Well, I met Ann and Betty who are doctors, and Cathy who is a nurse and Diana and Fiona who are professors, but I haven't made up my mind.

(10) a. (ne-nun) **etten/enu**-uysa-hako-**na** kyelhonhay-to.kwaynchanh-e.
you-TOP WHAT/WHICH-doctor-with-OR marry-can-DEC
'You are allowed to marry any doctor (of those you have been dating).'
b. (ne-nun) **amwu**-uysa-hako-**na** kyelhonhay-to.kwaynchanh-e.
you-TOP AMWU-doctor-with-OR marry-can-DEC
'You are allowed to marry any doctor.'

(11) a. (ne-nun) **etten/enu**-uysa-hako-**lato** kyelhonhay-to.kwaynchanh-e.
you-TOP WHAT/WHICH-doctor-with-EVEN marry-can-DEC
'You are allowed to marry any doctor (of those you have been dating).'
b. (ne-nun) **amwu**-uysa-hako-**lato** kyelhonhay-to.kwaynchanh-e.
you-TOP AMWU-doctor-with-EVEN marry-can-DEC
'You are allowed to marry any doctor.'

Empirically, regardless of whether *wh*-(N) combines with *-na* 'or' (10a) or *-lato* 'even' (11a), *wh*-(N) conveys that the mother gives John permission to marry one out of the contextually salient doctors, i.e., out of the doctors that John has had a blind date with, namely, Ann and Betty. In contrast, in the cases where *amwu*-(N) combines with *-na* 'or' (10b) or *-lato* 'even' (11b), the mother is not committed to the two doctors but gives John the more general permission to marry a doctor and all possible doctors are a marriage option for John.

The last piece of evidence suggesting a difference in domain size between *amwu*-(N) and *wh*-(N) comes from (negative) existential sentences. When combined with the particle *-to* 'also, even,' both roots are in principle possible in a negative episodic sentence, as in (12). But, if the negative sentence is existential, as in (13), a contrast between *amwu*-(N)*-to* and *wh*-(N)*-to* arises: *amwu*-(N)*-to* is grammatical in (13a), but *wh*-(N)*-to* is deviant in (13b).[10]

---

[10]As an internal reviewer pointed out with example (i), the Korean sentences in (13) do not have as many restrictions as the English existential sentences do. It is probably because unlike English, the Korean language does not employ a fixed construction to express existence. Therefore, (13) is not the existential construction in Korean, the counterpart to *there*-construction, but is the most appropriate translation of the English sentence "There is no one in the classroom." My point is, in translating that sentence, we can observe a difference between employing *amwu-to* and using *wh-to*, as in (13).

(i) kyosil-ey ku salam-to eps-e.
classroom-LOC that person-also not.exist-DEC
'That person is not in the classroom either.'

Also, a workshop participant suggested that (13) gets better if *nwukwu-to* 'who-EVEN' is replaced by *etten*-N-*to* 'what-N-EVEN' as in (ii) below. However, to me, when the *wh*- root *etten*- is placed in the determiner position as in (ii), the sentence stops conveying existence anymore (just as

(12) a. John-un **amwu-**koki-**to** mek-ci.anh-ass-ta.
J.-TOP AMWU-meat-EVEN eat-NEG-PAST-DEC
'John didn't eat any meat'.
b. John-un **etten-**koki-**to** mek-ci.anh-ass-ta.
J.-TOP WHAT-meat-EVEN eat-NEG-PAST-DEC
'John didn't eat any meat'.

(13) a. kyosil-ey **amwu-to** eps-e.
classroom-LOC AMWU-EVEN not.exist-DEC
'There isn't anyone in the classroom.'
b. *kyosil-ey **nwukwu-to** eps-e.
classroom-LOC WHO-EVEN not.exist-DEC

As is well known, weak quantifiers are ambiguous between a proportional (partitive) reading and a cardinal (non-partitive) reading (Milsark 1974). For instance, the NP *many/some superheroes* in (14) can be interpreted in two ways, as in (15a) and (15b). On the so-called proportional reading, the NP is equivalent to the partitive NP *many/some of the superheroes* (15a). On the cardinal reading, the NP means "many/some in number" (15b). Crucially, when an indefinite occurs in an existential sentence, it cannot take on the partitive reading, but is only given the cardinal reading, as exemplified in (16).

(14) Many/Some superheroes are playing in our neighbor's garden.

(15) a. Many/Some of the superheroes are playing in our neighbor's garden.
b. A high/Some number of superheroes are playing in our neighbor's garden.

(16) There exist some superheroes.
≠ Some of the superheroes exist, as opposed to others.
= Some number of superheroes exist.

The fact that the partitive reading of a weak indefinite is blocked in an existential sentence is arguably the reason why *wh*-(N)-*to* is marginal in (13b). If we assume that *wh*-(N)-*to* in (13b) takes on the partitive reading while *amwu*-(N)-*to* in (13a) takes on the cardinal reading, the contrast in (13) can be accounted for on the same grounds as in (17). That is, (13a) and (13b) can be paraphrased as in (17a) and (17b) below, respectively. Due to the conflict of the partitive reading of *wh*-(N)-*to* with the existentiality of the sentence, *wh*-(N)-*to* is judged marginal in (13b), just as (17b) is judged marginal.

(17) a. There is not even one person in the classroom.
b. *There is not even one of the people in the classroom.

(Footnote 10 continued)

(i) does), but is interpreted as having a universal quantifier scoping over negation. Why then *wh*- in argument position in (13b) cannot scope over negation goes beyond the extent of the current paper.

(ii) ?kyosil-ey **etten-haksayng-to** eps-e.
classroom-LOC WHAT-student-EVEN not.exist-DEC
"For every$_D$ student x, x is not in the classroom."

Assuming that partitivity can be treated as a form of familiarity or specificity, as proposed by Enç (1991), *wh*-(N)'s taking on the partitive reading indicates that *wh*-(N) selects a specific or contextually salient domain of individuals. By contrast, *amwu*-(N) does not pick such a specific domain, and is interpreted on the cardinal reading in an existential sentence.

These three sets of data strongly suggest that the root *amwu*-(N) is a morphological incarnation of DW, ranging over an open or widened domain. In contrast to this, the other root *wh*-(N) ranges over a specific or regular domain. From the fact that both of the two roots—regardless of whether they introduce a widened or a regular domain—can induce polarity sensitivity, we conclude that the source of polarity sensitivity in these items is not DW, but something else.

3 Two Sources for Free Choice in Korean

Given that DW cannot be the source for polarity sensitivity, what is responsible for polarity sensitivity in Korean? Having eliminated from the core value(s) of PSIs the difference in domain size of the indefinite roots, we argue that the culprit is the particles that are combined with the indefinite roots, namely, *-to* 'also/even,' *-lato* 'even,' and *-na* 'or,' as in (18). Due to space limitations, I will only deal with FCIs, i.e., *amwu/wh*-(N)-*lato* and *amwu-/wh*-(N)-*na* in this paper. In Sect. 3.1, I will show that it is the particles *-lato* and *-na* that produce free choiceness of these items; without these particles, no FC-ness arises. In Sects. 3.2 and 3.3, respectively, I introduce a simplified version of Choi's (2007) analysis for each particle. It will be shown that both of the particles commonly yield, directly or indirectly, a "no singling out" effect or "no matter wh-" reading as an inference. This "no singling out" or "no matter wh-" reading triggered by the particles forms the common core of FCIs in Korean.

(18) Two sources of polarity sensitivity in Korean

Sources / Korean PSIs	**EVEN** (*-to, -lato*)	**OR** (*-na*)
NPI	√	*
FCI	√	√

3.1 *The Two Sources:* -na *'or' and* -lato *'even'*

Now, let us take a closer look at the particles at issue, i.e., *-na* and *-lato*. When these particles combine with a common noun, they mean *or* and *even*, respectively. For example, in (19), *-na* conjoins two nouns *khephi* 'coffee' and *cha* 'tea,' and the accusative marker *-lul* attaches to the whole disjunctive phrase. This gives rise to the epistemic effect that John drank coffee or tea and *I don't know which*. In contrast to this, in (20), where another instance of *-na* attaches to the whole disjunctive phrase instead of the accusative marker, a FC reading arises such that John likes coffee and tea and he does not care which—both coffee and tea—can be an option for John. These two examples show that *-na* is parallel to English *or* in the sense that both of them can generate an epistemic or a free choice effect.[11]

(19) Epistemic effect
John-un khephi-**na** cha-lul masi-ess-ta
John-TOP coffee-OR tea-ACC drink-PAST-DEC
'John drank coffee or tea – I don't know which one John drank.'

(20) Free choice effect
John-un khephi-**na** cha-**na** cohaha-n-ta
John-TOP coffee-OR tea-OR like-GEN-DEC
'(Lit.) John likes any of coffee and tea – He likes both.'

Turning to the particle *-lato*, we can see in (21) that when *-lato* associates with a common noun, the noun is focused and two kinds of presuppositions, namely, scalar presupposition (or ScalarP) and existential presupposition (or ExistP) are generated, just as English *even* does (Rooth 1985; Karttunen and Peters 1979; Wilkinson 1996). Note importantly that the focused constituent in (21) is interpreted as denoting a most likely alternative among the focus alternatives, while the other EVEN particle *-to* evokes a least likely scalarP, as shown in (22).

(21) *-lato* as evoking the most-likely presupposition (Choi 2005)
John-i [i-mwuncey]$_F$-**lato** phwul-myen, ku-lul honnay-ci.ahn-ulkkey.
J.-NOM this-problem-EVEN solve-if he-ACC admonish-NEG-will
'If John solves at least this problem, I will not admonish him.'
a. ScalarP: This problem is the **easiest** problem for John to solve.
b. ExistP: There is some problem other than this problem that John didn't solve.

(22) *-to* as evoking the least-likely presupposition
John-i [i-mwuncey]$_F$-**to** phwul-myen, swuhak.swuep-ul tut-ci.anh-ato.tway.
J.-NOM this-problem-EVEN solve-if math.class-ACC take-NEG-can
'If John solves even this problem, he can skip the whole math course.'
a. ScalarP: This problem is the **hardest** problem for John to solve.
b. ExistP: There is some problem other than this problem that John solved.

Importantly, the particles *-na* and *-lato*, when combined with one of the indefinite roots *amwu-*(N) and *wh-*(N), induce FC-ness (see Tables (2) and (3)). In (23) and (24), *-lato* items and *-na* items function as FCIs; they correspond to English *any* in meaning and show restricted distribution, appearing in modal sentences (23a, 24a) while banned in (non-agentive) episodic sentences (23b, 24b).[12]

[11] Refer to Alonso-Ovalle (2006) and references therein, as for the two effects of *or*.

[12] The point here is that both *-na* FCIs and *-lato* FCIs are inherently not happy in an episodic sentence. More specifically, they are banned in a non-agentive episodic sentence, as in (23b) and (24b), where the particles' presuppositions are not fulfilled. However, as mentioned in footnote 4, *-na* FCIs can be rescued with an agent's volitional action being present, because agentivity enables the presupposition of *-na* to be satisfied. See the analysis of (38) in Sect. 3.2.

(23) a. **Amwu-/nwukwu-na** ku-il-ul ha-l.swu.iss-ta.
AMWU-/WHO-OR the-job-ACC do-can-DEC
'Anyone can do the job.'
b. ***Amwu-/nwukwu-na** nemeci-ess-ta. (Example from Lee 1996)
AMWU-/WHO-OR fell-PAST-DEC
'(Lit.) Anyone fell.'

(24) a. **Amwu-/nwukwu-lato** ku-il-ul ha-l.swu.iss-ta.
AMWU-/WHO-EVEN the-job-ACC do-can-DEC
'Anyone can do the job.'
b. ***Amwu-/nwukwu-lato** nemeci-ess-ta.
AMWU-/WHO-EVEN fell-PAST-DEC
'(Lit.) Anyone fell.'

If the particles are eliminated, then a case marker must be inserted by default according to the Korean morphology system, as illustrated in (25) and (26). The absence of the particles *-na* and *-lato* causes either ungrammaticality to arise (25a, 26a)[13] or FC-ness not to occur (25b, 26b). This clearly shows us that it is the particles *-na* and *-lato* that produce FC-ness.

(25) a. *John-un amwu-koki-**lul** mek-ci.anh-ass-ta.
J.-TOP AMWU-meat-ACC eat-NEG-PAST-DEC
b. John-un etten-koki-**lul** mek-ci.anh-ass-ta.
J.-TOP WHAT-meat-ACC eat-NEG-PAST-DEC
'John didn't eat some (specific) meat'.

(26) a. *Amwu-**ka** ku-il-ul ha-l.swu.iss-ta.
AMWU-NOM the-job-ACC do-can-DEC
b. nwukw'-**ka** ku-il-ul ha-l.swu.iss-ta.
WHO-NOM the-job-ACC do-can-DEC
'Somebody can do the job.'

So far, I have argued that the difference in domain size of the indefinite roots *amwu-*(N) and *wh-*(N) does not play an essential role in triggering polarity sensitivity. I also have shown that the two particles, i.e., *-na* 'or' and *-lato* 'even,' induce free choiceness. Then, the question is whether it is possible to make a unified account of these two particles. Lee et al. (2000), while trying to make a uniform analysis of *amwu*-PSIs, consider *amwu-*(N)*-na* as introducing a scalar meaning that associates with the same likelihood scale as the one with *-lato* 'even.' They claim that all of the particles *-to*, *-lato*, and *-na* are "concessive" operators that make their focus associates denote the least likely entity on a likelihood scale. In contrast to this, I contend that the EVEN particles *-to/-lato* and the disjunctive particle *-na* must be treated separately, in a similar vein to Rullmann's (1996) point:

> Although the proposals by Kadmon and Landman (1993) and Lee and Horn (1994) are similar in certain ways, they also differ in some respects. In K&L's analysis, the notion of scale does not play any role. Widening just refers to the replacement of the set denoted by

[13]*Amwu-* becomes ungrammatical when it combines with a case marker. Kim and Kaufmann (2006) link this ungrammaticality to *amwu-*'s not being able to occur as a free-standing indefinite that receives a specific or non-specific interpretation.

> the CN by a superset; the elements of these sets do not have to be ordered on a scale. In K&L's theory there also is no sense in which *any* is associated with an endpoint of a scale. (Rullmann 1996: 336)

I argue that EVEN-based items and disjunction-based items should not be analyzed in the same way because the disjunctive particle *-na* 'or' has nothing to do with the likelihood scale. As shown in (27), items like *even* that operate on a likelihood scale can usually co-occur with so-called minimizers, e.g., *lift a finger*. The particle *-lato* can also combine with the minimizer *sonkalak hana kkattakha-*, the Korean counterpart to *lift a finger*, as illustrated in (28). However, *-na* 'or' cannot combine with the minimizer, as in (29). It shows us that the particle *-na* cannot play with the likelihood scale, and thus the *-na*-based FCIs *amwu-/wh-*(N)*-na* cannot fall under the same semantics as the *even*-based FCIs *amwu/wh-*(N)*-lato*.

(27) John couldn't even lift a finger.

(28) John-i **sonkalak** **hana-lato** kkattakha-myen cham coh-kess-ta.
J.-NOM finger one-EVEN lift-if very pleased-FUT-DEC
'If John even lifts a finger, I'll be very pleased.'

(29) a. *John-un **sonkalak** **hana-na** kkattakha-ci.anh-ass-ta.
J.-TOP finger one-OR lift-NEG-PAST-DEC
b. *John-i **sonkalak** **hana-na** kkattakha-myen cham coh-kess-ta.
J.-NOM finger one-OR lift-if very pleased-FUT-DEC

In the next two sections, I will introduce two independent semantic analyses for the particles *-na* and *-lato*, which will reveal mechanisms of how the FC-ness of *-na* FCIs and *-lato* FCIs comes about. The semantics of *-na* will extend von Fintel's (2000) account of *-ever* of the "indifference" use of *-ever* free relatives. The semantics of *-lato* will build on Guerzoni's (2003, 2005) decompositional analysis of the German EVEN item *auch nur*.

3.2 *The* -na *Source*

Choi (2007) argues that the contribution of the particle *-na*, when it combines with *amwu-* or *wh-*, is to trigger an **essential link** between the property of the NP headed by *-na* and the VP property.[14] In (30), the presence of *-na* employs an implication that there is an essential link between "being a linguistics student" and "knowing Chomsky," regardless of whether the particle combines with *amwu-* or *wh-*. This essential link creates the FC reading, "It doesn't matter who the linguistics students

[14] This is inspired by Dayal's (1995) observation that all instances of English *any* convey an "it-can't-be-an-accident" reading, as exemplified in (i).

(i) a. Anybody who is in Mary's semantics seminar is writing a paper on NPIs.
b. #Anybody who is in Mary's Field Methods course is writing a paper on NPIs.

are; every linguistics student knows Chomsky." The regular universal quantifier *motu-* 'every, all' combined with the nominative marker *-ka* does not necessarily carry such an implication, as shown in (31).

(30) **amwu-/etten**-enehakkwa-haksayng-**ina** Chomsuki-lul a-n-ta.[15]
AMWU/WHAT-linguistics-student-OR Chomsky-ACC know-PRES-DEC
'Any linguistics student knows Chomsky.'

(31) **motun**-enehakkwa-haksayng-**i** Chomsuki-lul a-n-ta.
ALL-linguistics-student-NOM Chomsky-ACC know-PRES-DEC
'Every linguistics student knows Chomsky.'

Notice that a similar essential or causal link can be found with the "indifference" use[16] of *-ever* FRs. Consider (32). In contrast to the plain FR *who* in (32b), *-ever* in (32a) adds that there was an essential link between "being at the top of the ballot" and "winning the election." From this, an inference arises that it does not matter to the nature of yesterday's election who was at the top of the ballot and that the person who was at the top of the ballot won. Take another example in (33). Here again, *-ever* FR in (33a) means that "being at the top of the ballot" and "getting Zack's vote" are in an essential relation, from which an inference obtains that it does not matter to the agent Zack who was at the top of the ballot. The only difference between the essential implications in (32a) and (33a) is what is the locus such an essential meaning is oriented to: it is attributed to an external locus in (32a) ("external indifference," Tredinnick 2005) while oriented to an agent in (33a) ("agent indifference," Tredinnick 2005; Choi 2005).

(32) a. In yesterday's election, whoever was at the top of the ballot won.
b. In yesterday's election, who was at the top of the ballot won.

(33) a. Zack voted for whoever was at the top of the ballot.
b. Zack voted for who was at the top of the ballot.

[15]More natural examples are the following, where *-na* FCIs are placed in a floating quantifier position.

(i) Enehakkwa-haksayng-(un) **amwu-/nwukwu-na** Chomsuki-lul a-n-ta.
Linguistics-student-(TOP) AMWU/WHO-OR Chomsky-ACC know-PRES-DEC
'Any linguistics student knows Chomsky.'

They pattern like many quantifiers and numerals in Korean, which prefer a floating quantifier position, as illustrated in (ii); (iia) sounds less natural than (iib).

(ii) a. ??yel chengnyen-i cim-ul nal-ass-ta.
ten young.man-NOM baggage-ACC deliver-PAST-DEC
'Ten young men delivered baggage.'
b. chengnyen-(i) yel-i cim-ul nal-ass-ta.
Young.man-(NOM) ten-NOM baggate-ACC deliver-PAST-DEC
'Ten young men delivered baggage.'

[16]Note that *wh-ever* can also convey an ignorance reading, like in (i). The *-na*-based FCIs lack this kind of reading. See also footnote 17.
(i) *Whatever Arlo is cooking has a lot of garlic in it.* (von Fintel 2000).

This essential link, renamed "external/agent indifference," is well captured in von Fintel's (2000) account. von Fintel (2000) analyzes the role of *-ever* in sentences like (32a) and (33a) as introducing a presupposition of counterfactual variation, adopting Dayal's (1997) insight that *-ever* FRs bring a layer of quantification over possible worlds. In his formulae for sentences containing an *-ever* FR (34), an *-ever* FR associates with its modal base F, its NP property P, and Q which is the property of the rest of the sentence. The presupposition of variation of *-ever* operates on a set of worlds of F, which can be either epistemic or counterfactual modal. When an *-ever* FR takes on an indifference reading, F is always counterfactual. As shown in (34a), a sentence containing an *-ever* FR asserts that the thing that has P is Q in the actual world, meaning that *-ever* FRs are basically definite descriptions (Jacobson 1995; Dayal 1997). To this, *-ever* adds the presupposition (34b) that in all worlds (of modal base F) that are different from the actual world only with respect to the referent of the *-ever* FR, the asserted proposition has in w' whatever truth value it has in the actual world w_0.

(34) *Whatever* (w_0) (F) (P) (Q)
   a. Asserts: $Q(w_0)(\iota x.P(w_0)(x))$
   b. Presupposes: $\forall w' \in min_{w0}\ [F \cap \lambda w'.\iota x.P(w')(x) \neq \iota x.P(w_0)(x)]$:
      $Q(w')(\iota x.P(w')(x)) = Q(w_0)(\iota x.P(w_0)(x))$

Applying (34) to (32a) and (33a), we obtain the interpretations (35) and (36), respectively. Whether external indifference or agent indifference arises depends on pragmatic factors. That is, the presupposition (35b) together with the context makes it most appropriate that the person's identity was not important to the nature of the election, i.e., external indifference. Also, from the presupposition (36b) in the context, one can most plausibly infer that Zack the agent did not care about the person's identity. Hence, agent indifference. I omit more details of his account here; refer to von Fintel (2000) and Tredinnick (2005) for further details and discussions.

(35) a. Assertion: In w_0, the person who was at the top of the ballot in w_0 won.
   b. Presupposition: In each world w', a counterfactual world of w_0, if someone else had been at the top of the ballot in w', the person who was at the top of the ballot in w' won in w' iff the person who was at the top of the ballot in w_0 won in w_0.

(36) a. Assertion: In w_0, Zack voted for the person who was at the top of the ballot in w_0.
   b. Presupposition: In all counterfactual worlds w' minimally different from w_0 in which someone different is at the top of the ballot, Zack voted in w' for the person at the top of the ballot in w' iff he voted in w_0 for the person at the top of the ballot in w_0.

Now let us see how the presupposition of variation in von Fintel's analysis can lead to the FC reading in *-na* FCIs. Choi (2007) gives *-na* FCIs the formulae in (37) by extending von Fintel (2000). Two important differences are observed between *-na* FCIs and *-ever* FRs. First, *-na* FCIs are indefinites whose basic quantification is existential, whereas *-ever* FRs are definite. Therefore, the assertion (37a) means that an individual x having P also has Q. Second, while the presupposition of *-ever* has as its modal base either the counterfactual or epistemic modal, the presupposition of *-na* always operates on the counterfactual worlds.[17] Accordingly, the presupposition indicates that in all counterfactual worlds w' where the set of x's is not the same as the one in w_0, the asserted proposition has in w' whatever truth value it has in the actual world w_0.[18]

(37) *wh-/amwu-*(N)*-na* (w_0) (F) (P) (Q)
  a. Asserts: $\exists x\ [P(w_0)(x) \wedge Q(w_0)(x)]$
  b. Presupposes: $\forall w' \in min\text{-}_{w0}\ [F \cap \lambda w''.P(w'')(x) \neq P(w_0)(x)]$:

$$\exists x[P(w')(x) \wedge Q(w')(x)] = \exists x[P(w_0)(x) \wedge Q(w_0)(x)]$$

To start with a simple case, let us consider (38). This sentence conveys that John chose a book indifferently without caring about its identity. That is, an essential link holds between "being a book" and "being chosen by John." What needs to be captured here is (i) it is not all books, but some that John picked up and (ii) the book (s) that John chose could be any book because John did not care about its identity.

(38) John-un **amwu-/?mwusun**[19]-chayk-**ina** cip-ese congi-wi-ey noh-ass-ta.
  J.-TOP AMWU-/WHAT-book-OR pick.up-and paper-on-LOC put-PAST-DEC
  'John picked up a random book and put it on the pile of paper.'

Applying (37) to (38) yields the formulae (39). The assertion (39a) ensures that John picked up some book(s), but not all. The presupposition (39b) says that if a set of books had been different, the same thing, i.e., John's picking up a book from that different set would have happened. This presupposition together with the context makes it most plausible to infer an agent-oriented indifference reading;[20] even if a different set of books had been given, John would have chosen a book out of the set because John did not care about what kind of a book it could be. This indifference part reads as a FC meaning, namely, "any book could be a picking-up option for John."

---

[17]For ignorance, the Korean language employs the *wh*-root combined with a question ending *-nka*, as illustrated in (i).

(i) pakk-ey **nwukwu-nka**-ka iss-ta
  outside-LOC WHO-Q-NOM exist-DEC
  '(I think/guess) there is somebody outside.'

[18]van Rooij (2008) analyzes sentences having English *any* as counterfactual donkey sentences.

[19]Admittedly, obtaining an existential reading with *wh-N-na* is much harder than *amwu-N-na*, and Kim and Kaufmann (2006) and Yun (2011) characterize *nwukwu-na* 'who-or' as being always universal. However, I think that while *nwukwu-na* 'who-or' may be pretty much grammaticalized and almost always universal, other '*wh*-N-*na*' items like *mwues-ina* 'what-or' or *etten-salam-ina* 'what-person-or' can be interpreted existentially depending on the context.

[20]Agent-oriented indifference is inferred only if a volitional agent is available (Choi and Romero 2008).

(39) a. Assertion: $\lambda w_0.\ \exists x.book(x,w_0)\ \&\ pick\text{-}up(j,x,w_0)\ \&\ put\text{-}on\text{-}pile(j,x,w_0)$
b. Presupposition: $\lambda w_0.\forall w' \in min_{w0}.[F \cap \lambda w''.\ \{x:book(x,w'')\} \neq \{x:book(x,w_0)\}]$: $\exists x.book(x,w')\ \&\ pick\text{-}up(j,x,w')\ \&\ put\text{-}on\text{-}pile(j,x,w') = \exists x.book(x,w_0)\ \&\ pick\text{-}up(j, x,w_0)\ \&\ put\text{-}on\text{-}pile(j,x,w_0)$[21]

Now let us consider a more complex case where a given sentence contains an operator, namely, a universal quantifier. In (40), *amwu*-(N)-*na* appears in the antecedent of the operator *motwu* 'every.' (40) is ambiguous between the external indifference reading (40a) and the agent indifference reading (40b). Under the external indifference reading, even a small amount of meat, regardless of its kind, caused those kids who ate it to have an upset stomach, because, say, all meat there was rotten. "*Amwu-/wh*-meat-*na*" is interpreted as an existential quantifier as in the "even a small amount of meat …" part. On the other hand, under the agent-oriented reading (40b), the reason why those kids got an upset stomach is because they were indifferent or indiscriminative as to what kind of meat to eat. Their indifferent/indiscriminative behavior is understood to mean that their eating repetitively and exceedingly or their eating many kinds of meat caused them to get an upset stomach. Notice that "*amwu-/wh*-meat-*na*" here is taken to denote plural indefinites (e.g., a large amount of meat or many kinds of meat).

(40) **amwu**-koki-**na** mek-un aitul-un motwu
AMWU-meat-OR eat-REL kids-TOP ALL
paythal-i na-ss-ta.
stomach_upset-NOM occur-PAST-DEC
(a) 'Every kid who ate some meat had an upset stomach, no matter what kind of meat it might have been.'
(b) 'Every kid who ate meat without caring about its identity had an upset stomach.'

We account for this ambiguity regarding the locus of the indifference presuppositions and the quantificational force in terms of different presupposition projections, as Tredinnick (2005) does for *wh-ever*. In order to analyze (40), first, the formulae (37) are revised to have the syntax (41), in which the operator is applied to the sentence containing *-na* FCIs. Then, the sentence that contains an operator and *-na* FCIs conveys the assertion (42a). For instance, sentence (40) is analyzed to have assertion (42b).

---

[21]One way to represent the DW action of *amwu-* that we discussed in Sect. 2 would be like (i), where the domain of *amwu-* is a superset of the regular contextual domain C. The widened domain of *amwu-* can create a more emphatic reading, but I argue that what is crucial to induce FC-ness is (ib), the presupposition of variation.

(i) ***amwu***-(N)-*na* (w_0) (F) (P) (Q)
a. Asserts: $\exists x\ [C'(w_0)(x) \wedge P(w_0)(x) \wedge Q(w_0)(x)]$
b. Presupposes: $\forall w' \in min\text{-}_{w0}\ [F \cap (\lambda w''.P(w'')(x) \wedge C'(w'')(x) \neq P(w_0)(x) \wedge C'(w_0)(x))]$: $\exists x[P(w')(x) \wedge C'(w')(x) \wedge Q(w')(x)] = \exists x[\ P(w_0)(x) \wedge C'(w_0)(x) \wedge Q(w_0)(x)]$
c. Presupposes: $C \subseteq C'$, where C is the "normal" relevant domain.

(41) ϕ [*wh-/amwu-*(N)*-na* (w_0) (F) (P) (Q)]

(42) a. Asserts: [[ϕ *wh-/amwu-*(N)*-na* (w_0) (F) (P) (Q)]]
b. $\lambda w_0.\ \forall x\ [kid(x,w_0)\ \&\ \exists y.meat(y,w_0)\ \&\ eat(x,y,w_0)]\ [upset\text{-}stomach(x,w_0)]$

Now let us consider the presupposition of *-na*. Basically, when an operator is present in the sentence containing *-na* FCIs, *-na*'s presupposition of variation can either project over the operator or accommodate inside the operator. If the former is the case, the presupposition will be (43a), where the part of variation, i.e., "$\forall w' \in min_{w0}\ [F \cap \lambda w''.P(w'') \neq P(w_0)]$," is over the operator ϕ. An application of (43a) to (40) yields (43b), where the portion of variation (underlined) is projected over the universal quantifier. This is paraphrased: if a set of meat is different in w' from the one in w_0, every kid who eats meat out of (x, w') has an upset stomach in w' iff those who eat meat out of (x, w_0) have an upset stomach in w_0. Namely, regardless of the kind of meat x, every kid who eats x gets an upset stomach. Hence, FC-ness arises, oriented to an external locus.

(43) With an operator & global projection
a. Presupposes: $\underline{\forall w' \in min_{w0}\ [F \cap \lambda w''.P(w'') \neq P(w_0)]}$:
[[ϕ *wh-/amwu–*(N)*-na* (w') (F) (P) (Q)]] = [[ϕ *wh-/amwu–*(N)*-na* (w_0) (F) (P) (Q)]]
b. Presupposition: $\lambda w_0.\ \underline{\forall w' \in min_{w0}\ [F \cap (\lambda w''.\{y:meat(y,w'')\} \neq \{y:meat(y,w_0)\})]}$:
$\forall x\ [kid(x,w')\ \&\ \exists y.meat(y,w')\ \&\ eat(x,y,w')]\ [upset\text{-}stomach(x,w')]$
$= \forall x\ [kid(x,w_0)\ \&\ \exists y.meat(y,w_0)\ \&\ eat(x,y,w_0)]\ [upset\text{-}stomach(x,w_0)]$

On the other hand, the presupposition of counterfactual variation can be accommodated inside the operator. When this local accommodation occurs, the presupposition is interpreted as if it is a part of the assertion, as represented in (44a). Applying (44a) to (40), we obtain (44b), where the presupposition of variation (underlined) is interpreted inside the restriction of the universal quantifier. This reads that in w_0, every kid x to whom the following two things happened got an upset stomach: (i) x eats some meat and (ii) in all counterfactual worlds w' where the identity of the set of meat is different from the one in w_0, x eats some meat. Under this reading, the agent x eats meat no matter what kind of meat it is, and the locally accommodated presupposition is construed like a verbal modifier, meaning the agent eats a large amount of meat indifferently/indiscriminately. This corresponds to the agent-oriented reading in (40b), explaining the FC-ness of *-na* FCIs.

(44) Local presupposition accommodation
a. [[ϕ]] ([[*wh-/amwu-*(N)*-na* (w_0) (F) (P) (Q)]] = 1 $\wedge$ $\underline{\forall w' \in min_{w0}\ [F \cap \lambda w''.\ P(w'') \neq P(w_0)]}$: [[*wh-/amwu-*(N)*-na* (w') (F) (P) (Q)]] = [[*wh-/amwu-*(N)*-na* (w_0) (F) (P) (Q)]])
b. $\lambda w_0.\forall x[kid(x,w_0)\ \&\ \exists y.meat(y,w_0)\ \&\ eat(x,y,w_0)\ \&\ \underline{\forall w' \in min_{w0}\ [F \cap (\lambda w''.\ \{x: meat\ (x,w'')\} \neq \{x:meat(x,w_0)\})]} \rightarrow eat(x,y,w') = eat(x,y,w_0)]\ [upset\text{-}stomach\ (x,w_0)]$

So far, we have seen that *-na* adds a presupposition of counterfactual variation, which leads to a FC reading that can be oriented either to an external locus or an agent. I will turn to the semantics of the particle *-lato* in the next section.

3.3 *The* -lato *Source*

The particle *-lato* has been analyzed as a normal-*even* (Lee et al. 2000), a wide-scope *even* (An 2007), or an NPI-*even* (Choi 2005, 2007; Lim 2017). Giannakidou and Yoon (2011) claim that the *even* meaning of *-lato* in *amwu/wh-*(N)-*lato* gets almost bleached due to grammaticalization and thus *-lato* has no scalar meaning anymore. In this section, I will show that *-lato* displays a behavior deviating from a run-of-the-mill *even*, and present a NPI-*even* account of *-lato* à la Guerzoni (2003, 2005), where the three presuppositions—an existential, a scalar, and an exclusive presuppositions—that are evoked by *-lato* have distinct scope properties.

As is well known, *even* is ambiguous in DE contexts like (45) (Karttunen and Peters 1979; Rooth 1985). That is, *Syntactic Structures* in (45) can be interpreted as the hardest book or the easiest book. Rooth (1985) proposes that the ambiguity is lexical; apart from the normal *even*, there is an NPI-*even* that occurs in the same contexts that license NPIs. (46) and (47) illustrate the presuppositions evoked by the normal *even* and the NPI-*even*, respectively.

(45) It's hard to believe that John even understands $[\text{Syntactic Structures}]_F$.

(46) Normal *even*
a. ScalarP: SS is the least likely (i.e., hardest) book for John to understand.
b. ExistP: There is some book other than SS that John understood.

(47) NPI-*even*
a. ScalarP: SS is the most likely (i.e., easiest) book for John to understand.
b. ExistP: There is some book other than SS that John didn't understand.

We saw in Sect. 3.1 that *-lato* introduces a most likely presupposition in DE contexts like (21), repeated in (48). Based on this observation, Choi (2005) proposed that *-lato* is an NPI-*even*. However, there are several important differences between the run-of-the-mill NPI-*even* and Korean *-lato* (Lim 2017). First, while NPI-*even* can occur in negation, *-lato* is prohibited in an episodic negation as in (49). In addition, while NPI-*even* only occurs in DE contexts, *-lato* can appear in FC contexts as well, as illustrated in (50).[22]

(48 = 21) *-lato* as evoking a most-likely presupposition

John-i	$[\text{i-mwuncey}]_F$-**lato**	phwul-myen,	ku-lul	honnay-ci.ahn-ulkkey.
J.-NOM	this-problem-EVEN	solve-if	he-ACC	admonish-NEG-will

'If John solves at least this problem, I will not admonish him.'
a. ScalarP: This problem is the **easiest** problem for John to solve.
b. ExistP: There is some problem other than this problem that John didn't solve.

(49)

*	John-i	<u>i-mwuncey-**lato**</u>	phwul-ess-ta.
	J.-NOM	this-problem-EVEN	solve-PAST-DEC

[22]When *-lato* items occur in modal contexts, they can denote either a most likely entity as in (50), or a least likely individual (see An 2007; Lim 2017). I leave the analysis of the least likely reading of *-lato* for future work.

(50) ne-(nun) mwul-i**lato** masi-eya.han-ta.
you-NOM water-EVEN drink-should-DEC
'You should at least drink water (while there could be other more favorable beverages for you to drink).'

The scope theory (Karttunen and Peters 1979; Wilkinson 1996) cannot deal with *-lato* properly, as Gurezoni (2003, 2005) argues with the corresponding German item *auch nur*. The proponents of the scope theory treat the so-called NPI-*even* as normal *even* taking wide scope over a DE operator. Such an analysis may work for English *even*, as the two presuppositions of *even*, as in (51a), do not clash with each other. Sentence (51a) evokes an ExistP (51c), where *even* in *even 10 children* takes wide scope over a DE operator *if*. In addition, the ScalarP (51b) also takes wide scope over *if*. These two presuppositions do not contradict each other and provide the interpretation that even if you have 10 children, you do not receive child support.

(51) a. If you even have 10 children, you are refused child-support.
b. ScalarP: "Ten children" is the least likely number of children for you to be refused child-support.
c. ExistP: There are some number x of children other than ten such that if you have x children you are refused child-support.

However, such an approach does not apply to *-lato*. If *-lato* were a wide scope *even*, sentence (52), which is a Korean translation of (51a), must be judged grammatical too. However, (52) is ungrammatical, because "ten children" here is intuitively meant to denote the most likely number of children that you would have, not the least likely number. This shows that Korean *-lato* cannot be treated as a wide-scope *even* under the simple scope theory. Originally, (51a) is an example of Guerzoni (2003, 2005), with which she contrasted the German *even* item *auch nur* as in (53) and argued for a revised scope theory for *auch nur*. Observing the similar behavior of *-lato* in (52) and *auch nur* in (53), I attempt to apply Guerzoni's account to analyzing *-lato*.

(52) *ai-ka yel-myeng-i**lato** iss-umyen, ne-nun cengpwupoco-lul pat-cimosha-nta.
kid-NOM ten-CL-EVEN have-if you-TOP c.support-ACC receive-NEG-DEC
'(Lit.) If you even have10 children, you cannot get child-support.'

(53) *Wenn du auch nur 10 Kinder hast, wird dir die Kinderbeihilfe verweigert.
'If you even have 10 children, you are refused child-support.'

Guerzoni (2003, 2005) proposes that the *even* items like *auch nur* introduce a most-likely ScalarP that targets an embedded proposition (e.g., the antecedent of a conditional) and gets interpreted locally while triggering an ExistP that targets the unembedded one and gets interpreted outside a DE operator. That is, the ScalarP of *auch nur* in (53) (and possibly of Korean *-lato* in (52)) is analyzed as being most-likely and gets computed inside the antecedent of *if*, as shown in (54a). (54a) tells that 10 children is the most likely number of children to have, which does not make sense. The infelicitous ScalarP (54a) allows us to account for the ungrammaticality of (53).

(54) Scalar presupposition à la Guerzoni (2003)
 a. ScalarP: The likelihood of having 10 children exceeds the likelihood of having n children. (⊥)
 b. ExistP: There is some number n other than 10 that if you have n children you are refused child-support.

To develop an analysis of *-lato*, let us explore Guerzoni's account in more detail. From the fact that German *auch nur* is morphologically complex, Guerzoni (2003) proposes to decompose the German item. *Auch nur* is decomposed into two focus particles: an existential or additive particle *auch*, which introduces an ExistP as in (55), and an exclusive particle *nur*, which evokes an exclusive presupposition (ExclP) as in (56). Since the ExistP and the ExclP inherently cannot help contradicting with each other, as shown by the underlined portions in (55) and (56), Guerzoni suggests that while the ExistP targets a larger proposition, the ExclP as well as the ScalarP of *nur* targets an embedded proposition.

(55) a. $[[auch]]^{w}(C)(p)$ is defined iff $\underline{\exists q[q \in C \wedge q \neq p]} \wedge q(w)=1$ *Additivity*
 b. If defined, then $[[auch]]^{w}(C)(p) = p(w)$

(56) a. $[[nur_2]]^{w}(C)(p)$ is defined iff (i) $\underline{\neg\exists q \in C\ [q \neq p} \wedge q(w)=1]$ *Exclusivity*
 And (ii) $\forall q \in C\ [q \neq p \rightarrow p >_{likely/insignificant...} q]$ *Scalarity*
 b. If defined, then $[[nur_2]]^{w}(C)(p) = p(w)$ *Factivity*

To see this, consider (57), whose LF is given in (58). The ExistP of *auch* in (58a) is formulated globally by (covertly) moving *auch* above the operator *niemand* to the top at LF, so that the ExistP does not clash with the ExclP in (58b), which is formulated below *niemand* with no movement at LF. The most-likely scalarP arising from *nur* is also formulated with no movement. In this way, no presupposition clash arises, and the sentence is predicted to be grammatical.

(57) Niemand hat auch nur die Maria getroffen.
 Nobody has also only the Mary met.
 'Nobody even met Mary.'

(58) LF: [**auch** [niemand$_1$ [[**nur** [t$_1$ hat [[die Maria]$_F$]$_F$ getroffen]]]]]
 a. ExistP: There is someone different from Mary that nobody met.
 b. ExclP: There is nobody except Mary that g(1) met.
 c. ScalarP: Mary is the most likely person to meet.

Guerzoni's account basically predicts that *auch nur* can be licensed as long as an intervening operator (like *niemand* in (58)) sits between *auch* and *nur* at LF to ameliorate their presuppositions' clash.[23] This analysis can easily be extended to *-lato* because every environment licensing *-lato* has an operator in it, such as a conditional, a universal quantifier, modal operators, and the generic operator. But a

[23]Since German *auch nur* is not licensed in modal contexts, Guerzoni treats the modal operators distinctly from DE operators (Guerzoni 2003, 2005). In contrast to this, Korean *-lato* is perfectly fine in modal statements.

more intriguing question relevant to this paper is how to obtain the free choiceness of *-lato* FCIs under the current analysis.

Now let us see how Guerzoni's account can be extended to account for the licensing condition and FC-ness of *-lato* FCIs. First, consider example (59), where *amwu-/wh-*(N)*-lato* appear in the antecedent of a conditional. The sentence reads: even if you eat a small amount of meat or a most available kind of meat, you are not a vegetarian. A la Guerzoni (2005), I analyze *-lato* as evoking a most-likely ScalarP (60a) and an ExclP (60b), both of which target an embedded proposition. In addition, following Lahiri (1998), *amwu-*(N) and *wh-*(N) are interpreted as denoting "some N," as opposed to "a few N" or "many N." Then, the ScalarP reads that some meat is most likely or most insignificant amount of meat, which perfectly makes sense. The ExclP tells that you eat only some meat, not more. To this, *-lato* also introduces an ExistP (60c) that targets a larger proposition.[24] Thanks to the intervening operator *-myen* 'if,' no presupposition clash arises between the ExclP and the ExistP.

(59)	**amwu-/etten**-koki-**lato**	mek-umyen,	ne-nun	chaysikka-ka	an-i-ta.
	AMWU-/WHAT-meat-EVEN	eat-if	you-TOP	vegetarian-NOM	not-be-DEC

'No matter what meat it may be, if you eat it, you are not a vegetarian.'

(60) The presuppositions of *-lato* à la Guerzoni (2003, 2005)
  a. ScalarP: *Amwu/etten koki* (x), i.e., some meat (x) is the most likely/insignificant (amount of) meat for you to eat.
  b. ExclP: There is nothing but some meat (x) that you eat.
  c. ExistP: There is some other (amount of) meat (y) such that if you eat y, you are not a vegetarian.

With the three presuppositions of *-lato*, sentence (59) can be paraphrased as follows: "If you eat even the smallest amount of meat or even the most insignificant type of meat like crabmeat, then you're not a vegetarian." While there are other more significant alternatives (y) available, even the most likely or most insignificant amount/type of meat may be considered to see if you are not a vegetarian. This gives rise to the inference that the identity of meat does not matter to proving that you are not a vegetarian. In other words, every amount or type of meat can be an option to verify you are not being a vegetarian. Hence, FC effects obtain.

As mentioned above, *-lato* FCIs can occur in modal contexts such as possibility modal sentences like (61). Intuitively, what seems to be conveyed by sentence (61) is the reading in (62), where *amwu/wh-*meat(x) seems to be a least likely item, not most likely. Then, how can we obtain the least likely reading like (62) within the current analysis of *-lato* whose ScalarP is most-likely.

[24] Lee (1996) sees *-lato* as a derived morpheme from a concessive or hypothetical clause, *-i-ta-to* (copula-DEC-EVEN). Also, Lim (2017) proposes that *-lato* can be decomposed into two independent scope-taking components: *-la* as corresponding to 'only' and *-to* to 'even'. This paper, however, is not concerned with breaking down the particle but only suggesting that the presuppositions of the particle take different scopes.

(61) John-un **amwu-/etten**-koki-**lato** mek-eto.tw-ay. *Possibility*
J.-TOP AMWU-/WH-meat-EVEN eat-can-DEC
'John is allowed to eat any meat: every meat is a possible eating option for John.'

(62) *Amwu/etten koki* (x) is the least likely type of meat for John to be allowed to eat.

In order to see what kind of presuppositions *-lato* really triggers in modal sentences, consider (63). Clearly, in (63), *-lato* associates with the easiest problem, but not with the hardest problem. The easiest problem is the **most likely** problem for John to solve. But still, sentence (63a) conveys some sort of a least-likely reading, such that John's solving the easiest problem is the **least likely** thing for the speaker to allow to happen, which may be parallel to (62).

(63) a. John-un swiwun-mwuncey-**lato** pwul-eto.tw-ay.
J.-TOP easy-problem-EVEN solve-can-DEC
'John is allowed to solve even the easiest problem.'
b. #John-un elyewun-mwuncey-**lato** pwul-eto.tw-ay.
J.-TOP hard-problem-EVEN solve-can-DEC
'John is allowed to solve even the hardest problem.'

I propose that this "least-likely" ScalarP from the speaker's perspective can be captured by positing that the ExclP of *-lato* is locally projected.[25] Note that in Guerzoni (2003), all of the three presuppositions of *auch nur* are supposed to project globally, a point in which our revised analysis of *-lato* differs. On our revised analysis of *-lato*, the ExclP is locally projected, unlike the two other presuppositions. For instance, the three presuppositions triggered by *-lato* in (63a) can be shown in (64).

(64) a. ScalarP: "That John solves the easiest problem" is the most-likely alternative.
b. ExclP: John solves nothing but "the easiest problem."
c. ExistP: There is some y different from the easiest problem such that the speaker allows John to solve y.
d. Assertion (together with any locally computed presupposition): It is allowed that John solves the easiest problem and nothing else.

Given that there is permission from the speaker to solve other problems, if the speaker allows John to solve the easiest problem and nothing better than that, we can infer that John's solving the easiest problem is the last thing that the speaker wants. Hence, a FC flavor obtains that for every alternative problem y, John is

[25]This local projection of ExclP was suggested to me by Maribel Romero. Exactly how to motivate the local projection is left open for future research, but it seems to have a broader impact on NPI-*even*'s crosslinguistically, because a group of NPI-even's appears in modal sentences and imperatives that typically license FCIs. For instance, Spanish NPI-*even*, *siquiera,* can occur in an imperative sentence like the following:

Comete siquiera este trocito.
Eat-IMPER-CL NPI-even this little-piece
"Eat at least / if nothing else this little piece." (Maribel Romero, p.c.)

allowed to solve y. What is crucial here is that the ExclP is locally projected under the modal.

In a similar fashion, I propose that the three types of presuppositions play a role in the modal sentence (61) containing *amwu-/wh-*(N)-*lato*, repeated below. The three presuppositions that *-lato* evokes in (61) are given in (65). As before, the ExistP targets a larger proposition containing the modal, while the ScalarP and the ExclP are formulated inside the modal.

(65) a. ScalarP: *Amwu/etten koki* (x), i.e., some meat (x) is the most likely/insignificant (amount/kind of) meat for John to eat.
b. ExclP: There is nothing different from *amwu/etten-koki* (x) that John eats.
c. ExistP: There is some other (amount/kind of) meat (y) such that John is <u>allowed</u> to eat y.
d. Assertion (together with locally projected presupposition): It is allowed that there is <u>no different</u> *amwu/etten-koki* (x) that John eats.

The combination of the three presuppositions says "Given that there is permission from the speaker to eat some other (amount/kind of) meat, the speaker allows John to eat the most insignificant (amount/kind of) meat <u>and nothing better than that.</u>" It yields the revised assertion in (66).

(66) $\lambda w_0.\exists w' \in \text{Deo}(w_0)$ [John eats *amwu/wh*-meat(x) <u>and no other meat</u> in w'].

Imagine a situation where John's mother says the sentence in (61). The speaker normally wants John to eat more or better meat. Thus, it is inferred from (66) that "John's eating the most insignificant (amount/kind of) meat and nothing better than that" is the least likely alternative for the speaker to permit. Hence, a FC flavor obtains that for every alternative meat y, John is allowed to eat y.

4 Similarities and Differences Between the Two Types of FCIs

So far, we have discussed that Domain Widening proposed in K&L is not essential in introducing FC-ness in Korean. Also, we have seen that the particles *-na* 'or' and *-lato* 'even' trigger a presupposition or presuppositions from which a FC reading "the identity of FCIs' referents does not matter; every member is not singled out but equally considered" is derived. In this section, I go over similarities and differences between the FC-ness of *-na* FCIs and *-lato* FCIs.

To illustrate, let us compare (67) and (68). In (67), *-na* FCIs in the antecedent of a conditional can be ambiguous. On the first reading (67a), the FC or indifference reading is interpreted locally (i.e., agent indifference). So the interpretation will be "If the type of meat does not matter to you (= the agent) and consequently you eat meat indiscriminately, then you are not a kosher Jew." On the second reading (67b), the indifference reading projects higher up (i.e., external indifference) and derives the interpretation: "No matter what (kind of) meat x is considered (i.e., the identity of meat does not matter), you are not a vegetarian if you eat x."[26] In contrast, *-lato* FCIs in (68) do not allow the "kosher Jew" continuation; only external indifference reading obtains as in (68b).

(67) a. **amwu-/etten**-koki-**na** mek-umyen,ne-nun utayin-i an-i-ta.
AMWU-/WH-meat-OR eat-if you-TOP Kosher.Jew-NOM not-be-DEC
'If you eat just ANY meat without caring about what kind of meat it is, you are not a Kosher Jew.'

b. **amwu-/etten**-koki-**na** mek-umyen,ne-nun chaysika-ka an-i-ta.
AMWU-/WH-meat-OR eat-if you-TOP vegetarian-NOM not-be-DEC
'No matter what meat it may be, if you eat it, you are not a vegetarian.'

(68) a. #**amwu-/etten**-koki-**lato** mek-umyen, ne-nun utayin-i an-i-ta.
AMWU-/WH-meat-EVEN eat-if you-TOP Kosher.Jew-NOM not-be-DEC

b. **amwu-/etten**-koki-**lato** mek-umyen, ne-nun chaysika-ka an-i-ta.
AMWU-/WH-meat-EVEN eat-if you-TOP vegetarian-NOM not-be-DEC
'No matter what meat it may be, if you eat it, you are not a vegetarian.'

From the contrast between (67) and (68), we identify that whereas *-na* FCIs can produce both external indifference and agent indifference, *-lato* FCIs' presuppositions are always interpreted globally, making only external indifference available. In addition, this difference of *-na* FCIs and *-lato* FCIs with respect to the orientations of FC effects is closely linked to their quantificational interpretations. When these FCIs take on an external indifference reading (67b, 68b), they are interpreted as an existential quantifier (e.g., a piece of meat). However, when a *-na* FCI takes on an agent indifference reading like (67a), it is interpreted as a plural indefinite (e.g., many kinds of meat) because the agent indifference reading implies the agent's indiscriminative action, which can be construed that the agent's action was repetitive and thus he ate a lot of or many kinds of meat. This iterative action makes the FCI interpreted quasi-universally.[27]

Then, what would be the difference between the external indifference interpretations of *-na* FCIs and *-lato* FCIs (i.e., (67b) vs. (68b))? In (67b), meat(x) denoted by *-na* FCIs may or may not be contextually marginal (kind of) meat. In contrast to

---

[26]To get this reading, a pause is needed between the *-na* FCIs and the verb.

[27]This is why Horn (2000) considers only the instance of stressed *any* in the Kosher Jew example (ia) to be a FCI because he thinks stressed *any* here is interpreted as a universal quantifier due to its "indiscriminacy." He treats *any* in the vegetarian example (ib) as an NPI. Under the current analysis, however, both instances of stressed *any* would be considered FCIs, whose FC effect is either locally interpreted in (ia) or globally projected in (ib).

(i) a. If you eat ANY meat, you are not a vegetarian.
b. If you eat ANY meat, you are not a kosher Jew. (Example from Horn 2000)

this, *-lato* FCIs in (68b) always go down to the endpoint entity of a likelihood scale, and thus they denote the most likely or insignificant kind/amount of meat for you to eat. In this way, *-lato* FCIs always accompany scalarity in meaning, while *-na* FCIs do not necessarily involve a scalar meaning.

One last thing to note is a common point that the two types of FCIs share, namely, that their FC-ness is never canceled. For some type of FCIs such as German *irgendein* and English *any*, their FC effects are reported to disappear in DE contexts (Kratzer and Shimoyama 2017).

(69) Mary musste **irgendeinen** Mann heiraten.
Mary had-to irgend-one man marry
'Mary must marry any one man: it doesn't matter who he is.'

(70) Ich bezweifle, dass sie je **irgendjemand** einladen durfte.
I doubt that she ever irgend-one invite could
'I doubt that she was ever allowed to invite anybody.'

Comparing (69) and (670), we can see that the FC component "it doesn't matter…" in (69) disappears in DE contexts like (70). *Irgendjemand* in (70) is simply an existential quantifier, taking narrow scope under *bezweifle* 'doubt.' In contrast to this, the FC-ness of *-na* FCIs and *-lato* FCIs are hard-wired, never defeasible. Consider again (67) and (68). The two types of FCIs appear in a DE context and their indifference readings do not disappear but are either locally accommodated (67a) or globally projected (67b, 68b).

In this section, we observed three differences and one common point between *-na* FCIs and *-lato* FCIs, as summarized in (71) and (72).

(71) Differences
a. Orientations of FC effects: *-na* FCIs can give rise to external indifference and agent indifference while *-lato* FCIs allow external difference only.
b. Quantificational force: *-na* FCIs can be interpreted either existentially or quasi-universally, whereas *-lato* FCIs are interpreted only existentially.[28]
c. Scalarity: *-lato* FCIs always involve a likelihood scale while *-na* FCIs do not.

(72) A common point
The FC effects of both types of FCIs are never cancelable.

[28]This is except for the cases where the two FCIs appear in generic sentences. In (i), both FCIs receive universal force form the generic operator.

(i) a. amwu-/etten-say-na na-n-ta
AMWU-/WH-bird-OR fly-GEN-DEC
'Any birds fly.'
b. amwu-/etten-say-lato na-n-ta
AMWU-/WH-bird-EVEN fly-GEN-DEC
'Any birds fly.'

5 Conclusion

In this paper, I argued that domain widening proposed in K&L does not form a core part of polarity sensitivity in languages like Korean, given that the indefinite root *amwu-* is an incarnation of proper DW in Korean and is not indispensable to form FCIs in Korean. Furthermore, I showed that free choiceness in Korean is derived from the two types of particles: the scalar focus particle *-lato* and the disjunctive particle *-na*. By taking a lexical-semantic and compositional approach, we identified that the particles' presuppositions produce the FC reading "The identity of a FCI does not matter," which reads then as "Every member of the set denoted by a FCI is not singled out but equally considered." Also, depending on their lexical-semantic properties, their FC effects display differences with respect to orientations of FC-ness, quantificational force, and scalarity. However, they are similar in that their FC effects are hard-wired, never cancelable.

Acknowledgments I would like to express my deepest gratitude to Maribel Romero for her insights and valuable guidance throughout the course of my Ph.D and this paper. I also thank Chungmin Lee for constant encouragement. Thanks also go to the reviewers and all the CIL workshop participants.

References

Alonso-Ovalle, Luis. 2006. *Disjunction in Alternative Semantics*. Ph.D. dissertation, University of Massachusetts at Amherst, Amherst: MA.

An, Dukho. 2007. On the distribution of NPIs in Korean. *Natural Language Semantics* 15: 317–350.

Chierchia, Gennaro. 2006. Broaden Your Views: Implicatures of Domain Widening and the ''Logicality'' of Language. *Linguistic Inquiry* 37: 535–590.

Choi, Jinyoung. 2005. Another type of free choice effect: Korean Amwu N-Lato. In *Proceedings of the 24th West Coast Conference on Formal Linguistics*, ed. J. Alderete, C.-H. Han and A. Kochetov. Somerville, MA: Cascadilla Proceedings Project.

Choi, Jinyoung. 2007. *Free Choice and Negative Polarity: A Compositional Analysis of Korean Polarity Sensitive Items*. Ph.D. dissertation, University of Pennsylvania.

Choi, Jinyoung, and Maribel Romero. 2008. Rescuing Existential Free Choice in Episodic Sentences. In *Empirical Issues in Syntax and Semantics*, ed. O. Bonami and P. Cabredo-Hofherr, 77–98. http://www.cssp.cnrs.fr/eiss7. ISSN: 1769-7158.

Dayal, Veneeta. 1995. Licensing any in non-negative/non-modal contexts. *Proceedings of SALT* 5: 72–93.

Dayal, Veneeta. 1997. Free relatives and *Ever:* Identity and free choice readings. *Proceedings of SALT* 7: 99–116.

Dayal, Veneeta. 1998. *Any* as inherently modal. *Linguistics and Philosophy* 21: 433–476.

Enç, Murvet. 1991. The semantics of specificity. *Linguistic Inquiry* 21(1): 1–25.

Farkas, Donka F. 2005. Free choice in Romanian. In *Festschrift for Larry Horn*, ed. G. Ward and B. Birner.

von Fintel, Kai. 1994. *Restrictions on quantifier domains*. Ph.D. dissertation, University of Massachusetts, Amherst.

von Fintel, Kai. 2000. *Whatever, SALT 10: 27–39*. Ithaca, NY: Cornell University.

Giannakidou, Anastasia. 1998. *Polarity Sensitivity as (Non)Veridical Dependency*. Amsterdam, the Netherlands and Philadelphia, US: John Benjamins.

Giannakidou, Anastasia. 2001. The meaning of free choice. *Linguistics and Philosophy* 24: 659–735.

Giannakidou, Anastasia, and Yoon Suwon. 2011. Referential vagueness and negative polarity: evidence from Greek and Korean. *CLS* 38.

Guerzoni, Elena. 2003. *Why even ask? On the pragmatics of questions and the semantics of answers*. Ph.D. dissertation, MIT.

Guerzoni, Elena. 2005. When even is also only. *Paper presented at Workshop on Polarity from Different Perspectives*, NYU.

Horn, Laurence. 2000. Any and ever: Free choice and free relatives. In *Proceedings of the 15th Annual Conference of the Israeli Association for Theoretical Linguistics*, 71–111.

Jacobson, Pauline. 1995. On the quantificational force of English free relatives. In *Quantification in Natural Language*, ed. Bach et al. Kluwer.

Jayez, Jacques, and Lucia Tovena. 2005. When 'Widening' is too narrow. In *Proceedings of the Fifteenth Amsterdam Colloquium*, 131–136.

Kadmon, Nirit, and Fred Landman. 1993. Any. *Linguistics and Philosophy* 16:353–422.

Karttunen, Lauri, and Stanley Peters. 1979. Conventional implicature. In *Syntax and Semantics* 11: *Presuppositions*, ed. by Choon-Kyu Oh, and Daniel Dinneen, 1–56. New York: Academic Press.

Kim, Minjoo, and Stefan Kaufmann. 2006. Domain restriction in freedom of choice: A view from Korean Indet-na items. In *Proceedings of Sinn und Bedeutung* 11, E. Puig-Waldmueller (ed.), Barcelona: Universitat Pompeu Fabra, pp. 375–389.

Kratzer, Angelika, and Junko Shimoyama. 2017. Indeterminate pronouns: The view from Japanese. In *Contrastiveness in Information Structure, Alternatives, and Scalar Implicatures*, eds. Chungmin Lee, Ferenc Kiefer, and Manfred Krfika, 123–143. Springer.

Krifka, Manfred. 1994. The semantics and pragmatics of weak and strong polarity items in assertions. *SALT* 4: 195–219. DMLL, Cornell University.

Krifka, Manfred. 1995. The semantics and pragmatics of polarity items. *Linguistic Analysis* 25: 209–257.

Lahiri, Utpal. 1998. Focus and negative polarity in Hindi. *Natural Language Semantics* 6: 57–123.

Lee, Chungmin. 1996. Negative polarity items in English and Korean. *Language Sciences* 18: 505–523.

Lee, Chungmin, Daeho Chung, and Seungho Nam. 2000. The Semantics of amwu N-to/-irato/-ina in Korean—arbitrary choice and concession. *Language and Information* 4(2).

Lee, Young-Suk, and Laurence Horn. 1994. *Any as Indefinite Plus Even*. Ms. Yale University.

LeGrand, Jean. 1975. *Or and any: The semantics and syntax of two logical operators*. Ph.D. dissertation, University of Chicago.

Lim, Dongsik. 2017. The semantics of *-lato* in Korean. In *Contrastiveness in information Structure, Alternatives, and Scalar Implicatures*, eds. Chungmin Lee, Ferenc Kiefer, and Manfred Krfika, 203–226. Springer.

Milsark, Gary. 1974. *Existential sentences in English*. Ph.D. dissertation. M.I.T.

Musolino, Julian, and Andrea Gualmini. 2004. The role of partitivity in child language. *Language Acquisition*.

Nakanishi, Kimiko. 2006. The semantics of *even* and negative polarity items in Japanese. In *Proceedings of the 25th West Coast Conference on Formal Linguistics*, ed. Donald Baumer, David Montero, and Michael Scanlon, 288–296, Somerville, MA: Cascadilla Proceedings Project.

van Rooij, Robert. 2008. Towards a uniform analysis of *any*. *Natural Language Semantics* 297–315.

Rooth, Mats. 1985. *Association with focus*. Ph.D. dissertation, University of Massachusetts, Amherst.

Rullmann, Hotze. 1996. Two types of negative polarity items. *Proceedings of NELS* 26: 335–350.

Szabolcsi, Anna. 2004. Positive polarity-negative polarity. *Natural Language and Linguistic Theory* 22(2): 409–452.
Tredinnick, Victoria. 2005. *On the semantics of free relatives with –ever*, Ph.D. dissertation, University of Pennsylvania.
Wilkinson, Karina. 1996. The scope of *Even*. *Natural Language Semantics* 4: 193–215.
Yun, Jiwon. 2011. On the meaning of wh-(N)-ina and wh-(N)-itun in Korean. *Language Research (Ehakyenkwu)* 47: 191–218.

Expletive Negation and Polarity Alternatives

Yoonhee Choi and Chungmin Lee

Abstract This study investigates the nature of licensing predicates of expletive negation (ExN) and the role of ExN in Korean/Japanese and French. Recently, ExN-licensing predicates have been analyzed as a subcase of nonveridicality (Knüppel 2001 cited from Godard 2004; Choi and Lee 2009; Yoon 2009, 2013), which introduces polarity alternatives (p and $\neg p$) of an embedded complement (Hamblin 1973; Martin 1987; Giannakidou 1997 among others). However, not all nonveridical predicates license ExN. We account for this overgeneration problem of nonveridicality by restricting ExN-licensing predicates to the predicates whose meaning are neg-raisers or can be lexically decomposed into opinion neg-raisers, which are involved in the belief case. On the other hand, in Korean and Japanese, epistemic predicates which are not nonveridical in the sense of Giannakidou (1997) license ExN. We solve the problem by assuming veridicality-suspension by virtue of the question complementizer. This paper analyzes the complement containing ExN in parallel with the positively biased negative question, and argues that regardless of its semantic expletive reading, it implicates that the attitude holder holds a bigger belief of the embedded proposition p than $\neg p$. The analysis solves the 'double negation effect' with the predicates *douter 'doubt'* and *nier 'deny'* in French and the frozen expression of ExN with epistemic predicates in Korean and Japanese.

Keywords Expletive negation (ExN) • Modality • Q-complementizer • Subjunctive mood • Nonveridicality • Polarity alternatives • Negative question • Attitude holder's belief

Y. Choi (✉) · C. Lee
Seoul National University, Seoul, Republic of Korea
e-mail: youni@snu.ac.kr

C. Lee
e-mail: clee@snu.ac.kr

C. Lee et al. (eds.), *Contrastiveness in Information Structure, Alternatives and Scalar Implicatures*, Studies in Natural Language and Linguistic Theory 91, DOI 10.1007/978-3-319-10106-4_9

1 Introduction

Expletive Negation (ExN) is said to be 'nonnegative' in that it does not affect the meaning of its sentence truth-conditionally. Let us consider the French example given in (1).[1]

(1) Je crains que vous **ne** preniez froid. (F)
I fear that you **ExN** catch-SUBJ cold
'I fear that you may catch a cold.'

In the literature, ExN is analyzed based on two views: the expletive view and the negative view. The first view argues that ExN is semantically and morphologically unnecessary, and does not have negative force. For instance, Dubois et al. (1994:191) notes:

> We call items which are empty in meaning *expletive words* (negative adverb...).[2]

Le Nouveau Petit Robert 1 dictionary (1993:864) also defines ExN as:

> What is used without necessity for the meaning or the syntax of the sentence.[3]

This expletive view, however, is not satisfactory in two respects. First, it does not comply with the principle of compositionality (Frege), which says that "the meaning of a whole is a function of the meanings of its parts and their mode of syntactic combination." Second, if ExN is expletive, its restricted distribution is not accounted for.[4] Noam Faust (p.c.) points out that the above two arguments are weak. His counterexample is that the English *there* in the *there*-construction is expletive, but it also shows restricted distribution. However, the English *there* in the *there*-construction contributes to the syntactic combination of the sentence. If *there* is omitted, the sentence becomes ill-formed. Likewise we assume that the ExN has its own function, which we will deal with in Sect. 4.1

Other linguists, on the other hand, take the negative view. As in the above example in (1), the licensing predicates of ExN in French include adversative predicates such as *craindre* 'fear.' For this reason, Jespersen (1917) claims that ExN has the full negative force and analyzes it as paratactic negation. He notes (Jespersen 1917:75, cited from Joly 1972:33):

[1] The following glosses are used in this paper: ACC = accusative case, COMP = complementizer, Qcomp = question complementizer, Fcomp = factive complementizer, DECL = declarative mood, EN = embracing negation, ExN = expletive negation, IMP = imperative mood, IND = indicative mood, MOD = modal, NEG = negation particle, NOM = nominative case, PST = past tense, PostP = postposition, PRES = present tense, PROG = progressive aspect, Rcomp = reportative complementizer, REL = relativizer, SUBJ = subjunctive mood, TOP = topic marker.

[2] "On appelle *mots explétifs* (adverbe de negation...) des termes vides de sens...."

[3] "Qui est usité sans necessité pour le sens ou la syntaxe d'une phrase."

[4] The distribution of ExN will be dealt with in the following section.

> A negative is placed in a clause dependent on a verb of negative import like *deny*, *forbid*, *hinder*, *doubt*. The clause here is in some way treated as an independent sentence, and the negative is expressed as if there had been no main sentence of that particular kind.

For instance, the French example given in (2a) should be understood as having the same meaning as that in (2b).

(2) a. Je crains qu'il **ne** vienne.
I fear that he ExN come-SUBJ
'I fear that he may come.'
b. Il ne viendra pas, je le crains.
He not will-come not, I it fear
'He will not come, I am afraid of it.'

Joly (1972:33–4), however, refutes this argument. His crucial claim is based on his intuition that the sentence (2a) is generally understood as 'I fear that he may come,' and not as in (2b). Agreeing with Joly's intuition, we think that Jespersen's negative view of ExN is too strong. On the other hand, Damourette and Pichon (1911–1940, cited from Martin 1987:67) proposes a discordance analysis where ExN indicates a discordance between 'what the subject wants' and 'what seems to be probable.' For example, in the above example (2a), the subject expresses that '(s) he does not want him to come.' The discordance analysis of ExN, however, raises at least two problems. First, it is unclear why some but not all negative predicates do not license ExN. For instance, as Martin (1987) notes, the French negative predicate *regretter* 'regret' does not license ExN. Second, in Korean and Japanese, ExN can occur with some 'sentimentally' positive predicates which do not convey undesirability implicature.[5,6]

Meanwhile, van der Wouden (1994) classifies ExN as an NPI which is licensed by a negative operator in a higher clause. Consider the French example (3).

(3) Je ne crains pas qu'il (*ne) fasse cette faute.
I EN fear NEG that-he (*ExN) make-SUBJ that error
'I am not afraid he will make that mistake.' (van der Wouden 1994:113)

In (3), the apprehensive predicate *fear* cannot license ExN in the scope of negation. He accounts for this phenomenon by positing a 'double negation effect.' He argues that since the verb *craindre* 'fear' is an NPI-licensing operator, it thus loses its negative property under negation. However, this account raises another

[5]'Sentimentally' is added in front of the term 'positive', since 'positive' may give the impression of being opposite to the notion of 'nonveridicality'.

[6]For positive licensing predicates of ExN in Korean and Japanese, see Yoon (2009, 2013).

problem. The French dubitative predicate *douter* 'doubt' licenses ExN only in the scope of negation or in interrogative forms.[7] Consider (4).

(4) Je ne doute plus que la vraie dévotion **ne** soit la source du repos
I EN doubt NEG that the true devotion ExN be-SUBJ the source of rest
'I do not doubt at all that true devotion is the source of rest.' (van der Wouden 1994:113)

He (1994:113) notes that "verbs such as *to doubt* that do not trigger paratactic negation (i.e. expletive negation),[8] may 'inherit' this property from negation." However, it is unclear why the same reasoning does not apply to the adversative predicate *craindre* 'fear.' According to Hoeksema and Klein (1995), both *craindre* 'fear' and *douter* 'doubt' are DE contexts.

Finally, Muller (1991:410) notes that French ExN-licensing contexts contains a negative part such as 'X = Y (NEG)' in their meanings. For instance, *craindre* p 'fear' means *souhaiter que ne pas* p 'request if not p.' While this negative view cannot be extended to ExN in Korean and Japanese, it is noticeable that he deals with an interaction between ExN-licensing predicates and polarity, which are 'double negation effect.' We will deal with the above problems in the following sections.

From the data presented above, it appears that neither the expletive view nor the negative view can account for the property of ExN. In order to account for ExN-licensing predicates, we adopt Hamblin (1973) and Giannakidou (1997), and assume that ExN-licensing predicates are best characterized as an inducer of non-veridicality relevant to the attitude holder's view of an embedded proposition (Choi and Lee 2009; Yoon 2009, 2013). The nonveridical analysis of ExN-licensing predicates accounts for Korean and Japanese data where nonveridical positive predicates (e.g., *ship-ta* (K) 'seem,' *para-ta* (K)/*nozo-mu* (J) 'hope') license ExN, contra van der Wouden (1994). While the nonveridical analysis is not new, this paper discusses the over-generation and under-generation problem of the non-veridicality as well. In addition, we provide a new perspective in studies of the function of ExN. In our analysis, ExN functions as a negation in a question, and the embedded complement with ExN is analyzed as a positively biased negative question both in syntactic makeup and pragmatic implicature. Thus, the whole embedded complement with ExN implicates that the attitude holder holds a higher belief toward p than $\neg p$. Our analysis of ExN is different from the previous studies in that we deal with its pragmatic implicature, regardless of its semantic expletive

[7]Some examples that show that *douter* 'doubt' licenses ExN might be found with a Google search.

(i) ? Je doute que cette liste ne soit disponible. (F)
I doubt that this list ExN be-SUBJ available.
?'I doubt that this list is available.' (example found on google by Mingya Liu (p.c.))

In fact, the acceptability of ExN with the predicate *douter* and its polarity seems to be controversial. However, we take Muller (1991:389) and van der Wouden (1994) where ExN is absent after the words of dubitation such as *douter* 'doubt' and *nier* 'deny' when it is not in the scope of negation.

[8]The underlined part is our addition.

interpretation. Our pragmatic approach solves the 'double negation effect' pointed out by Muller (1991) and van der Wouden (1994) where negative predicates such as *douter* 'doubt' and *nier* 'deny' in French can license ExN only in the scope of negation or in interrogative forms.

The paper is structured as follows. Section 2 presents the distribution of ExN. Section 3 characterizes predicates that license ExN, focusing on the data from Korean and Japanese, and deals with the over-generation and under-generation problem of the nonveridicality. Section 4 shows the role of ExN in Korean, Japanese, and French and deals with its pragmatic condition. Section 4 discusses degrees of belief of the attitude holder in the statements which have a different complementizer type respectively and provides a formal analysis.

2 The Distribution of ExN

The distribution of ExN shows cross-linguistic variation. In the Romance languages, ExN appears generally in the complement clause of some adversative predicates (e.g., *fear*, *deny*, *prevent*), comparatives of inequality, and certain conjunctions (e.g., *before*, *without*, *unless*), as shown in (5)–(7) respectively.

(5) Adversative predicates
   a. Il faut empêcher qu'elle **ne** vienne. (French)
      It must prevent that she ExN come-SUBJ
   'We must stop her from coming.'
   b. Timeo **ne** ueniat. (Ancient Latin)
      (I) fear ExN il come-SUBJ
   'I fear that he may come.' (S. Deleani & J.M.Vermander, 1975, cited from Park, 2008)

(6) Comparatives of inequality
   Il est plus riche qu'on **ne** le pense. (French)
   He is more rich that we ExN it think-IND
   'He is richer than we think.'

(7) Conjunctions
   Aidez -moi avant que tu **ne** partes. (French)
   Help-IMP me before you ExN leave-SUBJ
   'Help me before you leave.'

Among the above contexts, apprehensive predicates are the most typical ExN-licensing contexts cross-linguistically. Consider the examples in Korean (K), Japanese (J).

(8) ney -ka kamki-ey keli.ci -nun **anh** -ul -kka kekcengha -go.iss -ta.(K)
   you-NOM cold-PostP catch -TOP ExN -MOD-Qcomp fear -PROG -DECL

(9) anata-ga kaze-o hiki -wa shi **nai** -ka(-to) shimpaishi -te.i -ru. (J)
you-NOM cold-ACC catch -TOP do -ExN -Qcomp fear -PROG -DECL
(8-9) '(I) fear that you may catch a cold.' [(Lit.) 'I fear 'won't you catch cold?]
(Choi and Lee 2009)

In order to provide a unified analysis of the above contexts, van der Wouden (1994) argues that the licensing contexts of ExN in the Romance languages are a subset of downward entailment (DE) contexts. However, as mentioned above, ExN-licensing predicates in Korean and Japanese do not always belong to DE contexts. ExN can be triggered by the psychological verb *siph-ta* (K) 'seem,' the epistemic verb *sayngkakha-ta*(K)/*omo-u* (J) 'think,' the intensional usage of *chac-ta* (K)/*saga-su* (J) 'look for,' and the desire predicate *prara-ta*(K)/*nega-u* (J) 'hope,' as shown in (10)–(13).[9] With the ExN-licensing predicates, the Q-complementizer (Qcomp) *–kka* in Korean is always accompanied by the conjecture modal marker (MOD) *-(u)l*, whereas in Japanese only Qcomp *–ka* appears and MOD is covertly present.[10]

(10) ku ai -ka oyemtoyn-mwul-ul masi.ci -**anh** -ass -ul -kka siph -ta. (K)
the child-NOM polluted -water-ACC drink **-ExN** -PST-MOD -Qcomp seem-DECL
'It seems (to me) that the child may have drunken polluted water.'

(11) a. hyencay chwucengha-ko.iss-nun piyong-kwa emchengnan
currently estimate -PROG-REL cost -with significant
- chai -ka na.ci -**anh**-ul -kka sayngkakha-n-ta. (K)
- difference -NOM show -**ExN**-MOD -Qcomp think -PRES-DECL
'I think that (the cost) may be significantly different from what we estimate currently.'
b. kare-ga kaze-o hiiteru.no.dewa -**nai** -ka(-to) omot -te.i -masu. (J)
he -NOM cold-TOP catch -**ExN** -Qcomp think -PROG -DECL
'I think that he may catch a cold.'

(12) a. na -lul towu-l.swu.iss-nun salam-i iss.ci -**anh** -ul -kka chac -ko.iss -ta.(K)
b. watashi-o tetsuda - e -ru hito -ga i -**nai** -(u)ka(-to) sagashi -te.i -ru.(J)
me -ACC help -can -REL man-NOM exist -**ExN**-MOD -Qcomp look.for-PROG-DECL
(12a-b)'(I) am looking for a man who may be able to help me.' (Yoo et al. 2008)

[9]Yoon (2009, 2013) argues that the expletive negation in Korean and Japanese cannot occur with opinion predicates (*think, believe*).

[10]In fact, *-kka* is an underlying semantic quasi-Qcomp; a real syntactic Qcomp is licensed by a higher interrogative verb such as *mut-ta* 'ask' (see Lee 1988). Therefore, we believe that the conjectural/presumptive epistemic marker *–(u)l*, together with Qcomp*–kka*, came to be licensed by the licensing epistemic or apprehensive verbs. Some grammaticalization seems to have occurred.

(13) a. pal-kang cengtouy sengcek-ul naynta-myen kanungha.ci **-anh** -ul -kka
Quarter-final approximately result-ACC make-if be possible **-ExN**-MOD-Qcomp
-pala-ko.iss-ta. (K)
-hope-PROG-DEC
'I hope that it will be possible for Korea to make it to the quarter finals (of the world cup)'.

b. ame-ga hur.a -nai -ka(-to) negat-te.i-masu[11]. (J)
rain-NOM come **-ExN** -Qcomp(-Rcomp) hope-PROG-DECL
'I hope that it will rain.' (J)

In addition to the data in Korean and Japanese, we found that volitional predicates in French can also trigger ExN in combination with *ne…que* 'only.'[11]

(14) On ne peut qu' *espérer/attendre/souhaiter/desirer/vouloir* que la guerre ne s'arrête enfin.
we *ne* can *que* hope /expect /hope /wish /want that the war ExN stop finally
'(Lit.) We can only wish that the war would end finally.'
(Muller 1978:10 cited in Martin1987:72)

Since *only* can license NPIs in English, one might think that these contexts are DE. However, we could not find other positive predicates that can trigger ExN even in combination with *ne…que* 'only' in French. The licensibility of ExN in example in (14) seems to be due to the volitional predicates which are nonveridical. The above Korean, Japanese, and French examples suggest that the licensing contexts of ExN should not be restricted to DE contexts. In the next section, we will characterize the ExN-licensing contexts. However, in Korean and Japanese, ExN appears in more restricted contexts than French, i.e., in some predicates. For this reason, this paper will deal with only ExN-licensing predicates.

3 Characterization of ExN-Licensing Predicates

3.1 Nonveridical Analysis of ExN-Licensing Predicates and Problems

In the previous section, we have seen that neither the expletive view nor the negative view of ExN can account for ExN-licensing contexts. Recently, the ExN-licensing predicates have been analyzed as having nonveridical characteristics (Knüppel 2001 for French, Choi and Lee 2009; Yoon 2009, 2013 for Korean among others). Zwarts' (1995:287) definition of nonveridicality is as follows:

[11]A native speaker told me that adding the Rcomp *-to* after Qcomp *–ka* is more natural in written Japanese. We assume that in spoken Japanese, *-to* can be covertly added by a pause.

(15) Nonverdicality

"Let O be a monadic sentential operator. O is said to be veridical just in case Op⇒p is logically valid. If O is not veridical, then O is nonveridical. A nonveridical operator is called averidical iff Op ⇒ ~p is logically valid."

Based on this definition, nonveridicality can be characterized as having wider property than DE (Giannakidou 1997). The extended view accounts for the licensing predicates of ExN in Korean and Japanese. In addition, the nonveridicality gives an answer for the adversative predicates which do not trigger ExN. For instance, the French predicate *regretter* 'regret' does not license ExN because it is a factive predicate.

However, there is an under-generalization problem: epistemic predicates like *think* and *believe* in Korean and Japanese license ExN as shown in (16)–(17), whereas the French counterparts do not.[12]

(16) a. taywha -ka ohay -lul phwu-nun choysenuy pangpep-i **-ani**
communication-NOM misunderstanding-ACC solve-REL best way -be **-ExN**
-l -kka sayngkakha-n -ta.
-MOD - Qcomp think -PRES-DECL
'I think that communication may be the best way to solve misunderstanding.'

b. muri -de -wa **-nai** -ka(-to) omot-te.i -ru.
impossibility -DEC-TOP **-ExN**-Qcomp think -PROG -DECL
'I think that it may be impossible.'

(17) a. olhkey sa -nun kes -eytayhan haytap-ul cwu -l.swu.iss.ci **-anh** -ul -kka
justly live-REL thing -about answer-ACC give-possible **-ExN** -MOD-Qcomp
-mit -go.iss -ta.(K)
believe -PROG-DEC
'I believe that (it) may give an answer to the question of how to live justly.'

b. hontou-wa tsuyoi.n.za **-nai** -ka(-to) shinjin-te.i -masu. (J)
reality-TOP strong -ExN-Qcomp believe-PROG -DECL
'I believe that (he) may be strong in fact.'

While epistemic predicates such as *mit-ta* (K)/*shinji-ru* (J) 'believe' and *sayn-kakha-ta* (K)/*omo-u* (J) 'think' in Korean and Japanese can license ExN, the English counterpart *believe* and *think* are analyzed as veridical with respect to the attitude holder in the sense of Giannakidou (1997:111). With regard to this problem, we will follow Hooper (1975, cited in Marques 2010:138) that the predicates such as *think* and *believe* are nonfactive, i.e., nonveridical even with regard to the attitude holder. This position seems to follow from Zwarts' (and ultimately Montague's

---

[12]In the sense of Giannakidou (1998; 2011), epistemic verbs such as *believe, think,* and *imagine* are veridical. She mentions: "When it comes to sentence embedding, Giannakidou 1998, 1999 argues that epistemic attitudes are veridical. For *x believes that p* to be true, it must be the case that *x*, the main clause subject, is committed to the truth of the embedded proposition *p*." (Giannakidou 2011:26).

(1974) nonveridicality definition). Unlike in French, the predicate *believe* in Portuguese can select both the indicative and the subjunctive as shown in (18a–b).

(18) a. Acredito que a Maria està doente.
Believe-I.SG. that the Maria **is-IND** ill
b. Acredito que a Maria esteja doente.
Believe-I.SG. that the Maria **is-SUBJ** ill
'I believe that Maria is ill.' (Marques 2010:145)

Marques (2010:144–5) mentions that the subjunctive mood can occur under epistemic predicates depending on the attitude holder's degree of belief: the indicative mood in (18a) indicates a high degree of belief whereas the subjunctive mood in (18b) a lower belief. From the Portuguese examples given in (18), we can assume that the veridicality of the epistemic predicates relevant to the attitude holder's view can be suspended by virtue of the subjunctive mood in Portuguese, which we will call 'veridicality-suspension.' In the same vein, the veridicality-suspension can occur with epistemic predicates in Korean/Japanese when they take a Qcomp. The suspension of veridicality solves the under-generation problem in Korean and Japanese.

On the other hand, there is an over-generation problem: not all nonveridical predicates license ExN. For instance, the nonveridical adversative predicates *pwulkanungha-ta* (K)/*dekina-i* (J) 'impossible' in Korean and Japanese do not license ExN.

(19) a. *pi-ka o.ci **-anh**-ul-kka pwulkanungha-ta
rain-NOM come - **ExN**-MOD-Qcomp impossible-DEC
b. *ame-ga hur.a **-nai**-kka dekinai-da.
rain-NOM come **-ExN**-Qcomp impossible-DEC
'Int. It is possible that it will rain.'

In order to solve the over-generation problem, we will compare nonveridical predicates with neg-raising predicates. We found that all neg-raising predicates are ExN-licensing predicates in Korean and Japanese. The classification of neg-raising predicates by Horn (1989:323) recurs in (20). Compare neg-raising predicates illustrated in (20) with ExN-licensers in Korean and Japanese given in (21).

(20) Neg-raiser predicates in English (Horn 1989:323)
a. Opinion: *think, expect, believe, suppose, guess*
b. Intension/volition *want, intend*
c. Perception/probability: *appear, seem, be likely*
d. Judgment *be supposed to, be desirable, advise, suggest*

(21) The licensing predicates of ExN in Korean and Japanese

a. Opinion	*sayngkakha-ta*(K)/*omo-u*(J) 'expect', *mit-ta*(K) 'believe', *ceyanha-ta*(K)/*taiansu-ru*(J) 'propose', *cimcakha-ta*(K)/ *suisokusu-ru*(J) 'guess'
b. Intension/volition	*para-ta*(K)/nozo-mu(J) 'want', *chac-ta*(K)/*saga-su*(J) 'look for'
c. Perception/probability	*siph-ta*(K) 'seem' (only when the speaker is an attitude holder)
d. Apprehension /dubitation	*twuryep-ta*(K)/*osoroshi-i*(J) 'fear, afraid', *kekcengha-ta*(K) /*shimpaisu-ru*(J) 'worry', *uysimha-ta*(K)/*utaga-u*(J) 'suspect/not doubt'

Apprehensive and dubitative predicates given in (21d) are not neg-raising predicates in a strict sense. However, in Sailer (2006:400), dubitative predicates can be extended to neg-raising opinion predicates since they can be decomposed into "think ~ not." In a similar way, apprehensive predicates can also be analyzed as "believe and want ~ not" as van der Wouden (1994:111) has already noted. Namely, ExN-licensing predicates in Korean and Japanese are, thus, neg-raising predicates or can be decomposed into opinion neg-raising predicates. Clearly, an epistemic verb *know* is not a neg-raiser and its equivalents *al-ta* (K) and *shi-ru* (J) 'know' in Korean and Japanese are not neg-raisers, not permitting Qcomp, and therefore are not ExN-licensers (however, see footnote 14 for an exceptional nonfactive complementizer for *al-ta*).

Although further studies should be done on the relationship between neg-raising predicate and ExN-licensing predicates, it appears that neg-raising predicates and ExN-licensing predicates are involved in the belief of the attitude holder. Tovena (2000:339) mentions that "neg-raising sentences express epistemic attitudes with respect to *p*, when there is no way to logically prove that *p* is true." While the class of neg-raising predicates are not uniformly accounted for semantically, Tovena (2000) said that neg-raising predicates are connected with evaluative use.[13] Her account predicts that the nonveridical predicates, such as *unable* or *impossible* in Korean and Japanese cannot license ExN because they do not have evaluative use.[14] Like ExN-licensing predicates, neg-raising is also related with mood. For instance, in Spanish, a neg-raising reading is available only with the embedded verb in the subjunctive mood as in (22a) but not with one in the indicative mood as in (22b).

[13]Yoon (2013) also argues that ExN-licensing predicates in Korean and Japanese have an evaluative function. But she inadequately excludes 'think'/'believe' from ExN-licensing predicates.

[14]On the other hand, *impossible* in French licenses ExN in a negative form, such as "il n'est pas impossible que Paul ne soit venu (it is not impossible that Paul might come)." But Muller (1978:81) mentions that it conveys an apprehensive menaing such as "il est à craindre que Paus ne soit veun (it is feared that Paul might come)."

(22) a. No cree que sea inteligente.
not believe that is-SUBJ intelligent
'He doesn't believe that he is intelligent.'
b. No cree que es inteligente.
not believe that is-IND intelligent
'He doesn't believe that he is intelligent.' (Tovena 2000:347)

According to Tovena (2000:347), the subjunctive mood in the Romance languages in general have "noncommittal reading" which she views as "the feature of neg-raising sentences." Namely neg-raising reading is involved only in the attitude holder's stance. We think that the noncommittal reading is a kind of nonveridicality relevant to the attitude holder. Interestingly, the neg-raising predicates can take two types of complementizers in Korean and Japanese. The same holds for dubitative predicates in the two languages. Depending on the complementizer type, neg-raising and dubitative predicates can express the attitude holder's stance toward the complement clause. When these predicates take the Rcomp *–ko* (K) or *–to* (J) after declarative or the Fcomp *–kes* (K)/*-koto* or *–no* (J) 'that,'[15] the attitude holder believes that complement clause is true. Therefore, with those complementizers in Korean and Japanese, the complement clause cannot trigger ExN and the negation particles *ahn-* (K) and *nai* (J) in the examples in (23)–(26) are interpreted as negative.

(23) na-nun John-i cwuk.ci -**anh**-ass-ta -ko mit -nun -ta. (K)
I-TOP John-NOM die **-NEG-PST-**DECL -Rcomp believe-PRES-DECL
'I believe that John is not dead.'

(24) machigai.ja -**nai**-to shinji -te.i -ru. (J)
be wrong -**NEG**-Rcomp believe-PROG-DECL
'(I) believe that (it) is not wrong'

(25) na-nun Yuna-ka kenkangha.ci -**anh** -un -**kes** -ul kekcengha-go.iss-ta.(K)
I-TOP Yuna-NOM be healthy-**NEG** -REL **-Fcomp** -ACC worry-PROG-DECL
'I am worried that Yuna is not healthy.'

[15]*-Kes* (K) can be interpreted as either the clausal complementizer 'that' or the general nominal entity 'the thing', and is used mainly with factive predicates in Korean. The same goes for *–koto/-no* (J) (Fcomp). The apprehensive adjective/verb *twuryep-ta* 'fear/be afraid'/*kekcengha-ta* 'worry' can make a proposition formed with a factive *-kes* complementizer. On the other hand, without ExN, neg-raising epistemic predicates in K and J typically take the reportative COMP (Rcomp) –*ko* (K) and *-to* (J). The Rcomp does not presuppose the truth of the complement clause in an actual world, but the factivity holds to the attitude holder in the subject position. On the other hand, the inherently factive verb *al-ta* (K) and *shiru* (J) 'know' cannot license ExN. In this connection, see Lee and Hong (2015) and their citation of Lee (1978) for Korean. Lee (1978) notes that *al-ta* 'know' can be either factive or nonfactive depending on whether it takes a *–kes-ul* 'Fcomp-ACC' or *–kes-uro* 'Fcomp-DIRECTIVE' in the complement. The latter becomes a neg-raiser, as shown in the experiment, but it cannot be accommodated in ExN. Therefore, we assume that the Qcomp is crucal for licensing ExN.

(26) boku-wa Akiko-ga genki.ja -nai-**no** -oshimpai-shi-te.i-ru. (J)
I -TOP Akiko-NOM be health **-NEG-Fcomp** -ACC worry-PROG-DECL
'I am worried that Akiko is not healthy.'

On the contrary, when neg-raising predicates take a Qcomp *-kka* (K)/ *-ka* (J) 'whether,' they can license ExN since the Qcomp together with the presumptive modal *–ul* triggers an epistemic modality, which is essential to nonveridicality. The same goes for apprehensive predicates. The meanings of the statements given in (27) and (28) remain the same regardless of the presence or absence of ExN.

(27) na-nun etten silswu -lato ha. (ci-**anh**) -ass **-ul -kka** twuryep-ta. (K)
I-TOP any mistake-even do -ExN -PST -MOD -Qcomp afraid -DECL
'(I) am afraid that I might made a mistake.' (K)

(28) kare -ga shiken-ni ochiru (-no de -wa **nai**) **-ka(-to)** shimpaishi-te.i -ru.
he -NOM exam DAT fail -Comp -TOP ExN -Qcomp worry -PROS -DECL
'(I) am worried that he might fail the exam.' (J)

However, unlike the other neg-raising predicates, the opinion predicates, such as *sayngkaha-ta* (K)/*omo-u* (J) 'think' prefer the presence of ExN. In addition, the predicates *mit-ta* (K) and *shinji-ru* (J) 'believe' take ExN obligatorily in the scope of Qcomp as shown in (29a–b).

(29) a. ku-ka cal ha-l.swu.iss. *(ci **-anh**) -ul **-kka** mit -go.iss -ta.
he-NOM well do-can ***(-ExN)** -MOD **-Qcomp** believe -PROG -DECL
'(I) believe that he can do (it) well.'
b. kare-ka ko -re-ru *(n.ja. **nai**) **-ka(-to)** shinji -te.i -ru.
he -NOM come -can-DECL *(**ExN**) **-Qcomp** believe-PROG -DECL
'(I) believe that he can come.'

While both epistemic and apprehensive predicates are involved in the belief state, epistemic predicates seems to impose a ranking on the two epistemic worlds where *p* and not *p* are respectively true. From the data in Koran and Japanese, it seems that ExN has something to do with the attitude holder's belief state. We will discuss this problem in Sect. 4.

3.2 *The Analysis of ExN-Licensing Predicates*

In the previous section, we have mentioned that the ExN is licensed by nonveridicaity which is conveyed by an interaction with ExN-licensing predicates and the Qcomp or the subjunctive mood. Adopting Hamblin (1973) and Giannakidou (1997), we also propose that the ExN-licensing predicates generate propositional polarity alternatives of their complement (cf. Martin 1987 for possible world analysis of ExN in French). In Hamblin question semantics (1973), the polar question denotes a set of possible answers, i.e., polarity alternatives. Each polarity alternative is assigned in each possible world which is an attitude holder's epistemic world. In order to define the nonveridicality in terms of epistemic modality, we will adopt Giannakidou's (1997:108) formalization of nonveridicality in context.

(30) **Nonveridicality in context** Giannakidou's (1997:108)[16]
A model $M_E(X)$ in a context *c* is a set of worlds W' ⊆ W(*c*) associated with an individual x, representing worlds compatible with what x believes.

In this model, $M_E(X)$ represents "the epistemic status of an individual X" and W (*c*) stands for "collections of worlds." In other words, $M_{(x)}$ requires an individual as a locus of judgment of the truth value of a model. Given this definition, we can now characterize ExN-licensing predicates in terms of nonveridicality. However, since ExN occurs in embedded sentences, the truth value of the proposition *p* can be evaluated with respect to the attitude holder or with respect to the speaker.[17] For instance, in a sentence like 'Jacob is worried that Lucy might come (modified from Giannakidou 1997:109), the complement proposition 'Lucy comes' can be either true or false in the speaker's epistemic world (Giannakidou 1997:109). On this point Giannakidou (1997:109) mentions that the truth value of *p* under intensional predicates is relevant only to 'the subject' of the matrix clause, and not to the speaker. While we agree with her, we will use the term 'the attitude holder' instead of 'the subject of the matrix clause', because in case of the psych predicates *siph-ta* 'seem,' *twuryep-ta* 'fear/be' 'afraid' in Korean, it is always the speaker who holds the attitude without 'the speaker' realized in the utterance. In addition, in French, ExN can occur in impersonal statement, such as "la crainte que Marie **ne** témoigne au procès est manifeste (the fear that Marie may testify during the proceedings is manifest). (Muller 1978:82)" Muller (1978:82) notes that with ExN, the statement is read as "someone is worried that Marie may come to testify." Namely, there is a hidden attitude holder. If there is not ExN, que 'that' can be interpreted as a relative, and the statement is read as 'Marie showed a fear during the testimony.' Therefore, ExN is crucial to indicate an attitude holder. Therefore, it could be said that the predicates that license ExN convey nonveridicality relevant to the attitude holder's view. By adopting Giannakidou's formalization (1997), we provide a formalization of the nonveridicality relevant to the attitude holder's view with respect to ExN-licensing predicates.

(31) The nonveridicality relevant to the attitude holder's view
a. $\| p \|_{ME(AH),\, g} \neq 1$, where the function *g* is ExN-licensers with Qcomp (in K and J) or the subjunctive mood (in French).
b. The function *g* evaluates a complement proposition as nonveridical with respect to the attitude holder $M_{E(AH)}$.

[16]We changed *what x knows* into *what x believes* in Giannakidou (1998:108)
"A model M(X) in a context *c* is a set of worlds W' ⊆ W(*c*) associated with an individual x, representing worlds compatible with what x *knows*."

[17]We thank Lucia Tovena for pointing out this problem with ExN-licensing predicates (p.c.).

However, as mentioned above, ExN in Korean and Japanese is mandatory with the epistemic predicate 'believe.' It seems that while the epistemic predicates in Korean can express a degree of belief, its lexical meaning persist in only one state of belief. We will relate this issue with the function of ExN in the next section.

4 The Function of ExN: A Unified Analysis in Korean, Japanese, and French

4.1 ExN and Positively Biased Questions

In this section, we propose that the interpretation of ExN exhibits the same pattern as that of positively biased negative questions both in syntactic makeup and in pragmatic implicature. The crucial point of our proposal is that ExN has its own function pragmatically: ExN implicates the attitude holder's positively biased belief toward *p*. For this proposal, we will provide some evidence.

First, "the conjunction *-ciman* 'but' requires the second conjunct to be contrasted with the first conjunct." (Han 1998:243) In the following examples, while the statement in (32a) is acceptable, the one in (32b) is not acceptable. The reason why (32a) is acceptable is that the second conjunct is a negative tag question '*didn't he?*' expresses the speaker's expectation toward the positive answer. In (32a–b), due to the conjunction *but*, the second conjunct should have an opposite polarity bias to the first conjunct which is negative, i.e., positive bias.

(32) a. John said that he didn't finish the paper, **but** didn't he?
b. # John said that he finished the paper, **but** didn't he? (Han 1998:243)

Likewise, in the Korean example (33), the statement with ExN in the second conjunct is acceptable because it expresses the speaker's biased belief toward the positive proposition, whereas the one without ExN is not.

(33) ilkiyeypo -nun nayil pi-ka an -o.n -ta -ko
weather forecast -TOP tomorrow rain-NOM NEG-come -DECL-Rcomp
-ha-yss **-ciman**, na-nun nayil pi-ka o.*(**ci anh**)-ul-kka siph-ta.
-say-PST **-but** I-TOP tomorrow rain-NOM come*(**ExN**)-MOD-Qcomp seem-DECL
'The weather forecast said that it will not rain tomorrow, but it seems to me that it may rain tomorrow.'

If ExN is omitted, the statement is not acceptable.

Second, embedded complement clauses having ExN cannot license strong NPIs. One might say that NPIs are not licensed by the ExN since it is expletive. Then why is ExN interpreted as expletive? We would like to highlight the same syntactic makeup between the complement clause with ExN in Korean and Japanese and negative rhetorical questions. We assume that ExN is a negation and the embedded complement clause is a question. Han (2002:223) indicates that "NPIs are not licensed by rhetorical negative yes-no questions" because negative rhetorical questions are interpreted as positive assertions. Consider Han's example:

(34) a. *Didn't John visit anyone? (rhetorical interpretation)
b. ¬ [¬ (John visited anyone.]]
c. *John visited anyone. (Han 2002:223)

Likewise embedded complement clause having ExN in Korean cannot license the strong NPI *amwuto* 'anyone.'[18]

(35) * amwu-to o.ci ahn -ul -kka kekceng-i -ta.
Who -even(NPI) come ExN -MOD -Qcomp fear -be -DECL
(Int.) 'I fear that nobody will come'

The interpretation of the statement in (35) is available only when *ahn* 'not' is read as negative such as in 'I am afraid that nobody will come.' Our argument is different from the simple expletive account of ExN, because in our analysis, ExN functions fully 'negatively' in the scope of the Qcomp. The ExN and its interaction with the Qcomp is necessitated to capture the process of the expletive interpretation. As Han (2002) shows, the combination of the DE context and the interrogative form results in a positive assertion. Since we view interrogative forms as having DE force, we agree with Han in this point. In our analysis, ExN can be viewed as negation (DE force) and the complement clause with the Qcomp as an interrogative form. This phenomenon can be accounted for by means of the principle of 'presumption of innocence', which is used in order to judge the truth value in logic, where 'innocent' means 'true'. The principle says that "one is considered innocent until proven guilty."[19] Thus, the embedded complement clause having ExN and Qcomp is considered to be true, since its truth value cannot be proven due to nonveridicality originated from Qcomp as well as MOD.[20]

We will now compare rhetorical questions and embedded complement clauses with ExN. Let us consider Ille's three discursive features of rhetorical questions given in (37). However, since rhetorical questions are related to interactions between the speaker and the hearer, the following three features are applied to the cases where the attitude holder of the statement having ExN is the speaker.

---

[18] The weak NPI wh-*(N)-lato* 'any N' can appear in the complement clause with ExN due to the nonveridicality.

(i) nwukwu-lato o.ci ahn -ul -kka kekcengha-ko.iss -ta.
Who -even come ExN -MOD -Qcomp fear PROG-DECL
'I am worried that someone might come'

[19] http://en.wikipedia.org/wiki/Presumption_of_innocence.

[20] We owe our account to Tovena (2000), where neg-raising is analyzed as failure in negation. Tovena (2000:349) views that "a 'neg-raised sentence' conveys an epistemic attitude towards the proposition expressed by the subordinate clause. The hedge consists in making it clear that a certain conclusion is compatible with the current information state, but cannot be proven."

(36) The discursive features of rhetorical questions (Ille 1994:64)[21]
(a) Rhetorical questions can be followed by responses of agreement and disagreement.
(b) Rhetorical questions can function as valid answer to genuine questions.
(c) Rhetorical questions functioning as answers can often be interpreted as argumentative.

As for the feature (36a), statements with embedded complement clauses having ExN can be followed by responses of agreement and disagreement. Consider examples in Korean and French. It is important to note that the responses of agreement given in (37b) and (37b) are related with the attitude holder's biased belief toward the complement proposition. If the statement with ExN expressed low-likelihood in Korean or undesirability in French, the responses of agreement with supporting pieces of evidence for the complement proposition would not be possible, contra Yoon (2013).

(37) a. Yuna -ka pihayngki-lul nohci. ci -**anh**-ass -ul-kka kekcengtoy-n-ta.
Yuna -NOM plane -ACC miss -ExN-PST-MOD-Qcomp worry-PRES-DECL
'(I) am worried that Yuna may have missed the plane.'
b. **maca**, nwun-ttaymwuney taypwupwunuy konghang pesu-ka wunhayngchwiso toy-ess-tay.
Right, snow-because of most of airport bus-NOM cancel be-PST-Rcomp
'You are right; most airport buses have been cancelled due to snow.'

(38) a. Je crains que Yuna **n**'ait loupé son avion
I fear that Yuna ExN has-SUBJ missed her plane.
'I am worried that Yuna may have missed the plane."
b. **Tu as raison**, avec la tempête de neige, la plupart des bus qui mènent à l'aéroport
you are right, with snowstorm, the most of bus which take to the airport
- ont été annulés" (p.c. Margot Colinet)
- have been cancelled.
'You are right; most airport buses are cancelled due to snowstorm.'

With regard to the features (36b–c), the embedded complement clause with ExN can function as an answer to genuine questions. As an answer to the question 'do you think our new program will work?' the following statements with ExN are very natural as an answer. The counterpart statements without ExN cannot function as an answer to this question.[22] Consider (39a–b).

---

[21]One of the features of rhetorical questions that is not applied to the embedded complement with ExN is that "rhetorical questions can only be quoted, but not reported or represented." (Ille 1994:64) The embedded complement with ExN can be followed by the Rcomp *–ko* (K) or *–to*(J) either covertly or overtly, except for *ship-ta* (K) 'seem' and *twuryep-ta* 'be afraid' which take only the first person speaker in the subject position.

[22]Note that if the higher predicate does not appear, the answer *kocen-ul ha. *(ci -**anh**) -ul -kka* is fine but remains as a rhetorical question, which has a real negation. We will present some detailed relations between ExN and rhetorical question in a sequel paper.

(39) a. kocen-ul ha. *(ci -**anh**) -ul -kka (siph-ta). (K)
struggle-ACC do *(-ExN) -MOD-Qcomp (seem-DECL)
'(It seems that) (we) might struggle with it.'
b. kocen-ul ha. ?(ci -**anh**) -ul -kka (kekcengi-ya). (K)
struggle-ACC do ?(-ExN) -MOD -Qcomp (worry-DECL)
'(I am afraid that) (we) might struggle with it.'

We will also provide examples which support our argument in French. First, we will consider the licensing predicate *nier* 'deny'. It is important to note that ExN is triggered only when the predicate *nier* 'deny' is in the scope of negation or question. As shown in (40) if the predicate *nier* 'deny' in the scope of negation does not take ExN, the statement conveys an interpretation that the attitude holder has a neutral belief of the complement clause. Namely, the attitude holder's degree of belief of *p* and not *p* is 50:50. Therefore, a continuation that "but I don't admit it either' can be added as shown in (40)."

(40) Je ne nie pas qu'il soit intelligent, mais je ne l'admet pas non plus.
I EN deny NEG que he be-SUBJ intelligent, but I EN it admit NEG either
'I don't deny that he is intelligent, but I don't admit it either.' (Muller 1991: 408)

However, when the predicate *nier* 'deny' in the scope of negation takes ExN, the statement conveys the attitude holder's biased belief toward *p*. For this reason, the continuation of 'but I don't admit it either' is not possible due to a contradiction between the implicature that the attitude holder has a positively biased belief that he is intelligent and the semantic meaning of the continuation. If ExN conveys undesirability, the statement in (41) would be possible.

(41) *Je ne nie pas qu'il **ne** soit intelligent, mais je ne l'admet pas non plus.
I EN deny NEG que he **ExN** be-SUBJ intelligent, but I EN it admit NEG either
'I don't deny that he is intelligent, but I don't admit it either.' (Muller 1991:408)

Second, questions having the predicate *deny* in the matrix clause and ExN in the complement clause as in (42) are understood as positively biased rhetorical questions, whereas the ones without ExN as in (43) express a genuine request for information.

(42) Peut-on nier qu'il **ne** soit intelligent?
can we deny that he ExN be-SUBJ intelligent
'Can we deny that he is intelligent?' (Rhetorical interpretation: he is intelligent.)

(43) Peut-on nier qu'il soit intelligent, ou doit-on simplement en douter?
can we deny that he be-SUBJ intelligent, or should we simply it doubt
'Can we deny that he is intelligent or should we simply doubt it?' (Muller 1991:408)

The expletive *ne* can be used for rhetorical effect in yes-no questions as well.

(44) Qui *ne* souhaite partir en vacances?
who ExN wishes leave on holidays
'Who (on earth) doesn't want to go on holiday?' (Rowlett 1998:28)

Thirdly, Muller also shows that *ne pas ignorer que* 'not be ignorant that' in French can trigger ExN in the seventeenthth century.

(45) Je n'ignore pas qu'il **n'**ait voulu me nuire.
I EN not know NEG que he **ExN** have-SUBJ wanted me harm
'I am not ignorant of the fact that he wanted to do me harm.' (Muller 1991:409)

Since *ne pas ignorer* can be read as *not not-know* (≒*know*), the example is in line with the epistemic predicate *sayngkakha-ta* (K)/*omo-u* (J) *think*, which prefers to take ExN in Korean and Japanese, and supports our argument that ExN conveys the attitude holder's belief toward *p*. Also, Muller (1991: 386) notes that the statement with French predicate *craindre* 'fear' conveys "positive scalar orientation" with ExN whereas the one without ExN does not.

(46) a. Je crains que Paul ne soit riche, et même très riche.
I fear that Paue ExN be-SUBJ rich, and even very rich.
'I fear that Paul might be rich, and even very rich.'
b. *Je crains que Paul soit riche, et même très riche.
I fear that Paue be-SUBJ rich, and even very rich.
(Int.) 'I fear that Paul might be rich, and even very rich.' (Muller 1991:386)

The same observation is found in Korean data.

(47) Yuna-ka tachi. ??(ci **-anh**) -ul -kka kekcengtoy-n-ta.
Yuna-NOM get hurt ??(-ExN) -MOD -Qcomp fear -PRES–DECL.
- Simcie acwu manhi
- Even very much
'(I) fear that Yuna might get hurt, and even very much.'

Finally, we have checked an intuitive difference with regard to presence and absence of ExN with two French statements having *craindre* 'fear' as a main verb with French native speakers.

(48) a. Je crains qu'il ne vienne.
I fear that he ExN come-SUBJ.
b. Je crains qu'il vienne.
I fear that he come-SUBJ.
'I fear that he might come.'

While most French native speakers did not find a difference between the two statements, six of them[23] said that the statement with ExN in (48a) conveys the

[23]Two of them are linguists, and four of them are nonlinguists.

attitude holder's biased belief toward his coming whereas the one without ExN in (48b) is neutral. Namely, (48a) can be interpreted as "unfortunately I think he's coming."

In sum, we can assume that the complement clause with ExN implicates the attitude holder's biased belief toward *p* in Korean, Japanese, and French. We summarize the function of ExN in its interaction with nonveridicality coming from Qcomp or the subjunctive mood in (50).

(49) The Function of ExN
(i) *Biased belief marker* toward *p* in the attitude holder's belief state, where $\{p, \neg p\}$ is a set of polarity alternatives of the embedded complement clause, which are induced by nonveridicality with respect to the attitude holder.
(ii) The ExN implicates that the attitude holder holds a higher belief toward *p* than $\neg p$.

The function of ExN in our analysis, thus, solves the 'double negation effect' puzzles observed in van der Wouden (1994). Recall that while the dubitative predicate, such as *douter* 'doubt' in French is a DE context, it can license ExN only in the scope of another external DE operator. The lexical meaning of *doubt p* 'not believe p' results in a contradiction to the implicature which ExN conveys, i.e., higher belief toward *p*. On the other hand, the predicate *craindre* 'fear' in French cannot license ExN if it is in the scope of DE. The same is applied to apprehensive predicates in Korean. Consider (50).

(50) *Nayil pi -ka o.ci **-anh** -ul -kka twuryep -ci.**anh** -ta.
Tomorrow rain -NOM come **-ExN** -MOD-Qcomp afraid **-NEG** -DECL
(Int.) 'I am not afraid that it might rain tomorrow.'

The ungrammaticality of the example in (50) can be accounted for due to the contradiction between the lexical meaning of *twuryep-ta* 'fear/be afraid' in the scope of negation and the implicature which ExN conveys. According to van der Wouden (1994), the predicate *fear* has the following lexical meaning.

(51) *fear* X = believe that X will be the case and hope that X will not be the case.
(van der Wouden 1994:111)

Due to negation, the interpretation of statement in (50) is that 'it is not the case that the attitude holder believes that it will rain tomorrow or that the attitude holder hopes that it will not rain'. In contrast, the ExN in (50) conveys an implicature that 'the attitude holder believes that it will rain tomorrow' at the same time. Therefore, the whole sentence results in a contradiction. As mentioned above, the double negation effect in French is not accounted for by means of undesirability. In Korean and Japanese, however, the dubitative predicates sometimes seems to license ExN not in the scope of negation. The reason for this is that there is no morphological distinction between *doubt* and *suspect* in Korean and Japanese. The meaning of 'doubt that *p*' can be paraphrased as 'not believe that *p* is true.' On the other hand, the meaning of '*suspect* that *p*' is to 'believe that *p* is true.' Namely, the meaning of *doubt* is totally opposite to that of *suspect* from the perspective of belief. Thus, when the dubitative predicate in Korean and Japanese is used as the meaning of *suspect*, it licenses ExN regardless of the presence of an external DE operator. Consider the examples in (52)–(53).

(52) ku-ka palam-ul phiwu.ci **-anh** -ass **-ul** **-kka** uysimha-ko.iss-ta. (K)
He-NOM cheat-ACC do **-ExN**-PST-MOD-Qcomp suspect -PRES-DECL
'(I) suspect that he cheated on me.'

(53) watashi-wa kare ga usotsuki de-wa **nai** **-ka**(-to) utagatte-i-masu. (J)
I -TOP he NOM liar DECL-CT **ExN** -Qcomp suspect-PRES-DECL
'I suspect that he is a liar.'

There is no contradiction between the lexical meaning of '*suspect* that *p*,' which is 'believe that *p* is true,' and the meaning conveyed by ExN 'believe that *p* is true.'

4.2 The Pragmatic Conditions of ExN

This section deals with the pragmatic conditions, where ExN can occur. Due to the subjunctive mood or the Qcomp, the embedded complement clause with or without ExN can occur only in the situation, where a low degree of certainty is presupposed by the contexts. Consider the scenario 1. 9 out of 9 Korean native speakers said that the two statements are all unnatural in this situation.

(54) Scenario 1: According to the National Weather Service, the chance of showers is about 80 % tomorrow. Showers will continue into the evening, with a 90 % chance of rain.

(55) a. # nayil pi -ka o -l -kka kekcengtoy-n-ta.
tomorrow rain -NOM come-MOD-Qcomp fear - PRES-DECL
'I am worried that it will rain tomorrow.'
b. # nayil pi -ka o.ci **-anh** -ul -kka kekcengtoy-n-ta.
tomorrow rain -NOM come **-ExN** -MOD -Qcomp fear -PRES-DECL
'I am worried that it will rain tomorrow.'

In contrast, the statement with ExN in (55b) is acceptable under the following scenario 2 given in (56) whereas the statement without ExN in (55a) is not natural.

(56) Scenario 2: the speaker is supposed to go to South Beach in Miami this weekend for vacation. The weather forecast predicts sunshine tomorrow and it is sunny right now. She has already booked dinner outside. But she also knows that it is hurricane season and the Hurricane Dolly may change course. Moreover, it is very windy outside, etc.

In scenario 2, there are two different information sources which affect the attitude holder's belief state: the hearsay/reported information (presupposed information) and inferring/reasoning information inferred by the attitude holder (cf. Kratzer 2002). The two polarity alternatives *p* and ¬*p* are compatible with each other based on different indirect, i.e., nonvisual conversational information. However, it seems that the reported information, i.e., weather forecast seems to be more 'objective[24]' and reliable than the information inferred by the attitude holder, in that the former is established by science and technical equipment, such as weather measuring instruments, etc. Nevertheless, the attitude holder wants to place a higher possibility on her inferring conversational information, and believes that it will rain tomorrow. Hence in scenario 2, the statement with ExN in (55b) can be preceded by the concessive adverb *nevertheless*. For this reason, Yoon (2013) argues that the ExN indicates the low-likelihood of the context, which is below 50 %. However, unlike the scenario in (56), ExN does not always require a low-likelihood of the context. Let us consider this in scenario 3.

(57) Scenario 3: Yuna had physical education and she had 100 dollars. She put it in the pocket of her backpack because she thought that she might lose it during the session. After she came back to the classroom she could not find the money. Most students whisper that Arron is the most likely person to have stolen her money, and they even found some evidences. Arron is Yuna's best friend. Judging from the circumstantial evidences, it is the most likely that Arron stole her money. Yuna says:

(58) na-**to** Arron-i ton -ul humchi.ci -**anh**-ass -l **-kka** kekcengtoy-n-ta.
I-**additive** Arron-NOM money-ACC steal -**ExN** -PST-MOD-**Qcomp** worry-PRES -DECL
'I am also worried that Arron might have stolen the money.

In scenario 3 above, where the likelihood for Arron to steal Yuna's money in the context is higher than 50 %, the statement with ExN can naturally occur as in the scenario 3. In Yuna's belief state, the proposition p that 'Arron stole her money' which is based on hearsay/reported (objective) information, is more probable than a proposition $\neg p$ which is based on the attitude holder's former belief that Arron will not steal her money. In this case, the additive particle *–to* 'also' should be put, which indicates that the attitude holder's current belief corresponds to the given context. The above scenarios lead us to additional pragmatic stipulations which are related to the context where ExN appears. We assume that ExN is acceptable only when the attitude holder has an opposite belief to the presupposed context ($\neg p$), and that the attitude holder has her/his own belief based on her/his own information source which is favorable for p. For this reason, we suggest that ExN can function only when one of the following pragmatic conditions given in (59) and (60) is satisfied.

(59) Pragmatic condition of ExN 1
In the given context, the probability of $\neg p$ is higher than p, and in an attitude holder's epistemic world w', the probability of p is higher $\neg p$.

(60) Pragmatic condition of ExN 2
In an attitude holder's epistemic world w', the probability of $\neg p$ was higher than p, and in an attitude holder's epistemic world w', the probability of p is higher $\neg p$.

[24]John Lyons (1977, cited by Kratzer 2002) distinguishes two kinds of epistemic modality, objective and subjective.

A possible explanation of the pragmatic condition of ExN comes from Han (2002). Han (2002:215) accounts for the interpretation of yes-no rhetorical questions by means of the Gricean maxim of Quantity:

(61) Make your contribution as informative as required.

In Han (2002:215), "the informativeness is relative to the individual's degree of belief in a certain proposition p in a given context c." Han (2002:215) mentions:

> I speculate that when a speaker is formulating a question to find out whether p or $\neg p$, s/he formulates the question in the form of the proposition that would be the most informative if it turned out to be true. This means that if a question has the form $\neg p$?, the speaker believes that $\neg p$ is the most informative proposition if it turned out to be true. This in turn means that in such a context, the speaker believes that it is likely that p holds. In other words, the likelihood that a speaker will use a negative question $\neg p$? is equal to the speaker's assessment of the probability of p.

In the same vein, if an attitude holder uses a form $\neg p$? (combination of ExN and Qcomp) in the embedded complement clause, $\neg p$ is the most informative proposition if it turned out to be true. This means that the context or his/her former belief is involved in $\neg p$, and the attitude holder believes that it is likely that p holds, in spite of the context or his/her former belief $\neg p$.

4.3 *Degree of Belief*

In Sect. 3.1, we have mentioned that the apprehensive/dubitative predicates can be decomposed into opinion neg-raising predicates in their lexical semantics. This section shows how different degrees of belief toward the complement proposition p are conveyed by the opinion predicate *sayngkaha-ta* 'think' and the apprehensive predicate *kekcengha-ta* 'worry' in interaction with two different complementizers, i.e, the Rcomp *–ko* after the declarative or the Fcomp *–kes* (with a 'be worried'), and the combination with MOD+ExN+Qcomp. Let us consider the first case.

(62) a. Yuna -nun Arron-i pemin-i -la -ko sayngkakha-go.iss-ta.
Yuna-TOP Arron-NOM criminal-be -DECL -Rcomp think -PROG-DECL
'Yuna thinks that Arron is a criminal.'

b. Yuna-nun Arron-i pemin-i **-n** **-kes** **-ul** kekcengha-go.iss-ta.
Yuna-TOP Arron-NOM criminal-be -REL **-Fcomp** **-ACC** worry -PROG-DECL
'Yuna is worried that Arron is a criminal.'

The statement with the predicate *sayngkaha-ta* 'think' having the Rcomp *–ko* after declaratative in (62a), implicates that the complement proposition 'Arron is a criminal' is true in all epistemically accessible worlds of Yuna. Therefore, the Rcomp *–ko* after declaratative is veridical with regard to the attitude holder. Hence, Yuna's belief state can be formalized as follows. The formalization used in (63) is taken from Kratzer's (2009) seminar on modality.[25]

[25]Seminar ppt 6. http://cpr.nicod.free.fr/Texte/A.Kratzer_6.pdf.

(63) Yuna's belief state with the Fcomp *–kes* or the Rcomp *–ko* 'that' complementizer:
λs[belief(Yuna)(↓s) &∀s'[s' ∈ f(s) → criminal(Arron)(s')]]
(where 'belief(Yuna)(↓s)' means that 's is a belief state whose holder is Yuna.')

Likewise, apprehensive predicates can take the Fcomp *–kes*, and it presupposes the factivity of the complement clause that Arron is a criminal. However, unlike the opinion predicate *sayngkaha-ta* 'think,' the target of the belief or the fear tends to be a 'harmful future event' contextually inferred from the factivity of the complement. Hence, the statement in (62b) is read as factive such as 'Yuna is worried because Arron is a criminal.' For this reason, we assume that the apprehensive predicates are special cases which tend to accommodate inferred future event as a target of the fear even if its compliment clause is factive. Therefore, apprehensive predicates are usually interpreted as nonveridical, and this is why they are cross-linguistically exemplified as an ExN-licensing predicate.[26] Namely, apprehensive predicates are inherently nonveridical predicate.[27] Nevertheless, the nonveridical inference resulted from the factive complement of apprehensive predicates cannot license ExN in Korean and Japanese. We conclude that ExN is licensed only by directly conveyed nonveridicality of its complement. The same goes for apprehensive predicates in French. Muller (1991: 408) notes that the statement below in (64) can convey either factive reading which is a cause of the fear such as 'Mary is worried because Paul came to see her yesterday' or nonveridical reading of its complement clause, such as 'Mary is worried about whether or not Paul came to see her yesterday'. However, only the latter case can license ExN.

(64) Marie se tourmente de **ce que** Paul **ne** soit venu la voir hier.
Marie worry about what Paul ExN be-SUBJ come her see yesterday.
'Mary is worried about whether or not Paul came to see her yesterday.'

Let us now consider the statements with ExN and Qcomp, namely nonveridical reading of the complement clause with the predicate *sayngkakha-ta* 'think,' and *kekcengha-ta* 'worry' in Korean given in (65a)–(65b).

---

[26]The apprehensive predicate in Yiddish also licenses ExN. (Choi and Lee 2009)

(i) di tsvey hob-n moyre ge-ha-t es zol im **nit** shat-n zum gezunt. (Y)
the two have-3PL fear have-PTCP it shall he.DAT ExN harm-INF to.DEF.ART health
'Both of them were afraid that it would harm his health.' (Bjoern Hansen, Ms)

[27]In Korean, there is a special complementizer *–(u)l-kka.po.a* '(for fear) that' which is used only with apprehensive predicates.

(i) Pi-ka o -l.kka.bo.a kekcenha -ko.iss-ta.
Rain-NOM come -Comp fear -PROG-DEC
'(I) am worried that it will rain.'

However, the statements with comp *–(u)l-kka.po.a* '(for fear) cannot license ExN. Further studies should be done to account for this phenomenon.

(65) a. Yuna-nun Arron-i pemin-i **an -i -l -kka** sayngkakha-go.iss-ta.
Yuna-TOP Arron-NOM criminal-NOM **ExN- be-MOD- Qcomp** think -PROG-DECL
'Yuna thinks that Arron might be a criminal.'

b. Yuna-nun Arron-i pemin-i **an -i -l -kka** kekcengha-go.iss-ta.
Yuna-TOP Arron-NOM criminal-NOM **ExN- be-MOD- Qcomp** worry -PROG-DECL
'Yuna is worried that Arron might be a criminal.'

As expected, Yuna's degree of belief never meets 100 % due to the presence of MOD and Qcomp. However, according to our previous proposal, the above statements with ExN + MOD + Qcomp implicates a higher degree of Yuna's belief of the proposition that Arron is a criminal than the proposition that Arron is not a criminal. In order to investigate approximate intuitive degree of belief of the statements with ExN + MOD + Qcomp, we tested an intuitive percentage of the attitude holder's belief in the two statements given in (65a) and (65b) with 34 native speakers.[28] While most speakers mention that Yuna's degree of belief toward the proposition that Arron is a criminal is higher than 50 %, their intuitions are slightly different. Twenty-eight speakers out of 34 (82.4 %) said that the degree of belief with the predicate *sayngkakha-ta* 'think' is higher than that with the predicate *kekcengha-ta* 'worry.' On the other hand, 6 speakers out of 34 (17.6 %) said that the degree of belief with the statement with the negative predicate 'worry' is higher because when the attitude holder worries about something, (s)he presupposes its happening. On average, Yuna's degree of belief with the statement with the predicate *sayngkakha-ta* 'think' is 75.75 %, whereas that with the predicate 'worry' is 61.79 %.[29] With the predicate *sayngkakha-ta* 'think' in (65a), the degree of Yuna's belief is more than 50 % and less than about 75 %, whereas with the predicate *kekcengha-ta* 'worry' in (65b), it is about more than 50 % and less than about 60 %. The reason why degree of belief of the predicate *kekcengha-ta* 'worry' is lower than that of the predicate *sayngkakha-ta* 'think' seems to be its inherently nonveridical characteristics. At any rate, the crucial point here is that ExN indicates a higher belief of *p* regardless of the predicate type. Based on the result, Yuna's belief state with ExN + MOD + Qcomp can be formalized as follows. The formalizations used in (66)–(67) are modified from Kratzer's (2009) seminar on modality.

[28]In the original test, the attitude holder was 'I'.

[29]The result of the test.

The degree of belief of the statements with ExN+MOD+Qcomp (%)											
	(66a)	(66b)		(66a)	(66b)		(66a)	(66b)		(66a)	(66b)
1	70-80(75)	70-80(75)	**10**	80	60	**19**	75	50	**28**	51	60
2	50	70	**11**	80-90	50-60	**20**	70	45	**29**	80	80
3	80-90(85)	70	**12**	80-90	80-90	**21**	80	50	**30**	90	50
4	90	90	**13**	80	50	**22**	90	80	**31**	50	50
5	80	70	**14**	60	90	**23**	49	51	**32**	50	60
6	90	50	**15**	75	50	**24**	80	50	**33**	80	50
7	80	50	**16**	80	60	**25**	90	10	**34**	80	50
8	80	90	**17**	70	50	**26**	80-90	50	**TATAL**	**75.73**	**61.79**
9	100	70	**18**	60	90	**27**	70	90			

(66) Yuna's belief state with the positive predicate 'think' and ExN+MOD+Qcomp in Korean:
λs [belief(Yuna)($\downarrow$s)& $\exists$s'[s'$\in$f(s) & criminal(Arron)(s') $\underline{\&\ 50<\text{degree(Yuna)(s)}<75}$]]
(where 'belief (Yuna)($\downarrow$s)' means that 's is a belief state whose holder is Yuna' and degree(Yuna)(s) indicates a degree of Yuna's belief state.)

(67) Yuna's belief state with the negative predicate 'worry' and ExN+MOD+Qcomp in Korean:
λs [belief(Yuna)($\downarrow$s)& $\exists$s'[s'$\in$f(s) & criminal(Arron)(s') $\underline{\&\ 50<\text{degree(Yuna)(s)}<60}$]]

A hierarchy of degree of belief of the attitude holder by means of the complementizer type in Korean is given in (68).

(68) *sayngkakha-ta* 'think' with Rcomp after the declarative (100%) > *sayngkakha-ta* 'think' (50%~75%) / *kekcengha-ta* 'worry' ExN+MOD+Qcomp *anh-ul-kka* (50%~60%) > *sayngkakha-ta* 'think'/ *kekcengha-ta* 'worry'

In sum, ExN conveys an implicature which reveals a degree of belief of the attitude holder which is not 100 %. For this reason, ExN can be viewed as a kind of cognitive strategies which expresses an attitude holder's mitigated degree of belief.

5 Conclusion

This chapter proposed that ExN-licensing predicates in Korean, Japanese, and French have the property of nonveridicality relevant to the attitude holder's view. The under-generation problem of nonveridicality, i.e.. why some predicates which are not 'nonveridical' (in the definition of the earlier ExN dealing authors) can license ExN is accounted for by the veridicality-suspension by virtue of the combination of presumptive/conjectural MOD and question complementizer Qcomp, replacing reportative Rcomp in those predicates with no ExN, in Korean and Japanese. The over-generation problem, i.e., why some nonveridical predicates cannot license ExN is solved by restricting the predicates to neg-raisiers or opinion neg-raiser holders in their lexical meaning which is involved in the degree of belief, which is weaker than that in the factive epistemic verb *know* and its equivalents. This chapter also provides a new perspective in studies of ExN: ExN implicates the attitude holder's positively biased belief. Furthermore, we analyze embedded complement clauses having ExN in parallel with negative rhetorical questions, which we believe are the underlying source of expletive negation. We also compared different degrees of belief in statements built with different complementizer types by a native speakers' survey. This chapter mainly deals with case studies in Korean, Japanese, and French, but possibly provides a clue for some novel cross-linguistic generalizations and principles of the phenomenon. Thus, we need more extensive cross-linguistic data to fully verify the function of ExN in the future.

Acknowledgments An earlier version of this paper was presented at the CIL18 Workshop on Contrastiveness in Information Structure and/or Scalar Implicatures (2008). We thank the participants of the workshop for their questions, comments, and discussion. We are also grateful to

Lucia Tovena, Manfred Krifka, Mingya Liu, Pierre Larrivée, Fumitake Ashino, Margot Colinet, Noam Faust, and Brain Butler for their help, advice, and comments. All the inadequacies remaining are ours. This work was partly supported by the Korean Government through the NRF (Excellent Scholar) Grant 100-20090049, awarded to the second author.

References

André, Joly. 1972. La négation dite "explétive" en vieil anglais et dans d'autres langues indo-européennes. In *Etudes anglaises*, 20(1): 30–44. Paris: Klincksieck.

Choi, Yoonhee, and Lee, Chungmin. 2009. Adversative predicates: with reference to nonveridicality and expletive negation. In *Proceedings of 18th congress of international linguists 2008 (CIL 18)*.

Damourette Jacques et Edouard Pichon. 1911–1940. *Des mots à la pensée. Essai de grammaire de la langue française*. D'Artrey, Paris.

Dubois, Jean, et al. 1994. *Dictionnaire de linguistique et des sciences du language*. Larousse.

Giannakidou, Anastasia. 1997. *The landscape of polarity items*. Groningen Dissertations in Linguistics, University of Groningen.

Giannakidou, Anastasia. 2011. (Non)veridicality and mood choice: subjunctive, polarity, and time. In *Tense across Languages* ed. Musan, R., and Rathert, M. De Gruyter.

Godard, Danièle. 2004. French negative dependency. In *Handbook of French Semantics*. CSLI Publications.

Hamblin, Charles Leonard. 1973. Questions in Montague English. In *Foundations of language* 10: 41–53.

Han, Chung-hey. 1998. Deriving the interpretation of rhetorical questions. In *Proceedings of the 16th west coast conference on formal linguistics* (WCCFL 16). 237–253. CSLI. Stanford.

Han, Chung-hey. 2002. Interpreting interrogatives as rhetorical questions. *Lingua* 112: 201–229.

Hoeksema, Jacob, and Klein, Henny. 1995. Negative predicates and their arguments. *Linguistic Analysis* 25: 146–180.

Hooper, Joan. 1975. On assertive predicates. In *Syntax and Semantics 4*. ed. Kimball, J. 91–124. New York: Academic Press.

Horn, Laurence. 1989. *A natural history of negation*. CSLI Publications.

Ille, Cornelia. 1994. *What else can I tell you? A pragmatic study of english rhetorical questions as discursive and argumentative acts*. Ph.D. dissertation. Stockholm. Sweden: University of Stockholm, Almqvist & Wiksell International.

Jespersen, Otto. 1917. Negation in English and other languages. In *Selected wings of Otto Jespersen*. George Allen & Unwin Ltd.

Kratzer, Angelika. 2009. Modality in context. In *Handout of context & content*. Lecture in Paris.

Knüppel, Veronika. 2001. *Die Syntax der Negation im Französischen*. Tübingen Niemeyer.

Lee, Chungmin. 1988. Speech act terms and mood indicators (in Korean). *Acta Linguistica (Hungarica)* 39: 127–141.

Lee, Chungmin. 1978. *The analysis of al-ta 'know' (in Korean)*. 60–65. Yusimhoy: Maum. Seoul.

Lee, Sungbom, and Hong, Seungjin. 2015. An experimental study of neg-raising in Korean. In *Negation and polarity: experiemental perspectives*. LCAM Series ed. Larrivee, P., and Lee, C., Springer.

Lyons, John. 1977. *Semantics*, vol. 2. Cambridge: Cambridge University Press.

Manfred, Sailer. 2006. *Don't Believe* in Underspecified Semantics—Neg raising in lexical resource semantics. In *Empirical issues in syntax and semantics 6*. ed. Bonami, O., and Cabredo Hofherr, P., 375–403.

Marques, Rui. 2010. Modality, Context Change Potential and Mood selection, In *Modality and Mood in Romance: Modal interpretation, mood selection, and mood alternation*. ed. Becker, M., and Remberger, E. 133–161. La Linguistische Arbeiten 533, Niemeyer/de Gruyter.

Martin, Robert. 1987. *Langage et Croyance—Les <Universe de Croyance> dans la theorie sémantique*. Pierre Mardaga.

Montague, Richard. 1974. *Formal philosophy. selected papers of Richard montague*. Edited and with an introduction by Thomason, Richmond H. New Haven/London: Yale University Press.

Muller, Claude. 1978. La négation explétive dans les constructions complétives. *Langue française* 39: 76–103.

Muller, Claude. 1991. *La Négation en Français*. Droz: Genève.

Park, Dongyeol. 2008. L'étude sur NE dit "explétif"-L'étude sur la psychomécanique de NE au point de vue de la linguistique historique et comparative-. *Enseignement de Langue et Littérature Française* 28: 217–240.

Rey-Debove, Josette and Rey, Alain. 1993. *Le Nouveau Petit Robert, dictionnaire de la langue française 1*. Le Robert.

Rowlett, Paul. 1998. *Sentential negation in French*. Oxford University Press.

Tovena, Lucia. 2000. Neg-raising: negation as finite failure?. In *Perspectives on negation and polarity items*. ed. Hoeksema, J., Rulmann, H., Sanchez Valencia, V., and van der Wouden, T., 331–356. John Benjamins.

Yoo, Sejin, Choi, Yoonhee, and Chungmin Lee. 2008. Aspectual meanings of the verb *chac-ta* 'look for/find' in Korean. *Korean Linguistics 52. The Society of Korean Linguistics* (Korean), 153–188.

Yoon, Suwon. 2009. Expletive negation in Japanese and Korean. In *Japanese/Korean linguistics 18*. ed. den Dikken, M., and McClure, W., 423–434. Stanford: CSLI Publications.

Yoon, Suwon. 2013. Parametric variation in subordinate expletive negation: Japanese/Korean vs. others. *Journal of East Asian Linguistics* 22(2): 133–166.

van der Wouden, Ton. 1994. *Negative context*. Groningen dissertations in linguistics. University of Groningen.

Zwarts, Frans. 1995. Nonveridical contexts. *Linguistic Analysis* 25(3–4): 286–312.

On the Distribution and the Semantics of the Korean Focus Particle *–lato*

Dongsik Lim

Abstract The Korean focus particle *–lato* carries the implication similar to that of English *even*, but its distribution is different from English *even* or *even*-like items in other languages (German *auch nur,* Italian *anche solo*, etc.). In this paper, I analyze *–lato* in parallel with *auch nur* or *anche solo*, by decomposing it into the covert exclusive particle similar to English *merely* and the additive particle *–to*, which is similar to *also*. Furthermore, to account for the difference between *–lato* and *auch nur* or *anche solo*, I assume that *–to* in *–lato* introduces an additive presupposition weaker than that of *also*, *auch* or *anche*.

Keywords *–lato* • *even* • Weak additivity • Exclusivity • Factivity • Scalarity

1 Introduction

The Korean focus particle *–lato* has been widely discussed by various authors (Lee 1996; Lee et al. 2000; Choi 2007, among others) due to its unique distribution and implication. The following examples exhibit the characteristic properties of *–lato*. First, *–lato* associates with focus (Rooth 1985), and carries a scalar implication apparently identical to that of English *even*:

This paper is a revised and extended version of Lim (2009) and Lim (2010). I would like to thank audiences at 17th Japanese/Korean Linguistics Conference and CIL 18, as well as Jinyoung Choi, Barry Schein, and Roumyana Pancheva, for their comments and suggestions. I also thank Chungmin Lee and an anonymous reviewer for helpful comments. Special thanks go to Elena Guerzoni for detailed comments and extensive discussions. All remaining errors are mine, of course.

D. Lim (✉)
Department of English Education, Hongik University, Seoul, South Korea
e-mail: dongsik.lim@gmail.com

C. Lee et al. (eds.), *Contrastiveness in Information Structure, Alternatives and Scalar Implicatures*, Studies in Natural Language and Linguistic Theory 91, DOI 10.1007/978-3-319-10106-4_10

(1) a. Mary-ka John-ekey [sakwa]$_F$–lato cwuessta-nun kes-un sasil-i anita.
Mary-Nom John-Dat apple-*lato* gave-Rel Comp-Top fact-Nom Neg
'It is not the case that Mary even gave [apples]$_F$ to John.'
b. Mary-ka [John]$_F$-ekey-lato sakwa–lul cwuessta-nun kes-un sasil-i anita.
Mary-Nom John-Dat-*lato* apple-Acc gave-Rel Comp-Top fact-Nom Neg
'It is not the case that Mary even gave apples to [John]$_F$.'

(1a), where *–lato* associates with *sakwa* 'apple,' carries the implication that apples are the most likely objects for Mary to give to John, just like its English counterpart, where *even* associates with *apples*. Similarly, the implication of (1b) is that John is the most likely person to receive apples from Mary, the same implication as what its English counterpart carries.

Second, the distribution of *–lato* is similar to that of Negative Polarity Items (hereafter NPIs) like *any* or *lift a finger*. (2) shows *–lato* is not acceptable in plain affirmative sentences, and (3) shows it is acceptable in the scope of long-distance negation.

(2) a. ??John-un [sakwa]$_F$-lato mekessta.
John-Top apple-*lato* ate
b. #John ate any apple.

(3) a. Mary-ka [sakwa]$_F$–lato mekessta-nun kes-un sasil-i anita.
Mary-Nom apple-*lato* ate-Rel Comp-Top fact-Nom Neg
'It is not the case that Mary even ate apples.'
b. It is not the case that Mary ate any apples.

Things become complicated, however, when we notice that *–lato* is different from run-of-the-mill NPIs in two crucial respects. First, as (4) shows, *–lato* is not acceptable in the immediate scope of negation, which is different from *any*:

(4) a. #John-un [sakwa]$_F$-lato mek-cianh-ass-ta.
John-Top apple-*lato* eat-Neg-Past-Decl
b. John did not eat any apple.

Second, *–lato* is licensed in a significant number of contexts where NPIs are known to be unacceptable, including under modals, as shown in (5):

(5) John-un [Bill]$_F$-i-lato manna-yaha-n-ta.
John-Top Bill-L-*lato* meet-necessary-Pres-Decl
'John must meet even/at least Bill.'

In this paper, I claim that, a la Guerzoni's (2003, 2006) analysis of German *auch nur* '(lit.) also only' and Italian *anche solo* '(lit.) also only,' and Nakanishi's (2006) analysis of Japanese *–dake-demo* '(lit.) only even,' *–lato* needs to be decomposed into two independent scope-taking components. Specifically, I propose that *–lato* consists of the covert exclusive particle corresponding to English *just* or *merely*, which carries the exclusive and 'most likely' presuppositions, and another particle which carries a weaker additive presupposition than *auch*, *anche*, and *–demo*, requiring the existence of the *non-false* alternatives to the assertion instead of true ones.

This paper is organized as follows. Section 2 provides some background of the discussion: in this section I review the standard analysis of focus particles and overview two theories of *even*—scope theory and lexical ambiguity theory. Section 3 illustrates one of previous proposals where *–lato* is analyzed as a counterpart of the Rooth's (1985) $even_{npi}$, and shows why this proposal does not work. Section 4 reviews An's (2007) analysis of *–lato* in terms of scope theory, and shows that the simple application of the scope theory to *–lato* does not work. In Sect. 5, I review Guerzoni's (2003, 2006) analysis of so-called $even_{npi}$s in other languages (including German *auch nur* and Italian *anche solo*), according to which *auch nur* and *anche solo* can be analyzed as *also* + *only*. However, we will also see in this section that *–lato* is different from *auch nur* or *anche solo*, in the sense that they show different distributions. In Sect. 6, I will present my own proposal, according to which *–lato* can be decomposed into the covert exhaustive particle corresponding *only* and the overt additive particle *–to* corresponding to *also*. Here, I will also suggest that the additive introduced by *–to* in *–lato* is weaker than what is usually assumed, in that it only requires that there is a non-false alternative to the assertion rather than a true alternative. In Sect. 7, I will briefly deal with the problem of the free-choice effect of *–lato*, and in Sect. 8, I conclude the paper.

2 Focus Particles and Two Theories of *even*

Focus particles in English and other languages typically introduce additive (e.g., English *also*), exclusive (e.g., English *only*), and/or scalar implications (e.g., English *even* and *only*).[1]

(6) a. Additivity: I met also Mary ≈> I met someone in addition to Mary
b. Exclusivity: I met only Mary ≈> I met nobody other than Mary
c. Scalarity: I met even Mary ≈> For me to meet Mary was less likely/more surprising…

In each sentence the content of a particular implication being introduced depends on the position of the focus. For example, (7a) carries the implication that Mary is the least likely person for me to introduce to Bill, and (7b) carries the implication that Bill is the least likely person for me to introduce Mary to.

(7) a. I even introduced $[\text{Mary}]_f$ to Bill
b. I even introduced Mary to $[\text{Bill}]_f$.

Rooth (1985) accounts for this phenomenon as follows. Focus particles take propositional scope; the focus in their scope triggers a set of alternatives of the whole argument of the relevant particle, which is obtained by substituting the denotation of the focused constituent with objects of the same semantic type; focus particles quantify over a contextually salient subset C of their complement's focus value as defined above. An example with *even* is given in (8):

---

[1]Following Horn (1969), I assume that *only* is truth-conditionally exclusive, and introduces the factivity of the assertion and a scalar presupposition. *Also* and *even* introduce an additive/existential presupposition. A scalar presupposition usually does not appear independently, but always accompanies other presupposition.

(8) a. I met even $[\text{Mary}]_F$.
b. LF: even [I met Mary]
c. C = {I met Mary, I met Bill, I met John, ...}

Among all focus particles, *even* has received a lot of attention because of its unexpected behavior in the scope of negation. In affirmative sentences *even* introduces a scalar presupposition (which I will call a least likely presupposition) and an existential (or additive) presupposition, which compare the proposition without *even* (henceforth prejacent) and the alternatives in the contextually salient subset C of the focus value.

(9) a. Assertion: I met Mary.
b. Existential (additive) presupposition: I met someone other than Mary.
c. Scalar presupposition: Mary is the least likely person for me to meet.

The problem is that, unlike what the standard theory of presupposition projection predicts, under surface local negation, the scalar presupposition of *even* appears to be different (which I will call a most likely presupposition), as indicated in (10).[2]

(10) John did not even meet $[\text{Mary}]_F$.
Assertion: John did not meet Mary.
Existential Presupposition: There is some other x different from Mary such that John did not meet x.
Scalar Presupposition: Mary was the most likely for John to meet.

Two proposals have been made to account for this difference. The first proposal also known as the scope theory of *even*, is found in Karttunen and Peters (1979). Karttunen and Peters (1979) claims that *even* unambiguously introduces the presupposition that its prejacent is the least likely in C (see lexical entry for *even* in 11). In addition to this Karttunen and Peters (1979) view *even* as a positive polarity item (PPI), that is an item which obligatorily takes wide scope over local negation at LF (as shown in 12). The resulting scalar presupposition ultimately entails that the focus is the least likely item to make the proposition with negation true. This is equivalent to a most likely presupposition, as in (12).

(11) $[[\textit{even}]]^w(p)$ is defined iff $\exists q \neq p \in C \wedge q(w) = 1 \wedge \forall q \neq p \in C, p <_{\text{likely in } w} q$
If defined, $[[\textit{even}]]^w(p) = 1$ iff $p(w) = 1$

(12) John did not meet even $[\text{Mary}]_F$.
LF: [even [neg [John met Mary]]]
Assertion: John did not meet Mary.
Existential Presupposition: There is some x different from Mary such that John did not met x.
Scalar Presupposition: Mary is the least likely x for John not to meet.
$\Longleftrightarrow$ Mary is the MOST likely for John to meet.

The second proposal, which is also known as the lexical ambiguity theory, was first presented in Rooth (1985). The lexical ambiguity theory assumes that *even* is

[2]For brevity, hereafter let us call the scalar presupposition in (11) a least likely presupposition, and the scalar presupposition in (13) a most likely presupposition.

lexically ambiguous between the *even* PPI we saw in (11) and the *even* NPI in (13) contributing the opposite presuppositions, namely, a different existential presupposition and a most likely presupposition, as shown in (15).

(13) $[[even_{npi}]]^{w}(p)$ is defined iff $\exists q \neq p \in C \wedge q(w) = 1 \wedge \forall q \neq p \in C, \underline{p >_{likely\ in\ w} q}$
If defined, $[[even_{npi}]]^{w}(p) = 1$ iff $p(w) = 1$

(14) John met even $[\text{Mary}]_f$.
LF: [even_{ppi} [John met Mary]]
Assertion: John met Mary.
Existential Presupposition: There is some x different from Mary such that John met x.
Scalar Presupposition: Mary is the least likely x for John to meet.

(15) John did not meet even $[\text{Mary}]_f$.
LF: [neg [even_{npi}[John met Mary]]]
Assertion: John did not meet Mary.
Existential Presupposition: There is some x different from Mary such that John did not meet x.
Scalar Presupposition: Mary is the MOST likely for John to meet.

One apparent argument in support for the lexical ambiguity theory (and therefore against the scope theory) is that some languages other than English, such as German, Italian, Dutch, and Greek, employ two different sets of expressions, which appear to correspond to Rooth (1985)'s $even_{ppi}$ and $even_{npi}$ in their meaning and distribution, respectively (Rooth 1985; Rullmann 1997; Herburger 2001; Giannakidou 2007). For example, German *sogar* '(lit.) even' is banned in the local scope of negation and introduces a least likely presupposition, (like 11) while *auch nur* '(lit.) also only' appears to show NPI-like distribution and introduces a most likely presupposition (like 13). Italian *addirittura* '(lit.) even' and *anche solo* '(lit.) also only' exhibit the same pattern. (The relevant examples are given in 16 and 17, quoted from Guerzoni 2003: Chap. 4).

(16) John even greeted Mary.
German: Der Hans hat sogar /*auch nur [die Maria] $_f$ begruesst.
The John has even/also only the Mary greeted.
Italian: Giovanni ha addirittura / *anche solo salutato $[\text{Maria}]_f$.
John has even/also only greeted Mary.
Presupposition: Mary was the least likely person to be greeted by John.
& There was somebody other than Mary to be greeted by John.

(17) Nobody even greeted Mary.
German: Niemand hat auch nur / *sogar $[\text{die Maria}]_f$ begruesst.
No one has also only/even the Mary greeted.
Italian: Nessuno ha salutato anche solo/addiritura $[\text{Maria}]_f$.[3]
No one has greeted also only/even Mary.
Presupposition: Mary was the most likely person to be greeted by John.
& Someone else was not greeted.

[3]In Italian both *anche solo* and *addiritura* is fine under the overt local negation. But *anche solo* introduces a most likely presupposition, whereas *addiritura* introduces a least likely presupposition.

From (16) and (17), one might conclude that *auch nur* is equivalent to Rooth's NPI-*even* in (13) and *sogar* equals is equivalent to Karttunen and Peters' original PPI-*even* (but see Guerzoni 2003, 2006 for arguments against this conclusion). The following section provides arguments showing that an analysis of *–lato* as equivalent to (13) is incorrect.

3 *–lato* as *even*$_{\mathbf{npi}}$—Why and Why Not

We have already seen some examples suggesting that *–lato* seemingly corresponds to Rooth's (1985) *even*$_{npi}$: it is not acceptable in episodic affirmative sentences (see 2), but acceptable in the scope of negation (see 3). (18–20) shows two further pieces of seemingly supporting evidence. First, *–lato* is acceptable under some entailment-reversal environments (including downward-entailment and Strawson-entailment in the sense of von Fintel 1999), like under the scope of *nollap-* 'be surprised', downward-entailing quantifiers like *kikkeshaya* 'at most,' and comparatives/*before* clauses. Second, *–lato* combines with semantically weak foci, which is compatible with the most likely presupposition, like the one triggered by *even*$_{npi}$.

(18) Na-nun John-i kwuk [han]$_f$ / #[payk]$_f$ swukalak-i-lato mekessta-nun sasil-i nollapta.
I-Top John-Nom soup one / 100 spoon-L-lato ate-Rel fact-Nom be surprised.
'I am surprised that John even ate one spoon of soup.'

(19) Kikkeshayya sey myeng-uy sonyen-i ppang [han]$_f$ /#[payk]$_f$ cokak-i-lato mek-ess-ta.
At most three CL-Poss boy-Nom bread one / 100 CL-i-lato eat-Past-Decl
'At most three boys even/at least ate one/100 piece of bread'

(20) [han]$_f$ /#[yel]$_f$ salam-i-lato te o-ki ceney kutul-un ttena-ass-ta.
one /10 man-L-lato more come-Comp before they-Top depart-Past-Decl
'Before even/at least one more man came, they departed'

This view has several problems, however. First, as shown in (4), *–lato* is not acceptable under local negation. Second, *–lato* is allowed under some contexts where NPIs are not acceptable, including modals (see 5) and attitude predicates (21).

(21) Na-nun John-i kwuk [han]$_f$ / #[payk]$_f$ swukalak-i-lato mekessta-ko mitnunta.
I-Top John-Nom soup one / 100 spoon-L-lato ate-Comp believe
'I believe that John even ate one spoon of soup.'

Finally, in yes/no questions *–lato* triggers an obligatory negatively biased interpretation, which cannot be accounted for in terms of *even*$_{npi}$ analysis (see Guerzoni 2003, 2004). The bias effect is illustrated in (22):

(22) John-i [il]$_f$ talle-lato peless-ni?
John-Nom one dollar-*lato* earned-Q
'Did John make (even) a single dollar?'
Bias: John did not make any money.

We can see yes-no questions with *–lato* are negative-biased by putting them under contexts in which the speaker is clearly unbiased, and seeing whether these questions are felicitous or not:

(23) (Recently John got a job from a company I did not know before, and I had no idea about whether that company is good or not, or whether that company makes a lot of profit every year or not. Therefore I ask a close friend of John's…)
a. (ku il-ul hayse) John-i ton-ul pel-ess-ni?
(that job-Acc doing-by) John-Nom money-Acc make-Past-Q
'(By having that job) did John earn some money?'
b. #(ku il-ul hayse) John-i $[\text{il}]_{\text{f}}$ talle-lato pel-ess-ni?
(that job-Acc doing-by) John-Nom 1 dollar-lato make-Past-Q
'(By having that job) did John make (even) a single dollar?'

This shows that in the neutral context the question with a semantically weak item and *–lato* cannot be used felicitously, which indicates that these questions are negatively biased. This is also confirmed by the fact that yes-no questions with *–lato* cannot be answered by 'yes' in a plain intonation, and can only be used with emphasis.

(24) (Recently John got a job from a company which is very small and has not earned much profit last year. I also knew that John is very lazy. Therefore I ask a close friend of John's…)
a. (ku il-ul hayse) John-i $[\text{il}]_{\text{f}}$ talle-lato pel-ess-ni?
(that job-Acc doing-by) John-Nom 1 dollar-lato make-Past-Q
'(By having that job) did John make (even) a single dollar?'
b. kulem, pelessci. (with emphasis)[4]
'Yes, (he) did.'
c. #ung, pelesse. (plain intonation)
'Yes, (he) did.'
d. ani, mos pelesse.
'No, (he) didn't.'

As argued in Guerzoni (2003, 2004), this cannot be accounted for by simply assuming that *–lato* is an NPI, like the lexical ambiguity theory, but can only be accounted for by theories based on the scope theory.[5]

So far we saw that the lexical ambiguity theory does not work for Korean *–lato*, which leads us to consider the option of the scope theory of *even* to *–lato*. Moreover, the facts regarding *–lato* in questions indicate that the direction to look into for a solution is LF scope. Therefore this is what we turn to next. First, in the next section, we will evaluate the simple-minded extension of the scope theory of *even*, and conclude that it cannot account for Korean *–lato*, either, by reviewing An (2007). This will lead us to consider more complex variants of the scope theory.

---

[4]In this example I use two forms of 'yes' in Korean: *kulem* and *ung*. It is unclear why, but for most Korean speakers, with emphasis the former is more likely to be used.

[5]A reviewer pointed out that the negative bias effect of yes-no questions with *-lato* disappears when there is no focal accent/intonational cue on the lexical item associated with *-lato*. It seems to be the case, but since in this paper I treat *-lato* as a focus particle associated with intonational focus, I do not take the case into consideration where *-lato* is not associated with any intonational cue.

4 The Simple Scope Theory Does not Work: An (2007)

In an attempt to give a unified account for Korean *–lato* and *–to* based on the scope theory, An (2007) assumes that *–lato*, as well as *–to*, introduces the same scalar and existential presupposition as *even* PPI.

(25) $[[to/lato]] = \lambda C_{<st,t>}.\lambda p_{<st>}:\forall q_{<st>}[q \in C \;\&\; q \neq p \rightarrow q >_{likely} p].p$ (An 2007: 322)

Assuming the lexical entry above, An (2007) claims that the limited distribution of *–lato* can be accounted for in terms of constraints in its scope possibilities. However, it turns out that in order to account for all the relevant facts relative to the distribution of *–lato* in terms of scope restrictions, An (2007) is committed to a rather implausible if not incoherent set of constraints on the scope of *–lato*. Let's see why.

First, to account for the unacceptability of *–lato* under local negation, An (2007) assumes that *–lato* must take narrow scope with respect to negation:

(26) a. *[John]$_F$-i-lato an o-ass-ta. (An 2007: 329)
John-L-lato Neg come-Past-Decl
'Even John did not come'
b. LF: [Neg [lato [John came]]]

Recall, however, that *–lato* is acceptable under long-distance negation, where it is compatible only with a semantically weak focus (the example is repeated below)

(27) a. Mary-ka sakwa [han]$_F$ kay-lato mek-ess-ta-nun kes-un sasil-i ani-ta.
Mary-Top apple one CL-lato eat-Past-Decl-Comp-Top fact-Nom not-Decl
'It is not the case that Mary ate even one apple'
b. #Mary-ka sakwa [payk]$_F$ kay-lato mek-ess-ta-nun kes-un sasil-i ani-ta.
Mary-Top apple 100 CL-lato eat-Past-Decl-Comp-Top fact-Nom not-Decl
'It is not the case that Mary ate even one hundred apples'

Since An (2007) assumes that *–lato* introduces a least likely presupposition, this can only be the case if *–lato* is forced to scope above negation. Given this, An (2007) claims that *–lato* cannot move over a local negation but can move over a long-distance negation. Since local (in fact clause internal) movement is universally better tolerated by the grammar than long-distance ones, the above statement cannot be right.

Moreover, this cannot be an issue of local versus nonlocal negation, because *–lato* is acceptable in the environment of other entailment reversal expressions, both distant (28) and local (29):

(28) John-un Mary-ka sakwa [hana]$_F$-lato mek-ess-ta-nun sasil-ey nola-ess-ta.
John-Top Mary-Nom apple one-lato eat-Past-Decl-Rel fact-Dat be surprised-Past-Decl
'John was surprised that Mary ate even one apple'

(29) Kikkeshayya sey myeng-uy sonyen-i ppang [han]$_F$ cokak-i-lato mek-ess-ta.
At most three CL-Poss boy-Nom bread one CL-i-lato eat-Past-Decl
'At most three boys even/at least ate one piece of bread'

An's (2007) account for the unacceptability of *–lato* in affirmative sentences and the negative bias *–lato* triggers in questions like (30) is based on the assumption that *–lato* must take scope above the entailment-reversal and *wh*-trace operators.

(30) (ku il-ul hayse) John-i [il]$_{F}$ talle-lato pel-ess-ni?
(that job-Acc doing-by) John-Nom 1 dollar-lato make-Past-Q
'(By having that job) did John make (even) a single dollar?'

From the discussion above, we end up with the following set of constraints: i) *–lato* obligatorily takes wide scope relative to the local entailment-reversal expressions (with the mysterious exclusion of negation which would also be entailment reversal), ii) *–lato* obligatorily takes wide scope relative to all long-distance entailment reversal expressions. This is very stipulative at best.

Let us return to the local negation case in (26) (repeated below as 31)

(31) a. *[John]$_{F}$-i-lato an o-ass-ta. (An 2007: 329)
John-L-lato Neg come-Past-Decl
'Even John did not come'
b. LF: [Neg [lato [John came]]]

Even if we grant that *–lato* must scope under negation, why should this make *–lato* unacceptable here? According to An (2007), this unacceptability is due to pragmatics; since *–lato* introduces a least likely presupposition, (31) presupposes that John is the least likely person to come and asserts that John did not come, and since it is natural for the least likely person not to come, we do not have any reason to use the particle *–lato* under local negation. This account is very dubious, however, in light of the fact that assertions that are presupposed to be very likely occur all the time in language.

Moreover, An's (2007) stipulations lead us to the incorrect prediction that *–lato* should be unacceptable in (31) where *–lato* appears under local negation, which in turn is in the scope of other scope-taking elements occurring at the same time. See (32):

(32) John-un sakwa [hana]$_{F}$-lato mek-cianh-ulkes-ita.
John-Top apple one-lato eat-Neg-Fut-Decl.
'John will not eat even one apple'

(32) is acceptable for Korean native speakers. However, if we hold the stipulation that *–lato* takes narrow scope with respect to negation this leads to a pragmatically unacceptable statement: *–lato* should take narrow scope under local negation, but at the same time, it should take wide scope over the future/modal operator, which already takes wide scope over the negation.

Finally, An's (2007) assumptions regarding the semantics of *–lato* and its scope in interrogatives lead us to the incorrect predictions in examples like the following example:

(33) John-i *Syntactic structures*-lato ilk-ess-ni?
John-Nom *Syntactic Structures*-lato read-Past-Q
'Did John read even *Syntactic Structures*?'

According to An (2007), because *–lato* introduces a least likely presupposition, and is forced to scope above the trace of *whether*, to the extent that *Syntactic Structures* is interpreted as a least likely book for anyone to read, the question should be biased towards the affirmative answer (see An's discussion). In general, however, even if *Syntactic Structures* is the least likely item in the context, we do not get a question with positive bias, but the sentence is judged as unacceptable. For most Korean speakers, the sentence is felicitous only when *Syntactic Structures* is regarded as the book most likely to be read, and the question is negatively biased.

All discussions made in this section show that the simple scope theory like what is suggested in An (2007) actually does not work for the correct analysis of *–lato*. In the following sections, we will see a variant of scope theory of *even*, and how this variant accounts for the distribution and the semantics of *–lato*.

5 Second Trial: *–lato* Versus *auch nur* and *anche solo*

–lato actually shares some semantic and distributional properties with German *auch nur*, Italian *anche solo*, or Japanese *-dake-demo*. Following examples show similarities between *–lato* and *auch nur, anche solo, or -dake-demo*, and the differences between them and English *even*. First, unlike English *even*, *–lato*, as well as *auch nur, anche solo*, and *-dake-demo*, is not acceptable in the local scope of negation, as already mentioned in the introduction.

(34) a. #John-un [sakwa]$_f$-lato mek-cianh-ass-ta.
John-Top apple-*lato* eat-neg-Past-Decl
b. #Hans kann nicht auch nur [Italienisch]$_f$. (German)
Hans knows not also only Italian (Schwarz 2005)
c. ohn-wa [sono hon]$_f$-dake-demo yom-ana-katta. (Japanese)
John-Top that book-only-even read-Neg-Past (Nakanishi 2006)

Furthermore, *–lato* does not associate with semantically strong foci, unlike English *even*, but similarly to *auch nur, anche solo,* and *-dake-demo*.

(35) a. John-un Mary-ka sakwa [han} / #[paek]$_f$ kay-lato
John-Top Mary-Nom apple one /100 CL-*lato*
mek-ess-ta-nun sasil-ey nola-ess-ta.
eat-Past-Decl-Rel fact-Dat be surprised-Past-Decl
'John was surprised that Mary ate even one apple / 100 apples'
b. Es hast mich überrascht dass die Maria auch nur die [einfachste]$_f$ /
It has me surprised that the Maria also only the easiest /
#[schwierigste]$_f$ frage beantworten konnte.
hardest question answer could (German: Guerzoni 2006)

Facts considered above lead us to consider about Guerzoni's (2003, 2006) proposal about *auch nur* and *anche solo*, and Nakanishi's (2006) proposal about *-dake-demo*.

5.1 *Guerzoni's (2003, 2006) Analysis on* auch nur *and* anche solo

Guerzoni (2003, 2006) proposes that the *even*-like semantics and restricted (NPI-like) distribution of items like *auch nur* or *anche solo* is the consequence of the composition and scope of their evident subcomponents. In her proposal, *auch nur*, *anche solo*, and their cross-linguistic cognates can be analyzed compositionally as a combination of two particles: the additive particle (36) (like *also*) and the scalar exclusive particle in (37) (corresponding to *only*), consisting of three different components—factivity, scalarity, and exclusivity (Guerzoni 2003: 175).

(36) $[[$*auch/anche/also*$]]^{w}$(C)(P) is defined iff some proposition in C $\neq$ p is true in w.

(37) $[[$*nur/solo/only*$]]^{w}$(C)(P) is defined iff
(i) p(w) = 1 — factivity
(ii) p is the most likely/insignificant proposition in C — scalarity
If defined, then (iii) $\sim\exists q \neq p$ in C that is true (unless p entails q) — exclusivity

Guerzoni (2003, 2006) also assumes that in German and Italian, *nur/solo* is underspecified relative to whether the prejacent is presupposed and exclusivity asserted or the other way around. Guerzoni labels this second option *nur*$_2$/*solo*$_2$:

(38) $[[$*nur*$_2$/*solo*$_2]]^{w}$(C)(p) is defined iff
(ii) p is the most likely/insignificant proposition in C — scalarity
(iii) there is no other q in C that is true (unless p entails q) — exclusivity
If defined, then (i) $[[$*nur*$_2$/*solo*$_2]]^{w}$(C)(p) is true iff p(w)=1 — factivity

Guerzoni argues that the unacceptability of *auch nur* or *anche solo* in plain affirmative sentences and a number of other linguistic contexts is due to the contradiction between their presuppositions emerging when the particles associate with the same focus and take the same scope (see 39), whereas the clash is resolved when *auch* or *anche* scopes outside entailment reversal expressions at LF (see 40).

(39) #Hans hat auch nur [[die Maria]$_f$]$_F$ getroffen.
LF: [auch [nur$_2$ [Hans hat [[die Maria]$_f$]$_F$ getroffen]]]
Presupposition due to *nur*$_2$: Hans met no x different from Mary &
& Mary was the most likely for him to meet.
Presupposition due to *auch*: Hans met someone different from Mary.

(40) Niemand auch nur [[die Maria]$_f$]$_F$ getroffen.
LF: (iii) auch [niemand$_1$ (ii) 1 [nur [t$_1$ [[die Maria]$_f$]$_F$ getroffen]]]
Presupposition of *auch*: There is some x $\neq$ M. that nobody met x.
Presupposition of *nur*$_2$ at (ii): There is no x $\neq$ M. that everybody met x
& Mary was the most likely for everyone to meet.

5.2 –lato *as* Also + Only*: Preliminary Evidence*

One part of my proposal about *–lato* is that, in parallel with Guerzoni's analysis of *auch nur /anche solo*, *–lato* can be decomposed into a covert exclusive particle, corresponding to Guerzoni's *nur_2/$solo_2$*, and an additive particle *–to*. In the following subsection I will provide some preliminary evidence supporting my proposal.

5.2.1 Morphological Complexity of *–lato*

Overtly, *–lato* contains the particle *–to,* comparable to English *even/also,* and the affix *–la*, which also features in Korean as combined with the conditional marker *–myen* in *-lamyen* and the contrastive marker *–ya* in *–laya*:

(41) *–la* + {*myen, to, ya*}

a.	John-i-la-myen	ku il-ul	ha-lswuiss-ta.
	John-L-*la*-COND	that work-Acc	do-be able to-Decl
	"If he is John, he can do that work."		
b.	John-i-la-to	ku il-ul	ha-lswu-iss-ta.
	John-L-*la*-also	that work-Acc	do-be able to-Decl
	"Even if he is John, he can do that work."		
c.	John-i-la-ya	ku il-ul	ha-lswuiss-ta.
	John-L-*la*-Cont	that work-Acc	do-be able to-Decl
	"(roughly) Only John can do that work."		

Each particle, *-myen*, *-to*, and *–ya* can be used in isolation in Korean. In addition, *-man* can appear before *–lato*, forming *–manilato*, but cannot co-occur with *–to*, forming *–manto* as shown in (42):

(42)

a.	wain [han]$_F$ can-(man)-i-lato	masi-myen	ku-nun haykotoy-lkes-ita.
	wine one CL-only-L-*lato*	drink-Cond	he-Top get fired-Fut-Decl
	"Even if he drinks one glass of wine he will get fired."		
b.	**wain [han]$_F$ can-man-to*	*masi-myen*	*ku-nun haykotoy-lkes-ita.*
	wine one CL-only-*to*	drink-Cond	he-Top get fired-Fut-Decl

It is plausible to account for the facts given in (41) and (42) by assuming that *-la* in *–lato* signals the presence of a covert exclusive *–man_2*, corresponding to English *merely* and Guerzoni's *nur_2/$solo_2$*, but semantically different from the overt *-man* (corresponding to Guerzoni's *nur_1/$solo_1$*).[6]

[6]Chungmin Lee and Jiyoung Shim (p.c.) pointed out the difference between *-lato* and *-man-i-lato*, and Elena Guerzoni and Maria-Luisa Zubizarreta (p.c.) suggested to me to make it clear the difference between the covert exclusive particle and the overt *–man*.

5.2.2 Concessive Conditionals with Two Variants

The second set of facts leading to a decompositional analysis involves nonfactive concessive conditionals. Bennett (1982) pointed out that concessive conditionals can be classified into two types: those which carry the implication that the consequent is true no matter what, and those which do not. For example, (43) carries the implication that I will take a walk no matter what, whereas (44) does not carry the implication that John would be fired in any case (that is, if John drank no alcohol, he would not be fired). In this paper I call concessive conditionals like (43) factive concessive conditionals, and concessive conditionals like (44) non-factive concessive conditionals.[7]

(43) Even if it rains I will take a walk.
(44) (John's boss is puritanical, so she prohibits any alcohol in her company, and she also prohibits her employees to drink any alcohol)
Even if John drank a glass of wine, he would be fired.

In Korean, concessive conditionals are expressed in the following way.

(45) (i) attaching the additive particle *–to* the antecedent of a conditional instead of the conditional marker *–myen*.

If concessive conditionals are non-factive, then there are two more ways to express the concessive conditionals:

(46) (ii) by attaching the conditional marker *–myen* to the antecedent, and putting *–lato* on the focus in the antecedent.
(iii) by attaching *–to* the antecedent, and putting –man on the focus in the antecedent.

These three ways to express concessive conditionals are shown in (47a, 48a), (47b, 48b), and (47c, 48c), respectively.

(47) a. photocwu [han]$_f$ can-ul masi-e-to ku-nun haykotoy-lkesi-ta.
wine one glass-Acc drink-L-Also he-Top get fired-Fut-Decl
'Even if he drank one glass of wine he would get fired'
Cf.) photocwu [han]$_f$ can-ul masi-myen ku-nun haykotoy-lkesi-ta.
Wine one glass-Acc drink-Cond he-Top get fired-Fut-Decl
'If he drank one glass of wine he would get fired.'
b. photocwu [han]$_f$ can-i-lato masi-myen ku-nun haykotoy-l kes-i-ta.
wine one glass-L-lato drink-Cond he-Top get fired-Fut-Decl
c. photocwu [han]$_f$ can-man masi-e-to ku-nun haykotoy-l kes-i-ta.
wine one glass-Only drink-L-Also he-Top get fired-Fut-Decl

[7]Bennett (1982) employs the term 'standing-if' and 'introduced-if' to refer to non-factive concessive conditionals and factive concessive conditionals, respectively.

(48) a. ai [han]$_F$ myeng-ul nah-a-to ywuka ciwen-ul pat-ul swu iss-ulkesi-ta.
child one CL-Acc give birth-L-Also child support-Acc get-be able to-Fut-Decl
'Even if you have one child you can get the child support'
b. ai [han]$_F$ myeng-i-lato nah-u-myen ywuka ciwen-ul pat-ul swu iss-ulkesi-ta.
child one CL-L-lato give birth-L-Cond child support-Acc get-be able to-Fut-Decl
c. ai [han]$_F$ myeng-man nah-a-to ywuka ciwen-ul pat-ul swu iss-ulkesi-ta.
child one CL-Only give birth-L-Also child support-Acc get-be able to-Fut-Decl

Interestingly, if the focus is semantically strong, only (i) is possible (49a), and (ii) and (iii) are not. Therefore (49b) and (49c) are unacceptable for most Korean speakers, or do not have the same meaning as (49a) at best. This indicates that *–lato*, as well as *–man*, is incompatible with the semantically strong item.

(49) a. ai [yel]$_F$ myeng-ul nah-a-to ywuka ciwen-ul pat-ulswueps-ulkesi-ta.
child ten CL-Acc give birth-L-Also child support-Acc get-not be able to-Fut-Decl
'Even if you have ten children you cannot get the child support'
b. #ai [yel]$_F$ myeng-i-lato nah-u-myen ywuka ciwen-ul pat-ulswueps-ulkesi-ta.
child ten CL-L-lato give birth-L-Cond child support-Acc get-not be able to-Fut-Decl
c. #ai [yel]$_F$ myeng-man nah-a-to ywuka ciwen-ul pat-ulswueps-ulkesi-ta.
child ten CL-Only give birth-L-Also child support-Acc get-not be able to-Fut-Decl

The examples above show that *–lato* can be paraphrased into *–man* and *–to* in non-factive conditionals, and both of *–lato* and *–man* can only combine with the semantically weak focus.

Turning to factive concessive conditionals, as shown in (50), they can be expressed only by (i), and not by (ii) or (iii), as shown in (50a), (50b), and (50c), respectively.

(50) a. pi-ka [o-a]$_F$-to na-nun sanchayk-ul ha-keyss-ta.
rain-Nom come-L-Also I-Top walk-Acc do-Fut-Decl
'Even if it rains I will take a walk'
b. #[pi]$_F$-lato o-myen na-nun sanchayk-ul ha-keyss-ta.
rain-lato come-Cond I-Top walk-Acc do-Fut-Decl
c. #[pi]$_F$-man o-a-to na-nun sanchayk-ul ha-keyss-ta.
rain-Only come-L-Also I-Top walk-Acc do-Fut-Decl

This can be explained if we follow Guerzoni and Lim's (2006) suggestion, where in factive concessive conditionals, the focus of *even* is associated with the phonetically null head, which expresses the polarity of the sentence. Assuming that the position of this null head is as high as C, and as Höhle (1992) suggested, that this null head is realized as intonational prominence of the main predicate, of the auxiliary verb, or of negation, in (50b) and (50c) the focus is different from (50a), with *–lato* or *–man* overtly being adjacent with the focus.

Summarizing the discussion above, in nonfactive concessive conditionals, *–lato* is equivalent to *–man* and *–to*, which suggests to us that *–lato* can also be decomposed into the exclusive *–man* and the additive *–to*.

5.3 Why **–lato** *Is not* **auch nur** *or* **anche solo***—Difference in Distribution*

Even though there are striking similarities between *–lato*, on the one hand, and *auch nur* and *anche solo*, on the other hand, there are significant differences between them, which prevent us from applying Guerzoni's proposal to *–lato* without any revision. Most of all, as pointed out in the introduction, *–lato* is licensed under attitude predicates and non-counterfactual modals (relevant examples are repeated below).

(51) Attitude: belief

a. Na-nun John-i [Bill]$_F$-eykey-lato cenhwaha-ess-ta-ko mit-nun-ta.
I-Top John-Nom Bill-Dat-lato make a phone call-Past-Decl-Comp believe-Pres-Decl
'I believe John even called Bill'

b. na-nun John-i pap [han]$_f$ swutkalak-i-lato mek-ess-ta-ko mit-nun-ta.
I-Top John-Nom meal one spoon-L-lato eat-Past-Decl-Comp believe-Pres-Decl
'I believe John even ate one spoon of meal'

c. ??na-nun John-i pap [yel]$_f$ kulus-i-lato mek-ess-ta-ko mit-nun-ta.
I-Top John-Nom rice ten bowl-L-lato eat-Past-Decl-Comp believe-Pres-Decl
'I believe John even ate ten bowls of meal'

(52) Modal: possibility (epistemic)

a. John-i sakwa [han]$_f$ kay-lato mek-ess-ul kanungseng-i iss-ta,
John-Nom apple one CL-lato eat-Past-Rel possibility-Nom exist-Decl.
'It is possible that John ate even one apple'

b. #John-i sakwa [100]$_f$ kay-lato mek-ess-ul kanungseng-i iss-ta.
John-Nom apple 100 CL-lato eat-Past-Rel possibility-Nom exist-Decl.
'It is possible that John ate even one hundred apples'

This shows that Korean *–lato* is different from German *auch nur* or Italian *anche solo*, because it is reported that neither *auch nur* nor *anche solo* appear under these contexts (Guerzoni 2006: 17):

(53) a. Ich glaube #(nicht) dass du auch nur die Maria begrüsst hast.
I believe not that you also only the Mary greet have

b. #Es ist möglich dass der Hans auch nur die Maria begrüsst.
It is possible that the Hans also only the Mary greets.

6 Solving the Puzzle

To account for the apparently contradicting facts, I would like to propose that the difference between *–lato* and *auch nur/anche solo* is due to the fact that *-to* in *–lato* carries presuppositions different from the ones that *also/auch/anche* carry. The lexical entries for the covert exclusive particle *–man*$_2$ and the additive particle *–to* are shown in (54) and (55), respectively.

(54) $[[\textit{-man}_2]]^w(C)(p) = [[\textit{nur}_2/\textit{solo}_2]]^w(C)(p)$ is defined iff

(i) p is the most likely/insignificant proposition in C	scalarity
(ii) there is no other q in C that is true (unless p entails q)	exclusivity
If defined, then $[[\textit{nur}_2/\textit{solo}_2]]^w(C)(p)$ is true iff p(w)=1	factivity

(55) $[[\textit{-to}]]^w(C)(p)$ is defined iff

(i) $\exists q\, [q \in C \wedge q \neq p] \wedge \underline{q(w) \neq 0}$	(weak) additivity
(ii) p is the LEAST likely proposition in C	scalarity
If defined, then $[[\textit{-to}]]^w(C)(p) = p(w)$	

In this proposal, *-man*$_2$ shares the same lexical entry as Guerzoni's *nur*$_2$/*solo*$_2$, but *-to* is different from *auch/anche/also* in two respects. First, as in (55ii), *-to* introduces the same scalar presupposition as Karttunen and Peters' (1979) *even*, unlike what has been assumed about other additive particles like *also*. Second, the additive presupposition of *–to* is weaker than the additive presupposition of *auch/anche/also*, in that it only requires that there be an alternative proposition different from the prejacent which is *not false* (i.e., either *true* or *undefined*), while *auch* requires the existence of a true alternative. In the following subsections I will show how this lexical difference explains the distribution and meaning of *–lato*.

6.1 Simple Affirmative Sentences

Let us begin with the simple affirmative sentence (56).

(56) ??John-un [Bill]$_F$-i-lato manna-ess-ta.
John-Top Bill-L-*lato* meet-Past-Decl
(Intended reading: 'John even met [Bill]$_F$.')

My account predicts that (56) is unacceptable because of the contradiction between the presupposition of the covert exclusive particle *–man*$_2$ and that of the overt additive particle *–to*, like Guerzoni's account for *auch nur/anche solo*. However, I claim that, unlike *auch nur/anche solo*, presuppositions in contradiction in *–lato* are the scalar ones rather than the existential ones. (57) shows this point.

(57) Scalarity
LF:

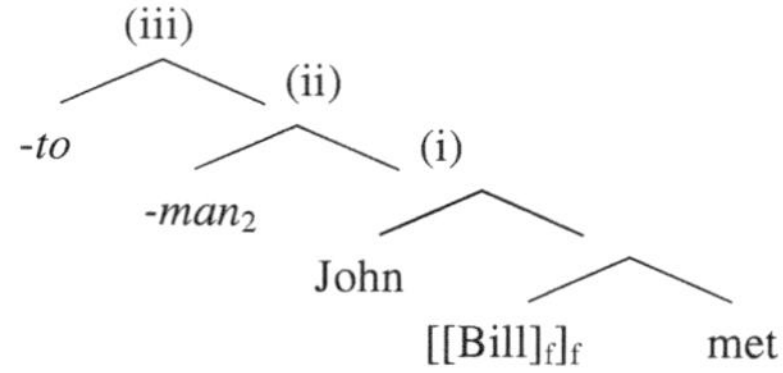

(i): $[[(i)]]^{o}(w) = 1$ iff John met Bill in w
$[[(i)]]^{f}(w) = \{\lambda w.\ J.\ \text{met } x \text{ in } w\text{: } x \in D_e\}$
(ii): $[[(ii)]]^{o}(w)$ is defined if B. is the MOST likely for J. to meet in w
(iii): $[[(iii)]]^{o}(w)$ is defined iff
B. is the MOST likely person in w for J. to meet. (from *man*$_2$)
AND B. is the LEAST likely person in w for J. to meet. (from *–to*) (⊥)

In (57), since the two focus particles take essentially the same scope, in (iii), we derive the scalar presupposition that Bill is the most likely person for John to meet, due to the presence of *–man*$_2$; and at the same time, we also derive the scalar presupposition that Bill is the least likely person for John to meet, because of the presence of *–to*. Therefore, we get the presupposition clash.

On the other hand, (58) shows, unlike in *auch nur* or *anche solo*, there is no clash between the exclusive presupposition of *–man*$_2$ and the additive presupposition of *–to* due to the weakness of the latter.

(58) (Weak) additivity and exclusivity
LF:

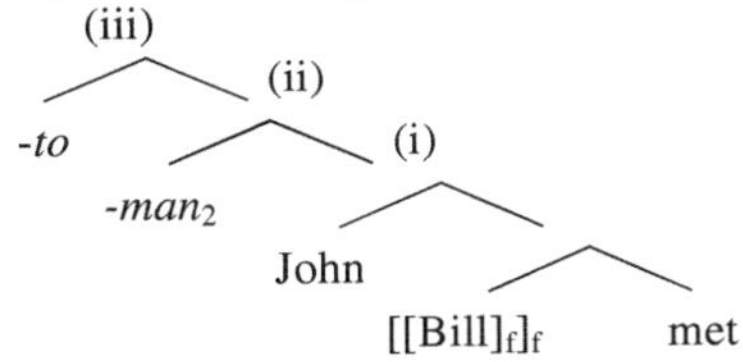

(i): $[[(i)]]^{o}(w) = 1$ iff John met Bill in w
$[[(i)]]^{f}(w) = \{\lambda w.\ J.\ \text{met } x \text{ in } w\text{: } x \in D_e\}$
(ii): $[[(ii)]]^{o}(w)$ is defined iff $\sim \exists x \neq$ B. s.t. J. met x
$[[(ii)]]^{f}(w) = \{\lambda w\text{: } \sim \exists y \neq x$ s.t. J. met y in w. John met x in w: $x \in D_e\}$
(iii): $[[(iii)]]^{o}(w)$ is defined iff
John met no one different from Bill (from *man*$_2$)
AND for some $x \neq$ Bill, [λw': John met no one $\neq$ x.
John met x](w) = 1 or undefined (from *–to*)

The focus value of (i) in (58) is a set of alternatives determined by the focus on *Bill*. Turning to (ii), the interpretation of this constituent comes with the definedness condition introduced by *man*$_2$ that is that John met Bill and no one else. Given this, the focus value of this same constituent is going to be a set of alternatives, each coming with a similar definedness condition. Specifically, each alternative is defined iff John met no individual different from the one substituted for Bill in that alternative. Given this, and given that the assertion entails that John met Bill, all alternatives different from the prejacent will turn out to be undefined, a situation that trivially satisfies the weak additive presupposition of *–to*, hence no clash. Therefore, we can safely conclude that, within this analysis, scalarity is the only factor ruling out (56).

This conclusion leads us to a very interesting and novel prediction: if we can construct examples where the relative scope of the two particles makes the scalar presuppositions of *–to* and *–man*$_2$ compatible, we expect that example to be grammatical. The prediction is correct, as this is exactly what happens when moving *–to* outside the scope of modals, attitude predicates, and long-distance negation. As an illustration, in the following subsection I will show how the presupposition clash between two scalar presuppositions can be resolved via movement in modalized sentences.

6.2 Modals

Consider the following example.

(59) John-i [Bill]$_f$-i-lato manna-totoy-n-ta.
John-Nom Bill-L-*lato* meet-may-Pres-Decl
'John may meet even Bill.'

The additive presupposition of *–to* and the exclusive presupposition of the hidden *-man*$_2$ are going to be compatible with each other, regardless of the position of *–to* at LF. (60) shows that two scalar presuppositions are compatible each other if *–to* moves above the modal.

(60) Scalarity
LF:

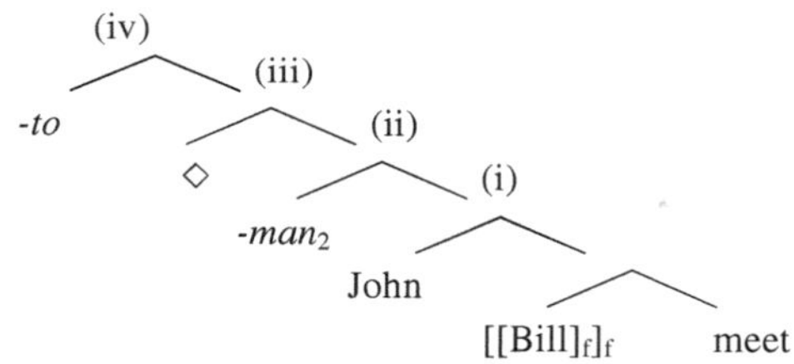

(i): $[[(i)]]^o(w) = 1$ iff John meet Bill in w
$[[(i)]]^f(w) = \{\lambda w.$ John meet x in w: $x \in D_e\}$
(ii): $[[(ii)]]^o(w)$ is defined iff $\sim \exists x \neq$ Bill such that John meet x
$[[(ii)]]^f(w) = \{\lambda w: \sim \exists y \neq x$ s.t. John met y in w. John meet x in w: $x \in D_e\}$
(iii): $[[(iii)]]^o(w)$ is defined iff B. is the most likely for J. to meet in w
If defined, $[[(iii)]]^o(w) = 1$ iff J. is allowed to meet B. in w.
$[[(iii)]]^f(w) = \{\lambda w$: B. is the most likely person for J. to meet in w. $\exists w'$, John is allowed to meet x in w': $x \in D_e\}$
(iv): $[[(iv)]]^o(w)$ is defined iff
B. is **the most likely person for J. to meet in w (due to *–man*$_2$)**
AND B. is **the least likely person for J. to be allowed to meet (due to *-to*).**

As in (60), the two scalar presuppositions are 'Bill is the most likely person for John to meet in w' (due to man_2) and 'Bill is the least likely person for John to be allowed to meet in w.' (due to *to*) One can easily think about a scenario where these presuppositions are simultaneously true, like (61):

(61) John is an interviewer of a local newspaper, and it is typically prohibited for interviewers to get close to the secret agents. Bill, one in John's neighborhood, is indeed a secret agent. However, since Bill happens to be John's closest neighbor, it is really hard for John to avoid Bill.

In this situation, it is true that (among the neighbors) Bill is the most likely person for John to meet, given the locations of their respective homes, and yet it is also true that Bill is the least likely person (among the neighbors) for John to be allowed to meet, due to their respective professions.

The same reasoning can be applied to necessity modals and attitude predicates, since one can also think about scenarios where Bill is the most likely person for John to meet as well as the least likely person for John to be required to meet, or for some to believe that John met him, etc.

6.3 *Quantifiers*[8]

The discussion about modals raises another problem about quantifiers. Modals can be considered quantifiers over possible worlds, and under modals the clash between scalar presuppositions of *–man* and *–to* can be resolved, we might also expect that the presupposition clash of *–lato* should be resolved under usual quantifiers, such as *nwukwunka* 'someone' or *motun* 'every.' This prediction is not borne out, however. (i) is still unacceptable even though *–lato* appears under the scope of the quantifier *nwukwunka* 'someone':

(61) # nwukwunka-ka	$[\text{Mary}]_F$-lato	manna-ess-ta.
someone-Nom	Mary-*lato*	meet-Past-Decl

This problem may be resolved if we adopt Heim's (1988) theory of presupposition projection under the scope of quantifiers, according to which a universal presupposition is derived in the scope of quantifiers. For example, in Heim (1998), the lexical entry for *some* is (62).

(62) $[[\text{some}]] = \lambda P.\lambda Q$: $\forall x P(x)$, $x \in \text{Dom}_Q$. $\exists y[P(y) \& Q(y)]$

(63) shows why under this lexical entry the presupposition clash emerges.

[8]The problem in this subsection was originally pointed out by Daniel Büring (p.c.).

(63) LF:

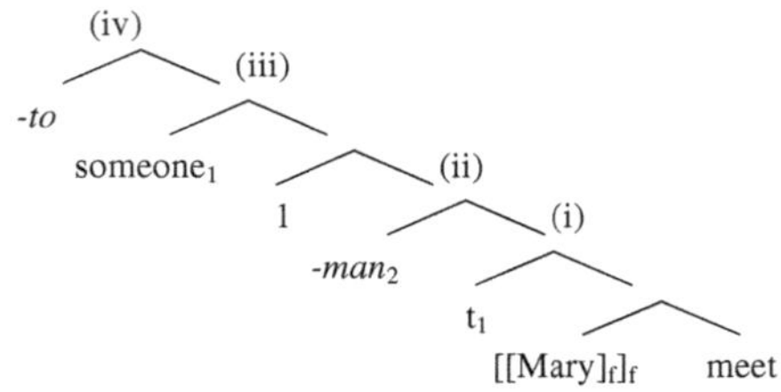

Assertion at (i): λw. g(1) met Mary in w
Assertion at (ii): λw.g(1) met Maryin w
Presupposition at (ii): g(1) met no one different from Mary (exclusive presupposition of *-man$_2$*)
& Mary was the most likely for g(1) to meet. (scalar presupposition of *man$_2$*)
Assertion at (iii): Someone met Mary
Presupposition at (iii): Everyone met no one different from Mary (exclusive presupposition of *man$_2$*)
& Mary was the most likely for everyone to meet (scalar presupposition of *man$_2$*)
Assertion at (iv): Someone met Mary
Presupposition at (iv): Everyone met no one different from Mary (exclusive presupposition of *man$_2$*)
& Mary was the most likely for everyone to meet (scalar presupposition of *man$_2$*)
& There was someone x different from Mary such that if everyone met no one different from that person, and if x was most likely for everyone to meet, then someone met x (weak additive presupposition of *to*)
& Mary was the least likely for someone to meet (scalar presupposition of *to*)

In Heim's (1988) theory of presupposition projection, under quantifiers a universal presupposition is projected. This assumption is applied to (63), where presuppositions introduced by *–man$_2$* in (ii) are projected in (iii), the variable g(1) is replaced by universal quantifiers, resulting in presuppositions that everyone met no one different from Mary (exclusive one), and Mary was the most likely person for everyone to meet (scalar one). The scalar presupposition of *–man$_2$* therefore clashes with the scalar presupposition introduced by *–to* (these two presuppositions are underlined in 63): according to the scalar presupposition introduced by *–man$_2$* Mary was the most likely for everyone in the domain to meet, whereas according to the scalar presupposition introduced by *–to* Mary was the least likely for someone in the domain to meet.

6.4 Local Negation

In this last subsection I would like to return to the case of *–lato* under local negation.

(64) a. #John -un [aiskhulim]$_f$-i-lato mek-cianh-ass-ta.
John-Top ice cream-L-*lato* eat-neg-Past-Decl
b. John did not eat any ice cream. (English)

Why does local negation matter? While the analysis proposed so far explains most cases of unacceptability of *–lato* in terms of an unavoidable conflict between the two scalar presuppositions of *–to* and *–man,* respectively, in cases like (64) the scope of *–to* above negation could in principle resolve the contradiction. Given this, facts like (64) still await an explanation. Here I adopt Nakanishi's (2006) proposal on Japanese *–dake-demo* 'only even.' The following example (from Nakanishi 2006: 290) shows that *–dake-demo*, like *–lato*, is unacceptable under local negation.

(65) *John-wa [sono hon]$_F$-dake-demo yom-ana-katta.
John-TOP that book-only-even read-NEG-PAST
(Intended reading: 'John even read [that book]$_f$.')

Nakanishi (2006), whose view on *–dake-demo* is otherwise fully parallel to Guerzoni's (2003, 2006) analysis of *auch nur* and *anche solo*, provides a convincing explanation for cases like (65), which is missing in Guerzoni's theory (and in fact is not applicable in the analysis of German and Italian). Nakanishi notes that Japanese negation always takes scope under *–dake* 'only' and *-demo* 'even,' as shown in (66) and (67), respectively.

(66) (from Nakanishi 2006: 291, ex. 7)
John-wa [Hon A]$_F$-dake yom-ana-katta.
John-Top Book A-only read-Neg-Past
'John did not only read Book A.'
(= John read everything except Book A)

(67) (from Nakanishi 2006: 291, ex. 8)
a. John-wa [Hon A]$_F$ {-mo/-demo} yonda-wake-de-wa-nai.
John-TOP Book A {even/-even} read-it is not the case
'It is not the case that John even read Book A.'
b. LF: [not [even C [John read [Book A]$_F$]]] ¬ > even

Given this, Nakanishi (2006) argues that both *–dake* and *–demo* in *–dake-demo* take wide scope over local negation, and the clash between two scalar presuppositions remains unresolved when they both combine with the negative proposition. (68) shows Korean *–man* also always takes wide scope over negation:

(68) John-un [Barriers]$_f$-man an ilk-ess-ta.[9]
John-Top *Barriers*-only neg read-Past-Decl
'John read everything except *Barriers*' Only > Neg, *Neg > Only

Based on this, I propose that local negation always takes narrow scope with respect to *–lato*, which makes it impossible to resolve the presupposition clash by moving *–to* in *–lato* to take a different scope from *–man*$_2$.

---

[9]To avoid confusion here I use so-called short-form negation in Korean. In the case of long-form negation, the scope between *–man* and negation varies depending on the intonational cue.

John-un Barriers-*man* *ilk-cianh-ass-ta.*
John-Top *Barriers*-only read-neg-Past-Decl
a. *John-un* *[*Barriers*]$_f$-man* *ilk-cianh-ass-ta.*
'John read everything except *Barriers.*' Only > Neg
b. *John-un* Barriers-*man* *ilk-[ci]$_f$anh-ass-ta.*
'John read not only *Barriers* (but other books).' Neg > Only

Since *–lato* is accompanied with an intonational cue, we may still conclude that both particles in *-lato* always takes wide scope over local negation.

7 *–lato* and Free-Choice Effect

In this section I would like to briefly discuss the cases where *–lato* shows free-choice effect. As thoroughly examined in Choi (2007), *–lato* can combine with *amwu* 'any' or other wh-quantifiers like *nwukwu* 'someone/who', *mwues* 'something/what' or *etten* 'certain/which', behaving like free-choice (FC) items *any* NP in English, as indicated in the interpretation of (69):

(69) John-un amwu/etten-koki-lato mek-elswuiss-ta.
John-Top any/what-meat-lato eat-may/can-Decl
'John is allowed to eat meat: every meat is a possible eating option for John.'
(Choi 2007: 318)

Choi (2007) pointed out that the decompositional analysis of *–lato* given in this paper does not capture the FC flavor of *amwu* (NP) *lato*. For example, the presuppositions introduced by *–lato* with the lexical entry given above are shown in (70) where, according to her, we cannot derive the FC effect.

(70) a. LF:[- *to* [◇ [-man [John eats *amwu-/wh*-meat]]]]
b. ExclP of *–man* : John eats nothing different from *amwu-/wh*-meat
c. ScalarP of *–man*: *Amwu-/wh*-meat is the most likely meat for John to eat.
d. ScalarP of *–to*: *Amwu-/wh*-meat is the least likely for J. to be allowed to eat.
e. Weak Additivity of *–to*: There was an x different from *amwu-/wh*-meat such that if John eats nothing different from *amwu-/wh*-meat, and if x was the most likely meat for John to eat, then John is allowed to eat x.
(Choi 2007: 315ff)

To solve this problem, Choi (2007) claims, in parallel with Guerzoni's (2003, 2006) analysis of *auch nur* and *anche solo* (and therefore mine), that *–lato* introduces three different presuppositions: the exclusive one, the additive one, and the scalar one. Unlikely to those analyses, however, Choi (2007) also claims that: (i) *–lato* does not introduce a weak additive presupposition, but the (standard) additive presupposition, and ii) the exclusive presupposition is not projected globally, but is accommodated locally. For instance, in Choi (2007), the presupposition introduced by *–lato* in (69) will be as (71):

(71) a. ScalarP: *Amwu/etten koki* (x), i.e., some meat (x) is the most likely or insignificant (amount/kind of) meat for John to eat.
b. ExclP: There is nothing different from *amwu/etten-koki* (x) that John eats.
c. ExistP: There is some other (amount/kind of) meat (y) such that John is allowed to eat y.
d. Assertion (together with locally projected presupposition): It is allowed that there is no different *amwu/etten-koki* (x) that John eats.
(Choi 2007: 318)

Even though in Choi's (2007) framework the FC effect of *amwu* (NP) *lato* may be accounted for, she does not give us a satisfactory explanation of the behavior of *–lato* in general. First of all, as already pointed out by Choi (2007) herself, it is unclear in her analysis what motivates the local accommodation of the exclusive presupposition introduced by *–lato* in modal contexts. Furthermore, Choi's (2007) analysis does not seem to derive the negatively biased yes/no questions. If local accommodation occurs in each of possible answers (in this case, the positive answer and the negative answer),[10] it seems that these accommodated alternatives do not show any clash with the existential presupposition, which is essential to derive the negative bias in Guerzoni's (2003, 2004) analysis (since the exclusive presupposition is accommodated).

One candidate to capture the FC effect in terms of our decompositional analysis is to adopt Chierchia's (2006) proposal of the free-choice items, where the FC items and polarity-sensitive items are analyzed in terms of the domain widening, scalar implicatures, and the alternative sensitive operators corresponding to *only*. More investigations are yet to be done, and at this point we do not know how the free-choice effect of *amwu* (NP) *lato* and *wh-lato* can be derived in our decompositional analysis of *–lato*.

8 Conclusion

In this paper, I argued that*–lato* can be decomposed into two subparts, the covert *–man*$_2$ and the overt *–to*, following decompositional analysis of alleged NPI *even*s, like *auch nur* or *anche solo*. Furthermore, I also argued that *–to* in *–lato* introduces the additive presupposition weaker than that of *also, auch* or *solo*. This decompositional analysis can account for the unique distribution and the semantics of *–lato*, without stipulating any NPI-like behavior.[11] Many questions still remain unanswered, such as the apparent association of *–lato* with either a most likely item and a least likely item, and the recent discussion of *–lato* made by Ginnakidou and Yoon (2011, 2012),[12] but I leave these for future research.

References

An, D.-H. 2007. On the distribution of NPIs in Korean. *Natural Language Semantics* 15: 317–350.

Chierchia, G. 2006. Broaden your views: Implicatures of domain widening and the "Logicality" of Language. *Linguistic Inquiry* 37: 535–590.

Choi, J. 2007. *Free choice and negative polarity: A compositional analysis of korean polarity sensitive items*. Doctoral Dissertation, University of Pennsylvania.

von Fintel, K. 1999. NPI-Licensing, Strawson entailment, and context dependency. *Journal of Semantics* 16: 97–148.

Giannakiou, A. 1998. *Polarity sensitivity as (Non)veridical dependency*. Amsterdam, Netherland and Philadelphia, US: John Benjamins.

[10]Following Guerzoni (2003, 2004), we assume Hamblin's (1973) and Karttunen's (1977) semantics of questions.

[11]Lee (1996, 1999, 2003) analyzes *–lato* in terms of concessivity, but I do not have space and time to review them in this paper – I hope to investigate this issue further in the consequent works.

[12]I thank the anonymous reviewer for raising these issues.

Giannakidou, A. 2007. The landscape of *EVEN*. *Natural Language & Linguistic Theory* 25: 27–81.
Giannakidou, A., and Suwon Yoon. 2011. Referential vagueness and negative polarity. CLS 47.
Giannakidou, A., and Suwon Yoon. 2012. *Weakening and reanalysis of EVEN in non-emphatic negative polarity items: evidence from Greek and Korean*. Manuscript: University of Chicago and University of Texas Arlington.
Guerzoni, E. 2003. *Why even ask? On the pragmatics of questions and the semantics of answers*. Doctoral Dissertation, MIT.
Guerzoni, E. 2004. *Even*-NPIs in Yes/no questions. *Natural Language Semantics* 12: 319–343.
Guerzoni, E. 2006. Scalarity in focus: Scalar participles in romance & germanic languages. Handout presented in University of Konstanz, February 13, 2006.
Guerzoni, E., and D. Lim. 2006. *Even if*, factivity, and focus. In *Proceedings of Sinn und Bedeutung*, E. Puig-Waldmüller, Vol. 11, 276–290.
Hamblin, C.L. 1973. Questions in Montague grammar. *Foundations of Language* 10: 143–152.
Heim, I. 1988. On the projection problem for presuppositions, In *Proceedings of the Second West Coast Conference on Formal Linguistics*, D. Flickinger et al., 114–125. Stanford: Stanford University Press. (Reprinted In Steven Davis (ed.) 1991. *Pragmatics: A Reader*, pp. 397-405. Oxford: Oxford University Press).
Heim, I., and A. Kratzer. 1998. *Semantics in Generative Grammar*. London: Blackwell.
Herburger, E. 2001. The negative concord puzzle revisited. *Natural Language Semantics* 9: 289–333.
Horn, L. 1969. A presuppositional approach to *only* and *even*. *In Proceedings of the Chicago Linguistic Society* 5: 98–107.
Höhle, T.N. 1992. Über Verum-Fokus im Deutschen. *Linguistische Berichte, Sonderheft* 4: 112–141.
Karttunen, L., and S. Peters. 1979. Conventional implicature. In *Syntax and semantics 11: Presuppositions*, ed. C.-K. Oh, and D. Dinneen, 1–56. New York: Academic Press.
Lahiri, U. 1998. Focus and negative polarity in Hindi. *Natural Language Semantics* 6: 57–123.
Lahiri, U. 2006. Scope, presuppositions and dimensions of meaning: Some observations on scalar additive particles in English, Hindi and Spanish. Handout presented in Sinn und Bedeutung 11, Barcelona, Spain.
Lee, C. 1996. Negative polarity items in English and Korean. *Language Sciences* 18: 505–523.
Lee, C. 1999. Types of NPIs and nonveridicality in korean and other languages. In *Syntax at Sunset 2: UCLA Working Papers in Linguistics*, ed. G. Storto, Vol. 3.
Lee, C. 2003. Negative polarity items and free choice in Korean and Japanese: A contrastive study. *Bilingualism* 22: 1–48.
Lee, C., D. Chung, and S. Nam. 2000. The Semantics of *amwu* N-*to*/-*irato*/-*ina* in Korean—Arbitrary Choice and Concession. *Language and Information* 4: 107–123.
Lim, D. 2009. The Korean Focus Particle -*lato* and Weak Additivity. In *Proceedings of the 18th International Congress of Linguists*. Linguistic Society of Korea.
Lim, D. 2010. A decompositional analysis of the Korean Focus particle -*lato*. In *Japanese/Korean Linguistics 17*, ed. S. Iwasaki, H. Hoji, P.M. Clancy, and S.-O. Sohn. Stanford: CSLI Publications.
Nakanishi, K. 2006. The semantics of *Even* and negative polarity items in Japanese. In *Proceedings of the 25th West Coast Conference on Formal Linguistics*, ed. D. Baumer, D. Montero, and M. Scanlon, 288–296. Somerville, MA: Cascadilla Proceedings Project.
Rooth, M. 1985. *Association with focus*. Doctoral Dissertation, University of Massachusetts at Amherst.
Rullmann, H. 1997. *Even*, polarity and scope. In *Papers in experimental and theoretical linguistics*, ed. M. Gibson, G. Wiebe, and G. Libben, Vol. 4, 40–64.
Rullmann, H. 2003. Additive particles and polarity. *Journal of Semantics* 20: 329–401.
Schwarz, B. 2005. Scalar additive particles in negative contexts. *Natural Language Semantics* 13: 125–168.
Wilkinson, K. 1996. The scope of *Even*. *Natural Language Semantics* 4: 193–215.
Yang, I. 1973. *Semantics of delimiters*. *Language Research* 9: 84–121.

Negative Entailment, Positive Implicature and Polarity Items

Mingya Liu

Abstract In this paper, I argue that pragmatics plays a role in the (anti-)licensing of polarity items in addition to semantic notions such as downward monotonicity and anti-additivity. In the case of positive polarity items (PPIs), I argue that they can co-occur with the anti-additive quantifier *no N* if intonation or enriched context makes it a contrastive negation or denial. The anti-licensing fails due to a positive implicature (PI) that performs pragmatic licensing and it is to this PI that PPIs contribute their meaning. As for negative polarity items (NPIs), I focus on the case of *only* that is not straightforwardly downward monotonic but licenses NPIs. Following Horn (2002), I assume that *only* is semantically conjunctive and that it licenses NPIs by its exclusive entailment that is negative. In addition to Horn's arguments, I provide further arguments with domain-widening NPIs such as *any*, *ever* and minimizers that it is not to the prejacent but to the exclusive entailment that they contribute their domain widening (Kadmon and Landman 1993) function. In other words, the problem of *only* for NPI theories does not lie in the notion of downward monotonicity but in the compact packaging of two propositions with different monotonicity properties in one single sentence.

Keywords Polarity items • *Only* • Positive implicature • Negative exclusive entailment • Domain widening • Truth conditions

The study of polarity effects in natural language goes back at least as early as Bolinger (1960). There have been many fruitful results ever since, but none of them is perfect or exhaustive in its explanatory force. In this paper, I will compare two special cases in terms of polarity licensing, namely, one where the anti-additive quantifier *no N* fails to anti-license positive polarity items (PPIs) and the other where *only* licenses negative polarity items (NPIs). The central thesis is that polarity items can be pragmatically licensed, 'pragmatically' meaning beyond the logic of a

---

M. Liu (✉)
University of Osnabrück, Wachsbleiche 27, 49090 Osnabrück, Germany
e-mail: liu.mingya@uni-osnabrueck.de

C. Lee et al. (eds.), *Contrastiveness in Information Structure, Alternatives and Scalar Implicatures*, Studies in Natural Language and Linguistic Theory 91, DOI 10.1007/978-3-319-10106-4_11

single proposition, either by discourse or by the lexical semantics and pragmatics of the licensors.

In Sect. 1, I will discuss to what extent the parallelism between NPIs and PPIs is (un-)justified. In Sect. 2, I propose that if *no N* is used as contrastive negation or denial, a positive implicature (PI) arises in discourse that renders the presence of PPIs possible. I assume that an *only* sentence (without extra negation) entails a prejacent and an exclusive proposition and the two entailments contrast with each other in their logical properties, i.e. the exclusive is downward-entailing (DE) and the prejacent non-DE. This difference in polarity between the two entailments is the cause of all the complications that arise with *only* licensing NPIs. Strawson-DEness (von Fintel 1999) does not account for this fact, but is a consequence of it. My assumptions actually echo Atlas-Horn's two-entailment approach for *only*. However, I argue for a solution without turning to Horn's (2002, 2017) distinction between an asserted (i.e. at-issue) entailment and an inert (i.e. non-at-issue) entailment, namely, by admitting that NPIs such as *any*, *ever*, *lift a finger* contribute to a sentence's truth conditions by domain widening (Kadmon and Landman 1993), but only of the DE proposition in the case of *only*. It follows that *only* and *no N* license NPIs and PPIs respectively, the former by its complex lexical meaning and the latter by its collaboration with discourse into an un-anti-licensing context. A comparison between them and universal quantifiers is made in Sect. 4. The last section offers concluding remarks. Throughout the paper, examples are in English or in German.

1 NPI-PPI (A)Symmetry

NPIs are items that tend to only occur in negative contexts and PPIs are items that tend to only occur in positive contexts. For example, as (1) shows, the NPI *either* needs licensing by negation, as otherwise it would be unlicensed and the sentence would be ungrammatical; the PPI *too* is fine in an affirmative sentence, and would be anti-licensed by negation and the sentence would be at least odd. In all examples henceforth, boldfaced words are NPI licensors and underlined words are either NPIs or PPIs.

(1) a. *The King of France is* *(***not***) *bald,* <u>*either*</u>.
b. *The King of France is* (****not***) *bald,* <u>*too*</u>.

NPIs and PPIs also show oppositional behaviors towards external negation, i.e. what Karttunen and Peters (1979) call contradiction negation or what Horn (1989) calls metalinguistic negation. In (2), negation is not used descriptively (or truth-functionally), but metalinguistically to cancel the existence presupposition of the definite NP 'the King of France', namely, that there is a king of France, therefore, the NPI *either* is not licensed and the PPI *too* is not anti-licensed.

(2) a. *The King of France is* **not** *bald, *either—(because) there is no king of France.*
b. *The King of France is* **not** *bald, too—(because) there is no king of France.*

Due to this symmetry, NPI-licensing contexts are often taken as potential anti-licensors of PPIs. However, extending the theories of NPIs to PPIs does not always succeed, because these two categories do differ in certain nontrivial aspects, two of which I will discuss here.

First, many works on NPIs attempt to generalize the key logical property of their licensing contexts that include not only negation but a variety of other semantic or pragmatic environments. The most influential proposal is made by Ladusaw (1979), who marks NPI licensing contexts as downward entailing (DE), which covers *not*, n-words (*nobody, nothing, never*), *few, hardly, without*, conditionals, etc. (3) contains a formal definition with an example: *few*, as a function λu.few(u, call), is downward entailing as law students is a subset of students and (3a) entails (3b).

(3) A function *f* is downward entailing iff for all x, y in its domain such that x => y, f(y) => f(x).
a. ***Few*** *students called.* ⇒
b. ***Few*** *law students called.*

However, the DEness seems to be just necessary but insufficient to anti-license PPIs. As Szabolcsi (2004) points out, it is not DEness but anti-additivity (AA) that PPIs detest. (4) provides a formal definition and an illustration with the AA operator *no one*. In the examples cited in (5), *few* and *at most n* are both DE quantifiers while *not* and *no one* are both AA: they show different co-occuring possibilities with the PPI *someone*.

(4) A function *f* is anti-additive iff for all x, y in its domain such that $f(x \cup y) = f(x) \cap f(y)$
a. ***No one*** *sang or danced.* =
b. ***No one*** *sang and* ***no one*** *danced.*

(5) a. **John* ***didn't*** *call someone.*
b. ****No one*** *called someone.*
c. ***Few people*** *called* ***someone.***
d. ***At most five boys*** *called someone.* (Szabolcsi 2004: 414)

The second aspect where NPIs and PPIs differ is that sentences with unlicensed NPIs are ungrammatical and not repairable, as (6) shows, whereas sentences with anti-licensed PPIs are often only pragmatically odd, such as (7a) and (8a), and therefore repairable by intonation or enriched context, as shown by (7b) and the dialogue in (8b). Recent experimental studies also report different ERP components for positive and negative polarity violations that hint towards different mechanisms underlying the processing of NPIs and PPIs (Saddy et al. 2004; Yurchenko et al. 2013).

(6) a. **John ever came.*
b. **John is handsome at all.*

(7) a. ?*John did* ***not*** *already come.*
b. *John did* ***not*** *already come. In fact, he is quite late.*

(8) a. ?*John is* ***not*** *pretty handsome.*
b. A: *John is pretty handsome.*
B: *He is* ***not*** *pretty handsome. He is very handsome.*

To summarize, the co-occurrence of some PPIs with AA contexts seems not to be ruled out categorically: PPIs do appear with contrastive negation or denial. It is exactly these cases that the next section focuses on.

2 *No N*, Positive Implicature and PPIs

The intuition that a purely semantic approach would not work for PPIs is based on the observation that as (9) and (10) from German show, although *nobody/niemand* and *no N/kein N* are both AA operators, they show different behaviors in terms of PPIs (anti-)licensing. In both (9) and (10), the b-example sounds more natural than the a-example.

(9) a. ***Nobody*** *would rather stay on unemployment.*
b. ***No linguist*** *would rather stay on unemployment.*

(10) a. ***Niemand*** *bekräftigte die Notwendigkeit des Klimaschutzes.*
nobody asserted the necessity of the climate protection
'Nobody asserted the necessity of climate protection.'
b. ***Kein Politiker*** *bekräftigte die Notwendigkeit des Klimaschutzes.*
no politician asserted the necessity of the climate protection
'No politician asserted the necessity of climate protection.'

I propose that *kein F G* 'no F G' asserts $[\forall x(F(x) \rightarrow \neg G(x))]$ and can induce a positive implicature (PI) $[\exists x(\neg F(x) \wedge G(x))]$ that derivatively licenses the PPI in the G position. The PI is a conversational implicature and thus cancellable. It obtains for example by intonation or through enriched context such as contrastive negation in (11).

(11) a. ***No*** *[**linguist**] would rather stay on unemployment. Some [poets] do.*
b. ***Kein*** *[**Politiker**] bekräftigte die Notwendigkeit des Klimaschutzes,*
no politician asserted the necessity of the climate protection
einige [Wissenschaftler] allerdings schon.
some scientists though yet
'No politician asserted the necessity of climate protection, but some scientists did.'

Szabolcsi (2004) keeps contrastive negation or denial out of her generalization about PPIs: "PPIs do not occur in the immediate scope of a clausemate anti-additive operator AA-Op, unless [AA-Op > PPI] itself is in an NPI-licensing context" (Szabolcsi 2004: 419). This at least covers the three cases in (12): the PPI adverb *durchaus* 'quite' is anti-licensed in (12a). It is shielded from anti-licensing in (12b), as it is embedded in the adjective phrase and therefore not in the "immediate scope" of the anti-additive operator *niemand* 'nobody'. In fact, if we compute the logical form of (12b), it is clear that the PPI scopes out of the negative element. In the case of double negation such as (12c), they cancel each other out so that the PPI verb *bekräftigen* 'assert' still sounds fine in the sentence.

(12) I. Anti-licensing

a. ****Niemand*** *war mit dem Ergebnis durchaus zufrieden.*
nobody was with the result quite happy
'Nobody was quite happy with the result.'

II. Shielding: [∃x(x is quite useful)¬∃y(y was happy at x)]

b. ***Niemand*** *war mit dem durchaus brauchbaren Ergebnis zufrieden.*
nobody was with the quite useful result happy
'Nobody was happy with the quite useful result.'

III. Double negation

c. ***Niemand*** *bekräftigte* ***nicht*** *die Notwendigkeit des Klimaschutzes.*
nobody asserted not the necessity of the climate protection
'Nobody did not assert the necessity of climate protection.'

Nevertheless, Szabolcsi mentions Horn's (1989) analysis of denial as metalinguistic negation and Anastasia Giannakidou's suggestion that "denial counts extraclausal negation" (Szabolcsi 2004: 413). All in all, this leads to the conclusion that to account for cases such as (9)–(12), we need discourse logic involving either a preceding utterance (or a presupposed expectation) and the denial of it, or two utterances contrasting in polarity at the topic position. This means that although the PPI appears in a negative sentence, it should be interpreted in the logical form of a corresponding positive sentence. To put it informally, in (11b) the presence of the PPI verb *bekräftigen* 'assert' is justified as the event of asserting does exist although the agent is not any politician but some scientists. Similarly, in (11a) the predication with the PPI *would rather* is attributed to *poets*.

Based on these, I revise Szabocsi's generalization as in (13). (13i) covers the case of double negation. (13ii) is about pragmatic licensing of PPIs, for example by denial or contrastive negation.

(13) A PPI does not occur in the immediate scope of a clausemate AA operator, unless:
i. there is another negative operator available to cancel out the AA operator, or
ii. there is a positive implicature available to perform derivative licensing.

(14a) and (14b) show that if a contrastive focus (CF) intonation is applied to the NP, both sentences sound better than before as the speaker either denies, for instance, a presupposed utterance or an expectation that 'Students would rather speak Swabian' or 'Heidi Klum is quite pretty', or else implicates that some people other than students would rather speak Swabian or someone other than Heidi Klum is quite pretty.

(14) a. ***Kein*** *[Student]*$_{CF}$ *spricht lieber Schwäbisch.*

No student speaks rather Swabian.

'No student would rather speak Swabian.'

b. *[Heidi Klum]*$_{CF}$ *ist* ***nicht*** *durchaus hübsch.*

Heidi Klum is not quite pretty

'Heidi Klum is not quite pretty.'

I will now move to the case of *only* licensing NPIs and show that the mechanism involved there is very similar to that with contrastive negation un-anti-licensing PPIs, namely, both involve two propositions that contrast with each other in polarity at the topic position, where the polarity item is licensed at the proposition of appropriate polarity.

3 *Only*, Negative Entailment and NPIs

Only is one of the greatest puzzles in the theories of NPI licensing, as it licenses NPIs in its scope, taking *only PN/CN* (proper name/common noun) into consideration, but it is not, at least not straightforwardly, a DE position, as is shown in (15).

(15) a. ***Only*** *John ate vegetables for breakfast.* ≠> ***Only*** *John ate kale for breakfast.*

b. ***Only*** *John ever ate any kale for breakfast.*

In this section, I will discuss some available attempts and take my own standpoint, namely that an *only* sentence without extra negation in the scope of *only* entails two propositions, a non-monotonic 'prejacent' entailment expressed by the sentence without *only*, and a negative (i.e. DE, more accurately, anti-additive) 'exclusive' entailment involving a syntactically unpronounced element, as indicated in (16). It is due to the exclusive entailment that *only* is capable of licensing NPIs.

(16) *Only Peter lifted a finger to help.*

a. Peter helped. [Prejacent: non-DE]

b. Nobody other than Peter lifted a finger to help. [Exclusive: anti-additive]

3.1 Pseudo-antiadditivity, Strawson-dE, Downward Assertion

Atlas (1996) suggests that *only PN* is non-monotonic but pseudo-anti-additive. An operator is 'pseudo-anti-additive' if it meets the De Morgen conditions of "closure under finite unions, without being downwards monotonic" (Atlas 1996: 283), as illustrated below:

(17) a. ***Only** John smokes and **only** John drinks.* ⇒ ***Only** John smokes or drinks.*
b. ***Only** John smokes or drinks.* ≠> ***Only** John smokes and **only** John drinks.*

This proposal is problematic, as pseudo-anti-additive operators such as *some students*, *every student* or *at least three students* do not license NPIs in their scope (von Fintel 1999). With this as one of the arguments against the symmetrical (i.e. two-entailment) view on *only*, von Fintel (1999) advances an asymmetric semantics for *only*: the prejacent proposition is not entailed but presupposed in this view; *only* licenses NPIs in its scope due to the Strawson-DEness: "A function f of type $< \sigma, \tau >$ is Strawson-DE iff for all x, y of type σ such that x ⇒ y and *f(x) is defined*: f(y) ⇒ f(x)" (Fintel 1999: 104). To put it informally, (18a) Strawson-entails (18c), as the entailment holds only when the 'presupposition'—the prejacent proposition—of (18c), that is, (18b), also holds true.

(18) a. ***Only** John ate vegetables for breakfast.*
b. *John ate kale for breakfast.* (presupposition of the conclusion)
∴c. ***Only** John ate kale for breakfast.*

Truly, *only* licenses NPIs and *only* is Strawson-DE, but I am not convinced that *only* licenses NPIs due to its Strawson-DEness. In fact, I would rather drop the restriction 'Strawson' (although it is an important point by itself) and stay with the DEness, as it seems unnecessary to make the prejacent DE, as von Fintel does by putting the prejacent of the conclusion into the premises so that the prejacent turns DE as the exclusive proposition. The fact that *only* licenses NPIs in its scope has nothing to do with the prejacent but only with the exclusive. Strawson-DEness is therefore not an account but a consequence of the fact that *only* is semantically conjunctive, and it licenses NPIs in the negative exclusive proposition. The major flaw with the Strawson-DE approach to this problem is the assumption of a single-entailment semantics for *only*, which results in a forced attempt at accounting for its NPI licensing behavior in its entire meaning.

Horn (2002, 2017) also takes a symmetrical view, i.e. *only* is semantically conjunctive and non-DE. The two conjuncts, e.g. (16a) and (16b), are both entailments of (16), but only one, namely, in this case, (16b) is asserted while (16a) is "assertorically inert". The reason why *only* licenses NPIs, as he claims, is because "It's DOWNWARD ASSERTING, not DOWNWARD ENTAILING environments that license NPIs, or at least NPI *any/ever* and the minimizers" and *only* is downward asserting, as is the assertion (16b). That is to say, there is only a pragmatic asymmetry between the two entailments. Manfred Krifka pointed out (during the discussion of Horn's invited talk at CIL18) that this pragmatic asymmetry can be considered in terms of information packaging (also cf. Krifka 2007 in which he claims that focus, in association with *only*, can lead to truth-conditional differences). The basic idea is, in brief, that the negative contribution is prominent in the meaning of *only* and it is this part of meaning that licenses NPIs.

In the following, I will make my own proposal that is conjunctive in nature like Horn (2002, 2017) but does not turn to his distinction between asserted versus inert entailments.

3.2 The Current Proposal

Linebarger (1987) claims that the focus operator *only* in *Only Fs are G* licenses NPIs through a conventional implicature (CI) that is 'negative': $[\forall x(\neg F(x) \rightarrow \neg G(x))]$ and the NPI is contained in the G (topic) position. As she claims, this not only explains the fact that *only* licenses NPIs outside its focus but also that *only* licenses NPIs within its focus, that is, in the F position as well, as (19) illustrates.

(19) ***Only*** *those who had ever been invited came to the party.*

My proposal is inspired by Linebarger's account, but I will drop the notion of CI, as CIs are non-at-issue contents (Potts 2005) whereas the negative exclusive proposition contributes an at-issue meaning (Larry Horn, p.c.) or at least, not of an non-at-issue kind. Thus, I choose to stay with the more descriptive and less controversial distinction of the prejacent versus the exclusive. I assume that *only* is semantically conjunctive, that is, both the prejacent and the exclusive are conventional contents of the sentence, as neither of them is cancellable (cf. examples (49)/(50) in Horn (2011)). However, I will argue shortly that if NPIs are present in an *only* sentence, the prejacent entailment of the sentence needs some slight revision for both grammatical and truth-conditional reasons. The exclusive entailment is negative in that it has reversed polarity at both the restrictor and the scope position in relation to the prejacent.

3.2.1 Only the Doppelgänger

For simplicity, I assume that *Only a is G* and *Only Fs are G* have the same semantics and pragmatics, except that *only* induces a set of individuals as the set of the alternatives in the former, and a set of sets (properties) as the alternative set in the latter. The former has as its meaning the prejacent $[G(a)]$ and the exclusive $[\forall x(\neg(x = a) \rightarrow \neg G(x))]$ and the latter $[\exists x(F(x) \wedge G(x))]$ and $[\forall x(\neg F(x) \rightarrow \neg G(x))]$. With the two components conjoined, we get the entire meaning of e.g. *Only Fs are G* as in (20).

(20) Meaning of the (contrastive) focus operator *only*:
$[[\textit{Only Fs are G}]] = \langle [\exists x(F(x) \wedge G(x))] \wedge [\forall x(\neg F(x) \rightarrow \neg G(x))] \rangle$

That is, as a contrastive focus operator *only* expresses two propositions that contrast with each other at both the focus, i.e. F, and the topic, i.e. G, positions. The extensions of F and ¬F form together the entire target of domain of foci, restricted by context; the contrast at the G position is one of polarity. *Only* is therefore a 'Doppelgänger' as the affirmative and the negative parts of its meaning always go hand in hand. It is only and always halfway negative. The difference in logical properties between the two propositions is the cause of all the complications that arise with it in terms of NPI licensing. When negation intervenes in the first proposition such as *Only Fs are not G*, the other proposition turns positive at the topic position, that is $\langle [\exists x(F(x) \wedge \neg G(x))] \wedge [\forall x(\neg F(x) \rightarrow G(x))] \rangle$.

In Liu (2010), I proposed a different semantics for *only* with the aim of reducing it along *no* and *all* to universal quantification as they all license NPIs in their restrictor position, which is stated in in (21).

(21) The semantics of *only* (Liu 2010)
[[*Only Fs are G*]] = < $[\forall x(F(x) \rightarrow G(x))]$, $[\forall x(\neg F(x) \rightarrow \neg G(x))]$>

(20) and (21) differ in the semantic representation of the prejacent and the relation between the prejacent and the exclusive. I used Karttunen and Peters' (1979) labels, i.e. < ϕ^e, ϕ^i > with ϕ^e for a truth-conditional content and ϕ^i for a non-truth-conditional content, combined in a nonconjoined fashion. This is mistaken, as the prejacent and the exclusive are both entailments (i.e. not of separate meaning dimensions) and should thus be conjoined. This is corrected by the addition of the conjunction as in (20). In the following, I will address the question why the prejacent should be of existential nature rather than $[\forall x(G(x) \rightarrow F(x))]$ or $[\forall x(F(x) \rightarrow G(x))]$.

Consider the scenario in (22):

(22) Scenario: I invited Peter, Markus, Tom and Tom's wife and children and I say *a*.
a. ***Only*** *Tom came.*
b. ***Only*** *Tom came and nobody else.* (Tom was the only person who came.)
c. ***Only*** *Tom came. His wife and children did not.* (Tom was the only person of his family who came.)

If a speaker utters (22a), it seems that he or she can mean (22b) or (22c). (22b) is probably the preferred reading where *only* quantifies over the entire domain of individuals. However, this exhaustification does not come by the conventional meaning of the sentence but can vary by context. Thus, in some contexts, the speaker can exclude Peter and Markus from the quantification domain and mean, for example, (22c) by (22a). Therefore, the prejacent of (22a) is $[\exists x(x = tom \wedge G(x))]$ or G(tom) rather than for example, $[\forall x(G(x) \rightarrow x = tom)]$, which presents rather the meaning of *Tom was the only person who came*, that is, (22b).

The prejacent should not be $[\forall x(F(x) \rightarrow G(x))]$, either. Let's take the case of *only CN*. Talking about a group of 5 people 3 of whom I invited to my party (but only 2 of them came to the party) and 2 of whom I didn't, if I say *Only those who I had invited came to the party*, I don't mean to say all the 3 invited ones came (i.e. all those who I had invited came to the party) but mean to say all those who came were invited and nobody who was not invited came.

Finally, even though $[\forall x(\neg F(x) \rightarrow \neg G(x))]$ is logically synonymous to $[\forall x(G(x) \rightarrow F(x))]$ as $a \rightarrow b \equiv \neg a \vee b \equiv b \vee \neg a \equiv \neg b \rightarrow \neg a$, it is better to keep the negative operator in the exclusive, because *F* in the latter representation (for example, for *All Gs are F*) is not an NPI licensor but is one in the *only* sentence.

For a comparison, the semantics of *only* is stated below with that of *no* and *all.*

(23) The semantics of *only*, *no* and *all*
a. [[*Only Fs are G*]] = < $[\exists x(F(x) \wedge G(x))] \wedge [\forall x(\neg F(x) \rightarrow \neg G(x))]$>
b. [[*No Fs are G*]] = $[\forall x(F(x) \rightarrow \neg G(x))]$
c. [[*All Fs are G*]] = $[\forall x(F(x) \rightarrow G(x))]$

Only and *no* both license NPIs in their scope because it is also a negative position. The major difference is that *only* is semantically conjunctive. Thus, in (24), (24b), (24c) and the negative proposition by (24a) are logically equivalent.

(24) a. *Only those who had been invited came to the party.*
b. ***Nobody** who had**n't** been invited came to the party.*
c. ***Everyone** who had**n't** been invited did**n't** come to the party.*

3.2.2 Polarity Items and Truth Conditions

The major trick of my proposal is to assume that polarity items contribute to the truth conditions of a sentence. NPIs such as *any*, *ever* and minimizers contribute to the truth conditions of a sentence by domain widening (Kadmon and Landman 1993), by which they create a strengthening effect in the relevant utterance. With this assumption, (25a) is truth-conditionally not equivalent to (25b), as the presence of the NPI *any* widens the domain of what counts as breakfast. A glass of orange juice does not usually count as breakfast, but can possibly, and therefore (25c) is fine but (25d) is odd.

(25) a. *George did**n't** have breakfast today.*
b. *George did**n't** have any breakfast today.*
c. *George did**n't** have breakfast today, but drank a glass of orange juice.*
d. *?George did**n't** have any breakfast today, but drank a glass of orange juice.*

Similarly, since the presence of NPIs such as *ever* widens the interval of reference time, the truth conditions of the sentence are changed, as (26) shows.

(26) a. *Kim has**n't** had soup for breakfast, but only once in Korea ages ago.*
b. *Kim has**n't** ever had soup for breakfast, *but only once in Korea ages ago.*

The truth-conditional contribution by polarity items such as *already/yet*, *either/too*, *still/anymore* is a different story, namely, both elements of each pair contribute by their lexical pragmatics one and the same conventional presupposition (CP, cf. Potts 2005 for the difference between CPs and conversational presuppositions) that I maintain should be part of the sentence's truth-conditions but at the CP dimension separate from the at-issue core. The reason why I assume these words induce a CP rather than a CI is that q or r in (27)–(29) can be backgrounded (e.g. *Peter is supposed to be here, but he is not here yet*), whereas CIs are in general anti-backgrounding (Potts 2005).

(27) a. *Peter is already here.* <p, q>
b. *Peter is* ***not*** *here yet.* <¬p, q>
p: Peter is here.
q: Peter is supposed to be here.

(28) a. *Peter is still here.* <p, q>
b. *Peter is* ***not*** *here anymore.* <¬p, q>
p: Peter is here.
q: Peter was here.

(29) a. *Peter is here, too.* <p, q>
b. *Peter is **not** here, either.* <¬p, r>
p: Peter is here.
q: Someone other than Peter is here.
r: Someone other than Peter is not here.

Each sentence expresses two propositions of an at-issue and a CP kind. Take *already/yet* for example; (27a) and (27b) differ truth-conditionally in the polarity of the at-issue content, but not in the CP. The same is true with *still/anymore*. It is a bit more complicated with *too/either*, in that their CPs, (29q) and (29r) respectively, differ in polarity. The two propositions can be negated separately and thus there could be four possible results <p, q>, <¬p, q>, <p, ¬q> and <¬p, ¬q>. The third possibility obtains when negation is used metalinguistically to deny the conventional presupposition. The last combination is unavailable, as negation cannot be used truth-functionally and metalinguistically at the same time, in other words, the two propositions must be negated separately if they are to—this is strong evidence that p and q belong to different meaning dimensions. *Only* licenses NPIs of the *any-ever-lift a finger* type but not those of the *yet-either-anymore* type.

(30) a. ***Only** Kim had any soup for breakfast.*
b. ***Only** Kim has ever had soup for breakfast.*
c. ***Only** Kim lifted a finger to help with the cleaning up.*
d. *****Only** Kim had breakfast yet.*
e. *****Only** Kim had breakfast, either.*
f. *****Only** Kim is crazy about kimchi anymore.*

As I have already argued above, the first type of NPIs all contribute to the truth conditions of the sentence by domain widening. In the case of *only*, the truth-conditional contribution by these NPIs only occurs at the exclusive proposition.

(31) a. ***Only** Kim has had kimchi soup for breakfast.*
b. ***Only** Kim has ever had kimchi soup for breakfast.*

(31b) semantically expresses two things: <Kim has had kimchi soup for breakfast; Everyone other than Kim hasn't ever had kimchi soup for breakfast>. The first conjunct is not DE but the second is. Therefore, (31a) and (31b) actually entail (32a) and (32b) respectively.

(32) a. <Kim has had kimchi soup for breakfast ∧
Everyone other than Kim hasn't had kimchi soup for breakfast.>
b. <Kim has had kimchi soup for breakfast ∧
Everyone other than Kim hasn't ever had kimchi soup for breakfast.>

With these data and arguments, I want to show that the Strawson-DEness of *only* is the consequence of the fact that the two propositions expressed by an *only* sentence logically differ from each other, namely one is non-DE and the other is DE. The mechanism involved there, namely to put the 'presupposition' of the conclusion sentence into the premises as in (18) is but to make the prejacent DE so that both turn downward entailing. However, it is not a necessary move as NPIs are not licensed by the prejacent anyway.

Let me elaborate on the idea further:

(33) ***Only** Peter ate any vegetables.*
a. *<Peter ate any vegetables ∧ Everyone other than Peter didn't eat vegetables.>
b. *<Peter ate any vegetables ∧ Everyone other than Peter didn't eat any vegetables.>
c. ?<Peter ate vegetables ∧ Everyone other than Peter didn't eat vegetables.>
d. <Peter ate vegetables ∧ Everyone other than Peter didn't eat any vegetables.>

Only the NPI reading of *any* is relevant for the discussion here. (33a–b) are clearly wrong as the truth conditions of the sentence. (33c) is not quite wrong but it is rather the truth conditions of *Only Peter ate vegetables*. Similarly, as the dialogue that runs perfectly well shows: *After the party I was very disappointed that only Peter lifted a finger to help. In fact, he did most of the cleaning-up*, the domain widening by *lift a finger* does not target the proposition that Peter helped and in fact he could have been a big help. In other words, the NPI affects the negative proposition, namely *nobody else helped, not even lifted a finger to help and I was very disappointed at this.*

The most likely reason why *yet*, *anymore*, *either* do not work the same way is that they are different from NPIs *any*, *ever* and *lift a finger* in relation to negation. It is definitely not a question of their strength as NPIs, as *lift a finger* is a stronger NPI in English as *yet*; therefore, van der Wouden's (1997) classification fails to be explanatory here. Sentences such as **Anna is here yet/anymore/, either* are unavoidably ungrammatical as these NPIs require the modified propositions to be negative, in other words, these NPIs want grammatical licensing. The NPIs *any/ ever/lifted a finger*, though, can be licensed pragmatically, for example in adversatives such as *It is amazing that Kim has ever had any soup for breakfast*, and these NPIs are used to turn a negative utterance stronger in the assertoric tone. In brief, *yet/either/anymore* presuppose a negative proposition while *any/ever/lift a finger* strengthens a negative proposition. Moreover, take the minimizer *lift a finger* for example, if Peter helped, it follows that he at least lifted a finger to help. In other words, from the sentence *Only Kim lifted a finger to help*, *Kim lifted a finger to help* is trivially true, although the sentence is usually not assertable except in its literal meaning. As for *any* and *ever*, I don't know whether the fact that they can appear in the prejacent without contributing the domain widening function to the proposition has anything to do with their free choice reading. It is worth repeating that historically, *ever* did appear more frequently in affirmative sentences as an intensifier. I will leave this for future research.

The DEness of the exclusive gets lost if negation intervenes. The prejacent proposition turns DE but on the whole the DE still doesn't follow, so (34) does not entail that *Only Peter didn't eat any kale.* For the same reason as for (33c), (34c) is not really wrong but represents more accurately the truth conditions of *Only Peter didn't eat vegetables.* (The indices indicate the right licensor of an NPI when there are two potential licensors available.)

(34) ***Only*** *Peter* ***didn't***$_i$ *eat any*$_i$ *vegetables.*
 a. *<Peter didn't eat vegetables ∧ Everyone other than Peter ate any vegetables.>
 b. *<Peter didn't eat any vegetables; Everyone other than Peter ate any vegetables.>
 c. ?<Peter didn't eat vegetables ∧ Everyone other than Peter ate vegetables.>
 d. <Peter didn't eat any vegetables ∧ Everyone other than Peter ate vegetables.>

(35), however, entails *Not only Peter didn't eat any kale.* It is DE on the whole as both propositions it expresses as in (35a) are DE per se. Truth-conditionally speaking, (35) is synonymous to *Someone besides Peter didn't eat any vegetables, either.* Analogously, *Not only Peter ate vegetables* is truth-conditionally equivalent to *Someone besides Peter ate vegetables, too.* (36) is not a grammatical sentence, because neither proposition is able to accommodate the NPI *any*. This is so as *not only* is actually an additive operator, i.e. it does not make a negative context.

(35) ***Not only*** *Peter* ***didn't***$_i$ *eat any*$_i$ *vegetables.*
 a. <Peter didn't eat any vegetables ∧ Someone other than Peter didn't eat any vegetables.>

(36) ****Not only*** *Peter ate any vegetables.*
 a. *<Peter ate vegetables ∧ Someone other than Peter ate vegetables.>
 b. *<Peter ate vegetables ∧ Someone other than Peter ate any vegetables.>
 c. *<Peter ate any vegetables ∧ Someone other than Peter ate vegetables.>
 d. *<Peter ate any vegetables ∧ Someone other than Peter ate any vegetables.>

3.3 A Comparison with Horn (2002)

The semantics I propose for *only* in this paper differs from Horn's (2002) analysis in his pragmatic ordering of the two entailments. My solution does not turn to (while being compatible with) Horn's (2002, 2017) asserted/inert entailment distinction, but to a more straightforward trick, namely, to the composition of the entire sentence. It is plausible that whatever the contribution by the NPI *lifted a finger* is, this contribution is not made to the positive prejacent proposition—as otherwise the resulting proposition would be less informative than alternatives with the NPIs replaced by e.g. indefinites. The domain widening function (Kadmon and Landman 1993) of minimizer NPIs such as *any, ever, lift a finger* that occur with *only* only apply to the exclusive proposition. Correspondingly, it is at this proposition where these NPIs are licensed and where a strengthening effect arises.

Some people might criticize that my arguments here are circular, but such criticism would be due to a certain assumption about the nature of licensing between NPIs and their licensors, which is not yet entirely clear to me. But, if we admit the truth-conditional contribution of minimize NPIs that I have been talking about, we can know—logically—where an NPI is licensed by checking at which proposition its domain-widening function applies.

Moreover, although Horn's asserted/inert entailment distinction seems more explanatory for cases such as (37a) and many others (indeed), I see no reason for such a distinction in e.g. (37b). Therefore, the inference failure in (37a) arises not because *Peter helped* is not asserted but an assertorically inert entailment—as it can be asserted, shown in (37b)—per se, but because the matrix predicate—probably conversationally—only takes the negative content in its semantic scope. I say 'conversationally' as for example, if we change the embedded predicate from *help* to *stop*, the inference seems to follow in (37c).

(37) a. *I was disappointed that* ***only*** *Peter lifted a finger to help.* ≠>

I was disappointed that Peter helped and nobody else lifted a finger to help.

b. *I learned that* ***only*** *Peter lifted a finger to help.* =>

I learned that Peter helped and nobody else lifted a finger to help.

c. *I was disappointed that* ***only*** *Peter lifted a finger to stop you.* =>

I was disappointed that it was Peter and nobody else who stopped you. (I expected that somebody other than Peter would stop you, and was disappointed that it was not the case.)

To sum up, with the assumption that NPIs contribute truth-conditional meaning by what Kadmon and Landman (1993) call domain widening, it is then natural to claim that in an *only* sentence, NPIs are licensed at the negative exclusive proposition and it is to this content that they contribute their domain widening functions as part of the truth conditions of the entire sentence.

4 *Only*, *No* and *All*

No N works quite like the focus operator *only Ns*, except that *no N* expresses a negative proposition $[\lambda F.\lambda x.\neg\exists x(N(x) \wedge F(x))]$ and when used as contrastive negation, it can implicate a PI whereas *only* entails both a positive prejacent proposition and a negative exclusive proposition, in case the rest of the sentence has no extra negation.

(38) *Shall we start the wedding?*

a. ***Only*** *the bride is here.*

b. ***No*** *bridegroom is here.*

To a question such as (38), both (38a) and (38b) can serve a felicitous answer, namely, the wedding cannot be started due to the absence of the bridegroom. However, I don't think that we can apply the same analysis for *no N* and *only Ns*. First, the answerer of (38a) has to know both that the bride is here and the bridegroom is not here but that of (38b) has to know that the bridegroom is not here, not necessarily knowing whether the bride is here or not. Therefore, the information conveyed by the two sentences in (38) is not the same.

This is to certify that the exclusive induced by *only* is a conventional (i.e. context-independent) meaning component while the PI by *no N* is a conversational (context-dependent) one. The latter is cancelable while the former is not. Consider:

(39) *Shall we start the wedding?*
a. ***Only** the bride is here.* **The bridegroom is here as well.*
b. ***No** bridegroom is here. The bride is **not** here, either.*

This is why both the positive and negative meaning components for *only* should be of truth conditions, which is not the case with *no N*.

Coming back to the contrast between *no N* and *nothing/nobody* that we discussed in the second section, the reason why *nothing* or *nobody* tends not to induce such a PI like *no N* is that the N node presupposes the existence of an N-set or a contrastive ¬N-set. This is an insight from Atlas (1996: 272): "*All Fs* seems to 'presuppose' that there are Fs, while the absolute individual quantifier NP *Everything* does not", which he attributes to Strawson (1952). Therefore, *nothing/nobody* always serve an exhaustive answer concerning a certain domain of foci, while *no N* can but not necessarily. Observe (40):

(40) *Who came?*
a. ***Nobody** came. *But some students came.*
b. ***Nobody** came. ***No** professor, either.*
c. ***No** professor came. But some students came.*
d. ***No** professor came and **nobody** else, either.*

Analogously, in a discourse, *All Fs are Gs* or *Every F is G* does not exclude $[\exists x(\neg F(x) \wedge (\neg G(x) \vee G(x)))]$, while the same thing will be redundant to follow *everything/everybody* due to their exhaustivity regarding the targeted domain of foci.

(41) *Who came?*
a. ***Everybody** came. *Some professors came as well.*
b. ***Everybody** came. *Some professors didn't come.*
c. ***All** students came. Some professors came as well.*
d. ***All** students came. Some professors didn't come.*

All students came can serve an exhaustive answer if the domain of foci only contains a set of students, or an inexhaustive one if the domain of foci contains more than a set of students. If (41) is meant to ask about both students and professors, simply saying *All students came* can implicate that *not all professors came*, and for this reason (41c–d) are both coherent. However, such an implicative potential is much weaker than with *only Ns* or *no N*, as the latter two have negativity in their meaning which is normally parasitic on their corresponding positive contrast, while a positive utterance with *all Ns* does not have to take a negative correlate.

By comparison, *only* licenses NPIs both outside and inside its focus while *all Ns* does so only in its restriction but not in its scope, because the latter, i.e. G, is not DE and not even such at the derivative level (undefined in its polarity). Compare (42) with (19):

(42) *****All** Students have <u>ever</u> read the book.*

Concerning the fact that both NPIs and PPIs are fine in the restriction of universal quantifiers, I believe that *all* in *all Ns*, also a quasi-focus operator, licenses NPIs in its scope because of its DEness or anti-additivity. However, it is also to note that the part it indicates as the focus (the relative clause) carries a negative (conversational) implicature (NI), which can be strengthened by the presence of an NPI.

(43) ***All*** *the students who had* <u>*ever/already*</u> *read the book attended the lecture.*

In fact, the relative clause in (44) with the PPI *already* sounds more like part of the background information; in comparison, the relative clause with the NPI *ever* is salient. With *ever*, we get a stronger NI that there are students who did not read the book (whether they attended the lecture or not), while with *already*, we get a stronger PI that there are students who read the book (earlier than expected). The relative clause with *already* can function as the non-restrictive appositive, but not that with the NPI *ever*, which has to be in the restrictor of universal quantifiers.

(44) a. ***All*** *my students, who had* <u>*already*</u> *read the book, attended the lecture.*
b. ******All*** *my students, who had* <u>*ever*</u> *read the book, attended the lecture.*

To sum up, *all Ns* licenses both NPIs and PPIs, because it is not *all Ns* alone that contributes the NI, but the combination of *all Ns...NPI*, whereas the combination of *all Ns...PPI* does not necessarily do so. In other words, NPIs strengthen the existence of an NI while PPIs strengthen that of a PI. The same is true with *no N... PPI* versus *no N...NPI*, but the other way around, namely, due to the presence of PPIs, the former strongly implicates a positive content, a preceding utterance or an expectation for instance.

(45) a. ***No*** *student has* <u>*already*</u> *read the book on phonology.*
b. ***No*** *student has* <u>*ever*</u> *read the book on phonology.*

More generally, licensing and anti-licensing are not just a matter of the licensors' logical properties and the licensees' sensitivity, but also an effect of the two combined with each other. As (45b) indicates, an utterance with the NPI adverb *ever* is more emphatic than one without: this strengthening effect obtains due to the combination of a domain widening NPI in the affective domain of a negative element. NPIs such as *yet*, *anymore*, *either* do not have the same function although they need licensing by negation as well.

5 Conclusion

To conclude, polarity items can be pragmatically licensed, 'pragmatically' meaning that they can appear in one sentence but be licensed by another one with appropriate logical properties. NPIs are licensed both in and outside the focus of *only* due to its negative alter ego, i.e. the exclusive proposition, or Horn's asserted entailment, which is negative both at the focus and the topic positions. PPIs in anti-licensing such as AA contexts can be rescued through a PI, but only when the AA contexts are appropriate, that is, when they have the pragmatic force like *no N* (often with the help of intonation/discourse contrast) to induce such a PI, which is strengthened again by PPIs.

(46) The meaning of *only Ns*, *no N* and *all Ns*

	Truth-conditional	Non-truth-conditional
Only Fs are G	$<\exists x(F(x) \wedge G(x)) \wedge \forall x(\neg F(x) \rightarrow \neg G(x))>$	
No Fs are G	$\forall x(F(x) \rightarrow \neg G(x))$	Strongly implicates: $\exists x(\neg F(x) \wedge G(x))$
All Fs are G	$\forall x(F(x) \rightarrow G(x))$	Weakly implicates: $\exists x(\neg F(x) \wedge (\neg G(x) \vee G(x)))$

In the case of *only*, it is its exclusive entailment that performs the licensing of NPIs, whereas in the case of *no N*, it is a conversational positive implicature that performs the licensing or more accurately, the rescuing of PPIs. In the case of *all Ns*, the occurrence of NPIs in its restriction renders the weak (negative) implicature more prominent, whereas that of PPIs does not. This argues for a bi-directional view on polarity effects (at least for NPIs such as *any*, *ever*, *lift a finger*), that is, there is a pragmatic effect, e.g. the strengthening of a conversational implicature (in the case of universal quantifiers *all Ns*) or a negative entailment (in the case of *only*) by NPIs. As most research on polarity items focuses on sentence-level licensing, I want to call for future research at the discourse-level, especially regarding how the presence of polarity items in discourse affect sentence processing and reasoning.

Acknowledgments I am grateful especially to Laurence Horn and Frank Richter for their invaluable comments and also to Regine Eckardt, Sam Featherston, Doris Penka, Janina Radó, Manfred Sailer, Jan-Philipp Soehn for helpful discussions. I thank the audience of my presentation titled "Negative Implicature, Positive Implicature" at the workshop *Contrastiveness in Information Structure and/or Scalar Implicatures* at CIL18 in Seoul 2008, and the audience of my presentation titled "Universal Quantification and NPI Licensing" at Sinn und Bedeutung 14 in Vienna 2009. Many thanks also to Lucas Ogden for proofreading this paper. All remaining errors and shortcomings are of course my own responsibility. This research was funded by the *Landesstiftung Baden-Württemberg* and the *Deutsche Forschungsgemeinschaft*.

References

Atlas, Jay David. 1996. 'Only' noun phrases, pseudo-negative generalized quantifiers, negative polarity items, and monotonicity. *Journal of Semantics* 13: 265–328.

Bolinger, Dwight. 1960. Linguistic science and linguistic engineering. *Word* 16: 374–391.

Horn, Laurence R. 1989. *A natural history of negation*. University of Chicago Press.

Horn, Laurence R. 2002. Assertoric inertia and NPI licensing. *CLS* 38 Part 2, 55–82.

Horn, Laurence R. 2011. Only XL: The assertoric asymmetry of exponibles. In *Proceedings of Semantics and Linguistic Theory (SALT)*, eds. Cormany, Satoshi Ito and David Lutz, vol 19, 198–222. *eLanguage*.

Horn, Laurence R. 2017. *Almost* et al.: Scalar adverbs revisited. In *Contrastiveness in Information Structure, Alternatives, and Scalar Implicature*, eds. Chungmin Lee, Ferenc Kiefer, and Manfred Krfika, 283–304. Springer.

Kadmon, Nirit and Fred Landman. 1993. *Any*. *linguistics and philosophy* 16: 353–422.

Kfrikfa, Manfred. 2007. Basic notions of information structure. In *Interdisciplinary Studies on Information Structure 6*, ed. Caroline Féry, and Manfred Krifka, 13–56. Potsdam: Universitätsverlag.

Ladusaw, William A. 1979. *Polarity Sensitivity as Inherent Scope Relations*. Ph.d. thesis, University of Texas, Austin.

Linebarger, Marcia. 1987. Negative polarity and grammatical representation. *Linguistics and Philosophy* 10: 325–387.

Liu, Mingya. 2010. Universal Quantification and NPI Licensing. In Proceedings of *Sinn und Bedeutung* 14, Vienna, 273–288.

Potts, Christopher. 2005. *The Logic of Conventional Implicatures*. Oxford University Press.

Saddy, Douglas, Heiner Drenhaus, and Stefan Frisch. 2004. Processing polarity items: contrasting licensing costs. *Brain and Language* 90: 495–502.

Szabolcsi, Anna. 2004. Positive polarity—negative polarity. *Natural Language & Linguistic Theory* 22(2): 409–452.

van der Wouden, Ton. 1997. *Negative Contexts. Collocation, polarity and multiple negation*. Routledge, London and New York.

von Fintel, Kai. 1999. NPI licensing, strawson entailment, and context dependency. *Journal of Semantics* 16(2): 97–148.

Yurchenko, Anna, Dirk-Bart Den Ouden, Jack Hoeksema, Olga Dragoy, John C.J. Hoeks, and Laurie A. Stowe. 2013. Processing polarity: ERP evidence for differences between positive and negative polarity. *Neuropsychologia* 51(1): 132–141.

Disjunction and Implicatures: Some Notes on Recent Developments

Uli Sauerland

Abstract The paper considers three features of disjunction that played a role in recent discussions relating to the question of whether implicature computation is pragmatic and global or grammatical and local: Hurford's constraint, free choice inferences, and the mutual exclusivity of double disjunctions. The paper argues that both Hurford's constraint data and the free choice phenomena are consistent with a pragmatic, global approach to scalar implicatures if it is enriched with a lexical repair strategy. Furthermore to derive the mutual exclusivity of double disjunctions, a global approach taking scope over both disjuncts is necessary, since I show that local computation of scalar implicatures within on of the disjuncts would make wrong predictions. I conclude therefore that in the absence of other arguments for a grammatical approach, the pragmatic global account provides a better explanation.

Keywords Disjunction · Implicature · Scalar · Pragmatics · Semantics · Exclusivity

Use of disjunction often allows us to draw additional inferences about the speakers' belief: For example, (1) uttered by someone out of the blue would lead us to draw at least three additional inferences about the speaker. For one, we would infer that he did not see both Kyle and Ryan. Furthermore, we would infer that the speaker is neither certain that he saw Kyle nor that he is certain that he saw Ryan. What is certain is that he saw one of the two.

This paper was originally written up in 2009 and parts of it were presented at PARC in Palo Alto, California, and the Semantics Research Group at the University of Tokyo. I am very grateful for their helpful comments to the audiences at both venues and also to Ezra Keshet and Chungmin Lee. Since 2009, I have done more work on the comparison of pragmatic and grammatical approaches to scalar implicatures, and my more recent results speak against the pragmatic and in favor of the grammatical approach (see Sauerland 2011, 2014). This is consistent with the results in this paper since the convincing evidence comes from more complex examples than those considered here.

U. Sauerland (✉)
ZAS, Berlin, Germany
e-mail: uli@alum.mit.edu

C. Lee et al. (eds.), *Contrastiveness in Information Structure, Alternatives and Scalar Implicatures*, Studies in Natural Language and Linguistic Theory 91, DOI 10.1007/978-3-319-10106-4_12

(1) I saw Kyle or Ryan in the crowd.

What are the mental mechanisms deriving such inferences? This question is central question of the recent discussion targeting scalar implicatures as examples with disjunction have been crucial in this debate.

One of the leading questions in this debate is the following: Can the mechanism apply to constituents smaller than sentences? In work by Grice (1989) and work building on his intuitions, the computation of implicatures is tied to the act of speaking, the intentions of speakers, and the assumption that speakers act cooperatively. Therefore implicatures are assumed to be generally computed at the sentence level only, though this is not necessarily the only option even on a Gricean approach if speech acts can be embedded. Recent work has contrasted Grice's position with systems where implicature computation is not tied to speakers' intentions, but a purely grammatical procedure. This grammatical procedure could in principle apply to any subconstituent of a sentence structure—it can be applied *locally*. Since scalar implicature computation is semantically at least very similar to the meaning of *only*, namely exhaustification, work by Chierchia (2006), Fox (2007) and others has adopted the convention to mark constituents at which implicature computation applies with a silent operator abbreviated either as *O* (for *only*) or *Exh* (for *Exhaustification*). In this paper, I adopt *Exh*. As far as I am aware of, while it is generally acknowledged that constraints govern the distribution of *Exh*, a proposal for the distribution of *Exh* is still forthcoming. At this point, what especially Chierchia et al. (2008, 2009) claim to have shown, though, is that *Exh* can occur in embedded positions and they therefore reject Grice's connection of implicature to speaker intention. The phenomenon of *Exh* applying below the sentence level is also referred to as *local* implicature computation, as opposed to *global* computation at the sentence level.

This paper discusses two potential arguments against a Gricean account of implicatures due to Chierchia et al. (2009) (see also Chierchia et al. 2008; the Hurford's constraint data) and Fox (2007) (the Free choice data). The two classes of data are illustrated in (2) and (3) respectively.

(2) *Hurford's constraint datum* (Hurford 1974; Gazdar 1979):
Mary read some or all of the books.

(3) *Free choice datum* (Kamp 1973):
You may eat the cake or the ice-cream.

Chierchia et al. (2008) claim that the account of these two classes of data requires local computation of implicatures. I take objection to this claim. In the following section I address Hurford's constraint. I show that local implicature for each disjunct is in general not attested, but only global implicature computation. In particular, I argue that the another class of data—the generalized xor data (*xor* for exclusive *or*)—have been mistakenly taken to argue for a local analysis of implicatures, while in fact the opposite is the case: only the global analysis can account for these data. The Hurford's constraint data therefore constitute an exceptional case, and I propose to account for them as such. In the second section of this paper, I turn to the free choice data. I first set out to clarify Fox (2007) argument: these data are actually not an argument in favor of a local account of scalar implicature, but rather the global analysis. However, Fox is correct to point out that the free choice data are problematic the Gricean picture of entirely post-semantic implicature computation. However, Fox's argument depends entirely on the claim that free choice inferences are implicatures. On this issue, the current state of the art (Chemla 2009) says that implicatures and free choice inferences have different properties with respect to embedding under universal quantifiers. Therefore, I conclude tentatively that Fox's arguments do not threaten the global account. of implicatures.

1 Scalars Under Disjunction

I want to situate the discussion of the data involving Hurford's constraint in the context of the discussion of examples from Chierchia (2004) that were intensively discussed a few years ago (Sauerland 2004b; Spector 2005; van Rooij and Schulz 2004) (see also Keshet 2017). I want to call these data the *Generalized Xor* data for reasons that will become clear. I am to show that the generalized xor data require that the scalar implicatures of disjuncts cannot be locally computed in general. This conclusion then leads me to propose that the Hurford's constraint data are cases of a repair strategy.

Multiple disjunctions are a well known problem of the implicatures (McCawley 1993; Simons 1998). For expository purposes, consider an approach to the pragmatics of disjunction that assumes that disjunction is ambiguous between inclusive disjunction *or* and exclusive disjunction *xor*. Grice (1989) discusses and rejects this kind of approach, but it also fails in an instructive fashion with multiple disjunction like *(A or B) or C*. The salient attested interpretation of such examples is that exactly one of A, B, or C is satisfied as shown by the Venn diagram on the left in the following figure. But, this interpretation cannot be derived by the ambiguity-or-approach. The figure below illustrates *(A or B) xor C* and *(A xor B) xor C* which result in unintuitive interpretations.

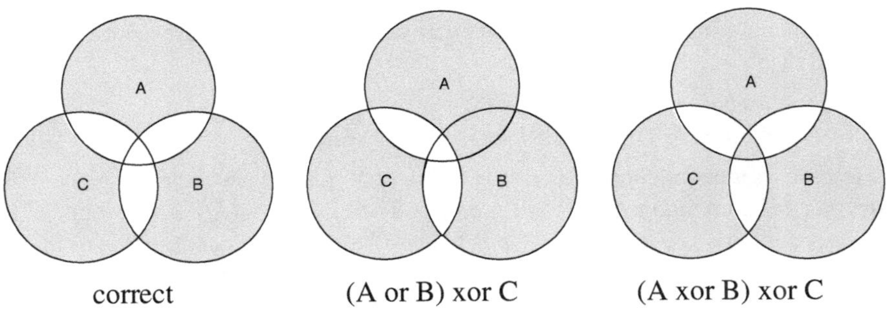

correct (A or B) xor C (A xor B) xor C

One may attempt to attack this problem by postulating a novel ternary exclusive disjunction operator that is defined to make the correct prediction. However, this is not a promising approach because the problem illustrated by multiple disjunction generalizes as Chierchia (2004) (as well as Bernhard Schwarz in unpublished work) discovered. One example demonstrating this from my own work (Sauerland 2004b) is (4). In (4), the weak scalar term *some* in the scope of disjunction triggers an implicature of *not all*, but this could not be derived correctly on a lexical ambiguity analysis. Specifically, if we postulated an ambiguity of *some* between *at least some* and *some and not all* in addition to the *or/xor* ambiguity of *or*, we would predict that (4) should be felicitous in the following scenarios: On the *xor* and *some and not all*-reading if Kai ate both the broccoli and all of the peas, and on the *xor* and *at least some*-reading, if Kai ate all of the peas and none of the broccoli.

(4) Kai had the broccoli or some of the peas last night.

The xor data argue for the global approach to implicatures. As far as I know, any published account of the xor data is global, even though the relevant data are discussed in much of the literature advocating a local approach to implicatures starting (Chierchia 2004; Sharvit et al. 2008; Gajewski et al. 2009). While this is as far as I can see largely due to confusion in the literature, there is some cause for this confusion: In unpublished work that preceded his 2004 paper (Chierchia 2004), Gennaro Chierchia attempted a solution of the xor data making use of a local implicature computation where implicatures are then not part of the sentence semantics, but projected. Specifically, Chierchia (2004) developed an account for *A or B or C* and (4) that made use of local implicature computation and assumed that local implicatures do not contribute to the semantic meaning of a sentence. In the published paper, Chierchia still appeals to this intuition, for example when he writes that "implicatures are projected upwards and filtered out or adjusted". However, the published version of Chierchia's work and all current work on the local approach has not executed this intuition of Chierchia's—and for good reasons, as I'll show below—but instead has adopted the semantic *exh*-operator. The *exh*-operator contributes an exhaustivized meaning to compositional semantics, rather than contributing subject to a implicature projection procedure. A first version of the exhaustification operator is given in (5). The subscript T of *exh* must denote a set of alternative propositions to S (the scope of *exh*). The content of T is determined jointly by context and by S itself.[1] Exhaustification means that all the alternatives from T are false except for those entailed by S.

(5) Exhaustification (preliminary version):
$[\![exh_T S]\!] = (S \wedge \forall S' \in A\ ((S \nrightarrow S') \vee \neg S)$

In case of a disjunction *A or B*, Chierchia et al. (2009) and others assume T to equal the set containing *A or B* and *A and B*. Therefore $exh_T(A \vee B)$ is predicted to be equivalent to *A xor B*. Therefore, it is plain to see that local computation of implicatures as in $exh_T(exh_T(AorB)orC)$ is equivalent to *(A xor B) xor C*, and therefore in general makes the wrong predictions for multiple disjunctions.

[1]For example, T may defined as the set of scalar alternatives of S, i.e. those expressions derivable from S by replacement of scalar expressions with the alternatives. Or it may denote the subset of contextually relevant scalar alternatives.

The problem with multiple disjunctions on the localist approach stems from the fact that the exh-operator contributes to compositional meaning. As I pointed out above, if this assumption was abandoned it may be possible to compute implicatures locally in the case of multiple disjunction. But, there would be a cost. Namely, there is another set of data that are generally taken to show that local implicatures can contribute to compositional semantics. Some of these facts have been first discussed by Cohen (1971). Geurts (2009) provides a lucid summary. (6) illustrates implicatures drawn in the scope of negation (all from Chierchia et al. (2008)):

(6) a. Joe didn't see Mary or Sue; he saw both.
b. It is not just that you can write a reply. You must.
c. I don't expect that some students will do well, I expect that all students will.

In the examples in (7) implicatures are drawn locally in other downward entailing environments (also from Chierchia et al. (2008))

(7) a. If you take salad or dessert, you pay $20; but if you take both, there is a surcharge.
b. Every professor who fails most students will receive no raise; every professor who fails all of the students will be fired.

Crucially, the implicature is part of the content the downward entailing operator applies to in all of this case. If the localist approach would find a solution for the multiple disjunction data along the lines of a separate projection mechanism for implicatures as sketched above, it would lose an account of these data.

The global approach, on the other hand, can account for the xor data rather straightforwardly. I briefly sketch the approach I proposed in Sauerland (2004b) (cf. Spector (2005)). It is based on the assumption that the logically strongest information is most cooperative at least in the contexts where scalar implicatures arise. It assumes like the local approach a notion of scalar alternative, which informs the system as to which of the stronger alternatives it should consider. It furthermore assumes that discourse participants make a competence assumption about speakers: those speakers have definite opinion on every scalar alternative of a statement they make. The competence assumption divides scalar implicatures into two classes: those that can be derived without it, and those that can only be derived with it. The former I called *primary implicatures* and the latter *secondary implicatures*. For illustration, consider the case of multiple disjuction *(A or B) or C*.[2] I assume there that the alternatives to a disjunction *A or B* are not only the conjunction *A and B* but also the individual disjuncts *A* and *B* (see also Katzir (2007)). Then the set of scalar alternative to *(A or B) or C* is as shown in (8):

(8) A, B, C, A and B, A and C, B and C, (A and B) and C, A or B, A or C, B or C, (A or B) or C

The primary implicatures are derived from this set by prefixed each of them with the operator 'the speaker is not certain that' and testing whether this statement is

[2]Note that while this case is discussed in the 2004 paper, the exposition there is actually erroneous.

compatible with the assertion the speaker just made. In this case, it is only incompatible for the assertion itself *(A or B) or C*. Hence, we arrive at the primary implicatures in (9), where 'the speaker is not certain that' is abbreviated as $\neg K_S$.

(9) $\neg K_S$ A, $\neg K_S$ B, $\neg K_S$ C, $\neg K_S$ (A and B), $\neg K_S$ (A and C), $\neg K_S$ (B and C), $\neg K_S$ (A and B) and C, $\neg K_S$ (A or B), $\neg K_S$ (A or C), $\neg K_S$ (B or C)

Furthermore, secondary implicatures are derived by prefixed a scalar alternative with the operator 'the speaker is certain that not' (or alternatively by reasoning from the primary implicature '$\neg K_S \psi$' and the competence assumption '$K_S \psi or K_S \neg \psi$' for a scalar alternative ψ). Naturally a secondary implicature will only be drawn if it is compatible with the assertion and the primary implicatures. The resulting secondary implicatures are the three below

(10) $K_S\neg$ (A and B), $K_S\neg$ (A and C), $K_S\neg$ (B and C), $K_S\neg$ (A and B) and C

It is easy to verify that this derives the desired result by glancing back at the Venn diagrams at the beginning of this section.

Hence, multiple disjunctions are a strong argument in favor of the global approach. What about cases such as (6) and (7)? One important fact about these cases is that without adding a local implicature to the scope of the downward entailing operator, the sentences would all be contradictory. In an unpublished paper, Schwarz et al. (2008) test experimentally how frequently local implicatures are drawn in a downward entailing environment when this is not contraditory otherwise. They report that while for the positive case (11a), 64.7 % of their subject draw an exclusivity implicature, only 6.8 % do so in the downward entailing environment of (11b).

(11) a. Maria asked Bob to invite Fred or Sam to the barbecue.
b. Maria asked Bob not to invite Fred or Sam to the barbecue.

This indicates that local implicatures of the type in (6) and (7) are only drawn when the sentence otherwise violates a pragmatic constraint or prior belief. I conclude therefore that this is best described as a kind of repair strategy of a metalinguistic nature following Horn (1985), Geurts (2009).[3] In general, these can be represented by embedded speech act operators following Krifka (2001).

With this background, consider now the Hurford's constraint data. The argument in this case is based on the following constraint by Hurford (1974): A sentence that contains a disjunctive phrase of the form "S or S′" is infelicitous if S entails S′ or S′ entails S. (12) gives some examples for the application of Hurford's constraint:

(12) a. #Mary saw a dog or an animal.
b. #Mary saw an animal or a dog.
c. #Every girl who saw an animal or a dog talked to Jack.

[3] I am not considering in this paper a second class of examples with implicatures where the local implicatures may represent a strengthening of the global implicature since these are not directly linked to disjunction. See Sauerland (2004a), Russell (2006) and Geurts (2009) for discussion.

However, Gazdar (1979) noted a systematic exception to Hurford's constraint: scalar terms can occur with their stronger scale-mates Singh (2008 points out that there is an order restriction in such examples).

(13) a. Mary solved the first problem or the second problem or both problems.
b. Mary read some or all of the books.

In such examples, the literal meaning alone predicts that Hurford's constraint should be violated because the first disjunct *Mary solved the first problem or the second problem* is entailed by the second one *Mary solved both problems*. Rather than complicating the statement of Hurford's constraint, local implicatures provide a more elegant solution of the problem as Chierchia et al. (2008, 2009) correctly point out. In representation (14), Hurford's constraint is not violated, because the first disjunct is strengthened so as to not be entailed by the second disjunct since exh_T contributes the exclusivity implicature.

(14) Mary solved exh_T (the first problem or the second problem) or both problems.

But, local implicatures cannot be generally computed in multiple disjunctions as we saw above in the discussion of the xor data. While there have been no controlled experiments done on the generalized xor data, I doubt the percentage of local implicatures in the general case will be much greater than in the case of a downward entailing environment.

What then is the lesson to draw from the Hurford's constraint date. Note first, that in the case of these data, which we may represent abstractly as *(A or B) or (A and B)*, the same problem as with the generalized xor data doesn't arise: While *(A xor B) xor C* generally isn't equivalent to the intuitive meaning of *(A or B) or C*, *(A xor B) xor (A and B)* is equivalent to *A or B* because *A xor B* and *A and B* are disjoint. But, furthermore there is in this case as in the cases discussed in (6) and (7) a external factor, Hurford's constraint, that forces the computation of local scalar implicatures. Therefore, I think the correct conclusion to draw from data such as (13) is that local implicature computation is a repair strategy that is derived by speech act embedding and is only available when otherwise a constraint such as Hurford's is violated or the statement would contradict prior knowledge.

2 Free Choice Effects

Now let us turn to the second argument of Chierchia et al. (2008) supporting local implicature computation; the argument based on the free choice data. The basic observation of free choice Kamp (1973) is that (15a) and (15b) are naturally understood as synonymous.[4]

[4]The sentence also has a dispreferred second reading where it can be followed by *I don't know which* and the free choice effect is absent. I assume with the literature on the topic that this is a case of ambiguity and don't deal with this reading in the following.

(15) a. You may eat the cake or the ice-cream.
b. You may eat the cake and you may eat the ice-cream but not both.

This effect can be described by attributing to (15a) the two free choice inferences as shown in (16)[5]:

(16) You may/are allowed to eat the cake or the ice-cream.
$\rightsquigarrow$ You may/are allow to eat the cake.
$\rightsquigarrow$ You may/are allow to eat the ice-cream.

An important assumption of the argument by Chierchia et al. (2008) is that free choice inferences are implicatures. This argues against accounts of free choice inferences that derive them by changing the meaning of disjunction itself such as those of Zimmermann (2000) and Geurts (2005). The main argument to account for free choice inferences as implicatures is that these inferences disappear when the disjunction is embedded under negation (Kratzer et al. 2002, 2017; Alonso 2006). This is illustrated by (17), which does not mean that no one is allowed to eat the cake and the ice-cream, but has the stronger meaning that no one is allowed to eat either.

(17) No one is allowed to eat the cake or the ice-cream.

Assuming for now that this argument is sufficient to convince us that the free choice effect ought to be derived as an implicature, it provides another test where the global and the local can be compared. As Fox (2007) points out, the global approach fares badly on this comparison. This is very easy to see: If we use $\Diamond\,(p\ or\ q)$ as abbreviation for "You are allowed to eat the cake or the ice-cream", the primary implicatures predicted by the global approach as presented above are the following:

(18) a. $\neg K_S \Diamond$ p
b. $\neg K_S \Diamond$ q
c. $\neg K_S \Diamond$ (p and q)
d. $\neg K_S \Box$ (p or q)
e. $\neg K_S \Box$ p
f. $\neg K_S \Box$ q
g. $\neg K_S \Box$ (p and q)

Of these, (18a) and (18b) contradict the free choice inferences. Therefore, the global approach not only fails to predict the free choice inferences, but in fact predicts their negations.

The local approach as presented above doesn't do much better. We can apply exhaustification in $\Diamond\,(porq)$ at two point; below and above $\Diamond$. If we apply it in both places, the result is $Exh_T(\Diamond\,(pxorq))$. If we assume that the scalar alternative to $\Diamond$ is the necessity operator $\Box$, we arrive at $\Diamond\,(pxorq)$ and $\neg\Box\,(pxorq)$. While this does not contradict both free choice inferences, the result is too weak to derive the free choice inferences.

[5] I put aside here the question whether this effect arises with indefinites to and how general it is.

The system Fox advocates is a hybrid of the local and global systems presented above with some innovations of his own. It adopts from the local approach mainly the assumption that implicature computation is a grammatical process and contributes to truth conditions. Therefore implicature computation on Fox's approach takes place before sentence pragmatics applies, and this avoids the conflict between primary implicatures and the free choice inference we observed in (18). In all other respects, Fox's procedure is a global process for the reason just discussed. However, the global can also not be $Exh_T(\Diamond\,(porq))$: This would predict just the implicatures $\neg\Diamond\,(pandq)$ and $\neg\Box\,(p \text{ or } q)$, not the free choice inferences.

Fox's solution is to revise exhaustification generalizing my proposal (Sauerland 2004b), which I summarized in the previous section. Fox adopts the assumption that the alternatives of a disjunction are not just conjunction, but also individual disjuncts. Since then the alternatives aren't linearly ordered, this has the consequence that potential implicatures can contradict each other. Indeed in the simplest case of disjunction, such a contradiction arises: If both alternatives to (19a) are negated, the resulting implicatures (19a) and (19b) contradict the assertion.

(19) John talked to Mary or Sue.
  a. John didn't talk to Mary.
  b. John didn't talk to Sue.

In my proposal, potential primary implicatures were filtered so as to not contradict the assertion and potential secondary implicatures such as to not contradict either the assertion or the primary implicatures. While this addresses the case in (19) indirectly, the filtering procedure would not directly say anything about a case like (19), where the individual implicatures don't contradict the assertion, but taken together they do. Fox proposes a more general procedure that avoids problems arising from logical relationships between conjunctions of potential implicatures and the assertion. He introduces the notion of *innocent excludability* as defined in (20) to this end:

(20) q is *innocently excludable* given T and p iff.
  for any maximal subset $S \subset T$ such that $\{\neg\phi \mid \phi \in S\}$ is consistent with p, $q \in S$

Innocently excludable alternatives are those that will not contradict the assertion when negated even in conjunction with other potential implicatures. The exhaustivity operator is then defined as in (21) to negate exactly the innocently excludable alternatives

(21) $[\![Exh]\!](T)(p)(w) \Leftrightarrow p(w) \wedge \forall q \in T(q$ is innocently excludable given T and $p \rightarrow q(w) = 0)$

As an example, consider simple disjunction as in (19), abbreviated here as $A \vee B$. The alternatives are shown in the graph in (22). There are two maximal subsets of the set of alternatives such that their negations are consistent with the assertion, and both are indicated in the graph. Only elements of their intersection are innocently excludable, i.e. only $A \wedge B$. In this way, the approach predicts the exclusivity implicature.

(22)

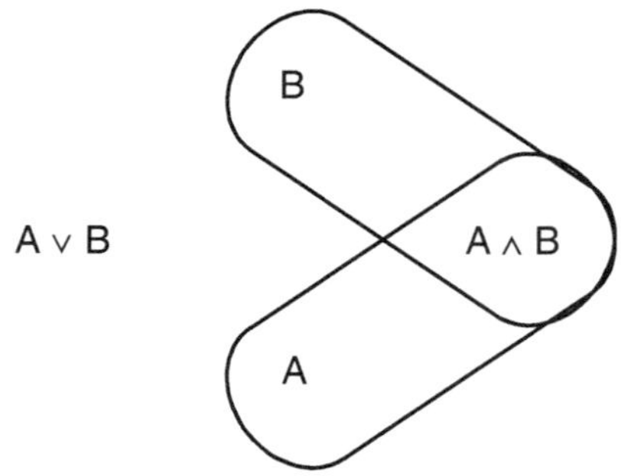

Note that the approach does not capture the primary, uncertainty implicatures such $\neg K_S A$ and $\neg K_S B$ for (22). So it needs to be supplemented with a Gricean mechanism to derive these.

Now consider Fox's derivation of free choice effect using (23) as the paradigmatic example which I'll abbreviate as $\Diamond(p \vee q)$. The result of exhaustification at the sentence level is computed right below (23), where the arrows indicate entailment relations. I did not include alternatives with $\Box$ in the graphic in (24) because these all are innocently excludable, and the implicature $\neg\Box(p \vee q)$ results. From the alternatives with $\Diamond$ shown in (24), the implicature $\neg\Diamond(p \wedge q)$ is derived.

(23) You may eat the cake or the ice-cream.

(24)

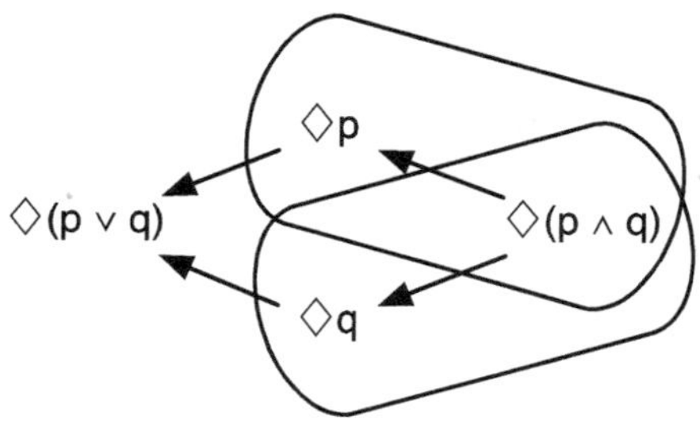

Fox (2007) accounts for free choice by second order exhaustification (cf. Kratzer et al. 2002; Spector 2007). Second order exhaustification represents a recursive application of the Exh-Operator as shown in (25). Note that Fox assumes that for the primary exhaustification in the scope of the secondary exhaustification, the set of alternatives T is the same for each alternative considered by the secondary exhaustification.[6]

(25) Exh(T′)(Exh(T)(You may eat the cake or the ice-cream)), where $T' = \{Exh(T)(\phi) \mid \phi \in T\}$

[6]One consequence of this is that higher order exhaustification always lives on the partition of logical space introduced by the elements of T. i.e. if two worlds occupy the same cell of this partition, no higher order exhaustification of will distinguish between the two worlds. This entails that if T is finite, at some level n of higher order exhaustification of level n, level $n+1$ and any greater level will be equivalent.

The alternatives to be considered for second level in this case are shown in (26), where again the arrows indicate entailment. The result of second order exhaustification in this case differs from the of first order exhaustification because both $\Diamond p \wedge \neg \Diamond q$ and $\Diamond q \wedge \neg \Diamond p$ are innocently excludable.

(26)

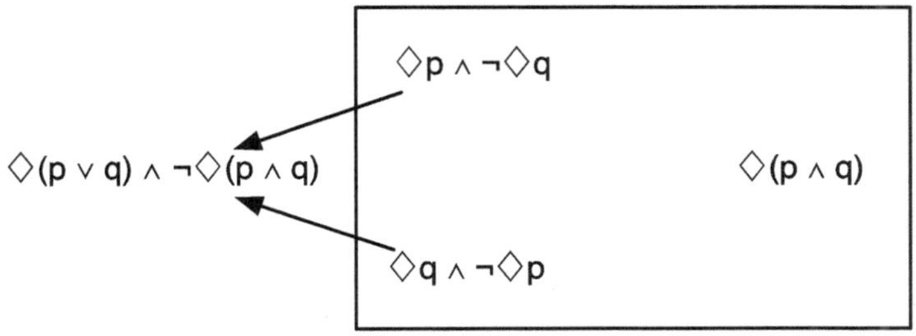

Therefore, two new implicatures are predicted by second order exhaustification, namely $\neg(\Diamond p \wedge \neg \Diamond q)$ and $\neg(\Diamond q \wedge \neg \Diamond p)$. Given that the assertion states that $\Diamond$ (p $\vee$ q), these two implicatures amount to exactly the desired free choice inferences: $\Diamond$ p and $\Diamond$ q.

Note that Fox's approach also provides an account for the generalized xor data discussed in the previous section. There we saw that other versions of a local approach don't predict the right implicatures for the xor data. Fox's system in this case essentially adopts the global solution of Sauerland (2004b). Consider for example the case in (27):

(27) Kai had the broccoli or some of the peas.

Abbreviating this sentence to $A \vee \exists x Bx$, (28) shows the alternatives Fox assumes for the examples, and computes which are innocently excludable. In this case, there are two different maximal sets that could be all negated and still be consistent with the assertion. Therefore, only the alternatives included in both sets are innocently excludable. This predicts the implicatures $\neg$ (A $\wedge$ $\exists$xBx) and $\neg$ ($\forall$xBx) as desired.

(28)

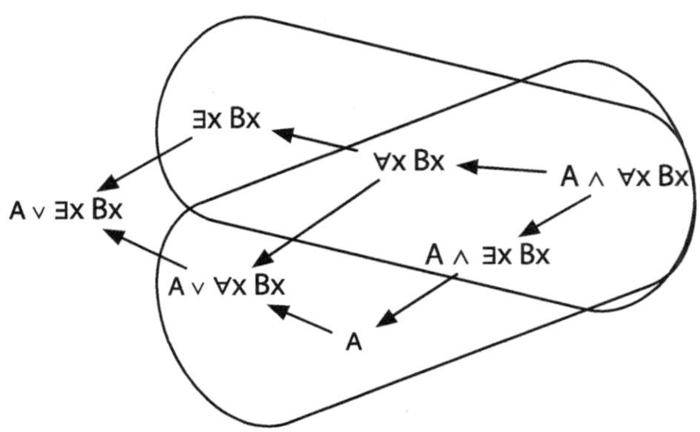

It is easy to verify that Fox's approach also makes the correct prediction for the multiple disjunction case.

Note though that Fox's approach in this case applies exhaustification globally, and would indeed make wrong predictions if it was applied locally: Consider the representation in (29), where the second line uses the same abbreviations as we did previously.

(29) exh_T (Kai had the broccoli or exh_U some of the peas)
exh_T (Bx ∧ exh_U (∃x Bx))

The alternative set U of the second Exh-operator in (29) consists of $\exists xBx$ and $\forall xBx$. Therefore local exhaustification yields $\exists xBx \wedge \neg(\forall xBx)$. The alternative set of the higher exhaustification operator is as shown in (30). Note that only $A \wedge \exists xBx \wedge \neg(\forall xBx)$ is innocently excludable.

(30)

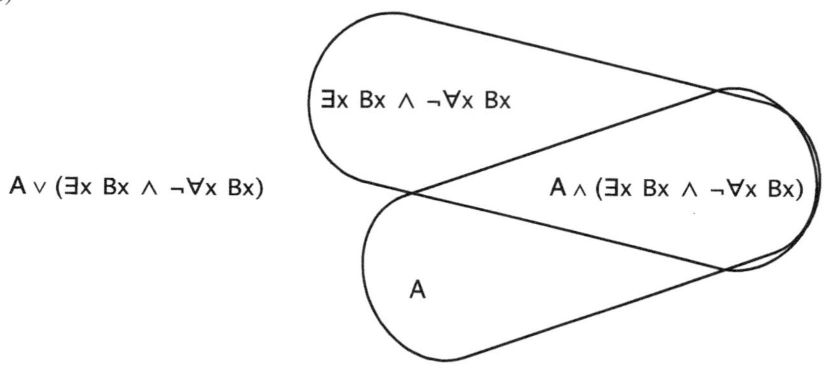

Exhaustification therefore results in the following interpretation.

(31) $(A \vee (\exists x\, Bx \wedge \neg(\forall x\, Bx))) \wedge \neg(A \wedge \exists x\, Bx \wedge \neg(\forall x\, Bx))$

This is equivalent to the following disjunction where it is easy to see that the third disjunct, $A \wedge \forall xBx$, does not capture part of the intuitive interpretation of the generalized xor sentences.

(32) $(\neg A \wedge \exists xBx \wedge \neg(\forall xBx)) \vee (A \wedge \neg\exists xBx) \vee (A \wedge \forall xBx)$

To sum up this chapter, I have shown that the free choice data represent a potential problem not for the global approach to implicatures, but for the assumption that implicatures and free choice inferences are all due to the same pragmatic mechanism. In fact, Fox's account of implicatures is crucially global in the relevant sense. The argument against the Gricean account of implicatures Fox makes therefore is entirely dependent on the question whether free choice inferences should be accounted for in the same way as other implicatures or not. As noted above, approaches that build free choice inferences into the meaning of disjunction (Zimmermann 2000; Geurts 2005) do not account for free choice inferences as implicatures and in the case of free choice items we find that the free choice inferences are grammaticalized. The implicature account of free choice inferences rests on the observation by Kratzer et al. (2002) in (17) that free choice inferences do not arise when disjunction occurs in the scope of negation. However, there are other ways of accounting for this fact: it could be that the disjunction of Zimmermann or Geurts is a positive polarity item, while in downward entailing environments disjunction must receive the meaning of logical disjunction. This would predict differences between free choice inferences and scalar implicatures. The next paragraph discusses some emerging evidence for such differences.

At the time I was working on this paper, Chemla (2009) presented new experimental data casting further doubt on the assumption that free choice inferences are regular implicatures. Specifically, Chemla experimentally compares the strength as an inference of a universal implicature as in (33) with that of a universal free choice inference as in (34).

(33) a. *Premise:* Everyone passed most of his exams.
b. *Inference tested:* No one passed them all.

(34) a. *Premise:* Everybody is allowed to give me the dissertation or the commentary.
b. *Inference tested:* Everybody can choose which of the two he will give to the teacher.

As Chemla reports, there is a significant difference. Namely, the universal implicature (33) is judged as less strong than the universal free choice inference in (34b) (see page 17 of Chemla's paper). Chemla rightly notes that his result casts doubt on the link between scalar implicatures and free choice inferences. Note that Chemla's result would be exactly predicted by the account sketched in the previous paragraph: The absence of a universal implicature in (33) argues further against the local approach to implicatures, but confirms the global approach that only predicts the implicature that not everyone passed all of his exams for (33a). Furthermore a universal free choice is predicted if the free choice inference is part of the lexical meaning of disjunction.

3 Conclusion

In this paper, I considered some current work on the interaction of implicature computation and disjunction. In particular, I addressed data from Hurford's constraint and data from free choice that Chierchia et al. (2008) discuss in their interesting paper. Specifically, they claim that these data provide support for a local approach to implicatures. The data from Hurford's constraint, in particular, are taken to show that local implicature computation applies to each disjunct of a disjunction. However, I show in Sect. 1 that in general an account that assume local implicature computation for each disjunct faces problem with the xor data, for instance multiple disjunction. In these cases, local implicatures are intuitively never available and therefore local implicature computation must be blocked. I have concluded therefore that the data involving Hurford's constraint raised by Chierchia et al. (2008, 2009) are cases where we see a repair strategy at work, which may well be metalinguistic in the form of an embedded speech act.

The second kind of criticism of the global approach I have addressed is that of Fox (2007) based on free choice inferences. As I have shown, Fox's criticism does not actually directly adhere to the local/global distinction, but in fact his approach must crucially be global as well. Rather Fox's argument targets the question whether implicature computation is entirely pragmatic, or at least partially semantic. While this is an interesting argument, I have shown that Fox's assumption that free choice inferences are implicatures is at least worth further examination. If the assumption is dropped—and recent experimental data by Chemla (2009) suggest doing so—the global approach to implicatures can account for all the data straightforwardly.

References

Alonso-Ovalle, Luis. 2006. Disjunction in alternative semantics. Doctoral Dissertation, University of Massachusetts at Amherst, Amherst, MA.

Chemla, Emmanuel. 2009. Universal implicatures and free choice effects: experimental data. *Semantics and Pragmatics* 2: 1–33.

Chierchia, Gennaro. 2004. Scalar implicatures, polarity phenomena, and the syntax/pragmatics interface. In *Structures and beyond*, ed. Adriana Belletti, 39–103. Oxford, UK: Oxford University Press.

Chierchia, Gennaro. 2006. Broaden your views: implicatures of domain widening and the "logicality" of language. *Linguistic Inquiry* 37: 535–590.

Chierchia, Gennaro, Danny Fox, and Benjamin Spector. 2009. Hurford's constraint and the theory of scalar implicatures: evidence for embedded implicatures. Semanticsarchive.

Chierchia, Gennaro, Benjamin Spector, and Danny Fox. 2008. The grammatical view of scalar implicatures and the relationship between semantics and pragmatics.

Cohen, Jonathan. 1971. Some remarks on Grice's views about the logical particles of natural language. In *Pragmatics of natural languages*, ed. Y. Bar-Hillel, 50–68. Dordrecht: Reidel.

Fox, Danny. 2007. Free choice and the theory of scalar implicatures. In Sauerland and Stateva (2007), 71–120.

Gajewski, Jon, and Yael Sharvit. 2009. In *Defense of the Grammatical Approach to Local Implicatures*. University of Connecticut, Ms. http://web2.uconn.edu/sharvit/Gajewski-Sharvit-15may2009.pdf.

Gazdar, Gerald. 1979. *Pragmatics: Implicature, Presupposition, and Logical Form*. New York, N.Y.: Academic Press.

Geurts, Bart. 2005. Entertaining alternatives: disjunctions as modals. *Natural Language Semantics* 13: 383–410.

Geurts, Bart. 2009. Scalar implicature and local pragmatics. *Mind and Language* 24: 51–79.

Grice, Paul. 1989. *Studies in the Way of Words*. Cambridge, Mass.: Harvard University Press.

Horn, Laurence R. 1985. Metalinguistic negation and pragmatic ambiguity. *Language* 61: 121–174.

Hurford, James R. 1974. Inclusive or exclusive disjunction. *Foundations of Language* 11: 409–411.

Kamp, Hans. 1973. Free choice permission. *Proceedings of the Aristotelian Society, New Series* 74: 57–74.

Katzir, Roni. 2007. Structurally-defined alternatives. *Linguistics and Philosophy* 30: 669–690.

Keshet, Ezra. 2017. Scalar implicatures with alternative semantics. In *Contrastiveness in Information Structure, Alternatives, and Scalar Implicatures*, eds. Lee Chungmin et al., 261–279. Springer.

Kratzer, Angelika, and Junko Shimoyama. 2002. Indeterminate pronouns: the view from Japanese. In *Proceedings of the third Tokyo conference on psycholinguistics*, ed. Yukio Otsu, 1–25. Tokyo: Hituzi Syobo.

Kratzer, Angelika, and Junko Shimoyama. 2017. Indeterminate pronouns: the view from Japanese. In *Contrastiveness in Information Structure, Alternatives, and Scalar Implicatures*, eds. Lee Chungmin et al., 123–143. Springer.

Krifka, Manfred. 2001. Quantifying into question acts. *Natural Language Semantics* 9: 1–40.

Lee, Chungmin, Ference Kiefer, and Manfred Krifka, ed. 2017. *Contrastiveness in Information structure, Alternatives, and Scalar Implicatures*. Heidelberg, Germany: Springer.

McCawley, James D. 1993. *Everything that Linguists have Always Wanted to Know About Logic*. Chicago, Ill.: University of Chicago Press, 2nd edition.

Russell, Ben. 2006. Against grammatical computation of scalar implicatures. *Journal of Semantics* 23: 361–382.

Sauerland, Uli. 2004a. On embedded implicatures. *Journal of Cognitive Science* 5: 103–137.

Sauerland, Uli. 2004b. Scalar implicatures in complex sentences. *Linguistics and Philosophy* 27: 367–391.

Sauerland, Uli. 2011. The computation of scalar implicatures: pragmatic, lexical, or grammatical? *Language and Linguistics Compass* 6: 36–49.

Sauerland, Uli. 2014. Intermediate scalar implicatures. In *Pragmatics, semantics and the case of scalar implicatures*, ed. Salvatore Pistoia-Reda. Basingstoke, UK: Palgrave Macmillan.

Sauerland, Uli, and Penka Stateva (eds.). 2007. *Presupposition and Implicature in Compositional Semantics*. Basingstoke, UK: Palgrave Macmillan.

Schwarz, Florian, Charles Jr. Clifton, and Lyn Frazier. 2008. Strengthening 'or': effects of focus and downward entailing contexts on scalar implicatures. UMass Amherst.

Sharvit, Yael, and Jon Gajewski. 2008. On the calculation of local implicatures. In *Proceedings of WCCFL 26*, ed. C. Chang and H. Haynie, 411–419. Somerville, Mass: Cascadilla Press.

Simons, Mandy. 1998. "or": issues in the semantics and pragmatics of disjunction. Doctoral Dissertation, Cornell University, Ithaca, N.Y.

Singh, Raj. 2008. On the interpretation of disjunction: asymmetric, incremental, and eager for inconsistency. *Linguistics and Philosophy* 31: 245–260.

Spector, Benjamin. 2005. Scalar implicatures: exhaustivity and Gricean reasoning. In *Questions in Dynamic Semantics*, ed. Maria Aloni, Alastair Butler, and Paul Dekker, 225–250. Elsevier.

Spector, Benjamin. 2007. Aspects of the pragmatics of plural morphology: On higher-order implicatures. In Sauerland and Stateva (2007), 243–281.

van Rooij, Robert, and Katrin Schulz. 2004. Exhaustive interpretation of complex sentences. *Journal of Logic, Language, and Information* 13: 491–519.

Zimmermann, Thomas Ede. 2000. Free choice disjunction and epistemic possibility. *Natural Language Semantics* 8: 255–290.

Scalar Implicatures with Alternative Semantics

Ezra Keshet

Abstract This paper explores interactions between the alternative semantics of Kratzer and Shimoyama (2002) and the embeddable exhaustive operator Exh proposed to handle embedded implicatures (Chierchia 2004; Fox 2004, 2007). The proposal is that when Exh applies to single alternative propositions (instead of complete, matrix-level sets of alternatives), it can generate correct scalar implicatures while avoiding several problems proposed in prior literature. The problems solved include implicature generation when a quantifier appears in a disjunction (Chierchia 2004) and when a sentence includes complex quantifiers like "more than two" (Krifka 1999).

Keywords Scalar implicatures · Exhaustive operator · Alternative semantics

1 Introduction

This paper examines several challenges to the standard Horn Scale analysis of scalar implicature and proposes a new system that addresses these challenges, based on the Alternative Semantics of Kratzer and Shimoyama (2002).

2 Standard Analysis

One standard account of scalar implicature proposes that scalar items are associated with linguistically available scales, called Horn Scales after Horn (1972). To generate implicatures for a sentence containing a scalar item, one must consider the alternative sentences where the scalar item has been replaced with an item from its scale. All such sentences that are stronger are implicated to be false. For a sentence ϕ,

---

E. Keshet (✉)
University of Michigan, Ann Arbor, USA
e-mail: keshet@alum.mit.edu

C. Lee et al. (eds.), *Contrastiveness in Information Structure, Alternatives and Scalar Implicatures*, Studies in Natural Language and Linguistic Theory 91, DOI 10.1007/978-3-319-10106-4_13

the set of alternative sentences $Alt(\phi)$ is given in (1), and the implicatures generated are given in (2)[1]:

(1) $Alt(\phi) = \{\phi' : \phi$ contains scalar item s and ϕ' is the same as ϕ except that s is replaced with an item from the Horn Scale for $s\}$

(2) Implicatures Generated: $\forall \phi' \in Alt(\phi) \,.\, (\phi' \Rightarrow \phi) \rightarrow \neg\phi'$

For example, an implicature for (3a) is given in (3b) is as follows:

(3) a. Paul read three books. $\rightsquigarrow$
b. Paul did not read four books.

The scalar item *three* is part of the Horn Scale consisting of at least the natural numbers, so the relevant alternatives to (3a) are those sentences where *three* is replaced with another number as follows:

(4) Horn Scale for *three*: $\{$*one, two, three, four, five, ...*$\}$

(5) *Alt(Paul read three books)* =

$$\left\{\begin{array}{c} \textit{Paul read one book},\ \textit{Paul read two books}, \\ \textit{Paul read three books},\ \textit{Paul read four books}, \\ \textit{Paul read five books},\ \ldots \end{array}\right\}$$

Since *Paul read four books* is such an alternative and furthermore entails (3a), the implicature is generated that Paul did not read four books:

(6) *Paul read four books.* $\Rightarrow$ *Paul read three books.*

(7) $\therefore$ *Paul did not read four books.* (by 2)

3 Challenges

This standard approach does not generate the correct results in every case, however. For the remainder of the paper, I will concentrate on two instances where the standard proposal fails. These cases will motivate a new approach to scalar implicature, detailed in Sect. 6 below.

3.1 Comparative Problem

When a scalar item like *three* is embedded in a comparative expression, the implicature it normally gives rise to in a simpler context often disappears. For instance, (8a) does not actually generate the implicature in (8b)[2]:

---

[1]Note that if ϕ itself (or another scalar item with the same meaning as ϕ) were a member of $Alt(\phi)$ the entailment in (2) would have to be asymmetric entailment.

[2]This is explicitly pointed out by Krifka (1999), but assumed in many earlier works, such as Horn (1985).

(8) (after Krifka 1999)
  a. Paul read more than three books. $\not\rightsquigarrow$
  b. Paul did not read more than four books.

However, if you were to go through the exact steps of the standard proposal used above, you would generate this (fallacious) implicature. *Paul read more than four books* is a stronger alternative of (8a) as defined in (1):

(9) *Alt*(*Paul read more than three books*) =

$$\left\{\begin{array}{c} \textit{Paul read more than one book},\ \ \textit{Paul read more than two books}, \\ \textit{Paul read more than three books},\ \ \textit{Paul read more than four books}, \\ \textit{Paul read more than five books},\ \ \ldots \end{array}\right\}$$

(10) a. *Paul read more than four books.* $\Rightarrow$
  b. *Paul read more than three books.*

Therefore, by (2):

(11) *Paul did not read more than four books.*

This incorrect prediction is a challenge to be overcome by any theory of scalar implicature.[3]

3.2 Disjunction Problem

In order to handle the implicature generated by a disjunction, the standard approach considers *or* to be part of a Horn scale also containing *and*. This yields the alternatives in (13) for the sentence in (12):

(12) Paul read *The New York Times* or *The Washington Post*.

(13) $Alt(12) = \left\{\begin{array}{l} \textit{Paul read The New York Times or The Washington Post}, \\ \textit{Paul read The New York Times and The Washington Post} \end{array}\right\}$

With this alternative set, the correct implicature is derived: Paul did not read *The New York Times* and *The Washington Post*.

Another case where the standard proposal makes an incorrect prediction was pointed out by Chierchia (2004) and discussed in detail by Sauerland (2004b). The problem is that when one clause of a disjunction contains a scalar item, the standard account predicts that the other clause of the disjunction be implicated to be false.[4] For instance, (14a) is predicted incorrectly to have the implicature in (14b).

---

[3]Lee (2010) points out that there is a reading of a comparative sentence like (10a) where the numeral—*three* in this case—is accommodated from previous discourse, and the only scalar term is the phrase *more than*. In this reading, the implicature generated is something like *Paul did not read many more than three books*. However, there is also a reading where the numeral *three* is truly new information. For instance, the person uttering (10a) could only have enough information to say for sure that Paul read three, but there is inconclusive evidence that he may have read more books. It is this reading that I will focus on below.

[4]Sauerland (2004b) points out that a version of this problem, involving disjunction within disjunction, was noted by McCawley (1993) and Simons (2000).

(14) a. Paul read *The New York Times* or some of the books. $\not\rightsquigarrow$
b. Paul did not read *The New York Times*.

The reasoning goes as follows. Sauerland (2004b) argues that the set of alternatives for sentences containing two scalar items is the set of all sentences where either or both items are replaced by items from their respective Horn scales. Such a set of alternatives for (14a) is given in (16). Notice, then, that (17a) is a stronger alternative to (14a).

(15) Horn Scale for *some*: {*some*, *most*, *all*}

(16) *Alt*(*Paul read The New York Times or some of the books*) =

$$\left\{\begin{array}{l} \textit{Paul read The New York Times or some of the books,} \\ \textit{Paul read The New York Times or most of the books,} \\ \textit{Paul read The New York Times or all of the books,} \\ \textit{Paul read The New York Times and some of the books,} \\ \textit{Paul read The New York Times and most of the books,} \\ \textit{Paul read The New York Times and all of the books} \end{array}\right\}$$

(17) a. *Paul read The New York Times or all of the books.* $\Rightarrow$
b. *Paul read The New York Times or some of the books.*

Therefore, by (2):

(18) *Paul did not read The New York Times or all of the books.*

And if you apply DeMorgan's Law:

(19) *Paul did not read The New York Times and Paul did not read all of the books.*

Therefore (taking the first clause of the conjunction):

(20) *Paul did not read The New York Times.*

Once again, this fallacious prediction should be avoided in a theory of scalar implicature.

4 Intuitive Proposal

To address these challenges, I will start with a simple observation, which is also found in Kratzer (2005).[5] First, it has been noted that scalar sentences including the word *only* and having focus on their scalar item roughly paraphrase the strengthened meanings of the same sentences without *only* (Fox 2004). (The strengthened meaning is the meaning of the original sentence plus its scalar implicatures.) For instance, (21) roughly paraphrases the strengthened meaning of (3a):

[5] Kratzer (2005) proposes a similar line of attack, especially for the comparative puzzle, in her 2005 LSA Summer Institute handout. I have tried to expand this analysis to other puzzles and flesh out the technical details.

(21) Paul only read **three** books.

Building on this idea, the observation I will base my analysis on is that paraphrases where the indefinite quantifier takes scope over the rest of the sentence seem to avoid the problems mentioned above. Such a scenario is schematized in (22), where the indefinite SCALAR is existentially closed at the top of the sentence (assuming that an indefinite is some kind of existential quantifier):

(22)

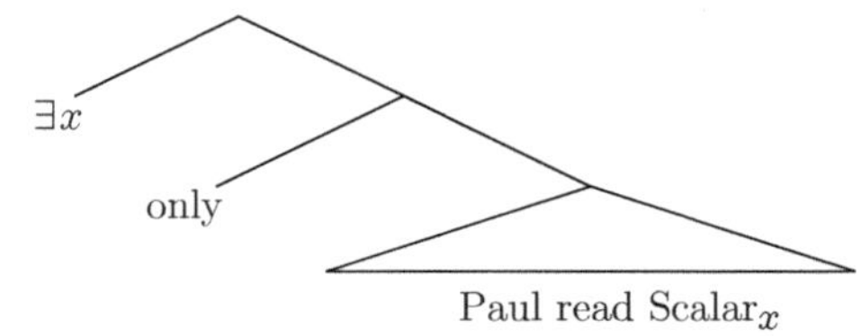

Indeed, paraphrases that force a high scope reading for the indefinite quantifier seem to match the expected strengthened meaning of sentences with scalar implicatures:

(23) a. Paul read three books.
b. There is a group x of (exactly) three books: Paul only read x.

(24) a. Paul read some books.
b. There is a group x that is a proper subset of the books: Paul only read x.

(25) a. Paul read *War and Peace* or *The Brothers Karamazov*.
b. There's a group x containing one book, which is either *War and Peace* or *The Brothers Karamazov*: Paul only read x.

Also, in the comparative and complex disjunction cases, the paraphrases seem to match the actual strengthened meanings more closely than the meanings generated by the standard proposal:

(26) a. Paul read more than two books.
b. There is a group x of more than two books: Paul only read x.

(27) a. Paul read *The New York Times* or some of the books.
b. There is a group x such that x is the group containing only *The New York Times* or x is a proper subset of the books: Paul only read x.

Having made this observation, the question arises of how a structure suggested by these paraphrases can be implemented syntactically and semantically. The next section presents some background work that will provide the basis for the proposal given in Sect. 6.

5 Background

In this section, I will adapt a system proposed by Kratzer and Shimoyama (2002). In their system, the normal semantic values for many items of type σ (or $\langle \sigma t, t \rangle$) are replaced by sets containing items of type σ. For the remainder of the paper, I will refer to such items as being of type $\{\sigma\}$ or subsets of D_σ. For instance, a simple indefinite such as *a book* has the following denotation:

(28) $[\![\textbf{a book}]\!] = \{x \in D_e : x \text{ is a book}\}$ (type $\{e\}, \subseteq D_e$)

The phrase *a book* denotes the set of individuals that are books.

5.1 Hamblin Functional Application

In the Kratzer and Shimoyama system, these denotation sets combine pointwise with predicates via the following composition rule:

(29)

$\alpha_{\{\tau\}}$ [$\beta_{\{\langle\sigma,\tau\rangle\}}$ $\gamma_{\{\sigma\}}$]

$\{b(c_1), b(c_2), \ldots, b(c_n)\}$ [$\{b\}$ $\{c_1, c_2, \ldots, c_n\}$]

(30) *Hamblin Functional Application*
If α is a branching node with daughters β and γ, and $[\![\beta]\!] \subseteq D_{\langle\sigma,\tau\rangle}$ and $[\![\gamma]\!] \subseteq D_\sigma$, then $[\![\alpha]\!] = \{a \in D_\tau : \exists b \exists c[b \in [\![\beta]\!] \ \& \ c \in [\![\gamma]\!] \ \& \ a = b(c)]\}$.

Basically, the rule applies each of the predicates in set β to each of the individuals in set γ. The results of these operations form the set α.

For instance, in the example below, the singleton set representing the denotation of the verb *read* combines with the set representing the meaning of the phrase *a book*:

(31)

read a book
{*read War & Peace*, *read The Brothers Karamazov*, ...}

read {*read*} — **a book** {*War & Peace*, *The Brothers Karamazov*, ...}

This new set, a set of predicates, can combine with another at the next level up:

(32)

Paul read a book
{*Paul read W&P*, *Paul read TBK*, ...}

Paul {*Paul*} — **read a book** {*read W&P*, *read TBK*, ...}

This process continues, until at the the top of a sentence you are left with a set of propositions.

5.2 Sentential Quantifier

The normal meaning of the sentence *Paul read a book,* however, is not a set of propositions, but a single proposition. The correct meaning is obtained in this system by applying the sentential quantifier ∃ (using the standard Functional Application Rule):

(33) $[\![\exists\alpha]\!] = \{\lambda w' \,.\, \exists p[p \in [\![\alpha]\!] \;\&\; p(w') = 1]\}$ for $[\![\alpha]\!] \subseteq D_{st}$

∃ takes a set of propositions and returns a singleton set containing the proposition that is true when one of the original propositions in the set is true.[6]

5.3 Plural Individuals

Another bit of background machinery that the proposal below requires is the idea of plural individuals. Plural individuals (Link 1983) represent the mereological sums of singular individuals in D_e and have some properties analogous to sets (e.g., cardinality, part-of and proper part-of relations, and membership). Using this concept, we can now define the words of our example sentence:

(34) a. $[\![\textbf{books}]\!] = \{x \in D_e : x \text{ is two or more books}\}$ (type $\{e\}$)
b. $[\![\textbf{three}]\!] = \{x \in D_e : |x| = 3]\}$ (type $\{e\}$)
c. $[\![\textbf{read}]\!] = \{[\lambda y \in D_e \,.\, \lambda x \in D_e \,.\, x \text{ reads } y\}$ (type $\{\langle e, \langle e, t\rangle\rangle\}$)
d. $[\![\textbf{Paul}]\!] = \{Paul\}$ (type $\{e\}$)

Note that the standard Predicate Modification rule (Heim and Kratzer 1998) will work correctly on sets of alternatives:

(35)

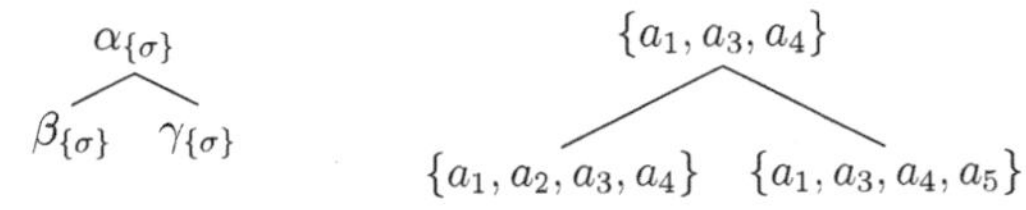

(36) *Predicate Modification*
If α is a branching node with daughters β and γ, and $[\![\beta]\!] \subseteq D_{\{\sigma\}}$ and $[\![\gamma]\!] \subseteq D_{\{\sigma\}}$, then $[\![\alpha]\!] = [\![\beta]\!] \cap [\![\gamma]\!]$.

This is the rule used to combine *three* and *books* to form the set of all groups of three books.

Now we can derive the complete meaning of a simple sentence:

(37) $[\![\exists$ **Paul read three books.**$]\!] = 1$ iff a statement in the following set is true: $\{$Paul read x : x is the sum of exactly three books$\}$.

---

[6]Kratzer and Shimoyama (2002) also propose generalized quantifiers that take sets of individuals. I believe that the presence of such a quantifier would have the same effect as reversing the order of an exhaustive operator and sentential quantifier—see Sect. 7.1.

5.4 Context

The last concept that the new proposal requires is a particular (but not unusual) notion of context. Every sentence is assumed to be uttered in relation to a subset of D_{st} that I will call the focus set, which can be thought of as the Hamblin denotation of the question under discussion.[7] For instance, the question in (38a) might set up the focus set in (38b):

(38) a. What did Paul read last night?
b. {Paul read *War and Peace* last night, Paul read *The Brothers Karamazov* last night, Paul read *The New York Times* last night, Paul read *W&P* ⊕ *NYT* last night, … }

Lee (2006) notion of a Potential Topic also comes in handy for describing the context of a potential scalar implicature by specifying exactly what can replace the *wh*-word(s) in the question under discussion. For instance, the Potential Topic for the context given in (38) would specify the reading material being considered in the current context, so {*War and Peace, The Brothers Karamazov, The New York Times, …*}.

6 Proposal

With the system outlined in the previous section in place, I can now describe the actual proposal. The idea is that scalar implicatures arise when a sentence contains a silent exhaustive operator (Fox 2004; see also Groenendijk and Stokhof 1984; Krifka 1995) which scopes below the existential closure of indefinites (Heim 1982; Kratzer and Shimoyama 2002) and disjunction (Rooth and Partee 1982).

My definition of the exhaustive operator *Exh* (adapted from those referenced above) is:

(39) $[\![Exh]\!] = \{[\lambda p \in D_{st} \,.\, \lambda w' \in D_s \,.\, p(w') \,\&\, \forall f \in F\ [f(w') \rightarrow\ (p \Rightarrow f)]]\}$, where F is the focus set.

When taking a proposition p, *Exh* means that p (often called the prejacent) is true and the only true propositions in the focus set are those that are entailed by p.

Proponents of an operator like *Exh* claim that it is simply missing in cases where implicatures are missing or canceled. Also, as opposed to a sentence-level implicature generation mechanism like that outlined in Sect. 2, a syntactic exhaustive operator can apply in embedded contexts. For the rest of the paper, I will assume *Exh*; but see Chierchia et al. (2008) for an extensive discussion of these issues and Geurts (2009, 2010); Giannakidou and Quer (2013) for criticism of the approach.

---

[7] As far as I can tell, this idea goes back to Collingwood (1940), as quoted in von Fintel (1995):

(i) Every statement that anybody ever makes is made in answer to a question (p. 14).

See also Roberts (1996).

Imagine that there are three choices of reading material in the focus set established by the question in (40a): *War and Peace*, *The New York Times*, and *The Brothers Karamazov*. Given this focus set, the meaning comes out as follows:

(40) a. What did Paul read last night?
b. $\exists$*Exh* Paul read *War & Peace* and *The Brothers Karamazov*.
c. A statement from this set is true:
{Paul read *War & Peace* $\oplus$ *The Brothers Karamazov* but not *The New York Times*.}

War & Peace and The Brothers Karamazov denotes the mereological sum ($\oplus$) of the two books mentioned. The exhaustive operator strengthens the meaning of the proposition in the following way: the alternative proposition where Paul read the third available piece of reading material, namely *The New York Times*, is asserted to be false.

This definition differs from most definitions of the overt exhaustive operator *only* in that the plain meaning of the prejacent is asserted to be true, rather than presupposed.[8] This cannot be the only difference, however, since there are positions where I have assumed *Exh* is benign that are essentially ungrammatical for *only*:

(41) *Paul only read more than three books last night.

As Lee (2010) points out, this sentence only has a meaning if *three* is stressed—and then it actually does implicate something like *Paul did not read more than four books*. The claim, then, is not that *Exh* is identical to *only*, only that it is similar.

6.1 Numerals

Consider a simple scalar sentence containing a numeral, in relation to the focus set in (42):

(42) {Paul read *War and Peace* last night, Paul read *The Brothers Karamazov* last night, Paul read *Crime and Punishment* last night, Paul read *The New York Times* last night, Paul read *W&P* $\oplus$ *NYT* last night, ...}

(43) a. Paul read three books last night.
b. There's a group x of three books: Paul only read x last night.

The intuitive paraphrase for the strengthened meaning of (43a) is given in (43b). This paraphrase entails that among the sentences in the focus set, the only true sentences are those where Paul read nothing other than some group of three books[9].

---

[8] An anonymous reviewer notes that Geurts (2009) terms this "M-ONLY."

[9] In relation to the focus set in (42), this sentence generates, among others, the implicature that Paul did not read *The New York Times*, since *The New York Times* is not a book. Please note that this sentence would be a fine answer to the question *How many books did Paul read last night?*. However, given this different question, the implicature that Paul did not read *The New York Times* would not be generated, since the sentence *Paul read The New York Times last night* would not be in the relevant focus set.

Finally, we can see how such a paraphrase is possible. The existential that scopes above all else comes from the ∃ operator. This is possible in the Kratzer and Shimoyama system even without proposing that the indefinite itself moves in the syntax.[10] A fuller derivation is given below:

(44) a. $\exists$*Exh* Paul read three books last night.
b. $\exists Exh$ {Paul read x last night : $x \in [\![\textbf{book}]\!]$ & $|x| = 3$}

By Hamblin Functional Application, you combine *Exh* and the set pointwise:

(44) c. $\exists$\{*Exh* Paul read x last night : $x \in [\![\textbf{book}]\!]$ & $|x| = 3$}

Now, if we assume there are only four books under discussion:

(44) d. One of these statements is true:

$$\left\{\begin{array}{l}\text{Paul only read } b_1 \oplus b_2 \oplus b_3,\\ \text{Paul only read } b_1 \oplus b_3 \oplus b_4,\\ \text{Paul only read } b_1 \oplus b_2 \oplus b_4,\\ \text{Paul only read } b_2 \oplus b_3 \oplus b_4\end{array}\right\}$$

6.2 *Some*

Similarly, in a sentence with the scalar item *some,* the desired result is obtained with the following new definition[11]:

(45) $[\![\textbf{some of the}]\!] = [\lambda X \subseteq D_e.\{x \in X : \exists y \in X[y \not< x]\}]$
(type $\langle\{e\},\{e\}\rangle$)

This definition operates on a set and therefore is applied using normal Functional Application. It basically returns its argument set minus the largest element, defined in terms of the plural individual part-of relation. A richer definition of *some of the books* might include the fact that it only includes groups containing a small proportion of the books, but for the purpose of deriving the simple *not all* implicature, this definition suffices.

In our four-book world the meanings of the terms are as follows:

(46) a. $[\![\textbf{books}]\!] =$

$$\left\{\begin{array}{l} b_1 \oplus b_2, b_1 \oplus b_3, b_1 \oplus b_4, b_2 \oplus b_3, b_2 \oplus b_4, b_3 \oplus b_4,\\ b_1 \oplus b_2 \oplus b_3, b_1 \oplus b_3 \oplus b_4, b_1 \oplus b_2 \oplus b_4, b_2 \oplus b_3 \oplus b_4,\\ b_1 \oplus b_2 \oplus b_3 \oplus b_4 \end{array}\right\}$$

---

[10] An anonymous reviewer points out that there is another system which allows similar existential closure over indefinites without movement: the choice-function analysis of Ruys (1993); Reinhart (1997); Winter (1997). The choice between the Kratzer and Shimoyama system and the choice-function system is not crucial to the analysis presented here.

[11] The constituent structure assumed here is simplified for presentation purposes. See Sauerland and Yatsushiro (2004) for a discussion of the true structure of such phrases.

b. $[\![\textbf{some of the books}]\!] = \left\{ \begin{array}{l} b_1 \oplus b_2, b_1 \oplus b_3, b_1 \oplus b_4, b_2 \oplus b_3, b_2 \oplus b_4, b_3 \oplus b_4, \\ b_1 \oplus b_2 \oplus b_3, b_1 \oplus b_3 \oplus b_4, b_1 \oplus b_2 \oplus b_4, b_2 \oplus b_3 \oplus b_4 \end{array} \right\}$

The group including all four books is the only one missing from this second set.

This definition basically builds the "some-but-not-all" meaning into the definition of the determiner. Now, one early objection to this definition might be that it could not handle contexts where the implicature is missing, for instance:

(47) Paul read some of the books. In fact, he read all of them.

This is not a problem, though. Note what the sentence means when the exhaustive operator is absent:

(48) a. $\exists$ Paul read some of the books last night.
b. $\exists$ {Paul read x last night : $x \in [\![\textbf{some of the books}]\!]$}

This meaning simply makes no claim about the sum of all books; therefore it is not false in a world where Paul read all of the books. Similarly, it makes no claim about him reading or not reading any magazines or newspapers.

Once the *Exh* is added, however, we derive the strengthened meaning:

(49) a. $\exists$*Exh* Paul read some of the books last night.
b. $\exists \left\{ \begin{array}{l} \text{Paul only read } b_1 \oplus b_2, \\ \text{Paul only read } b_1 \oplus b_3, \\ \text{Paul only read } b_1 \oplus b_4, \\ \text{Paul only read } b_2 \oplus b_3, \\ \text{Paul only read } b_2 \oplus b_4, \\ \text{Paul only read } b_3 \oplus b_4, \\ \text{Paul only read } b_1 \oplus b_2 \oplus b_3, \\ \text{Paul only read } b_1 \oplus b_3 \oplus b_4, \\ \text{Paul only read } b_1 \oplus b_2 \oplus b_4, \\ \text{Paul only read } b_2 \oplus b_3 \oplus b_4 \end{array} \right\}$

This means that one group of books not containing all the books is such that Paul read only that group. If magazines or newspapers were added to the focus set, then Paul is asserted to have not read those items either.

6.2.1 Some + Plural Problem

This example warrants a small excursus into another problem encountered by some other systems for scalar implicature. Some systems generate the following fallacious implication:

(50) Paul read some of the books. $\rightsquigarrow$ Paul did not read more than two books.[12]

[12]This problem appears in Sauerland (2004a). Danny Fox (p.c.) pointed out the application here.

Groenendijk and Stokhof (1984) have this problem due to the fact that their exhaustive operator limits meanings to the set of minimal possible answers. Example (51) shows the set of minimal values of the plural indefinite *some of the books* in a four-book world; this set happens to be equivalent to *exactly two of the books*:

(51) $$\left\{\begin{array}{l}\{b_1, b_2, b_1 \oplus b_2\},\\ \{b_1, b_3, b_1 \oplus b_3\},\\ \{b_1, b_4, b_1 \oplus b_4\},\\ \{b_2, b_3, b_2 \oplus b_3\},\\ \{b_2, b_4, b_2 \oplus b_4\},\\ \{b_3, b_4, b_3 \oplus b_4\}\end{array}\right\}$$

If such a set includes a group of three books, such as in (52), it will necessarily be a superset of one of the sets in (51), because if you read a group of books, you also read all subgroups of that group:

(52) $\{b_1, b_2, b_3, b_1 \oplus b_2, b_2 \oplus b_3, b_1 \oplus b_2 \oplus b_3\}$

Just for completeness, notice that any smaller set, such as the set in (53) will not satisfy the pluralness of the indefinite:

(53) $\{b_1\}$

Fox (2007) runs into the same problem for a slightly different reason. His exhaustive operator works on maximal exclusions, where a maximal exclusion is the largest set of alternatives that can be excluded by an exhaustive operator without falsifying the prejacent. For *some of the books,* every maximal exclusion must leave out one group of books of size two in order not to falsify the pluralness of the prejacent. However, any group of size three or greater can safely be included in all maximal exclusions without falsifying the prejacent. Since under this theory the propositions in the intersection of all maximal exclusions are implicated to be false, there is no group of size three or greater that will satisfy the exhaustified meaning.

As shown in the section above, the new system described in this paper does not suffer from this problem. *Some of the books,* even when strengthened by the exhaustive operator, is compatible with groups of books of size greater than two.

6.3 Comparatives

Turning now to the first of the challenges mentioned in Sect. 3 above, Kratzer (2005) suggests how an analysis along these lines might solve the comparative problem. To see how it works in the current framework, consider this definition for the comparative expression *more than two*:

(54) $[\![\textbf{more than two}]\!] = \{x \in D_e : |x| > 2\}$ (type $\{e\}$)

The denotation of *more than two* is simply the set of all plural individuals of cardinality greater than two.

In our world with only four books, this meaning applies as follows:

(55) a. $\exists Exh$ Paul read more than two books last night.
b. $\exists Exh$ {Paul read x last night : $x \in [\![\textbf{book}]\!]$ & $|x| > 2$ }
c. $\exists${Exh Paul read x last night : $x \in [\![\textbf{book}]\!]$ & $|x| > 2$ }
d. $\exists \left\{ \begin{array}{l} \text{Paul only read } b_1 \oplus b_2 \oplus b_3, \\ \text{Paul only read } b_1 \oplus b_3 \oplus b_4, \\ \text{Paul only read } b_1 \oplus b_2 \oplus b_4, \\ \text{Paul only read } b_2 \oplus b_3 \oplus b_4, \\ \text{Paul only read } b_1 \oplus b_2 \oplus b_3 \oplus b_4 \end{array} \right\}$

As shown in (57b), the sentence *Paul read more than two books last night* denotes a set of propositions of the form *Paul read x last night*—where x is replaced by each group of books having more than two elements. Next, the exhaustive operator applies pointwise to this set of propositions, yielding the exhaustified versions of the original propositions. Last, the existential closure applies to this set, asserting that one of these exhaustified propositions is true. In other words, one group containing more than two books is such that Paul read only that group.

Since we are exhaustifying over specific groups of books and only then applying the existential closure, this approach does not run into the same problem as the standard analysis. For instance, the group of four books $b_1 \oplus b_2 \oplus b_3 \oplus b_4$ is among the possible groups that Paul may have read. In fact, any appropriate group might have been read, including groups of size four, five, six, or even more, depending on how many books are in the context.

Interestingly, a completely parallel derivation works for a downward-entailing comparative[13]:

(56) $[\![\textbf{fewer than three}]\!] = \{x \in D_e : |x| < 3\}$ (type $\{e\}$)

(57) a. $\exists Exh$ Paul read fewer than three books last night.
b. $\exists Exh$ {Paul read x last night : $x \in [\![\textbf{book}]\!]$ & $|x| < 3$ }
c. $\exists${Exh Paul read x last night : $x \in [\![\textbf{book}]\!]$ & $|x| < 3$ }
d. $\exists \left\{ \begin{array}{l} \text{Paul only read } b_1, \\ \text{Paul only read } b_2, \\ \text{Paul only read } b_3, \\ \text{Paul only read } b_4, \\ \text{Paul only read } b_1 \oplus b_2, \\ \text{Paul only read } b_2 \oplus b_3, \\ \text{Paul only read } b_3 \oplus b_4, \\ \text{Paul only read } b_1 \oplus b_4 \end{array} \right\}$

This structure derives the strengthened meaning that Paul read exactly one or exactly two books last night.

[13] Uli Sauerland (p.c.) pointed out this example.

6.4 Disjunction Problem

Taking the standard meaning of *or* as set union, we can tackle the disjunction problem[14]:

(58) $[\![\textbf{or}]\!] = [\lambda X \subseteq D_\sigma \,.\, \lambda Y \subseteq D_\sigma \,.\, X \cup Y]$ (type $\langle\{\sigma\}, \langle\{\sigma\}, \{\sigma\}\rangle\rangle$)

Or also applies to sets (using normal Functional Application); it takes two sets and returns their union. For instance, the meaning for a sentence with two singleton indefinites is derived as follows:

(59) a. ∃*Exh* Paul read *The New York Times* or *The Boston Globe* last night.
b. ∃{*Exh* Paul read *x* last night : *x* ∈ {*The New York Times*, *The Boston Globe*}
c. $\exists \left\{ \begin{array}{l} \text{Paul only read } \textit{The New York Times} \text{ last night,} \\ \text{Paul only read } \textit{The Boston Globe} \text{ last night} \end{array} \right\}$

The derivation is the same when one of indefinites has more alternatives in its denotation set:

(60) a. ∃*Exh* Paul read *The New York Times* or some of the books.
b. $\exists \left\{ \begin{array}{l} \text{Paul only read } \textit{The New York Times}, \\ \text{Paul only read } b_1 \oplus b_2, \\ \text{Paul only read } b_1 \oplus b_3, \\ \text{Paul only read } b_1 \oplus b_4, \\ \text{Paul only read } b_2 \oplus b_3, \\ \text{Paul only read } b_2 \oplus b_4, \\ \text{Paul only read } b_3 \oplus b_4, \\ \text{Paul only read } b_1 \oplus b_2 \oplus b_3, \\ \text{Paul only read } b_1 \oplus b_3 \oplus b_4, \\ \text{Paul only read } b_1 \oplus b_2 \oplus b_4, \\ \text{Paul only read } b_2 \oplus b_3 \oplus b_4 \end{array} \right\}$

This meaning is merely the union of the sets for the sentences with *The New York Times* and the sentences with *some of the the books,* which is then closed with one ∃ operator. Once again, the problem with the standard analysis does not arise, since we exhaustify each of these alternatives separately before applying existential closure.

7 Further Issues

7.1 Order of Operators

One question that often arises in reference to null operators is their distribution. The simplest answer is that the operator, *Exh* in this case, can appear anywhere where it is

[14]It is crucial for this analysis that the existential force of *or*, like that of the indefinites, be able to scope above the exhaustive operator. See Alonso and Ovalle (2006) for more discussion of disjunction in Alternative Semantics.

not prevented from occurring by some outside factor. To maintain this position, it is necessary to show what happens when the exhaustive operator appears in positions other than those shown above.

As it turns out, many positions for *Exh* simply fail due to incompatible types: *Exh* requires a set of propositions, so it cannot combine with, for instance, a *DP* or a *PP*, or any other phrase whose meaning does not evaluate to a set of propositions.

One position where *Exh* could conceivably apply, however, is before a sentence where the ∃ has already been added.[15] This possibility does not seem to cause any trouble, though. In simple cases, this "wrong" order derives the same meaning as the right order:

(61) a. *Exh*∃ Paul read *The New York Times*.
b. Paul only read *The New York Times*.

In more complex cases, the meaning derived is contradictory. In the following structure, for instance, the exhaustive operator generates the truth conditions paraphrased in (66c).

(62) a. *Exh*∃ Paul read three books.
b. One of these statements is true:

$$\left\{\begin{array}{l}\text{Paul read } b_1 \oplus b_2 \oplus b_3, \\ \text{Paul read } b_1 \oplus b_3 \oplus b_4, \\ \text{Paul read } b_1 \oplus b_2 \oplus b_4, \\ \text{Paul read } b_2 \oplus b_3 \oplus b_4\end{array}\right\}$$

And all of these statements are false:

$$\left\{\begin{array}{l}\text{Paul read } b_1, \\ \text{Paul read } b_2, \\ \text{Paul read } b_3, \\ \text{Paul read } b_4, \\ \text{Paul read } b_1 \oplus b_2, \\ \text{Paul read } b_2 \oplus b_3, \\ \text{Paul read } b_3 \oplus b_4, \\ \text{Paul read } b_1 \oplus b_4, \\ \text{Paul read } b_1 \oplus b_2 \oplus b_3, \\ \text{Paul read } b_1 \oplus b_3 \oplus b_4, \\ \text{Paul read } b_1 \oplus b_2 \oplus b_4, \\ \text{Paul read } b_2 \oplus b_3 \oplus b_4, \\ \text{Paul read } b_1 \oplus b_2 \oplus b_3 \oplus b_4\end{array}\right\}$$

The way that the exhaustive operator is defined, it will assert the negation of all of the sentences in the focus set—except those entailed by the prejacent. In this case, the prejacent (∃ *Paul read three books*) does not entail any of the statements in the focus set. Therefore, every focus-set proposition is asserted to be false according to the definition of *Exh*. However, this yields a contradiction, since if they are all

[15]Notice that as defined above, ∃ returns a set of propositions; the assumption is that the interpretation procedure can handle such singleton sets of propositions.

false, then the prejacent itself cannot be true. Assuming that such contradictions are avoided in the semantic system, this derivation would be ruled out.[16]

7.2 The Symmetry Problem

One additional interesting consequence of the system presented in this paper is that it avoids another major problem of neo-Gricean methods of computing scalar implicatures, dubbed the *Symmetry Problem* by von Fintel and Heim (2005). In calculating the scalar implicatures for a sentence like *Paul read some of the books* using Horn scales, one alternative we considered was (63), because *all* is on the same scale as *some* and (63) is stronger—it entails the original sentence. By negating this alternative, we derive the implicature that Paul did not read all of the books.

(63) Paul read all of the books.

However, why is *all* on the Horn scale for *some* but not *some but not all*? If *some but not all* were on the scale, then (64) would be a stronger alternative. But if we negated the meaning of (64), we would derive the implicature that Paul did not read all of the books—the opposite of the attested implicature.

(64) Paul read some but not all of the books.

The question is why is *all* on the Horn scale for *some* but not *some but not all*.

Several proposals to solve this problem exist. Matsumoto (1995) claims that members of the same Horn scale must share monotonicity features. Katzir (2007) refutes this claim and instead proposes a complexity metric on scale-mates. Notice though, that this question simply does not arise in the new system. The alternatives used in the new system are all members of the focus set, whose meaning derives from the independently motivated question under discussion. These alternatives are not quantified, but mention instead simple groups of individuals, like *Paul read* $b_1 \oplus b_2 \oplus b_3$. Therefore, their negations will always rule out groups of individuals, never rule groups in, like the negation of (64).

7.3 Negation

The interaction of implicatures with negation and other downward-entailing environments is quite a complex topic and mostly beyond the purview of this paper. This subsection will, however, indicate how the proposal presented above fares with respect to certain key cases involving indefinites inside of downward-entailing envi-

[16]Giannakidou and Quer (2013) criticize this type of approach.

ronments.[17] Consider the sentence in (65) (inspired by von Stechow and Zimmermann 1984):

(65) Paul didn't (even) read three books.

This case can certainly receive an adequate meaning under the system presented above. Consider the following derivation for (65) (assuming a plausible focus set):

(66) a. *Exh*¬∃ Paul read three books.

b. $\neg\exists \left\{ \begin{array}{l} \text{Paul read } b_1 \oplus b_2 \oplus b_3, \\ \text{Paul read } b_1 \oplus b_3 \oplus b_4, \\ \text{Paul read } b_1 \oplus b_2 \oplus b_4, \\ \text{Paul read } b_2 \oplus b_3 \oplus b_4 \end{array} \right\}$

c. None of these statements is true:

$\left\{ \begin{array}{l} \text{Paul read } b_1 \oplus b_2 \oplus b_3, \\ \text{Paul read } b_1 \oplus b_3 \oplus b_4, \\ \text{Paul read } b_1 \oplus b_2 \oplus b_4, \\ \text{Paul read } b_2 \oplus b_3 \oplus b_4 \end{array} \right\}$

And one of these statements is true:

$\left\{ \begin{array}{l} \text{Paul read } b_1, \\ \text{Paul read } b_2, \\ \text{Paul read } b_3, \\ \text{Paul read } b_4, \\ \text{Paul read } b_1 \oplus b_2, \\ \text{Paul read } b_2 \oplus b_3, \\ \text{Paul read } b_3 \oplus b_4, \\ \text{Paul read } b_1 \oplus b_4, \\ \text{Paul read } b_1 \oplus b_2 \oplus b_3, \\ \text{Paul read } b_1 \oplus b_3 \oplus b_4, \\ \text{Paul read } b_1 \oplus b_2 \oplus b_4, \\ \text{Paul read } b_2 \oplus b_3 \oplus b_4, \\ \text{Paul read } b_1 \oplus b_2 \oplus b_3 \oplus b_4 \end{array} \right\}$

The meaning derived is that Paul read one or two books, but no more—a plausible strengthened meaning for (65).

Crucial to this derivation, however, is the order in which the operators apply. Above, the exhaustive operator applies to a structure where negation has already applied. If, on the other hand, the exhaustive operator were to apply below negation, the derivation would not fare so well:

(67) a. ¬∃*Exh* Paul read three books.

b. $\neg\exists \left\{ \begin{array}{l} \text{Paul only read } b_1 \oplus b_2 \oplus b_3, \\ \text{Paul only read } b_1 \oplus b_3 \oplus b_4, \\ \text{Paul only read } b_1 \oplus b_2 \oplus b_4, \\ \text{Paul only read } b_2 \oplus b_3 \oplus b_4 \end{array} \right\}$

This order of operators derives the strengthened meaning for (65) that Paul read fewer than three books or more than three books, but not exactly three books. Currently, I

---

[17] Uli Sauerland (p.c.) suggested the addition of this section.

have no proposal to rule out this errant meaning other than to stipulate that negation must take scope beneath the exhaustive operator.[18]

7.4 Conclusion

This paper has presented a new way to analyze scalar implicatures that solves some challenges to other theories. The proposal uses well-known linguistic machinery to build a new theory: a focus set to define alternatives instead of Horn Scales, existential closure to get the correct scope, and contradiction avoidance to motivate this scope.

Acknowledgement Thanks to Danny Fox, Irene Heim,Gennaro Chierchia, Kai von Fintel, Tamina Stephenson, Uli Sauerland, the members of the MIT Workshop on Syntax and Semantics, Fall 2005, and the participants of SALT 16. A previous version of this paper appears in the proceedings of SALT 16.

References

Alonso-Ovalle, L. 2006. *Disjunction in alternative semantics*. Ph.D. thesis, University of Massachusetts Amherst.

Chierchia, G. 2004. Scalar implicatures, polarity phenomena, and the syntax/pragmatics interface. In *Structures and Beyond*, ed. A. Belletti, 39–103. Oxford, UK: Oxford University Press.

Chierchia, G., D. Fox., and B. Spector. 2008. The grammatical view of scalar implicatures and the relationship between semantics and pragmatics. In *Handbook of Semantics*. New York, NY: Mouton de Gruyter.

Collingwood, R.G. 1940. *An Essay in Metaphysics*. Oxford University Press.

von Fintel, K. 1995. A minimal theory of adverbial quantification. Unpublished draft Ms. MIT, Cambridge, March. http://urlciteseer.ist.psu.edu/vonfintel96minimal.html.

von Fintel, K., and Heim, I. 2005. *Pragmatics Lecture Notes. Notes for Class Taught at MIT*.

Fox, D. 2004. Implicatures and exhaustivity. Handout from class at USC. http://web.mit.edu/linguistics/www/fox/.

Fox, D. 2007. Free choice and the theory of scalar implicatures. In *Presupposition and Implicature in Compositional Semantics* ed. U. Sauerland and P. Stateva, 71–120.

Geurts, B. 2009. Scalar implicature and local pragmatics. *Mind & Language* 24 (1): 51–79.

Geurts, B. 2010. *Quantity Implicatures*, Cambridge University Press.

Giannakidou, A., and Quer, J. 2013. Exhaustive and non-exhaustive variation with free choice and referential vagueness: Evidence from Greek, Catalan, and Spanish Lingua.

Groenendijk, J., and Stokhof, M. 1984. Studies in the semantics of questions and the pragmatics of answers. Ph.D. thesis, University of Amsterdam.

Heim, I. 1982. *The semantics of definite and indefinite noun phrases*. Ph.D. thesis, Univeristy of Massachusetts, Amherst.

Heim, I., and A. Kratzer. 1998. *Semantics in Generative Grammar*. Oxford: Blackwell.

[18] An anonymous reviewer suggests an additional wrinkle: the DP *three books* may also scope above negation. I assume that in that case, the DP raises above negation, and Exh may apply as usual to the transformed structure.

Horn, L. 1972. On the Semantic Properties of Logical Operators in English. Ph.D. thesis, UCLA.
Horn, L. 1985. Metalinguistic negation and pragmatic ambiguity. *Language* 61 (1): 121–174.
Katzir, R. 2007. Structurally-defined alternatives. *Linguistics and Philosophy* 30 (6): 669–690.
Kratzer, A. 2005. *LSA Class Notes*.
Kratzer, A., and J. Shimoyama. 2002. Indeterminate pronouns: The view from Japanese. In *The Proceedings of the Third Tokyo Conference on Psycholinguistics*, ed. Y. Otsu, 1–25. Hituzi Syobo: Tokyo.
Krifka, M. 1995. The semantics and pragmatics of polarity items. *Linguistic Analysis* 25: 209–257.
Krifka, M. 1999. At least some determiners aren't determiners. In *The Semantics/Pragmatics Interface from Different Points of View. Current Research in the Semantics/Pragmatics Interface*, ed. K. Turner, Vol. 1, 257–291. Elsevier Science B.V.
Lee, C. 2006. Contrastive topic/focus and polarity in discourse. In *Where Semantics Meets Pragmatics*, CRiSPI 16, ed. K. von Heusinger and K. Turner, 381–420. Elsevier.
Lee, C. 2010. Information structure in pa/sn or descriptive/metalinguistic negation: With reference to scalar implicatures. In *Contrasting Meaning in Languages of the East and West*, ed. D. Shu, and K. Turner, 33–73. Berne: Peter Lang.
Link, G. 1983. The logical analysis of plurals and mass terms: A lattice-theoretical approach. In *Meaning, Use and Interpretation in Language*, ed. R. Bäuerle, C. Schwartze, and A. von Stechow, 302–323. Berlin: Mouton de Gruyter.
Matsumoto, Y. 1995. The conversational condition on Horn scales. *Linguistics and Philosophy* 18 (1): 21–60.
McCawley, J. 1993. *Everything that Linguists Have Always Wanted to Know about Logic but Were Ashamed to Ask*, University of Chicago Press.
Reinhart, T. 1997. Quantifier scope: How labor is divided between qr and choice functions. *Linguistics and philosophy* 20 (4): 335–397.
Roberts, C. 1996. Information structure in discourse: Towards an integrated formal theory of pragmatics. *Working Papers In Linguistics—Ohio State University Department of Linguistics*, 91–136.
Rooth, M., and B. Partee. 1982. Conjunction, type ambiguity and wide scope or. In *Proceedings of the First West Coast Conference on Formal Linguistics*, ed. D. Flickinger, M. Marken, and N. Wiegand. Stanford University.
Ruys, E.G. 1993. *The Scope of Indefinites, LEd.*
Sauerland, U. 2004a. On embedded implicatures. *Journal of Cognitive Science* 5 (1): 107–137.
Sauerland, U. 2004b. Scalar implicatures in complex sentences. *Linguistics and Philosophy* 27: 271–316.
Sauerland, U., and K. Yatsushiro. 2004. A silent noun in partitives. *Proceedings-NELS* 34: 505–516.
Simons, M. 2000. *Issues in the Semantics and Pragmatics of Disjunction*. Garland Pub.
von Stechow, A., and T.E. Zimmermann. 1984. Term answers and contextual change. *Linguistics* 22 (1): 3–40.
Winter, Y. 1997. Choice functions and the scopal semantics of indefinites. *Linguistics and Philosophy* 20 (4): 399–467.

Part III
Quantificational Expressions

Almost et al.: Scalar Adverbs Revisited

Laurence R. Horn

Abstract The division of labor between semantic and pragmatic aspects of the *almost, barely,* and other proximatives has been a bone of contention ever since Sadock's (1981) proposal that *a almost ϕ'd* is true if a in fact *ϕ'd*: *Chris almost died* entails that Chris approached dying while merely conversationally implicating that Chris didn't die. Given that *barely ϕ = almost not ϕ*, *Dana barely survived* would likewise on the same account implicate, not entail, that Dana in fact survived. While additional support has been marshaled for this "radical pragmatic" line, one persistent problem acknowledged by Sadock and not dispelled since is the resistance of the *almost ϕ → not ϕ* implication to cancelation. New evidence for and against Sadock's approach and competing analyses of the proximatives is considered and a solution presented.

Keywords Almost • Assertoric inertia • Downward entailment • Implicature, conversational • Inverted readings (of proximatives) • Negative polarity • Pragmatic intrusion • Proximatives • Un-nouns

1 The Proximal and the Polar

Thirty-odd years ago, the young leader of a fanatical cadre of radical pragmaticists circulated an underground manifesto calling for the overthrow of the bourgeois establishment's analysis of *almost.* In the published version of his manifesto, Sadock (1981, p. 257) posed the central question this way:

> A sentence of the form *almost P,* in which *almost* is a verb phrase modifier, is used as if it meant, among other things, "not P." For example, someone who says *Sam almost died* would be taken as indicating that Sam didn't die...But what is the nature of the connection between the English word *almost* and the negative proposition?

L.R. Horn (✉)
Yale University, P.O. Box 208366, New Haven, CT 06520-8366, USA
e-mail: laurence.horn@yale.edu

C. Lee et al. (eds.), *Contrastiveness in Information Structure, Alternatives and Scalar Implicatures*, Studies in Natural Language and Linguistic Theory 91, DOI 10.1007/978-3-319-10106-4_14

The starting point for any analysis of *almost* is the recognition that in uttering (1) I commit myself in some sense to (1a) and (1b).

(1) It almost rained.
  a. It came close to raining.
  b. It did not rain.

Following the practice of Sevi (1998) and Horn (2002a), I refer to these aspects of the meaning of *almost* sentences as the proximal and polar components, respectively. But are these implications created equal? Sadock offers three, or 3½, answers to his question, the traditional symmetricalist view in (2A), the moderate asymmetricalist view in (2B) (available in two flavors), and the radical asymmetricalist view in (2C):

(2) A. (1b) is *entailed* by (1); (1) = (1a) and (1b) and is F if (1b) is false.
  B_1. (1b) is (logically) *presupposed* by (1); (1) is neither T nor F if (1b) is false.
  B_2. (1b) is *conventionally implicated* or pragmatically presupposed by (1); (1) is "strictly speaking true" but inappropriate if (1a) is true and (1b) known to be false.
  C. (1b) is *conversationally implicated* by (the utterance of) (1); (1) is T but misleading if (1a) is true and (1b) false. The inference from (1) to (1b) is a scalar implicature.

It is the radical pragmatic view in (2C) that Sadock endorsed: if you know (1b) is false, it's misleading to assert (1), given the maxim of quantity. Hence, it is *(mirabile dictu)* true that 2 + 2 almost equals 4. I will argue here that in some respects Sadock's approach is too radically pragmatic and in others not radically pragmatic enough.

2 Proximatives: What Has (Almost) Been Learned

I now turn to a review of some of what has been learned in the 30 years since Sadock's manifesto—and what has been unlearned. We begin with a brief note on the problems surrounding the characterization of the proximal component. Typically, it is viewed in terms of reference to possible worlds: *almost P* entails that P is "not far from being true" (Ducrot 1973), that it is "true in a possible world not very different from the real world" (Sadock 1981), or true in "a world which is almost not different from the actual world" (Rapp and von Stechow 1999). But note the problem with circularity (is (1a) really distinct from (1)?) and consider the problems posed for any possible worlds account by sentences like *Planets travel in almost circular orbits* (Atlas 1984, p. 357) or 0.3333 *almost equals* 1/3 (Sevi 1998, p. 18) —or, most eloquently, by Sadock's observation that 961 *is almost a prime number*

> might be adjudged true because the only blot on 961's record as a prime number is the sad fact that it is the square of 31. If this one little fact were not true, then 961 would be a prime number. The imaginary world in which 961 is a prime number is not very different from the

real world in the nontechnical sense that only one proposition has to changed to gain access to it, but of course it is *very* different from our world in the technical sense than it is an inconsistent world and lacks mathematics. (Sadock 1981, p. 259)

Two more bits of standard wisdom on *almost* that appear periodically in the literature are its role in arguments for lexical decomposition and intervention in polarity licensing. But, while the varying scope possibilities for *almost* has been used to argue for decomposing causatives as in *I almost killed John* based on the availability of separate readings like "I almost did something that caused John to die," "I did something that caused John to become almost dead," etc. (as in Morgan 1969; McCawley 1973), Dowty (1979, Sect. 5.4) finds the evidence unconvincing and Rapp and von Stechow (1999) reject the corresponding scope argument for German *fast.* The common wisdom is that *almost* co-occurs with universals but not indefinites or existentials and thus serves as a reliable diagnostic for free choice as opposed to than NPI *any.* Such claims date back to Carlson (1981) and have since entered received wisdom.

As pointed out by Horn (1972), free choice *any,* like other universal determiners, may be modified by adverbs like *almost* or *nearly.* (Hoeksema 1983, p. 409)

We know that in general, FC-*any* can be modified by almost (just as other universal quantifiers can). Crucially, such modification…is rejected in downward entailing contexts like negation. (Zepter 2003, p. 234)

More recently, Penka cites the purported impossibility of **I didn't see almost any student* (2006, (2b), (31), (35)) as evidence for an intervention constraint blocking NPI licensing across *almost* (cf. Horn 2000b, Sect. III). Along the same lines, *almost* is periodically claimed to be a positive polarity item blocked from the scope of negation (e.g. Klein 1997, p. 87; Rapp and von Stechow 1999, p. 197; Horn 2000b, p. 87). But in fact, as noted in Horn (2005, pp. 198–99), clauses with *doesn't {know/have} almost any, don't like almost any, NEG almost a single CN,* et al. are readily googlable:

(3) In a story that didn't see almost any coverage here,…
Global warming: we didn't see almost any snow in the winter
I didn't see almost any of the movies so I'm going by who I think is a good actor
I'm in the 5th week and i didn't see almost any results.
I don't pay almost a single cent for any of my art work
I do not know almost a single individual of talent who is not too busy…

Crucially, however, *almost* semantically scopes over negation in such cases, so that *not almost any* = *almost no.* The standard constraint can thus be retained provided it applies at a more abstract level than that of the surface string.

Almost is often assumed, at least tacitly, to share its semantics (whatever they are) with its adverbial "kin"; in particular the distribution of *almost* is taken to be essentially identical to that of *nearly, just about, damn near, virtually,* or *pretty much* (Sadock 1981; Morzycki 2001; Horn 2002a). But in fact, *nearly* is largely excluded from taking negative focused expressions (cf. van Dongen 1921 on

{Almost/#Nearly} nobody was there); other differences between *almost n* and *nearly n* (for cardinal *n* focus) seem to involve speaker expectations (Sadock 2007).

Another standard assumption—made by Morzycki (2007) and Atlas (2007), following (2A)-type symmetricalists, lexicographers, and butchers—is to equate *almost* with *not quite*. The *American Heritage Dictionary,* as endorsed by Atlas, glosses *almost* as "slightly short of, not quite, nearly". The "nearly" gloss doesn't quite work, but is "not quite" at least nearly successful? As the marketing slogan for Boar's Head deli meats puts it, "Almost Boar's Head Isn't Boar's Head"—that is, it's not *quite* Boar's Head even when it pretends to be. But as Sadock (1981, p. 263) points out, *almost but not quite* is not as redundant it would be if the two adverbials were synonymous; indeed, as Sadock also recognizes, the adversative *but* indicates that *almost* and *not quite,* far from mutual paraphrases, are at odds. This is reinforced by the frequently encountered tendency to repeat an *almost* to register the rhetorical contrast with *not quite:*

(4) a. I almost felt sorry for Sonterra. Almost but not quite.
(Linda Lael Miller (2003), *Don't Look Now,* p. 223)
b. "You almost make it sound all right."
"Almost. Not quite."
(exchange on Law & Order, NBC-TV, about shading the truth)
c. [Following a day of breathtaking adventures including an encounter with the Pope, Herr Doktor Professor Moritz-Maria von Igelfeld reflects that…]
the life of a diplomat, or even a schismatic if it came to it, could be almost as fulfilling as life as a professor of Romance philology. Almost, but not quite.
(Alexander McCall Smith (2004), *The Finer Points of Sausage-Dogs*)

Now we come to the interdefinability of *barely* with *almost not,* assumed in many treatises on proximatives (Ducrot 1973; Sadock 1981; Horn 2002a) but challenged in many others (Atlas 1997; Amaral 2007; Ziegeler 2008) on cross-linguistic grounds and the basis of the differential role played by expectation for the two proximatives. This issue aside, both adverbs have been assigned similar conjunctive (2A)-style expansions in the literature, as seen in (5) and (6), either or both of which are endorsed, mutatis mutandis, by Hitzeman (1992), Atlas (1997), Sevi (1998), and Rapp and von Stechow (1999). (For a tabular display of the various descriptive options advocated, cf. Horn 2002a, p. 60.)

(5) *Lee almost passed*: $\neg$[Lee passed] $\wedge$ CLOSE-TO [Lee passed]
(6) *Lee barely passed*: [Lee passed] $\wedge$ CLOSE-TO $\neg$[Lee passed]

3 Problems with (a)Symmetry

The primary argument for a conjunctive analysis of the polar implication has always been its apparent non-cancelability. The contrast in (7) (=Sadock 1981, (23), (25))

(7) a. ?Not only did Bill almost swim the English Channel, he did swim it.
b. Not only did Bill eat some of the cake, he ate all of it.

does render an implicature-based analysis problematic. On the other hand, the conjunctionalist must cope with the troublesome fact that *barely VP* (despite its positive polar component) licenses negative polarity items, while *almost VP* (despite its negative polar component) does not:

(8) a. She barely {budged/slept a wink/touched a drop/spoke to anyone}.
b. #She almost {budged/slept a wink/touched a drop/spoke to anyone}.

But notwithstanding its NPI-licensing ability, *barely* cannot be a downward entailing or non-veridical operator, given its polar entailment, i.e., the fact that *It barely rained* entails *It rained.* Note that cancelation is difficult, even with an epistemic rider:

(9) a. #It barely rained and in fact (it's possible) it did not.
b. #It almost rained and in fact (it's possible) it did.

The resolution of this conflict I have urged elsewhere (Horn 2002a, 2009b) is to accept that while the polar component of the meaning of *barely VP* and *almost VP* is indeed entailed, it is not asserted—assertorically inert—predicting the quasi-negative behavior of the relevant clauses. Thus, the conjunctive analysis (2A) is correct…almost.

A particularly dramatic illustration of the contrast between asserted and non-asserted entailments comes from Sadock's contrast between *almost* and *not quite*, two approximatives that on the current view are equivalent at the level of what they entail while differing as to what they assert. This is displayed in the table in (10), adapted from Schwenter (2002), who extends the distinction and analysis to Spanish.

(10) *almost* versus *not quite*:

	Entailed	Asserted
Proximal component (*almost*)	+	+
Polar component (*almost*)	+	–
Proximal component (*not quite*)	+	–
Polar component (*not quite*)	+	+

Thus consider the difference between *It's too bad you almost died (—now you'll need a long difficult recovery)* and *It's too bad you didn't quite die (—now I'll have to finish you off…).* Given that what is relevant for negative polarity licensing is not downward entailment as such but downward *assertion* (with inert entailments disregarded), we predict the contrast in (11):

(11) I {never quite/*almost} made it all the way through any of those papers.

Another reflex of assertoric asymmetry is the interation of approximatives. In the following example, from Alexander McCall Smith's 2011 novel *The Forgotten Affairs of Youth,* the philosopher Isabel Dalhousie has just introduced a visiting philosopher colleague from Australia to her fortyish cousin Katrina, an administrative assistant at the University of Edinburgh who Isabel hopes will help them track down Jane's biological parents, former graduate students at the university there. The administrator is delighted to learn that the visitor hails from Melbourne.

> "Jane is with us from Melbourne. She's at the Humanities Institute."
> Katrina smiled warmly. "Melbourne! I went there three years ago. I watched the tennis. The Australian Open."
> "Katrina is a keen tennis player," exclaimed Isabel. "Almost played for Scotland."
> "A hundred years ago," said Katrina. "And not all *that* almost. Almost almost, I'd say."

In saying she almost almost played for Scotland, Katrina is (modestly) insisting that she (only) came close to coming close to doing so, thereby reaffirming (rather than canceling out) the polar component, i.e., that she didn't play. On the other hand, if a hit man sheepishly confesses that he didn't quite not quite kill his target, he's saying that he inadvertently did kill the target that he was under orders to merely frighten, the two asserted negatives here canceling out.

The rhetorical negativity of *barely* and positivity of *almost,* as posited by Ducrot (1973) and supported by Sadock (1981) and Jayez (1987), is left unexplained by a pure (2A)-type symmetricalist analysis. Thus, it's *good* news if my laptop is *almost* working and *bad* news if it's *barely* working, even though it's in the latter case that it actually functions. Similarly, compare:

(12). a. The tank is almost half full—so {let's drive on/#we'd better stop for gas}.
b. The tank is barely half full—so {we'd better stop for gas/#let's drive on}.

although the tank in (12a) has less gas in it than the one in (12b).

Another asymmetry between polar and proximal components, as Ziegeler (2000) observes, is that the former cannot support causal explanation. Thus in (13), kimchi could only have been an insufficient lure to attract me, not the ultimate deterrent.

(13) I almost moved to Korea because of the kimchi.

As for *barely,* its behavior as an NPI licenser derives from its downward assertive character: the polar entailment is transparent to polarity licensing. In fact, as the usenet posting in (14) shows, NPI licensing correlates with the invocation of a negative scale.

(14) The typical airline bathroom barely accommodates one person, much less two.

The rhetorical negativity of *barely* thus stands in opposition to its veridicality, whence the force of adversative *but* to mark this opposition while reversing the rhetorical direction of the utterance, as seen in (15a) (from a 2006 Luanne Rice novel *Sandcastles*) and in the "*barely but* sandwich" in (15b) (from "Grey's Anatomy", ABC TV, 5/08).

(15) a. Sissela meowed from the bed above and Agnes barely heard. But *Brendan* did and after another kiss he pulled slightly away to look up.
b. He's alive. Barely, but...he's alive.

4 Inverted Readings and the Permeable Polar Membrane

The polar component of *almost* and *barely* clauses is more peripheral to the primary force of proximatives, learned later than the proximal component (Amaral 2007) and more evanescent. In particular, the polar (negative) component is subject to flip-flopping in some contexts to yield "inverted" readings while the proximal component never is (Horn 2002a, p. 65; Schwenter 2002; Amaral and Schwenter 2007; Amaral 2007, p. 25; cf. also Ziegeler 2006, Sect. 4.7.1 and especially Amaral 2007 on the role of context).

Inverted readings were first recognized in the case of the Mandarin Chinese particle transliterated as *cha-yidiar* or *chadianr* and literally glossed as "miss-a-little" (Li 1976; Biq 1989). While its ordinary interpretation is "almost", when it scopes over a negative predicate it can be rendered as either "almost not" (="barely") or as "almost", with the negation essentially pleonastic, as in (16(ii)):

(16) *Wo chadianr mei chi.* (i) 'I almost didn't eat', 'I barely ate'
I miss-a-little not eat (ii) 'I almost ate' [= Wo chadianr chi le]

The non-compositional pleonastic reading is the only one emerging in certain contexts:

(17) *Wo chadianr mei zhuangdao qiang.* (i) #'I almost didn't bump into the wall'
I miss-a-little not bump-to wall (ii) 'I almost bumped into the wall'

Similarly, in Spanish (Schwenter 2002; Pons Bordería and Schwenter 2005), negation under *por poco* "almost" can—and in certain contexts must—be interpreted pleonastically, as in (19b(ii)), rather than compositionally, as in (19b(i)):

(18) a. *Por poco sale.* 'She almost left'
b. *Por poco no sale.* 'She almost didn't leave'

(19) a. *Por poco se mata.* 'She was almost killed'
b. *Por poco no se mata.* (i) #'She almost wasn't killed'
(ii) 'She was almost killed'

In general, *casi* "almost" does not permit the inverted readings of *por poco;* Pons Bordería and Schwenter (2005) attribute this to diachronic differences in the history of the two approximatives and subtle pragmatic distinctions in expressiveness between them. In any case, Valencian Spanish contains a limited use of "inverted" *casi* explored by Schwenter (2002). Someone trying to squeeze out of her car after parking on a narrow street is forced to wait as many cars go past. When she is finally able to escape, she sighs "*¡Casi salgo!*"—literally, "I almost get out", but meaning "I barely/finally got out." Someone else, impatiently awaiting his friend at the auditorium door, sees her arrive a minute before the session starts and exclaims *¡Casi llegas!* "You just barely made it!" (lit., "You almost arrive!"). In such cases, all restricted to simple present tense and utterance-initial occurrence, *casi p* clearly does not entail *~p,* since the truth of *p* is obvious in the context, but is essentially equivalent to *apenas* "barely." In other words, *casi (p)* here = canonical *casi* + *no* (*p*), as in the standard Spanish expostulations *¡Casi no salgo!; ¡Casi no llegas!*

Thus too, Swiss German *fasch* is normally equivalent to the standard *fast* "almost," but also has an inverted "barely" sense emerging in relevant contexts. And in English, a *near miss* can be either a goal barely missed or a disaster barely averted, i.e., nearly a non-miss, as in the case of air traffic collisions. Prescriptivists lambaste this latter, non-compositional interpretation, as in William Safire's objection to "the overuse of *near"* in his 2 January 2005 "On Language" column in the New York Times Magazine:

> It became controversial with *near miss,* a nonsensical version of *near thing;* some of us patiently but uselessly pointed out that the writer meant "near hit." *Near miss* has since entrenched itself as an idiom. (Idioms is idioms, and I could care less.)

Similarly, Bill Pidto referred on ESPN's SportsCenter (24 August 2001) to "Greg Norman, best known for his massive collapse in "96 and his other near misses." But elsewhere, depending on the context, a near miss *is* nearly a miss:

> [Headline:] Martin's **near miss**
> Great Britain curling skip Rhona Martin almost missed the [Salt Lake City] Winter Olympics because of a stomach problem…
> (http://news.bbc.co.uk/winterolympics2002/hi/english/curling)

Finally, we come to *the* permeable polar membrane represented by the distribution of the *un-noun* (Horn 2002b, 2005). These come in two flavors, the first of which is the Class A un-noun. A Class A unX is a non-member of the category X which, while lacking one or more criterial properties of category members, nevertheless shares salient functional attributes with them and effectively coerces a superset category of which both X and unX are members. The "sponsor" item for this class is the *un-cola,* introduced in a 1967 advertising campaign for the soft drink 7-Up; its intended interpretation posits a set (i.e., that of soft drinks) encompassing both colas and 7-Up, which is why *un-cola* wouldn't have been as successful for promoting chocolate milk or beef jerky, which are by any definition not colas. Additional examples of Class A un-nouns appear in (20)

(20) The *Class A un-noun*: a Class A unX is *Almost* an X

un-hit
Un-hit of the week: Cardinals pitcher Garrett Stephenson came into last Saturday's game with Atlanta 1 for 36 at the plate. Then he lined what looked like a single to right. But Brian Jordan charged, fielded it and threw him out at first.
(Baseball "Week in Review" column by Jayson Stark at espn.com, 11 August 2000)

unmartini
Photo caption: *UNMARTINI*—A Ginger Citrus Snap, with pomegranate seeds, at Tabla (*New York Times* 20 Jan. 1999, F1, "The Aperitif Moment: Sip or Flinch")

unpotato
Photo caption: THE *UNPOTATO*: Jerusalem artichokes are roasted with thyme at Craft. (*NYT* 14 March 2001, F3)

unpublications
The main *unpublications* of H.P. Grice
(Heading for column in bibliographic addendum to Grandy and Warner's 1986 festschrift for Grice, facing page listing "The publications of H.P. Grice")

unturkey (and *unbird*)
The Great *UnTurkey*. Let One of Now and Zen's featherless friends be the centerpiece of Your Holiday table! This impressive creation is completely vegan and offers 5 solid pounds of boneless eating (enough for 8 hungry adults)! Made of delicately flavored tender seitan, dressed in a delectable "skin" made from yuba (beancurd skin), …this innovative creation will delight vegetarians and non-vegetarians alike. This frozen "*unbird*" comes fully cooked, and needs only reheating to be enjoyed. (ad for Now and Zen, San Francisco, November 1999)

If a Class A un-X is almost (but not quite) an X, a Class B un-X is an X, but not a particularly good representative of its category. Note that whatever we think of the designated *un-place* New Jersey, it is most certainly a place, just as un-sheets are sheets.

(21) The *Class B un-noun*: a Class B unX is *Barely* an X

uncollege
Even though many Mids (=Midshipmen, i.e., US Naval Academy undergraduates) refer to their school with bemused affection as "the *uncollege*", it remains one of the great bastions of "old college spirit" in its pristine form. (Washington Post, 22 November 22, 1977, D1, "Navy Revives College Spirit For The Game")

unbank
Banking on the *Unbanks*: Tellerless Wonders Are Reinventing Small-Business Lending (Headline, *NYT* February 4, 1999)

un-place (referring to E.B. White's essay "Here is New York")
And what he made just as clear was that any place else was just, well, any place else. Or perhaps an *un-place*. The closest of these is New Jersey.
(Charles Strum, "Garden State? The Image is Closer to Crab Grass", NYT Arts Section, 27 October 1996, p. 33)

unsheets
Now that the big names in bedding—Cannon, Fieldcrest and J. P. Stevens—are bringing out their own versions of *unsheets,* suggestible types can go see natural (unbleached, untreated cotton sheets) displayed…in department stores around town. (Liz Logan, "New Bed Linen," NYT 10 October 1991, Home p. 1)

unwoman
label for infertile women, feminists, lesbians, nuns, etc. in Margaret Atwood's 1985 dystopian novel *The Handmaid's Tale* who are exiled to the colonies as slave labor

Summarizing, we can say that an *A*-class unX is not an X (≈ is almost/not quite an X), while a *B*-class unX is technically an X (but just barely an X). In some cases, however, it's hard to tell: is an *unbreakfast* (e.g., an eel and egg sushi roll consumed at 7:00 a.m.) a breakfast (because of its timing) if just barely, or almost a breakfast but not quite (given its structure)? What of the politician's sleazy illocution in "If I've offended anybody, I apologize"? or "I'm sorry if I hurt the feelings of anyone who can't take a joke"? Lakoff (2000, p. 31) employs *un-apologies,* "*apologies*" (with scare quotes), and *apologies* (without them) to refer interchangeably to this phenomenon. And, speaking of politics, what of those infamous disputed Floridian ballots? Americans of both blue and red stripe may have acknowledged that these were not ideal exemplars of their class, but the 2000 (un)election hinged on whether those dimpled, chad-hung *unvotes* were in fact votes or (as it turns out) not.

As we have seen, while proximatives entail and assert their proximal component, the polar component is more of a semi-permeable membrane. An early account of this variable permeability is given by Harder and Kock (1976), who insightfully invoke Ducrot's notion of argumentation theory for dealing with the negative orientation of *barely,* but—like the *almost* = *not quite* brigade—succumb to the temptation of dictionary-hugging. Of sentences like (22a) they write,

(22) a. Roderick barely kissed Honoria.
b. Roderick kissed Honoria.

> In terms of truth conditions, *barely* is strangely ambiguous. The *Shorter Oxford English Dictionary* lists as one of extant meanings "Only just; *hence,* not quite…". According to this description, *barely* entails, in (22a), either that Roderick kissed Honoria, or that he did not kiss her—we do not know which. The serious consequences of this confusion would be even more obvious, e.g., in a criminal case where Roderick was charged with rape, and where a witness made the statement *Roderick barely raped Honoria.*
> (Harder and Kock 1976, p. 28)

But any such ambiguity is far more plausible for *hardly* (cf. Amaral and Schwenter 2007) as in *Roderick hardly kissed Honoria* than for *barely.* Harder and Kock find that it is "in any case clear that (22a) is always argumentatively stronger than (22b)," but this is untenable without a specification of what conclusion these statements are presented as arguments *for.* It appears that despite its promise, the Harder-Kock theory can hardly penetrate the polar membrane. We turn now to other perspectives on the slippery status of the polar component of proximatives.

5 The Implicature Line Revisited

We now review one non-argument for, and offer one new argument against, the (2C)-type conversational line on the polar component.

5.1 The Non-redundancy Argument

> A second fact that lends support to the idea that "not *P*" is a conversational implicature (of *almost P*) is that it can be reinforced—it can be made explicit without producing redundancy. Consider (22) as an answer to the question *Did Bill swim the English Channel?*
> (Sadock 1981, p. 263; cf. Sadock 1978, p. 293)

(22) Almost, but not quite.

But, as shown in Horn (1991) and contra Sadock (1978), informationally redundant propositions can be asserted as long as they introduce a rhetorical opposition (Anscombre and Ducrot 1983), typically signaled as above by *but*. Thus, we have (23a–d), where the *but* clause is semantically entailed/presupposed yet felicitously assertable:

(23) a. I don't know why I love you, but I do.
b. Obama barely won the nomination, but he did win.
c. It's odd that dogs eat cheese, but (eat cheese) they do.
d. I'm sorry I said it, but (say it) I did.

This does not show that *almost P-ing* is semantically distinct from *not quite P-ing,* but it does vitiate Sadock's non-redundancy argument for the implicature analysis.

5.2 *The Subset Diagnostic: A Griceogloss for Entailment Versus Implicature*

For a new argument for why the relation between *almost P* and *not P* cannot be (just) conversational implicature, pace Sadock (1981) and Ziegeler (2000, 2006, 2008), consider the distribution of reduced assertions in a variety of cases. When dealing with clear instances of conversational implicature, we get the inclusive readings.

(24) a. 20 students tried to solve the problem. [*includes those who succeeded*]
b. 20 students solved most of the problems. [*includes whoever solved them all*]
c. 20 students don't drink much. [*includes any who don't drink at all*]

Thus, if 5 students managed to solve the problem, they constitute 5 of the 20 who tried to solve it, if 5 students solved them all, the total is again 20, and if 5 are teetotalers, again we have just 20 in all. But now compare the case of proximatives, or the related example with *only* (see Horn 2002a, 2009b, and discussion below):

(25) a. 20 students almost solved the problem. [*excludes those who succeeded*]
b. 20 students barely passed the test. [*excludes those who failed*]
c. 20 students solved only the last problem. [*excludes any who solved none*]

If (25a) is true and 5 students solved the problem, we have a total of (at least) 25 students—the 5 who succeeded and the 20 who almost did; (25b) and (25c) are parallel. This supports the view that conversational implicature does not suffice for the polar component of proximatives. What of conventional implicature (as on the ($2B_2$)-style analysis of *almost/presque* in Jayez and Tovena 2008)? While it is difficult to find testable examples, it is instructive that the 20-student set in (26a) includes the subset of masochistic students who deliberately seek out food they find painful to eat, and that in (26b) includes the subset who were given the answers ahead of time, suggesting that neither variety of implicature suffices to handle the polar implication.

(26) a. 20 students find kimchi painfully spicy but attended CIL 18 anyway.
b. 20 students managed to pass the test.

The patterns discerned in this section thus constitute a GRICEOGLOSS to distinguish those meaning components that are entailed (even as assertorically inert entailments) from those that are conversationally implicated.

6 Scales Versus Rank Orders: The Coercion Effect

As we have seen, there is a palpable distinction between the behavior of the polar implication and that of classic scalar implicatures:

(27) a. ?Not only did Bill almost swim the English Channel, he did swim it.
b. Not only did Bill eat some of the cake, he ate all of it.

(28) A: It almost rained yesterday.
B: #Yes, in fact it did rain.

(29) A: It's likely it will rain tomorrow.
B: Yes, indeed it's certain it will.

This asymmetry is a problem for the claim that *almost P* : *P* : : *some* : *all.* But what if *almost P* : *P* : : *sick* : *dead*? We would be dealing then not with a true scale but a rank order (cf. Horn 2000a and references cited therein). See (30) for a notational differentiation and (31) for additional examples of rank orders:

(30)

true scales:	*rank orders:*
<scalding, hot, warm>	«felony|misdemeanor|tort»
<certain, likely, possible>	«win|place|show»
<loathe, hate, dislike>	«dead|sick»

(31)

«general|colonel|lieutenant|sergeant|private»	«married|engaged»
«full professor|associate prof.|assistant prof.»	«full house|flush»
«senior|junior|sophomore|freshman»	«A|B|C|D|F»
«a ϕ'd| a almost ϕ'd»	«a didn't ϕ| a barely ϕ'd»

In a scale of the form <Y, X>, …Y… unilaterally entails …X…: if it's hot, it's warm; in a rank order ≪Y|X≫, …Y… unilaterally entails …¬X…: if they're married, they're *not* engaged; if he's a colonel, he's *not* a lieutenant. Similarly, if she's a full professor, it's false that she's an assistant professor—although it's true that she's *at least* an assistant professor. Similarly, compare these exchanges between players in (non-wild card) poker, where having a full house outranks but precludes having a flush:

(32) A: Do you have a flush?
B: {No/#Yes} (in fact) I have a full house.

(33) A: Do you have at least a flush?
B: {Yes/#No} (in fact) I have a full house.

Not only (as opposed to *not just)* distinguishes between true scales, as in (27b), and rank orders, as in (34):

(34) a. #Not only are we engaged, we're married.
b. This is not {just/#only} a one-night stand, it's true love.

As noted above, *S is at least P* differs crucially from *S is P* in its truth conditions and illocutionary potential. Thus consider the exchanges in (35) and (36):

(35) a. Is your daughter a sophomore?
b. No/#Yes, (in fact) she's a junior.

(36) a. Is your daughter at least a sophomore?
b. Yes/#No, (in fact) she's a junior.

The fact that *Amy is a sophomore* can be false when *Amy is at least a sophomore* is true is consistent with the account of *at least* in Geurts and Nouwen (2007), on which *A[my] is at least a sophomore* is assigned the logical form in (37).

(37) $\Box$ [sophomore (a) $\vee$ junior (a) $\vee$ senior (a)] $\wedge$ and $\Diamond$ [junior (a) $\vee$ senior (a)]

The effect of *at least* is to coerce a rank order into an acting (virtual) scale; (36a), unlike (35a), induces a disjunction between the item in question and "higher"/ "better" alternative values = *Is your daughter a sophomore-or-more?*

This effect is the other side of the coin from the effect of focus in cases of "pragmatic intrusion", the tendency for pragmatically derived "enriched" meanings within an embedded context to contribute compositionally to what is said (cf. Cohen 1971; Levinson 2000; Carston 2002; Recanati 2004). It is argued by Horn (2004, 2006, 2009a), King and Stanley (2005), and Geurts (2009) that in such cases as (38), originally from Levinson 2000,

(38) a. Eating *some* of the cake is better than eating *all* of it.
b. Because the police recovered *some* of the missing gold, they will later recover it *all*.
c. Because the police recovered *some* of the missing gold, the thieves are expected to return later for the *rest*.

the double processing or retroactive accommodation is triggered by the role of focus on the scalar elements and by the minimal contrast. While *some* is normally compatible with *all* (to eat all of the cake is a fortiori to eat some of it), in the context of (38) the two are placed in opposition, and *some* is taken as amounting to *some but not all*. Focus alone is not enough to trigger reprocessing, as seen in (39):

(39) a. #Because the police recovered *some* (i.e., only some) of the missing gold, the thieves are expected to return later.
b. #Because it's *warm* out (i.e., warm but not hot), you should still wear a shirt.
c. #Because you ate *some* of your gruel (i.e., and not all), you get no dessert.

In cases like (38), focusing a weak scalar item in a contrastive context can effectively coerce scales into rank orders, just as *at least* coerces rank orders into ordinary scales, whence the contrast between being at least almost finished (which is compatible with finishing) and being almost finished (which is not). Or is it?

7 On Being Almost Dead Versus Almost Ready for Dinner

> "You thought something would change?"
> "She almost died."
> "Almost dying changes nothing. Dying changes everything."
> —exchange on "House" ABC TV, 17 December 2008

As we have seen, the paraphrase relation between *almost* with *not quite* assumed by some lexicographers and even some linguists and philosophers fails to account for the rhetorical difference between the two proximatives (see Sect. 3). On the account supported here, this difference is attributable to the fact that *almost* and *not quite* share their entailments but differ at the level of what they assert. Now consider the contrast between them in the context of (40):

(40) A: So dinner is {(?)almost/#not quite} ready, right?
B: Yes, in fact it *is* ready.

Accounting for the impossibility of *not quite* here is not the problem: to assert that dinner is not quite ready is to assert that it's not ready, whence the contradiction. But if the statement that dinner is almost ready *entails* (even though it does not *assert*) that it is, why is the positive response at least marginally possible (if not impeccable) in this case? Similarly, many speakers have no problem with the exchange in (41), while the apparently parallel cases in (42) and (43) seem far less acceptable.

(41) A: Is your dissertation almost ready to file?
B: (?)Yes, (in fact) {it *is* ready/it's *completely* ready}.

(42) A: Is Fredo almost dead?
B: #Yes, (in fact) he's *totally* dead.

(43) A: Did you almost kill Sollozzo at the restaurant?
B: #Yes, (in fact) I *did* kill him.

And, as we might expect, the cancelation facts yield a similar contrast:

(44) A: (?)Dinner is almost ready, and in fact it *is* ready. (cf. (7a) above)
B: #Fredo is almost dead, and in fact he *is* dead.

While there are several factors affecting the robustness of the polar implication and its cancelability, including the aspect of the predicate and the desirability of the outcome (cf. Ziegeler 2006, 2008; Amaral 2007), one consideration is that if dinner is almost ready in the actual world, it will be ready soon in all the inertia worlds determined in the context (cf. Dowty 1979, p. 148), while death is not similarly projectible from near death as a default future. Furthermore, it must be acknowledged that at least in our culture, whether a dinner or a dissertation is ready or not is of considerably less import than the metabolic difference between being dead versus not dead. Thus, *almost P* is sometimes (virtually) compatible with *P* and sometimes incompatible with *P*, depending in part on the significance of the distinction (as the waggish Paul Grice might have put it) between *P*-ing and not *P*-ing.

8 A not so Distant Cousin: The Pragmatic Asymmetry of *Only*

Disputes on the relative status of the two components of *only* clauses predate the related questions for the proximatives by a millennium or so. Since the 13th century, symmetricalists from Peter of Spain to Atlas (1993 et seq.), for whom (45a) essentially unpacks into the conjunction of (45b + c), have squared off against asymmetricalists (Geach, McCawley, Horn, et al.), for whom (45a) entails the negative (exclusive) component (45c) but at most presupposes or implicates the positive (prejacent) component (45b); cf. Horn (1996), Atlas (1996) for history and references.

(45) a. Only love counts.
b. Love counts.
c. Nothing distinct from love counts.

Like the polar component of *barely/almost VP,* the prejacent of *only NP* is entailed, pace Ippolito (2006, 2008) and van Rooij and Schulz (2007):

(46) a. #Only Sue passed the test, and (possibly) even she did not.
b. #Only the President can end the war—indeed, nobody can.

While semantically conjunctive and non-downward entailing, however, *only XP* and *only n CN* phrases license NPIs (pace Atlas 1993 et seq., Giannakidou 2006), trigger subject-aux inversion, and produce scale reversal, very much like its proximative cousin *barely:*

(47) a. *(Only) Dana {would ever eat any of that stew/drank a drop/slept a wink}.
b. *(Only) in stories does a dropped glass betray agitation. (Graham Greene)
c. *(Only) a fool would even eat a bite of that jellyfish risotto.

The semantic and pragmatic parallel between cross-categorial *only* and VP-modifying *barely* is especially striking here. The scale reversal attested in (47c) and in (48) is a diagnostic of the rhetorically negative character of semantically non-monotonic particles.

(48) *Patient's boyfriend*: "You can't do this. We lived together. We were going to have kids. You barely even know her."
Patient's mother: "Apparently neither did you." ("House" episode, 9/07)

Even the *barely but* sandwich of (15b) has a partial analog with *only*, as Galway Kinnell illustrates in his 1985 poem "Prayer" (formatting in original):

Whatever happens. Whatever
what is is is what
I want. Only that. But that.

Another parallel property shared by the polar component of proximatives and the prejacent of *only* is their predilection for taking wide scope with respect to complement-embedding emotives, i.e., the Karttunen and Peters (1979) diagnostics (but see Atlas 2002, 2007 for another view). What I just discovered in (49) is that

Gore came close to winning, or Bush to losing, or that the tax cuts won't help the non-wealthy. The propositions—that Gore lost, that Bush won, or that the wealthy benefit—scope out of the discovery. Similarly, what's bemoaned in (50) is the near thing or the exclusion, not the polar or prejacent implication.

(49) a. I just discovered that {Gore almost won/Bush barely won} the 2000 election.
b. I just discovered that the tax cuts will help only [$_F$the wealthy].

(50) a. It's too bad that {Hillary almost won/Barack barely won} the nomination.
b. It's too bad that the tax cuts will help only [$_F$the wealthy].

On the assertoric inertia account (Horn 2002a, 2009b), it's downward asserting, not downward entailing, environments that license NPIs—or at least *ever,* polarity *any,* and the minimizers. The Karttunen and Peters (1979) scopal diagnostics for presupposition or conventional implicature can be redefined as diagnosing material outside the scope of assertion. For Giannakidou (2006, 2012), on the other hand, *only* and emotive factives are "renegade" NPI licensers in languages like English. This conclusion is based partly on the fact that in languages such as Greek, NPIs are not licensed in such contexts (Giannakidou 1998, 2006):

(51) *Monon i Theodora idhe {ti Roxani/*kanenan}.*
only the Theodora saw-3SG the Roxanne/anybody
'Only Theodora saw {Roxanne/anybody}' (Giannakidou 1998: 154)

In addition, Giannakidou stresses the fact that *only* clauses are veridical and the fact that they don't license all NPIs. But first, as we have seen with *barely,* veridicality is not a deal-breaker as long as the relevant entailment is assertorically inert, and second, licensing isn't a binary affair in that *only* is a relatively weak trigger, as has been recognized at least since Horn (1970). Even those restrictive polarity items that Giannakidou (2006, 2012) sees as requiring overt negative licensers (as in her examples in (52)) do not always require them, as seen in (53):

(52) a. *Only Bill came either.
b. *Only Bill is all that intelligent.
c. *Only Bill arrived until Friday.

(53) a. Few of *my* friends could make it here either.
b. If he's all that smart, why isn't he rich?
c. I'll be damned if I'll quit until I absolutely have to.

Do languages like Greek require downward entailment as opposed to downward assertion to rule out (52) and similar sentences? No—for two reasons. First, DEness is not necessary for licensing in Greek. Disjunctive and *want*-contexts permit unstressed *kanenas,* as Giannakidou (1998) has documented; cf., e.g., (54), courtesy of Jason Merchant (p.c.):

(54) *I bike kanenas mesa i afisame ta fota anamena.*
lit. "Either n-one came in or we left the lights on"

(Note the impossibility of the corresponding sentence in English: **Either anyone came in or…*)

Second, DEness is not always sufficient. *At most n,* unlike *only n,* establishes a true downward entailing environment: if at most 5 students passed, then at most 5 students got A. (Notice that this is a question of actual DEness, not the Strawson DEness proposed for *only* in von Fintel 1999.) Yet, the equivalent expression to *at most* fails to license even weak NPIs in Greek (Anastasia Giannakidou, p.c.):

(55) **To poli pende fitites ipan tipota.* "At most 5 students said anything"

Thus, we see that in Greek, *at most n* and *only n* are equivalently *non*-licensers, while in English they're equivalently (medium-strength) licensers (cf. De Decker et al. 2005), so it can't be DEness as such that's relevant in either case.

On their conjunctive epistemic analysis of *at most n,* Geurts and Nouwen (2007) would unpack (56a) into a conjunction of (56b) and (56c).

(56) a. At most 30 people have proved this theorem.
b. It is (epistemically) possible that 30 people have proved this theorem
c. for $n > 30$, ¬[It is possible that *n* people have proved this theorem]

The obvious question arises under this analysis: Why is *at most n* an NPI licenser, given the conjunctive and hence apparently non-monotonic expansion in Geurts and Nouwen (2007)? Notice that as seen in (57), the quasi-negative behavior of *at most n* nominals is shared by that of the upper bounding proposition in (56c) but not by that of the positive epistemic proposition in (56b).

(57) a. At most 30 people have ever proved this theorem.
b. *It is possible that 30 people have ever proved this theorem.
c. It is not possible that more than 30 people have ever proved this theorem.

The key, as with the cases of *almost, barely,* and *only,* is to recognize that symmetry in the semantics may conceal a crucial asymmetry at the level of what is asserted. Because the entailment in (56b) is assertorically inert, *at most n* asserts only the negative proposition in (56c) and thus counts as effectively downward monotonic.

One more example of conjunctive asymmetry in licensing: while (as García-Álvarez 2009 points out) exceptives like *nobody but X* and *everybody but Y* entail both the generalization and exception, so that (58a) entails (58b, c) and (59a) entails (59b, c), *nobody but* licenses NPIs, given that the exception entailment of (58c) is assertorically inert, but *everybody but* does not.

(58) a. Nobody here but Kim has (ever) been to Tokyo.
b. Nobody here who isn't Kim has been to Tokyo.
c. Kim has been to Tokyo.

(59) a. Everybody here but Kim has (*ever) been to Tokyo.
b. Everybody here who isn't Kim has been to Tokyo.
c. Kim hasn't been to Tokyo.

9 Concluding Remarks

For Stalnaker (1978), an assertion is a proposal to change the context: a potentially controversial move to reduce the context set—the set of possible worlds constituting the "live options"—or equivalently a proposal to add the content of what is asserted to the common ground. I have proposed here, and in more detail in Horn (2002a), that the apparent tension between the evidence for the semantic symmetry of the meaning *almost* and *barely* and the evidence for their rhetorical asymmetry can be resolved by distinguishing what is (simply) entailed from what is (not just entailed but) asserted. Material in the former category counts as inert, and as transparent with respect to a wide range of linguistic diagnostics, including the "subset" diagnostic or Griceogloss introduced in Sect. 5.2.

Additional experimental evidence has recently been provided for this conclusion by Amaral (2007), the results of whose studies demonstrate that

> the "proximal" component is the asserted contribution of approximatives adverbs and plays a crucial role in textual coherence, whereas the "polar" component is entailed, and hence added to the Common Ground, but not asserted. In particular, the results obtained for *almost* show that the "polar" component, as understood by the Conjunctive Analysis, cannot adequately capture the full range of interpretations of this adverb.
>
> (Amaral 2007, p. 347)

Amaral's dissertation also provides a careful elaboration of the norms invoked by proximatives like *almost* and *barely,* which we have not been able to touch on here. While I would dispute the suggestion on the part of some analysts that the positive affect associated with proximatives is truth-conditionally relevant (so that for *a almost ϕ'd* to be true, being closer to ϕ must count as better or more positively relevant for the speaker than being less close to ϕ), there is often, as Robert van Rooij (p.c.) points out, a palpable element of subjective or assessment or rhetorical affect involved, though arguably more for *barely* than for *almost:*

(60) a. Robin {almost survived/almost perished in} the explosion.
b. Dana {barely survived/#barely perished in} the explosion.

In his important thesis on proximatives, Sevi (1998) defends a formally symmetric (2A)-style conjunctive analysis for the proximal and polar components: *almost p* entails (and asserts) *not p* and *barely* entails (and asserts) *p.* At the same time, he acknowledges, the polar assertion is "somehow 'backgrounded' or less 'prominent'" than the proximal assertion (1998, p. 32). That is, "*almost* is 'positive' and *barely* is 'negative' in some sense" (1998, p. 34). But how and in what sense? This is the question we have sought to address here for the proximatives (and their exclusive cousins).

Like *barely, only NP* on the proposed account is neither downward entailing nor non-veridical. This would predict it shouldn't license NPIs, and indeed it doesn't in Greek, but in English its veridicality and non-monotonicity are overridden by downward assertion (in which assertorically inert components are disregarded), a property that is evidently irrelevant for Greek. Disjunctions, on the other hand, are not NPI triggers in English, where non-veridicality is insufficient for licensing NPIs. We thus obtain a parameterized account of polarity licensing to allow for cross-linguistic variation: (non-)veridicality must be invoked to account for the distribution of polarity items in some languages (Greek, Bengali), while downward assertion is relevant in others (English, Swedish).

Sentences based on *almost VP, barely VP, only NP, no X but NP, at most n CN,* and other quasi-conjunctive expressions *entail* both conjuncts of the relevant expansion but *assert* only one of those conjuncts (the other being assertorically inert). Recognizing this asymmetry at the pragmatic level enables us to capture asymmetries reflected (inter alia) by NPI licensing, scalar orientation, inversion, and discourse negativity while avoiding the contradictions incurred by a semantically asymmetric account. Like Atlas (2002, p. 12), I "remain as unconvinced as ever that downward entailment can explain the distributional data of NPI licensing," but the fault, I have argued, lies not with the "downward" but with the "entailment."

Acknowledgments Earlier versions of different subsets of this material were presented in Tel Aviv (June 1999), Chicago (January 2000), Berlin (March 2001), Tokyo (May 2001), Reading (September 2001), UMass (October 2001), Yale (April 2002), Chicago (April 2002), Pomona (April 2005), Potsdam (December 2005), Swarthmore (April 2006), Anaheim (January 2007), Leysin (March 2007), and Chicago (May 2007). Some of this material appears in a different form in Horn (2011). I am grateful to commentators at those occasions and that of the scalar workshop at CIL 18 organized by Chungmin Lee, and I am indebted to Barbara Abbott, Patricia Amaral, Jay Atlas, Kent Bach, Ariel Cohen, Bart Geurts, Anastasia Giannakidou, Janet Hitzeman, Jack Hoeksema, Michael Israel, Jason Merchant, Robert van Rooij, Scott Schwenter, Mandy Simons, Su-won Yoon, Debra Ziegeler, and an anonymous reviewer for their thoughts and comments and in particular to Jerry Sadock for his inspiration. Of course, only I am responsible for any errors. For insightful recent treatments of the semantics, the scalar directedness, and the cross-categorial nature of *almost, barely,* and their cross-linguistic analogs, see Penka (2006), Ziegeler (2006, 2008), Nouwen (2006), and Amaral (2007, 2010). See also Liu, this volume, for a different take on some of the issues explored here.

References

Amaral, Patricia. 2007. The meaning of approximative adverbs: Evidence from European Portuguese. Ohio State University dissertation.

Amaral, Patricia. 2010. Entailment, assertion, and textual coherence: the case of *almost* and *barely*. *Linguistics* 43: 525–545.

Amaral, Patricia and Scott Schwenter. 2007. The contextual dependence of inverted approximatives. In *Paper presented at 8th Semantic Fest*, Stanford University.

Anscombre, Jean-Claude, and Oswald Ducrot. 1983. *L'argumentation dans la langue*. Bruxelles: Pierre Mardaga.

Atlas, Jay D. 1984. Comparative adjectives and adverbials of degree. *Linguistics and Philosophy* 7: 347–377.

Atlas, Jay D. 1993. The importance of being 'only': Testing the neo-Gricean versus neo-entailment paradigms. *Journal of Semantics* 10: 301–318.

Atlas, Jay D. 1996. 'Only' noun phrases, pseudo-negative generalized quantifiers, negative polarity items, and monotonicity. *Journal of Semantics* 13: 265–332.

Atlas, Jay D. 1997. Negative adverbials, prototypical negation, and the De Morgan taxonomy. *Journal of Semantics* 14: 349–368.

Atlas, Jay D. 2002. NPI licensing and overcoming assertoric inertia. Paper given at One Day Only, Groningen, 8 May 2002. http://staff.science.uva.nl/~pdekker/Only/Literature/Atlas2.pdf.

Atlas, Jay D. 2007. On a pragmatic explanation of negative polarity licensing. In *Pragmatics*, ed. N. Burton-Roberts, 10–23. Houndmills: Palgrave Macmillan.

Biq, Yung-O. 1989. Metalinguistic negation in Mandarin. *Journal of Chinese Linguistics* 17: 75–94.

Bordería, Salvador Pons, and Scott Schwenter. 2005. Polar meaning and 'expletive' negation in approximative adverbs: Spanish *por poco (no)*. *Journal of Historical Pragmatics* 6: 262–282.

Carlson, Gregory. 1981. Distribution of free choice *any*. *CLS* 17: 8–23.

Carston, Robyn. 2002. *Thoughts and utterances: The pragmatics of explicit communication*. Oxford: Blackwell.

Cohen, L. Jonathan. 1971. Some remarks on Grice's views about the logical particles of natural language. In *Pragmatics of natural language*, ed. Y. Bar-Hillel, 50–68. Dordrecht: Reidel.

De Decker, Paul, Erik Larson, and Andrea Martin. 2005. Polarity judgments: an empirical view. Poster for "Polarity from Different Perspectives" workshop, NYU, March 2005.

Dowty, David. 1979. *Word meaning and montague grammar*. Dordrecht: D. Reidel.

Ducrot, Oswald. 1973. *La preuve et le dire*. Paris: Maison Mame.

García-Álvarez, Ivan. 2009. Generality and exception: A study in the semantics of exceptives. PhD dissertation, Stanford University.

Geurts, Bart. 2009. Scalar implicature and local pragmatics. *Mind and Language* 24: 51–79.

Geurts, Bart and Rick Nouwen. 2007. *At least* et al.: The semantics of scalar modifiers. *Language* 83: 533–59.

Giannakidou, Anastasia. 1998. *Polarity sensitivity as (non-)veridical dependency*. Amsterdam: John Benjamins.

Giannakidou, Anastasia. 2006. *Only*, emotive factives, and the dual nature of polarity dependency. *Language* 82: 575–603.

Giannakidou, Anastasia. 2012. Negative and positive polarity items. In *Semantics: An international handbook of natural language meaning*, eds. K. von Heusinger, C. Maienborn, and P. Portner, vol. 2, 1660–1712.

Grandy, Richard, and Richard Warner (eds.). 1986. *Philosophical grounds of rationality: intentions, categories, ends*. Oxford: Clarendon Press.

Harder, Peter, and Christian Kock. 1976. *The theory of presupposition failure*. Copenhagen: Akademisk Forlag.

Hitzeman, Janet. 1992. The selectional properties and entailments of 'almost'. *CLS* 28: 225–238.

Hoeksema, Jack. 1983. Negative polarity and the comparative. *NLLT* 1: 403–434.

Horn, Laurence. 1970. Ain't it hard (anymore). *CLS* 6: 318–327.

Horn, Laurence. 1972. On the semantic properties of logical operators in english. UCLA dissertation.

Horn, Laurence. 1991. Given as new: When redundant affirmation isn't. *Journal of Pragmatics* 15: 313–336.

Horn, Laurence. 1996. Exclusive company: Only and the dynamics of vertical inference. *Journal of Semantics* 13: 1–40.

Horn, Laurence. 2000a. *Pick a theory (not just any theory): Indiscriminatives and the free choice indefinite*. In *Negation and Polarity*, eds. L. Horn and Y. Kato, 149–92. Oxford: Oxford University Press.

Horn, Laurence. 2000b. *any* and *(-)ever:* Free choice and free relatives. *IATL* 15: 71–111.

Horn, Laurence. 2002a. Assertoric inertia and NPI licensing. CLS 38. *Part* 2: 55–82.

Horn, Laurence. 2002b. Uncovering the un-word: A study in lexical pragmatics. *Sophia Linguistica* 49: 1–64.

Horn, Laurence. 2004. Implicature. In *The handbook of pragmatics*, ed. L. Horn and G. Ward, 3–28. Oxford: Blackwell.

Horn, Laurence. 2005. An un-paper for the unsyntactician. In *Polymorphous linguistics: Jim McCawley's legacy*, ed. S. Mufwene, et al., 329–365. Cambridge: MIT Press.

Horn, Laurence. 2006. The border wars: A neo-Gricean perspective. In *Where semantics meets pragmatics*, ed. K. von Heusinger and K. Turner, 21–48. Oxford: Elsevier.

Horn, Laurence. 2009a. WJ-40: Implicature, truth, and meaning. *International Review of Pragmatics* 1: 3–34.

Horn, Laurence. 2009b. *ONLY* XL: The assertoric asymmetry of exponibles. In *Proceedings of SALT XIX*, 198–221.

Horn, Laurence. 2011. Almost forever. In *Pragmatics and autolexical grammar in honor of Jerry Sadock*, ed. E. Yuasa, et al., 3–21. Amsterdam: Benjamins.

Ippolito, Michela. 2006. Remarks on *only*. In *Proceedings of SALT XVI*.

Ippolito, Michela. 2008. On the meaning of *only*. *Journal of Semantics* 25: 45–91.

Jayez, Jacques. 1987. Sémantique et approximation: Le cas de *presque* et *à peine*. *Lingvisticæ Investigationes* 11: 157–196.

Jayez, Jacques and Lucia Tovena. 2008. *Presque* and *almost:* How argumentation derives from comparative meaning. In *Empirical Issues in Syntax and Semantics 7,* eds. B. Olivier and P. Cabredo Hofherr, 217–239.

Karttunen, Lauri, and Stanley Peters. 1979. Conventional implicature. In *Syntax and semantics 11: Presupposition*, ed. C.-K. Oh, and D. Dinneen, 1–56. New York: Academic Press.

King, Jeffrey and Jason Stanley. 2005. Semantics, pragmatics, and the role of semantic context. In *Semantics vs. pragmatics,* ed. Z. Szabó, 111–64. Oxford: Clarendon.

Klein, Henny. 1997. Adverbs of *Degree in Dutch*. U. of Groningen dissertation.

Lakoff, Robin. 2000. *The Language War*. Berkeley: University of California Press.

Levinson, Stephen. 2000. *Presumptive meanings: The theory of generalized conversational implicature*. Cambridge: MIT Press.

Li, Charles. 1976. A functional explanation for an unexpected case of ambiguity (S or ~S). In *Linguistic studies offered to Joseph Greenberg*, vol. 3, ed. A.M. Devine and L. Stephens, 527–535. Saratoga: Anma Libri.

McCawley, James. 1973. Syntactic and logical arguments for semantic structures. In *Three dimensions in linguistic theory,* ed. O. Fujimura, 259–376. TEC: Tokyo.

Morgan, Jerry. 1969. On arguing about semantics. *Papers in Linguistics* 1: 49–70.

Morzycki, Marcin. 2001. *Almost* and its kin. *SALT XI,* 225–38.

Nouwen, Rick. 2006. Remarks on the polar orientation of *almost.* In *Linguistics in the Netherlands 2006,* eds. J. van der Weijer and B. Los. Amsterdam: John Benjamins. http://semanticsarchive.net/Archive/DcyMzAyO/almost.pdf.

Penka, Doris. 2006. Almost there: the meaning of *almost.* In *Proceedings of Sinn und Bedeutung 2005,* eds. C. Ebert and C. Endriss, 275–86.

Rapp, Irene, and Arnim von Stechow. 1999. *Fast* 'almost' and the visibility parameter for functional adverbs. *Journal of Semantics* 16: 149–204.

Recanati, François. 2004. *Literal Meaning*. Cambridge: Cambridge U. Press.

Sadock, Jerrold. 1978. On testing for conversational implicature. In *Syntax and semantics 9: Pragmatics*, ed. P. Cole, 281–297. New York: Academic Press.

Sadock, Jerrold. 1981. Almost. In *Radical pragmatics*, ed. P. Cole, 257–271. New York: Academic.

Sadock, Jerrold. 2007. *Nearly* and *almost*. Language Log posting, 24 June 2007. http://158.130.17.5/~myl/languagelog/archives/004640.html.

Schwenter, Scott. 2002. Discourse context and polysemy: Spanish *casi*. In *Romance philology and variation: Selected papers from the 30th linguistic symposium on romance languages*, ed. C. Wiltshire, and J. Camps, 161–175. Amsterdam: John Benjamins.

Sevi, Aldo. 1998. A semantics for *almost* and *barely*. M.A. thesis, Tel Aviv U.

Stalnaker, Robert. 1978. Assertion. In *Syntax and semantics 9: Pragmatics*, ed. P. Cole, 315–332. New York: Academic Press.

van Dongen, W.A. 1921. Almost and nearly. *Neophilologus* 6: 184–207.

von Fintel, Kai. 1999. NPI-licensing, Strawson-entailment, and context-dependency. *Journal of Semantics* 16: 97–148.

van Rooij, Robert, and Katrin Schulz. 2007. Only: Meaning and implicature. In *Questions in dynamic semantics*, ed. M. Aloni, et al., 193–223. London: Elsevier.

Zepter, Alex. 2003. How to be universal when you are existential: Entailment along a scale. *Journal of Semantics* 20: 193–236.

Ziegeler, Debra. 2000. What *almost* can reveal about counterfactual inferences. *Journal of Pragmatics* 32: 1743–1776.

Ziegeler, Debra. 2006. *Interfaces with aspect*. Chapter 4, *Proximative aspect*. Amsterdam: John Benjamins.

Ziegeler, Debra. 2008. Running the gauntlet on the proximatives debate: a response to recent challenges Unpublished ms., National U. of Singapore.

Interpretations of Numerals and Structured Contexts

Jae-Il Yeom

Abstract It has been assumed that the interpretation of a numeral *n* is determined as part of a scalar implicature, but there is a lot of evidence against it. First, numerals do not form a semantic scale but a pragmatic scale. Second, sometimes a numeral *n* is interpreted as 'at least *n*' or 'at most *n*', but the meaning of at least/most is not part of the meaning of a numeral. The meaning of a numeral is determined contextually. The basic principle is that we should make a statement as informative as possible. In making a statement informative, we consider two scales: one is the basic scalarity of largeness between numerals and the scalarity of likelihood. The two scales apply to two different regions with respect to a quantifier. The informativeness from the basic scalarity requires the numeral mentioned to be the maximal number of elements involved when each member in the quantifier domain is considered. And the alternative sentences with the numeral replaced with an alternative numeral are ordered by the informativeness from the unlikelihood scalarity, making the number mentioned a limit value among the maximal numbers of the elements involved in the meaning of the quantifier. The limit number *n* is taken to be 'at least n' or 'at most n'. If no overt quantifier is involved, a universal quantifier over epistemic alternatives is provided by the support conditions of the sentence.

Keywords Numeral • Scalar implicature • Likelihood • At least • At most • Quantification domain • Informativeness

J.-I. Yeom (✉)
Hongik University, Seoul, South Korea
e-mail: jiyeom@hongik.ac.kr

C. Lee et al. (eds.), *Contrastiveness in Information Structure, Alternatives and Scalar Implicatures*, Studies in Natural Language and Linguistic Theory 91, DOI 10.1007/978-3-319-10106-4_15

1 Introduction

Grice (1975)'s maxim of quantity consists of the following two sub-maxims:[1]

- Make your contribution as informative as is required for the current purposes of the exchange.
- Do not make your contribution more informative than is required.

The maxims apply to utterances with scalar expressions, which include numerals. In this tradition, a numeral *n* is assumed to have the semantic meaning of 'at least *n*'. On the other hand, it gets the interpretation of 'exactly *n*', because the speaker is supposed to follow the maxim of quantity: the speaker would mention a larger number if he or she could assert a stronger statement with a larger number, even if the number in the sentence really means 'at least *n*'. Therefore mentioning the number *n* means that the number is the largest one with which the speaker can make a statement truthfully. In the following example, the semantic meaning of (1a) is (1b) and (1c) is a scalar implicature. So we conclude that (1d) is what is intended by the speaker.

(1) a. John has three children
b. John has at least three children.
c. NOT(John has more than three children)
d. John has *exactly three* children.

However, this way of reasoning is easily refuted by other statements with numerals. Cf. Horn (1992, 1996), Koenig (1991), Atlas (1992), etc. Numerals are different from other scalar terms:

(2) A: Are many of your friends linguists?
B: ?No, all of them are.
B′: Yes, (in fact) all of them are.

(3) A: Do you have three children?
B: No, four.
B′: ?Yes, (in fact) four.

We generally assume that if all of your friends are linguists, it is also true that many of your friends are. Thus when you make an affirmative answer to the question of whether many of your friends are linguists, you can claim that all of your friends are. But after you deny that many of your friends are linguists, you cannot very naturally claim that all of your friends are. In contrast, after you deny that you have three children, you can claim that you have four children, as shown in (3B). But after you assert that you have three children, it is awkward to claim that you have four children, as shown in (3B′). You may think of a situation in which the discourse becomes appropriate, but it is important that there are cases where the discourse can be inappropriate. This implies that a numeral *n* may not mean 'at least *n*'.

---

[1]The original maxim of quantity mentions the factor of relevance to the context. Later this factor is more or less ignored and informativeness is emphasized more, and the maxim has got other names like the Q-principle (Horn 1984; Levinson 1987) or the principle of volubility.

A more convincing example is like the following:

(4) a. ??Neither of us liked the movie – she hated it and I absolutely loved it. (Horn 1996, 316)
b. Neither of us have three kids – she has two and I have four.

Loving a movie entails liking it. If neither of us liked the movie, neither of us loved it. On the other hand, having four children does not entail having three, as (4b) shows. This would be surprising if *three children* had the semantics of 'at least three children'. This shows that numerals do not constitute a semantic scale.

A second argument against the semantic interpretation of a numeral *n* as 'at least *n*' is that a numeral *n* can have the 'at most *n*', 'at least *n*' or 'exactly *n*' interpretation, depending on the context. Sadock (1984, 143) and Carston (1998) give some examples involving modality of possibility in which a numeral has an 'at least' or 'at most' interpretation:

(5) a. That golfer is capable of a round of 100 (and maybe even 90/*110).
b. Women with two preschoolers are eligible for the welfare benefit.

In (5a), the number 100 is interpreted as 'at most 100'. This allows the possibility of a round of 90. In (5b), the number *two* has 'at least' interpretation because people with more preschoolers are more likely to get the welfare benefit.

When necessity is involved, a numeral tends to have 'at least' interpretation:

(6) a. In Britain you have to be 18 to drive a car.
b. Mary needs three A's to get into Oxford.

The expressions *have to* and *need* involve the meaning of necessity, and the numerals indicate minimal requirements.

Breheny (2008) shows that the interpretation of a numeral is completely dependent on background knowledge:

(7) No one who has three children is happy.

In (7), the quantifier *no one* introduces a downward-entailing context, but the numeral has three possible readings, depending on background knowledge. In a context where more children implies more stress, the numeral is likely to have 'at least' interpretation. In a context where more children implies more benefits, it is more likely to have 'at most' interpretation. Having four children is taken to be the minimal requirement to get some benefits. We can also think of a context where a specific number of children, say, three children for some reason, make their parents unhappy. In this context the numeral *three* is interpreted as 'exactly three'. Breheny (2008) discusses this example to see if monotonicity affects the interpretation of a numeral, and it is shown that the main factor of determining the interpretation of a numeral is background knowledge.

One thing to note in (7) is that the example involves quantification. When there is no quantification or modality involved, a numeral generally has an 'exactly' or, less likely, 'at least' interpretation.

(8) A: who has three children?
B: John has three children.
B′: John has three children, in fact he has five.

In this example, the numeral *three* seems to have an 'exactly' interpretation without the second sentence. But in B′'s response, it has 'at least' interpretation. This requires a context where having three children can be taken to be a minimal requirement for something and we need someone who can satisfy the requirement. One interesting fact is that in neither case can we get 'at most' interpretation. We cannot think of a context where such an interpretation is accepted.

We have seen that whether modality and quantification are involved or not can affect the interpretation of a numeral. Despite this generalization, there is an example discussed by Krifka (1999) in which a numeral has an 'at most' interpretation even without any quantification.

(9) In Guatemala, three percent of the population owns seventy percent of the land. (Krifka 1999)

In (9), there is no quantification involved. And the numeral *three* has an 'at most' interpretation, while *seventy* has an 'at least' interpretation. We have to be able to explain why numerals in general do not have 'at most' interpretations when there is no quantification involved. In addition, we have to explain why the numeral *three* in (9) has an 'at most' interpretation.

2 Previous Analyses

The problems with the classical analysis of numerals have been discussed by many linguists, including Carston (1998), Breheny (2008), Van Kuppevelt (1996a, 1996b), Horn (1992, 1996), Koenig (1991), Atlas (1992), etc. Among these, Carston (1998) claims that the meaning of a numeral is *underspecified*:

(10) X [THREE],
where the value of X is pragmatically determined. (cf. Recanati (1989))

In this interpretation, X can be 'at least', 'at most' or 'exactly', depending on the context the numeral is used. We have already seen that the interpretation of a numeral depends on the context where it is used, but simply saying that X is given by the context is not an explanation. We have to explain how the interpretation is determined and why modality or quantification affects the interpretation of a numeral.

Van Kuppevelt (1996a, 1996b) claims that the interpretation of a numeral also depends on whether it is in the topic or the comment part of the information structure of the utterance:

(11) How many children does John have?
a. He has three children.
b. *He has three children, in fact five.

(12) Who has three children?
  a. John has three children.
  b. John has three children, in fact five.

In (11), the numeral is in the focused part and gets the 'exactly' interpretation. This does not allow the possibility that John has more than three children. In (12), however, the numeral gets the 'at least' interpretation in the topic position of the sentence, which allows the possibility that John has five children. These examples show that interpretation of numerals is affected by information structure.

However, this explanation has some problems. First, it is not explained when an 'at most' interpretation is possible. The 'at most' interpretation does not seem to depend on information structure. A second problem is that this explanation is not empirically supported either. Krifka (1999) refutes van Kuppevelt's claim with the following example:

(13) A: How many children does Nigel have?
  B: Nigel has fourteen$_F$ children, perhaps even fifteen$_F$.

Even though the numeral *fourteen* is focused, it does not lead to 'exactly' interpretation: it still allows the possibility that Nigel has fifteen children.

Geurts (2006) gives a semantic analysis of numerals. He basically assumes that a numeral *n* is a predicate that applies to sum individuals, following Krifka (1999). In this usage, a NP with a numeral basically gets the 'exactly' interpretation:

(14) These are five cows.
(15) Five cows mooed.

In the first example, *five cows* only means 'exactly five cows', while in the second example *five cows* means 'exactly five cows' or 'at least five cows'.

He tries to explain an 'at least' interpretation by type-shifting, in terms of Partee (1986):

(16) a. $[\![n \text{ CN}]\!] = \lambda P\exists!x[\#(x) = n \;\&\; [\![\text{CN}]\!](x) \wedge P(x)]$
  b. $\lambda x[\#(x) = n \;\&\; [\![\text{CN}]\!](x)]$ (Quantifier Lowering)
  c. $\lambda P\exists x[\#(x) = n \;\&\; [\![\text{CN}]\!](x) \;\&\; P(x)]$ (Existential Closure)

He assumes that a numeral has the 'exactly' interpretation. Thus when a NP with a numeral is used as an argument, it is given the interpretation of (16a). By applying the rule of Quantifier Lowering to this, we can get the meaning of a NP with a numeral as a predicate, as given in (16b). And by applying Existential Closure to this, we can get the meaning of a NP with a numeral as an argument again, as given in (16c). This meaning is compatible with the situation in which *x* is more than *n*. This is how a numeral takes the 'at least' interpretation. By these derivations, Geurts tries to explain that a numeral can get an 'exactly' or 'at least' interpretation when a NP with a numeral is used as an argument, and that a numeral always has an 'exactly' interpretation when a NP with a numeral is used as a predicate.

Geurts explained the two meanings based on semantic type-shifting. However, one reading is missing: an 'at most' interpretation cannot be derived by semantic type-shifting. Instead, Geurts assumes that this interpretation is derived pragmatically, unlike the 'at least' interpretation. However, there is no evidence that 'at least' interpretations of numerals are semantically derived, while 'at most' interpretations of numerals are pragmatically derived. As will be shown below, interpretations of numerals are determined contextually. Moreover, even predicative uses of NPs with numerals can have 'at least' interpretations:

(17) These are five pills, if not six.

We normally assume that *five pills* here means 'exactly five pills', but in this example it is more plausible to assume that it has the 'at least' interpretation. So a numeral in a predicate use does not necessarily have the 'exactly' meaning.

In this paper, I am going to account for how a numeral is interpreted, on the basis of a pragmatic approach. To support my analysis, I am going to make several claims that are opposite to what some previous analyses of numerals claim. First, I show that numerals do not constitute a semantic scale, and claim that the meaning of 'at least/most' is not part of the meaning of a numeral. This means that the interpretation of a numeral is determined contextually. There are two kinds of informativeness based on two kinds of scalarity: the basic scalarity between numerals and a contextual scalarity of likelihood. The informativeness from the basic scalarity requires the speaker or hearer to consider the maximal numbers of elements in a domain of quantification. The informativeness from the contextual scalarity requires the speaker to provide a limit value in the set of the maximal numbers of elements considered in the quantification domain, and the limit number n is taken to be 'at least n' or 'at most n'. If no quantification is involved, quantification over epistemic alternatives is the default option.

3 Pragmatics in Using Numerals

3.1 Evidence Against Semantic Scalarity

First, I will show that numerals do not constitute a semantic scale. This means that a numeral n does not entail 'at least $n - 1$' in general. One piece of evidence is that a set of alternatives among numerals is determined contextually. Suppose that John juggles with balls, and that it is the more difficult to juggle with more balls. And for some reasons, it is impossible to juggle with an odd number of balls.

(18) A: Anyone who can juggle with more than six balls can participate in the competition. Does John juggle with six balls?
B: Yes, he does. He can even juggle with ten balls.

In this example, *six* means '*at least* six', but B's answer does not entail that John can juggle with five or seven balls. Note that the 'at least' interpretation does not have anything to do with semantic scalarity.

There is another example that supports that numerals do not constitute a semantic scale. Suppose that one boy ate three apples, and two boys ate two apples each (Krifka 1999).

(19) a. Three boys ate seven apples.
b. Two boys ate six apples.

In this context, (19a) does not entail (19b). From the context, we can say either that two boys ate four apples or that two boys ate five apples, but not that two boys ate six apples. Accumulation is not a semantic process. If numerals constitute a scale, the scalar set is determined in the context, not inherently in the language system.

Even though numerals constitute a pragmatic scale, there are many cases where they behave as if they constituted a semantic scale. This is related to the inclusion relation: for example, an event of reading six books includes an event of reading five books in general. But the relations between numerals can be restricted by the context: they are structured by the context. A sentence with a numeral '*five*' itself does not entail the corresponding sentence with the numeral '*six*'.

3.2 'At Least/Most' not Part of Semantics

In many of the previous analyses, the meanings like 'at least/most' are part of the meanings of numerals. However, there is evidence supporting that this is not actually the case. First, the same numeral may have different meanings depending on background knowledge. As I said, the interpretation of the numeral *three* in the following depends on which context the sentence is uttered in.

(7) No one who has three children is happy.

The numeral *three* has three interpretations: 'exactly three', 'at least three', and 'at most three'. However, the numeral itself does not seem to have the meaning of 'at least' or 'at most'.

One piece of evidence is that the three interpretations are always available, whether or not the relevant scales are semantic or pragmatic. {love, like} is a set of semantic alternatives:

(20) a. You must (at least) like studying math if you want to do well in math.
b. You may (at most) watch her dance, (but you may not dance with her).
c. No one who (at most) like studying math do well in math.
d. No one who (at least) like studying math fail in math.

In these examples, the expressions in parentheses indicate the possible interpretations of *like studying math*. It is implausible to assume that *like studying math* itself has the meaning of 'at least/most like studying math'. This shows that the meaning of 'at least' or 'at most' can be attached to any scalar term: it is not inherent part of the meaning of a numeral. It only comes from the context.

In (7), it is clear that directions of contextual scalarity are determined by *background knowledge* plus *the whole sentence*, and that contextual scalarity can be taken to be scalarity of informativeness: the less likely the utterance, the more informative it is. Suppose that more children implies more stress. Then ordering of being less likely is like the following with respect to numbers.

(21) 1 > 2 > **[3]** > … > n − 1 > n

This means that the smaller the number, the stronger the sentence becomes pragmatically. When a number x is mentioned in the sentence, it means that the *lower* limit number x such that no one who has x children is happy is three, so it gets the meaning of 'at least'.

In the same background knowledge, however, the direction of scalarity changes if we change the sentence. Consider the following sentence.

(22) People who have three children are happy.

Since having more children implies more stress, the ordering of the sentence being less likely to be true is like the following:

(23) n > n − 1 > … > **[3]** > 2 > 1 > 0

In this context the numeral *three* is taken to be the *upper* limit number such that people who have that number of children are happy. The numeral mentioned takes the meaning of 'at most three'.

Now we consider the two sentences with different background knowledge. Suppose that more children implies more prosperity. Then the direction of scalarity changes in relation to sentence (7).

(24) Ordering of being less likely: n > n − 1 > … > **[3]** > 2 > 1 > 0

Then the numeral gets the 'at most' interpretation. As for sentence (22), the direction of scalarity is reversed and the ordering of numerals is as follows:

(25) Ordering of being less likely: 1 > 2 > **[3]** > … > n − 1 > n

This indicates that the direction of scalarity changes with the whole utterance. Therefore the meanings like 'at least' and 'at most' must be associated with the whole sentence. So the meanings of the two sentences can be represented as follows:

(26) a. AT LEAST/MOST[No one who has three children is happy]
b. ATMOST/LEAST[People who have three children are happy]

That is, the numeral itself does not have the meaning of either 'at most' or 'at least', but rather the background knowledge plus the sentence as a whole determines the ordering of the (un)likelihood of the sentence. This, in turn, determines the meaning of the numeral by taking it as a limit value.

We can say a similar thing about sentences in which some kind of modality is involved. Suppose that people want to eat more apples. In this context, the numeral in the following sentence is interpreted as 'at most three'.

(27) You may eat three apples.

This is a permission statement. If people want to eat more apples, it is less likely to give a permission to have more apples. So the ordering of being less likely is the following:

(28) Ordering of being less likely: n > n − 1 > … > **[3]** > 2 > 1

In this respect, the larger the number, the stronger the permission becomes. So the number mentioned is taken to be the upper limit number such that the speaker can allow the hearer to eat that number of apples. This can be expressed as follows:

(29) AT MOST[You may have three apples]

Under the same background knowledge, the ordering of being less likely remains the same and sentence (30a) is understood as meaning (30b).

(30) a. You must have three apples.
b. AT MOST[You must have three apples]

Suppose that people want to solve fewer problems. Then it is less likely that permission or obligation statements are made with a smaller number. So the ordering of being less likely is like the following:

(31) Ordering of being less likely: 1 > 2 > **[3]** > … > n − 1 > n

In this context, the following statements in (32) are interpreted as those in (33) respectively.

(32) a. You may solve three problems.
b. You must solve three problems.

(33) a. AT LEAST[You may solve three problems]
b. AT LEAST[You must solve three problems]

4 Informativeness from the Basic Scalarity

I have discussed informativeness with respect to a pragmatic factor of being less likely. In some sense, uttering a sentence that is less likely to be true is uttering a pragmatically stronger sentence. This is the main factor that determines the meaning of a numeral. But in order for this account to make sense, we need to assume another scalarity. The traditional analysis of numerals is more concerned with a more basic kind of scalarity in numerals: that is, a larger number leads to a stronger statement than a smaller number. I have shown that there is no semantic scalarity among numerals, but pragmatically, an event of solving three problems includes an event of solving two problems in it, unless a case of solving two problems is excluded for some pragmatic reason.

(34) a. John must solve three problems.
b. $\boxdot\ \exists x[\#(x) \geq 3 \wedge \text{problems}(x) \wedge \text{solve}(j, x)]$
c. John must solve two problems.
d. $\boxdot\ \exists x[\#(x) \geq 2 \wedge \text{problems}(x) \wedge \text{solve}(j, x)]$

The meaning of sentence (34a) can be represented as in (34b): pragmatically it is supposed to mean that John must solve at least three problems. That is, the number must be the lower limit of the number of problems John solves. On the other hand, if John solves three problems in a deontic alternative, it is also true that John solves two problems in the same alternative. We can say the same thing about other deontic alternatives. Then we should be able to utter (34b) truthfully. In the current context, however, we cannot say that John must solve two problems. This is problematic, considering the fact that in some deontic alternatives John solves four or five problems but (34a) is uttered.

There are two regions in each of which the maximality and the lower limit can be captured separately. Take sentence (34a) for example. It involves a deontic operator, a quantifier over a relevant set of deontic alternatives. When we talk about the lower limit of the numbers of problems John solves, we are considering only the maximal number of problems John solves in each deontic alternative. Here the basic scalarity comes in. If there is an event of John solving three problems in a deontic alternative, it is also true that there is a subevent of John solving two problems in that deontic alternative. But we only consider the maximal numbers of problems John solves in the deontic alternatives. If the number mentioned in (34a) is understood as the lower limit, it is among those maximal numbers based on the scalarity of (un)likelihood. In the interpretation of the numeral '3', the basic scalarity of pragmatic inclusion applies to the number of problems John solves in each deontic alternative and determines the maximal number. The scale of unlikelihood orders alternative sentences with an alternative numeral, and the alternative numerals are taken to be the maximal numbers of problems John solves in each deontic alternative and determines the number mentioned as a limit value.

The same analysis can apply to cases of quantification over individuals. Consider (7) again. When more children means more stress, the sentence means that no one who have at least three children are happy. In the quantifier domain, we have people who have three children. A situation of having three children includes a sub-situation of having two children, but we only consider the maximal numbers of children the people in the quantification domain has. The number mentioned is taken to be the lower limit among the maximal numbers of children that people in the domain of quantification have.

The same distinction applies to cases where numerals have an 'at most' interpretation: the number mentioned is taken to be the upper limit, and it is the one in a set of maximal numbers.

(27) John may eat three apples.
$\Diamond\exists x[\#(x) \leq 3 \wedge apples(x) \wedge eat(j,x)]$ ($\Diamond$: may)

(35) John may eat two apples.
$\Diamond\exists x[\#(x) \leq 2 \wedge apples(x) \wedge eat(j,x)]$

(35) may follow from (27) pragmatically. Here again we only consider the maximal numbers of apples John eats in the deontic alternatives. 3 is the upper limit among them. The upper limit among the non-maximal numbers of apples people eat makes no sense. Since a situation of John eating four apples includes a situation of John eating three apples, (27) could open up the possibility that John may eat four apples. We can say the same thing about (7) with the numeral 3 having the 'at most *n*' interpretation.

The discussion so far indicates that the scalarity of unlikelihood applies to alternative sentences with an alternative numeral, whereas the basic scalarity among numerals themselves applies to each case in the quantification domain.

5 'At Least/Most' Interpretations and Domains of Quantification

Since the scalarity of unlikelihood applies to a set of alternative sentences that arise from alternative numerals in the sentence, the numeral itself does not have the meaning of 'at least' or 'at most'. This claim can be supported by cases where the meaning of 'at least/most' cannot directly apply to numerals. In some cases, if a sentence with a numeral has the 'at least/most' interpretation, we get the same meaning we can get by putting the corresponding expression 'at least/most' before the numeral.

(36) a. AT LEAST[John must solve three problems]
b. John must solve at least three problems.

(37) a. AT MOST[John may eat three apples]
b. John may eat at most three apples.

Here (36a) and (37a) are considered to have the same meaning as (36a) and (37a), respectively. When the two meanings are the same, the scalar readings of the numerals are salient.

However, there are cases where this is not the case. Consider the following cases.

(38) a. AT MOST[John must eat *three* apples]
b. ?John must eat at most three apples.

(39) a. AT LEAST[John may solve *three* problems]
b. ?John may solve at least three problems.

In these two pairs, the second sentences do not seem appropriate. The semantic scope relationship like 'AT LEAST/MOST[. . . *n* . . .]' is always possible even when [. . . at least/most *n* …] is not natural. This shows that even if a sentence with a numeral is interpreted with the meaning of 'at least' or 'at most', it does not mean that the numeral itself has the meaning of 'at least' or 'at most'.

Now we have to explain why these differences are observed between (36 and 37) and (38 and 39). To do this, we need to explain first what it means that a sentence is interpreted with the meaning of 'at least' or 'at most'. When a sentence includes a numeral, the use of a numeral introduces a set of alternative numerals, and hence a set of alternative sentences. If the original sentence includes a numeral in the scope of a quantifier, each alternative numeral is interpreted with respect to the domain of the quantifier in each alternative sentence. More specifically, each alternative numeral is interpreted with respect to a different domain of the quantifier, or with respect to a different nuclear scope of the quantifier with the same quantification domain, depending on whether the numeral occurs in the restrictor or the nuclear scope.

The alternative sentences are ordered with respect to unlikelihood. If a numeral has the 'at least/most' interpretation in the restrictor or nuclear scope of a quantifier over the numeral, the restrictor or nuclear scopes of more likely alternative sentences can be added to that of the original sentence, with the numeral actually mentioned as a limit value. This idea allows us to explain the differences between (36 and 37) and (38 and 39). In (36a), *must* has narrower scope than AT LEAST. This means that other alternative sentences with a larger number are more likely to hold. Then the nuclear scope of the quantifier *must* for the original sentence could be extended to cover the nuclear scopes of the alternatives with a larger number. The resulting meaning is the same as the meaning with the sentence with *three* replaced with *at least three*. This is why the numeral *three* is interpreted as meaning 'at least three'.

In (38a), on the other hand, *must* has narrower scope than AT MOST. This means that other alternative sentences with a smaller numeral are likely to hold. This means that the nuclear scope of the sentence actually uttered can be extended to cover the nuclear scopes of the alternative sentences with a smaller number. The resulting situation is that John eats three apples in some deontic alternatives and less than three apples in others. This is a situation in which the original sentence is false. In the resulting situation we could say that *John may eat three apples*, not that *John must eat three apples*. (38b) is odd just because there is no context in which the statement is appropriately uttered with *three* meaning 'at most three'.

The intended meaning can be expressed with the following sentence.

(40) John must eat three apples at most.

Here the expression *at most* is taken to be the operator equivalent to the operator of AT MOST at the beginning of a sentence. So the sentence means that the upper limit of the numbers of apples John must eat is three.

A similar reasoning can apply to cases where a permission statement is combined with *at least*. In (37a), *may* has narrower scope than AT MOST, which means that three is the upper limit of the numbers of apples John may eat. The nuclear scope of the sentence uttered can be extended to the nuclear scopes of the alternatives with a smaller number. This is the situation in which John eats three apples in some deontic alternatives and he eats less than three apples in other deontic alternatives. This is why we can say (37b) appropriately.

In (39a), on the other hand, *may* has narrower scope than AT LEAST, which means that other alternative sentences with a larger number are more likely to hold. Thus the nuclear scope of the sentence uttered can be extended to cover the nuclear scopes of the alternative sentences with a larger number. Thus in some deontic alternatives John solves three problems and in some deontic alternatives John solves more than three problems. Still it is possible that in some deontic alternatives John solves less than three problems. This is problematic because *three* in this situation is not a limit value: the meaning of 'AT LEAST' is lost. This is why (39b) is not an appropriate meaning.

In (41), a numeral occurs in the restrictor:

(41) AT LEAST/MOST[No one who has three_F children is happy]
= No one who has at least/most three children is happy.

The restrictor can be extended to cases with a larger number or a smaller number. In this case the appropriateness of the resulting reading is not affected by the quantifier. It just has the effect of extending the domain of quantification. Thus AT LEAST or AT MOST at the beginning of the statement can be transferred to the interpretation of the numeral.

So far I have shown that in obligation statements numerals can have ‘at least’ interpretations, and that in permission statements, numerals can have ‘at most’ interpretations. If obligation statements have ‘at most’ meanings or permission statements have ‘at least’ meanings, we cannot put *at least/most* before numerals, because there is no appropriate situation in which such statements with *at least/most* before numerals can be uttered appropriately.

6 Statements with no Quantification Apparently Involved

So far I have shown how numerals can get the meaning of ‘at least’ or ‘at most’ in the scope of a quantifier. However, a sentence with no quantifier involved can have the ‘at least’ interpretation in general, with some exceptional cases where a numeral get the ‘at most’ interpretation, as in (9). This implies that even in cases where no overt quantifier is involved, we need to assume that there is some kind of quantification involved. One such candidate is the universal quantification over epistemic alternatives. The quantifier comes from the support conditions of a statement:

(42) φ is supported in an information state s iff $\forall w \in s\ [\![\varphi]\!]^{w} = 1$.

A statement is supported in an information state iff it is true in every possible world in the information state. Thus all statements can be assumed to involve quantification over epistemic alternatives. We can also assume that the meaning ‘at least/most’ is related to lack of knowledge in some sense. Under the two assumptions, a statement uttered in a context is taken to be what the speaker can assert *at least* in the current information state. Thus the default ‘at least’ interpretation arises from epistemic necessity, just as obligation statements require numerals to have ‘at least’ interpretations.

Now consider (9) again. The statement is uttered in relation to the following pairs of alternative numerals.

(43) In Guatemala, *n* % of the population owns *m* % of the land.

strongest		←				
	<1,100>	<2, 100>	<3, 100>	<4, 100>	...	<100, 100>
↑	<1, 99>	<2, 99>	<3, 99>	<4, 99>	...	<100, 99>
|	...	...	...	...	...	
|	<1, 71>	<2, 71>	<3, 71>	<4, 71>	...	
	<1, 70>	<2, 70>	<3, 70>	<4, 70>	...	
	<1, 69>	<2, 69>	<3, 69>	<4, 69>	...	
	...	...	...	...	...	
	<1, 1>	...	...	...	...	<100, 1>
						weakest

The actual statement includes the pair <3, 70>, where 3 is the upper limit and 70 is the lower limit, compared with other possible statements the speaker can assert. Then does the sentence mean that in Guatemala, at least *n* % of the population owns at most *m* % of the land? The answer is negative. This should be accounted for.

In my analysis, the statement has the following meaning:

(44) □ [In Guatemala, 3 percent of the population owns 70 percent of the land]

Here □ is the universal quantification over epistemic alternatives. With the universal quantifier, the statement must be taken to be what can be asserted minimally at the current information state.

(45) AT LEAST[□ [In Guatemala, 3 percent of the population owns 70 percent of the land]]

This opens up the possibility that the statement can be strengthened further if the speaker gets to know more. Since the statement focuses on the concentration of wealth to a small group of people. Thus in a stronger statement, *n* might be smaller and *m* might be larger. That is, there are some epistemic alternatives in the information state in which less than 3 percent of the population owns more than 70 percent of the land. So *n* has 'at most' interpretation, while *m* has 'at least' interpretation. The numeral *n* can have the 'at most' meaning because the two numbers are inversely related in the scale of alternatives.

We can apply the same reasoning to the following sentence, if it can be taken to be what can be asserted minimally at the current information state.

(46) John ate three apples.
$n > n-1 > \ldots > [\mathbf{3}] > 2 > 1$
3 is the lower limit.

Even if the speaker can assert a weaker statement, the sentence does not mean that John ate at most three apples. The basic scalarity applies and we only consider the maximal number of apples John ate in each epistemic alternative. Applying the epistemic necessity to the statement, we can get the following meaning.

(47) AT LEAST[□ [John ate three apples]]

With the universal quantifier over epistemic alternatives, *three* takes the 'at least' interpretation, unless the numeral has the 'exactly' meaning.

7 So-Called 'Exactly' Interpretations

So-called 'exactly' readings obtain when all the other alternative numbers are excluded. There are two types of such cases. One is a case where scalarity lies in the background but it is known that other alternatives are not appropriate to assert, and the other is a case where the context is structured in a way that no scalarity is involved. In (48) the numeral *only three* is understood as having two meanings.

(48) John ate only three apples.

(48) means that John ate not more than three apples, or that the number of apples John ate is only three, not two or four. The former is a scalar reading, which is more plausible, and the latter is, less likely, a non-scalar reading. Even in the former case, we do not say that the numeral has 'at least/most' interpretation, because the speaker knows that John did not eat two or four apples. In neither case can we say that the numeral has different interpretations. This shows that so-called 'exactly' interpretations are obtained when the speaker knows that the other alternatives are excluded, regardless of whether numerals constitute scalar terms or not.

8 Conclusions

In this paper I have shown that numerals do not have 'at least/most' interpretations themselves. Such interpretations arise pragmatically when contexts provide such interpretations. Behind these interpretations lies directional likelihood with respect to numerals: the larger the numeral, the more or the less likely the whole sentence is to hold. In some sense, the less likely the statement, the more informative it is.

When we say that numerals constitute a scalar set, we are more concerned with the semantic strengths of them: something like 'the event of eating three apples includes the event of eating two apples', which has been the basic scalarity the previous literature on scalar implicatures has been more concerned with. But this plays a limited role in the interpretation of a numeral. The reason is that when we use a numeral, it is generally understood as the maximal numeral the speaker can say, unless the context is structured so that the maximal numeral is not relevant. When every numeral is relevant in the context, the interpretation of a numeral is determined by the informativeness from likelihood, by considering alternative numerals and alternative quantification domains for them. In cases where no explicit quantification is involved, we can assume that implicit universal quantification is involved over epistemic alternatives. This also can lead to some limit interpretation of the numeral mentioned in a statement, the lower limit in general.

References

Atlas, Jay D. 1992. Why 'three' does not mean 3: Scalar implicatures, truth-conditions, and meaning. Manuscript, Pamona.

Breheny, Richard. 2008. A new look at the semantics and pragmatics of numerically quantified noun phrases. *Journal of Semantics* 25: 93–139.

Carston, R. 1998. Informativeness, relevance, and scalar implicature. In *Relevance theory: Applications and implications*, ed. R. Carston, and S. Uchida, 179–236. Amsterdam: John Benjamins Publishing Co.

Geurts, Bart. 2006. Take "five": The meaning and use of a number word. In *Non-definiteness and plurality*, ed. S. Vogeleer, and L. Tasmowski, 311–329. Amsterdam/Philadelphia: Benjamins.

Grice, Paul. 1975. Logic and conversation. In *Syntax and semantics 3: speech acts*, ed. P. Cole, and J. Morgan, 41–58. New York: Academic Press.

Horn, Larry R. 1984. Toward a new taxonomy for pragmatic inference: Q-based and r-based implicature. In *Meaning, form, and use in context: Linguistic applications*, ed. D. Schiffrin, 11–42. Washington, DC: Georgetown University Press.

Horn, Larry R. 1992. Pragmatics, implicature, and presupposition. In *International encyclopedia of linguistics*, ed. W. Bright, 260–266. Oxford: Oxford University Press.

Horn, Larry R. 1996. Presupposition and implicature. In *The handbook of contemporary semantic theory*, ed. S. Lappin, 299–319. Oxford: Blackwell Publishers.

Koenig, Jean-Pierre. 1991. Scalar predicates and negation: punctual semantics and interval interpretations. In *Chicago linguistic society 27, part 2: Parasession on negation*, pp 140–155.

Krifka, Manfred. 1999. At least some determiners aren't determiners. In *The semantics/pragmatics interface from different points of view*, ed. K. Turner, 257–291. Oxford: Elsevier.

Levinson, Stephen C. 1987. Minimization and conversational inference. In *The pragmatic perspective*, ed. J. Verschueren, and M. Bertuccelli-Papi, 61–127. Amsterdam: Benjamins.

Partee, Barbara. 1986. Noun-phrase interpretation and type-shifting principles. In *Studies in discourse representation theory and the theory of generalized quantifiers*, eds. *Studies in Discourse Representation Theory and the Theory of Generalized Quantifiers.* Dordrecht: Reidel, pp 115–144.

Recanati, François. 1989. The pragmatics of what is said. *Mind and Language* 4: 295–329.

Sadock, Jerrold. 1984. Whither radical pragmatics? In *Meaning, form and use in context: Linguistic applications*, ed. D. Schiffrin. Washington: Georgetown University Roundtable, Georgetown University Press.

van Kuppevelt, Jan. 1996a. In defense of semantics: Scalar inferences as topic-dependent entailments. In *AAAI spring symposium on computational implicature: Computational approaches to interpreting and generating conversational implicature*, ed. et al BDE, Stanford University Press.

van Kuppevelt, Jan. 1996b. Inferring from topics: Scalar implicatures as topic-dependent inferences. *Linguistics and Philosophy* 19(4): 393–443.

Focus Particle *Mo* and *Many/Few* Implicatures on Numerals in Japanese

Chidori Nakamura

Abstract Japanese focus particle *mo* expresses scalar implicatures similar to English *even*. In the literature, these implicatures have been related to 'likelihood/expectation' of event occurrence. This paper investigates the 'numeral-CL-*mo*' construction where *mo* follows a numeral and means either *many* or *few*, and clarifies the nature of 'unlikeliness' given by *mo* in terms of the probability (Fernando and Kamp 1996) and the set of alternatives (Rooth 1985) of quantities. It is shown that (i) syntactic categories and the scope of *mo* determine possible interpretations, and (ii) the conventional implicature of *mo*, together with the order of probabilities, provides *many/few* interpretations.

Keywords Scalar implicature • Quantity • Many • Focus • Particle • Monotonicity • Probability

1 Introduction

Japanese postpositions *mo*, *sura*, *sae*, *demo*, called focus particles, express scalar implicatures similar to *even* in English, and their implicatures have been analyzed in the literature with regard to 'likelihood' or 'expectation' for the occurrences of events/propositions (Numata 1986, etc.). Among these focus particles, *mo* productively makes various 'conventional implicatures' (Grice 1975; Karttunen and Peters 1979), when following or preceding a case marker. While the sentence without *mo* in (1) simply means 'ten students came,' the first *mo* in (2) expresses either *also* or *even* and the second *many*, so as to implicate 'others than students came' and 'ten is many' respectively.[1]

[1]The NP-focus *mo* such as in (2) is generally known as the focus particle of 'addition' similar to *also*, but it occasionally means *even* within a certain environment created by a context, lexical item, strong stressed intonation, etc. For the descriptive classification of the meanings/usages of *mo*, which is beyond the scope of this paper, refer to e.g. Numata (1986), Sadanobu (1995). Numata (1995) gives a summary of the various classifications of *mo* in the literature.

C. Nakamura (✉)
Ritsumeikan University, Kyoto, Japan
e-mail: chidori@fc.ritsumei.ac.jp

C. Lee et al. (eds.), *Contrastiveness in Information Structure, Alternatives and Scalar Implicatures*, Studies in Natural Language and Linguistic Theory 91, DOI 10.1007/978-3-319-10106-4_16

(1) *Gakusei-ga juu-nin ki-ta.*
student-NOM ten-CL come-PST
'Ten students came.'

(2) *Gakusei-mo juu-nin-mo ki-ta.*
student-NOM.*mo*.also/even ten-CL-*mo*.many come-PST
'Ten students also came. / Even ten students came.' (Ten is many.)

This paper deals with the 'numeral-classifier-*mo*' constructions ('*n*-CL-*mo*,' henceforth), where *mo* follows quantities and means either *many* or *few* depending on its environment; and clarifies how the *many/few* interpretations and the scale of likelihood/expectation are determined.

It is known that the interpretations of focused numbers are affected by the polarity of sentences, for they are interpreted as *many* in affirmatives such as in (3), but *few* in quantifier negations as in (4).

(3) *Gakusei*-ga *juu-nin-mo ki-ta.*
student-NOM ten-CL-*mo*.many come-PST
'Ten students came.' (Ten is many.)

(4) *Gakusei-ga juu-nin-mo ko-nakat-ta.*
student-NOM ten-CL-*mo*.few come-NEG-PST
'Less than ten students came.' (Ten is few.)

Polarity, however, does not explain sentences such as (5), where *mo* inside the conditional indicates *few* without negation.

(5) *Gakusei-ga futari-mo kure-ba juubunda.*
student-NOM two_person-*mo*.few come-COND enough
'If only about two students come, it's enough.' (Two is moderate.)

For the unified account of these, Sect. 2 considers syntactic categories and the scope (Karttunen and Peters 1979) of *mo*, together with the monotonicity (Barwise and Cooper 1981 etc.) of quantities.

As for the meaning or implicature of the '*n*-CL-*mo*,' the *many* and *few* interpretations, as well as *even*,[2] have been explained in the literature in connection with 'likelihood' (Nakanishi 2006; Yamamori 2006 etc.) or 'expectation' (Numata 1986; Yamanaka 1991; Sadanobu 1995 etc.): so to say, they are either 'unlikely many' or 'unlikely few' different from expectations. This unlikeliness, which has been considered to be the reason behind the *many/few* interpretations and can also be seen in the examples above, seems to be crucial if we want to give *mo* a single meaning rather than the distinct meanings of *many* and *few*.

[2]Regarding the meaning of *even*, Rooth (1985) employed a unary predicate unlikely'(*p*) on propositions *p*, while Krifka (1991) adopted a probability relation $<_p$, whose left proposition is less/least probable. But the semantic contents of these notions are not clearly given.

However, it is not clear in the literature how unlikeliness determines the likely quantities, since any quantity can be 'likely' depending on the situation. If one says *Only ten came*, 'more than ten' is likely; but in *As many as ten came*, it is 'less than ten.' That is, the unidirectionality of expected quantities is not given by unlikeliness alone, and there seems to be no explanation as to why, for instance, *n*-CL-*mo* in the affirmative sentence (3) indicates only smaller quantities as likely ones. The notion of likelihood should be elaborated to the extent the unidirectionality of likely numbers is uniquely determined. And if the likelihood scale is the cause of some co-occurrence restrictions of *mo* such as in '*Gakusei-ga *hitori-mo kita* (As many as one student came)' (Yamanaka 1991; Nakanishi 2006; Yamamori 2006 etc.), the semantics of *mo* must explicitly show how *mo* blocks *hitori* (one person), as *one* can be the unlikely number if the speaker's estimation is *zero*. Also, it is not clear why *n*-CL-*mo* can co-occur with phrases such as *yosoodoori* (as expected) and *itsumodoori* (as usual), for they seem to be contrary to the lexical meaning of 'unlikeliness/unexpectedness.'

As a solution to these problems, a single conventional implicature to various quantifier-focus *mo*-phrases is presented in Sect. 3, making use of the probability function (Fernando and Kamp 1996) and the set of alternatives (Rooth 1985) of quantities, where the controversial 'unlikeliness' is determined as the probabilities among the possible worlds.

Additionally, the correlation between the three meanings of *mo*, addition, scale, and *many/few*, such as seen in (2), is briefly considered in Sect. 3.4. There seems to be no necessity that the same morpheme, *mo*, is used for them, since in other languages they are expressed by elements different from each other; but it is still possible to see the common parts of their interpretations, for explaining the cognation of the three meanings of *mo*.

2 Scope and Monotonicity

In the '*n*-CL-*mo*' construction, *mo* gives an interpretation of either *many* or *few* to the focused number as in the following examples. In each case, the number of people coming or not coming is the same, *ten*, i.e., $|A \cap B| \geq 10$, or $|A \cap B| < 10$, where *A* stands for an NP (set of students), *B* a VP (set of coming individuals), and *n*-CL-*mo*, which is a determiner in Generalized Quantifier Theory, specifies the relation between *A* and *B* (Barwise and Cooper 1981; Zwarts 1983). The interpretations of *n*-CL and *n*-CL-*mo* in affirmatives are regarded as ambiguous between '*n or more*' and '*exactly n*,' if not specified.

When the focus particle *mo* precedes a case or other postposition,[3] this pre-case *mo* is invariably interpreted as *many* in both affirmative and negative sentences as

---

[3]The pre-case *mo* here, which appears always within an NP, is called a 'fuku joshi' or 'juntai joshi' in Japanese.

shown in (6) and (7). The difference between affirmation in (6) and VP negation in (7) does not affect the interpretation of *mo*.

(6) *Gakusei* *juu-nin-mo-ga* *ki-ta*.
student ten-CL-*mo*.many-NOM come-PST
'Ten students came.' (Ten is many.)

(7) *Gakusei* *juu-nin-mo-ga* *ko-nakat-ta.*
student ten-CL-*mo*.many-NOM come-NEG-PST
'Ten students were absent.' (Ten is many.)

By contrast, *mo* of post-case,[4] which follows a case postposition or adverbial, expresses *many* in affirmations but *few* in quantifier negations as seen in (3) and (4), repeated here.

(3) *Gakusei*-ga *juu-nin-mo* *ki-ta.*
student-NOM ten-CL-*mo*.many come-PST
'Ten students came.' (Ten is many.)

(4) *Gakusei-ga* *juu-nin-mo* *ko-nakat-ta.*
student-NOM ten-CL-*mo*.few come-NEG-PST
'Less than ten students came.' (Ten is few.)

This correspondence of syntactic categories and *many/few* interpretations can be stated as (8) below.

(8) Syntactic categories and interpretations of *mo*.
(i) pre-case *mo* in affirmation/negation: *many*
(ii) post-case *mo* in affirmation: *many*
(iii) post-case *mo* in negation: *few*

Since the *many* interpretation of pre-case *mo* is fixed irrespective of environment, this *mo* may be regarded as a kind of postfix in NPs and its meaning, *many*, can be stated in the lexicon. On the other hand, the different interpretations of post-case *mo* seem to be explained in terms of polarity, for negation provides the *few* interpretation; but the polarity does not explain the conditional sentences such as (5) seen earlier. Here the notion of monotonicity (Barwise and Cooper 1981 etc.), either increasing or decreasing, deserves consideration, as both negation and conditionals affect monotonicity.

In the light of the monotonicity in the scalar entailments, or logical material implications, of focused numbers, the rules of (9) can be seen: if *n* is increasing in an environment, *mo* gives it a *many* reading, but *few* if decreasing. Negation and conditionals are operators which reverse monotonic directions, thus providing environments for *few* interpretations.

---

[4]This post-case *mo* is regarded as a 'kakari joshi,' a kind of genuine focus postposition in Japanese.

(9) Monotonicity and interpretation of *n*-CL-*mo*.
(i) increasing *n*-CL: *n* is *many*
(ii) decreasing *n*-CL: *n* is *few*

Accordingly, *mo* indicates *many* in (3) *Gakusei-ga juu-nin kita* (Ten students came), for it logically implies 'gakusei-ga kyuu-nin kita (nine students came)'; but *few* with quantifier negation in (4) *Gakusei-ga juu-nin ko-na-kat-ta* (Less than ten students came) which implies 'gakusei-ga juuichi-nin ko-nakat-ta (less than eleven students came).' The same applies for pre-case *mo*, which provides *many* interpretations for both affirmation in (6) and VP negation in (7); since the negation in VP does not affect the monotonicity outside VP, and *Ten students were absent* implies 'nine students were absent.' Thus, (9) explains both pre-case and post-case *mo*.

Considering here the scope of the focus particle *mo*, various interpretations are explained in terms of scope ambiguity: focus particles should have the scope for a proposition in which the alternatives of a focused element are embedded (Karttunen and Peters 1979; Rooth 1985), and this scope determines the monotonicity.

In the examples below, following Karttunen and Peters (1979), the focus is indicated by capital letters and the scope of focus by [ ]. In (10) and (11), the different scopes assigned by each context produce different interpretations.[5] If the scope excludes conditional subordinator *ba* as in (10), the numeral has increasing monotonicity and means *many*; whereas with inclusion of the conditional, the numeral is decreasing and means *few* as in (11).

(10) [*Gakusei-ga JUU-NIN-mo kure*]*-ba totemo ureshii.*
student-NOM ten-CL-*mo*.many come-COND very happy
'If as many as ten students come, I'm very happy.' (Ten is many.)

(11) [*Gakusei-ga JUU-NIN-mo kure-ba juubunda*].
student-NOM ten-CL-*mo*.few come-COND enough
'If only about ten students come, it's enough.' (Ten is few.)

The scope ambiguity also explains different interpretations in quantifier negations below. The bigger scope which includes negation in (12a) creates the decreasing monotonicity, thus a *few* interpretation, while the smaller scope without negation in (12b) does not change the increasing monotonicity and provides a *many* interpretation.[6,7]

---

[5]It is known that the scope of a focus particles is affected by the lexical meanings of words, contexts, phonological intonation, etc. For a description of the various scopes taken by *mo* in written texts, see Numata and Jo (1995).

[6]The same scope assignment as in (12b) applies if *mo* is followed by the focus particle *wa* of contrast, as in [*Gakusei-wa JUU-NIN-mo-wa atsumara*]*-nakat-ta.* (Ten students did not gather. ten: many).

[7]This paper does not deal with the negation of assertion, such as [*Gakusei-ga JUU-NIN-mo kita*]*-n-ja-nai. Juu-nin-shika konakatta-nda.* (It is not that as many as ten students came. Only ten came); since regardless of the construction/scope, any element in a sentence can be negated by *n-ja-nai* (it is not that), including conventional implicatures such as the *many mo* here.

(12) a. [*Gakusei-wa JUU-NIN-mo atsumara-nakat-ta*].
student-TOP ten-CL-*mo*.few gather-NEG-PST
'Less than ten students gathered.' (Ten is few.)

b. [*Gakusei-wa JUU-NIN-mo atsumara*]*-nakat-ta.*
student-TOP ten-CL-*mo*.many gather-NEG-PST
'Less than ten students gathered.' (Ten is many.)

Likewise, when both reversing operators, i.e., negation and conditional, appear in a single sentence, either one of *many* and *few* is chosen according to the scope, as seen in (13) below.

(13) a. [*Gakusei-ga JUU-NIN-mo atsumara-nakere*]*-ba kono-kurasu-wa*
student-NOM ten-CL-*mo*.few gather-NEG-COND this-class-TOP
hirake-nai.
open-NEG
'If as few as ten students don't gather, we can't offer the class.' (Ten is few.)

b. [*Gakusei-ga JUU-NIN-mo atsumara*]*-nakere-ba kono-kurasu-wa*
student-NOM ten-CL-*mo*.many gather-NEG-COND this-class-TOP
hirake-nai.
open-NEG
'If as many as ten students don't gather, we can't offer the class.' (Ten is many.)

c. [*Gakusei-ga JUU-NIN-mo atsumara-nakere-ba kono-kurasu-wa*
student-NOM ten-CL-*mo*.many gather-NEG-COND this-class-TOP
hirake-nai].
open-NEG
'If as many as ten students don't gather, we can't offer the class.' (Ten is many.)

In (13b) and (13c), two different scope assignments are possible for a single *many* interpretation, the smaller affirmative one and the bigger conditional one, since the conditional which follows negation reverses the decreasing monotonicity to increasing.[8]

Thus, it can be concluded here that it is the scope of *mo* that determines the choice of *many* or *few* interpretations. The interpretations in sentences can be summed up as follows: Negation and conditional, which are reversing operators, change monotonicity within the scope of *mo*, so that among the sentences seen earlier, only negative or conditional sentences can be ambiguous between *many* and

[8]Subordinate clauses other than conditionals do not reverse monotonicity, so that the biggest scope does not affect the interpretation. To take a simple example, in *Juu-nin-mo kita koto-wa/node yokatta* (It was good that/because as many as ten people came), *mo* expresses invariably *many* irrespective of the scope, as opposed to the conditional *kure-ba* (if come).

few according to the scope of *mo*. Affirmative sentences and VP negations should have only *many* interpretations, for they have no reversing operators affecting monotonicity of quantity. As well, the pre-case *mo*, which cannot scope over quantifier negation, indicates invariably the *many* interpretation.

Next, in the following section, the semantic content of both *many* and *few* readings is examined.

3 The Semantic Content of *n*-CL-*mo*

3.1 Unexpectedness, Moderation, and the Co-occurrence Restriction

As seen earlier in the introduction, the *many/few* interpretations are considered to be related to 'unlikeliness' or 'unexpectedness' in the literature. In addition to this, Numata (1986), Sadanobu (1995) point out that *mo* in conditionals as in (5) is used for 'softening' or 'moderating' quantities.

(5) *Gakusei-ga futari-mo kure-ba juubunda.*
student-NOM two_person-*mo*.few come-COND enough
'If only about two students come, it's enough.' (Two is moderate.)

The number *two* above is 'few,' for it can co-occur with *seizei* (few); and if modified by, e.g., *itsumodoori* (as usual) or *yosoodoori* (as expected), it is regarded as an 'expected' number within the speaker's estimation. Thus the notion of 'unlikeliness' or 'expectation' without clear definition does not seem to explain these sentences.

Moreover, *n*-CL-*mo*, different from the quantifier *takusan* (many), very often focuses on the number *two* if the speaker has expected numbers fewer than *two*, i.e., *one* or *zero*, as in (14); but it never co-occurs with the number *one* or an 'additive determiner' (Zwarts 1996),[9] which designates the least quantities, even if the speaker has expected *zero* as in (15).

(14) *Gakusei-ga futari-mo ki-ta.*
student-NOM two_person-*mo*.many come-PST
'Two students came.' (Two is many.)

(15) *Gakusei-ga *hitori-mo ki-ta.*
student-NOM one_person-*mo* come-PST
'One student came.' (One is many/few.)

[9]A function f from Boolean algebra B to B^* is said to be additive iff for each two elements X and Y of the algebra $B{:}f(X \cup Y) = f(X) \cup f(Y)$. A determiner such as *one* in '*One student came*,' which is a function on NPs, is called an additive determiner.

By contrast, with both a quantifier and negation as in (16), *mo* occurs with the smallest number to compose a negative polarity item (NPI), so that 'anti-additivity' (Zwarts 1996)[10] in the least quantity in negative environments does not obstruct *mo*.

(16) *Gakusei-ga* *hitori-mo* *ko-nakat-ta.*
student-NOM one_person-*mo*.few come-NEG-PST
'Not a single student came.' (One is few.)

These co-occurrence restrictions on determiners should also be explained by the semantic content of *n*-CL-*mo*. In the following Sect. 3.2, the notion of probability, *many*, and *few* are defined, and in Sect. 3.3 the unified interpretation of 'quantifier-*mo*' is shown.

3.2 'Many' and Probability

The correlation of the notions of *many* and 'expectation' has been studied in the literature (Barwise and Cooper 1981; Keenan and Stavi 1986; Partee 1988 etc.) for clarifying the meaning of quantifier/determiner *many* in English as in *Many students came*, since unstated quantities which satisfy *many* are determined according to expectations within contexts. Regarding the two different readings/reasons of *many*, a cardinal one and a proportional one, Partee (1988) claims (17), where some number *n* in a weak cardinal reading and some fraction *k* (between 0 and 1) in a strong proportional reading are determined by a fixed context, thus extensionally.

(17) (i) cardinal reading: $many(A,B)$ iff $|A \cap B| > n$
(ii) proportional reading: $many(A,B)$ iff $|A \cap B| > k \cdot |A|$

As opposed to this simple extensionality, Fernando and Kamp (1996) present intensionalized interpretations of *many*, considering how different expectations determine the values of *n* and *k* in a given context. They claim that '*n C*'s are many when $|C|$ could well have been $< n$,' and define the interpretations of the determiner *many* as follows:

(18) $\text{Many}\, x(\varphi,\psi)$ iff $\bigvee_{n\geq 1}((\exists_{\geq n}x)(\varphi \wedge \psi) \wedge n\text{-is-many}_x(\varphi,\psi))$

where φ and ψ represent the set *A* and *B* above respectively. $(\exists_{\geq n}x)(\varphi \wedge \psi)$ gives an existential claim 'there are at least *n x*'s which are φ and ψ in the actual world,' and $n\text{-is-many}_x(\varphi,\psi)$ concerns expectation or probability of *n*.

[10]A function *f* from Boolean algebra *B* to *B** is said to be anti-additive iff for each two elements *X* and *Y* of the algebra $B{:}f(X \cup Y) = f(X) \cap f(Y)$. A determiner such as *no* in '*No student came*,' which is a function on NPs, is called an anti-additive determiner.

The cardinal reading of *many* is given by substituting n-IS-MANY$_x$ in (19) below for n-is-many$_x$ above.

(19) n-IS-MANY$_x(\chi)$ iff "it is probable that $(\exists_{<n}x)\chi$"
iff $p(\{w:|\chi|_{x,w} < n\}) > c$.

$|\chi|_{x,w}$ is defined as $|x{:}\chi$ in $w|$ and the probability function p on sets of worlds counts the number of possible worlds accessible in the model where the number of χ-x's is less than n. The values of p and c are fixed in the model independently of χ, and if a value of the probability function is greater than c, it is probable; thus the notion of 'probable' is defined here within the possibility throughout accessible worlds.

The proportional reading on the other hand, is defined as

(20) n-is-many$_x(\varphi,\psi)$
iff "it is probable, given there are $|\varphi|_x$ φ-x's, that $(\exists_{<n}x)(\varphi\wedge\psi)$"
iff $p(\{w:|\varphi\wedge\psi|_{x,w} < n\} \mid \{w:|\varphi|_{x,w} = |\varphi|_x\}) > c$,

where the conditional probability $p(X|Y)$ of X given Y, and c determine a probable number, which can be different from the probable number in the cardinal reading, according to the number of φ-x's.

These notions of probabilities can be used for the n-CL-*mo* constructions as the resolution of the controversial 'unlikeliness' seen earlier. First of all, the determiners n-CL and $\neg n$-CL in verbal/adjectival/nominal predicate sentences are defined to fix the existential readings of n, as below.

(21) n-CL$_x(\varphi,\psi)$ iff $(\exists_{\geq n}x)(\varphi\wedge\psi)$
iff $|\varphi\wedge\psi|_x \geq n$.

Since n-CL is a weak intersectional determiner, it can be regarded as a unary predicate applied to $\varphi\wedge\psi$. And $|\varphi\wedge\psi|_x$, where no world is specified, represents the cardinality of x's which are $\varphi\wedge\psi$ in the actual world. If n is *five*, it means 'there are at least five x's which are φ and ψ.' The interpretation of n-CL is ambiguous between 'exactly n' and 'at least n' if not stated explicitly: the 'exactly n' readings in those predicate sentences which are given by conversational implicatures are cancelable (Grice 1975; Gazdar 1979), so that the literal meaning of n-CL ought to be 'n or more.' Accordingly, the default interpretation of cardinal determiners in verbal/adjectival/nominal predicate sentences such as *Gakusei-ga go-nin ki-ta* (Five students came) assures us of monotonic reasoning, as contrasted to cleft-like sentences such as *Kita gakusei-wa go-nin-dat-ta* (It was five students who came), which force 'exactly n' readings. (21) does not represent interpretations in cleft sentences, where *mo* rarely appears.

The negation within the negative determiner $\neg n$-CL ranges over only the determiner, so that $(\neg(\exists_{\geq n}x))(\varphi\wedge\varphi)$, and this negative determiner is defined as a complementary determiner of n-CL as below.

(22) $\neg n\text{-CL}_x(\varphi,\psi)$ iff $(\exists_{<n}x)(\varphi \wedge \psi)$
iff $(|\varphi \wedge \psi|_x < n)$.

If n is *five*, (22) says 'there are less than five x's which are φ and ψ.'

The interpretations of n-CL-*mo* and $\neg n$-CL-*mo* with the cardinal interpretation of *many* can now be defined as follows:

(23) $n\text{-CL-mo-MANY}_x(\varphi,\psi)$ iff $n\text{-CL}_x(\varphi,\psi) \wedge n\text{-IS-MANY}_x(\varphi \wedge \psi)$
iff $(\exists_{\geq n}x)(\varphi \wedge \psi) \wedge$ "it is probable that $(\exists_{<n}x)(\varphi \wedge \psi)$"
iff $|\varphi \wedge \psi|_x \geq n \wedge p(\{w : |\varphi \wedge \psi|_{x,w} < n\}) > c$.

n-CL-*mo*, which has a *many* interpretation, is regarded here as a new predicate n-CL-mo-MANY, and its interpretation is given as a conjunction of n-CL and Fernando and Kamp's n-IS-MANY. If n is *five*, (23) says 'there are at least five x's which are φ and ψ, and it is probable that less than five x's are φ and ψ.' In the same manner, negative determiner $\neg n$-CL-*mo*, which has a *few* interpretation, is defined as $\neg n$-CL-mo-FEW, a conjunction of $\neg n$-CL and a new predicate n-IS-FEW as below.

(24) $\neg n\text{-CL-mo-FEW}_x(\varphi,\psi)$ iff $\neg n\text{-CL}_x(\varphi,\psi) \wedge n\text{-IS-FEW}_x(\varphi \wedge \psi)$
iff $(\exists_{<n}x)(\varphi \wedge \psi) \wedge$ "it is probable that $(\exists_{\geq n}x)(\varphi \wedge \psi)$"
iff $|\varphi \wedge \psi|_x < n \wedge p(\{w : |\varphi \wedge \psi|_{x,w} \geq n\}) > c$.

If n is *five*, (24) says 'there are less than five x's which are φ and ψ, and it is probable that five or more x's are φ and ψ.'

The proportional *many*/*few* readings are also gained if the predicates n-IS-MANY and n-IS-FEW above are replaced by proportional ones as follows:

(25) $n\text{-CL-mo-many}_x(\varphi,\psi)$
iff $n\text{-CL}_x(\varphi,\psi) \wedge n\text{-is-many}_x(\varphi \wedge \psi)$
iff $(\exists_{\geq n}x)(\varphi \wedge \psi) \wedge$"it is probable, given there are $|\varphi|_x$ φ-x's, that $(\exists_{<n}x)(\varphi \wedge \psi)$"
iff $|\varphi \wedge \psi|_x \geq n \wedge p(\{w : |\varphi \wedge \psi|_{x,w} < n\} \mid \{w : |\varphi|_{x,w} = |\varphi|_x\}) > c$.

If n is *five*, (25) means 'there are at least five x's which are φ and ψ, and it is probable that less than five x's are φ and ψ, provided the number of φ-x's is the same as that in the actual world.' The negative counterpart is given in the same manner as below.

(26) $\neg n\text{-CL-mo-few}_x(\varphi,\psi)$
iff $\neg n\text{-CL}_x(\varphi,\psi) \wedge n\text{-is-few}_x(\varphi \wedge \psi)$
iff $(\exists_{<n}x)(\varphi \wedge \psi) \wedge$"it is probable, given there are $|\varphi|_x$ φ-x's, that $(\exists_{\geq n}x)(\varphi \wedge \psi)$"
$|\varphi \wedge \psi|_x < n \wedge p(\{w : |\varphi \wedge \psi|_{x,w} \geq n\} \mid \{w : |\varphi|_{x,w} = |\varphi|_x\}) > c$.

Thus far the appropriate interpretations for each *n*-CL-*mo* and ¬*n*-CL-*mo* are presented. However, the above definitions do not give the fundamental reason why *mo* expresses *many* in a positive determiner, but *few* in a negative determiner, since it is not explained how the direction of probable elements, i.e., $(\exists_{<n}x)(\varphi \wedge \psi)$ in (23) and (25), or $(\exists_{\geq n}x)(\varphi \wedge \psi)$ in (24) and (26), is determined. This problem is considered next.

3.3 Alternatives in Quantity

Focus particles indicate the existence or nonexistence of other elements than focused elements through 'conventional implicatures' (Grice1975; Karttunen and Peters 1979). In order to capture this function of *mo*-phrases, the set of alternatives (Rooth 1985) and the focused subexpression (Fernando and Kamp 1996) and replacement of alternatives are defined as follows.

A determiner Q in $Qx(\varphi, \psi)$ is a relation between x-extensions $\{x: \varphi\}$ and $\{x: \psi\}$ of φ and ψ. Q^a_e is a determiner obtained by replacing e in Q by a, where e is a focused subexpression in Q, $\mathcal{A}$ is a set of alternative quantities, a is an alternative in $\mathcal{A}$, and $a, e \in \mathcal{A}$. Q is made up of a quantity, weak cardinal or strong proportional, which co-occurs with *mo*; e is either a part or the whole of the Q; and $\mathcal{A}$ consists of only quantities resembling e in 'the most similar worlds modulo *a/e* (Fernando and Kamp 1996).'[11]

Then, *mo*-phrases of quantity, which express probability and *many/few*, are interpreted as in (27).[12]

(27) $Q\text{-mo}_x(\varphi, \psi)$

iff "$Qx(\varphi, \psi)$, and for some a other than e in Q, it is probable $Q^a_e x(\varphi, \psi)$ but not $Qx(\varphi, \psi)$"

iff $Qx(\varphi, \psi) \wedge \exists a((a \neq e) \wedge p(\{w: Q^a_e x(\varphi, \psi)\}) > c > p(\{w: Qx(\varphi, \psi)\}))$.

In the second conjunct, $\exists a((a \neq e)$ assures the existence of an alternative, i.e., some other quantity than the focused one, and the following

$$p(\{w: Q^a_e x(\varphi, \psi)\}) > c > p(\{w: Qx(\varphi, \psi)\})$$

---

[11]The clarification of the notions of 'resemble' and 'similar world' is beyond the scope of this study; and it is simply assumed here 'if *Q-mo* is made up of a number, $\mathcal{A}$ also consists of numbers or proportions whose cardinality is calculable within the same cardinality of φ,' adopting the postulation in Fernando and Kamp (1996) 'the switch *a/e* (regarding the alternation χ^a_e) could be viewed intensionally as moving to a most similar world modulo *a/e*.'

[12]For displaying the scope and focus of *mo* seen in Sect. 2, $Q\text{-mo}_x(\varphi, \psi)$ in (27) can be replaced by $\text{mo}(Q_F x(\varphi, \psi))$, where *mo*'s scope is shown by ( ), the focus by F. Thus, $Q\text{-mo}_x(\varphi, \psi)$ iff $\text{mo}(Q_F x(\varphi, \psi))$. But the former concise one is used here for simplicity.

determines unidirectionality of alternatives, employing the probability function and c and the relation '> (is greater than)' seen in Sect. 3.2. Here, 'it is probable' is defined as 'higher probability than c' as in Fernando and Kamp (1996), and another definition 'it is not probable' as 'lower probability than c' is added.

Probabilities of propositions with quantities in $\mathcal{A}$ themselves constitute a weak partial order (transitive, reflexive, antisymmetric), together with a relation '$\geq$ (is greater than or equal to).' For instance, probability of 'four or more students come' should be the same or higher than that of 'five or more students come' in every model/context, as the latter materially implies the former in each world; their probabilities are the same if there is no possible world in which 'exactly four students come' is satisfied. The actual interpretation of *Q-mo* is always obtained in accordance with this probability order of quantities, as *Q-mo*'s conventional implicature cannot change the logical entailments.

To put it differently, the strong partial order with > in (27) is identical to the conjunction of a weak partial order with $\geq$ and an unequal relation $\neq$:

$$\begin{aligned} & p(\{w: Q_e^a x(\varphi,\psi)\}) > c > p(\{w: Qx(\varphi,\psi)\}) \\ & \equiv (p(\{w: Q_e^a x(\varphi,\psi)\}) \geq c \geq p(\{w: Qx(\varphi,\psi)\})) \wedge \\ & \quad (p(\{w: Q_e^a x(\varphi,\psi)\}) \neq c \neq p(\{w: Qx(\varphi,\psi)\})). \end{aligned}$$

Thus, the interpretation of *Q-mo* contains the weak partial order which is identical to the probability order of quantities except c. This congruity explains why the monotonicity between logical implications of numerals is crucial for *many/few* interpretations as seen in Sect. 2.

In (27), $(a \neq e)$ is actually not needed: since their probabilities are different, they cannot be the same. Thus, (27) can be replaced by (27)' below, which is identical to (27) but the redundant $(a \neq e)$ is omitted.

(27)' $Q\text{-mo}_x(\varphi,\psi)$

iff "$Qx(\varphi,\psi)$, and for some a other than e in Q, it is probable $Q_e^a x(\varphi,\psi)$ but not $Qx(\varphi,\psi)$"

iff $Qx(\varphi,\psi) \wedge \exists a(p(\{w: Q_e^a x(\varphi,\psi)\}) > c > p(\{w: Qx(\varphi,\psi)\}))$.

To gain the interpretation that 'alternative numbers are likely but the focused number is unlikely,' which gives only probable alternatives, c is placed between probabilities of e and a. For if there is no c,

$$p(\{w: Q_e^a x(\varphi,\psi)\}) > p(\{w: Qx(\varphi,\psi)\}$$

simply indicates the existence of another possible quantity in either direction of the order without the 'probable' property. *Q-mo* without c can choose the appropriate direction by the given partial order between probabilities in quantities, e.g., probability of 'four or more φ-x's are ψ' is the same or higher than that of 'five or more

φ-x's are ψ'; but it cannot specify 'likely' or 'unlikely' quantities according to the speaker's estimation.

Likewise, if not the probability of the focused number e, then

$$p(\{w: Q_e^a x(\varphi, \psi)\}) > c$$

expresses only 'an alternative number is likely,' and does not have the information 'the focused number is unlikely.' It allows

$$p(\{w: Qx(\varphi, \psi)\}) > p(\{w: Q_e^a x(\varphi, \psi)\}) > c,$$

where e cannot be a maximal/minimal element in the order created by *mo*, thus 'unidirectional alternation from the focused number' is lost.

Here only the cardinal reading of *many* is employed, since it is enough for choosing appropriate alternatives. Though the quantity in Q can be proportional, such as *gojup-paasento* (50 %) or *sanbun-no-ichi* (one third), *Q-mo* can choose appropriate alternatives, since in any world the probability of, for instance, *yonjup-paasento* (40 %) is the same or higher than that of *gojup-paasento* (50 %). If c is taken as intentional, thus flexible in *Q-mo* according to subjective expectations of the speaker, the proportional reading, given the number of φ-x's, provides one of the reasons why the focused number is unlikely.

The interpretation of *Q-mo* above provides the unidirectionality for both positive and negative polarity, regarding both *n*-CL-*mo* and ¬*n*-CL-*mo* defined in (21) and (22) in Sect. 3.2 as Q's. If, for instance, e is *five* and $\mathcal{A}$ consists of numbers, the following interpretations in (28) and (29) are given to them respectively.

(28) $\text{5-CL-mo}_x(\varphi, \psi)$
$= (|\varphi \wedge \psi|_x \geq 5) \wedge \exists a(p(\{w: |\varphi \wedge \psi|_{x,w} \geq a\}) > c > p(\{w: |\varphi \wedge \psi|_{x,w} \geq 5\})).$

Provided e is *five*, a is chosen from numbers *one* to *four* as being probable in the possible worlds, making use of the transitive probability order in $\mathcal{A}$. If the sentence is *Gakusei-ga go-nin-mo kita* (As many as five students came), the interpretation amounts to 'it was probable that fewer than five students came, but in fact five students, which was not probable, came.' Thus, (28) has both the interpretations, *many* and unlikeliness. If *five* appears in the negative determiner ¬*n*-CL-*mo* as in

(29) $\text{5-CL-mo}_x(\varphi, \psi)$
$= (|\varphi \wedge \psi|_x < 5) \wedge \exists a(p(\{w: |\varphi \wedge \psi|_{x,w} < a\}) > c > p(\{w: |\varphi \wedge \psi|_{x,w} < 5\})),$

the numbers more than *five* are chosen as being probable. The sentence *Gakusei-wa go-nin-mo ko-nakat-ta* (Less than five students came) indicates 'it was probable more than five students came, but in fact, less than five, which was not probable, came.'

Considering here the co-occurrence restrictions seen earlier in (15) *Gakusei-ga *hitori-mo kita* (One student came), the reason behind the additive restriction on *n*-CL-*mo* is obvious: if e constructs an additive determiner in a context such as *one* *person,* no a's which satisfy *Q-mo* exist in $\mathcal{A}$. Due to the transitive probability order, no numerals can have higher probability than *one person*. And the least quantity *zero*, which is free from the transitive order and possibly the most probable number in the speaker's estimation, cannot create an adverbial quantifier such as **zero-nin* (zero person), thus the substitution mechanism blocks it. Accordingly, 1-CL-*mo* never appears in affirmative sentences such as **hitori-mo kita* (one person came), while 2-CL-*mo* in (14) and ¬1-CL-*mo* in (16) are possible if the probable numbers are *one* and *more than one* respectively. This is the reason why '*one*-CL-*mo*' only amounts to an NPI in Japanese.

The meaning of *mo* presented here seems to provide the same interpretation of *many* as Fernando and Kamp's *n*-is-many by way of a slightly different semantics. The difference is that the *many* interpretation in adverbial *many* is expressed by the likeliness of the complementary event, i.e., the proposition created by the negative determiner '$< n$,' which amounts to the negation of '$\geq n$.' As '$< n$' and '$\geq n$' make complementary events and c is assumed to be big enough, there is no need to express the unlikeliness of '$\geq n$.' On the other hand, *Q-mo* here provides the likeliness/unlikeliness only through the substitution of alternatives, thus '$\geq n$' does not evoke '$< n$,' but the transitive order of probabilities creates the same interpretation.

This substitution mechanism correctly specifies alternative quantities within other monotonic environments created by conditionals as in (30), where *mo* has the widest scope.[13]

(30) $\text{Q-mo}_x((\varphi,\psi) \to \omega)$
iff "$Q_x(\varphi,\psi) \to \omega$, and for some a other than e in Q, it is probable $Q^a_e x(\varphi,\psi) \to \omega$, but not $Q_x(\varphi,\psi) \to \omega$"
iff $(Q_x(\varphi,\psi) \to \omega) \wedge$
$\exists_a(p(\{w{:}Q^a_e x(\varphi,\psi) \to \omega\}) > c > p(\{w{:}Q_x(\varphi,\psi) \to \omega\}))$.

Since *mo* ranges over conditionals, the likely quantities are determined within the whole $(\varphi,\psi) \to \omega$. If e is *five* and $\mathcal{A}$ consists of numbers, it means

(31) $\text{5-CL-mo}_x((\varphi,\psi) \to \omega)$
$= (|\varphi \wedge \psi|_x \geq 5 \to \omega) \wedge$
$\exists_a(p(\{w{:}\ |\varphi\wedge\psi|_{x,w} \geq a \to \omega\}) > c > p(\{w{:}\ |\varphi\wedge\psi|_{x,w} \geq 5 \to \omega\}))$

where the likely numbers should be more than *five*. If the sentence is *Gakusei-ga go-nin-mo kure-ba juubunda* (If only about five students come, it is enough), with the widest scope of *mo*, (31) amounts to 'it is probable if more than five or six or seven… come, it's enough; but in fact, if five come it's enough, which is not probable in other situations.' It indicates *five* as moderation, and the *five,* which is 'not probable' here, can co-occur with the speaker's estimation 'five will come,'

[13]As well as (27), $\text{Q-mo}_x((\varphi,\psi) \to \omega)$ here means $\text{mo}(Q_F x(\varphi,\psi) \to \omega)$, where the scope and focus of *mo* are explicitly shown.

thus with *itsumodoori* (as usual) or *yosoodoori* (as expected), if one can imagine many other possible worlds which are different from the estimation. The 'probable' here is determined on the number of possible worlds.

Provided Q is 10-CL or ¬10-CL, the *many/few* interpretations in sentences seen in Sect. 2 are correctly given. Only the sentence (12b), where the scope of *mo* is smaller than the quantifier negation, is hard to explain with the definitions of the negative determiner and *Q-mo* above, since *mo* cannot be negated by the wider scope negation, and a single predicate such as *Q-mo* here can hardly demonstrate the interaction of scope. This is left for the future study.

3.4 'Many/Few,' 'Even,' and 'Also'

Lastly, the correlation of the three meanings of *mo* seen in the introduction, addition *also*, scalar *even*, and *many/few*, is briefly considered here.

If the literal meaning of determiner Q is eliminated from the interpretation of *Q-mo* in (27) to see the conventional implicature of *mo*, it is 'for some other a than e in Q, it is probable $Q_e^a x(\varphi, \psi)$, but not $Qx(\varphi, \psi)$,' thus,

$$\exists a((a \neq e) \wedge p(\{w: Q_e^a x(\varphi, \psi)\}) > c > p(\{w: Qx(\varphi, \psi)\})).$$

This indicates 'the existence of some other alternative that is more probable than the focused one,' and this interpretation is identifiable as the meaning of the NP-focus scalar *mo*, which means *even* following nouns/individuals, for it also designates some other alternatives as probable, as in *John-mo kita* (Even John came). It can be assumed that these *mo* have the same conventional implicature which employs the weak/strong partial order of probabilities, or the preorder of alternatives, but only the domains of focused elements or alternatives are different from each other: if the domain is a set of individuals, it means *even*, if a set of quantities *many* or *few*. The complementary distribution also suggests they can be the same.[14]

In addition, the interpretation above amounts to

$$\exists a((a \neq e) \wedge Q_e^a x(\varphi, \psi) \wedge p(\{w: Q_e^a x(\varphi, \psi)\}) > c > p(\{w: Qx(\varphi, \psi)\})),$$

where 'the existence of alternatives in the actual world' is expressed by $Q_e^a x(\varphi, \psi)$. The existence is brought by the logical implications of quantified sentences, e.g., 'four or more students come' has higher probability than 'five or more students come,' because the former is logically implied by the latter. Thus, the interpretation of *Q-mo* includes an existential claim of alternatives in the actual world, which is

[14]It is not claimed here that NP-focus *mo*'s behavior is explained only by this conventional implicature, since its occurrence with NPs is rather limited, and syntactic/semantic differences between the focus particles of NP-*even*, i.e., *mo, sura, sae, demo, made*, etc., require further elucidation.

the same as the existential interpretation of addition *mo*, i.e., *also*, as in *John-mo kita* (John also came). In the case of scalar NP-focus *mo*, however, the existence of probable alternatives is assured not in the actual world but in the possible worlds; since 'John came' does not logically imply 'others came,' and it is possible to say *John-mo kita-noni hokani daremo ko-nakat-ta* (Even John came, but no others came).

This common interpretation, i.e., the existence of alternatives in either the actual world or possible worlds, can be one of the reasons why the same *mo* is used for both the existential and scalar readings; since it is natural to assume that the similarities between interpretations support the cognation of different meanings of the same morpheme.

4 Conclusion

This paper, examining the *many* and *few* interpretations on numerals with the focus particle *mo*, showed how the two readings are reduced to a single conventional implicature of *mo*.

First, the numeral-classifier-*mo* was divided into two different syntactic categories: pre-case *mo* and post-case *mo*. In both cases, the scope of *mo*, which determines the increasing or decreasing monotonicity, gives an interpretation of either *many* or *few*.

Then, the semantic content of the *n*-CL-*mo* and ¬ *n*-CL-*mo*, i.e., the *Q-mo*, was presented making use of the probability function (Fernando and Kamp 1996), the set of alternatives (Rooth 1985), and the focused subexpression (Fernando and Kamp 1996). The 'unlikeliness' behind *many/few* interpretations is created by *mo*'s scalar implicature, which concerns the probabilities of event occurrences throughout the possible worlds, possibly aside from the speaker's estimation in the real world. Thus, the reason for the unidirectionality of likely/expected quantities is explained by the logical nature of this implicature, for it creates the same transitive order as the entailments between quantities. And the substitution mechanism in *Q-mo*, which assures the various *many/few* interpretations, including with negation and conditionals, gives also the semantic account for *mo*'s co-occurrence restrictions such as **hitori-mo kita* (one person came).

Finally, as for the correlation between the three meanings of *mo*, addition, scale, and *many/few*, the rough sketch showed that the common parts of the three interpretations seem to support the cognation of these *mo*'s.

Acknowledgments The author greatly thanks the reviewers and participants of the workshop 'Contrastiveness in Information Structure and/or Scalar Implicatures' in CIL 18, for the helpful comments and suggestions.

References

Barwise, Jon, and Robin Cooper. 1981. Generalized quantifiers and natural language. *Linguistics and Philosophy* 4: 159–219.

Fernando, Tim, and Hans Kamp. 1996. Expecting many. *Semantics and Linguistic Theory (SALT) VI*, 53–68.

Gazdar, Gerald. 1979. *Pragmatics*. New York: Academic Press.

Grice, H.Paul. 1975. Logic and conversation. In *The Logic of Grammar*, ed. D. Davidson, and G. Harman, 64–75. Encino: Dickenson.

Karttunen, Lauri, and Stanley Peters. 1979. Conventional implicature. In *Presupposition (Syntax and Semantics 11)* ed. C. Oh et al., 1–56. Academic Press.

Keenan, Edward L., and Jonathan Stavi. 1986. A semantic characterization of natural language determiners. *Linguistics and Philospophy* 9(3): 253–326.

Krifka, Manfred. 1991. A compositional semantics for multiple focus constructions. In *Informationsstruktur und Grammatik* ed.J. Jacobs (Linguistische Berichte, Sonderheft 4), 17–53.

Nakanishi, Kimiko. 2006. Even, only and negative Polarity in Japanese. *Semantics and Linguistic Theory (SALT) XVI*, 138–155.

Numata, Yoshiko. 1986. Toritateshi (Focus particles). In *Iwayuru Nihongo Joshi no Kenkyū (The study on the So-called Japanese Particles)*, ed. K. Okutsu, et al., 105–225. Tokyo: Bonjinsha.

Numata, Yoshiko. 1995. 'Mo' in modern Japanese (Gendai nihongo no 'mo'). In *'Mo' no Gengogaku (Linguistics of 'Mo')* eds. Tsukuba Nihongo Forum, 13–76. Tokyo: Hituzi Syobo.

Numata, Yoshiko, and Kenbin Jo. 1995. Toritateshi 'mo' no fookasu to sukoopu (Focus and scope of the focus particle 'mo'). In *Nihongo no Syudai to Toritate (Topic and Focus in Japanese)*, ed. T. Masuoka, et al., 175–207. Tokyo: Kurosio Publishers.

Partee, H.Barbara. 1988. Many quantifiers. In *Proceedings of the Fifth Eastern States Conference on Linguistics (ESCOL)*, ed. J. Powers, et al., 383–402. Columbus: Ohio State University.

Rooth, Mats. 1985. *Association with Focus*. Dissertation, Amherst: University of Massachusetts.

Sadanobu, Toshiyuki. 1995. Shinteki purosesu kara mita toritateshi 'mo' 'demo' (Focus particles 'mo' and 'demo' viewed from the cognitive process). In *Nihongo no Syudai to Toritate (Topic and Focus in Japanese)*, ed. T. Masuoka, et al., 227–260. Tokyo: Kurosio Publishers.

Yamamori, Yoshie. 2006. *Nihongo no genryoo hyoogen no kenkyuu (Study on Japanese determiners)*. Tokyo: Kazamashobo.

Yamanaka, Mieko. 1991. 'Mo' no gan i ni tsuite saikoo -suuryooshi + mo o chuushin ni- (On the implicature of 'mo': reconsideration focusing on the quantifier phrase of 'mo'). *Kansai Linguistic Society* 11: 21–30.

Zwarts, Franz. 1983. Determiners: A relational perspective. In *Studies in Modeltheoretic Semantics*, ed. A. ter Meulen, 37–62. Dordrecht: Foris.

Zwarts, Franz. 1996. A hierarchy of negative expressions. In *Negation: Notion in Focus*, ed. H. Wansing, 169–194. Berlin: De Gruyter.

Scales and Non-scales in (Hebrew) Child Language

Leah R. Paltiel-Gedalyovich and Jeannette Schaeffer

Abstract This paper reports adult and child knowledge of the generalized scalar implicature (GCI) of disjunction, the non-scalar 'Allover' GCI and the particularized no-contrast implicature. The contributions of scales, generalization, and relational complexity to the developmental difficulty of phenomena at the semantic–pragmatic interface are discussed. Results show that children as old as 9 years do not demonstrate adultlike knowledge of the scalar GCI of disjunction or the no-contrast PCI, while the 'Allover' GCI is demonstrated at 5 years. We conclude that the quaternary level relational complexity of the later developing implicature and the ternary level complexity of the earlier developing implicature, as analyzed by Halford et al. (1998) Relational Complexity Metric, can account for this developmental pattern, and not scales or generality.

Keywords First language acquisition • Semantic–pragmatic interface • Implicatures • Relational complexity

1 Introduction

This paper reports results from experiments on adult and child knowledge of one type of scalar implicature (based on the <*and*, *or*> scale) and two types of non-scalar implicatures (the first the no-contrast implicature based on the reference set {*but*, *and*} and the second based on reference sets of attributes—the 'Allover' implicature). The results show that even at the age of 9, six Hebrew-speaking children do not yet have adultlike knowledge of either the scalar or non-scalar

L.R. Paltiel-Gedalyovich (✉)
Early Childhood Centre, Mizpeh Ramon, Israel
e-mail: leah.gedalyovich@gmail.com

J. Schaeffer
Department of Literature and Linguistics, University of Amsterdam, Amsterdam, Netherlands
e-mail: j.c.schaeffer@uva.nl

C. Lee et al. (eds.), *Contrastiveness in Information Structure, Alternatives and Scalar Implicatures*, Studies in Natural Language and Linguistic Theory 91, DOI 10.1007/978-3-319-10106-4_17

implicatures of coordination. However, they do calculate the non-scalar 'Allover' implicature from the age of 5 years. We argue that for children, it is the relational complexity of the semantic and pragmatic relations involved (as measured by the relational complexity metric suggested by Halford et al. 1998) that determines the age of calculation of a given implicature.

When investigating children's performance on conversational implicatures, we examine three issues which we consider to influence the developmental difficulty of each implicature. The first is the participation of a scale in the implicature: is there a difference in the difficulty of scalar and non-scalar implicatures? Crosslinguistically, the majority of investigations into child acquisition of implicatures have been into scalar implicatures with relatively late ages being reported (e.g., Papafragou and Musolino 2003). Note, however, that at least one non-scalar implicature has also been found to develop relatively late (e.g., Noveck and Chevaux 2002). Crucially, we consider acquisition to be demonstrated by behavior which does not differ significantly from adult behavior. Thus, results as high as 80 % or even 90 % adultlike responses are not considered to indicate acquisition if the adult control group provided responses significantly higher.

The second issue is the generalized versus particularized nature of the implicature. Levinson (2000) expands the Gricean concept of generalized conversational implicatures (GCIs), defining these inferences as the default interpretation of an utterances, as opposed to particularized conversational implicatures (PCIs) which are dependent on specific contexts. In the current investigation we examine the relative difficulties of GCIs versus PCIs. Crosslinguistically, the majority of implicatures which have been investigated are GCIs. Note that there are difficulties which arise in investigating the development of PCIs due to their nonuniform appearance in adult communication (Paltiel-Gedalyovich 2008).

The third and final issue bearing on the acquisition of implicatures is the complexity of processing the specific implicature phenomena. Differences in the age of acquisition of various implicatures may be independent of scalar involvement or of generalization and dependent on the complexity of the specific implicature as expressed by the relation which it involves. Crosslinguistically, allusion has been made to processing difficulty of various implicatures resulting from the processing of reference sets (e.g., Reinhart 1999); however, no detailed explanation has been provided for differences in the difficulty of various phenomena. We make use of Halford et al. (1998) relational complexity metric to provide a detailed analysis of the complexity of each implicature investigated, and thus predict and account for differences in developmental ages. We argue that non-adultlike child behavior is not related to the involvement or non-involvement of a scale, nor to whether the implicature is particularized or generalized, but rather to the complexity of the specific implicatures

We view adult behavior as a crucial factor in interpreting child acquisition data. Adult behavior serves as the reference point for determining 'correct' (= adultlike) and 'incorrect' (= non-adultlike) responses. We therefore report and discuss adult as well as child data.

2 Scales Versus Non-scales

We take scalar implicatures to be those implicatures that are calculated based on Horn's entailment scales (Horn 1976), while non-scalar implicatures include those calculated based on reference sets or non-scales (e.g., Levinson 2000). Entailment relationships existing between the members of the set determine whether the set is a scale or not. In scales, there is a unidirectional entailment relationship between the members of the reference set. In non-scales, there is either no entailment relationship or a bidirectional entailment relationship between set members. Thus, the scalar implicature calculated with the use of disjunction involves rejection of the truth of conjunction based on the scale <*and*, *or*>, where disjunction entails conjunction but not vice versa.

The non-scalar no-contrast implicature calculated from the use of the non-contrastive *and* involves rejection of contrast based on the reference set {*but*, *and*}. This is a non-scale; although *but*, which includes contrastive meaning, is more informative than *and*, the truth of each of the members of the set entails the truth of the other.

The use of a bare attribute, say the color *blue*, gives rise to an 'Allover' implicature specifically, 'blue allover' (Harnish 1991). This implicature is calculated by considering a set of unordered alternates {*blue, red, green, yellow*...}. The use of one member of the set in an utterance implicates that the other members of the set are false, i.e., uttering *blue* gives rise to the implicature that none of the other colors are true of the described object. So *red* will be false and therefore, *blue and red* will be false. In the view adopted here, scales are formed by single terms. So, although *blue and red* entails *blue*, and not vice versa, the reference set {*blue and red*, *blue*} is not considered a scale, but a pseudoscale (see Levinson 2000).

There is no specific developmental prediction which arises directly from the involvement of non-involvement of an entailment scale. Accounts which discuss the complexity of processing reference sets (e.g., Reinhart 1999) do not distinguish between the difficulty in processing an ordered set of the type representing a scale versus processing a non-ordered set of the type representing a non-scalar reference set.

3 Generalized Versus Particularized Implicatures

We adopt Levinson's (2000) version of the theory of generalized implicatures. According to this theory, GCIs are default interpretations arising with every utterance of a term which evokes the implicature. Cases in which the GCI is not apparent in the interpretation are considered to be the result of a cancelation of the GCI. (Note that some researchers, working for instance within the context of Relevance Theory, have challenged the default nature of implicatures which have hitherto been taken to be generalized, e.g., Bott and Noveck 2004).

The implicature arising with the use of disjunction is considered to be a generalized conversational implicature or GCI (Levinson 2000), while we take the no-contrast implicature to be a particularized conversational implicature (PCI), since the absence of contrast in *and* is context dependent and not part of the default interpretation. Uses of *and* may give rise to many other implicatures, for example an implicature of sequence based on the maxim of manner giving the interpretation that the first conjunct precedes the second conjunction chronologically. This is shown in (1). *And* can also give rise to an implicature of causality as demonstrated in (2).

(1) Implicature of sequence arising from conjunction
'The boy put on a coat *and* went outside.'
Implicature: he put on his coat before he went outside.

(2) Implicature of causality arising from conjunction
'The boy slipped and fell.'
Implicature: slipping caused the fall

Levinson (2000) suggests that the 'Allover' implicature may also be a GCI and we adopt this view.

Here, too, there is no specific developmental prediction which arises from the theory of GCIs. There is no definitive reason to predict that a GCI will be harder or easier than a PCI. However, there are three points which should be considered. First, the variable nature of PCIs may provide children with less exposure to them and inconsistent evidence regarding when they arise. Second, determining adultlike performance in children for PCIs may prove difficult since the adults themselves will calculate these implicatures inconsistently and the target for child development will be therefore unclear. Finally, children's inconsistent calculation of GCIs may reflect their miscategorization of the implicatures as PCIs.

4 Relational Complexity of (Some) Implicature Phenomena

The relational complexity of each of these implicatures may be determined using the relational complexity metric proposed by Halford et al. (1998). According to this metric the complexity of a given skill is determined by the number of elements which must be processed simultaneously. A developmental sequence indicating at which age each level of relational complexity is mastered is suggested and presented here in (3).

(3) Ages of mastery of different levels of relational complexity

Level of relational complexity	Age of mastery
Unary	1 year
Binary	2 years
Ternary	5 years
Quaternary	11 years

4.1 Relational Complexity of the Scalar Implicature of Disjunction

Within this framework, the scalar implicature based on the scale <*and*, *or*> is assigned quaternary level complexity, a level hypothesized by Halford et al. (1998) to be acquired only by age 11 years. The application of the relational complexity metric to this scalar implicature is illustrated in (4).

(4) Processing of scalar implicature based on <*and, or*>

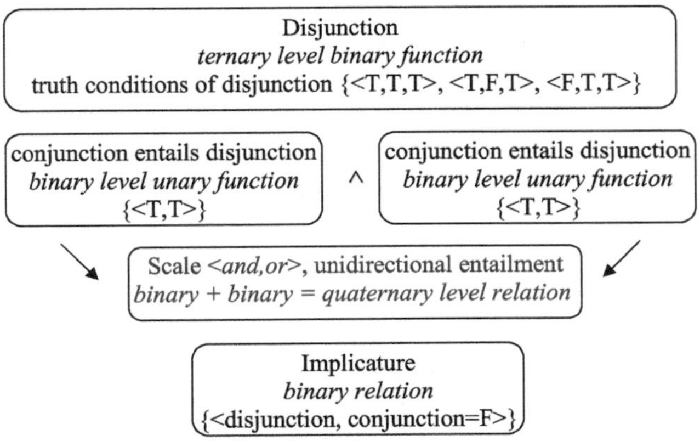

If we apply the model given in (4) to the utterance *Bigbird is wearing a coat* **or** *a scarf* the result is as follows. The utterance itself is a *ternary* level binary function as interpretation involves application of the truth conditions of disjunction, the set of ordered sets {<T,T,T>, <T,F,T>, <F,T,T>} to the truth values of the conjuncts involved (*Bigbird is wearing a coat* and *Bigbird is wearing a scarf*).[1]

[1]Coordinated sentences are given a lower complexity in Halford et al. (1998) own analysis; however, we see the current analysis as more accurate and supported by behavioral results. Ternary level complexity is predicted to be acquired by 5 years, and this is the age at which children have been shown to demonstrate knowledge of the truth conditions of the coordinators (Paltiel-Gedalyovich 2003).

The next step involves the scale <*and*, *or*>. We have unidirectional entailment which is the conjunction (a *ternary* level binary function based on the truth conditions of conjunction, the set of ordered sets {<T,T,T>}) of 'conjunction entails disjunction' and the negation of 'disjunction entails conjunction.' Entailment can be seen as *binary* level relation based on the ordered set <T,T> where the truth of one sentence (a disjunction) yields a guarantee of the truth of a second sentence (a conjunction). In order for the entailment relation to be unidirectional, the second condition must also hold, namely the negation of an entailment relationship such that conjunction entails disjunction. Negation is seen as a *binary* level unary function, as represented by the set of ordered sets {<T,F>, <F,T>}. Thus we have binary level negation having scope over *binary* level entailment.

The *ternary* level conjunction of the *ternary* level binary function of disjunction couples with the *ternary* level binary function of the unidirectional entailment yields a *quaternary* level relation.

4.2 The Relational Complexity of the No-Contrast Implicature of and

The relational complexity of the non-scalar no-contrast implicature based on {*but*, *and*} is quaternary because the relational complexity of the contrast relation of *but* is in itself quaternary. This application of the relational complexity metric is based on Winter and Rimon's (1994) analysis of *but*, shown in (5).

(5) Winter and Rimon's (1994: 370) analysis of the contrast of but
presupposition of but: **p** implies *not* (**r**) and **q** implies **r**

The application of the relational complexity metric to this analysis is given in (6).

(6) Processing of the contrast relation of *aval*/but

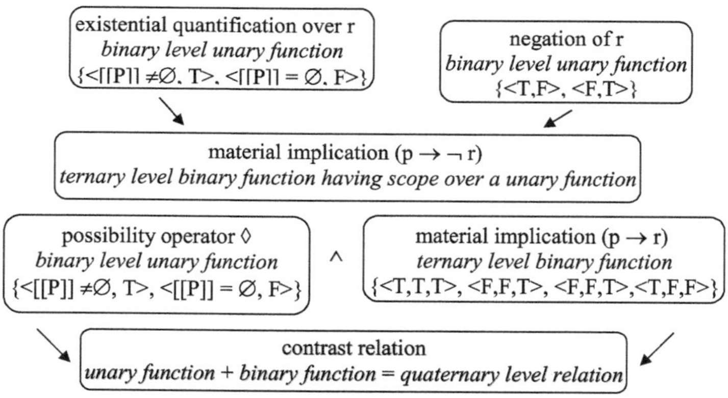

If we consider the utterance *The man hates cucumbers but eats a lot*, the analysis of the complexity of the utterance based on (6) would be as follows.

The utterance itself as conjunction is a *ternary* level binary function based on the set of ordered sets {<T,T,T>, <T,F,F>, <F,T,F>, <F,F,F>, the truth conditions of conjunction.

In addition, there is an expectation arising from the first conjunct, *The man hates cucumbers* of a material implication, specifically, ‘if the man hates cucumbers then it is not the case that he eats a lot of cucumbers.’ This material implication is a *ternary* level binary function, the set of ordered sets {<T,T,T>, <T,F,F>, <F,T, T>, <F,F,T>}.

The conjunction of the *ternary* level binary function, the conjunction, and the *ternary* level binary function of the implication yields (at least) a *quaternary* level relation, for the contrast relation. This would then feed into the implicature.

4.3 The Relational Complexity of the Allover Implicature

Finally, the relational complexity of the allover implicature calculated with the use of attributes is ternary as shown in (7).

(7) Relational complexity of the allover implicature

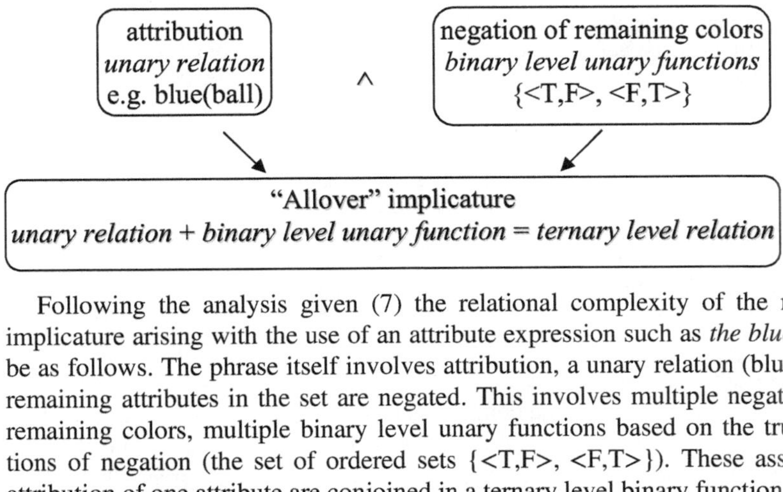

Following the analysis given (7) the relational complexity of the non-scalar implicature arising with the use of an attribute expression such as *the blue ball* will be as follows. The phrase itself involves attribution, a unary relation (blue(x)). The remaining attributes in the set are negated. This involves multiple negation of the remaining colors, multiple binary level unary functions based on the truth conditions of negation (the set of ordered sets {<T,F>, <F,T>}). These assertions of attribution of one attribute are conjoined in a ternary level binary function (based on the truth conditions of conjunction, {<T,T,T>, <T,F,F>, <F,T,F>, <F,F,F>}. Thus, the implicature is considered to have ternary level complexity.

Ternary level relations are predicted to be acquired by 5 years (Halford et al. 1998).[2]

5 Experimental Predictions

Returning to the three issues which arose in the introduction, we can formulate experimental predictions in each area.

First, consider the question of scale versus non-scale. As far as adult behavior is concerned, there are no discriminating predictions based on this issue. For the children, the presence/absence of a scale itself may not predict developmental difficulty. The processing of any kind of implicature scalar or non-scalar requires the comparison with some sort of reference set. There is no reason to suppose on face value that a scalar reference set requires greater processing ability than a non-scalar contrastive reference set. Note, however, that a scale is analyzed as quaternary (requiring the quaternary level conjunction of entailment and negation of entailment constituting unidirectional entailment). Since quaternary level processing is considered to be mastered only at 11 years, we can formulated the predictions in (8) regarding scales and non-scales.

(8) Predictions for adult and child processing of scales and non-scales
   (a) There will be no difference in the frequency of adults' calculation of the scalar implicature of disjunction (as evidenced by their rejection of disjuncts as descriptions of pictures where both disjuncts are true), and the frequency of adults' calculation of the non-scalar implicatures of no-contrast (as evidenced by their rejection of the use of neutral *and* in cases where there is no contrast between the conjuncts) or the allover implicature (as evidenced by their preference for a wholly attributed object over a partially attributed object).
   (b) (i) Children's calculation of the quaternary level scalar implicature (as evidenced by their rejection of disjuncts as descriptions of pictures where both disjuncts are true) will not reach adultlike levels until the age of 11.
   (ii) Children's calculation of the non-scalar implicatures cannot be predicted based solely on the absence of the scale, although in general all other things being equal this calculation should occur earlier than for scalar implicatures since the processing of a scale is quaternary.

Now consider the question of the generalized nature of implicatures. According to the theory of GCI, GCIs are the default, typical interpretation of an expression in the absence of a special context, while PCIs arise only in specific contexts. The implicature associated with disjunction is considered to be a GCI, arising in all uses of disjunction and only canceled in particular contexts. As described above, we

[2]It has been suggested to us anonymously that the negation of the remaining colors has a greater ternary complexity. An alternative analysis would be that there is a double negation, *not blue* resulting in a binary relation having scope over a binary relation which yields a quaternary level relation. We would, however, argue that the first analysis is more accurate, but that the multiple negations are chunked, thus reducing their combined complexity.

hypothesize that the allover implicature, like the scalar implicature of disjunction, is a GCI, while the no-contrast implicature of conjunction is a PCI. For adults there is a clear prediction that their performance on tasks requiring the calculation of a GCI will be very consistent, far more consistent than their performance on PCIs. These predictions are summarized in (9).

(9) Predictions for adults:
   (a) Adults will reject violations of the scalar GCI close to 100 % of the time
   (b) Adults will interpret use of a bare attribute as completely attributed, calculating the non-scalar allover GCI close to 100 % of the time
   (c) Adults will show variability in rejection of violations of the no-contrast PCI

For children, the consistency of the adult responses provides a very clear developmental target. Otherwise, the generalized or particularized nature of an implicature should have no bearing on the developmental difficulty of the implicature. In the present case, the GCI of disjunction being quaternary will be predicted to develop only at 11 years while the allover GCI will be predicted to develop by 5 years. The no-contrast PCI of non-contrastive conjunction will also be predicted to develop only at 11 years, as this implicature is also quaternary. In short, we hypothesized that the acquisition of implicatures would be dependent on the relational complexity of the implicatures and be independent both of the nature of the reference set and whether the implicature is generalized or particularized, resulting in the predictions in (10).

(10) Predictions for children:
   (a) Children are not predicted to reject violations of the quaternary level scalar GCI before the age of 11 years
   (b) Children are predicted to interpret use of bare attribute as completely attributed, calculating the ternary level non-scalar 'Allover' GCI from the age of 5
   (c) Children will not reject violation of the quaternary level non-scalar no-contrast PCI before the age of 11 years

The third and final issue we raised was the question of the relational complexity of the implicature phenomena involved. As is clear from the discussion to this point, we find this to be the crucial point in formulating developmental predictions for the implicatures. If we momentarily disregard the questions of scales and generalization we can derive the predictions given in (11).

(11) Predictions for children based on relational complexity alone:
   (a) Children are not predicted to reject violations of the quaternary level no-contrast implicature consistently before the age of 11 years.
   (b) Children are not predicted to reject violations of the quaternary level implicature associated with disjunction consistently before the age of 11 years.
   (c) Children are not predicted to reject violations of the ternary level allover implicature before the age of 5 years.

We now turn to the experiments developed to test these predictions.

6 The Experiments

6.1 Experiment 1—Investigating the Scalar Implicature Associated with Disjunction

6.1.1 Procedures

In order to test predictions knowledge of the GCI of disjunction and the no-contrast PCI, we carried out a variant of the Truth Value Judgment Task (Crain and Thornton 1998). Children participated in individual sessions in their homes or kindergarten/school settings. Adults participated in individual sessions in their homes. A total of 141 typically developing monolingual Hebrew-speaking children aged 2;7 to 9;6 and 17 monolingual Hebrew-speaking adults were asked to judge the acceptability of a puppet's descriptions of pictures prepared using the Creative Wonders Sesame Street Art Workshop (Henson Productions Inc. 1995).

One condition tested calculation of the GCI based on the scale <*and*, o>.[3] There were 10 target items and 5 filler items. The target items were true descriptions of the stimulus pictures using *o* with both disjuncts true. The filler items were false disjunctions. In each case the experimenter described the picture to the participant and to the puppet and then asked the puppet to describe the picture. The participant was then asked to judge the appropriateness of the puppet's description. For descriptions judged to be unacceptable, the participant was asked to 'teach' the puppet the correct description. The items were mixed with two other conditions and organized in two different random presentation orders with approximately half of the participants presented with each presentation order. Sample target and filler items appear in (12) and (13), respectively.

(12) Target item eliciting calculation of the scalar GCI based on scale <*and*, *or*>:
Picture stimulus: Cookie Monster eating cookies and holding a balloon.
Experimenter description: *hine ugifletset. hu maxzik balon. hu oxel ugijot.*
Here Cookie-monster.he holds balloon. He eats cookies.
'Here's Cookie-monster. He's holding a balloon. He's eating cookies.'
Puppet's description: *ugifletset maxzik balon o oxel ugiyot*
Cookie-monster holds balloon *or* eats cookies
'cookie monster is holding a balloon *or* eating cookies.'

(13) Filler item
Picture stimulus: Bigbird standing near a table which holds a drink and a sandwhich.
Experimenter description: *hine tsiporet. hi lo shota mits, hi lo oxelet senvich.*
Here Bigbird.she no drinks juice she no eats sandwhich
'Here's Bigbird. She's not drinking juice, she's not eating a sandwhich.'

Puppet's description: *tsiporet shota mits o oxelet senvich.*
Bigbird drinks juice or eats sandwhich
'Bigbird is drinking juice or eating a sandwhich.'

---

[3]This was part of a larger experiment into semantic and pragmatic knowledge of coordinators. Only the relevant conditions are reported here.

6.1.2 Results and Discussion

As predicted, adults consistently rejected true picture descriptions violating the scalar GCI associated with disjunction (97.1 % of the time). This supports the prediction that as a GCI, this implicature will be consistently calculated by adults. The scalar nature of the implicature was not predicted to influence the consistency of the adults' responses and therefore will be discussed by comparison with performance on non-scalar implicatures below. In terms of complexity, the complexity of the implicature was analyzed as quaternary, within the predicted processing abilities of adults.

Even the oldest children failed to calculate the GCI with adult level consistency. Their rejection of the stimulus items ranged from 11 % rejection for the 3 year olds, increasing gradually to 50.5 % rejection for the 9 year olds. Even the oldest children's responses differed significantly from the adult responses ($F(7,115) = 13.07$, MS error = 11.623, $p < 0.05$). The fact that the adults calculated this implicature as a GCI provides a clear target for child acquisition such that the children's inconsistent performance can be interpreted as immature language development. The source of the children's difficulty is predicted by the complexity of the specific implicature, analyzed as quaternary, and thus predicted to develop only at 11 years. The involvement of a scale in the implicature in itself did not lead to a prediction of non-adultlike behavior, and therefore in itself does not account for this result.

6.2 *Experiment 2—Investigating the Non-scalar Implicature Associated with Non-contrastive Conjunction*

6.2.1 Procedures

A further condition of this same experiment testing calculation of the non-scalar, no-contrast PCI based on the set {*but, and*}. This second condition deals with the non-scalar particularized implicature based on the non-scale of contrastive conjunction represented in Hebrew by *aval*, and what we may call neutral, conjunction, the Hebrew *ve*. Participants and materials were the same as for the previous condition; however, this time the target items involved the use of *ve* to coordinate two contrasting conjuncts while the filler items used *aval* to coordinate two contrasting conjuncts. Examples of target and filler items appear in (14) and (15), respectively.

(14) Target item the No-Contrast PCI based on reference set {*but*, *and*}:
Picture stimulus: Hungry dog walking away from bone
Experimenter's description:
hine kelev. hu raev. hu ohev etsem. hu mashir et haetsem. muzar!
here dog. he hungry. he likes bone. he leaves 'et' the-bone. strange.
'Here's a dog. He's hungry. He likes bones. He leaves the bone. Strange!'
Puppet's description: *hakelev raev ve mashir et haetsem*
The-dog hungry *and* leaves 'et' the-bone
'The dog is hungry *and* leaves the bone.'

(15) Filler item
Picture stimulus: Man eating a large pile of cucumbers.
Experimenter's description:
hine ish. haish sone melafefonim. hu oxel harbe melafefonim. muzar!
here man. The-man hates cucumbers. he eats many cucumbers. strange.
'Here's a man. The man hates cucumbers. He eats lots of cucumbers. Strange!'
Puppet's description: *haish sone melafefonim aval oxel harbe.*
The-man hates cucmbers *but* eats many.
'The man hates cucumbers but eats alot.'

6.2.2 Results and Discussion

As predicted, the adults rejected the use of the less informative *ve/and* when the contrast allowed the use of the more informative *aval/but*, but only 50 % of the time, thus demonstrating that they calculate the implicature based on the non-scale PCI optionally. This does not indicate chance levels, but rather individual differences with individual participants consistently (>80 % of the time) calculating/failing to calculate the implicature. This is consistent with prediction that the no-contrast implicature is a PCI.

The majority of the children failed to demonstrate knowledge of the contrastive nature of *aval/but* in that they accepted the use of *aval/but* in non-contrastive coordinations. Thus, they showed no preference for the more informative *aval/but* in contexts where contrast was indicated (20 % rejection of the less informative *ve/and*). The children's failure to calculate the non-scalar no-contrast PCI we interpret as, a product of the difficulty of calculating the contrastive meaning of *aval/but* which is considered quaternary. In this case, the children do not see *aval/but* as more informative than *ve/and* and no implicature is calculated. Of those children who did demonstrate knowledge of the contrast of *aval/but*, only one (of 5) calculated the no-contrast PCI. Conclusions about children's knowledge of particularized implicatures such as this are difficult to draw due to the inconsistency of adult calculation of these implicatures.

6.3 *Investigating the 'Allover' Implicature Associated with Some Adjectives*

6.3.1 Procedures

In order to test knowledge of the 'Allover' implicature associated with some adjectives, we carried out a pointing task with 38 typically developing monolingual Hebrew-speaking children aged 2;11–12;0 and 12 adults on their knowledge of non-scalar conversational implicatures in a pointing task. Participants heard target picture descriptions in two sets. The first set included 10 items using colors and the second set included 18 items using other attributes. The target items were equally divided between two experimental conditions: in the first the target picture was a completely attributed object compared with a partially attributed object and two other distracters, in the second the target picture was a partially attributed object compared with three distracters. Each set also included filler items where the items where different objects of different colors/attributes were depicted. Children were pre-tested for knowledge of the colors and attributes before testing. Examples of experimental items for the 'allover' and 'partially' appear in (16) and (17), respectively, while a sample filler item appears in (18).

(16) Target item for Non-scalar 'Allover' GCI – 'allover' condition
Picture display of four balls: blue striped ball, all blue ball, all green ball, blue middle changing to green border
Stimulus: *tari li et hakadur hakaxol*
show me 'et' the-ball the-blue
'show me the blue ball.'

(17) Target item for partially condition
Picture display of four shirts: red shirt with yellow circle, green shirt with red circle, red shirt gradually changing to blue, green shirt with floral square on one shoulder
Stimulus: *tari li et haxultsa hapirxonit*
show me 'et' the-shirt the-flowery
'Show me the flowery shirt.'

(18) Filler item
Picture display of four objects: red ball, black giraffe, black parakeet, green hat
Stimulus: *tari li et ha-dZiraffa ha-xamuda*
show me 'et' the-giraffe the-cute
'Show me the cute giraffe.'

6.3.2 Results and Discussion

As predicted, adults calculated the 'Allover' GCI consistently for colors, selecting the completely attributed object picture 100 % of the time, and slightly less consistently for attributes, selecting the completely attributed object picture 99 % of the time. The consistency of the allover implicature supports the existence of at least one type of default non-scalar implicature, much the same as that of default scalar implicatures (cf Levinson 2000).

Children in the 5–6 year old age group exhibited adultlike preference for a completely attributed object 90 % for attributes and 95 % of the time for colors. The result for colors did not differ significantly from the adults' results ($p > 0.05$); however, for the other attributes, this result was marginally significantly different from the adults ($p = 0.57$) and adult consistency was only obtained by the 7–8-year-old group 9p > 0.05). The later acquisition of the attribute adjectives is attributed to the later lexical acquisition of these types of adjectives (see e.g., Berman 2004).

7 General Discussion and Conclusions

The first question we asked related to the scalar versus non-scalar nature of implicatures: Are scalar implicatures more difficult and therefore later acquired than non-scalar implicatures, simply because scales themselves are difficult to process? In the studies reported here, for adults, the fact that an implicature includes a scale rather than a non-scale, or vice versa, does not appear to have an effect on the pattern of calculation of the implicature since one scalar and one non-scalar implicature were calculated consistently. In other words, even if scales are more difficult than non-scales, their difficulty is well within the abilities of adults.

As for children, is it the presence of a scale that makes an implicature difficult for children? In the studies reported here, one scalar (that of disjunction) and one non-scalar (the no-contrast) implicature were not mastered even by the oldest children participating in the study (the 9–year-old group). There was also evidence from the non-scalar 'Allover' implicature that at least one type of non-scalar implicature is acquired relatively early. Taking these two points together we may conclude that the presence of a scale suggests a more difficult implicature, but the absence of a scale in itself does not guarantee that the implicature will be easy/early developing. For non-scalar implicatures the difficulty of the relations involved in the lexical/semantic content of the utterance appears to determine the difficulty and age of acquisition. The late development of the no-contrast implicature can be explained in terms of the late development of the underlying (semantic) contrastive meaning of the coordinator *aval*/but and the later age of calculation of the 'Allover' implicature for denominal and resultative adjectives. In terms of the implicature, there is no difference in the difficulty of calculation of the 'Allover' implicature for color adjectives and for denominal and resultative adjectives. The greater difficulty of the calculating the implicature for these adjectives results from the greater difficulty of the adjectives themselves. This is evidenced by the later comprehension and spontaneous use of these types of adjectives in Hebrew child language (e.g., Berman 2004). For scalar implicatures, even given relatively simple lexical/semantic content, such as the semantic meaning of conjunction/disjunction, the implicature itself is complex.

The second question we asked regarded the acquisition of generalized versus particularized implicatures. This question was found to distinguish adult behavior. GCIs were calculated far more consistently than PCIs. There was primarily variation between individuals such that adult participants could be divided into two groups: those who consistently calculated the PCI and those who consistently failed to calculate the PCI. Yet, there was also some (20 %) variation within individuals. This amount of variation although clearly not at chance levels differs from the approximately <5 % variation found in the calculation of the GCIs.

The implications for the child data are not clear. We found that one GCI and one PCI were acquired relatively late with adultlike behavior not obtained even by the oldest participants, while one GCI was mastered at a relatively young age (5–6 years). At first glance this may appear to suggest that PCIs are mastered late while the mastery of GCIs is variable, dependent on some other factor. It is possible that PCIs are more difficult to acquire just because of their inconsistent nature. The input to children regarding the calculation of these implicatures will be inconsistent and even contradictory, and therefore more difficult to learn. Furthermore, regarding the inconsistent calculation of the GCI, it could be argued that the children know the implicature but are not aware that it is generalized and therefore calculate it only optionally. We find this explanation to be contradictory since it results in particularized implicatures being both easier and harder at the same time. Thus, we consider that the generalized or particularized nature of an implicature is insufficient to predict its difficulty or age of acquisition.

Thus, viewing our data in terms of the first two questions yields equivocal results. We now turn to our third question. Is the determining factor in the acquisition of implicatures the complexity of the relations involved? Of the three implicatures studies, two were considered to have quaternary relational complexity, as determined by Halford et al. (1998) relational complexity metric. As predicted by their high complexity level, these implicatures were not demonstrated to be calculated by the oldest children participating in the studies, aged 9 years. Similarly, the implicature which was demonstrated by 5–6 year olds is analyzed as having ternary level complexity, a complexity level predicted to be mastered by 5 years. Thus, of the three possible factors we suggested as possible explanations for the developmental pattern for three implicatures, the relational complexity of the implicature phenomena provides the best account for the children's data.

We cannot explain the late acquisition of the no-contrast PCI in terms of a specific difficulty with scales or with GCIs so we suggest that either the processing of the quaternary level relation is too difficult for these children (and note the difficult step in the process is the unilateral entailment). As far as the non-scalar PCI of contrastive conjunction, we saw individual differences within the adult group. For children, it appears that the problem here is not with non-scales being difficult, or of a PCI versus a GCI, but rather related to difficulty due to specific complexity of the contrastive meaning, before the stage of implicature calculation. This explanation is supported by the fact that for those children who did demonstrate knowledge of the contrastive meaning the results were very similar to the adults. Finally, the difficulty the children under the age of 5 showed appears to be related to the ternary complexity of the relation. Ternary level relations are predicted to be mastered by 5 years. Of course, here, too, it could be argued that they are not aware of the generalized nature of the implicature, but since the age matches the prediction based on the relational complexity metric, the processing difficulty explanation seems more likely.

In summary, Hebrew-speaking adults consistently calculate generalized implicatures, both scalar implicatures, such as that of disjunction, and non-scalar, such as the 'allover' implicature. Furthermore, Hebrew-speaking adults calculate a particularized implicature far less consistently. Finally, the consistency of the adult responses does not appear to be related to the involvement of a scale in the implicature.

For children, the age at which they master calculation of implicatures appears to be a result of the relational complexity of the phenomenon and not related to the participation of a scale, or to the generalized or particularized nature of the implicature

Concluding, the results from these experiments exemplify the calculation of quantity implicatures using both entailment scales and non-scales; however, the consistency of calculation of the GCIs is much greater than the calculation of PCIs. Children's knowledge of these implicatures are argued to be adultlike dependent upon the complexity of the relations involved. The ages of acquisition found are consistent with the complexity of the skills being acquired as determined by Halford et al. (1998) relational complexity metric given above, 5 years for the ternary non-scalar GCI and 11 years for the quaternary scalar GCI and no-contrast PCI.

But there are many questions which remain to be answered. Some of these relate to the limited number of implicatures investigated to date. Are there scalar implicatures which can be demonstrated in the preschool years? If so, this would challenge the analysis of the scale as contributing quaternary level complexity to scalar implicatures. What is the complexity of other implicatures? Particularly, we need more investigations of non-scalar implicatures. Regarding the generality of implicatures, which implicatures show crosslinguistic generalization and which do not, and why? And regarding the complexity of various implicatures, is the complexity of some implicatures so great as to account for adult inconsistency? At what age do children actually become adultlike in their calculation of the more complex implicatures? We need data from older children—and we are in the process of collecting these data for the implicatures investigated here.

Acknowledgments This work is partially based on Leah's doctoral thesis (2003) completed under the supervision of Dr. Jeannette Schaeffer and Prof. Nomi Shir. This work was partially supported by grant no. 4-2004 from the National Institute for Psychobiology in Israel to Dr. Jeannette Schaeffer, and by a 2007 Summer Excellency Fellowship to Dr. Leah Paltiel-Gedalyovich from the Zlotowski Center for Neurosciences. Thanks to Professor Yishai Tobin who kindly presented an earlier version of this paper at CIL18 in Seoul.

References

Berman, R.A. 2004. Between emergence and mastery: The long development route of language acquisition. In *Language Development Across Childhood and Adolescence*, ed R.A. Berman. Amsterdam/New York: John Benjamins.

Bott, L., and I.A. Noveck. 2004. Some utterances are underinformative: The onset and time course of scalar inferences. *Journal of Memory and Language* 51(3): 437–457.

Crain, S., and R. Thornton. 1998. *investigations in universal grammar: A guide to experiments in the acquisition of syntax and semantics*. Cambridge, Mass: MIT Press.

Halford, G.S., W.H. Wilson, and S. Phillips. 1998. Processing capacity as defined by relational complexity: Implications for comparative, developmental and cognitive psychology. *Behavioral and Brain Sciences* 21(6): 803–831.

Harnish, R. 1991. Logical form and implicature. In *Pragmatics* ed S. David, pp. 316–364. Oxford: Oxford University Press.

Henson, J. 1995. *Creative Wonders Sesame Street ArtWorkshop*. Henson Productions, Inc.

Horn, L.R. 1976. *On the semantic properties of logical operators in English*. Bloomington, Indiana.: Indiana University Linguistics Club.

Levinson, S. 2000. *Presumptive Meanings*. Cambridge, Mass: MIT Press.

Noveck, Ira A., and Florelle Chevaux. 2002. The pragmatic development of *and*. In *BUCLD 26 Proceedings*, ed. Badbara Skarabella, et al., 453–463. Somerville, MA: Cascadilla Press.

Paltiel-Gedalyovich, L.R. 2003. Towards an explanation of first language acquisition of Hebrew coordination. Unpublished doctoral dissertation: Ben-Gurion University of the Negev.

Paltiel-Gedalyovich, L.R. 2008. Response uniformity distinguishes semantics from pragmatics: Evidence from Hebrew coordination and implications for interpreting child language data. Presented at Workshop on Experimental Pragmatics/Semantics, DGfS conference, Bamberg, 27–29 Feb 2008.

Papafragou, A., and J. Musolino. 2003. Scalar implicatures: experiments at the semantics-pragmatics interface. *Cognition* 86: 253–282.

Reinhart, T. 1999. The processing cost of reference-set computation: Guess patterns in acquisition. *OTS Working Papers*, Utrecht.

Winter, Y., and M. Rimon. 1994. Contrast and implication in natural language. *Journal of Semantics* 11: 365–406.

Part IV
Questions and Speech Acts

Negated Polarity Questions as Denegations of Assertions

Manfred Krifka

Abstract The paper offers a new proposal for so-called high negation in questions like *Isn't there a vegetarian restaurant around here?* It develops a theory of speech acts that allows for certain semantic operators, like negation, to scope over them. It is argued that high negation is negation over an assertion (here, 'there is a vegetarian restaurant around here'), and that the question is a request by the speaker to refrain from asserting that proposition. In doing this, the speaker checks whether the addressee would exclude that there is a vegetarian restaurant around here. This rhetorical move is justified under certain circumstances, which explains the biases that have been observed with such questions, and also with questions with low negation such as *Is there no vegetarian restaurant here*? The paper also introduces a more fine-grained notion of polarity questions; in addition to the standardly assumed "bipolar" questions that present two propositions, one being the negation

Precursors of this paper were presented at the 18th Amsterdam Colloquium 2011, at the University of Wuppertal, at ZAS Berlin, at the University of Frankfurt/Main in 2012 (Network meeting "Questions in Discourse"), and at Semantics and Linguistic Theory (SALT22) in Chicago. I gratefully acknowledge support by the DFG (SFB 632 "Information Structure") and by the Bundesministerium für Bildung and Forschung (Förderkennzeichen 01UG0711; responsibility for the content of this publication remain with the author). Readers should be aware of my later paper, Krifka (2015), that develops a different take on high negation questions within the general overall framework. Specific thanks to inspiring discussions with colleagues at the occasion of these presentations, in particular David Beaver, Manfred Bierwisch, Andreas Haida, Joachim Jacobs, Horst Lohnstein, Sophie Repp, Uli Sauerland, Rob van der Sandt, Paul Portner, Tue Trinh, Hubert Truckenbrodt, Susanne Uhmann, Henk Zeevat, Malte Zimmermann, and Ede Zimmermann.

I dedicate this paper to the memory of Susanne Anschütz, the resourceful guardian of linguistics in Germany at the DFG, who passed away in February 2012.

M. Krifka (✉)
Leibniz-Zentrum Allgemeine Sprachwissenschaft (ZAS), Humboldt-Universität zu Berlin, Berlin, Germany
e-mail: krifka@rz.hu-berlin.de

C. Lee et al. (eds.), *Contrastiveness in Information Structure, Alternatives and Scalar Implicatures*, Studies in Natural Language and Linguistic Theory 91, DOI 10.1007/978-3-319-10106-4_18

of the other, it also assumes "monopolar" questions that present just one proposition, and hence allow for the expression of a bias.

Keywords Negation • Speech act • Assertion • Questions • Polarity questions • Question bias • Common ground

1 Introduction: Negated Polarity Questions

Since Ladd (1981), negation in questions continued to be a challenge for semantics and pragmatics. Ladd observed that questions like (1) are systematically ambiguous:

(1) *Isn't there a vegetarian restaurant around here?*
  a. Speaker wants confirmation that there is a vegetarian restaurant here.
  b. Speaker wants confirmation that there is no vegetarian restaurant here.

Prosody might shift the interpretation into one or the other direction, and particles have a similar effect: adding *too* shifts the interpretation toward (a), adding *either* shifts it toward (b). Reading (b) can also be expressed by *Is there no vegetarian restaurant around here?* In other languages, the two interpretations tend to be expressed in morphosyntactically different ways, as, e.g., in German (cf. Büring and Gunlogson 2000), where the readings (1)(a) and (b) tend to be expressed as in (2)(a) and (2)(b).

(2) a.

Gibt	*es*	*hier*	*nicht*	*ein*	*vegetarisches*	*Restaurant*	*?*
exist-3SG	it	here	NEG	INDEF.SG	vegetarian	restaurant	

b.

Gibt	*es*	*hier*	*k-ein*	*vegetarisches*	*Restaurant*	*?*
exist-3SG	it	here	NEG-INDEF.SG	vegetarian	restaurant	

'Is there no vegetarian restaurant here?'

Another difference was pointed out in Repp (2009, 2013): If negation precedes the additive particle *auch*, hence has scope over it, we get the interpretation corresponding to (a); if negation follows, and hence the particle has scope over negation, we get the interpretation corresponding to (b).

(3) a. *Schläft Peter nicht auch?*
  'Doesn't Peter sleep too?'
  b. *Schläft Peter auch nicht?*
  'Doesn't Peter sleep either?'

Romero and Han (2004) discuss differences in other languages. In Korean, negation in the (a) reading is expressed by an auxiliary (long form negation), whereas (b) is expressed with a short form negation:

(4) a. *Suni-ka coffee-lul masi-ess.ci anh-ni?*
Suni-NOM coffee-ACC drink-PAST NEG-Q
'Didn't Suni drink coffee?'

b. *Suni-ka coffee-lul an masi-ess-ni?*
Suni-NOM coffee-ACC NEG drink-PAST-Q
'Didn't Suni drink coffee?'

Ladd proposes that the two readings of (1) are due to a scope difference of negation, something that is made plausible by the German examples. In (b), the scope of negation is internal to the proposition that is questioned, whereas in (a), it is "somehow outside the proposition under question." I will call this structure **negated polarity question**.

Ladd sees that the assumption of a negation outside of a proposition "raises some fairly major difficulties for logical representation," as it is not clear how negation, a propositional operator, should be interpreted outside of the proposition. Indeed, Ladd's observation has turned out to be a major challenge to semantic theory, especially for the way how semantics and pragmatics interact.

In this paper, I will propose a novel solution to the interpretation of negated polarity questions. I will do so in the context of other question types, like declarative questions as in *There is a vegetarian restaurant around here?* (cf. Gunlogson 2002). The solution is rooted in a general theoretical framework for speech acts in which they are analyzed as transitions between commitment spaces (cf. Cohen and Krifka 2011). In essence, "outer" negation will be analyzed as an instance of speech act denegation that we also find in cases like *I don't promise to come*. Such speech act denegation express that a speaker refrains from performing a speech act (here, the promise to come). I will argue that in the case of (1) with outer negation, the speaker asks whether the addressee would refrain from making the assertion that there is a vegetarian restaurant around here. It will be shown that this explains the various biases that have been observed with such sentences.

The paper will proceed as follows: In Sect. 2, I will give a short overview of existing accounts of negated polarity questions and their problems.[1] In Sect. 3 I will present the framework for the interpretation of speech acts that the analysis proposed here uses. Section 4 shows how assertions and reactions to assertions work in this framework, and Sect. 7 discuss how regular questions work, in particular constituent questions and simple polarity questions like *Is there a vegetarian restaurant around here?*. Section 8 then turns to declarative questions like *There is a vegetarian restaurant around here?*, Sect. 9 to biased polarity questions like *Is there no vegetarian restaurant here?*. After these preliminaries, we will be able to explain, in Sect. 10, negated polarity questions like *Isn't there a vegetarian restaurant around here?*

In addition to looking at a wider range of polarity questions, I will also develop an explanation of the sometimes quite confusing answer patterns that polarity

[1]The current paper was finished in 2012, and could not take into account two recent publications on the topic, AnderBois (2011) and Sudo (2013).

questions with and without outer or inner negations engender. Furthermore, I will point out the role of the so-called incredulity contour in the construction of biases of such questions.

2 Previous Accounts

Ladd (1981) pointed out a puzzle, and it took a number of years till the first attempts at a solution appeared. Here, I will discuss four such accounts. I should mention that I cannot do full justice to these works here. My main goal is to characterize their basic approach and point out certain problems with them.

There is one account that essentially treats negation in negated polarity questions such as propositional negation, contrary to Ladd's intuition, by van Rooij and Šafařová (2003). It assumes that if a polarity question based on a sentence *p* that denotes a proposition p, the proposition p should have a greater "pragmatic utility" than ¬p. In the case of (1) under the interpretation (a), the question is based on the negation of the sentence *There is a vegetarian restaurant around here*, hence the proposition $\neg\varphi = \neg$ 'there is a vegetarian restaurant around here' should have a greater "pragmatic utility" than the proposition φ. This explains the pragmatic bias of negated polarity questions: If the speaker thinks that it is likely that φ, then learning that $\neg\varphi$ would be of high utility, as it would help to detect, and correct, a blatant error in the speaker's assignment of probabilities to propositions.

One major problem of this account is that it does not explain the high syntactic position of negation in cases like (2)(a). According to van Rooij and Šafařová, the negation in negated polarity questions is simple propositional negation. Ladd's proposal that the negation in (1) under reading (a) is outside of the proposition also explained why it is not compatible with negative polarity items like *either*; this prediction appears to be lost under van Rooij and Šavařovás account.

The second account to be discussed is Romero and Han (2004), cf. also Romero (2006). It assumes that preposed negation in questions results in the availability of a VERUM operator, as proposed in Höhle (1992) for cases of predicate focus and *do*-support. VERUM is an epistemic operator that relates to the strength with which a proposition should be added to the common ground; VERUM(p) states that the proposition p should be added "for sure" to the common ground CG, that is, the speaker considers the evidence for p as high. The two readings of sentences with high negation in (1) result from a scopal ambiguity of negation with VERUM, which is expressed in the underlying propositions as follows:

(5) a. ¬VERUM(φ): 'It is not for sure that φ should be added to the CG'
b. VERUM(¬φ): 'It is for sure that ¬φ should be added to the CG'

Romero and Han assume, following Hamblin's framework for questions, that polarity questions arise from a proposition p by forming a set of propositions {p, ¬p} as possible answers. In the case at hand, we get interpretations (6)(a), (b) for the two readings of (1), to be contrasted with reading (6)(c) for the simple question *Is there a vegetarian restaurant around here?*

(6) a. $\{\neg\text{VERUM}(\varphi), \text{VERUM}(\varphi)\}$
b. $\{\text{VERUM}(\neg\varphi), \neg\text{VERUM}(\neg\varphi)\}$
c. $\{\varphi, \neg\varphi\}$

In (1) under reading (a), the speaker has a bias toward φ. The interpretation (6)(a) captures this: The speaker already tends toward φ and now asks whether φ can be assumed with a high degree of certainty. Conversely, in (1) under reading (b), the speaker has a bias toward $\neg\varphi$ and asks, according to (6)(b), whether $\neg\varphi$ can be assumed with a high degree of certainty. In contrast, the question *Is there a vegetarian restaurant around here?* lacks such bias, which is captured by (6)(c).

Romero and Han's analysis explains the high syntactic position of negation in (1)(a). It makes sense of the intuition that this negation is interpreted outside of the proposition, and it gives a decent explanation of the pragmatic bias of the interpretations of (1)(a, b). However, the analysis also has its problems. First, there is no account how the negation preposed to an auxiliary makes available the VERUM operator (to be sure, VERUM can arise by other means, e.g. by the sentence adverb *really* and by focus on a negation). Second, it is unclear how the bias in questions like *Is there no vegetarian restaurant around here?* originates, which appears to be similar to (1)(b). Romero and Han discuss such sentences where focus is on the negation, but focus on the negation is not required to obtain this bias. Furthermore, notice that VERUM is essentially a pragmatic operator that indicates what should be done with a proposition in conversation (e.g., add it to the common ground with a particular strength). But then it is actually not clear what negating VERUM(φ) means, as negation is a propositional operator, and VERUM(φ) is not obviously a proposition. The nonpropositional status of VERUM(φ) is not quite clear in Romero and Han's account, as they render it technically as a modal statement, similar like 'it is sure that φ', or 'φ should definitely be part of the common ground'. But if this is to be taken seriously, then we have a problem, as questions based on *it is sure…* and questions with outer negation are not equivalent, as the following example shows:

(7) *They say that it is raining, but I don't quite believe that.*
a. *Is it certain that it is raining?*
b. *#Isn't it raining?*

The third account has been developed by Asher and Reese, see Reese (2007) and Asher and Reese (2007). In this account, negated polarity questions are complex speech acts; they are combinations of assertions and questions, just like tag questions (*There is a vegetarian restaurant around here, isn't there?*) and rhetorical questions based on emphatic negative polarity items (*Is there even a SINGLE vegetarian restaurant around here?*). For such combinations, the authors provide for speech act combinations with a dot operator, like ASSERTION · QUESTION. In such combined speech acts, Gricean principles link one speech act type to the other. In the case of negated polarity questions, Asher and Reese assume that these questions are basically assertions, and that the question part adds to that assertion a request for acknowledgment, for confirmation, or for contradiction.

The theory of Asher and Reese explains the lack of NPIs, which do not occur in assertions without being licensed by an operator-like negation. It also explains why negated polarity questions pass certain tests for assertions proposed by Sadock (1971, 1974). For example, *after all* marks assertions, but can also occur in negated polarity questions:

(8) *We can go out here.*
  a. *After all, there is a vegetarian restaurant around here.*
  b. **After all, is there a vegetarian restaurant around here?*
  c. *After all, isn't there a vegetarian restaurant around here?*

One problem, however, is that Asher and Reese's account does not explain how a negation in a polarity question, in particular a syntactically high negation, leads to the assertive component of the question. Also, the explanation of the effect of combining ASSERT and QUESTION is not really worked out in their theory.

The most recent account is due to Repp (2013). Repp assumes that in addition to Romero and Han's operator VERUM there is an operator FALSUM that, like VERUM, indicates the status of a proposition relative to the common ground: they are "common ground managing" operators. Repp assumes that the outer negation reading of (1) is not an instance of negation scoping over VERUM, but rather that negation expresses the FALSUM operator, which states that the degree of strength with which the proposition should be added to the common ground is zero. This is the same operator that occurs in denials, a certain type of reactive speech act. Repp analyzes negated polarity questions as questions that ask whether the degree to which a proposition should be added to the common ground is zero, that is, whether the addressee would deny the proposition. For example, in (1)(a), the speaker asks the addressee to decide between the options FALSUM(φ) and $\neg$FALSUM(φ). Evidence for this analysis over the one by Romero and Han comes from the following answer pattern in German:

(9) S_1: *Gibt es hier nicht ein vegetarisches Restaurant?*
  S_2: *Doch, ich glaube schon, aber ich bin mir nicht sicher.*
  "Yes, I think there is, but I'm not sure."

Under Romero and Han's proposal, the speaker S_1 in (9) would ask the addressee S_2 to identify the option $\neg$VERUM(φ) or VERUM(φ); an answer marked by *doch* would identify VERUM(φ), that is, that φ should be added for sure to the common ground. However, as (9) shows, the speaker is not committed to that high degree of certainty. Under Repp's account, a *doch*-answer identifies the option $\neg$FALSUM(φ), and this is compatible with a reduced degree of certainty.

Under Repp's account, there is no problem with interpreting negation as a non-propositional operation, as it is assumed that high negation is interpreted as FALSUM; what we would have to account for is why negation can either express propositional negation or FALSUM. The distributional difference between negated polarity questions and questions based on *sure* observed in (7) does not constitute a problem for Repp either. However, there is a problem, which is directly linked to the predictive advantage over Romero and Han: If a question like (9)(S_1) is answered affirmatively, by *ja*, without any modification, then according to my intuition this is not just understood as the weak commitment that ¬FALSUM(φ) would indicate. Rather, a simple affirmative answer indicates a commitment to the proposition φ, without modification. As Repp has shown that Romero and Han's analysis as VERUM(φ) does not work either, an obvious conclusion is that negated polarity questions do not address the strength of the answerhood condition at all. Assuming that the question itself asks for strong or weak answers appears to be on the wrong track.

In the following, I will present a novel solution that takes Ladd's insight of a syntactically high negation in negated polarity questions seriously. It follows the accounts of Romero and Han and of Repp, in assuming that negation scopes over a speech act related operator, but it also provides for a theory for what it means for speech acts to be "negated." It takes on the suggestion of Asher and Reese that negated polarity questions combine a question with an assertion, and it provides a precise account how this combination can be understood.

3 A Framework for the Interpretation of Speech Acts

Speech acts have been analyzed in a variety of ways, e.g., as expressing beliefs, or as moves in language games, or as intentions to communicate. Here, I will assume a "normative" approach to speech acts: Speech acts create **commitments** by the interlocutors. That speech acts change commitments has been proposed by a wide variety of authors, for example by Hamblin (1971), Stalnaker (1978), Gazdar (1981), Alston (2000), and Gunlogson (2001), and is discussed more recently in Harnish (2005) and Beyssade and Marandin (2006). For example, in the speech act of asserting a proposition φ, the speaker takes on a commitment to be responsible for the truth of φ, and in the speech act of a promising the speaker takes on a commitment to act in a particular way in the future. Such commitments have social consequences. For example, in the case of an assertion the speaker has to present evidence for φ if asked for, and can be held liable for the truth of φ.

More formally, speech acts can be seen as enacting **changes of commitments**, and linguistic forms that are conventionally related to a certain speech acts can be seen as **functions from input commitments to output commitments**. The current proposal follows Cohen and Krifka (2011), which models the development in the commitments in form of a game tree, but there are important differences in detail. It is also inspired by the account in Merin (1994), where speech acts are seen as transitions between states of automata.

Let c be a representation of the commitments, rendered in some formal language, that have accumulated up to the current point in discourse. This will be called **commitment state**. Then the **update** of c with a speech act $A_{S1,S2}$ by the speaker S_1 directed to the addressee S_2 can be represented as in (10), where $com_c(A_{S1,S2})$ is the set of commitments introduced when the speech act A is performed by S_1_S_2 at the commitment state c.

(10) Update of c with speech act $A_{S1,S2}$, where S_1: Speaker, S_2: Addressee:
$c + A_{S1,S2} = c \cup com_c(A_{S1,S2})$

Updating c by $A_{S1,S2}$ consists of adding the commitments expressed by the act $A_{S1,S2}$ to the commitment state c that represents the commitments at the current point in conversation c, where the commitments that are generated by $A_{S1,S2}$ might depend on c (as in the case of context-sensitive, "particularized" conversational implicatures). See Fig. 1 for a graphical representation.

Typically, updates like c + A indicate that $com_c(A)$, the new commitments expressed by A, are not already present in c (more precisely, $c \cap com_c(A) \neq \emptyset$), otherwise there would be no point in performing A in the first place (the "first principle" in Stalnaker 1978). However, we would not want to express this as a strict condition for updates, *pace* Hamblin (1971); rather, it should follow from Gricean reasons, perhaps as a consequence of the Maxim of Manner, "Be brief!" In fact, Speakers repeat themselves, and often with good reason, as they might assume that the commitments expressed by the speech act already be there, but still have to be stressed and made salient.

It should be stressed that A is not a concrete speech act, or a speech act **token**, but rather an abstract operation that can be used to perform speech acts—a speech act **type**. The speech act type can be rendered as a function $\lambda c[c + A]$, a function from commitment states to commitment states. If a speaker applies A to a specific commitment state c, the commitments of speaker and/or addressee change, and an actual speech act ensues. This change of commitments is actually a change of the world itself. This was observed in Szabolcsi (1982), who treated speech acts as functions from worlds to worlds.

Commitment states, and transitions between commitment states, are not sufficient to represent all conversational acts. One case in point is **speech act denegation** (cf. Searle 1969):

(11) *I don't promise to come.*

Following Hare (1970), such denegations are explicit refusals to perform a certain speech act, here the commissive speech act expressed by *I promise to come*, which adds the commitment of the speaker to come. To model denegations, we have to consider the possible future developments of commitment spaces. Cohen

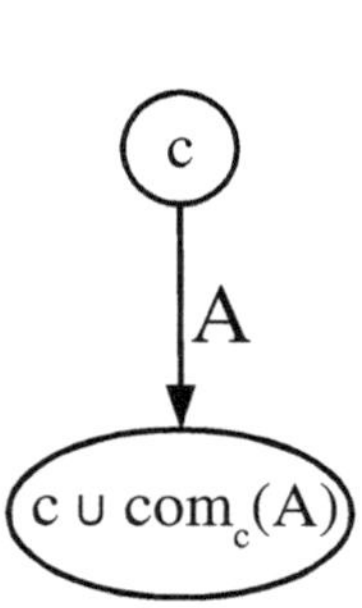

Fig. 1 Update of commitment state c by speech act A

and Krifka (2011) introduce the notion of **commitment spaces** to model such admissible continuations of commitment states. We assume that commitment spaces are sets of commitment states that are **rooted** in a (non-empty) commitment state with respect to the relation of continuation.

(12) C is a commitment space iff
a. C is a set of commitment states;
b. $\exists c \in C\ \forall c' \in C\ [c \neq \emptyset \wedge c \subseteq c']$

In the given model, the root of a commitment space is its intersection, provided that it is nonempty; we will write $\surd C$ instead of $\cap C$. The update of a commitment space C with a regular speech act A then can be defined as in (13), and illustrated as in Fig. 2.

(13) $C + A = \{c \in C \mid \surd C + A \subseteq c\}$

Now, denegation of a speech act A can be represented as excluding the speech act A from a commitment space C. The resulting set of commitment states is a commitment space, with the same root as the original commitment space, cf. (14) and illustrated in Fig. 3.

(14) $C + {\sim}A = C—\{c \mid \exists c'[c' + A] \subseteq c\}$

Cohen and Krifka (2011) assume a less restrictive version of denegation: $C + {\sim}A = C + A$, the complement of $C + A$. This is because denegations of speech acts

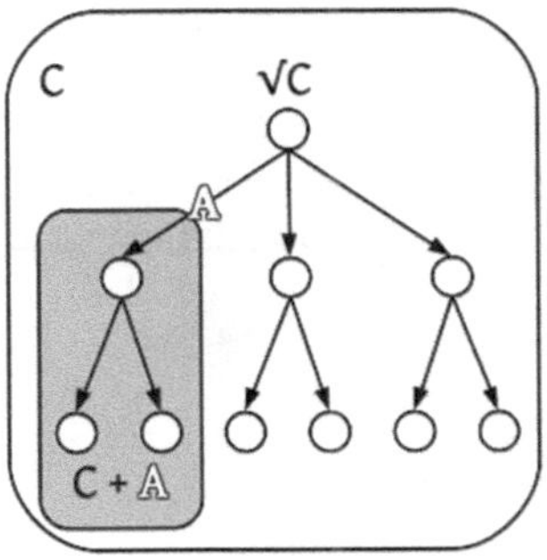

Fig. 2 Update of commitment space C with speech act A; $\surd C$: root of C

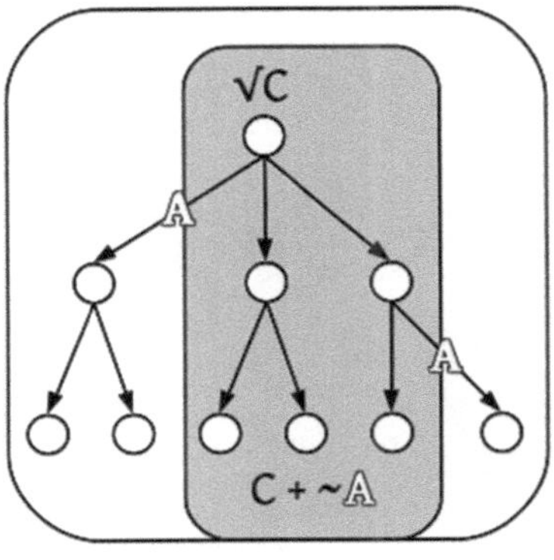

Fig. 3 Denegation of commitment space with ~A

can be retracted: *I don't promise to come. But if you really insist, I might change my mind.* However, performing A after a denegation of A can also be considered a case of nonmonotonic update, similar to asserting that it is not raining after asserting that it is raining, due to a change of mind. So, a stronger version of denegation appears to be justified, and it will be assumed here.

One might ask here why denegation is expressed by the same morpheme as propositional negation, namely, *not* or *n't*, clitized to the highest auxiliary. This is part of a more general phenomenon: Expressions that are used to express speech acts can often also be used to describe speech acts (cf. Krifka 2001a). In the case at hand, we can describe (11) as *the speaker did not promise to come.*

Denegation obviously is not a simple move in the speech act game, which is reflected by the fact that it does not change the root of a commitment space. But it restricts the admissible future moves. It is as if, in a game of chess, a stronger player promises the weaker player not to use the queen. As a restriction on future moves, it is a **meta speech act** (cf. Cohen and Krifka 2011). Such restrictions of future conversational moves can be expressed in a wide variety of ways—for example, *I wouldn't bother you further if you give me one last hint to solve this puzzle.* This is because we can freely talk about conversational moves, just as we can talk about other things in the world. But I would like to claim that denegation is a somewhat special way to talk about conversation; it can be given a particularly simple interpretation, similar to conjunction and conditionalization of speech acts. Hence, it should be part of the speech act algebra.

Commitment spaces develop during conversation. This is captured by assuming **commitment space developments** as the proper structures at which speech acts are interpreted. A commitment space development is a **sequence** of commitment spaces $\langle C_0, C_1, \ldots, C_n \rangle$, where C_n is the current commitment space, and $C_0, \ldots C_{n-1}$ are the preceding commitment spaces. The update of a commitment space development by a speech act is then defined as in (15), and illustrated in Fig. 4.

Fig. 4 Commitment space development

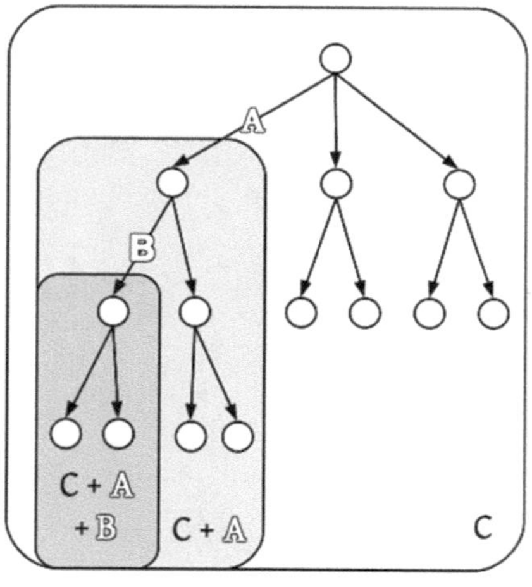

(15) $\langle ..., C\rangle + A = \langle ..., C, C + A\rangle$

The notion of commitment space development allows us to record every move in the conversational game. It might very well be that this representation is too fine grained; ultimately, only the last few moves in a commitment state development are accessible for straightforward discourse manipulation, and everything else is collapsed into the last commitment space. We will be concerned here with the phenomena that need to look back just one step (namely, the REJECT operation discussed below). But there are strategies of discourse development that clearly need to look farther back, e.g., the discourse trees involving contrastive topics in Büring (2003).

Commitment space developments also distinguish different paths that lead to the same commitments and to the same commitment spaces. The updates of a commitment state do not form a tree; that is, it might be that $c + A + B = c + B + A$, depending on the context-sensitivity of the acts A and B. Consequently, update of commitment spaces do not form a tree either; it might be that $C + A + B = C + B + A$. However, commitment state developments record these different ways of reaching the same commitment state, or commitment space: The developments $\langle C, C + A, C + A + B\rangle$ and $\langle C, C + B, C + B + A\rangle$ are different.

4 Assertions and the Notion of Common Ground

In the preceding section, we have laid the grounds by introducing the notions of commitment states, commitment space, and commitment space development. We now can turn to the treatment of specific speech acts. In this section, we will deal with assertions and various ways to react to them.

I assume that assertion expresses not one, but two commitments. In asserting a proposition, the speaker first expresses a commitment to the proposition, and then the speaker calls on the addressee to be also committed to that proposition, with the result that the proposition becomes part of the common ground. Here, I would like to propose that this is a two-stage process.

In the first move, the **speaker expresses a commitment** to stand behind the proposition asserted. That is, the speaker is to be held responsible for the truth of the proposition. This means that the speaker has to provide evidence for its truth, if asked for, and can be blamed to be a liar if the asserted proposition turns out to be false. I will write "$[S_1: \varphi]$" for "S_1 is liable for the truth of φ." We could also specify the addressee of this liability, which will be skipped here.

In the second move, the speaker expresses an expectation that the **addressee accepts the truth** of φ, that is, to treat it as **common ground**, as part of what the interlocutors take to be true, and of which they mutually know that they take to be true. This component of assertions has been stressed, e.g., by Farkas and Bruce (2010).

Here, it will be implemented in the following way: For each commitment state c, there is a common ground CG(c) that consists of a set of propositions that are mutually taken to be true. This set CG(c) contains all elements of c, that is, all commitments that are present in c. For example, after S_1 asserts φ, the commitment [S_1: φ] will become an element of c, and it will also be an element of CG(c), as it is mutually known that S_1 is committed to C. In general, we have:

(16) $c \subseteq CG(c)$

Furthermore, a proposition φ may become part of the common ground if one speaker asks the other to treat it as such. I will write "[$\varphi \in$ CG]" to express the commitment to treat φ as part of the common ground of the commitment state that this commitment is added to. As the common ground is shared between all speakers, reference to particular speakers can be omitted. But there is something special with the commitment [$\varphi \in$ CG]: If this is in a commitment state, and hence in the common ground of this commitment state, the proposition φ itself becomes part of the common ground of this commitment state.

(17) If [$\varphi \in$ CG] $\in$ c, then $\varphi \in$ CG(c)

There are other ways in which propositions may become part of the common ground—by accommodation or by being part of the shared cultural and world knowledge of the participants. We might be tempted to also assume that propositions that are easily inferrable are part of the common ground. But notice that the common ground is not closed under logical inference—this would be beyond the computational capacity of humans. Accepting easily inferrable propositions as part of the common ground will, by transitivity, lead to such super human common grounds. For this reason, I will assume that the common ground just contains things that are made explicit in the discourse, by commitments, by presuppositions, and by conventional and perhaps some conversational implicatures, such as scalar implicatures.

One requirement of the common ground is that it stays **consistent**. In particular, it is ruled out that a proposition φ and commitments like [S: $\neg\varphi$] or [S: BEL($\neg\varphi$)] are jointly part of the common ground. Furthermore, updating c with [$\varphi \in$ CG] comes with a **novelty condition**, namely that φ is not part of CG(c) already; otherwise, this request would be superfluous. I see this as a pragmatic condition following from Grice's maxim of relevance, and not as a strict semantic requirement for the interpretation of assertions.

With the condition that commitment states are contained in their common grounds (cf. (16)), what follows could well be formulated in terms of this extended notion of common ground. This will not be done here in order to highlight the role played by the commitments of the speakers, but everything that stated in the following could be rephrased in this way.

I will not go into details of syntax or prosody in the current paper, except for a few points. In particular, I will assume that propositions are reflected on the level of a syntactic category TP, which then are turned into speech acts by illocutionary operators, for which I assume a syntactic category Force Phrase, or ForceP (in the spirit of Rizzi 1997). The syntactic structure of an assertion then is as indicated in the following example:

(18) $[_{\text{ForceP}}\ [_{\text{ForceP'}}$ *ASS* $[_{\text{TP}}$ *there is a vegetarian restaurant here*]]]

This corresponds to the proposed structure of sentence radical and illocutionary operator in Stenius (1967), where the sentence radical is the TP, and the illocutionary operator is *ASS*. In addition, prosodic features express certain ways how sentences are interpreted in conversation. Here, I will make use of the tonal analysis of prosody of the TOBI system, which distinguishes between nuclear stresses like H* and L*, and edge tones for prosodic phrases like L-/H- and into national phrases like L% and H%, respectively.

The two steps that are involved in an assertion will be implemented as follows. Assume that S_1 utters an expression $[_{\text{ForceP}}$ *ASS* $[_{\text{TP}}\ \varphi]_{\text{H*}}]$ to S_2. With the declarative clause syntax (the syntactic operator *ASS*), the speaker S_1 expresses the commitment to the proposition, $[S_1: \varphi]$. The second commitment, $[\varphi \in \text{CG}]$, that the asserted proposition φ should become part of the common ground, is due to prosody, in particular the nuclear stress H* (cf. Pierrehumbert and Hirschberg 1990, Truckenbrodt 2012). Recall that $c + [\varphi \in \text{CG}]$ implicates that φ is not part of the common ground yet, $\varphi \notin \text{CG(c)}$. The nuclear accent H* stands in paradigmatic variation to L*, which does not express the condition $c + [\varphi \in \text{CG}]$, which can mean, among others, that S_1 thinks that φ is already part of the common ground, and that S_1 just reminds S_2 about it, as in (20) (notice that L* + L- will result in a rise after L*).

(19) *There's a vegeTArian REStaurant around here.*
H* H* L- L%

(20) *Of course we can find a decent place to eat. Just remember!*
There's a vegeTArian REStaurant around here.
L* L* L- L%

The position of the H* accents (there can be more than one of them) depend on the focus of the assertion, which is used to indicate alternatives (cf. Jacobs 1984 for the assumption that illocutionary operators can bind focus, and Rooth 1992 for the concept of alternatives). Even though this is of major importance for how discourse works, it will not be of special concern in this paper, to keep things simple.

Combining the two steps involved in assertions in one operator ASSERT, the proposed analysis of assertions can be rendered as follows:

(21)
$$\begin{aligned}
&\langle \ldots, C\rangle + \text{ASSERT}_{S1,S2}(\varphi)\\
&= \langle \ldots, C\rangle + [S_1{:}\ \varphi] + [\varphi \in \text{CG}]\\
&= \langle \ldots, C, C + [S_1{:}\ \varphi], C + [S_1{:}\varphi] + [\varphi \in \text{CG}]\rangle\\
&= \langle \ldots, C, \{c \in C \mid \sqrt{C} \cup \{[S_1{:}\ \varphi]\} \subseteq c\},\\
&\qquad \{c \in C \mid \sqrt{C} \cup \{[S_1{:}\ \varphi]\} \cup \{[\varphi \in \text{CG}]\} \subseteq c\}\rangle
\end{aligned}$$

The representation of the resulting speech act sequence can be illustrated as in Fig. 5. The initial commitment space is used to construct an intermediate commitment space with the condition $[S_1{:}\ \varphi]$ at its root, which differs from the root $\sqrt{C}$

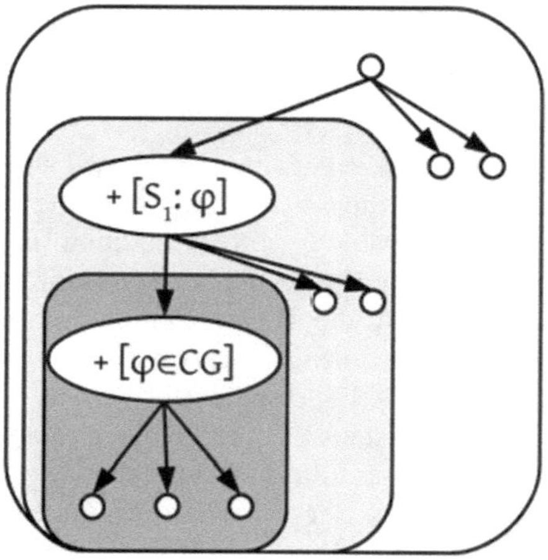

Fig. 5 Assertion of φ

by the liability of S_1 for φ. This is then followed by the commitment state with $[\varphi \in \text{CG}]$ at its root, which means that the proposition φ is now introduced in the common ground of the commitment state.

5 Reactions to Assertions: Acceptance and Rejections

The final commitment change in (21), $+ [\varphi \in \text{CG}]$, imposes a commitment on the interlocutors, to treat φ as common ground. Of course, the addressee S_2 has a say in this. S_2 can agree with this proposed commitment change, by uttering *aha*, or *okay*, or *mhm*, by nodding, or implicitly by lack of any reaction that would involve a rejection. This reaction by S_2–S_1 will be called **acceptance**, and to make things clear, I will propose an operation $\text{ACCEPT}_{S2,S1}$; it expresses that S_2 takes on the obligation imposed by S_1 on S_2 in the most recent conversational move:

(22) $\langle \ldots, C', C \rangle + \text{ACCEPT}_{S2,S1} = \langle \ldots, C', C \rangle$,
provided that C differs from C′ insofar as it contains an obligation imposed on S_2.

The addressee can also **reject** the imposed obligation, for which I assume an operation REJECT:

(23) $\langle \ldots, C', C \rangle + \text{REJECT}_{S2,S1} = \langle \ldots, C', C, [C' - C] \rangle$
provided that C differs from C′ insofar as it contains an obligation imposed on S_2.

Rejections have to be expressed overtly, of course, but there is no simple expression that expresses rejection and nothing else. The addressee S_2 must always indicate some reason for the rejection; this can be seen as a conventionalized

Fig. 6 REJECT + ¬BELIEVE(φ)

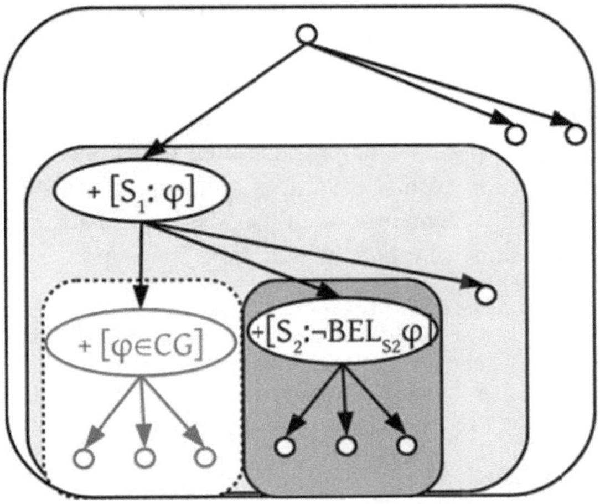

consequence from the general cooperation principle in communication. For example, S_2 can assert *I don't believe that.* The commitment [S_2: $\neg BEL_{S2}(\varphi)$] cannot be added to the commitment space C (effectively, to its root $\sqrt{C}$), as this would lead to a contradictory common ground, containing both φ and [S_2: $\neg BEL_{S2}(\varphi)$]. Hence, a rejection has to be performed first before the speaker can assert *I don't believe that.* See Fig. 6 for illustration.

Notice that it is just the last move that is rejected by the addressee. The first move, that the speaker is liable for the proposition, is not affected. This is to capture the fact that after a rejection, the first speaker remains liable for the proposition asserted; he or she could be accused to be a liar, for example, if it turns out to be false. We can express this due to the factorization of assertion into two components, one for the liability of the speaker for the proposition, one for the speaker's attempt to make the addressee treat the proposition as common ground.

We can explain Moore's paradox, the oddity of assertions like *It is raining but I don't believe it,* as follows: The second clause is inconsistent with the commitment expressed by the first clause, [$\varphi \in$ CG], and the reason for this lies with the speaker, the instigator of the action. In contrast, it is possible to construct valid instances of assertions like *It is raining, but you don't believe it* or *It is raining, even if you don't believe it*: The speaker still calls on the addressee to add the proposition to the common ground, but indicates that the addressee will reject this, resulting in the sole commitment of the speaker.

The common ground of the resulting commitment state in Fig. 6 contains the propositions [S_1: φ] and [S_2: $BEL_{S2}(\neg\varphi)$], but not the proposition φ itself. Hence, we distinguish between commitments of all participants, and discourse commitments for particular individuals (cf. also Hamblin 1971; Ginzburg 1995; Farkas and Bruce 2010).

Besides acceptance, there is another reaction to an assertion in which the addressee indicates his or her own commitment to the proposition in question.

This I take to be distinct from mere acceptance, and I will call this move **confirmation**. I assume that confirmations work typically by picking up a **propositional discourse referent** that was introduced by the assertion of the first speaker (see e.g. Asher 1993 for propositional discourse referents, and Krifka 2013 for a treatment of response particles as propositional anaphors). This discourse referent refers to the proposition of that assertion; syntactically, it corresponds to the sentence radical, the TP. Evidence for such propositional discourse referents comes from anaphoric expressions like *that*, which pick them up, as in the following example:

(24) S_1: *There is a vegetarian restaurant here.*
$\text{ASSERT}_{S1,S2}$('there is a vegetarian restaurant around here'),
sentence radical introduces a discourse referent
φ = 'there is a vegetarian restaurant around here'
S_2: *I believe that too.*
that picks up φ.

This propositional discourse referent is also taken up with reactions like *That's right*, as well as with the simple answers *Yes* or *Right*. I propose that *yes* has the same interpretation as *that's right*, that is, it **refers to a salient propositional discourse referent** and **asserts its proposition**. Cf. Kramer and Rawlins (2009) for an alternative view assumes that *yes* and *no* are remnants of ellipsis of full clauses like [*yes*].

(25) S_2 to S_1: *Yes./That's right.*
$\text{ASSERT}_{S2,S1}(\varphi)$, where φ: a salient propositional discourse referent.

(26) a. S_1: *There is a vegetarian restaurant here.*
introduces discourse referent for proposition φ
$\langle \ldots, C\rangle + \text{ASSERT}_{S1,S2}\ (\varphi)$
$= \langle \ldots, C\rangle + [S_1\text{: }\varphi] + [\varphi \in \text{CG}_{S1,S2}]$
$= \langle \ldots, C, C + [S_1\text{: }\varphi], C + [S_1\text{: }\varphi] + [\varphi \in \text{CG}_{S1,S2}]\rangle$, abbreviated as Γ
b. S_2: *Yes./That's right.*
$\Gamma + \text{ASSERT}_{S2,S1}(\varphi)$
$= \Gamma + [S_2\text{:}\varphi]\ (+ [\varphi \in \text{CG}_{S1,S2}])$

The last move, that the interlocutors treat φ as part of the common ground, is already satisfied, and hence can systematically be dropped for the interpretation of *Yes*. This is illustrated in Fig. 7. The common ground of the root of the resulting commitment space includes the commitments [S_1: φ], [S_2: φ], and the proposition φ itself.

Previous assertions can also be negated, or **denied**. Again, this is different from mere rejection by statements like *I don't believe that,* that do not necessarily express a commitment either way toward the proposition. With a **denial**, the addressee expresses a commitment toward the negation of the proposition that was asserted by the first speaker (cf. van der Sandt and Maier 2003). But just as the reaction *I don't believe that*, denials require a prior rejection of the conversational move of the first speaker, in particular, the attempt to make the second speaker treat the proposition as common ground. The reason is that φ and [S_2: $\neg\varphi$] cannot be both part of the CG

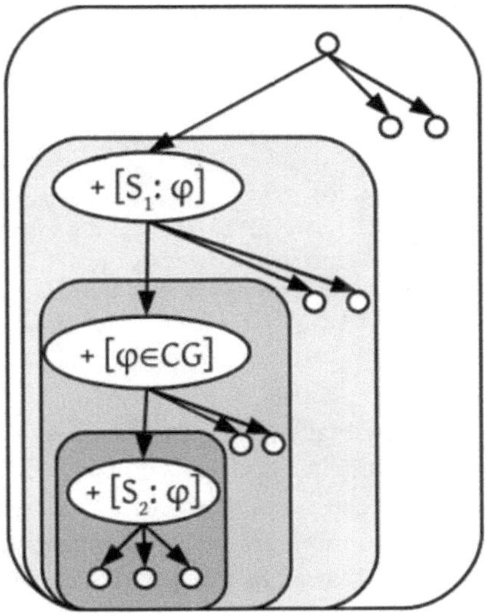

Fig. 7 Confirmation with *yes* and *no*

of a commitment state, hence a prior commitment [$\varphi \in$ CG] has to be rejected first before the commitment [S_2: $\neg\varphi$] can be entered.

We assume that the answer particle *no* picks out the propositional discourse referent introduced by the precedent sentence and asserts its negation, ASSERT ($\neg\varphi$). The use of *no* and equivalent phrases as denial is illustrated in (27) and in Fig. 8.

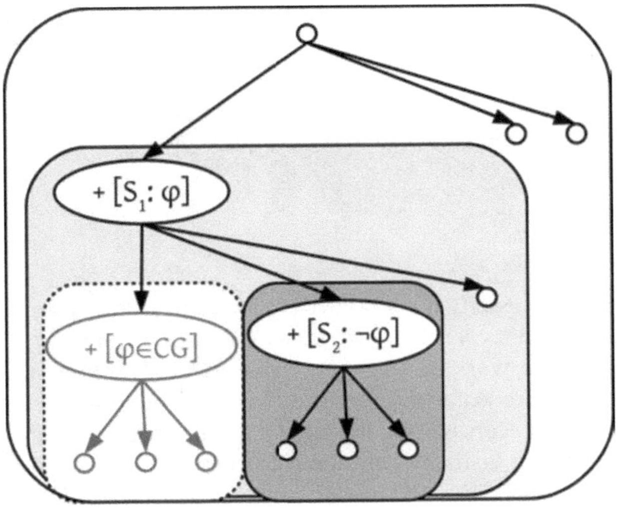

Fig. 8 Negation of an asserted proposition

(27) a. S_1: *There is a vegetarian restaurant here.*
introduces discourse referent for proposition
φ = 'there is a vegetarian restaurant around here'.
$\langle \ldots, C\rangle$ + $ASSERT_{S1,S2}$ (φ)
$\langle \ldots, C\rangle$ + [S_1: φ] + [$\varphi \in CG_{S1,S2}$]
= $\langle \ldots$, C, C + [S_1: φ], C + [S_1: φ] + [$\varphi \in$ CG]$\rangle$, abbreviated as Γ
b. S_2: *No./That's not true./No, there isn't.*
Γ + $ASSERT_{S2,S1}(\neg\varphi)$: not interpretable,
due to inconsistency of [$\varphi \in$ CG] and [S_2: $\neg\varphi$],
hence prior reject operation: Γ + $REJECT_{S2}$ + $ASSERT_{S2,S1}(\neg\varphi)$.
= $\langle \ldots, C\rangle$ + [S_1: φ] + [$\varphi \in CG_{S1,S2}$] + $REJECT_{S2}$ + [S_2:φ]
= $\langle \ldots$, C, C + [S_1: φ], C + [S_1: φ] + [$\varphi \in$ CG], * C + [S_1: φ],
C + [S_1: φ] + [S_2:$\neg\varphi$]$\rangle$

Notice that at the position marked * in the last line, the REJECT operation removes the last update, with [$\varphi \in$ CG], creating a commitment state at which then [S_2: $\neg\varphi$] can be interpreted. In a diagram:

The common ground of the resulting commitment state contains both [S_1: φ] and [S_2: $\neg\varphi$], that is, S_1 is liable for φ, and S_2 is liable for $\neg\varphi$. It will not contain φ or $\neg\varphi$. This is not a direct contradiction; it just means that φ is not part of the common ground. Often, one of the two liabilities will eventually have to be retracted if the participants choose to argue about this issue. Alternatively, the participants can agree to disagree, and turn to other points.

6 Reactions to Assertions of Negated Sentences

Before we turn to questions, it is worthwhile to consider affirmations and denials of assertions that are based on negated propositions, as in the following case:

(28) S_1: *There is no vegetarian restaurant around here.*

The reactions to such assertions is quite puzzling, both within a language and across languages. Consider the following answer options for English:

(29) a. S_2: *No, there isn't.*
b. S_2: *Yes, there isn't.*
c. S_2: *No, there is!*
d. S_2: *Yes, there is!*

Agreement to S_1's assertion in (28) is typically expressed by *no,* sometimes with a reduced clause, as in *no there isn't*, cf. (29)(a). But interestingly, it is also possible to express affirmation with *yes* and a clarifying reduced form as well, as in *Yes, there isn't* (cf. experimental data in Brasoveanu et al. 2013). Denial of S_1's assertion can also be expressed by *no* and *yes* with appropriate reduced forms.

This is not the place to discuss and compare the proposals that have been offered to account for this behavior of *yes* and *no* (see e.g. Cooper and Ginzburg 2011 and Brasoveanu et al. 2013 for recent proposals). Rather, I would like to sketch an account in which *yes* and *no* have exactly the same meaning as with non-negated antecedents. For this, it has to be assumed that clauses with sentential negations introduce **two** propositional discourse referents, one for the unnegated proposition, one for the negated propositions. Assuming that a negated declarative sentence radical has the structure $[_{\text{NegP}} \ldots [_{\text{TP}} \ldots]]$, where both TP and NegP are interpreted as propositions, then both NegP and TP should introduce propositional discourse referents, where the discourse referent of the NegP refers to the negation of the discourse referent of the TP. Evidence for the introduction of two propositional discourse referents comes from examples like the following. In (30), in (a) *that* picks up the TP proposition 'two plus two is five', and in (b) *that* picks up the NegP proposition ¬'two plus two is five'. In (31), *that* picks up the TP proposition 'Bill came to the party' in (a) and the NegP proposition ¬'Bill came to the party' in (b).

(30) a. *Two plus two isn't five. That would be a contradiction.*
b. *Two plus two isn't five. Everyone should know that.*

(31) a. *Bill didn't come to the party, even though everyone had expected that.*
b. *Bill didn't come to the party, and everyone had expected that.*

The answer patterns in (29) now can be explained under the assumptions that (28) introduces two propositional discourse referents, one the negation of the other, and that *yes* and *no* can apply to either one of these discourse referents.

(32) S_1: *There isn't a vegetarian restaurant around here.*
$[_{\text{ForceP}} [_{\text{Force}'}$ *ASS* $[_{\text{NegP}}$ *there*$_i$ $[_{\text{NegP}'}$ *is*$_j$*-n't* $[_{\text{TP}}$ e_i e_j *a vegetarian restaurant here*$]]]]]$
Introduces TP discourse referent φ = 'there is a vegetarian restaurant around here',
introduces NegP discourse referent ψ = ¬'there is a veg. restaurant around here'
$\langle \ldots, C\rangle + \text{ASSERT}_{S1,S2}(\psi) = \langle \ldots, C, C + [S_1{:}\ \psi], C + [S_1{:}\ \psi] + [\psi \in CG]\rangle$, abbr. as Γ.

Let us first consider the two agreeing reactions. They just differ in that *no* picks up the TP discourse referent φ, and *yes* picks up the NegP discourse referent ψ.

(33) a. S_2: *No, there isn't.*
$\Gamma + \text{ASSERT}_{S2,S1}(\neg\varphi)$
$= \langle \ldots, C, C + [S_1{:}\ \psi], C + [S_1{:}\ \psi] + [\psi \in CG], C + [S_1{:}\ \psi] + [\psi \in CG] + [S_2{:}\ \neg\varphi]\rangle$
b. S_2: *Yes, there isn't.*
$\Gamma + \text{ASSERT}_{S2,S2}(\psi)$
$= \langle \ldots, C, C + [S_1{:}\ \psi], C + [S_1{:}\ \psi] + [\psi \in CG], C + [S_1{:}\ \psi] + [\psi \in CG] + [S_2{:}\ \psi]\rangle$

The net effect of these two reaction is the same, as $\psi = \neg\varphi$. It is just that *no* picks out the TP discourse referent introduced by the S_1's assertion, and negates that proposition, whereas *yes* picks up the NegP discourse referent.

The two disagreeing reactions require a prior REJECT operation, which is visible by the protest prosody of such answers. Again, as $\neg\varphi = \psi$, the two changes of commitment spaces are effectively the same.

(34) a. S_2: *Yes, there is!*
Γ + $\text{REJECT}_{S2,S1}$ + $\text{ASSERT}_{S2,S1}(\varphi)$
= ⟨…, C, C+[S_1: ψ], C+[S_1: ψ]+[ψ ∈ CG], C+[S_1: ψ], C+[S_1: ψ]+[S_2: φ]+ [φ ∈ CG]⟩

b. S_2: *No, there is!*
Γ + $\text{REJECT}_{S2,S1}$ + $\text{ASSERT}_{S2,S1}(\neg\psi)$
= ⟨…, C, C + [S_1: ψ], C + [S_1: ψ] + [ψ ∈ CG], C + [S_1: ψ], C + [S_1: ψ] + [S_2: ¬ψ] + [¬ψ ∈ CG]⟩

While all these reactions are possible, *No there isn't* in (33)(a) appears to be the most straightforward; we can even skip the clarifying elliptic clause *There isn't* in this case. The reason is that the competing interpretation of *no* in (34)(b) is complex, as it involves the negation of the propositional discourse referent ψ, which is already negated. So, this interpretation of *no* is blocked by the simpler interpretation (33)(a). There is no clear blocking relationship between the *yes* answers. As the expression of interpretation (34) by *no* is blocked by the simpler interpretation of *no* as in (33), one could perhaps assume that (34) would rather be interpreted as *yes*, which should surface as a possible form according to the rules of Bidirectional Optimality Theory (cf. Jäger 2002), but it seems that it doesn't quite do that. In any case, as *yes* is ambiguous even after pragmatic reasoning, clarifying the meaning by an elliptical clause appears to be required.

As Brasoveanu et al. (2013) argue, clauses with negative determiners like *There is no vegetarian restaurant around here* have essentially the same syntactic structure as (32), and consequently induce the same answer patterns. They also point out that the syntactic form, and not just the interpretation, matters. For example, while *John didn't pass the test* induces the answer pattern discussed here, the logically equivalent assertion *John failed the test* is treated like the assertion of an ordinary non-negated proposition, and answers like *no, he did* or *yes, he didn't* are impossible.

It is well known that languages differ in their set of denial particles. For example, *doch* in German can be interpreted as REJECT + ASSERT(φ); this blocks the use of the particles *ja* and *nein* in (34), see (35).

(35) S_1: *Es gibt hier kein vegetarisches Restaurant.*
'There is no vegetarian restaurant here'.
S_2: *Doch (es gibt eines).* 'DOCH, there is one'.
(?) *Ja, es gibt eines.* 'Yes, there is one'.
(?) *Nein, es gibt eines.* 'No, there is one'.

In Romanian, according to Farkas and Bruce (2010), denials are marked by the particle *ba*, which is combined with the particles *nu* 'no' and *da* 'yes'. They illustrate the reactions to assertions as follows:

(36) a. S_1: *Ana a plecat.* 'Ana left'.
S_2: *Da./Da, a plecat.* 'Yes.'/'Yes, she left'.
S_2: *Ba nu, n-a plecat./*Nu, n-a plecat.* 'No, she didn't'.

b. S_1: *Ana nu a plecat.* 'Ana didn't leave'.
S_2: *Nu, n-a plecat.* 'No, she didn't leave'.
S_2: *Ba da./Ba a plecat./Ba da, a plecat.* 'You're wrong, she did'.

This answer pattern follows if we analyze *da* as ASSERT(φ), *nu* as ASSERT ($\neg\varphi$), and *ba* as an expression of REJECT. That is, *ba da* is REJECT + ASSERT (φ), and *ba nu* is REJECT + ASSERT($\neg\varphi$).

The well-known agreement/disagreement systems have just two particles. This is the case with Japanese *hai* and *iie*. In the current theoretical framework, *hai* expresses AGREE + ASSERT(ω) and *iie* expresses REJECT + ASSERT(ω), where ω is a propositional discourse referent—either a TP discourse referent like φ above, or a NegP discourse referent like ψ above.

7 Questions and Answers

We now turn to questions. Questions differ from assertions in two respects. First, they have a more complex sentence radical. There are two prominent families of theories, one assuming **functions into propositions**, the other assuming **sets of propositions**; see Krifka (2011) for an overview. While I think there are good theoretical reasons to use the former (cf. Krifka 2001b), here I will assume the simpler proposition set format, which was proposed in Hamblin (1973) and much subsequent work, e.g., Rooth (1992). The underlying idea is that the sentence radical of a question denotes the set of all propositions that are possible congruent answers to that question, regardless whether they are true or false. I assume that the syntactic category of **question radicals** is TPQ, as question radicals have a different syntax (e.g., they express *wh*-movement) and differ from assertion radicals in their semantic type (set of propositions instead of propositions). We find this sentence radical in **embedded questions** with *know* as the embedding predicate. Sentences with this structure can be interpreted along the following lines:

(37) a. *John knows where there is a vegetarian restaurant.*
b. Question sentence radical: *where there is a vegetarian restaurant.*
{'there is a vegetarian restaurant at l'| l $\in$ LOCATION}
c. *John knows* φ: $\forall p \in \varphi$[p is true $\rightarrow$ John knows that p]

That is, question-embedding *know* is derived from proposition-embedding *know*. (37)(c) states that *John knows* φ iff John knows the true propositions in φ, the set of propositions to which φ is interpreted. We can explain why *believe* does not embed questions: In the environment where 'know' is interpreted in (37)(c), the proposition p is true, allowing for the factive predicate 'know' instead of the non-factive *believe*. Also, we can derive that (37) implicates that there is a vegetarian restaurant: The propositions in the sentence radical are all of the form 'there is a vegetarian restaurant at l', where l is a location (where 'no where' is not a location), and the universal quantification in (37)(c) is understood to be nonvacuous. There is a stronger notion of knowing which also entails that for all false propositions p in φ, John knows that $\neg$p (cf. Groenendijk and Stokhof 1984, and subsequent work).

Root questions are formed by an illocutionary operator *QU* that takes a question sentence radical TPQ as an argument. In English, the *wh*-element moves to the specifier of the ForceP, and the head of the ForceP has to be occupied by an auxiliary or copula verb, leading to the following structure:

(38) $[_{\text{ForceP}}$ *where*$_i$ $[_{\text{ForceP}'}$ *QU-is*$_j$ $[_{\text{TPQ}}$ e$_i$ [*there* e$_j$ *a vegetarian restaurant* e$_i$]]]]

The second point in which questions differ from assertions is that with a question, the **speaker imposes on the addressee a restriction on future continuations** of the conversation. Only those continuations are admissible in which **the addressee makes an assertion that answers the question**. If φ is a question sentence radical, then a root question $[_{\text{ForceP}}\ QU\ [_{\text{TPQ}}\ \varphi]]$ is interpreted as follows:

(39) $\langle \ldots, C\rangle + QU_{S1,S2}(\varphi)$
$= \langle \ldots, C, C + QU_{S1,S2}(\varphi)\rangle$
$= \langle \ldots, C, \{\sqrt{C}\} \cup \{c \in C \mid \exists p \in \varphi[\sqrt{C} + [S_2\text{: } p]] \subseteq c\}\rangle$

The commitment state development will be extended by adding a new commitment state that consists of the root $\sqrt{C}$ of the previous commitment state C, and all the commitment states equal or following the update of the root with the liability of the second speaker for a proposition p, where p is a possible answer to the question. This is illustrated in the following example, with a root question that has undergone movement of the auxiliary *is*.

(40) S_1, to S_2: *Where is there a vegetarian restaurant?*
$\langle \ldots, C\rangle + QU_{S1,S2}(\{$'there is a vegetarian restaurant at l' $\mid l \in \text{LOCATION}\})$

Assuming that there are three relevant locations, Elm Street, Oak Street, and Maple Street, this amounts to (41), graphically represented in Fig. 9.

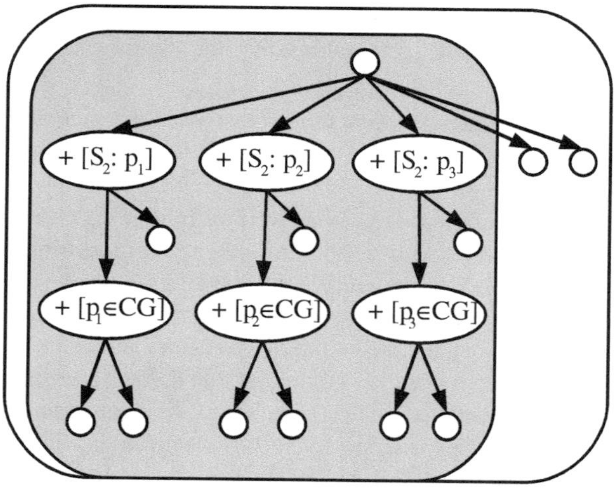

Fig. 9 Asking a constituent question

(41) $\langle ..., C\rangle + QU_{S1,S2}(\{$‘there is a veg. rest. on Elm St.’, ‘... Oak St.’, ‘... Maple St.’$\})$
$= \langle ..., C, \{\surd C\} \cup \{c \in C \mid \surd C + [S_2$: ‘... on Elm St.’$] \subseteq c$
$\vee \surd C + [S_2$: ‘... on Oak St.’$] \subseteq c$
$\vee \surd C + [S_2$: ‘... on Maple St.’$] \subseteq c\}\rangle$, abbreviated as Γ

The addressee S_2 can reject this imposition, e.g., by *I don't know*. This can be modeled, as usual, by REJECT followed by an assertion of the proposition ‘S_2 does not know where there is a vegetarian restaurant’. But the regular way to continue is for S_2 to make one of the assertions proposed by S_1, as specified in (42) and illustrated in Fig. 10. In doing so, S_2 will accept liability for one of the propositions, and in addition attempt to make it part of the common ground. The root $\surd C$ of the last commitment space is included here because the assertion by the second speaker has to be made with respect to that commitment state.

(42) S_2 to S_1: *There is a vegetarian restaurant on Oak street.*
$\Gamma + ASSERT_{S2,S1}(p_2)$,
$= \Gamma + [S_2: p_2] + [p_2 \in CG]$

The way how the proposition is referred to varies. There are term answers, like *On Elm street*, complete answers like *There is a vegetarian restaurant on Elm street*, or indirect answers, like *People say that there is a nice one on Elm street.* I will not go into the details of such answers here, but instead turn to polarity questions.

The sentence radical of polarity questions denotes a set of two propositions, one the negation of the other. This is what we find in embedded questions headed by the complementizer *whether*:

(43) *John knows whether there is a vegetarian restaurant around here.*
Sentence radical: {‘there is a veg. rest. here’, ¬‘there is a veg. rest. here’}
$\forall p \in$ {‘there is a veg. rest. here, ¬‘there is a veg. rest. here’}
[p is true $\rightarrow$ John knows p]

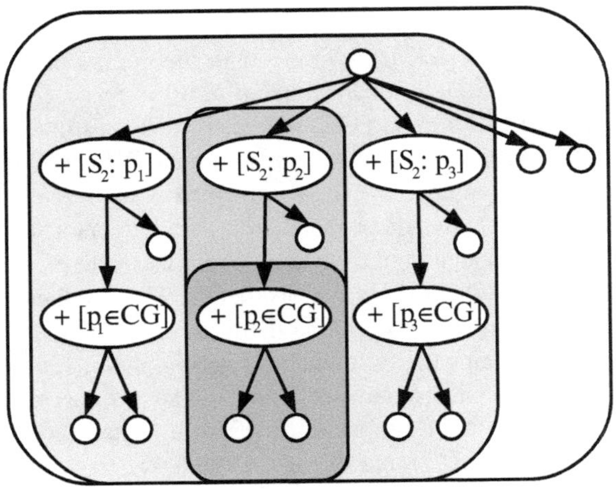

Fig. 10 Answering a constituent question

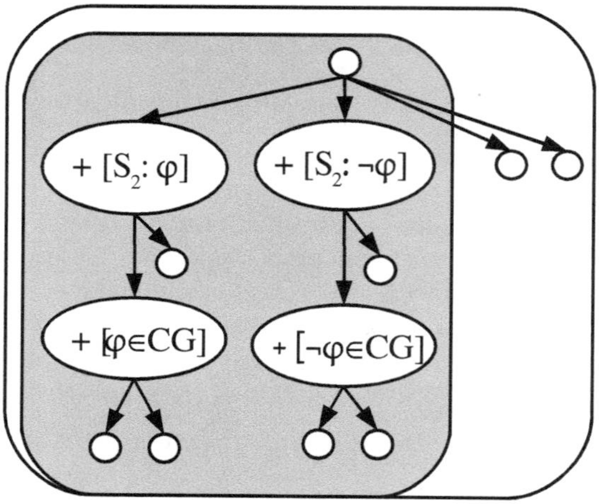

Fig. 11 Polarity question; QU($\{\varphi, \neg\varphi\}$)

The interpretation rule for polarity questions as speech acts is just the same as for constituent questions, cf. (39). Notice that, syntactically, we have auxiliary inversion, and *wh*-element *whether* drops. The following example and Fig. 11 illustrate this.

(44) S_1 to S_2: *Is there a vegetarian restaurant around here?*
With φ = 'there is a vegetarian restaurant around here':
$\langle \ldots, C\rangle + QU_{S1,S2}(\{\varphi, \neg\varphi\})$
$= \langle \ldots, C, \{\surd C\} \cup \{c \in C \mid \exists p \in \{\varphi, \neg\varphi\}[\surd C + S_2\text{: } p \subseteq c]\}\rangle$,
abbreviated as Γ.

Polarity questions can be rejected, but the categorical reaction to them is to answer them with *yes* or *no*. We can explain this by assuming that a question like *Is there a vegetarian restaurant here?* introduces a discourse referent for the proposition 'there is a vegetarian restaurant here'. If in the course of derivation of this question a TP [*there is a vegetarian restaurant here*] is formed, this is consistent with our previous treatment of assertions, where such TPs, as proposition-denoting expressions, introduce propositional discourse referents. We can indeed assume that the sentence radical of a polarity question is formed with the help of a TP and a wh-operator *whether* which takes a proposition p and delivers a set of propositions $\{p, \neg p\}$. This operator is spelled out as a complementizer with embedded questions but not in root questions. What is important is that the TP introduces a propositional discourse referent for p and not for $\neg$p, as there is no syntactic constituent corresponding to $\neg$p. This explains the following answering patterns; notice that *yes* and *no* pick up the propositional discourse referent, where *yes* asserts its proposition, and no asserts the negation of its proposition. This is just as with reactions to assertions. This is shown in (45) and in Figs. 12 and 13.

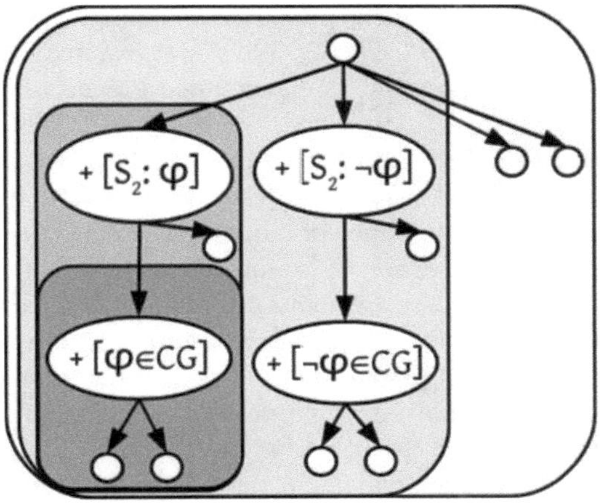

Fig. 12 Answer *Yes*

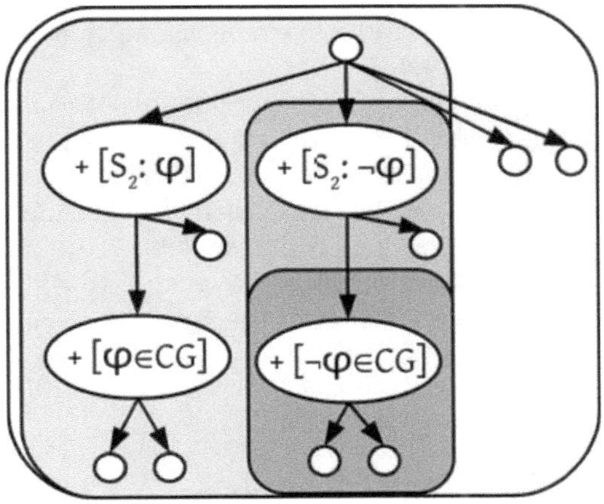

Fig. 13 Answer *No*

(45) S_1 to S_2: *Is there a vegetarian restaurant here?*
$[_{ForceP}$ $[_{ForceP'}$ *QU-is*$_i$ $[_{TPQ}$ $[_{TP}$ *there* e_i *a vegetarian restaurant here*]]]],
the TP introduces a propositional discourse referent
φ = 'there is a vegetarian restaurant here'
a. S_2: *Yes.*
$\Gamma + \text{ASSERT}_{S2,S1}(\varphi)$
$= \Gamma + [S_2\text{: } \varphi] + [\varphi \in \text{CG}_{S1,S2}]$
b. S_2: *No.*
$\Gamma + \text{ASSERT}_{S2,S1}(\neg\varphi)$
$= \Gamma + [S_2\text{: } \neg\varphi] + [\neg\varphi \in \text{CG}_{S1,S2}]$

It is worthwhile to point out a fundamental difference between assertions and questions. Assertions can be interpreted at the level of commitment states, c. If applied at commitment spaces C, they change the root $\sqrt{C}$, a commitment state. As such, assertions have an effect on the common ground of a commitment space, if we define the common ground of a commitment space as the common ground of its root: $CG(C) = CG(\surd C)$. We also can define the common ground of a commitment space development as the common ground of its last commitment space: $CG(\langle \ldots, C\rangle) = CG(C)$. In general, we will have: $CG(C) \neq CG(C + ASSERT(\varphi))$. Questions, on the other hand, cannot be interpreted at the level of commitment states, as they rather have an effect on the possible future development of commitment spaces. In our framework, questions do not change the root of a commitment space. With the exception of presuppositions or implicatures introduced by questions, the common ground remains the same: $CG(C) = CG(C + QU(\varphi))$. This reflects a distinction between **common ground content** and **common ground management** argued for in Krifka (2008): The common ground content is $CG(\Gamma)$, and operations on a commitment space development Γ that change $CG(\Gamma)$, like assertions, are operations on the common ground content. Common ground management, on the other hand, are operations that affect Γ without changing $CG(\Gamma)$. As we have seen, questions are one example of such operations; as questions may be indicated by the focus of assertions, this kind of focus contributes to common ground management as well. Another example is topic, which is arguable a speech act in its own right (cf. Krifka 2001a).

The treatment of questions proposed here also offers a straightforward account of certain shifts of indexical expressions such as the interpretation of evidential particles (cf. e.g. Zimmermann 2004 about German *wohl*, expressing uncertainty of speaker in assertions and uncertainty of addressee in questions) or so-called conjunct person marking (cf. Hale 1980 about Newari verb agreement, identifying the speaker with assertions and the addressee with questions). In the proposed system, questions are essentially assertions by the addressee, hence the indicated shifts appear quite natural.

8 Declarative Questions

We now turn to a type of question that comes with the syntax of declarative sentences, but whose prosody, with a final rise, indicates the question interpretation. Gunlogson (2002) calls them **declarative questions**.

(46) *There is a vegetarian restaurant here?*

Declarative questions differ from standard polarity questions insofar as they express a certain bias of the speaker. For example, in a job interview, a question like *Have you been convicted of a felony?* is fine, but a question like *You have been convicted of a felony?* is decidedly odd, as it suggests that there is evidence that the underlying proposition may well be true.

While the bias of declarative questions is generally acknowledged, it hasn't been discussed that the nature of the bias depends on the precise nature of the prosodic contour. With a simple rise (e.g., L* H- H%), the speaker has independent evidence that the proposition is true, assumes that the addressee has more definite knowledge, and wants to check with the addressee whether the proposition is indeed true. But such questions can also be uttered with a fall-rise, the so-called **incredulity contour** identified in Pierrehumbert and Hirschberg (1990), here assumed to be L* L- H%, here rendered with "!?." In this case, the speaker expresses doubt that the proposition is true, and challenges the addressee to assert it.

I assume that in either case, declarative questions can be rendered similar to polarity questions, except that they **propose only one continuation to the addressee**—the assertion of the proposition. We can call such questions **monopolar** questions, to distinguish them from the **bipolar** questions that are commonly assumed. The addressee can either take up this proposal by the first speaker and assert the proposition, for example with *yes*, or reject it and react with a different assertion, for example with *no*, which would assert the negation of the proposition.

How does this interpretation come about? I assume that declarative questions are exactly what their syntax tells us: They are assertions. At the same time, they are what their prosody tells us: Their final rise H%, together with the L* nuclear accent, marks them as questions. The final rise can be seen in the way suggested by Merin and Bartels (1997), as indicating that the speaker offers a choice to the addressee, whereas L* can be seen as indicating the lack of expression of the speaker that the addressee should take the proposition as part of the common ground.

There is no evidence for any question sentence radical in declarative questions. For example, declarative questions cannot be embedded; at least, *John knows (that) there is a vegetarian restaurant around here?* cannot be distinguished from a declarative question with an embedded proposition. Therefore, I assume that declarative questions are not expressed by QU, but by an operator **REQUEST**. This operator is **applied to a speech act** (a commitment change potential), not to a proposition, or set of proposition. If REQUEST(A) is performed at a commitment space development by a speaker S_1 to an addressee S_2, then S_1 restricts the continuations to those that start with a performance of A by the addressee, S_2.

(47) $\langle \ldots, C\rangle + \text{REQUEST}_{S1,S2}(A) = \langle \ldots, C, \{\surd C\} \cup C + A_{S2,S1}\rangle$

If A is an assertion, we have the following:

(48) $\langle \ldots, C\rangle + \text{REQUEST}_{S1,S2}(\text{ASS}(\varphi))$
$= \langle \ldots, C, \{\surd C\} \cup C + \text{ASS}_{S2,S1}(\varphi)\rangle$
$= \langle \ldots, C, \{\surd C\} \cup C + [S_2\text{: } \varphi]\rangle$

The conversational effect of a request of an assertion is illustrated in Fig. 14. Syntactically, a REQUEST act should contain another speech act, like an assertion. That is, we assume that ForceP can be recursive: $[_{\text{ForceP}}$ *REQUEST* $[_{\text{ForceP}}$ *ASS* $[_{\text{TP}}\ \varphi]]]$. I have assumed here that the REQUEST operator just embeds the effect of the *ASS* operator, that is, the commitment $[S_2\text{: } \varphi]$, as declarative questions lack the H* tone that is responsible for the second commitment, $[\varphi \in \text{CG}]$.

Fig. 14 Asking a declarative (monopolar) question

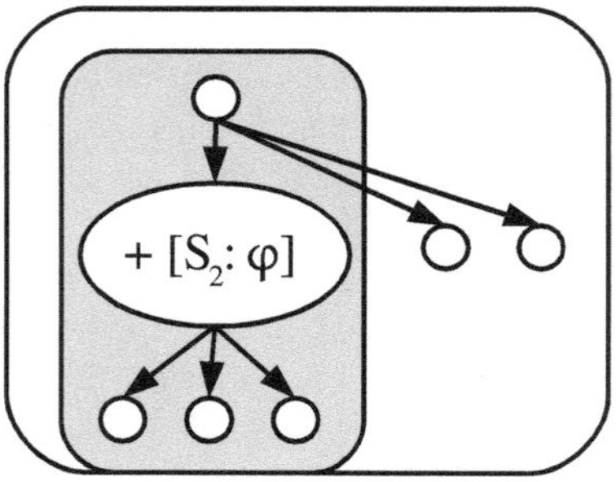

The reactions to a declarative question are illustrated in the following example, where *REQUEST* is realized by the specific prosodic contour, and does not have a syntactic exponent.

(49) S_1 to S_2: *There is a vegetarian restaurant here?*
REQUEST $[_{\text{ForceP}}\ [_{\text{ForceP}'}$ *ASS* $[_{\text{TP}}$ *there is a vegetarian restaurant here?*$]]]$
introduces φ = 'there is a vegetarian restaurant here'
$\langle ..., C\rangle + \text{REQUEST}_{S1,S2}(\text{ASS}(\varphi)) = \langle ..., C, \{\surd C\} \cup C + [S_2{:}\ \varphi]\rangle$, abbreviated as Γ
a. S_2 to S_1: *Yes.*
$\Gamma + [S_2{:}\ \varphi] + [\varphi \in \text{CG}]$
b. S_2 to S_1: *No.*
$\Gamma + \text{REJECT} + [S_2{:}\ \neg\varphi] + [\neg\varphi \in \text{CG}]$

These two answers are illustrated in Figs. 15 and 16.

The bias of declarative questions against a background in which φ and $\neg\varphi$ are considered equally plausible arises as follows: The speaker has a choice between a regular polarity question involving QU, which presents both options equally, and

Fig. 15 Answering a declarative question with *yes*

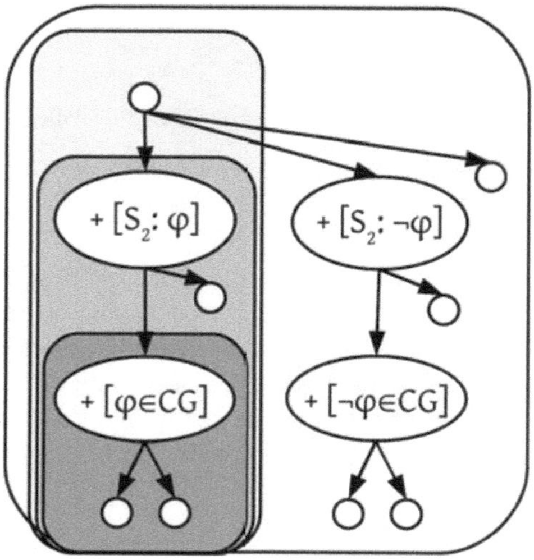

Fig. 16 Answering a declarative question with *no*

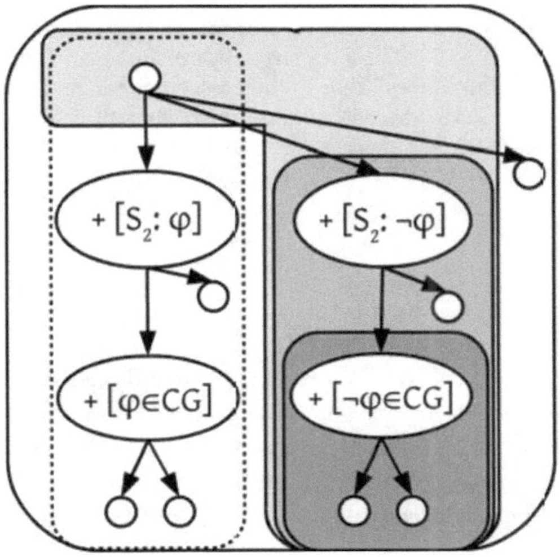

REQUEST, which just presents the φ option. The reason for the second option is to indicate that the two options are not considered equal. The asymmetry in declarative questions also shows up in the fact that assertion of φ is easier than assertion of $\neg\varphi$, as the latter requires a prior REJECT operation. In this way, the speaker can make it "easy" for the addressee to answer a question in one way. Hence, the bias of declarative questions comes about as a **conversational** implicature.

In the case of declarative questions with **incredulity contour**, there is a **conventional** implicature that the speaker does not believe that the addressee will be able to perform the indicated assertion. We can assume an operator I-REQUEST here that works like REQUEST but in addition carries this conventional implicature. As a result, the suggested move is a challenge imposed by the first speaker. Such conventional implicatures can be seen as hints in a conversational game. They are not proper moves in their own right, but nevertheless influence the course of actions, just as, e.g., hints in a card game. In the following, I will mark moves that are meant as a challenge by double underlining.

(50) S_1 to S_2: *There is a vegetarian restaurant here?!*
$\langle \ldots, C\rangle$ + I-REQUEST$_{S1,S2}$(ASS(φ))
= $\langle \ldots, C\rangle + \underline{\underline{\{\surd C\}}} \cup \underline{\underline{C+[S_2\text{: } \varphi]}}\rangle$

The reply patterns are essentially similar as to cases of REQUEST, except perhaps that they have a more emphatic prosody.

It is to be expected that declarative questions can also be constructed on the basis of sentence radicals that are themselves negated.

(51) S_1 to S_2: *There is no vegetarian restaurant around here?*
There isn't any vegetarian restaurant around here?
Introduces propositional discourse referents
φ = 'there is a vegetarian restaurant here',
$\psi = \neg$ 'there is a vegetarian restaurant here'
$\langle ..., C\rangle$ + $\text{REQUEST}_{S1,S2}(\text{ASS}(\psi))$, = $\langle ..., C, \{\sqrt{C}\} \cup C+[S_2{:}\ \psi]\rangle$, abbreviated as Γ.

a. *No (there isn't).*
$\Gamma + [S_2{:}\ \neg\varphi] + [\neg\varphi \in CG]$

b. *Yes, there isn't.*
$\Gamma + [S_2{:}\ \psi] + [\psi \in CG]$

c. *No, there is!*
Γ + REJECT + $[S_2{:}\ \neg\psi] + [\neg\psi \in CG]$

d. *Yes, there is!*
Γ + REJECT + $[S_2{:}\ \varphi] + [\varphi \in CG]$

We find the four answer possibilities that we have already identified in reactions to assertions based on negated sentences, cf. Sect. 6. The most straightforward answer is *no*, with interpretation (a). The operator *no* has to express negation, and negating φ is easier than negating ψ, as the latter would involve double negation (recall that $\psi = \neg\varphi$), and in addition a REJECT operation. Hence (a) is preferred over (c). As (b) would express the same as (a), the answer *yes* would rather be interpreted as in (d). But this preference appears to be only weak, and *yes* typically will have to be specified by elliptical clauses, as in *Yes, there is*. In German, *doch* is used in this case, lexically expressing REJECT and assertion of the negation of an accessible propositional discourse referent; this corresponds to option (c) above.

In closing this section, I would like to point out that the theory developed here allows for a novel way of representing questions with question tags, which also express bias questions.

(52) S_1: *There is a vegetarian restaurant around here, isn't it?*

Such questions can be expressed as proposing first a commitment of S_1 to the truth of the proposition. It then restricts the legal moves to either $[\varphi \in CG]$, where φ is accepted as part of the common ground, or to the move $[S_2{:}\ \neg\varphi]$, a move of the other speaker to assert the negation of φ. Hence, S_1 offers S_2 a way to negate φ without first undergoing a reject operation. In this sense, assertions with question tags are more conciliatory than regular assertions.

9 Biased Polarity Questions

I have argued that there is a REQUEST operator that can be applied to an assertion, and that is expressed by prosodic means, H%. In this section, I would like to argue that **REQUEST can also be expressed syntactically,** in a similar way as QU, by triggering head movement of auxiliary verbs or copulas. That is, I assume that a question like *Is there a vegetarian restaurant around here?* does not only have the interpretation in (44) but also the following one:

(53) S_1 to S_2: *Is there a vegetarian restaurant around here?*
$[_{\text{ForceP}}$ *REQUEST-is*$_i$ $[_{\text{ForceP}}$ *ASS*-e$_i$ $[_{\text{TP}}$ *there* e$_i$ *a veg. restaurant here?*]]]
$\langle \ldots, C\rangle$ + REQUEST$_{S1,S2}$(ASS('there is a vegetarian restaurant around here'))
= $\langle \ldots, C\rangle + \{\sqrt{C}\} \cup C+[S_2$: 'there is a vegetarian restaurant here']

The standard polarity question presents two options equally (φ and $\neg\varphi$); the REQUEST polarity question presents only one option, φ; the other option, $\neg\varphi$, can be asserted in a slightly more complex way, by applying a REJECT operation before. Normally, the simpler regular interpretation of polarity questions (44) blocks the REQUEST interpretation (53), and so is not easily detectable. But I will argue below that the REQUEST interpretation in English is detectable in certain contexts as well, cf. (65). And there is evidence for this interpretation coming from questions based on negated propositions, from questions marked with the incredulity contour, and from questions marked with *or not.*

As for questions based on negated propositions, it has been a puzzle for standard theories of polarity questions why they exist at all, as they should have exactly the same interpretation as questions based on non-negated propositions.

(54) S_1 to S_2: *Is there no vegetarian restaurant around here?*
(alternatively, *Isn't there any vegetarian restaurant around here?*)

As a standard polarity question expressed with QU, we predict a meaning of this expression that is exactly the same as with the simpler question, *Is there a vegetarian restaurant here?* Hence questions like (54) should be blocked. But they are, in fact, possible. And in addition to standard polarity questions, they express a bias; in our example, S_1 expects that there is vegetarian restaurant here. We can explain this by assuming an interpretation based on REQUEST, just as the declarative question based on a negated sentence radical, cf. (51).

(55) $\langle \ldots, C\rangle$ + REQUEST$_{S1,S2}$(ASS($\neg$'there is a vegetarian restaurant around here'))
= $\langle \ldots, C\rangle + \{\sqrt{C}\} \cup C+[S_2$: $\neg$'there is a vegetarian restaurant around here']

As before, the sentence radical introduces two propositional discourse referents, one for the TP, one for the NegP, and we find the same answer patterns as for the declarative question based on a negated sentence radical, discussed in (51).

A second case in which the REQUEST interpretation becomes detectable is under the incredulity contour, that is, when the operator I-REQUEST is applied:

(56) S_1 to S_2: *Is there a vegetarian restaurant around here?!*
$\langle \ldots, C\rangle$ + I-REQUEST$_{S1,S2}$(ASS(φ))
= $\langle \ldots, C\rangle + \underline{\underline{\{\sqrt{C}\}}} \cup \underline{\underline{C + [S_2: \varphi]}}$

As before (cf. (50)), double underlining signals that S_1 challenges S_2 to perform the speech act ASS(φ). That is, S_1 conventionally implicates that S_2 will probably not be able to perform it. This bias could not easily be explained on the basis of the standard derivation, which presents the two propositions φ, $\neg\varphi$ equally (with the exception that also a standard polarity question only introduces one propositional discourse referent, φ). So, the distinct interpretation of I-REQUEST is evidenced that polarity questions can be interpreted in a way that highlights one option.

A third case that poses problems for standard theories are questions with the question tag *or not.*

(57) S_1 to S_2: *Is there a vegetarian restaurant around here, or not?*

It is difficult to see how the tag *or not* is to be interpreted if the polarity question presents both options $\{\varphi, \neg\varphi\}$. We can assume that *or not* is either interpreted at the formation of the sentence radical of the question, leading to the interpretation $\{\varphi, \neg\varphi\}$, which then can be used as an argument to QU. Alternatively, we can assume that questions with question tags expresses REQUEST questions. Without going into details, if *or* corresponds to the union operation of commitment spaces, then (57) can be interpreted as follows:

(58) $\langle \ldots, C\rangle + \text{REQUEST}(\text{ASS}(\varphi) \vee \text{ASS}(\neg\varphi))$
$= \langle \ldots, C\rangle + \{\surd C\} \cup [C + [S_2{:}\ \varphi] \cup C + [S_2{:}\ \neg\varphi]]$

This leaves two options to the addressee S_2: to assert φ or to assert $\neg\varphi$, which are ranked equally. We have, effectively, the same requirement as with the regular polarity question, *Is there a vegetarian restaurant around here?* However, we now have two propositional discourse referents, φ and its negation ψ. Hence, the answer patterns become more difficult: Simple *yes* and *no* do not suffice, we need expanded answers like *yes, there is* or *no, there isn't.*

The two ways to construct polarity questions can be fruitfully applied to differences in the formation of such questions. For example, Chinese A-nonA-questions, which present two options equally and explicitly, can be seen as representing the question type (58), whereas questions marked with the particle *ma* either represent simple polarity questions or declarative questions (cf. Li and Thompson 1981). In German, polarity questions marked with the particle *denn* appear to mark REQUEST polarity questions, as they highlight one option as being of particular interest.

10 Negated Polarity Questions

We now return to the original problem of this article, the interpretation of high negation in polarity questions.

(59) S_1 to S_2: *Isn't there a vegetarian restaurant around here?*
(interpretation with high negation)

I propose that this is a **request question**, with a **denegation that scopes over the assertion operator**. This captures the high position of negation: The negation phrase actually embeds the force phrase of assertion. I assume the following structure:

(60) $[_{\text{ForceP}}$ *REQUEST* $[_{\text{NegP}}$ *is*$_i$*-n't* $[_{\text{ForceP}}$ *ASS* $[_{\text{TP}}$ *there* e_i *a vegetarian restaurant here*$]]]]$

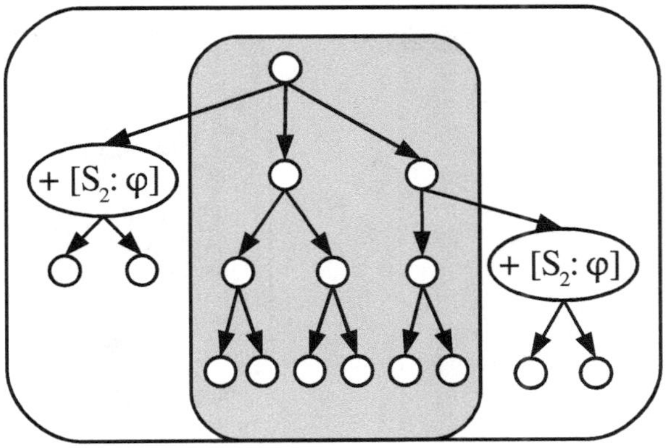

Fig. 17 *Isn't there a vegetarian Restaurant?* Denegation of Assertion

Here, negation is a speech act operator, meaning that the NegP in this case has the same type of interpretation as the ForceP. I propose the following interpretation for (59); cf. (14) for the interpretation of denegation, and Fig. 17 for illustration.

(61) $\langle \ldots, C\rangle$ + $\text{REQUEST}_{S1,S2}(\sim \text{ASS}(\varphi))$,
where φ = 'there is a vegetarian restaurant around here'
= $\langle \ldots, C\rangle + \sim \text{ASS}_{S2,S1}(\varphi)$
= $\langle \ldots, C, C - \{c \mid \exists c'[c' + [S_2: \varphi] \subseteq c\}\rangle$, abbreviated as Γ.

Negated polarity questions can also be uttered with incredulity contour, indicating that S_1 proposes a challenge to S_2 with the imposition to denegate the assertion of φ:

(62) S_1 to S_2: *Isn't there a vegetarian restaurant around here?!*
$\langle \ldots, C\rangle$ + $\text{I-REQUEST}_{S1,S2}(\text{ASS}(\varphi))$
= $\langle \ldots, C\rangle + \underline{\sim \text{ASS}_{S2,S1}(\varphi)}$
= $\langle \ldots, C\rangle + \underline{\sim [S_2: \varphi]}$

With questions like (59) and (62), S_1 asks S_2 whether S_2 would exclude the assertion of φ, where in (62) S_1 considers this as a challenge to S_2. Such questions can be rejected, as usual, with *I don't know*. They can also be answered with *yes* and *no*. These answers do not give rise to potential ambiguities as with polarity questions with propositional negation, as illustrated in (51). This is predicted, as in the case of polarity questions with high negation, only one propositional discourse referent can be introduced, namely φ. This is because negation is interpreted at the speech act level, which does not result in a second proposition. See the analysis in (63) and the illustrations in Figs. 18 and 19.

(63) S_1 to S_2: *Isn't there a vegetarian restaurant around here?*
(interpretation with high negation).
Introduces propositional discourse referent\
φ = 'there is a vegetarian restaurant around here'
a. *Yes (there is).*
Γ + REJECT + $[S_2: \varphi] + [\varphi \in \text{CG}]$
b. *No (there isn't).*
$\Gamma + [S_2: \neg\varphi] + [\neg\varphi \in \text{CG}]$

Fig. 18 S_1: *Isn't there a vegetarian restaurant here?* S_2: *Yes, there is*

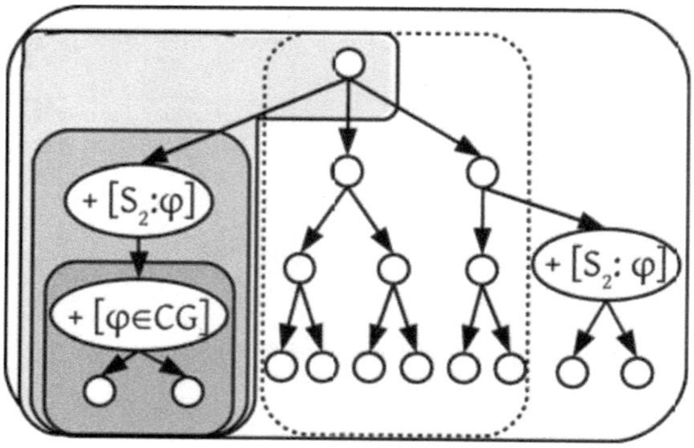

Fig. 19 S_1: *Isn't there a vegetarian restaurant here?* S_2: *No, there isn't*

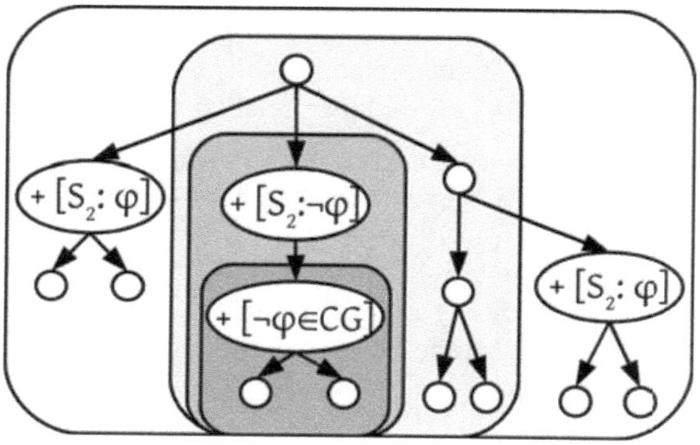

The answer *Yes (there is)* requires a reject operation because it cannot be interpreted directly at Γ, as the last commitment space has excluded S_2's assertion of φ. In contrast, the answer *No (there isn't)* is a regular move after a negated polarity question, as it does not require REJECT to be interpreted. One might ask why an arbitrary assertion by S_2, like *It is raining*, is not possible here; after all, it could be interpreted at the commitment state after the negated polarity question. The reason is that S_1 imposed a restriction for future moves of S_2 that S_2 either has to accept or to reject. An arbitrary assertion like *It is raining* does not count as an acceptance, as it would be compatible with later assertions of φ. The only way to exclude later assertions of φ is to assert the negation of φ.

Notice that qualified answers are possible, like *Yes, I think so, but I'm not sure*, yet a simple answer like *yes* will be an unqualified positive answer. This is in contrast to Romero and Han (2004), who assume that such an answer indicates strong evidence, and Repp (2013), who assumes that the answer would indicate weak evidence—see discussion of (9) above. There are two ways to model such qualified answers: Either by allowing high negation to exclude all kinds of modified assertions of φ; an answer like *Yes, I think so* would then pick out one of the excluded conversational moves. Or by assuming that such modified answers remain within the options presented by the person that asked the negated polarity question. At the current point, I will not go further into such evidentially modified answers.

Romero (pers. comm.) pointed out a potential problem with the analysis of negated polarity questions as denegations. It seems like a question like *Don't you promise to come?* should be analyzed as a request to denegate a promise to come. A possible reaction to that is *Correct.* However, it appears to be odd for the addressee to react to a negated polarity question like (63) with *Correct*, meaning that the addressee indeed excludes that assertion. This can be explained, however, as the overall intention of the speaker is to ask for confirmation for the proposition, and a reaction like *correct* would naturally support the speaker. In the case of negation into questions with incredulity contour, the reaction *Correct* would indeed state that the addressee is excluding the assertion, and thus it is willing to go along with the addressee.

One question that arises at this point is why high negation only arises when REQUEST is expressed syntactically, triggering interrogative syntax. The reason is that in case REQUEST is realized just by prosody, as in (49) and (50), there is no syntactic node at which negation can be expressed. Hence, a question like *There isn't a vegetarian restaurant around here?* can only be interpreted with narrow, propositional negation. Also, if we assume that REQUEST can be interpreted in syntax, triggering AUX movement just like the regular question operator QU,

For completeness, it should be mentioned here that negated polarity questions can be based on a sentence radical that is itself negated. This is evident if the latter negation is expressed by a negative determiner, like *no*. Consider the following example, which can be derived in a regular way, as REQUEST(~ASS(¬'there is a vegetarian restaurant there')). Notice that the first negation is denegation, whereas the second is propositional negation.

(64) *We can't suggest to go out to Fifth Street to our vegetarian friends.*
Isn't there no vegetarian restaurant there?

Let us now consider how, under the current theory, negated polarity questions get the bias they are reported to have. According to Büring and Gunlogson (2000), they do **not occur in a context that is biased to a positive answer**. This is illustrated with the following example, where negated polarity questions are compared with other question types that were discussed in this article.

(65) S_2: *There are all kinds of restaurants in this town, it won't be difficult to find something nice to eat out.*
a. S_1: *Is there a vegetarian restaurant here?*
b. S_1: *There is a vegetarian restaurant here?*
c. S_1: *#There is no vegetarian restaurant here?*
d. S_1: *#Is there no vegetarian restaurant here?*
e. S_1: *#Isn't there a vegetarian restaurant here?*
f. S_1: *Isn't there no vegetarian restaurant here?*

The negated polarity question (e) is odd here because from the context we cannot infer a reason for S_1 to find out whether S_2 would exclude the assertion of φ, that there is a vegetarian restaurant. S_2 had made it clear that presumably, there is one.

Simple polarity questions (a) and positive declarative questions (b) are possible. I would like to argue that the simple polarity question (a) actually is based on REQUEST, just like the declarative question (b), and hence is a monopolar question. This question is good in the context given because it suggests that there is a good possibility that φ, and the question REQUEST(ASS(φ)) is biased toward a positive answer: This is the option that the speaker presents to the addressee as the only regular continuation, whereas all other continuations require a prior REJECT operation. With these questions, S_1 double-checks if the context is indeed such that φ follows. Interestingly, the negated polarity question with negated sentence radical (f), though quite complex, is good as well. This is as predicted: Just as the context allows for S_1 to double-check whether φ is assertable, it allows to double-check whether the assertion of $\neg\varphi$ can be excluded.

Another observation by Büring and Gunlogson (2000) is that negated polarity questions do occur in a **neutral context** in which there is an interest in a positive answer. The following example gives again the fuller paradigm:

(66) S_1: *Remember, we were once at Mooswood restaurant, and we liked it a lot.*
a. *Is there a vegetarian restaurant in this town?*
b. *#There is a vegetarian restaurant in this town?*
c. *#There is no vegetarian restaurant in this town?*
d. *Is there no vegetarian restaurant in this town?*
e. *Isn't there a vegetarian restaurant in this town?*
f. *#Isn't there no vegetarian restaurant in this town?*

Here, (a) can be understood as a regular polarity question, suggesting both options φ and $\neg\varphi$ equally, which is predicted to be fine, given that the context is neutral with respect to the issue whether there is vegetarian restaurant in this town or not. For the same reason, (b) and (c) are bad because they select, for no good reason, the assertion of φ or the assertion of $\neg\varphi$ over the other. According to Büring and Gunlogson, the negated polarity question (e) is good in this case, where it is crucial that there is an expressed interest in the positive answer, φ. This can be explained if the speaker wants to check whether, under the neutral context, φ is an option to be considered. The rhetorical strategy behind this move is to appeal to the addressee to exclude certain options in order to find a solution, here the best restaurant choice. The negated polarity question, though complex, might be preferable to the standard polarity question (a), as that question suggests a sole interest in the issue whether φ or $\neg\varphi$. Answers (d) and (e) appear to be quite good in the given context as well. I assume that (d), like (c), is a REQUEST question, which asks the speaker to assert $\neg\varphi$. The strategy behind that is the same as with the negated polarity question (e), namely to check whether the option φ is to be considered. In contrast to (e), it does so by checking whether the addressee would assert $\neg\varphi$. The negated polarity question based on a negated sentence radical (f) is odd in this context. It would express an interest to exclude the option φ, but in the given context, this is not a "positive" option. However, it should be stressed that examples can be found where such sentences work fine, as they present a "positive" option:

(67) S_1: *The police still don't know much about this murder case. According to the evidence, Jones, Miller, and Smith could have done it.*
S_2: *Doesn't Miller have no proper alibi for the time of the murder?*

Büring and Gunlogson (2000) finally observe that negated polarity questions occur in contexts with a **negative bias** towards a positive answer. Again, we consider the larger paradigm of answers here:

(68) S_2: *As you don't eat meat, we can't go out in this town.*
a. S_1: *#Is there a vegetarian restaurant here?*
b. S_1: *#There is a vegetarian restaurant here?*
c. S_1: *There is no vegetarian restaurant here?*
d. S_1: *Is there no vegetarian restaurant here?*
e. S_1: *Isn't there a vegetarian restaurant here?*
f. S_1: *#Isn't there no vegetarian restaurant here?*

The context creates here a strong bias toward $\neg\varphi$, as it entails that φ is unlikely. This is not compatible with question (a) under its regular polarity reading, as this presents the proposition φ, $\neg\varphi$ equally. The REQUEST reading of (a) and the declarative question in (b) should be even worse, as they are biased toward the unlikely answer φ. In contrast, the declarative question in (c) and the REQUEST reading of the polarity question with negated sentence radical (d) are fine: The speaker S_1 double-checks whether the answer φ indeed is to be excluded. For the same reason, the negated polarity question (e) is fine. The negated polarity question based on $\neg\varphi$ is predictably bad, because in the context biased toward $\neg\varphi$ there is no obvious reason to check whether the speaker would exclude an assertion of $\neg\varphi$. It is remarkable that in all the good questions of (68), there is a strong tendency toward a realization with the incredulity contour (which should be marked by?!). This can be easily explained: The typical context in which double-checking that φ indeed is to be excluded is when S_1 has information that runs contrary to the bias that S_2 suggests, and hence S_1's questions will typically be challenges of S_2.

11 Conclusion

In this paper, I have presented a way how to interpret polarity questions with outer negation, as *Isn't there a vegetarian restaurant around here (too)?* I have argued that they are based on a REQUEST operation that asks the addressee to perform a certain speech act. In the case of negated polarity question, this speech act is a meta speech act: the denegation of the speech act *There is a vegetarian restaurant around here* (*too*). I have argued that the observed biases of such negated polarity questions follow from this assumption.

I have presented a theory for speech acts, especially for assertions and their denegation, and for questions. I have argued that in addition to the regular question based on the illocutionary operator QU, questions can also be based on the REQUEST operator. We find REQUEST in the case of biased questions, that is, with declarative questions like *There is a vegetarian restaurant around here?*, but also with polarity questions in certain contexts, and in particular with polarity questions with negated sentence radical, as in *There is no vegetarian restaurant around here?*

I have also presented a theory about the sometimes puzzling ways how speakers can react to assertions and answer polarity questions with *yes* and *no*. For one thing, I argued that we have to distinguish between the mere acceptance or rejection of assertions and reactions by *yes* and *no* that has signal independent evidence. Furthermore, I proposed that *yes* and *no* pick up propositional discourse referents introduced by assertions or questions. The various ways how *yes* and *no* can be used could be explained, under the assumption that when the sentence radical is negated, it introduces two discourse referents, one for the positive clause, and one for its negation.

The work presented here is preliminary in many respects. While I tried to be explicit about the underlying model of conversational game, which is based on the notion of commitment states, commitment spaces, and commitment space sequences, I glossed over the syntactic representation of speech acts. Also, I did not deal with other kinds of question bias, as with negative polarity items or the use of question tags. This, and other applications of the underlying framework of modeling conversation, has to wait for other occasions.

References

Alston, William P. 2000. *Illocutionary acts and sentence meanings.* Cornell University Press.

AnderBois, Scott. 2011. *Issues and alternatives.* Doctoral dissertation. Santa Cruz: University of California.

Asher, Nicholas, and Brian Reese. 2007. Intonation and discourse: Biased questions. *Interdisciplinary Studies on Information Structure* 8: 1–38.

Beyssade, Claire and Marandin, Jean-Marie. 2006. The speech act assignment problem revisited: Disentangling speaker's commitment from speaker's call on addressee. *Empirical Issues in Syntax and Semantics* 37–68.

Brasoveanu, Adrian, Donka Farkas and Floris Roelofsen. 2013. N-words and sentential negation: Evidence from polarity particles and VP ellipsis. *Semantics & Pragmatics* 6: 1–33.

Büring, Daniel and Gunlogson, Christine. 2000. Aren't positive and negative polar questions the same? *LSA Annual meeting*.

Büring, Daniel. 2003. On D-trees, beans, and B-accents. *Linguistics and Philosophy* 26: 511–545.

Cohen, Ariel, and Manfred Krifka. 2011. Superlative quantifiers as modifiers of meta-speech acts. *The Baltic International Yearbook of Cognition, Logic and Communication* 6: 1–56.

Farkas, Donka F., and Kim B. Bruce. 2010. On reacting to assertions and polar questions. *Journal of Semantics* 27: 81–118.

Gazdar, Gerald. 1981. Speech act assignment. In: Joshi, Aravind K. & Lynn, Bonnie, Webber, (eds). *Elements of discourse*. Cambridge: Cambridge University Press, 63–83.

Ginzburg, Jonathan. 1995. Resolving questions II. *Linguistics and Philosophy* 18: 597–609.

Gunlogson, Christine. 2001. *True to form: rising and falling declaratives as questions in English.* Doctoral dissertation. University of California, Santa Cruz.

Gunlogson, Christine. 2002. Declarative questions. *Proceedings of semantics and linguistic theory XII.* Ithaca, NY: Cornell University, 124–134.

Hamblin, Charles L. 1971. Mathematical models of dialogue. *Theoria* 37: 130–155.
Hare, R.M. 1970. Meaning and speech acts. *The Philosophical Review* 79: 3–24.
Harnish, Robert M. 2005. Commitments and speech acts. *Philosophica* 75: 11–41.
Höhle, Tilman N. 1992. Über Verum-Fokus im Deutschen. In *Informationsstruktur und Grammatik*, ed. Joachim Jacobs, 112–141. Opladen: Westdeutscher Verlag.
Jacobs, Joachim. 1984. Funktionale Satzperspektive und Illokutionssemantik. *Linguistische Berichte* 91: 25–58.
Jäger, Gerhard. 2002. Some notes on the formal properties of bidirectional optimality theory. *Journal of Logic, Language and Information* 11: 427–451.
Kramer, Ruth and Rawlins, Kyle. 2009. Polarity particles: an ellipsis account. *NELS 39*.
Krifka, Manfred. 2001a. Quantifying into question acts. *Natural Language Semantics* 9: 1–40.
Krifka, Manfred. 2001b. For a structured account of questions and answers. In *Audiatur vox sapientiae. A Festschrift for Achim von Stechow*, eds. Féry, Caroline and Sternefeld, Wolfgang, 287–319. Berlin: Akademie-Verlag.
Krifka, Manfred. 2008. Basic notions of information structure. *Acta Linguistica Hungarica* 55: 243–276.
Krifka, Manfred. 2011. Questions. In *Semantics. An international handbook of natural language and meaning*, ed. Maienborn, C.e.a.Berlin: Mouton de Gruyter.
Krifka, Manfred. 2013. Response particles as propositional anaphors. In *Semantics and Linguistic Theory (SALT)*, Vol. 23, ed. Todd Snider, 1–18. Washington, D.C.: LSA Open Journal Systems.
Krifka, Manfred. 2015. Bias in commitment space semantics: Declarative questions, negated questions, and question tags. In *Semantics and Linguistic Theory (SALT)* 25, eds. D'Antonio, Sarah, Moroney, Mary, and Little, Carol Rose, 328–345. Washington, D.C.: LSA Open Journal Systems.
Ladd, D. Robert. 1981. A first look at the semantics and pragmatics of negative questions and tag questions. In *Proceedings of the Chicago linguistic society,* 164–171. Chicago.
Li, Charles, and Sandra Thompson. 1981. *Mandarin Chinese: A functional reference grammar*. Berkeley: University of California Press.
Merin, Arthur and Bartels, Christine. 1997. Decision-theoretic semantics for intonation. In *Arbeitspapiere der SFB 340. Sprachtheoretische Grundlagen für die Computerlinguistik*. Stuttgart, Tübingen.
Merin, Arthur. 1994. Algebra of elementary social acts. In: *Foundations of speech act theory. Philosophical and linguistic perspectives*, eds. Tsohatzidis, Savas L, 234–266. London: Routledge.
Pierrehumbert, Janet, and Julia Hirschberg. 1990. The meaning of intonational contours in the interpretation of discourse. In *Intentions in communication*, ed. Philip R. Cohen, and Jerry L. Morgan, 271–311. Cambridge, Mass.: MIT Press.
Reese, Brian Jon. 2007. *Bias in questions*. Doctoral dissertation. Austin: University of Texas.
Repp, Sophie. 2009. *Negation in gapping*. Oxford University Press.
Repp, Sophie. 2013. Common ground management: Modal particles, illocutionary negation, and VERUM. In Expressives and beyond. Explorations of conventional non-truth-conditional meaning, eds. Gutzmann, Daniel and Gärtner, Hans-Martin, 231–274. Leiden: Brill.
Rizzi, Luigi. 1997. The fine structure of the left periphery. In *Elements of grammar*, ed. Liliane Haegeman, 281–337. Dordrecht: Kluwer.
Romero, Maribel, and Chung-hye Han. 2004. On negative yes/no questions. *Linguistics and Philosophy* 27: 609–658.
Romero, Maribel. 2006. Biased yes/no questions: The role of VERUM. *Sprache und Datenverarbeitung* 30: 9–24.
Rooth, Mats. 1992. A theory of focus interpretation. *Natural Language Semantics* 1: 75–116
Sadock, Jerold M. 1971. Queclaratives. *Chicago Linguistic Society* 7: 223–232.
Sadock, Jerrold M. 1974. *Towards a linguistic theory of speech acts*. New York: Academic Press.
Searle, John. 1969. *Speech acts*. An essay in the philosophy of language. Cambridge: Cambridge University Press.

Stalnaker, Robert. 1978. Assertion. In *Pragmatics*, ed. Peter Cole, 315–323. New York: Academic Press.

Stenius, E. 1967. Mood and language game. *Synthese* 17: 254–274.

Sudo, Yasutada. 2013. Biased polar questions in English and Japanese. In *Beyond expressives: Explorations in conventional non-truth-conditional meaning*, ed. Daniel Gutzmann, and Hans-Martin Gärtner, 275–296. Brill: Leiden.

Szabolcsi, Anna. 1982. Model theoretic semantics of performatives. In *Hungarian linguistics*, ed. Ferenc Kiefer, 515–535. Amsterdam: John Bejamins.

Truckenbrodt, Hubert. 2012. Semantics of intonation. In *Semantics: An international handbook of natural language and meaning*, Vol. 3, ed. Claudia Maienborn e.a., 2039–2069. Berlin: Walter de Gruyter.

van der Sandt, Rob and Emar Maier. 2003. Denials in discourse. *Michigan linguistics and philosophy.*

van Rooij, Robert and Marie Šafářová. 2003. On polar questions. In *Proceedings of Semantics and Linguistic Theory XIII.* Ithaca, NY: Cornell University, CLC Publications.

The Intonation of *Wh*- and Yes/No-Questions in Tokyo Japanese

Shinichiro Ishihara

Abstract The paper reports experimental results on the intonation of *wh*- and yes/no-questions in Tokyo Japanese, and discusses several implications for the semantic and phonological theories of focus. The intonation of declarative sentences, *wh*-questions, and yes/no-questions are systematically compared. The results show that the *wh*-question exhibits an F_0-prominence on the *wh*-phrase, while the yes/no-question exhibits an F_0-prominence on the verb. It is claimed that these prominences are both focus-oriented. This proposal fits the standard semantic theory of questions (Hamblin 1973) nicely. Phonological theories of focus prosody in Tokyo Japanese are compared in the light of the results. The interaction of the notions of focus and discourse-newness/givenness is also discussed.

Keywords Japanese · Wh-questions · Yes/no-questions · Intonation · Focus · Focus prosody · Verum focus

1 Introduction

The paper reports experimental results on the intonation patterns of *wh*- and yes/no-questions in Tokyo Japanese,[1] and discusses their implications for the semantic and phonological theories of focus.[2] Although there are several studies on the intonation of question sentences in Japanese (Maekawa 1991a, b, Maekawa 1997a, b, Ishihara 2003), there are a few pieces of missing information in each of these studies. In the experiment reported here, which is a follow-up on the previous studies,

---

[1] In this paper, we exclusively discuss Tokyo Japanese. For brevity, it will be referred to simply as "Japanese" hereafter.

[2] Here we adopt the definition of focus by (Krifka 2008: 247), which states that focus "indicates the presence of alternatives that are relevant for the interpretation of linguistic expressions".

S. Ishihara (✉)
Centre for Languages and Literature, Lund University,
BOX 201, 221 00 Lund, Sweden
e-mail: shinichiro.ishihara@ostas.lu.se

C. Lee et al. (eds.), *Contrastiveness in Information Structure, Alternatives and Scalar Implicatures*, Studies in Natural Language and Linguistic Theory 91, DOI 10.1007/978-3-319-10106-4_19

intonation patterns of *wh*-questions (WHQs), yes/no-questions (YNQs) and declarative (i.e., non-interrogative) sentences (DECLs) are systematically compared. The results show a three-way contrast in their F_0-realizations. The two question types exhibit an extra prominence on different locations in the sentence: on the *wh*-phrase in the case of WHQs, and on the verb in the case of YNQs.

These results can best be explained if we assume that both question types bear a focus on the respective element with prosodic prominence. This conclusion is in line with the previous discussions in the literature on the scope-prosody correspondence found in WHQs (Deguchi and Kitagawa 2002; Ishihara 2002, 2003, 2007; Hirotani 2005), and is also compatible with the semantics of questions (Hamblin 1973). Furthermore, the results are compared with another set of experimental results reported in Féry and Ishihara (2007), with regard to prosodic effects of givenness. The comparison of the results indicates that the focus assigned to a *wh*-phrase corresponds to what researchers call "identificational focus" (É. Kiss 1998), "contrastive focus" (Selkirk 2008), etc., and that the so-called "narrow focus"—a single discourse-new element surrounded by given material—behaves differently prosodically. This suggests that focus should be treated separately from newness/givenness, along the lines of Féry and Samek-Lodovici (2006), Selkirk (2008), and others.

The paper is organized as follows. In Sect. 2 previous literature on the intonation of WHQs and YNQs will be briefly reviewed. In Sect. 3 we present the experiment and its results. In Sect. 4 theoretical implications will be discussed based on the experimental results, first for the semantic theory of focus and questions (Sect. 4.1) and then for the phonological theory of focus (Sect. 4.2).

2 Previous Work on the Intonation of WHQs and YNQs

There are several experimental studies on the intonation of questions in Japanese. Even though they have revealed some of the crucial properties of the phenomena under discussion, there is still missing information yet to be investigated. We review some of the previous work, and clarify the main goal of the current experiment.

2.1 Wh-Questions

It has been reported that Japanese WHQs always exhibit a special intonation pattern (Maekawa 1991a, b; Deguchi and Kitagawa 2002; Ishihara 2002, 2003). Ishihara (2003) experimentally examined this intonation pattern, and compared it with that of declarative sentences (DECLs). Sample pitch contours of the DECL and WHQ are shown in Figs. 1 and 2, respectively.

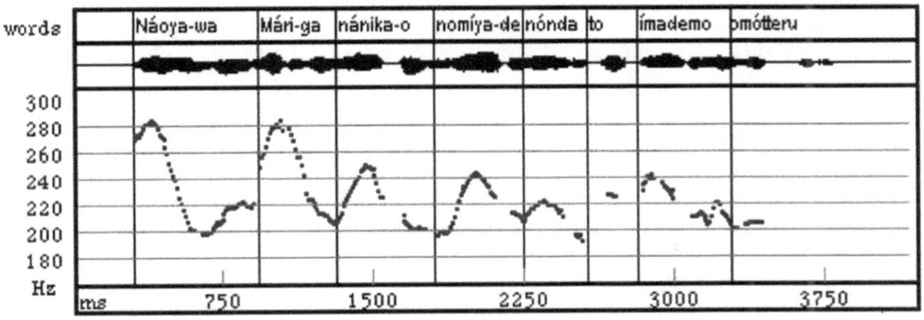

Fig. 1 Sample F_0-contour of DECL in (1a)

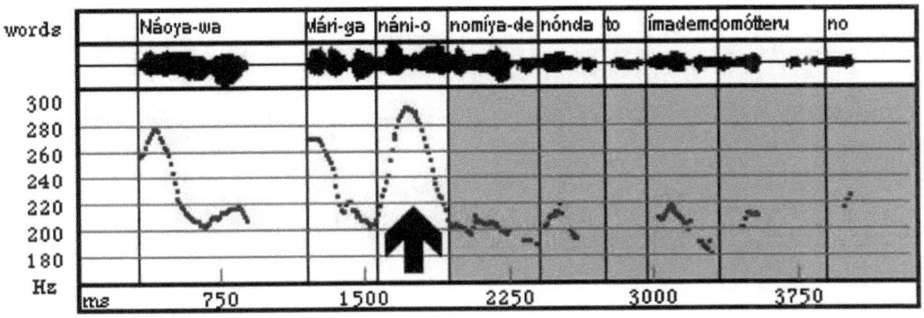

Fig. 2 Sample F_0-contour of WHQ in (1b)

(1) *Intonation of DECLs and WHQs* (Ishihara 2003, 53–54)

a. *DECL*
Náoya-wa [Mári-ga nánika-o nomíya-de nónda to] ímademo omótteru.
N.-TOP M.-NOM something-ACC bar-LOC drank that even.now think
'Naoya still thinks that Mari drank something at the bar.'

b. *WHQ*
Náoya-wa [Mári-ga ***náni****-o nomíya-de nónda to] ímademo omótteru* ***no****?*
N.-TOP M.-NOM what-ACC bar-LOC drank that even.now think Q
'What did Naoya still think that Mari drank at the bar?'

In the declarative sentence in Fig. 1, each word exhibits a clear F_0-peak.[3] In the *wh*-question in Fig. 2, there are two phenomena to be noted. First, the F_0-peak of the *wh*-phrase is realized higher compared to the non-*wh*-counterpart. Second, all the

[3]Japanese lexical items are categorized as either accented words or unaccented words. Only accented words exhibit an F_0-peak followed by a sharp fall, as shown in this example. For F_0-realization of unaccented words, see Pierrehumbert and Beckman (1988). For expository purposes, the examples used in this paper are composed of only accented words, unless noted otherwise. Lexical pitch accents are indicated by acute accents (′).

F_0-peaks following the *wh*-phrase are sharply reduced.[4,5] This is a typical intonation pattern for a sentence containing a focus. The F_0-peak of the focused phrase is raised, and the post-focal domain is radically reduced. In the case of WHQs, the *wh*-phrase always behaves as a focus. Following Ishihara (2003, 2007), we will call this special intonation pattern *focus prosody (FP)*, and the two phenomena found in an FP *focal* F_0*-rise* and *post-focal reduction*,[6] respectively.

(2) WHQs always exhibit a *focus prosody (FP)*

a. *Focal* F_0*-rise* on the *wh*-phrase
b. *Post-focal reduction* on the phrases following the *wh*-phrase

2.2 Yes/No-Questions

Compared to WHQs, there are not as many studies on the intonation of YNQs. Maekawa (1991a, b) compared the intonations of WHQs and YNQs, using sentences like those in (3). Sample pitch contours are given in Fig. 3.

(3) a. *WHQ*

náni-ga miéru?
what-NOM visible
'What can you see?'

b. *YNQ*

nánika miéru?
something visible
'Can you see anything?'

If we compare the pitch contours of the WHQ (Left) and the YNQ (Right) in Fig. 3, the F_0-peak of the *wh*-phrase in the WHQ is higher than the non-*wh*-counterpart in the YNQ, while the F_0-peak of the verb is lower in the WHQ than in the YNQ. These differences seem obvious at first, given that an FP is expected in WHQs (Sect. 2.1), because the higher F_0-peak on the *wh*-phrase and the lower F_0-peak on V in the WHQ could be attributed to focal F_0-rise and post-focal reduction, respectively.

It should be noted, however, that YNQs were not compared with declarative sentences in this study. It might be the case that YNQs not only lack FP effects, but also have additional effects that create the differences observed in Fig. 3, e.g., an F_0-lowering effect on the subject, or an F_0-raising effect on the verb. Therefore it remains unclear whether the differences between WHQs and YNQs come from the lack of FP effects or some additional effects in YNQs, or both. In order to find out whether

[4]Maekawa (1991b) reports that there was no significant F_0-rise on the *wh*-phrase, while the post-focal reduction was consistently observed. These results, however, appear to have been collected from a single speaker.

[5]In addition to the two phenomena described here, there is actually another difference between WHQs and DECLs, which is not clearly visible in the pitch track in Fig. 2 due to the nonoptimal quality of the pitch tracks. That is a rising intonation at the end of the question. As clearly shown in Figs. 3 and 4, this rising intonation is a property of both question types (WHQ and YNQ). See Sect. 3.3 below for more explanation.

[6]This terminology is originally introduced by Sugahara (2003).

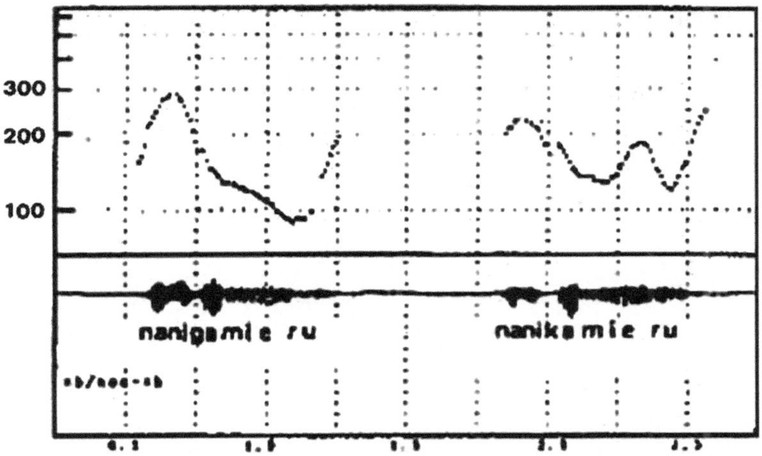

Fig. 3 Sample F_0-contours for a WHQ (*Left*) and a YNQ (*Right*) (Maekawa 1991a: Fig. 1)

YNQs have some special intonation, they have to be compared with a 'default' intonation contour—the contour of the DECL.

3 Experiment

In order to make a systematic comparison of the two question types and DECL, a new experiment was conducted. In this section, the details of the experiment and its results will be presented.

3.1 Stimuli

The three sentence types mentioned above (DECL/WHQ/YNQ) were tested as stimuli. Example (4) shows a sample triplet.

(4) a. *DECL (control)*
tookú-ni wáni-ga miéru
far-LOC crocodile-NOM visible
'I can see a crocodile far away.'

b. *WHQ*
tookú-ni náni-ga miéru?
far-LOC what-NOM visible
'What can you see far away?'

c. *YNQ*
tookú-ni wáni-ga miéru?
far-LOC crocodile-NOM visible
'Can you see a crocodile far away?'

The stimuli have either an adverbial or a topic subject at the beginning of the sentence, followed by an argument, and a verb.[7] Since the question particle *no* is omitted in all question sentences,[8] the question is indicated only by a question mark at the end of the sentence. Six sets of such minimal triplets were used as stimuli.

3.2 Methods

Data were collected from 12 subjects (5 female; 7 male). Stimuli (6 minimal triplets = 18 sentences) were mixed with 96 filler sentences (which were used as stimuli for other experiments). The whole set of sentences was divided into two groups and recorded in 2 different recording sessions. DECLs (=(4a)) and WHQs (=(4b)) were included in the first recording session, while YNQs (=(4c)) were included in the second session. There was at least a one-week interval between the two sessions.

Stimuli were pseudorandomized (so that two sentences in the same triplet would not be read in a row), and the entire stimulus set was read three times (in a different randomized order each time). This means that there were 18 samples (6 sentences × 3 times) per condition per subject.

Statistical analysis was done using R. For data analysis, the F_0-maximum and the F_0-minima before and after it were measured for the argument and the verb of each sentence. (The sentence-final rising contour was excluded in the calculation of the F_0-max for the verb.) The results shown in the next section were obtained by normalizing the results from all 12 subjects, using the following formula:

$$y = (x - R_2)/(R_1 - R_2)$$

with the two reference points (R_1, R_2) set to the mean value of F_0-peak of the argument and the mean value of F_0-valley after the verb, respectively.

3.3 Results

Figure 4 shows sample pitch contours of the argument and the verb in the three sentence types, overlapping each other. They show three different F_0-realizations.

There are three prosodic phenomena that have already been discussed in the literature, and these were in fact replicated in the sample contours. First, we observe *downstep* on the verb. We assume that the DECL (solid line) shows the 'default'

---

[7]Words used in the stimuli were all accented.

[8]In Japanese, the question particle is optional in the matrix clause (Yoshida and Yoshida 1996). In such a case, the question is only marked by the utterance-final rising intonation.

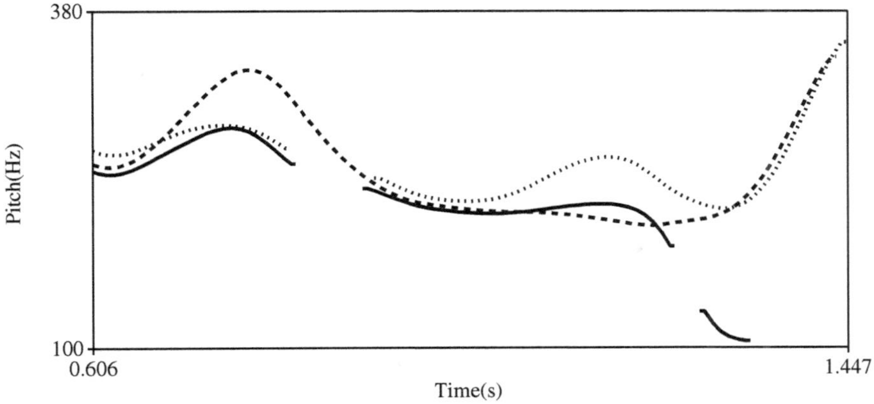

Fig. 4 Sample pitch contours of DECL (*solid line*), WHQ (*dashed line*), and YNQ (*dotted line*)

pitch contour, which is created according to the syntax-prosody mapping principle. The F_0-peak of the verb is usually realized lower than that of the immediately preceding phrase, due to downstep. Any standard syntax-prosody mapping principle (e.g., Selkirk and Tateishi 1991) groups the verb and the immediately preceding phrase into a single phonological phrase (henceforth *p-phrase*[9]). Within each p-phrase, downstep takes place after each (lexical) pitch accent.[10] Since the preverbal arguments in the stimuli are all lexically pitch accented, their lexical pitch accent triggers downstep, and lowers the F_0-peak of the verb.

Second, final boundary tones are different between the DECL and the two question types (cf. fn. 5). The DECL ends with an L% boundary tone, while both question types are marked by an H% boundary tone (Pierrehumbert and Beckman 1988).

Third, we can observe the FP effects in the WHQ, namely, a focal F_0-rise on the *wh*-phrase in the argument position and the subsequent post-focal reduction on the verb. The F_0-peak of the argument is clearly higher in the WHQ than in the DECL, and the F_0-peak of the verb in the WHQ is almost completely compressed.[11]

[9]This phrase has been referred to as either *Major Phrase* (Poser 1984; Kubozono 1993) or *intermediate phrase* (Pierrehumbert and Beckman 1988), in contrast to *Minor Phrase* or *accentual phrase*, respectively. However, Itô and Mester (2007, 2012) point out both conceptual and empirical problems of this distinction between the two levels of prosodic phrasing, and claim that this distinction is superfluous and can be dispensed with. Although the details of their account are not our concern here, we adopt Ito and Mester's (2007; 2012) framework, and hence use the general term *p-phrase*. See Itô and Mester (2007, 2012) for more discussion.

[10]In Japanese, downstep is triggered by a lexical H*+L pitch accent, that is, only accented words trigger downstep (Poser 1984; Pierrehumbert and Beckman 1988, among many others).

[11]This compression of the F_0-peak does not mean that lexical pitch accents are completely 'deaccented' or 'eradicated' in the post-focal domain, as sometimes (either explicitly or tacitly) assumed in the literature (Pierrehumbert and Beckman 1988; Deguchi and Kitagawa 2002). There is abundant evidence showing that lexical pitch accents are only less visible in the post-focal domain due to compression of the pitch range. See Maekawa (1994) and Sugahara (2003) for discussion.

Table 1 Comparison of DECL/WHQ/YNQ

	Argument	Verb	End
DECL (control)		Downstep	L%
WHQ	Raised	Downstep, lowered	H%
YNQ		Downstep, raised	H%

Now, the comparison we are most interested in here is the one between the DECL and the YNQ—the missing piece of the three-way comparison of DECL, WHQ, and YNQ. There are three important observations we can make. First, the F_0-peak of the argument phrase in the YNQ is just as high as that of the DECL. This suggests that there is no additional effect on the argument phrase of the YNQ. Second, more importantly, the F_0-peak of the verb in the YNQ is clearly higher than in the DECL. This indicates that there is an additional effect involved in the YNQ. This fact clarifies the unanswered question mentioned in Sect. 2.2, namely, whether the difference between WHQs and YNQs are solely due to the lack of the FP effects in YNQ, or YNQs also have additional effects of their own. Finally, the F_0-peak of the verb shows a downstep effect in the YNQ. Even though the F_0-peak of the verb is raised, it is still lower compared to the F_0-peak of the preceding argument. It appears that downstep is still in effect in the YNQ. The observed differences among DECLs, WHQs, and YNQs are summarized in Table 1.

Statistical analysis confirms the observations made above. Figure 5 shows the normalized mean of F_0-maxima and minima of the argument phrases and the verbs.

It is clear from Fig. 5 that the F_0-peak on the argument is higher in the WHQ, and that of the verb is higher in the YNQ than in the DECL (i.e., the control condition). These two contrasts are both statistically significant (F_0-max on the argument, WHQ versus DECL: 2-sided t-test[12]: $t(410.443) = -20.6322, p < 0.001$; F_0-max on the verb, YNQ versus DECL: 2-sided t-test: $t(415.018) = -18.6788, p < 0.001$).[13] As for the post-focal reduction in the WHQ, a statistically significant contrast between the WHQ and the DECL is found in terms of the amount of F_0-rise from the F_0-valley to the F_0-peak on the verb, i.e., the F_0-max minus the preceding F_0-min (2-sided t-test: $t(407.474) = 4.1711, p < 0.001$).

In sum, in the systematic comparison of DECLs, WHQs, and YNQs, we first confirmed (a) the FP effects in WHQs, which have been already claimed in the literature, and (b) an F_0-rise on the verb in YNQs.

(5) *Findings:*

a. WHQ: F_0-rise on the argument (*wh*-phrase) + F_0-lowering (= FP)

b. YNQ: F_0-rise on the verb

[12]If the variances of two samples are not equal, Welch's correction is made on the t-test.

[13]Both contrasts were statistically significant in all 12 subjects' individual data as well.

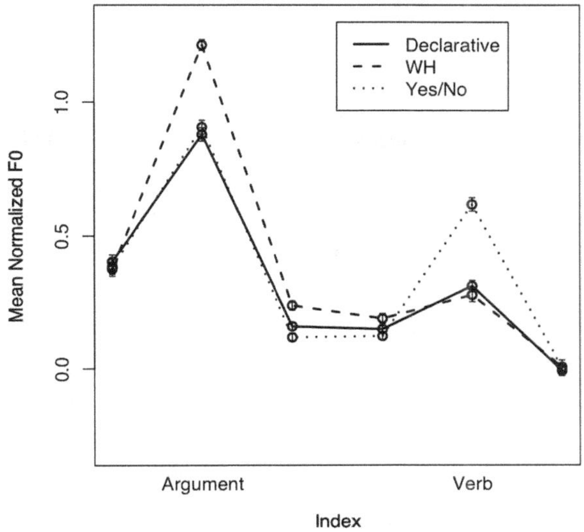

Fig. 5 Normalized mean F_0-maxima and minima of the argument phrases and the verbs in DECL (*solid line*), WHQ (*dashed line*), and YNQ (*dotted line*), with a 95 % confidence interval

In the next section, we propose that the F_0-rise in YNQs is also a focal prominence, and that this analysis is compatible with a standard semantic theory of questions. We also discuss implications for phonological theories of focus.

4 Discussion

In order to account for the findings above, we propose that the F_0-rise on V in YNQs is a prosodic realization of verum focus. That is, both WHQs and YNQs involve an FP. The difference is the location of the focus: it is on the *wh*-phrase in WHQs, while it is on the verb in YNQs. As will be shown below, this analysis allows us to treat WHQs and YNQs in a parallel fashion both semantically and prosodically.

(6) Prosodic prominence in WHQs/YNQs is a phonetic realization of focus.[14]

a. ***WHQ: Focus on WH***

nánı$_F$-ga miéru?
what-NOM visible
'What do you see?'

b. ***YNQ: (Verum) Focus on Tense***

wáni-ga miéru$_{VF}$?
crocodile-NOM visible
'Do you see a crocodile?'

[14]Just for expository purposes, verum focus will be distinguished with the subscript 'VF' ($_{VF}$), in contrast to other foci, which are marked by the subscript 'F' ($_F$). This does not mean that verum focus will be treated differently from other foci in terms of semantic or phonological computation.

4.1 Semantics

Here we discuss semantic aspects of WHQs and YNQs. It will be shown that our proposal that YNQs bear a focus on V goes well with the semantic theory of questions proposed by Hamblin (1973). Focus semantic value computed under Rooth's (1992) theory of focus derives correct semantic denotations for both WHQs and YNQs.

4.1.1 Location of Verum Focus

Before going into the discussion on the semantic theory of focus, we need to clarify the location of verum focus. In English, the verum focus is realized on Tense, as in *I do* $_{VF}$ *see something*. In Japanese, Tense is a verbal suffix, and hence morphologically incorporated in the verbal complex. Phonologically, the V-head and the T-head form a single prosodic word. This property may be captured syntactically by adopting the claim that V undergoes string vacuous head movement (V-to-T movement) in Japanese (Koizumi 2000; Miyagawa 2001).

(7) *V-to-T movement*

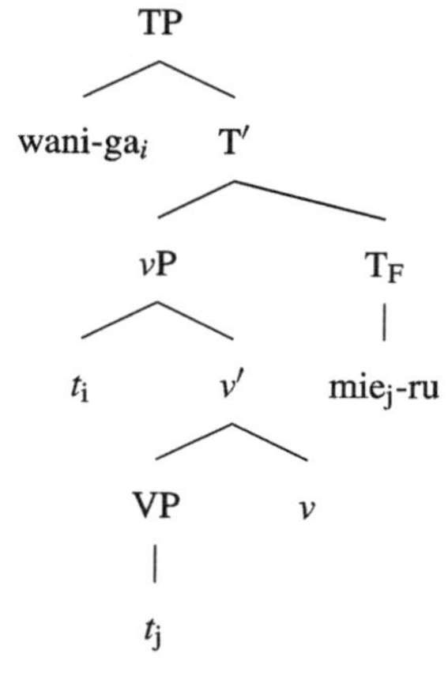

The following data suggest that V-T incorporation does in fact take place. An answer to a YNQ in Japanese requires a full, inflected verbal complex, and does not allow *do*-support.

(8) A: Taro-wa sono hon-o kat-ta no?
Taro-TOP that book-ACC buy-PST Q?
'Did Taro buy that book?'
B: Un, kat-ta yo. / *si-ta yo
yes buy-PST MOD do-PST MOD
'Yes (he) bought (it). / *Yes, (he) did.'
B′: Iya, kawa-nakat-ta yo. / *si-nakat-ta yo
no buy-NEG-PST MOD do-NEG-PST MOD
'No, (he) didn't buy (it). / *No (he) didn't.'

This does not mean, however, that Japanese never allows *do*-support. When a focus-sensitive particle, such as *mo* 'also/even', *dake* 'only', *koso* 'focus/emphasis', or *sae/sura* 'even', attaches to the root form of V, Tense will be realized separately from the V-root, with the help of *do*-support.

(9) Taro-wa [$_{VP}$ kuzira-o tabe]-sae si-ta.
Taro-TOP whale-ACC eat-even do-PST
'Taro even ate whale.'

In such a case, there is supposedly a focus associated with the focus particle, which may be assigned to either the object, the V-head, or the VP containing them, depending on the context. If we add a verum focus to this sentence (e.g., 'Taro did $_{VF}$ even eat [whale]$_F$.'), this verum focus seems to be realized on *si-ta* 'do-PST' and induces an FP, according to my own intuitions. Although this observation still needs to be confirmed empirically, it suggests that the verum focus is assigned to Tense.

Although the exact location of the verum focus in Japanese still needs to be studied further, we will assume that the verum focus is assigned to Tense, just like in English, and is realized on the V-T complex.

4.1.2 Semantics of Questions

The proposal that both WHQs and YNQs bear a focus is compatible with the standard semantic theory of questions and focus. According to Hamblin (1973), questions denote sets of propositions expressed by possible answers. In the case of the WHQ *What do you see?*, for example, it denotes a set of propositions of the form 'I see *x*', as shown in (10a). In the case of the YNQ *Do you see a crocodile?*, its denotation is a pair of propositions, namely, a positive and a negative answer to the question, as in (10b).

(10) a. *WHQ: set of possible answers*
⟦ What do you see? ⟧
= { *I see a crocodile, I see a piranha, I see John, ...* }
$= \{ see(I, x) \mid x \in E \}$
b. *YNQ: pair of possible answers*
⟦ Do you see a crocodile? ⟧
= { *I see a crocodile, I don't see a crocodile* }
$= \{ p \vee \neg p \mid p = see(I, crocodile)\}$

This set/pair of possible answers is derived from the *focus semantic value* (Rooth 1992) generated by the focus within the question. In the WHQ, the *wh*-phrase, the focus carrier, is replaced by a variable, and a set of propositions of the form 'I see *x*' will be produced by assigning individuals in the relevant context to this variable. In the same way, by assuming a verum focus on T (or the V-T complex in Japanese), a pair of propositions of the form 'I *x* see a crocodile' will be created as a focus semantic value for the YNQ. We assume here, following Beck (2006), that this focus semantic value is converted to the ordinary semantic value of the questions by the question particle (Q), as illustrated in (11):

(11) a. *WHQ*
$[\![\text{I see what}_F]\!]^f = \{\ see(I,x) \mid x \in E\ \}$
$[\![\text{Q [I see what}_F \text{]}]\!]^o = \{\ see(I,x) \mid x \in E\ \}$
b. *YNQ*
$[\![\text{I do}_{VF} \text{ see a crocodile}]\!]^f = \{\ p \vee \neg p \mid p = see(I, crocodile)\}$
$[\![\text{Q [I do}_{VF} \text{ see a crocodile]}]\!]^o = \{\ p \vee \neg p \mid p = see(I, crocodile)\}$

This means that the analysis proposed to account for the experimental results also correctly derives the wanted semantic interpretations for WHQs and YNQs.

4.2 Phonology

Returning to phonological aspects, there are two relevant issues to be discussed. The first issue is phonological theories of focus prosody in Japanese. Our proposal is *not* compatible with the widely adopted phonological theory of focus (Pierrehumbert and Beckman 1988) in which focus inserts a p-phrase boundary to block a downstep effect on the focused phrase. Rather, it is more in line with an alternative account in which focus only modifies pitch ranges and does not affect p-phrasing (Ishihara 2011). The experimental results support the latter analysis, along with other empirical evidence reported in the literature. The second issue is the interaction of 'focus' and the discourse-newness/givenness. A comparison of the experimental results of the current study with those of another experiment reported by Féry and Ishihara (2007) suggest that the 'focus' discussed in this paper and the discourse-newness/givenness have independent prosodic effects. This suggests that these notions should be kept apart in constructing a theory of focus.

4.2.1 Phonological Theories of Focus Prosody in Japanese

A widely accepted analysis of Japanese FP is that focus induces a p-phrase boundary to the left of the focused phrase, which, in effect, blocks downstep (Pierrehumbert and Beckman 1988; Nagahara 1994). If we combine this analysis and our proposal for YNQs (i.e., a focus is assigned on V), it would be predicted that the F_0-rise on V is a result of the cancelation of downstep at V. This prediction, however, is not compatible with the experimental results of the current study. As we discussed earlier (Sect. 3.3), the downstep effect is not completely canceled in YNQs. This means that our proposal is not compatible with this type of 'rephrasing' analysis.

This does not mean, however, that our proposal is not on the right track. The 'rephrasing' analysis mentioned above has been empirically challenged in several studies (Shinya 1999; Ishihara 2007, 2011, 2016). Ishihara (2016) showed experimentally that focus does not insert a p-phrase boundary, while a syntactic boundary does.[15] According to these studies, focus affects the pitch ranges of the focused phrase and the post-focal domain, but does not alter the prosodic phrasing.

Following this line of analysis, together with the assumption that both WHQs and YNQs involve an FP, the intonation patterns in the experimental results can be straightforwardly explained. The focus on the *wh*-phrase in WHQs and the focus on V in YNQs both trigger an FP. The focal F_0-rise raises the F_0-peak on the focused element. The subsequent post-focal reduction is only visible in WHQs, simply because there is no material following the focused V in YNQs.

4.2.2 Interaction with New-/Givenness

Finally, before we close our discussion, we reconsider the notion of 'focus,' and its interaction with the notion of newness and givenness. The notion of focus (vs. background) on the one hand and the notion of discourse-newness (vs. givenness) on the other are sometimes used interchangeably (at least partly), and sometimes used independently (again, at least partly). The question is whether they are two independent notions needed for a theory of focus, or should be treated uniformly.

Roughly speaking, there are two types of approaches to this question. One line of analysis makes no distinction between the notion of 'focus/background' and 'new/given,' or treats them within a single system (e.g., Rooth 1992; Schwarzschild 1999). Another approach is to postulate two types of foci, and make a clear-cut distinction between them (e.g., Rochemont 1986; É. Kiss 1998).[16]

To illustrate the question, let us look at the notions of 'wide/broad focus (WF)' and 'narrow focus (NF).' The distinction between them mainly depends on how much material in the sentence is discourse-given. When there is a single word that is discourse-new, this phrase is usually considered to be the 'narrow focus' of the sentence. A typical example would be an answer to a *wh*-question (e.g., Q: *What do you see?* A: *I see a* [*crocodile*]$_{NF}$). If a larger phrase or a clause is discourse-new, this phrase/clause is usually called the 'wide focus' (e.g., Q: *What did you do?* A: *I* [$_{VP}$ *saw a crocodile*]$_{WF}$). However, it is also well known that the WF/NF-contrast cannot simply be defined based on givenness. For example, a pronoun, which is intrinsically discourse-given, can also be focused (e.g., *I saw*[*HIM*]$_F$). The question is whether a typical 'narrow focus,' i.e., the single discourse-new element in a sentence ([*crocodile*]$_{NF}$), and a focus that is given ([*HIM*]$_F$) have the same focal status, and whether they are also realized in the same way prosodically.

In recent years several proposals have been made on this issue from a prosodic point of view in which these notions are treated independently (Féry and Samek-Lodovici 2006; Katz and Selkirk 2011; Selkirk 2002, 2008; Sugahara 2003), among

[15]Nor does focus delete p-phrase boundaries in the post-focal domain, contrary to the claim made in the 'rephrasing' analysis. See Ishihara (2011) for discussion.

[16]There are also approaches somewhere in between. Selkirk's (1995) F-marking theory, for example, is intended as a uniform theory, but is forced to assume an additional type of focus, when a given phrase needs to be focused. See Schwarzschild (1999) for details.

others. Féry and Samek-Lodovici (2006), for example, propose two independent OT-constraints, DESTRESS-GIVEN and STRESS-FOCUS. The former is responsible for prosodic effects of givenness, while the latter is responsible for prosodic effects of focus. This line of analysis treats the focus/background- and new/given-contrasts independently, because focus and givenness are independently marked.

(12) Féry and Samek-Lodovici (2006, 135)
  a. DESTRESS-GIVEN: A given phrase is prosodically nonprominent.
  b. STRESS-FOCUS: A focused phrase has the highest prosodic prominence in its focus domain.

We can examine the predictions of the two types of analyses above by comparing the data in this experiment with other data testing the wide/narrow focus contrast. Féry and Ishihara (2007) presented experimental data in which the phonetic realizations of wide and narrow focus were compared, using sentences like those in (13).

(13) a. *Wide Focus (WF):*
 Q: 'Why is Taro's face red?'
 A: tábun, [wáin-o nónda]$_F$ n da yo
  probably wine-ACC drank C COP MOD
  'Probably he drank wine.'
 b. *Narrow Focus (NF)*:
 Q: 'I wonder what Taro drank.'
 A: tábun, [wáin-o]$_F$ nónda n da yo

In the wide focus (WF) context, the VP of the answer sentence is discourse-new. In the narrow focus (NF) context, on the other hand, the preverbal argument phrase (subject or direct object) is the sole discourse-new element.

The WF sentence in (13a) can be considered to be parallel to DECL in our experiment, because both the argument and the verb are discourse-new in both experiments. If we consider NF to be parallel to a focus, we would expect the NF sentence to behave prosodically just like a WHQ: a focal F_0-rise on the argument followed by a post-focal reduction on V. That means that the F_0-peak on the argument would be expected to be higher in NF compared to WF, while that of the V would be lower.

However, Féry and Ishihara's (2007) results, shown in Fig. 6, suggest otherwise. Even though the F_0-peak on V shows the expected contrast between WF and NF (i.e., WF > NF), there is no significant difference on the F_0-peak of the argument phrase. This means that the NF shows a different contour from the WHQ in our data.

These results may be explained if we assume that there is no focus involved in a NF sentence like (13b), and that givenness triggers an F_0-lowering effect on V in the NF condition. That is, neither WF nor NF involves an FP. The WF condition exhibits the default pitch contour, while the NF condition only exhibits an F_0-lowering effect due to givenness. In the results of our study (Fig. 5), on the other hand, the WHQ exhibits an FP, independently of the givenness effect.[17] This interpretation of the

[17]For the effect of givenness in the post-focal domain, see Sugahara (2003).

Fig. 6 Normalized mean F_0-maxima and minima of the argument phrase and the verb in WF (*solid line*) and NF (*dashed line*), with a 95 % confidence interval

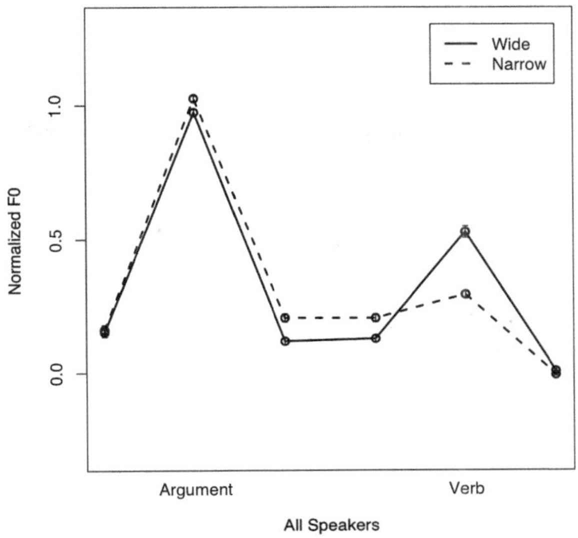

results supports the line of analysis in which prosodic effects of focus and those of givenness are distinguished (Féry and Samek-Lodovici 2006; Selkirk 2008).[18]

Since the two experiments were not designed with a direct comparison of their results in mind, this conclusion still needs to be confirmed empirically, possibly with another experiment specifically designed to test this question. Note, however, that the stimuli for the two experiments are quite similar in terms of the syntactic structure (Adverb-Argument-Verb). Furthermore, the data for the two experiments were recorded in the same recording sessions, using the same set of subjects. Given that the two experiments were performed under these almost identical conditions, the comparison between the results of the two experiments seems to indicate a clear difference that is worth paying some attention to.

5 Conclusion

In this paper, we discussed the intonation of WHQs and YNQs in Tokyo Japanese, based on experimental data. An empirical finding reported here is that while the WHQ exhibits an F_0-prominence on the *wh*-phrase (as already reported in many studies), the YNQ exhibits an F_0-prominence on the verb. This contrast was examined by systematic comparison of these question constructions with declarative sentences as a control condition.

[18]As an anonymous reviewer correctly points out, however, this interpretation of the results is incompatible with the standard analysis of the Question–Answer congruence (Rooth 1992). The issue seems not as simple as outlined here.

Theoretically, this contrast can best be explained by assuming a focus assigned to the *wh*-phrase in the case of a WHQ, and to the V-T complex in the case of a YNQ, that is to say, both WHQs and YNQs involve an FP. It was also shown that this unified account is compatible with the semantic theories of focus and questions. Regarding the prosodic realization of focus, the experimental data of the present study were compared with those from Féry and Ishihara (2007). It was shown that the FP found in WHQs is different from the intonation pattern of the so-called 'narrow focus,' a single discourse-new element in a sentence. It was suggested that the prosodic effects of focus (focal F_0-rise and post-focal reduction) and the prosodic effect of givenness (F_0-reduction) are independent.

Acknowledgments I would like to thank Caroline Féry, Andreas Haida, and an anonymous reviewer, as well as the audience at the Information Structure Workshop at the CIL18 Conference, for their comments and discussion. Thanks also go to Felix Engelmann and Juliane Böhme for their help on data annotation and analysis. All the remaining errors are mine.

References

Beck, Sigrid. 2006. Intervention effects follow from focus interpretation. *Natural Language Semantics* 14 (1): 1–56.

Deguchi, Masanori, and Kitagawa, Yoshihisa. 2002. Prosody and wh-questions. In *NELS 32: Proceedings of the North Eastern Linguistics Society, GLSA*, ed. Hirotani, Masako, 1, 73–92. Amherst, Amherst, Mass: University of Massachusetts.

É. Kiss, Katalin. 1998. Identification focus and information focus. *Language* 74: 245–341.

Féry, Caroline, and Ishihara, Shinichiro. 2007. Syntactic and prosodic realization of information structure in German, Hungarian, and Japanese. Paper presented at the Workshop on Prosody, Syntax, and Information Structure 3 (WPSI3).

Féry, Caroline, and Vieri Samek-Lodovici. 2006. Focus projection and prosodic prominence in nested foci. *Language* 82 (1): 131–150.

Hamblin, C.L. 1973. Questions in Montague grammar. *Foundations of Language* 10(1):

Hirotani, Masako. 2005. Prosody and LF: Processing Japanese wh-questions. Ph.D thesis, Amherst: University of Massachusetts.

Ishihara, Shinichiro. 2002. Invisible but audible wh-scope marking: Wh-constructions and deaccenting in Japanese. In *Proceedings of the 21st West Coast Conference on Formal Linguistics (WCCFL 21)*, ed. Line Mikkelsen, and Chris Potts, 180–193. Mass.: Cascadilla Press, Somerville.

Ishihara, Shinichiro. 2003. Intonation and interface conditions. Ph.D thesis, Massachusetts Institute of Technology. http://hdl.handle.net/1721.1/17020.

Ishihara, Shinichiro. 2007. Major phrase, focus intonation, and multiple spell-out (MaP, FI, MSO). *The Linguistic Review* 24: 137–167. doi:10.1515/TLR.2007.006.

Ishihara, Shinichiro. 2011. Japanese focus prosody revisited: Freeing focus from prosodic phrasing. *Lingua* 121 (13): 1870–1889. doi:10.1016/j.lingua.2011.06.008.

Ishihara, Shinichiro. 2016. Japanese downstep revisited. *Natural Language and Linguistic Theory* 34(4): 1380–1443. doi:10.1007/s11049-015-9322-8.

Itô, Junko, and Armin Mester. 2007. Prosodic adjunction in Japanese compounds. *Formal Approaches to Japanese Linguistics* 4 (FAJL4): 97–111.

Itô, Junko, and Armin Mester. 2012. Recursive prosodic phrasing in Japanese. In *Browsky Toni, Kawahara, Shigeto, Shinya Takahito*, ed. Marko Sugahara, 280–303. Prosody Matters: Essays in Honor of Elisabeth Selkirk, London: Equinox Publishing.

Katz, Jonah, and Selkirk, Elisabeth. 2011. Contrastive focus vs. discourse-new: Evidence from phonetic prominence in English. *Language* 87(4): 771–816.

Koizumi, Masatoshi. 2000. String vacuous overt verb raising. *Journal of East Asian Linguistics* 9: 227–285.

Krifka, Manfred. 2008. Basic notions of information structure. *Acta Linguistica Hungarica* 55 (3–4): 243–276.

Kubozono, Haruo. 1993. *The Organization of Japanese Prosody*. Tokyo: Kurosio Publishers.

Maekawa, Kikuo. 1991a. Perception of intonation characteristics of WH and non-WH questions in Tokyo Japanese. In *Proceedings of the 22nd International Congress of Phonetic Science*, 4, 202–205. Aix-en-Provence, France: Université de Provence.

Maekawa, Kikuo. 1991b. Tōkyō hōgen gimon-bun no intonēsyon [The intonation of question sentences in Tokyo dialect]. In *Proceedings of the 1991 PSJ Annual Convention*, 42–47. The Phonetic Society of Japan.

Maekawa, Kikuo. 1994. Is there 'dephrasing' of the accentual phrase in Japanese? *OSU Working Papers in Linguistics* 44:146–165.

Maekawa, Kikuo. 1997a. Effects of focus on duration and vowel formant frequency in Japanese. In *Computing Prosody: Computational Models for Processing Spontaneous Speech, chap 10*, Sagisaka Y, Campbell N, Higuchi N eds, 129–153. New York: Springer-Verlag.

Maekawa, Kikuo. 1997b. Nihongo gimonsi gimon-bun no intoneesyon [The intonation of the Japanese wh-question]. In *Bunpoo to onsei [Grammar and Sound], chap 3* ed. Onsei Bunpoo Kenkyuu-kai, 45–53. Tokyo: Kurosio Publishers.

Miyagawa, Shigeru. 2001. The EPP, scrambling, and wh-in-situ. In *Ken Hale: A Life in Language*, ed. Michael Kenstowicz, 293–338. Mass.: MIT Press, Cambridge.

Nagahara, Hiroyuki. 1994. Phonological phrasing in Japanese. Ph.D thesis, Los Angeles: University of California.

Pierrehumbert, Janet, and Mary Beckman. 1988. *Japanese Tone Structure*. Cambridge, Mass: MIT Press.

Poser, William J. 1984. The phonetics and phonology of tone and intonation in Japanese. Ph.D thesis, Massachusetts Institute of Technology.

Rochemont, Michael. 1986. *Focus in generative grammar*. Amsterdam: John Benjamins.

Rooth, Mats. 1992. A theory of focus interpretation. *Natural Language Semantics* 1: 75–116.

Schwarzschild, Roger. 1999. GIVENness, AVOIDF and other constraints on the placement of accent. *Natural Language Semantics* 7: 141–177.

Selkirk, Elisabeth. 1995. Sentence prosody: Intonation, stress, and phrasing. In *The Handbook of Phonological Theory*, ed. J.A. Goldsmith, 550–569. Oxford, UK: Blackwell.

Selkirk, Elisabeth. 2002. Contrastive *FOCUS* vs. presentational *focus*: Prosodic evidence from right node raising in English. In *Speech Prosody 2002*, ed. B. Bel, and I. Marlien, 643–646. Aix-en-Provence: France.

Selkirk, Elisabeth. 2008. Contrastive focus, givenness and the unmarked status of "discourse-new". *Acta Linguistica Hungarica* 55 (3–4): 331–346.

Selkirk, Elisabeth, and Tateishi, Koichi. 1991. Syntax and downstep in Japanese. In *Interdisciplinary Approaches to Language: Essays in Honor of S.-Y. Kuroda*, Georgopoulos, Carol, and Ishihara, Roberta eds, 519–543. Dordrecht: Kluwer Academic Publishers.

Shinya, Takahito. 1999. Eigo to nihongo ni okeru fookasu ni yoru daunsteppu no sosi to tyooon-undoo no tyoogoo [The blocking of downstep by focus and articulatory overlap in English and Japanese]. *Proceedings of Sophia Linguistics Society* 14: 35–51.

Sugahara, Mariko. 2003. Downtrends and post-FOCUS intonation in Japanese. Ph.D thesis, Amherst: University of Massachusetts.

Yoshida, Keiko, and Tomoyuki Yoshida. 1996. Question marker drop in Japanese. *ICU Language Research Bulletin* 11: 37–57.

Kolibri 360 GmbH
Ferdinand-Jühlke-Straße 7
99095 Erfurt, Deutschland
produktsicherheit@kolibri360.de